D1715189

Crossover Queries

John D. Caputo, *series editor*

PERSPECTIVES IN
CONTINENTAL
PHILOSOPHY

EDITH WYSCHOGROD

Crossover Queries

Dwelling with Negatives,
Embodying Philosophy's Others

FORDHAM UNIVERSITY PRESS
New York ∎ 2006

Library of Congress Cataloging-in-Publication Data

Wyschogrod, Edith.
  Crossover queries : dwelling with negatives, embodying philosophy's others /
Edith Wyschogrod.
    p.   cm.—(Perspectives in continental philosophy ; no. 52)
  Includes bibliographical references (p.   ) and index.
  ISBN 0-8232-2606-9—ISBN 0-8232-2607-7
  1. Philosophy, Modern.   2. Theology.   3. Ethics.   I. Title.   II. Series.
B804.W97   2006
190—dc22
                                                                    2006005903

Printed in the United States of America
08 07 06   5 4 3 2 1
First edition.

Contents

Acknowledgments

Permission to use the following previously published materials is gratefully acknowledged.

Chapter 1 appeared as "Intending Transcendence: Desiring God," in *Companion to Postmodern Theology*, ed. Graham Ward (London: Blackwell, 2001), 349–65.

Chapter 2 appeared as "Corporeality and the Glory of the Infinite in the Philosophy of Emmanuel Levinas," in *Incarnation*, Proceedings of the Conference of the Instituto di Studi Filosofici Enrico Castelli, 1998, vol. 63, nos. 1–3, 113–26.

Chapter 3 appeared as portions of Chapter 8 in Edith Wyschogrod, *Saints and Postmodernism: Revisioning Moral Philosophy* (Chicago: University of Chicago Press, 1990), 231–57.

Chapter 4 appeared as "Emmanuel Levinas and Hillel's Questions," in *Postmodern Philosophy and Christian Thought*, ed. Merold Westphal (Bloomington: Indiana University Press, 1999), 245–59.

Chapter 5 appeared as "Recontextualizing the Ontological Argument: A Lacanian Analysis," in *Lacan and Theological Discourse*, ed. Edith Wyschogrod, David Crownfield, and Carl Raschke (Albany: State University of New York Press, 1989), 97–118.

Chapter 6 appeared as "Heidegger, Foucault, and the Askeses of Self-Transformation," in *Foucault and Heidegger: Critical Encounters*, ed. Alan Rosenberg and Allen Milchman (Minneapolis: University of Minnesota Press, 2003), 276–94.

Chapter 7 appeared as "Blind Man Seeing: From Chiasm to Hyperreality," in *Chiasms: Merleau-Ponty's Notion of Flesh*, ed. Leonard Lawlor and Fred Evans (Albany: State University of New York Press, 2000), 165–76.

Chapter 8 appeared as "The Howl of Oedipus, the Cry of Héloïse: From Asceticism to Postmodern Ethics," in *Asceticism*, ed. Vincent Wimbush and Richard Valantasis (New York: Oxford University Press, 1995), 16–32.

Chapter 9 appeared as "From the Death of the Word to the Rise of the Image in the Choreography of Merce Cunningham," in *Philosophies of Religion, Art, and Creativity*, Proceedings of the Twentieth-Century World Congress of Philosophy, vol. 4, ed. Kevin I. Stoehr (Bowling Green, Ohio: Philosophy Documentation Center, 1999), 219–29.

Chapter 10 appeared as "Empathy and Sympathy as Tactile Encounter," in *The Journal of Medicine and Philosophy* 6 (1981): 23–41.

Chapter 11 appeared as "Levinas's Other and the Culture of the Copy," in *Encounters with Levinas*, ed. Thomas Trezise, special issue of *Yale French Studies*, 2004, no. 104:126–43.

Chapter 12 appeared as "From Neo-Platonism to Souls in Silico: Quests for Immortality," in *Rethinking Philosophy of Religion*, ed. Philip Goodchild (New York: Fordham University Press, 2002), 247–66.

Chapter 13 appeared as "The Semantic Spaces of Terror: A Theological Response," in *Religion in a Secular World: Violence, Politics, Terror*, ed. Clayton Crockett (Charlottesville: University of Virginia Press, forthcoming).

Chapter 14 appeared as "The Warring Logics of Genocide," in *The Palgrave Guide to Philosophy, Genocide and Human Rights*, ed. John K. Roth (Basingstroke, Hampshire: Palgrave Macmillan, forthcoming).

Chapter 15 appeared as "Incursions of Evil: The Double Bind of Alterity," in *Modernity and the Problem of Evil*, ed. Alan D. Schrift (Bloomington: Indiana University Press, forthcoming).

Chapter 16 appeared as "Memory, History, Revelation: Writing the Dead Other," in *Memory and History in Christianity and Judaism*, ed. Michael A. Signer (Notre Dame, Ind.: Notre Dame University Press, 2001), 19–34.

Chapter 17 appeared as "Exemplary Individuals: Towards a Phenomenological Ethics," in *Philosophy and Theology, Marquette University Quarterly* 1, no. 1 (1986): 9–31.

Chapter 18 appeared as "Interview with Emmanuel Levinas: December 31, 1982," in *Philosophy and Theology, Marquette University Quarterly* 4, no. 2 (1989): 105–18.

Chapter 19 appeared as "Postmodernism and the Desire for God: An E-mail Exchange," by Edith Wyschogrod and John D. Caputo, *Cross Currents* 48, no. 3 (1998): 293–310.

Chapter 20 appeared as "Heterological History: A Conversation," by Edith Wyschogrod and Carl Raschke, *Journal of Contemporary Religious Thought* 1, no. 2, http:www.jcrt,org.archives/01.2/wyschogrod_raschke.stml.

Chapter 21 appeared as "Between Swooners and Cynics: The Art of Envisioning God," in *Theological Perspectives on God and Beauty*, Rockwell Lectures Series (Harrisburg, Pa.: Trinity Press International, 2003), 66–85.

Chapter 22 appeared as "Facts, Fiction, *Ficciones*: Truth in the Study of Religion," presidential address, American Academy of Religion, *Journal of the American Academy of Religion* 62, no. 1 (1994): 1–16.

Chapter 23 appeared as "Eating the Text, Defiling the Hands: Specters in Arnold Schoenberg's Opera *Moses and Aron*," in *God, the Gift, and Postmodernism*, ed. John D. Caputo and Michael J. Scanlon (Bloomington: Indiana University Press, 1999), 245–59.

Chapter 24 appeared as "Killing the Cat: Sacrifice and Beauty in Genet and Mishima," in *Theology and Literature* 25, no. 2 (1993): 105–19.

Chapter 25 appeared as "The Art in Ethics: Aesthetics, Objectivity and Alterity in the Philosophy of Emmanuel Levinas," in *Ethics as First Philosophy*, ed. Adriaan T. Peperzak (New York: Routledge, 1995), 137–48.

Chapter 26 appeared as "The Moral Self: Emmanuel Levinas and Hermann Cohen," in *Daat: A Journal of Jewish Philosophy* 4 (Winter 1980): 35–58.

Chapter 27 appeared as "Autochthony and Welcome: Discourses of Exile in Levinas and Derrida," in *Derrida and Religion: Other Testaments*, ed. Yvonne Sherwood and Kevin Hart (New York: Routledge, 2005), 53–61.

Chapter 28 appeared as "Time and Non-Being in Derrida and Quine," in *Journal of the British Society for Phenomenology* 14 (May 1983): 112–26.

Chapter 29 appeared as "The Logic of Artifactual Existents: John Dewey and Claude Lévi-Strauss," in *Man and World* 14 (1981): 34–49.

Chapter 30 appeared as "The Mathematical Model in Plato and Some Surrogates in a Jain Theory of Knowledge," in *Civilizations*

East and West: A Memorial Volume for Benjamin Nelson, ed. E. V. Walter, Vytautis Kavolis, and Edmond Leites (Atlantic Highlands, N.J.: Humanities Press, 1985), 73–89.

Chapter 31 has not previously been published.

Chapter 32 appeared as "Fear of Primitives, Primitive Fears: Anthropology in the Philosophies of Heidegger and Levinas," in *Emotion and Postmodernism*, ed. Gerhard Hoffmann and Alfred Hornung (Heidelberg: Universitäts Verlag C. Winter, 1997), 401–20.

I should like to thank Mark C. Taylor for sharing his keen insights into many of the issues discussed here, John D. Caputo for his support of the present work, Adriaan T. Peperzak for his helpful observations concerning its content, Helen Tartar, without whose perceptive comments and indispensable editorial presence this work could not have gone forward, and Frank Shepherd for preparing the index for this volume.

Abbreviations

AE	John Dewey. *Art as Experience*. New York: Minton, Balch, 1934.
ARN	*The Fathers according to Rabbi Nathan*. Trans. Judah Goldin. Yale Judaica Series, vol. 10. New Haven: Yale University Press, 1955.
AT	Emmanuel Levinas. *Alterity and Transcendence*. Trans. Michael B. Smith. New York: Columbia University Press, 1999.
BL	Theodor Stcherbatsky. *Buddhist Logic*. 2 vols. *Bibliotheca Buddica*, vol. 26. Leningrad, 1932.
BPW	Emmanuel Levinas. *Basic Philosophical Writings*. Ed. Adriaan T. Peperzak, Simon Critchley, and Robert Bernasconi. Trans. Alphonso Lingis and Richard Cohen. Bloomington: Indiana University Press, 1996.
BT	Martin Heidegger. *Being and Time.* Trans. John Macquarrie and Edward Robinson. New York: Harper and Row, 1962.
C	Humberto R. Maturana. "Cognition." In *Wahrnehmung und Kommunikation*, ed. Peter M. Heil, Wolfram K. Köck, and Gerhard Roth (Frankfurt a. M.: Peter Lang, 1978), 29–49. Also available at http://www.enolagaia.com/M78bCog.html.

CCR	Peter Sloterdijk. *Critique of Cynical Reason.* Trans. Michael Eldred. London: Verso, 1988.
CJ	Immanuel Kant. *The Critique of Judgment.* Trans. J. H. Bernard. New York: Hafner Press, 1951.
CPP	Emmanuel Levinas. *Collected Philosophical Papers.* Trans. Alphonso Lingis. Pittsburgh: Duquesne University Press, 1987.
CS	Michel Foucault. *The Care of the Self.* Vol. 3 of *The History of Sexuality.* Trans. Robert Hurley. New York: Random House, 1988.
DA	Aristotle. *De Anima.* Trans. J. A. Smith. In *The Basic Works of Aristotle*, ed. Richard McKeon (New York: Random House, 1941).
DEHH	Emmanuel Levinas. *En découvrant l'existence avec Husserl et Heidegger.* Paris: Vrin, 1967.
DL	Julia Kristeva. *Desire in Language: A Semiotic Approach to Literature and Art.* Ed. Leon S. Roudiez. Trans. Thomas Gora, Alice Jardine, and Leon S. Roudiez. New York: Columbia University Press, 1980.
DNT	Jacques Derrida. "How to Avoid Speaking: Denials." Trans. Ken Frieden. In *Derrida and Negative Theology*, ed. Harold Coward and Toby Foshay (Albany: State University of New York Press, 1992), 73–77.
E	Michel Foucault. *Ethics, Subjectivity and Truth.* Vol. 1 of *Essential Works of Foucault 1954–1984.* Ed. Paul Rabinow. Trans. Robert Hurley. New York: The New Press, 1997.
EaN	John Dewey. *Experience and Nature.* Chicago: University of Chicago Press, 1929.
Écrits	Jacques Lacan. *Écrits: A Selection.* Trans. Alan Sheridan. New York: W. W. Norton, 1977.
EE	Emmanuel Levinas. *Existence and Existents.* Trans. Alphonso Lingis. Dordrecht: Kluwer, 1978.
EN	Emmanuel Levinas. *Entre Nous.* Trans. Michael B. Smith and Barbara Harshav. New York: Columbia University Press, 1998.
"Enigma"	Emmanuel Levinas. "Enigma and Phenomenon." In *BPW*, 65–78.
Enneads	Plotinus. *The Enneads.* Trans. Stephen MacKenna. New York: Pantheon Books, n.d.

EP	Richard Dawkins. *The Extended Phenotype: The Gene as the Unit of Selection.* Oxford: W. H. Freeman and Company, 1982.
FCM	Martin Heidegger. *The Fundamental Concepts of Metaphysics: World, Finitude, Solitude.* Trans. William McNeill and Nicholas Walker. Bloomington: Indiana University Press, 1995.
FL	Michel Foucault. *Foucault Live (Interviews 1966–84).* Ed. Sylvère Lotringer. Trans. John Johnston. New York: Semiotext(e), 1989.
FLPV	Willard Van Orman Quine. *From a Logical Point of View: Logico-Philosophical Essays.* 2d ed. New York: Harper and Row, 1961.
G	Jacques Derrida. *Of Grammatology.* Trans. Gayatri Chakravarti Spivak. Baltimore: The Johns Hopkins University Press, 1976.
GP	Moses Maimonides. *The Guide for the Perplexed.* Trans. M. Friedlander. New York: Dover Publications, 1956. Reprinted from the 2d ed., London: Routledge Kegan Paul, 1904.
Ideas	Edmund Husserl. *Ideas: General Introduction to Pure Phenomenology.* Trans. W. R. Boyce Gibson. New York: Collier Books, 1962.
MaA	Arnold Schoenberg. Libretto accompanying the Pierre Boulez and BBC singers and orchestra version of Schoenberg, *Moses and Aron.* Trans. Allen Forte. SONY, 1975/1982.
MT	Willard Van Orman Quine. "Meaning and Translation." In *The Structure of Language*, ed. Jerry A. Fodor and Jerrold Katz (Englewood Cliffs, N.J.: Prentice Hall, 1964), 460–78.
OB	Emmanuel Levinas. *Otherwise than Being; or, Beyond Essence.* Trans. Alphonso Lingis. The Hague: Martinus Nijhoff, 1981.
OG	Emmanuel Levinas. *Of God Who Comes to Mind.* Trans. Bettina Bergo. Stanford: Stanford University Press, 1998.
OS	Emmanuel Levinas. *Outside the Subject.* Trans. Michael B. Smith. Stanford: Stanford University Press, 1994.

PF	Søren Kierkegaard. *Philosophical Fragments*. Trans. Howard V. Hong and Edna H. Hong. Princeton: Princeton University Press, 1985.
PH	Julia Kristeva. *Powers of Horror: An Essay on Abjection*. Trans. Leon S. Roudiez. New York: Columbia University Press, 1982.
PLT	Martin Heidegger. *Poetry, Language, Thought*. Trans. Albert Hofstadter. New York: Harper and Row, 1971.
PML	Willard Van Orman Quine. "The Problem of Meaning in Linguistics," in *FLPV*, 47–64.
PN	Emmanuel Levinas. *Proper Names*. Trans. Michael B. Smith. Stanford: Stanford University Press, 1996.
PP	Maurice Merleau-Ponty. *Phenomenology of Perception*. Trans. Colin Smith. London: Routledge and Kegan Paul, 1962.
QCT	Martin Heidegger. *The Question Concerning Technology and Other Essays*. Trans. William Lovitt. New York: Harper and Row, 1977.
RC	Michel Foucault. *Religion and Culture*. Ed. Jeremy R. Carrette. New York: Routledge, 1999.
RL	Robert Bernasconi and Simon Critchley, eds. *Re-Reading Levinas*. Bloomington: Indiana University Press, 1991.
RRSJ	Hermann Cohen. *The Religion of Reason out of the Sources of Judaism*. Trans. Simon Kaplan. New York: Fredrick Unger, 1972.
SG	Richard Dawkins. *The Selfish Gene*. New York: Oxford University Press, 1976.
SL	Maurice Blanchot. *The Space of Literature*. Trans. and introd. Ann Smock. Lincoln: University of Nebraska Press, 1982.
SM	Claude Lévi-Strauss. *The Savage Mind*. Chicago: University of Chicago Press, 1960.
SO	Willard Van Orman Quine. "Speaking of Objects." In *The Structure of Language*, ed. Jerry A. Fodor and Jerrold Katz (Englewood Cliffs, N.J.: Prentice Hall, 1964), 446–59.
SoM	Jacques Derrida. *Specters of Marx: The State of the Debt, the Work of Mourning, and the New International*. Trans. Peggy Kamuf. New York: Routledge, 1994.

SP	Jacques Derrida. *Speech and Phenomena and Other Essays on Husserl's Theory of Signs*. Trans. David B. Allison. Evanston, Ill.: Northwestern University Press, 1973.
ST	St. Thomas Aquinas. *Summa Theologica*. In *Basic Writings of Saint Thomas Aquinas*, ed. Anton Pegis (New York: Random House, 1945).
TI	Emmanuel Levinas. *Totality and Infinity: An Essay in Exteriority*. Trans. Alphonso Lingis. Pittsburgh: Duquesne University Press, 1969.
TP	Gilles Deleuze and Félix Guattari. *A Thousand Plateaus: Capitalism and Schizophrenia*. Trans. Brian Massumi. Minneapolis: University of Minnesota Press, 1987.
"Transcendence"	Emmanuel Levinas. "Transcendence and Intelligibility." In *BPW*, 149–59.
TS	Michel Foucault. *Technologies of the Self: A Seminar with Michel Foucault*. Ed. Luther H. Martin, Huck Gutman, and Patrick H. Hutton. Amherst: University of Massachusetts Press, 1988.
UP	Michel Foucault. *The Use of Pleasure*. Vol. 2 of *The History of Sexuality*. Trans. Robert Hurley. New York: Pantheon Books, 1985.
VI	Maurice Merleau-Ponty. *The Visible and the Invisible*. Ed. Claude Lefort. Trans. Alphonso Lingis. Evanston, Ill.: Northwestern University Press, 1968.
WoD	Maurice Blanchot. *The Writing of the Disaster*. Trans. Ann Smock. Lincoln: University of Nebraska Press, 1986.
WP	Willard Van Orman Quine. *The Ways of Paradox and Other Essays*. Cambridge: Harvard University Press, 1976.

Crossover Queries

Introduction

Fixed bridges are firmly anchored structures that enable one to travel from one shore to another, whereas pontoon bridges are temporary connections that facilitate movement across a body of water. Cyberlinks arise anywhere and nowhere to create transitory ties joining images, sound bytes, and fragmentary messages. In the essays that follow, the risks and ambiguities, the unstable concatenations of contemporary thought as manifested in many and varied contexts—in the desire for transcendence and in meanings ascribed to corporeality, in critical dilemmas of ethical existence and in the status of philosophical inquiry itself—will be explored as expressions of negation loosely linked in a nexus of crossings.

The philosophy of Hegel describes the emergence of an all-encompassing Absolute that comes into being at the end of history, an ontological and logical vacuum that has sucked into itself all that is and sees itself as having brought to completion the work of historical and philosophical negation, thereby obviating the need for further inquiry into the labor of the negative. Still, one may ask, does not a work such as *Koheleth*, the biblical book of Ecclesiastes, not disclose in a more fundamental and unambiguous fashion the vanity of all things, the existence of a world from which meaning has been drained, thereby exposing the weariness of the world?[1] Without prescinding from the power of *Koheleth* to envision the world as vanity, we may nevertheless concede that Hegelian thought reflects an unending struggle with the negative, not only as intrinsic to each moment of Spirit's checkered history, but as the possibility of the nonexistence of the totality of all that is currently seen as world or as the maximal intensity of disvalue that can be attributed to the world. Still, in the end, is the sublation of the negative, its ultimate overcoming, not intrinsic to each moment of Spirit's history?

In the essays that follow, philosophical accounts of expressions of the negative are seen as a complex of crossings, no one of which is designed to endure but which, taken together, sway in the manner of fragile, loosely linked ropes that connect efforts to overcome manifestations of the negative to claims about its irrevocability. Such analyses need not be seen as signs of a postmetaphysical exhaustion but rather point to the need for further inquiry into theological, ethical, and aesthetic interpretations of negatives. New conceptual challenges to the understanding of negatives cannot be resolved by turning to positivism or linguistic analysis. There are few who today would hold to the narrow view that to be is to be the value of a variable. The limitations of defining analysis as a formal semantics or as the investigation of truth conditions as applied by the natural sciences to their objects of inquiry were already clearly grasped by the early Wittgenstein, who writes:

> At the basis of the whole modern view of the world lies the illusion that the so-called laws of nature are the explanations of natural phenomena.[2]

> People stop short at Natural Laws as at something unassailable as did the ancients at God and Fate. And they both are right and wrong. But the ancients were clearer, insofar as they recognized one clear terminus, whereas the modern system makes it appear as though everything were explained.[3]

Wittgenstein's reservations concerning the usefulness of the method of the natural sciences in interpreting other areas of experience cannot be dismissed, but his disclaimer may not simply be applied, mutatis mutandis, to the rapidly expanding interests of the sciences. What is called for is a reenvisioning of the negative, of the meaning of being and nonbeing.

Should a work that purports to be a philosophical work delving into significations of the negative not disclose its agenda by opening with a preface, a summary statement of the conclusions to be drawn from the arguments that the work expounds? Yet Hegel, who does not shy away from composing prefaces, warns that "whatever might appropriately be said about philosophy in a preface—say, a historical *statement* of the main drift and point of view, the general content and results, a string of random assertions and assurances about truth—none of this can be accepted as the way in which to expound philosophical truth."[4] Philosophy is for him a progressive unfolding of truth, a transformation of the love of knowing into actual knowing. Like Hegel's legendary owl of Minerva that flies at twilight, philosophy is the latecomer that arrives on the stage of history only at the close of an epoch. In sum, the preface to a philosophical work, like philosophy itself, is always already an afterword in that it could not have been written prior to the unfolding of its content, as Derrida has noticed. At the same time, the preface is also a prolegomenon to an always unfinished work, a work in progress. The prefatory remarks of this Introduction should be read in that light.

For Hegel, thought's development skips no steps. As a formative process, thought proceeds in accordance with necessary laws. However, far from appealing to what he regarded as an expression of an empty formalism, the identification of the negative with the falsity attributable to propositions, Hegel's view accords with that of an unlikely bedfellow, Wittgenstein, who asserts: "All propositions of logic say the same thing. That is nothing."[5] Hegel asserts that a regrettable "impatience demands the impossible, to wit, the attainment of the end without the means. . . . But the length of the path has to be endured . . . ; each moment has to be lingered over because each is itself a complete individual shape."[6] The World-Spirit is in no hurry. It has "the patience to pass through these shapes over the long passage of time and to take upon itself the enormous labor of world history."[7] Spirit's trajectory is not one of simple linear progress. Instead, each moment of its history implodes, collapses upon itself through the sheer force of the negative as the work of the understanding. "Death, if that is what we want to call this non-actuality, is of all things the most dreadful and to hold fast to what is dead requires the greatest strength. . . . It wins its truth only when in utter dismemberment it finds itself."[8] Unlike an individual who maintains that "something is nothing or that a proposition is false, and then having done with it, pass[es] on to something else," Spirit is the power that wins its truth only "by looking the negative in the face and tarrying with it."[9]

If Spirit is to tarry with the negative, so that its unfolding is thus contingent upon a continual undoing, can undoing itself, the labor of the negative, ever be undone? Unlike the optimistic philosophies of the Enlightenment that preceded the philosophy of Hegel, post-Hegelian existential thought does not undo or pass over nonbeing but, by focusing on the negative, reverses the injunction of an erstwhile popular song that one accentuate the positive and eliminate the negative. Heidegger and existential thinkers of his generation fasten upon the finality of death, upon facing up to the end. The *Angst* of human existence lived in anticipation of its coming to an end precludes the realization of Hegel's dream of crossing over, the conversion of nonbeing into being. Yet existential thought fails to dismantle the binary oppositions of being and nonbeing or of being-for-itself, the being of the subject, and being-in-itself, the being of things. Rather, it simply attributes primacy to the negative.

Although existential thinkers overturn the popular song's exhortation to accentuate the positive, they are in tune with its proscription not to "mess with Mr. In-between." It remains for postmodern thought not only to persist in tarrying with the negative but also to erect temporary conduits, to "mess with" betweens that lack fixed points of anchorage and that conform not to Hegel's model of mediation but to Nietzsche's vision of the between, "What is great in man is that he is a bridge and not an end: what can be loved in man is that he is an *overture* and a going under. I love those who do not know how to live for they are those who cross over."[10] Still, Nietzsche allows for at least a foothold, which permits the tightrope walker encountered by Zarathustra in his wandering to begin crossing over the void beneath even if, in the end, the walker lurches, and slips into the abyss.

These moments of negation and crossing wend their way errantly into new semantic spaces that can in part be envisaged as "the view from nowhere," Thomas Nagel's name for a centerless and featureless perspective, one that fails to mirror the qualitied experience of physical reality as it is lived by a corporeal subject.[11] Thus Nagel writes: "The physical world as it is supposed to be in itself contains . . . nothing that can appear to a particular point of view. Whatever it contains can be apprehended by a general rational consciousness that gets its point of view from whatever perceptual point of view it happens to view the world from."[12] In ethics as in metaphysics, the attraction of objectivity may lead one to prefer seeing and acting from a detached standpoint. Still, it is impossible to eliminate the subjective point of view. Nagel argues not for reconciling the subjective and objective perspectives, which would be impossible, but rather for learning to live with the discomfort of their difference.[13]

Before turning to the radically shifting perspectives of contemporary existence, to a "now" in flux and likely to dissipate in ongoing works of negation, I shall, in these introductory remarks, consider four interrelated moments of negation as presupposed by the sections that organize the content of this work: inquiries into transcendence, meanings attributable to the body, an ethics of otherness, the comparison of philosophies, and the relation of art to ethics. Consider first the theological moment as configured in Nietzsche's statement, at once amatory and belligerent: "I love him who chastens his god: for he must perish of the wrath of his god."[14] This moment of negation as it might be experienced today cannot be cordoned off from the cataclysms of history. The relation to an unalloyed transcendence can only be expressed in contemporary discourse as an erotics, a hope *per impossibile* to trump these cataclysms, as I seek to show in "Intending Transcendence: Desiring God."

The quest for a predicative language that would supplant the sheer ineffability of the divine name or, in Wittgenstein's phrase coined in another connection, that would show what cannot be said, finds consummate expression in Anselm's ontological argument, as I maintain in "Recontextualizing the Ontological Argument." The attempt to establish God's necessary existence can be seen as the coming to consciousness of the desire for a God who may be invoked in prayer but whose name resists explication. The initial triumph of Anselm's classical refutation of the arguments of the fool who denies God's existence and of the monk Gaunilo who applies Anselm's argument to a lesser entity gives way to the pathos of denial, to a refusal of access to the transcendent other, the ultimate source of joy. Efforts to show what cannot be said in phenomenological terms as a content of consciousness, as the object of an intention, express both a fundamental category mistake and an ineradicable hope.

The second moment is that of nihilatory force exerted in the interest of exterminating whole peoples to whom negative value is ascribed. There is no lack of ingenuity deployed in realizing this aim. Fueled always by an intricate web of cultural, economic, and political concerns, the strategies of annihilation—powerful technologies designed to eradicate a maximum number of persons in a minimum amount of time or, by contrast, a reliance upon simple weapons deployed against populations in impoverished areas as well as the destruction, in such regions, of the conditions that could sustain life—may vary. Elsewhere I have referred to an inclusive complex of the multiple manifestations of this nihilatory process as the "death event," in contrast to local enclaves of destruction or "death worlds," in which immediate qualitative experience is transformed into relations of utility and number.[15] In each case, the historian or observer may attempt to determine the social, political, and cultural circumstances that rendered possible this unmaking of worlds. Yet does observation, in this context, mean a view from nowhere? And is the view from nowhere as the adoption of objectivity, a view that precludes the observer's taking a stand, not itself a moral choice?

In this context, one must advert to the ambiguity embedded in the Hegelian dialectic of negation, in that the sublation of each moment issues in the next stage of Spirit's development—an ambiguity that opens a third moment of negation. In his comments on Adorno's account of the necessity for a negative dialectics after Auschwitz, Jean-François Lyotard takes up the issue of whether Auschwitz is a name for history's nadir moment, one that cannot be overridden, thus bringing to an end the possibility of an ongoing Hegelian dialectic. In contrast to death as the termination of individual existence, are we now in an era "of death without reversal, an end which is simply *the* end," including, in Hegelian terms, the end of the infinite? Are we not compelled to inquire "how can Auschwitz, something thought from the outside . . . (*an sich*), a referent placed only near itself (*an sich*) . . . be interiorized, suppressed as an unmediated position?"[16] Lyotard turns to Adorno's distinction between an "example," whose philosophical function is the illustration of an idea, and a "model," which names "a kind of 'para-experience,'" in which dialectics would encounter a kind of "non-negotiable negative" that would preclude the negation of a negative that would eventuate in a new moment of Spirit's development. In sum, Adorno construes this model as an existential ultimate that cannot morph into a concept.[17]

I would argue that Auschwitz is both a unique event and the name of a chasm that includes in its negativity Darfur, the Sudan, and Cambodia, the nadir events of the recent past and of the present. Can we assume that Auschwitz and subsequent events of mass extermination preclude, on the one hand, the realization of an infinite that ends as an Absolute all-encompassing totality and, on the other, what Hegel calls the "bad infinite," an infinite that presupposes there can be no terminal point, no completion in that there is always another ineluctable object beyond the horizon? According to Adorno, what remains after Auschwitz can only be detritus, waste. In considering the aporias of Hegelian dialectic in this connection, Derrida "risks," as Lyotard puts it, the proposition that Hegel failed to grasp the manner in which machines work, the fact that machines operate on the principle of loss, whereas speculation is, *per impossibile*, "a machine that gains."[18] Would a new understanding of historical reason as thus amended entail the unthinkable conclusion that the losses of nadir events could morph into positive outcomes, just as machines transform loss? Derrida's comment might be viewed as insensitive or frivolous but does in fact highlight the unviability of both the Hegelian speculative model of historical understanding, when viewed as a cumulative process, and the alternative model of a machinic integration already embedded in calculative reason, a model undermined by critics from Wittgenstein to existential and post-structuralist thinkers, including Derrida himself.

If the historian or observer is not to evade the analysis of nihilatory power in its multiple manifestations—mass extermination, artificially created famine, and terror—where is she to station herself in order to avoid the default position, that of the view from nowhere? Is it possible to stand inside these events after the fact by appealing to empathy? To be sure, empathic understanding may be useful as a penultimate strategy, but, at a more primordial level, empathy can be interpreted as an appropriation of the identity of the victim without having undergone her or his suffering. Problematic in still another sense is the historian's assumption through empathy of the identity of those who commit or facilitate committing acts of mass extermination, even in the interest of ascertaining what made these acts possible.

In "The Semantic Spaces of Terror," I consider the new discursive space of Terror as described by Derrida, a space in which, on his reading, technologically sophisticated weapons are deployed in the service of autochthonous and religious interests. It could be argued that this account is simply an extension of what has already been analyzed elsewhere as the degeneration of the meaning of being into an instrumental ontology, an understanding of being as the being of technology. But for Derrida the commodification of those who are members of a group and their depiction as demonic agents opens onto a field of warring sensibilities. Globalization and tele-technoscience, the merger of technology and information, are criticized by the practitioners of terror, who at the same time adopt the strategies generated by tele-technoscience in the interests of a repristinization envisaged in terms of religion and ethnicity. In the same essay, I discuss Dominique Janicaud's analysis of the ways in which the multiple languages of technology and information coalesce to form an overarching language, which (in the manner of Derrida) he calls "technodiscourse," a "rationality run wild" that has triumphed over antecedent modes of experience and is part of an older process, the transformation of knowledge into power. I hope to extend the depiction of the implosion of the rational, as first envisioned by Heidegger and more recently by Derrida and Janicaud, by extrapolating from the domain of information discourse itself a response to these phenomena that may override some of their undesirable outcomes.

The fourth moment of the negative can be seen as "an Ethic of ethics," which is contingent upon the otherness of the other person. As described in the philosophy of Emmanuel Levinas, the other person is given not as a phenomenon but as language, as a proscription against violence and, more radically, as a willingness to substitute oneself for another even in extreme situations where the life of another is at stake. Alterity functions as the ultimate, transcendental condition of ethics. Although the other person in her or his otherness functions as the transcendental condition of ethics, I shall use the lower case *o* when the referent is the human other while reserving the capital *O* for the divine Other. I include some earlier analyses of Levinas's thought not only because I believe that they remain in conformity with an ongoing and expanding body of recent scholarship but also and principally because such accounts must be revisited if recent conceptual innovations that challenge an ethics of alterity are to be understood. There can be no definitive interpretations of Levinas's thought, *ça va sans dire*. Thus, his work—its phenomenological roots, its trumping of metaphysics by an ethics of the other, its simultaneously critical and appropriative relation to Heidegger's philosophy, and its forging of links between Western philosophy and the Judaic tradition—must continually be consulted anew. Fresh challenges to an ethic of alterity—the impact of genetic research upon conceptions of altruism, new approaches by certain economic theories to the ways in which decisions are made, the infoculture as a model for thinking—necessitate fresh responses.

What is more, it might be asked how the generosity spurred by the advent of the other can comport with the notion of a postmodern self, the always already broken subject of postmodern discourse. While endorsing the abandonment of self-interest and the claim that the primacy of the other trumps moral rules, I argue that narratives depicting exemplary lives rather than rules have peremptory power, what J. L. Austin has called perlocutionary force. The lives of saints in many religious traditions may be described as sinful but bear no scars of this primordial postmodern fracturing. Can there be lives that exhibit both the magnanimity encountered in the texts and practices of religious traditions and the antinomian fracturing of postmodernity, what might be called "saints of depravity"? Are such figures not the subject of the fictions of Jean Genet, Jorge Borges, and Yukio Mishima, to name a few? Such saints do not serve as moral paradigms but rather exemplify the struggle to live out conflicting impulses of unconstrained desire and boundless altruism. To be sure, traditional practices of self-discipline may conform to Nietzsche's depiction of ascetic piety as expressing contempt for the body. Yet I maintain that the ascetic innovations of traditional modes of religiosity can change into a contemporary erotics, as Foucault, Deleuze, Kristeva and others try to show.

In his seminal work *Totality and Infinity*, Levinas depicts the moral self as emerging from a relatively comfortable ground of prior lived experience. In "Incursions of Alterity: The Double Bind of Obligation," however, I argue that a psychological brokenness must precede the emergence of a moral field if the advent of the other is to do its work. In this context, I turn to the double bind theory of Gregory Bateson, which depicts the warring imperatives confronted by individuals in childhood. In addition, I point to a formidable psychological barrier to heeding moral imperatives, an obstacle noted by some economists in the context of tracking consumer purchasing habits: the tendency to act in accordance with present satisfactions in preference to postponing satisfaction in the interest of future goods.

The efficacy of alterity as a moral force for Levinas presupposes that the other is a lived body as described by Husserl and elaborated upon by Merleau-Ponty, a body that is vulnerable and experiences pain. In the absence of sensate embodiment, of visceral encounters with the other, is the subject not consigned to the view from nowhere in which neither self nor other can arise as the presupposition of moral meanings? Bodies as they were envisaged in the period between the Renaissance and the nineteenth century could then be thought of as automata, machinelike beings that simulate the motions of living bodies. Jean-Claude Beaune argues that an automaton was understood as having "close links with living creatures in all its different manifestations . . . [imitating] them sufficiently well to generate a gratifying illusion about its own nature." What is more, Beaune contends, automata were often used in "investigating physical functions and providing surgical prostheses—a precursor of organ transplants."[19] Today, he concludes, the line between nature and culture is blurred, so that the automaton exists not only as machine but also as language, the technoscientific discourse that endows those who "know" with power. I would argue further that the longing for enhanced power is manifested in the general culture in the superheroes embodied in robots and action figures. In more sophisticated incarnations, ordinary humans are endowed with vastly expanded powers such as those hidden in and awaiting activation in the seemingly run-of-the-mill father, mother, and offspring in the movie *The Incredibles*.

Evolutionary biology would seem to belong to a sphere of objectivity even more remote from the lived body than that of the automaton. Geneticist Richard Dawkins explains that, according to a gene's eye view of the body, evolution takes place on behalf not of the organism but rather of its genes. Yet what appears to be the objectivity of the gene's eye view as a view from nowhere reflects a covert theological agenda that fissures the narrative of the selfish gene. In "From Neo-Platonism to Souls in Silico," I argue that the gene operates not merely as a force of continuity, the continuity of the species as depicted in "the grand narrative of evolutionary biology," but also may be interpreted as the return of a repressed theological narrative, a replay of the abstract, mathematized model of soul in a tradition extending from Pythagoras to neo-Platonism in which the soul's immortality is contingent upon its existence as number.

A preface cannot end but can only draw to a close as an inconclusive conclusion. As I have written elsewhere:

> Ceaseless talk—talk about genes as the retrieval bins of memory, about DNA as storage space for a world of self-replicating genes that serve as metaphors for the terror we feel before the nihilatory power of incurable disease [and mass extermination]. Talk about the commonalities of culture as linked to the materiality of brain states, about . . . beliefs and practices that transmit residual meanings, traces of a past that cannot be made present. Talk about shapes or moments as nontotalizable wholes and their permeability to one another, allowing them to implode in a nihil that is refractory to conceptual grasp. Talk about the relation of nonphilosophy, the conceptual spaces in which philosophy unfolds, as shedding light on philosophy itself.[20]

How are we to interpret pleasure and pain, flesh and spirit, God and revelation in the context of negatives and of crossing over? In the essays that follow, I have tried not to draw a map that, in postmodern language, precedes the territory but rather to move from island to island in an archipelago of concepts.

PART I

God: Desiring the Infinite

The Reason why God has no name, or is said to be above being named, is because his essence is above all that we can understand about God and signify in words.

. . . [W]e attribute to him simple and abstract names to signify his simplicity and concrete names to signify his subsistence and perfection; although both of these names fail to signify his mode of being, because our intellect does not know Him in this life as He is.

— **Thomas Aquinas,** *Summa Theologica*

God is the shortest distance between zero and infinity in either direction.

— **Alfred Jarry, "Concerning the Surface of God"**

The relation of referent to name is problematic in a unique way when the name of the referent is God. Transcendence may be envisaged as an excess that attaches to notions both of the infinite and of glory in a manner that bypasses the apophatic strategies of mysticism and of negative theology and expresses itself instead as an erotics of transcendence. Languages of art and ethics can become theological languages in which the thought of Husserl, Heidegger, Derrida, Lacan, de Certeau, and Levinas can function as influences and instruments of analysis.

Illustration: Visitors strolling through Christo and Jean-Claude *Gates* exhibit in Central Park, New York. Photograph by Meggie Wyschogrod.

Intending Transcendence
Desiring God

In what may seem a paradoxical claim, Edmund Husserl maintains that the "rich use of fancy" in art and poetry can contribute significantly to phenomenological philosophy conceived as a rigorous science. Phenomenology "can draw extraordinary profit" from the gifts of these arts, which "in the abundance of detailed features . . . greatly excel the performances of our own fancy," as Husserl declares (*Ideas*, 184). In consonance with this claim, it may be useful to turn (briefly) to contemporary Italian artist Francesco Clemente's *Inside/Outside*, an artwork that mimes the apophatic discourse of negative theology in its attempt to render visually that which resists representation, exteriority itself. An agglomeration of fourteen paper panels executed in pastel, watercolor, and ink, Clemente's work depicts a nude male figure behind horizontal and vertical bars, formed by green cloth strips that join the panels. The man's right arm is bent; his right index finger points to his left nostril; his left arm extends to link hands with another outstretched arm, that of a figure whose torso and head lie outside the confines of the work, an absent presence. The left half of the composition is broken only by the omnipresent squares formed by the green bars and by the long branch of a tree, which cuts across the work horizontally and brushes against the man's face. Frowning, the man appears to be inside, behind the bars, viewing the tree, which is outside. Upon closer inspection, inside and outside are indeterminable, continually exchanging places in a dizzying metaphor of immanence and transcendence.[1]

For Husserlian transcendental phenomenology, exteriority, or being that is "outside," is always (and already) being *for* an "inside," as though captured behind the green bars of Clemente's painting, an inside that is "a *self-contained system of Being*, as a system of *Absolute Being*, into which nothing can penetrate and from which nothing can escape" (*Ideas*, 139, emphasis in original). A veritable abyss separates the meanings of consciousness and of reality, Husserl declares. It is a virtual given of Husserl's *Ideas* that the spatiotemporal world has a merely secondary or relative sense in that it exists as being for a consciousness that posits it, that the field of physical nature is to be "switched off," and that what remains is the field of pure consciousness.

But if objects are grasped only as objects for an intending consciousness that reaches toward them and bestows meaning upon them, can there be anything that does not become an artifact of consciousness? Husserl's description of consciousness as absolute suggests that consciousness requires no real being outside itself, thereby vitiating the possibility of an exteriority that transcends the subject. As a philosophy of consciousness, phenomenology must sublate transcendence, for if it failed to do so, it would self-destruct as phenomenology. It would seem that a theology spawned by Husserlian phenomenology must necessarily be an immanentist theology. If prereflective religious experience is invoked to establish the existence of a transcendent object, not only is transcendence subordinated to the subject, but thought returns to a naive empiricism that credits philosophically unclarified experience with providing the warranty for transcendence.

In what follows, I shall argue that, in the face of these difficulties, Husserl attempts to perform the high-wire act of finding a place for transcendence while upholding the primacy of a consciousness that subordinates objects to itself. Thus phenomenology can be said both to succumb to and to elude a conception of being beyond the being of consciousness. Because, Husserl contends, consciousness as intentional bestows meaning, its objects are always (and already) discursive, so that conscious acts may be seen as textual practices. "Phenomenology," Ricoeur succinctly comments, "gambles on the possibility of thinking and naming . . . on that primordial discursivity of each subjective process" as well as on reflection.[2] If phenomenology's claim for the linguisticality of phenomena as constituted by consciousness is warranted, then even the wildest reaches of affect are always already discursive. But a transcendent Absolute that is beyond consciousness necessitates an apophatic theology that may be disclosed as an unremitting yearning *for* an absent Other or as a divestiture of self *on behalf of* an Other who, as Other, never appears. I shall maintain that, in his questioning of the primacy of the transcendental subject and in his description of the desire *for* God, Derrida's account of naming and negative theology is essentially transgressive, an *erotics* of transcendence. When the sheer contingency of fact leads neither to an eidetic science, to the certainty of an eidos that remains invariant through all of an object's variations, nor to an erotic desire for the Other, but rather to an alterity that is beyond consciousness, the way is open for a Levinasian *ethics* of transcendence.

Phenomenology's God

It is by now a truism of transcendental phenomenology that consciousness is intentional, that it points toward objects. A conscious intending act (*noesis*) is directed toward a "something" that is intended (*noema*). A physical or conceptual entity, as the object of an intention, cannot be posited apart from the act that intends it as the correlate of that act. A phenomenological description of intending acts is not to be confused with a psychological description of states of mind. The latter is undertaken from the standpoint of a naive faith in the givenness of the world in its plenary presence, what Husserl designates "the natural attitude," the apprehension of the world as real. Husserl insists that the phenomenological cordoning off of exteriority, of the existence of nature as outside in order to comprehend the being of consciousness, cannot be achieved through an empirical psychology. Only a suspension of the natural attitude, of the belief in the independent existence, the own-being of the world, by bracketing that existence or putting it out of play, assures access to the transcendental structure of consciousness (*Ideas*, 98).

Placing the actuality of the fact-world in brackets is not to be confused with the sophist's denial of the world. As Ricoeur points out, any such misapprehension is laid to rest in *Cartesian Meditations*. "I gain myself as the pure ego with the pure flux of my cogitations," Husserl alleges, so that, far from losing the world that has been placed in brackets, I retain the world as a world-for-me.[5] Similarly, bracketing is not to be confused with a skeptical doubt that is insufficiently radical because it is nothing but a modification of the natural attitude. It is, rather, a strategy that bars one "from using any judg-ment that concerns spatiotemporal existence" (*Ideas*, 100). Nor should bracketing be identified with the abstractions generated by the theoretical inquiries of natural science, in that such investigations transpire within the sphere of the natural attitude. The phenomeno-logical reduction or bracketing of the existing world, the *epoché*, can be viewed as a stratagem designed to outwit the realist illusion rather than to denigrate the world that it cordons off.

"Although we have suspended the whole world, things, living creatures, men ourselves included," Husserl concludes, "we have lost nothing, but have won the whole Absolute Being, which, properly understood, conceals in itself all transcendences, 'constituting' them" within consciousness (*Ideas*, 141). Far from spawning meaningless agglomerations, consciousness constitutes objective unities in every region of being. The modalities of consciousness—perceiving, think-ing, willing, wishing, and the like—constitute or prefigure "all possi-bilities and impossibilities of being" (*Ideas*, 232). Paul Ricoeur cautions, "Husserl will progressively abandon his earlier idealism so that the reduction as a reversion to a monadic ego will diminish to be replaced by a return to the prepredicative experience of the world."[4] Far from impugning the fact-world, Husserl affirms even at the con-clusion of the *Cartesian Meditations* that the phenomenological reduc-tion is undertaken in the interest of accounting for the way in which the world is experienced. Thus, he maintains:

> Phenomenological explication does nothing *but explicate the sense the world has for us all, prior to any philosophizing*, and obviously gets solely from our experience—*a sense which philosophy can un-cover but never alter*, and which, because of an essential necessity, not because of our weakness, entails (in the case of any actual experience) horizons that need fundamental clarification.[5]

Still, in the idealistic transcendental analyses of *Ideas* I, the "feel" of presentness and reality, of lived experience, is subordinated to acts of reflection about them, "acts of the second level" (*Ideas*, 141). Are we then to conclude that, despite shifting emphases, the being of con-sciousness remains absolute being, or are there grounds for maintain-ing that the notion of the being of consciousness can be viewed as itself subordinated to a transcendent absolute?

The paucity of theological reflection in Husserl's published work should not blind us to the importance of his remarks about God in

Ideas I. In a remarkable passage, Husserl asserts that God's absoluteness is different from that of absolute consciousness (*Ideas*, 174). Rudolf Boehm points out that, although consciousness may not require the support of actual beings in order to exist, "it might indeed require being sustained by another being and 'have its source in what is ultimately and truly absolute.'"[6] In an enigmatic statement that, on the face of it, would appear to sanction the primacy of consciousness, Husserl asserts: *"Immanent Being is . . . without doubt absolute in this sense, that in principle nulla 're' indiget ad existendum"* (*Ideas*, 137, emphasis in original). The Latin phrase originates in Descartes' definition of substance as that which requires nothing other than itself to exist.

It could be argued that, in a Husserlian context, the phrase acknowledges a difference between the being of consciousness and that of reality but that, for him, it is the being of consciousness that is absolute. It would then be possible to conclude that absolute consciousness is the sole substance and, as such, is analogous to the being of God. There is, however, room for an alternative interpretation. Just as Descartes does not apply the term *substance* univocally to God and other things, a corresponding disjunction can be detected in Husserl's surprising assertion that God "is an absolute in an entirely different sense than the absolute of consciousness."[7]

In a claim reminiscent of Kant's account of the purposiveness of nature in his third *Critique*, Husserl maintains that an intraworldly teleology may be discerned in organic life and in the development of human culture.[8] But if, as Husserl argues, the governing principle of that order derives from this immanent arrangement itself, world-being is regulated by a principle of internal ordering such that an internal teleological principle would be grounded in the immanence it is intended to explain and thus would be circular. "A world-god is impossible," Husserl says in a note to Section 51 (*Ideas*, 142). Such a god would not be exempted from the conditions governing spatial perception that would hold, "not only for us human beings, but also for [him in that] whatever has the character of a spatial thing, is intuitable only through appearances, as changing perspectively" (*Ideas*, 386).

Husserl asserts that there must be strategies to disclose transcendence apart from those appropriate to constituting thinglike realities. At the same time, phenomenological method cannot circumvent consciousness and still retain its identity as a philosophy of the subject. Although, in the same note in Section 51, Husserl seems unable to surrender the notion that the Absolute is "a research-domain proper to phenomenology" (*Ideas*, 143), his explication of divine transcendence suggests that phenomenology's dependence on consciousness can be bypassed. The Absolute transcends the world in a fashion different from that of the pure Ego, which is given as a unity accompanying all intraworldly presentations, a transcendence in immanence, he contends in Section 58 (*Ideas*, 157–60).[9] In contrast to the pure Ego, through which thought takes place and which radiates through its acts and is united immediately to consciousness, we come across another transcendence, says Husserl, which we know in mediated form. It stands "over and against the transcendence of the world as if it were its polar opposite. We refer to the transcendence of God" (*Ideas*, 157). He speaks of "a morphologically ordered world," which the natural sciences can apprehend, and claims to stand in awe before this extraordinary teleology. He goes on to say:

> It is not concrete actuality [*Faktum*] in general, but concrete actuality as the source of possible and real values extending indefinitely, which compels us to ask after the "ground." . . . What concerns us here . . . is that this existence should not only transcend the world but obviously also the "absolute" Consciousness. It would thus be an *"Absolute" in a totally different sense from the Absolute of Consciousness*, as . . . it would be a *transcendent in a totally different sense* from the transcendent in the sense of the world. (*Ideas*, 153)

It could be argued that, in relating the transcendental absolute to the absolute of consciousness, Husserl simply asserts their disconnection. Alternatively, the question of teleology could be seen as supplying the impetus to transcend phenomenological reflection upon the nature of fact and instead to account for the *order* of the fact-world by positing its grounding in transcendence in what might be seen as a version of standard teleological arguments.[10]

A more nuanced reading than either of these presupposes the inadequacy of a discursive consciousness, one that bestows meaning upon the fact-world, to account for a teleologically driven Absolute. Such an Absolute resists the semiotic pretensions of a language that is adequate to the phenomenological description of the fact-world but is unable to convey in predicative language the being beyond being of God. The being of such an Absolute has traditionally been conveyed in a language of negation, which speaks without speaking, an apophasis to which Husserl does not directly appeal and which derives its semantic power, as Derrida notes, from being "written completely otherwise." The language of negation is often preceded by a rhetoric of exhortation, of utterances addressing, beseeching, cajoling the unrepresentable God in expressions of erotic yearning. The quest for an Absolute whose hyperessentiality is felt as an absent presence demands the rhetoric of apostrophe, of an address to one that remains unseen.[11]

Absolute transcendence, which is disclosed by awe and wonder before the order of the world, can alternatively, Husserl asserts, lead to an ascent from reflection upon the nature of the individual *faktum* to thought about the ultimate purpose of the world, to what Husserl does not hesitate to designate as "value," even if in an unspecified sense (*Ideas*, 158). It is value that drives the quest to grasp the ground of intraworldly order rather than the converse.[12] (Were concrete actuality the causal ground of value, the naturalistic fallacy of a discredited old-style positivism would have been resurrected.) Has phenomenology then given way to axiology?

Far from surrendering the primacy of value, in a remark in the *Nachlass* Husserl subordinates ontology to the Good, maintaining: "The ultimate meaning of being [*Sinn des Seins*] is the Good, and that is the divine activity toward which the All of divine action is directed . . . God as will of the Good is ultimate reality.[13] This remark can be seen as premonitory of Levinas's repeated insistence that the Good beyond being, separate from the totality of essences, is the gift of Greek metaphysics. "The Good is Good in itself. . . . The place of the Good above every essence is the most profound teaching, the definitive teaching, not of theology but of philosophy" (*TI*, 102–3). I shall consider the *Spuren* of a transcendence that is on the way to both an erotics and an ethics of transcendence and for which Husserl's elusive remarks provide a prolegomenon.

The Ineffable Name and the Erotics of Transcendence

Although Anselm's *Proslogion* is hardly a document of negative theology, the entreaties suggesting a lover *in extremis* that precede the ontological argument offer a striking example of the affective tone of the pleas that may introduce such theologizing. "Thy face Lord do I desire . . . where should I seek thee who art absent?" Anselm cries out.[14] It is perhaps no accident that, in what can be seen as an inversion of the plea for the plenary presence of God, Nietzsche's Zarathustra speaks the language of an erotics of immanence that *ab origine* attests the absence of transcendence. Is Zarathustra's ineluctable yearning for eternity, for the ring of recurrence ("For I love you oh eternity"),[15] the erotic prolegomenon to what can be seen as the obverse of Anselm's argument, Nietzsche's celebrated claim that "If there were gods, how could I endure not to be a god! Hence there are no gods. Though I drew this conclusion, now it draws me."[16] Does Nietzsche's "being drawn" not *to* but *by* the conclusion of this argument reflect a solicitation that pulls one toward an absence different from that which is conveyed by the linguistic ruses of negative theology?

The question can be pursued by examining Derrida's account of God's name, an issue of particular interest to him in that terms such as *différance* and *trace* intrinsic to his own work have been identified (erroneously, he believes) with negative theology. Neither a genre nor an art, neither a concept nor a name, the term *negative theology* is used to designate disparate discourses loosely united by the claim that predicative language is inadequate to the beyond-being of God and that only negative attribution can be the preliminary to an intuition of God (*DNT*, 74). It can be objected that negative theology is speech that has no object, speech about nothing. Derrida responds that, in referring to negative theology's object, the objector is caught in the same bind as the advocate, in that she or he speaks simply for the sake of speaking, for nothing. Moreover, according to Derrida, "to speak for nothing is not: not to speak. Above all it is not to speak to no one" (*DNT*, 76). Thus, in considering the *Symbolic Theology of Dionysius*, Derrida suggests that there is something beyond the intelligible itself:

> In affirmative theology the logos descends from what is above downward to the last, and increases according to the measure of the descent toward an analogical multitude. But here, as we ascend from the highest to what lies beyond, the logos is drawn inward . . . [i]t will be wholly without sound and wholly united to the unspeakable.[17]

Derrida notes that Dionysius invokes a secret mystical discourse, on the one hand, and, on the other, a philosophical and demonstrative one. The crossing of these discourses with one another and with that of Derrida suggests revealed and secret messages that intersect and that both must and must not be divulged, a move of discursive assertion and self-divestiture that Derrida calls "denegation," "a negation that denies itself" (*DNT*, 95). Always (and already) dissimulating itself to the other, who putatively shares but cannot share it, the secret is inwardly fractured. Derrida denies that the secret is theological, yet (and this is the point to which we are heading) Derrida avers: "The name of God (I do not say God, but how to avoid saying God here, from the moment when I say the name of God?) can only be *said* in the modality of this secret denial" (*DNT*, 95).

The way in which apophasis is configured, Derrida contends, may rest on sheer autobiographical chance. Challenging Heidegger's obsession with the discourse of Angelus Silesius, who is not the best example of an apophatic mystic, Derrida explains the choice of Silesius as somehow pertinent to Heidegger's life.[18] Nevertheless, Derrida pointedly avoids discussing the apophasis found in the Jewish and Islamic traditions relevant to his own life, arguing that not to speak of them is itself a form of attestation. Yet it is precisely with regard to the missing traditions that one might apply Derrida's term "the logic of the supplement," the hidden presuppositions that drive his analyses, to his account of apophasis and denegation.[19]

Consider first the claim that negative theology's contention that God's excessive being cannot be conveyed in positive assertions tests the limits of language: "Of him there is nothing said that might hold."[20] Derrida fastens upon the exclusionary phrase *sauf le nom* ("except the name") as that which must be rescued and preserved. Although Angelus Silesius uses the term *Eigenschaft* rather than *Namen* in relation to God as pouring himself into creation, with this he means the name of God. What Silesius longs for, Derrida declares, is "to say God, such as he is, beyond his images, beyond this idol that being can still be, . . . to respond to the true name of God, to the name to which God responds and corresponds, beyond the name we know him by or hear."[21]

The work of Silesius as explicated by Derrida both conceals and reveals a crucial theological tenet of rabbinic discourse: the terms used to refer to God, his biblical names, are charged with the utmost sanctity. For the negative theologian, Derrida contends, the name erases itself before what it names, thereby safeguarding the named: "'The name is necessary' would mean that the name is lacking [*il y faut le nom*]. . . . Thus *managing to efface itself* it *itself will be safe, will be, save itself*" (emphasis in original).[22] According to a rabbinic text, those who know and guard, who save the secret name that cannot be pronounced, inherit this world and the next. "He who knows the secret, who is careful of it, who preserves it in purity, is loved by God and esteemed among men."[23] Another text suggests a way in which nondisclosure is also disclosure. When Moses asks God to reveal his sacred name, God replies that he is to be called in accordance with his acts: "When I judge my creatures, I am called Elohim or Judge" (Exod. 22:27); "when I punish my enemies, Lord of Hosts; when I suspend my judgment over man's sin, El Shaddai [Almighty God]; when I sit with the attribute of mercy, I am called the Compassionate One."[24] The name may be written but not read aloud, so that it is as utterance that the name remains secret. Although its thaumaturgical use is feared, the principal worry is that of violating the sanctity of the ineffable name, as attested in the claim "As the sanctification of the name is the supreme virtue or duty, so the profanation of the name is the supreme sin."[25] He who dares to pronounce the name will have no place in the world to come.

A crisis of language bound up with God's name, then, can be found in rabbinic thought, in the apophatics of negative theology, and, to an extent, in Husserl's account of what he acknowledges to be a crisis in phenomenology. This crisis is identified as the possibility of an empty intuition, whose meaning is not borne out by the plenary presence of what is intended. Similarly, apophatic statements announce from within language a forgetting of that which exists, an ontological amnesia that destabilizes the presuppositions of phenomenology itself.

In negative theology, that which is exterior to the apophatic moment, the prefatory address or hymn, saves and protects it in much the same way as the biblical name of God, which is not to be uttered, is protected by substituting the positive enumeration of God's deeds. In a gesture of denegation, the ineffable name that must not be pronounced is negated by the positivity of God's acts, acts that both are and are not who God essentially is. In negative theology, the impossibility of naming God attests to the limit of language in the face of God's hyperessentiality, whereas for rabbinic thought naming the God who cannot be named carries the penalty of irreparable privation, the loss of one's place in the world to come.

Does not the absence of affirmative discourse in effect affirm a nothingness, a void, that suggests atheism? Yet atheism affirms the most ardent desire for God. In an almost priapic surge toward the transcendent Other, the phrase *desire of God*, for Derrida, attests the ambiguity or equivocity of what Derrida calls a double genitive; the force of the preposition *of* suggests that God can become the one who desires, its subject, or the one desired, the object of God's love. In what could be envisaged as a gloss on the ambiguity of inside and outside as depicted in the Clemente work described earlier, the desire of God can mean my desire for the unreachable, transcendent God or *God's* desire for me. "Does it come from God in us, from God for us, from us for God?" But if, as Derrida claims, there can be no determination of self without an antecedent relation to another, "all reflection is caught in the genealogy of this genitive, a reflection on self, an auto-biographical reflection."[26] Thus, in naming the ineffable, God, one is named and the name denegated in an identity that cannot be conferred. But is not the "desire of God" a yearning for the unnameable, a desire for a kenosis that remains impossible, for a transcendence that can only be experienced as a failed immanence?

Transcendence Is Not a Failed Immanence

Can there be a relation to transcendence that resists phenomenology's claims to truth and certainty yet resorts neither to the apophatic stance of negative theology nor to denegation? Such a relation would avoid a desire that succumbs to the allure of its own futility. In desiring otherwise, it would retain the unbridgeable distance of an exteriority that does not cease to call into question the multiple manifestations of immanence.

In the quest for that which remains beyond experience, Levinas is drawn into language that is replete with traditional an-iconic resonances. Critical of phenomenology's privileging of visibility, Levinas maintains that "inasmuch as the access to beings concerns vision, it dominates those beings, exercises a power over them. A thing is given, offers itself to me. In gaining access to it, I maintain myself within the same" (*TI*, 194). Consciousness's reduction of alterity to the same reflects the dominance of thought as grounded in visibility that, in Husserlian phenomenology, reveals itself in intentionality, the directedness of consciousness toward objects as expressed in phenomenology's familiar apothegm: consciousness is always consciousness of. For Levinas, the subordination of the object to consciousness is unavoidable, a necessary condition for cognition and perception. When applied to the other, however, it constitutes an act of primordial violence. As a quest for that which is originary in the knowledge act, phenomenology falls back upon "the substantive, the nameable, the entity and the Same" essential to the construction of truth as determined by consciousness.[27] Nor is the sublation of alterity overcome by philosophies that proclaim the end of metaphysics: "The rear-guard work of this philosophy in retreat consists in deconstructing this so-called metaphysical language, which . . . is neither perception nor science" (*EN*, 78–79).

Despite these reservations, Levinas fastens upon Husserl's use of the term *living* as suggesting an aperture in phenomenology's appeal to the structures of consciousness as the ground of truth and certainty. Husserl's depiction of the prereflective experience of the I breaks into the equanimity of consciousness to awaken it, to rupture its self-presence. The lived that is a "lived for me" is a "transcendence in immanence" that unfreezes the hypostatized subject. This account of the fissuring of self opens the way for describing how the other person "tears me away from my hypostasis" (*EN*, 85–86). The relation of an I to another renders possible an awakening that is a "sobering up," in which the I is freed from its everyday indolence. Yet Levinas maintains that the exploration of the ethical implications of awakening lie outside the scope of Husserlian phenomenology, in that phenomenology's aim is to overcome an epistemological naïveté in the interest of ultimate truth and certainty.

Facing Up

Can there be a given that faces up to phenomenology's model of truth as a sublation of the other by resisting the cannibalization of the other? For Levinas, the face of the other, in showing itself always (and already) as a refusal to be contained in images or concepts, contests the sovereignty of the subject. Even in the contemporary culture of images, each face is never a mere datum of sense. An-iconic, exposed, vulnerable in its nudity, the face "speaks otherwise" than as a visual or tactile sensation. Nor can the face of the other be defined in terms of attributes that set it apart from the self, since comparison depends upon common categories.

For Levinas, the other is higher than the self. "The eye can conceive [the asymmetry between self and other] only by virtue of position, which as an above–below disposition constitutes the elementary fact of morality" (*TI*, 297). Could it not be objected that the entanglement in spatial metaphor renders alterity subject to phenomenological explication? Is Levinas not trapped by the language of description, without which he would fall back into apophatic discourse? "Above" and "below" in this context are not abstractions, as are terms that express value hierarchies: for example, "Magnanimity is better than parsimony."

For Levinas, spatial elevation expresses the pedagogic function of the Other as one's teacher. It is as elevation that the other looms over the self, mandating not only that the self assume responsibility for the other but that it surrender its interests, including its very life, on behalf of the other.[28]

Levinas also describes the other as "an epiphany" given "in expression, the sensible, still graspable, [that] turns into total resistance to the grasp."[29] The face yields itself to sensibility as a powerlessness that fissures the sensible. For Levinas, the other, divested of form, reveals her/himself as a surplus beyond the inevitable stasis of manifestation. But, in a crucial move, Levinas goes on to say: "The face speaks. . . . To speak is before all else this manner of coming from behind his appearance, from behind his form, an opening in the opening" (*DEHH*, 194, my translation). Images must give way to discourse, which now provides the warranty not only for individual actions but for social peace, peace among states. Violence is not a failure of social agreement but rather the result of a collapse of attentiveness to the command of alterity, a command that is an excess of sociality, "a proximity as the impossible assumption of difference . . . as impossible appearance" (*AT*, 138).

In an effort to disconnect the face from its status as a given whose veracity is attested by its perceptible presence, Levinas states that the face is in the track or trace of transcendence. Neither an image nor an intraworldly discursive sign, the trace disturbs the order of the world, means without meaning to mean, "intervenes in a way so subtle that it already withdraws unless we retain it" (*DEHH*, 208, my translation). The trace attests a past that can never be made present, a transcendence that has already passed by. Far from yielding an essence of the human or a universal moral law as a distillate of faciality, the face transcends images, remains exterior to them.

Levinas's shift from image to discourse can best be understood in the light of the biblical suspicion of images as adumbrated in rabbinic thought and Jewish philosophy. Thus Maimonides views the release of a figural imagination required in order to render theological truths accessible as disfiguring those truths through figuration itself. Compelled to account for the use of imagery in biblical discourse, he appeals to a property of verbal utterance, homonymy, in an effort to make sense of the dangerous but ineliminable visibility of the face in connection with God's countenance. If Moses is said to speak to God face to face (Deut. 5:4) and the face is a visible form, does it follow that, because faciality is attributed to God, that God is corporeal?

Maimonides responds by highlighting the ambiguity of faciality and by converting visibility into discourse. There is no doubt that the principal meaning of the word *panim* ("face") is "the presence and existence of a person." When Moses is said to have spoken with God face to face "without any intervening medium," Maimonides, as Levinas will do later, both proclaims and erases the face's materiality by transforming the visible into discourse:

> We read more plainly in another place, "Ye heard the voice of the words, but saw no similitude; only ye heard a voice" [Deut. 4.12]. The hearing of a voice without seeing any similitude is termed "face to face." Similarly in God's speaking to Moses is meant that Moses heard a voice [Num. 7:89]. (*GP*, 13)

It is noteworthy that, for Maimonides, a form of the word *panim* is used biblically to express time long past: "Of old [*le-phanim*] hast thou laid the foundation of the earth" (Ps. 102:25; *GP*, 53). Maimonides singles out yet another biblical meaning of the term *attention and regard*, as in "And a person receiving attention [*panim*]" (Isa. 3:3). This signification is retained in the blessing "The Lord turns his face to thee [i.e., lets his Providence accompany thee] and gives thee peace."[30] This metonymic dissemination of *panim* as signifying unmediated encounter, archaic time, a past that is irrecoverable, peace as the outcome of attention and regard for the person, expands the multiple meanings of alterity.

The Infinition of Transcendence

The surplus of meaning attested by the irruption of the face into the world of phenomena, Levinas asserts, "makes God come to mind" (*EN*, 131). Beyond being, unrepresentable, dazzling in his excessiveness, God singles out the self as responsible for the other. This divine extravagence is conveyed in the term *the infinite*. Understood in a Cartesian sense, the infinite is an idea that exceeds any idea one may have of it, an idea that compels thought to think beyond what it can think. "In relation to what should be its 'intentional correlate', [the idea] would be thrown off its course, not resulting in anything or arriving at an end" ("Transcendence," 156).

For Levinas, thought that occurs within the ambit of fulfillable intentionality is necessarily atheist because it cannot accommodate that which is in excess of itself, the infinite. Levinas is careful to contrast the inadequacy of a thought when understood as a deficit, as the failure of thought to fulfill its intentional aim, from what he calls "the deportation or transcendence beyond any end and any finality; the thinking of the absolute without this absolute being reached as an end" (ibid.). He also avoids thinking the infinite as the aim of a thought to think beyond the boundaries of a given concept in an effort to reconcile the possibility of "the more" to which it aspires with the fullness of the actual (*AT*, 58). Thus Levinas dissociates his view of the infinite from the potential infinite of Kant, who holds that for any finite number of X's selected, however large, there is a number of X's that is always greater. This view of the potential infinite contrasts with Descartes' account of the infinite as actual, which is intrinsic to his argument for God's existence.[31] Inwardization offers no solution to the problem of the excess of the infinite, since the finite would then *(per impossibile)* merge with the transcendent (*AT*, 75). Unlike the face, which remains haunted by a residuum of corporeality, the infinite must be envisaged in a/theophanic terms as other than what could appear.

Although God lays claim to the self, commands that it heed the suffering of the other, God is not to be understood teleologically as the final cause of one's actions. The infinite is, rather, a direction, a "toward-God," as Levinas would have it. Irreducible to the eschatological, which he sees as a yearning for persistence in being, the infinite interrupts the self's anxiety as a being-toward-death by transcending being, an event described by the traditional term "glory" (*EN*, 132). The excessiveness of the idea of the infinite precludes its originating in finite consciousness, so that it owes its impingement upon the self to God. The infinite is not connected to the finite through simple negation, but is rather a being-affected by the other, a relation beyond conceptual retrieval. At the same time, to understand the idea of the infinite as mere uncertainty would constitute a misreading of its irreducible originality (*EN*, 220).

■ ■ ■

If the relation to a transcendent other is one of irreducible exteriority, then Francesco Clemente's *Inside/Outside*, an artwork that is composed of images on linked paper panels and that spatially portrays the reciprocal negation of inside and outside, would seem to have little bearing upon the connection between an actual self and the other, an outside whose transcendence cannot be rendered visible. Yet the work's green bars, which separate and undo the separation of inside and outside, serve to highlight the nude male figure reaching for the hand of the other whose body lies outside the confines of the work and who remains invisible. Beyond concupiscence, each as other to the other is in the trace or track of a transcendence suggested by the proximity of the handclasp, a gesture of primordial generosity that is not a privation of presence but the "more" that lies beyond it. "Transcendence is no longer a failed immanence. It has the sort of excellence proper to Spirit: perfection or the Good" (*EN*, 221).

2

Corporeality and the Glory of the Infinite in the Philosophy of Levinas

In the opening line of Arnold Schoenberg's opera *Moses and Aron*, Moses stammers, "Only one, eternal, thou omnipresent one, invisible and inconceivable," thereby invoking a God who cannot appear, be pictured or mediated through images. The suspicion of theophany echoes a significant strand in Western theological thinking. Yet the lure of theophany, the appearing of God or a god to a human being, persists, as the protest of the Israelites in Schoenberg's opera attests: "To worship whom? Where is he? I see him not" (*MaA*, 61).

How is this conflict to be explicated if, as Levinas holds, God cannot be reduced to fit human conceptions, yet, at the same time, he sees ethics rather than metaphysics to be the discursive ground for theology? What is more, for Levinas, ethics in its primordial sense is to be understood not in terms of right conduct as determined by a moral theory or by social consensus but rather as an imperative that issues from another human being in her or his specificity. The otherness of the other person cannot be sublated and is construed as a species of an-iconic transcendence, which proscribes violence against another and (more strongly) commands one to assume responsibility for the other to the point of being willing to assume the perils of another's life, to become hostage for or to substitute oneself for that other. The submissiveness of the subject becomes, for Levinas, the condition of an ethics that has been theologized and a theology that has been ethicized.

Thus, for Levinas, philosophy must perform the high-wire act of showing how the other can be the determinant of the moral life without rendering the other as a phenomenon, as the sum of her or his properties as apprehended by perceptual or cognitive consciousness. To apprehend the other cognitively or affectively is to traduce the radical character of alterity, the insurmountable difference between self and other. Yet the failure to comprehend the other as incarnate, as a corporeal being subject to suffering and death, a human being in her or his *Leibhaftigkeit*, reflects an inability to grasp the other's vulnerability and destitution, the very source of her or his ethical appeal. If Levinas is to retain the transcendence of alterity while avoiding the pitfalls of noumenality, he must have recourse to phenomena that, as it were, erase their own phenomenality, images given empirically yet apprehended discursively in nonpredicative fashion. The other thus described is seen as a "phenomenon" having perlocutionary force, as demanding a response: the promise on my part to refrain from violence against and to assume responsibility for her or him. Ethics thus understood is prior to ontology, which, for Levinas, is bound up with the arena of freedom in which violence originates, that of history and the state.

In what follows, I shall consider briefly, by way of introduction, why Maimonides and Aquinas thought that sensory images fail to convey the meaning of transcendence and why they thought that, by contrast, intellectual understanding as exhibited in linguistic signs provides a necessary precondition for such apprehension. Levinas will be shown to have appropriated the an-iconicity of this tradition, while departing from its claims that insight into the divine nature can be obtained through rational intuition and inference. I shall then consider the ways in which tensions between corporeality and transcendence as generally manifested in Western theological tradition persist in Levinas's preempting and deconstructing of Husserlian phenomenology. These strains are most obvious in Levinas's description of the human face as incarnating ethical imperatives, but upon analysis they can also be seen when transcendence is troped as trace, the infinite, and illeity. Finally, I shall examine Levinas's use of the expression *the glory of the infinite* and shall argue that it points to a *process* of infinition rather than to a *property* of the infinite.

The Trouble with Images

Consider first Maimonides' description of the fear of images in relation to the unity and incorporeality of the divine nature, elements of which persist in Levinas's thought. So important are these attributes of God for Maimonides that his *Guide for the Perplexed* opens with a proclamation and defense of this idea. Struck by the biblical claim that God makes man in his image (Hebrew *zelem*; Gen. 1:26), Maimonides is driven to reinterpret the term *zelem*, the form or shape of a thing, so as to preclude its applying to anything material. If the form of God and man are homologous and the term *form* entails corporeality, as is generally assumed, then it might be concluded that denying God form and shape entails denying his existence. But, says Maimonides, the Hebrew term *toar* is used for form in its ordinary acceptance whereas *zelem* signifies essence. Thus the "specific form, [is] that which constitutes the essence of a thing, whereby the thing is what it is; the reality of a thing insofar as it is that particular being" (*GP*, 13). Thus interpreted, the biblical depiction of a theophanic event is made to conform to Aristotle's account of human form and that of his Mu'tazilite interpreters: what constitutes the essence of human beings, their form, is intellectual perception. Even when the term *zelem* is used biblically for idols, the context, Maimonides insists, shows that these idols are worshipped because of some idea they are thought to embody. If, however, there should be some doubt as to this univocity of meaning, Maimonides contends that the polysemic character of the term derives from its being a hybrid or homonym. In sum, what humans share with God is divine intellect and not corporeality. Although there is virtually no vestige of Maimonidean rationalism in Levinas's thought, we shall see that Maimonides' an-iconicity persists.

For Maimonides, then, the most serious theological error consists in imputing corporeality to God, an error that undergirds idolatry, the attribution of mediating agency to a particular form that is thought to represent God to his creatures (*GP*, 51–52). These errors are precipitated by the unfettering of a figural imagination that is required by ordinary mortals in order to render theological truths accessible but that disfigures this truth through figuration itself. But figuration does not leave the proscenium quietly, in that Maimonides concedes that prophecy requires the imaginative as well as the logical faculty, even if the rational faculty predominates. More important is Maimonides' turn to the theme of the face in his account of the expression "God's face," given that the face will play a key role in Levinasian ethics.[1] Forced to appeal to homonymy in an effort to make sense of the dangerous but ineliminable visibility of the face in connection with the biblical allusion to the divine countenance, Maimonides sees the face as both visible figure and theological trope.

If Moses is said to speak to God face to face (Deut. 5:4) and the face is a visible form, Maimonides asks, does it follow that because faciality is attributed to God that God is corporeal? He responds by highlighting the ambiguity of faciality and by converting visibility into discourse. On the one hand, Maimonides acknowledges that the Hebrew term *panim* ("face") is principally figural and generally refers to a certain physical part of a human being; on the other, he insists that *panim* has other meanings. A form of the word (*paneha*) connotes anger and is used to refer to God's wrath. But how is the term to be understood when its meaning is clearly "the presence and existence of a person," a corporeal sense that is retained when it is said that Moses spoke with God face to face "without any intervening medium"? Maimonides both proclaims and erases the face's materiality:

> we read more plainly in another place, "Ye heard the voice of the words, but saw no similitude; only ye heard a voice" (Deut. 4:12). The hearing of a voice without seeing any similitude is termed "face to face." Similarly, in God's speaking to Moses is meant that Moses heard a voice (Num. 7:89). (*GP*, 53)

Face to face, Maimonides continues, signals the absence of mediation:

> Thus it will be clear to you that the perception of the divine voice without the intervention of an angel is expressed by "face to face." In the same sense the word *panim* must be understood in "And my face [*panai*] shall not be seen (Exod. 33:23); i.e. my true existence, as it is, cannot be comprehended." (*GP*, 53)

In addition, the term has a temporal signification: "the word is also used as an adverb of time, meaning before. . . . 'Of old [*lephanim*] hast thou laid the foundation of the earth' (Ps. 102:25)" (*GP*, 53).

Maimonides points to yet another biblical meaning of the term, that is, "attention and regard," as attested in: "And a person receiving attention (*panim*)" (Isa. 3:3). Along the same lines, Maimonides claims, "The word *panim* ('face') has a similar signification in the blessing: 'The Lord turns his face to thee (i.e. . . . let[s] his Providence accompany thee) and gives thee peace'" (*GP*, 53). We shall see that the metonymic expansion of *panim* as signifying unmediated encounter, archaic time, and peace as the outcome of attention and regard for the person wend their way into Levinas's text as the relation with the other (*autrui*), a past or archaic time that is irrecoverable, and peace that issues from a social existence grounded in hospitality, welcoming the other.

The insistence upon divine incorporeality is continued in medieval Christian descriptions of divine perfection. I shall not enter into Aquinas's account of God as first mover and as full actuality, in conformity with his Aristotelean perspective. Of importance in the present context is Aquinas's contention that bodies cannot be noble and that God as the most noble of beings cannot be corporeal. Like Maimonides, Aquinas maintains that the biblical claim that humans are made in God's image refers not to corporeal but to intellectual likeness (*ST*, I, 3. 1. O.t.c.). Yet, because for Aquinas knowledge is a kind of seeing, the suspicion of images requires explanation. Rather than appealing to voice or audition, as does Maimonides, Aquinas turns to the mind's eye. For Aquinas, both sensible and intellectual vision require a certain inwardization, "the power of sight and the union of the thing seen with the sight. For vision is made actual only when the thing is seen in a certain way in the seer" (*ST*, I, 12, 2, O.c.t.).

The effort to adjudicate these incommensurables, what is seen and the faculty that apprehends it, raises the related question of outside and inside. In the case of physical objects, only the image of the object can be in the seer, not the object *in concreto*. Intellectual insight grasps intellectual objects in their own-being. But how can intellectual insight comprehend the essence of God, which, in the case of God, is his very existence? The superior cannot be comprehended by the inferior. Aquinas concludes: "To see the essence of God there is required some likeness in the visual power, namely, the light of glory strengthening the intellect to see God. . . . The essence of God, however, cannot be seen by any created likeness representing the divine essence as it is in itself" (*ST*, I, 12, 2 O.t.c.).

Unlike Maimonides, who appeals to metonymic expansion, Aquinas offers something like a phenomenology of double perception, for we shall see God as we see the life of another, as that "which is at once not known by sense, but at once together with sense, by some other cognitive power" (*ST*, I, 12, 3, reply obj. 2, 96). Thus divine presence is known by intellect "on the sight of and through corporeal things," as a result both of "the perspicacity of intellect" and from "the divine glory" that will affect the body after its final renewal. This doubleness and its sublation will be seen in Levinas's account of the face not in terms of an opposition between sense and intellect but rather as an-iconic shape, figuration that erases itself as it is apprehended, and as "expression" that commands me ethically.

Levinas, Phenomenology, and the "A/Theophany" of the Face

The tension between transcendence and the perceivable intrinsic to Husserlian phenomenology, a philosophical approach to which Levinas continually pays critical but appreciative homage, remains relevant to Levinas's own account of the relation between phenomenality and alterity from his earliest commentaries on Husserl and Heidegger to his complex late works on the relation of alterity to sensibility, proximity, and language.[2] Although the motifs through which this relation is interrogated may change, there is no shift in Levinas's thought that might be termed a radical *Kehre*. "Je ne suis pas Heidegger," he insisted.[3] Wary of Husserl's a-historicism, Levinas in his early comments on Husserl's theory of intuition contends that Husserl considers "everything sub specie aeternitatis."[4] Furthermore, if, as Levinas asserts, Husserl's transcendental phenomenology must be understood in terms of ontology, as Heidegger had seen, this claim would render transcendence pervious to ontological analysis and lead to the much-criticized position that God is a being, albeit the highest being.[5] Ontology is not ethics; rather ethics is now metaphysics, a term whose honorific meaning Levinas restores by initiating a supra-ontological metaphysics identified with the Good beyond being in Plato's sense.[6] At the same time, ethics is "discourse with God which leads above being" (*TI*, 297).

The matter is even more complex in that the reciprocal entanglement of phenomenality and transcendence involves the question of what is to count as philosophy. In his first essay on Levinas, "Violence and Metaphysics," Derrida comments:

> The complicity between empiricism and metaphysics [here meaning the rationalist and idealist traditions] is in no way surprising. By criticizing them, or rather by limiting them with one and the same gesture, Kant and Husserl had indeed recognized their solidarity. . . . But Empiricism always has been determined by philosophy, from Plato to Husserl as *nonphilosophy*: as the philosophical pretention to nonphilosophy.[7]

The deficiency attributed to empiricism as philosophy's other "when resolutely assumed" nonetheless contests philosophy. But, Derrida nevertheless concludes, "nothing can so profoundly *solicit* the Greek logos—philosophy—than the irruption of the totally-other."[8] Thus there is no bypassing the logocentrism of philosophy.

In the quest for that which both gives itself phenomenally yet remains exterior to experience, Levinas is drawn into language that is replete with traditional an-iconic resonances and critical of phenomenology's privileging of visibility. Thus Levinas maintains: "Inasmuch as the access to beings concerns vision, it dominates those beings, exercises a power over them. A thing is given, offers itself to me. In gaining access to it, I maintain myself within the same" (*TI*, 194). This dominance is manifested in Husserlian phenomenology in the operation of intentionality, the dynamic directedness of consciousness toward its object as expressed in phenomenology's familiar apothegm: consciousness is always consciousness of. For Levinas, when focused upon the other, the subordination of the object, a necessary condition for cognition and perception, constitutes an act of primordial violence, as if objectification of the other were virtually an act of ingestion.

Because it is both inside and outside the sphere of visibility, the human face resists such cannibalization. In contrast to Nietzschean masks, to Sartre's description of the face as signifying social role, or to Deleuze's account of the face as mechanism and icon of imperialistic force, for Levinas the face of the other is always given as a refusal to be contained in images or concepts. In a culture where one is assaulted by a plethora of images, each face among multiple faces is always already given in its nudity, "the nudity of the absolute openness of the Transcendent" (*TI*, 199). For Levinas, "It is neither seen nor touched—for in visual or tactile sensation the identity of the I envelops the alterity of the object, which becomes precisely a content" (ibid., 194), nor can the other's alterity be defined in terms of attributes that differ from one's own, for such comparison submerges the difference between self and other in common categories.

Yet spatial troping of alterity cannot be evaded: the other is always envisaged as situated higher than the self. "The eye can conceive [the asymmetery between self and other] only by virtue of position, which as an above-below disposition constitutes the elementary fact of morality" (ibid., 297). "Above" and "below" in this context are not abstractions, as, it might be argued, are value hierarchies—for example, courage is better than cowardice. It is as positionally elevated that Levinas envisages the other as one's teacher. Such pedagogy is not maieutic in the Socratic sense, in which case alterity would be a matter for recollection, nor is the truth of the teaching to be found in the unique character of the person of the teacher, as in Kierkegaard's interpretation of the teaching of Jesus. For Levinas, the semiotic properties of language persist in the teaching relation. For him, as for Augustine in the *De Magistro*, the poignant early dialogue with his son Adeodatus (rather than in the more sophisticated philosophy of language of the *De Doctrina Christiana*) linguistic meaning is inseparable from teaching.

Levinas also speaks of the other as "an epiphany," given "in expression, the sensible, still graspable, [that] turns into total resistance to the grasp" (*TI*, 197). The face expresses itself within sensibility but does so as a powerlessness that fissures the sensible. Thus Levinas writes:

> The presence [of the other] consists in *divesting* himself of the form which nevertheless manifests him. His manifestation is a surplus beyond the inevitable paralysis of manifestation. It is that which expresses the formula: the face speaks. . . . To speak is before all else this manner of coming from behind his appearance, from behind his form, an opening in the opening. (*DEHH*, 194, my translation)

It has been argued that not only the face but also Levinas's elaborate accounts of need and enjoyment, developed in Section II of *Totality and Infinity*, affirm exteriority, transport us beyond being, and reflect a break with the consciousness that represents.[9] Thus the face-to-face relation is not the only manifestation of a breach in thought and consciousness. I cannot enter here into complex analyses of the way in which the reductiveness of thought is broken by the challenge to representation posed by lived states that are neither cognitive nor perceptual. But it must be recalled that enjoyment and need, although characterized in Levinas's terms as "innocent," occlude both the rationality required for the implementation of justice, the obligation to all the others, and the self-divestiture mandated by the alterity of the face.

In the light of these various considerations, how is a certain cognitive dissonance already apparent in Aquinas's claim for the existence of "that which is at once not known by sense, but at once together with sense, by some other cognitive powers" (*ST*, I, 11, reply obj. 2) to be resolved? Or, if irresolvable, how are we to make sense of Levinas's positing the face as both epiphany and resistance to any mode of appearing? To resort to claims of primordiality would only be to return to the ontic/ontological distinction of Heidegger and thereby subordinate transcendence to ontology. Husserl's effort to develop "a science of essential Being (as eidetic science) [aimed at] establishing a knowledge of essences and absolutely no facts" (*Ideas*, 40) is equally unhelpful in construing alterity.

Yet phenomenological strategies are not difficult to discern in Levinas's account of the face. Consider Husserl's core claim that the "fact-world" as it is present to us is not to be denied or doubted but placed in brackets, subjected to the phenomenological *epochē*, which "completely bars [one] from using any judgment that concerns spatiotemporal existence" (*Ideas*, 100). The residue of this reduction is pure or transcendental consciousness, which remains unchanged by "phenomenological disconnection." It can be argued that for Levinas the face as percept or image must be "disconnected" from the face as signification, not in the interest of extracting a pure or absolute consciousness, but rather as showing that spatial configurations fail to disclose the meaning of the face, its discursiveness and ethical authority. "Speech cuts across vision," Levinas declares (*TI*, 195).

Although the modern subject is absent in Maimonides, it is tempting to find a precursor for such disconnection in his discussion of the multiple meanings of the face derived through its metonymic expansion and sublation as image. For Levinas, the face disconnected from iconicity is in the track or trace of transcendence. Neither an image nor an intraworldly discursive sign, the trace disturbs the order of the world, means without meaning to mean. "It intervenes in a way so subtle that it already withdraws unless we retain it" (*DEHH*, 208). Far from yielding an essence of the human or a universal moral law as a distillate of faciality, the face transcends images, remains exterior to them.

Claims for phenomenological method in Levinas's philosophy can be misleading if one takes them to imply that to bracket the image and render the face as an-iconic is to cordon off the sheer *existence* of the other, as the existence of the world is suspended in Husserl. In fact, what has been put out of play for Levinas is the ascription of transcendent *meaning* to the image, an anthropomorphism to which Maimonides, following biblical and rabbinic tradition, had strenuously objected. To bracket the *existence* of the other would dissolve the other's corporeality, the source of her or his ethical appeal as finite and vulnerable.

Yet it cannot be denied that substituting discursive signification for images constitutes an etiolation of bodiliness, of the very corporeality that must be preserved in the interest of ethics. A new view of language as itself a kind of embodiment, as so bound up with corpo-reality that it is only secondarily a predicative relation, is required. In contrast to the formal work of language characterized by Levinas as the joining of separate terms in a single theme, language is first and foremost an address, a solicitation by the other, who is "my inter-locutor" and, as such, escapes discursive thematization. For Levinas, language is primarily an interrogatory and imperative relation be-tween persons; both a questioning of selfhood, of what he terms "egoity," and an asymmetrical, authoritative relation of other to self. Levinas concludes that the formal structure of language, even if predicative, "announces the ethical inviolability of the other, and without any odor of the 'numinous,' his holiness" (*TI*, 195). Yet does not a certain sacrality attach to the other's body because it is the body that is prey to violence. Must the other not, in some sense, be her or his body in the manner of not being it, as Sartre might have put it? Thus, for Levinas, the body of the other is flesh and blood, but at the same time it is proscriptive and prescriptive discourse, the prohibi-tion against violence and the prescription of responsibility for another.[10]

Transcending the World

Whereas the phenomenological strategies just depicted may be useful in describing the face that both is and is not a phenomenon, is and is not an epiphany, do these strategies help when God is the object of inquiry? The paucity of theological reflection in Husserl's published work should not blind us to the importance of his remarks about God in *Ideas* I or to their suggestiveness for the Levinasian tropes of the infinite and illeity. In a note to section 51 in that work, Husserl claims that an intraworldly teleology may be discerned, especially in organic life and in the development of human culture, an assertion bound to provoke the question of whether the governing principle of that order can be derived from this immanent ordering itself or must instead be determined by an exterior Absolute. World-being, Husserl contends, must be relative to something more fundamental than any principle of internal ordering, because an internal teleological princi-ple would be grounded in the immanence it is intended to explain and thus would be circular. A world-god, he asserts, is impossible. At the same time, Husserl refuses to surrender the notion that the Absolute is "a research-domain proper to phenomenology" (*Ideas*, 51

n. 143). Although he suggests that there must be strategies to disclose the transcendent other than those appropriate to constituting
thinglike realities that cohere, Husserl asserts that phenomenological
method cannot circumvent consciousness and thereby remains a philosophy of the subject. His theological position would then seem to
be a variant of German idealism and thus of little use in explicating
Levinasian alterity.

Yet the explication of divine transcendence in *Ideas* section 58 suggests that consciousness has been bypassed. In contrast to the pure
Ego through which thought takes place, an Ego that radiates through
the acts of thought and is united immediately to consciousness, we
encounter another transcendence, which stands over and against the
transcendence of the world. As we saw in Chapter 1, Husserl, surprisingly, inquires after the ground of concrete actuality, after an Absolute in a totally different sense from the Absolute of Consciousness
and from the transcendent understood in the sense of the world.

Two points that can be juxtaposed profitably with Levinasian approaches to transcendence emerge from these comments. First, for
Husserl value (in an unspecified sense) drives the quest for the
ground of intraworldly order rather than the converse. Were concrete actuality the causal ground of value, the naturalistic fallacy of
a discredited, old-style positivism would have been resurrected. Second, for Husserl the Absolute transcends the world in a fashion different from that of the pure Ego (*Ideas*, 157). Given as a unity that
accompanies all presentations the pure Ego is, as suggested earlier,
intraworldly, a transcendence in immanence.[11]

To be sure, Levinas avoids value language, because of its Kantian
and Schelerian resonances. "The inquiries of Scheler into the objective world of values proceed from the same inspiration" as that of
Husserl, he insists (*DEHH*, 51). Yet Levinas's claim that the Good
as conceived in Greek metaphysics is separate from a philosophy of
essences suggests the difference between Absolute and absolute consciousness as depicted by Husserl. Unlike need, which is subject to
the dialectic of lack and replenishment, the Good is the object of a
desire that exceeds plenitude. "The place of the Good above every
essence is the most profound teaching, not of theology but of philosophy," Levinas insists (*TI*, 103). In a more Kant-like formulation than
Levinas might want to endorse, Husserl, in a remark in the *Nachlass*,
surprisingly subordinates ontology to the Good. He writes: "The ultimate meaning of being [*Sinn des Seins*] is the Good, and that is the
divine activity toward which the All of divine action is directed. . . .

God as will of the Good is ultimate reality."[12] Despite these tentative moves toward both the Good and radical transcendence, from Levinas's perspective Husserlian phenomenology can be seen to founder. If it ceases to be a philosophy of consciousness, it self-destructs as phenomenology; if, per contra, it remains phenomenological, it sublates transcendence.

For Levinas, one reason for this failure is reflected in phenomenology's incapacity to cope with an excess or surplus of signification. Mystical inwardization offers no solution to the problem of excess, since it can only be envisaged as a merging with the divine through interiorizing the Other. Instead, Levinas proposes a thought that recognizes its failure as thought by trying to think an ideatum that exceeds any idea that consciousness may have of it. Such is the Cartesian idea of the infinite. This idea "would somehow think beyond what it thinks. In relation to what should be its 'intentional correlate,' it would be thrown off its course, not resulting in anything or arriving at an end" ("Transcendence," 156). Levinas is careful to distinguish between the failure of a thought to fulfill its intentional aim and what he calls "the deportation or transcendence beyond any end and any finality; the thinking of the absolute without this absolute being reached as an end" ("Transcendence," 156). Thought that occurs within the ambit of an intentionality that can be fulfilled is necessarily atheist because it cannot think what is in excess of itself, the infinite. Unlike the face, the infinite must be envisaged as altogether other than that which appears and thus in a/theophanic terms. Such nonthought is the awakening of a psychism, an affectivity that must be distinguished from Heidegger's account of *Jemeinigkeit*, which is bound up with Dasein's death, an intraworldly event (ibid., 158).

Yet, contrary to what appears to be an a/phenomenological theology, Levinas's assertions about the nonappearing of the infinite are belied by a remarkable passage in the late (1984) essay just cited. Phenomenology is reintroduced both as a methodological safeguard against the loss of discursive meaning and in the interest of retrieving the "interhuman horizons" from which discourse emanates. Levinas writes: "The human or the interhuman intrigue . . . is the necessary 'mise en scène' from which . . . abstractions are detached in the *said* of words and propositions . . . an intrigue [that is] the fabric of ultimate intelligibility" (ibid.). In what seems to be an extraordinary volteface, the Husserlian notion of horizon is revived but it is now the staging for quite different concerns. The infinite remains an-iconic, but the thought of the infinite is realized a/conceptually in the ethical relation.

The Ancient of Days

The Maimonidean account of the face as a *zelem* or sign of transcendence has already been noted. For Levinas, Maimonidean epistemology would necessarily be seen as a return to a philosophy of representation, so that the manner in which transcendence and faciality are linked must be thought afresh. Turning to the notion of trace, Levinas describes the face as in the trace or track of a third (*DEHH*, 199). The notion of trace is invoked in part to elicit the time scheme of alterity, a time that cannot be made present, because presence belongs to the order of representation. The time of the trace can be uncovered by uncovering the way in which the trace incises itself into an order from which it must remain absent. Recall that the trace "means" by disrupting the order of the world in the way, as Levinas would have it, that the perfect crime destroys the trail that leads to its perpetrator. To leave a trace is "to pass by."

An imperfect analogy may be drawn with Peircean indexicals, signs that lose their role as signs if their objects are withdrawn but do not lose their sign-character in the absence of an interpretant or concept. In a graphic depiction, Peirce likens an indexical to "a piece of mould with a bullet hole in it as sign of a shot; for without the shot there would have been no hole; but there is a hole there, whether anybody has the sense to attribute it to a shot or not."[13] For Levinas, to be sure, the trace leads back to the absent object, one that can never be made present before consciousness and that cannot be made to conform to the time scheme of memory and representation (*DEHH*, 200). The primordial trace belongs to an archaic past or, even more radically, *is* the very passing toward an irrecoverable past "more distant than any past and than any future" (ibid., 201). Recall that, according to Maimonides' etymological tracking of the word *panim* ("face"), a form of the word is also an adverb of time (*le phanim*), meaning before in the sense of a past as ancient as the time of creation that can never be made present through memory or inference. For Levinas, the face is "read" as freeing or absolving one from the time scheme of everyday life and as time's giving way to a new time of requirement and obligation, the absolutely archaic time of the absolutely transcendent. If the time of transcendence is a past that cannot become present, it can be argued that, for Levinas, eschatological time does not in a key respect differ from the archaic past, so that past and future are nondifferent, a problem that lies beyond the scope of the present paper.

Because the pastness of the face can never be rendered visually or notionally present, Levinas avoids the iconic resonances of Maimonides' *zelem elohim* as well as those of Aquinas's *imago dei*. He refers instead to illeity as the origin of the other's alterity. He writes: "God who has passed is not the model of which the face would be the image. To be in the image of God does not mean to be the icon of God but to find oneself in his trace." Levinas concludes that to move Godward, as it were, "is to go toward the others who are held in the trace" (ibid., 202).

By resorting to the third-person pronoun *il* rather than to *tu*, the French for "Thou," Levinas eschews the language of intimate relation, thereby distinguishing himself from the interpretation of the divine/human encounter as depicted by Martin Buber. In the intimacy of relation, the radical transcendence of the other gives way to a between that is the space of dialogue and that for Buber is, as it were, the playing field of religious encounter. What is more, the time scheme of relation is that of an eternal present rather than that of an irrecuperable past. Bypassing the language of encounter, Levinas refers to what signifies supra-ontologically as enigma.[14] Having neither the transparency of a problem, a puzzle that lends itself to possible solution, nor the opaqueness of mystery (Gabriel Marcel's terms), the enigma signifies in the mode of uncertainty. "Perhaps is the modality of an enigma, irreducible to the modalities of being and certainty." Issuing from illeity, "enigma is the way of the Ab-solute, foreign to cognition . . . because it is already too old for the game of cognition . . . [and] imposes a completely different version of time" ("Enigma," 75). Levinas adds that the movement of going beyond being toward the immemorial past is called the idea of the infinite, an "infinite that is an unassimilable alterity, a difference and absolute past . . . with respect to everything that is contemporized with him who understands" (ibid.).

Levinas's philosophy of religion may be viewed as a meditation upon the reciprocal relations of enigma, illeity, and the idea of the infinite, as brought together through a past that can never be made present. To understand these terms in conjunction with traditional concepts would go against the grain of the a/conceptual interpretation mandated by the text. Yet is it not possible to think of epistemic, ontological, and axiological approaches to transcendence as being in the trace of enigma, illeity, and the infinite, not as equivalences of the latter but rather as approaches placed under siege, as it were, by these Levinasian tropes?

Incarnation and the Glory of the Infinite

For traditional philosophies of religion, the divine/human relation may be depicted as requiring the transfiguration of corporeality such that divine glory is the agent and the glorified body the result of this transformation. Recall that, for Aquinas, divine presence is known by intellect "on the sight of and through corporeal things," as a result both of "the perspicacity of intellect" and from "the divine glory" that will affect the body after its final renewal. For Levinas, glory disrupts the cognitive subject, transcends its intraworldly imbrication in facts and states of affairs, and opens subjectivity to an excess of Goodness that exceeds intellectual comprehension.

In a surprising move, Levinas adopts the language of glory to describe not the apprehension of divine presence but rather the suspension of the conatus to know or do, to become pure receptivity or passivity, a subject who places her or himself at the disposal of the other. "Glory is but the other face of the passivity of the subject," he insists (*OB*, 144). Yet far from embodying an intellectual vision in the Thomistic sense, the subject is "a seed of folly, already a psychosis" (*OB*, 142). Open to the point of total defenselessness, the subject who is for another is described as wholly and unreservedly sincere. Unlike Sartre, for whom sincerity is in bad faith because it imagines that it can, *per impossibile*, be in good faith, for Levinas sincerity is incapable of dissimulation, scandalizes in its assumption of limitless responsibility.

But the passive subject runs the risk of pride in its very passivity, so that passivity reverses itself and becomes active. Thus the subject must remain vigilant, redouble its passivity such that no act could arise from it. Subjectivity must give itself as Saying, by which Levinas means discourse prior to actual speech, to predicative language or to essence, the precondition that makes possible the subsequent thematization of language in what is termed "the said." Saying points to the glory of infinity, a glory that resists phenomenality, an entrapment in immanence. The glory of the infinite leaves the subject no place to hide. The evasion of responsibility described by Sartre in the context of politics is rendered moot before the infinite. On the one hand, the glory of the Infinite traumatizes egoity, expels the subject from itself as self-presence; on the other, glory is the outcome of that trauma, the willingness of the subject to substitute him/herself for another. "The anarchic identity of the subject," says Levinas, "is flushed out without being able to slip away" (*OB*, 144). The one who, in self-giving, says to the other, "Here I am," placing her/himself at the other's disposal, bears witness to the infinite. By intertwining transcendence and immanence, Levinas is able to assert: "The Infinite does not appear to him that bears witness to it. On the contrary, the witness belongs to the glory of the Infinite." Yet he goes on to say, "It is by the voice of the witness that the glory of the Infinite is glorified" (ibid., 146). In a movement of reversal in which outside becomes inside, Levinas claims that the exteriority of the infinite is interiorized, rendered subjective, a move that would appear to endorse the inwardization he elsewhere roundly condemns as mystification. But Levinas sees no contradiction: the infinite is an outside that maintains its exteriority, even when inwardized, in that glory persists in the internalized infinite as disrupting thematization and "giving sign" to the other. In a visual metaphor rare in Levinas's accounts of transcendence, the glory of the infinite is described as dazzling and arousing adoration ("Transcendence," 157). One might ask whether the glory of the infinite is not a mere pleonasm, in that glory adds nothing to the infinite, to which nothing *could* be added. But if glory is Saying, substituting oneself for another, taking responsibility for the other, proclaiming peace or proscribing violence, and if infinition is this process, as Levinas thinks, then glory is the dynamism of the infinite.

3

Postmodern Saintliness
Ecstasy and Altruism

What must saintliness be if we are to think of it as postmodern? Does the term *postmodernism* not refer to a dizzying array of ever-shifting significations attributable to aesthetic styles and cultural practices? I shall focus upon postmodernism as a revolt against modes of rationality that make foundational claims, that is, as an attack upon what Jean-François Lyotard calls "grand narratives," by which he means comprehensive epistemological schema, as well as all-encompassing theories of emancipation. In preference to the logics of modernity in their idealist and empiricist expressions, postmodern thinkers embrace what I should like to call an epistemic erotics, one in which desire is both a critical instrument and a means of production.

As a social and cultural practice, postmodernism can pit social epistemology against commonsense arguments that endorse altruistic action. By highlighting extreme situations in the twentieth century, it brings into high relief the contrast between the radical altruism of those who place themselves at the disposal of the other, become hostage to the other, and those who respond with tepid benevolence or, worse yet, contribute to harming others.

Three charges have been leveled against postmodernism: the first is that it attacks the lawful; the second, that it assaults the past; and the third, that it unmakes the subject or self. Critics of postmodernism argue that in unburdening itself of nomological structure it has thrown away morality, that in shedding the past it has created a historical vacuum, which totalitarianism can occupy, and that in attacking the self or subject it has opened the possibility for an abuse of the other because there is in *sensu strictu* no other and no self to be held responsible. Is postmodernism not an expression of moral decadence rather than a solution to the problem of decline?

Consider postmodernism's antinomianism, its attack on the lawful. Some postmodernists hold thought to be captive to a politics that shapes it, so that thought qua thought is discredited when one rejects the politics in which it is embedded. This is stated in an extreme form by Deleuze and Guattari: "Thought as such is already in conformity with a model that it borrows from the State apparatus, and which defines for it goals and paths, conduits, channels, organs, an entire *organon*" (*TP*, 374). Behind this critique is the historical example of the radical injustice of National Socialism and what Deleuze and Guattari believe to be elements of fascism that infiltrate many contemporary states. "From thought to *l'univers concentrationnaire*" appears to be the political motto of those who see in the old metaphysics an urgent need for a new politics.

Less radical is the notion that thought qua thought is "legitimated" but separated from morality, and the latter cordoned off as undesirable. Thus Peter Sloterdijk writes:

> Under a sign of the critique of cynical Reason, enlightenment can gain a new lease on life and remain true to its most intimate project: the transformation of being through consciousness. To continue enlightenment means to be prepared for the fact that everything that in consciousness is mere morality will lose out against the unavoidable amoralism of the real. (*CCR*, 82)

Both types of antinomianism, that of Deleuze and Guattari and that of Sloterdijk, are manifestations of the will to ecstasy, both texts the work of postmodernism in its empirical, ecstatic form. The will to joy, the "transformation of being through consciousness," is, for Sloterdijk and Deleuze and Guattari, the "telos" of metaphysics. Joy is to be enhanced by contributions from the arsenal of modernism, so that the machinic is harnessed to the flesh. Such ecstasy is expressed, for example, in the new worldwide culture of music—rock, new wave, and their successors—in which the body as a whole is both sensorium and medium for aesthetic expression. I have argued that Deleuze and Guattari's antinomianism derives from an account of desiring production that conceals a metaphysical monism beneath the differential and pluralistic character of their version of the real. I shall not go over this ground again, except to notice that the single-minded quest for ecstasy by way of a hidden monism is bound up with a coercive seam in the otherwise an-archic postmodernism of Deleuze and Guattari.

Sloterdijk's antinomianism results not only from a broken meta-physics but also from a broken politics, in that two quite different and opposing political wills are the starting point of his work. On the one hand, there is the postmodern expression of the will to joy de-rived from Nietzsche; on the other, there is as the work's immediate backdrop, the historical experience of National Socialism, which Sloterdijk unequivocally rejects. His use of Nietzsche, which stems from the first consideration, is modified by the second. "It was per-haps Nietzsche's theoretical recklessness that allowed him to believe that philosophy can exhaust itself in provocative diagnoses without . . . thinking seriously about therapy" (CCR, 206).

Yet is there not a danger in the fact that postmodernism draws upon the immediate past? And once "morality" has been repudiated and eclecticism enjoined as a principle of selection, does not a strange contiguity and juxtaposition of elements become likely? Sloterdijk's repudiation of National Socialism is strongly voiced in his work. It is hard to imagine a more forceful expression of revulsion than his endorsement of Adorno's remark "All culture after Auschwitz, in-cluding the penetrating critique of it, is garbage" (CCR, 287). Yet a quasi-unconscious deployment of a Fascist detritus fissures this criti-cal discourse.[1] In the context of a discussion of Hitler's SS as Death's Head (Todtenkopf) units, for example, he writes:

> Fascism is the vitalism of the dead . . . embodied in [Western culture] in vampire figures that, for lack of their own life force, emerge as the living dead among the not yet extinguished to suck their energy into themselves. Once the latter are sucked dry they too become vampires. Once they become devitalized they crave the vitality of others. (CCR, 286)

Does the contagion of vampirism spread to its victims, so that all become vampires? Does Sloterdijk know that vampirism was attrib-uted to Jews, and does he intentionally reverse this discourse by at-tributing it to the SS? If so, how can one explain the contagion that allows the "disease" to be attributed to its victims? Who are the vic-tims? People in general, the German populace, which accepted Na-zism, the victims of the SS? The ambiguities of Sloterdijk's discourse persist within the ambit of his broader quest for ecstasy.

Ecstatic postmodernism's ambiguities arise in part from its failure to go deep enough and in part from its wresting from the ruins a metaphysics that will allow for the return of an all-encompassing unity—not, of course, without first paying homage to topographical difference (Deleuze) or the "kynical" absurd (Sloterdijk). It is noteworthy that there is no mention, critical or otherwise, in Sloterdijk's work of the discourse of alterity, beginning with the dialogical philosophies of Martin Buber, Eugen Rosenstock-Huessy, and Gabriel Marcel, or of the recent analysis of this tradition by Michael Theunissen.[2] Suffice it to say that ambiguity pervades the discourse of postmodern ecstatics insofar as alterity remains an absence that is absent from this discourse.

Julia Kristeva's work is especially disquieting in this regard. Repelled by National Socialist discourse, she is nevertheless led by the ecstatic, empirical thrust of her thought to bring this discourse into closest contiguity with the language of ecstasy or *jouissance* in a way that ultimately renders it nearly impossible to discriminate between them.

Rejecting the inside/outside and self/other dichotomies, Kristeva develops a phenomenology of the abject, a new psychological type that experiences itself as the discarded refuse, the trash, of the psyche. Neither an object (objects provide a locus for the establishment of homologous meanings) nor an other (others flee signification altogether), Kristeva's abject is a liminal being. "What is abject, the jettisoned object, is radically excluded and draws me towards the place where meaning collapses" (*PH*, 2).[3] Thus, for example, the infant who rejects its food as separating it from its desire for its parents identifies with the loathed object, spits it out, and in ejecting the food ejects itself (*PH*, 3). It will, Kristeva contends, continue to see itself as something loathsome because the ego and the superego have driven it away. Hounded into exile, as it were, "from its place of banishment, the abject does not cease challenging its master. Without a sign it beseeches a discharge, a convulsion, a crying out" (*PH*, 2). It is not difficult to interpret saintly anorexia, as described by Donald Weinstein and Rudolph M. Bell, as a version of saintly abjection. The saint can be viewed as an abject, loathsome to herself/himself but taken up into the compensatory love of God. This interpretation would reduce the role of alterity, the appeal of the other's destitution in saintly life, to an endless quest to overcome abjection.

Kristeva argues that in abjection a certain uncanniness appears. It comes to acquire independent existence, whereas its origin is forgotten. "[I]t harries me as something radically separate, loathsome. Not me, not that. But not nothing either. A weight of meaninglessness about which there is nothing insignificant and which crushes me. On the edge of non-existence and hallucination" (*PH*, 2). Compounded of Kierkegaard's dread as well as Freud's and Heidegger's *Unheimlichkeit*, Kristeva's uncanniness nevertheless differs from uncanniness as conceived by any of them in that the abject's lack is not allowed to subsist. Thus, in her interpretation of Freud's famous case of little Hans, no sooner does the child recognize the phallic lack of his mother and perhaps himself than it is replaced with the horse, "a hieroglyph having the logic of metaphor and hallucination" (*PH*, 35). Little Hans creates, in the manner of the abject, what is absent. The principle of hieroglyphic substitution opens the possibility for "the subject of abjection" to develop a language of her/his own and, as such, to be "eminently productive of culture. Its symptom is the rejection and reconstruction of languages" (*PH*, 45).

Abjection challenges theories of the unconscious that are sustained by negation. The abject, unable to locate herself/himself, unsituated, self-exiled, becomes a "deject." Like Deleuze's nomad, Kristeva's abject asks not "Who am I?" but "Where am I?" and, like the schizo-revolutionary, is "a deviser of territories" (*PH*, 8). To be sure, for Kristeva it is "a space that is never *one*, nor *homogeneous* nor *totalizable*" (*PH*, 8), a place of exclusion upon which the abject/deject will live her or his *jouissance*. Despite this affirmation of difference, Kristeva has strayed onto the pleasure plateaus of Deleuze and Guattari, onto the territory of a body without organs, a body without alterity which, on the one hand, is declared to be nontotalizable but, on the other, is the hypostatic pleroma of *jouissance*. This homogeneity is attested in her treatment of the other, that other who no longer has a grip on the stray: the abject/deject is an *Auswurf* (my term), a castaway, which enters "an abominable real . . . through jouissance" (*PH*, 9). The *jouissance* of abjection is without alterity, the ecstasy that comes from a repeated iteration of self-loathing. Like the other empirical ecstatics, Kristeva's is a broken discourse, one in which the plenum becomes not a nihil but the abject's sick and sickening plane of *jouissance*. The abject, repugnant to others and having no "clean and proper" self, replaces the desired Other with internal fluids such as urine or blood (*PH*, 53). An older phenomenology of qualities — Sartre's analysis of the sticky, for example — is now applied to the abject's plane of ecstasy.[4]

Kristeva relates this analysis of psychological abjection to the history of religions, which she interprets as a nexus of collective expressions of abjection — paganism or Greek religion, Judaism and

Christianity each having its own means of purifying the abject (*PH*, 17). Mark C. Taylor observes that her analysis "recalls Hegel's tripartite interpretation of religion."[5] Unlike in Hegel, however, in Kristeva the dialectical relation of Western religious patterns does not culminate in their resolution:

> Advancing from the Greek, through the Jewish, to the Christian, the sacred is transformed from exteriority to interiority. While the Greek suffers the sacred from without and the Jew encounters it in and through willful transgression, the Christian experiences the sacred as an outside that is inside, forever faulting his identity.[6]

For Kristeva, arguing against Hegel, the tension between Greek and Jew is not reconciled in Christianity. The Hegelianism rejected in the irreconcilability of religious oppositions reenters through the backdoor in Kristeva's understanding of the historical route taken by abjection. Thus, she maintains, the move from a naive and unmediated paganism, matrilinear in character, is succeeded by biblical Judaism's fear of a matrilineal power that could threaten the paternal Law and its distribution of the categories of pure and impure (*PH*, 91). What is extruded, the maternal, does not disappear but builds a victimizing and persecuting machine by ascribing sanctity to a people and segregating it from the nations of the world (*PH*, 112). The theme of exclusion is further elaborated in the Christian conception of sin and retribution, in which the righteous are cordoned off from the sinners and the whole played out as a scenario of eternal bliss and eternal punishment. This, in turn, leads to the "final" stage of Kristeva's dialectic: "the catharsis par excellence called art," which purifies and is "destined to survive the historical forms of religion" (*PH*, 17). Sin, Kristeva claims, is transcended when, as Nietzsche revealed, it becomes integral to the beautiful (*PH*, 122).

Although Kristeva's discourse breaks with Hegel on the matter of the dialectical sublation of religious moments, she replicates Hegel's ordering of Western religions. In his analysis of Hegel's early theological writings, Taylor shows that, for Hegel, Old Testament religion is not merely dialectically overcome but despised as representing the nadir of Spirit. Hegel declares: "How were [the Jews] to recognize divinity in a man, poor things that they were, possessing only a consciousness of their misery, of the depth of their slavery, of their opposition to the divine?"[7] Yet, for Kristeva, because abjection is subversive there is a certain *pli* or fold in her analysis that distinguishes it from the early Hegel's description of Judaism as the religion of stones and fecal matter.[8] Despite this difference, Kristeva writes:

> In opposition to Apollonian . . . Greek corporeality, flesh here signifies according to two modalities: on the one hand, close to Hebraic flesh (*basar*), it points to the body as eager drive confronted with the law's harshness; on the other, it points to a subdued body, a body that is pneumatic since it is spiritual, completely submersed into divine speech in order to become beauty and love. (*PH*, 124)

Biblical monotheism, argues Kristeva, is to be exorcised by a Christianity that is the last stage before the *jouissance* of aesthetic quietism.

There is in this account a forgetting of postmodernism's perspectivalism. Kristeva fails to notice that, although Exodus, for example, may have been interpreted by classical Christianity through the symbolics of prefigurement, for Jews it is an epic of freedom, and, to a considerable extent, has become so for Afro-Americans, against the ground of a quite different metaphysics.

The matter is even more complex, because Kristeva goes on to declare that one of Christianity's insights is that both "perversion and beauty" belong to the same libidinal economy. It would seem that, for Kristeva, the multiple modes of expressing abjection are determined not by moral concerns when these concerns are proscriptive but, as in Genet, through transformation into beauty: "sin is the requisite of the Beautiful . . . the Law of the Other becomes reconciled with Satan" (*PH*, 122). Not the surrender of nomological discourse to the discourse of the Other but rather the *aestheticization* of the Law is, for Kristeva, therapeutic, both at a psychological and at a metaphysical level. The joker or wild card (Derrida) and the simulacrum (Deleuze and Guattari), which might be invoked as tropes for the saint as quick-change artist of social and personal transformation, could be borrowed by Kristeva to describe the being that belongs to the Other. But the implication to be drawn from Kristeva's account of the Other is that the Other is a floating signifier to be transformed into beauty. Her discussion of the abject is a double discourse: an explanation of abjection in its many forms but also a subtle endorsement of it through a certain break in the discourse of abjection. This manifests itself in a particularly puzzling way in her extended analysis of Céline.

Céline's anti-semitism, and Kristeva's treatment of it, is an exceedingly complex matter, and my remarks will bear only on its relevance for the problematics of saintly life. There is, on the one hand, Kristeva's exposure of Céline the "Fascist ideologue," who rages against Jewish monotheism and displaces this by fascist mystic positivity. And yet Kristeva, through an almost invisible conceptual slippage, avers: "It is impossible not to hear the liberating truth of [Céline's] call to rhythm and joy, beyond the crippling constraints of a society ruled by monotheistic symbolism and its political and legal repercussions" (PH, 179). To be sure, "the liberating truth" is bound up with "the deadliest of fantasies" (PH, 174), as Céline's pamphlets show. Yet she asks:

> Do not all attempts . . . at escaping from the Judeo-Christian compound . . . to return to what it has repressed . . . converge on the same Célinian anti-Semitic fantasy? And this is so because . . . the writings of the chosen people have selected a place, in the most determined manner, on that untenable crest of manness seen as symbolic fact—which constitutes abjection. (PH, 180)

The entire discourse of the chapter "'Ours to Jew or Die'" is written with an abhorrence of fascism that is at the same time a lure, a willing subjection to its seductive power that not only discloses it but speaks with pleasure its transgressive and unspeakable discourse through the mouth of another.

Yet it could be argued that a concept of saintly existence shows itself in Kristeva's work apart from her analysis of abjection. Lacan, she insists, connects saintliness to the psychoanalyst (PH, 27), the witness to abjection, to its decoding, and to its cathartic explosion in the patient. If this is so, a further question must be asked: "Who is the analyst?" Not the psychoanalyst but the writer of genius is the "master" analyst, who reaches the point where writing transcends itself: "the sublime point at which the abject collapses in a burst of beauty that overwhelms us—and that 'cancels our existence' (Céline)" (PH, 210). It is the writer, Céline, who appropriates the discourse of abjection in its most violent form and who transforms it into beauty.[9]

It is not inapposite in the context of Kristeva's transcendence of abjection through its aestheticization to recall Kierkegaard's admonition to envision existence as a starting point to "reason from existence not towards existence, whether moving in the palpable realm of fact or in the realm of thought" (*PH*, 31). The consequences of this aestheticization for the existence of the other cannot be ignored, since abject/deject is not only "a hieroglyph" marked by the sign of negation but a flesh and blood existent, for whom this negation is nihilation.[10] To bestow a shadowy existence on the other is to exert the power of negation.

Kristeva's docetic side, her failure to treat the other as a creature of flesh and blood, leads indirectly to a certain general inattentiveness to the distribution of discourse, to the question "Says who?," the liberating question of postmodernism posed compellingly by Foucault and Sloterdijk, among others. She explicates the abjection of paganism, Judaism, and Christianity and the abjection described in Céline's fascist idiolect but forgets that men and women who wield or lack power, who kill or are killed, are both the objects of these discourses and their controllers. In the context of contemporary history, to be an abject of another, not least an abject in the writing of Céline, is to be implicated not in a speculative but in an actual chain of death.

The preference for a joy beyond pleasure, for an ecstaticism that is different from solicitude, shows itself elsewhere in Kristeva's work in her preference for the madonnas of Giovanni Bellini over those of Leonardo Da Vinci on the grounds that, in the distanced look of Bellini's Virgin, "unlike the . . . solicitude in Leonardo's paintings . . . [there is] ineffable jouissance." It seems that there is in Bellini's madonnas "a shattering, a loss of identity, a sweet jubilation where she is not" (*DL*, 247).

The maternal space found in Bellini's virginal images points to a *jouissance* that has been transfigured into an exquisite inward joy, one that expresses the docetic dimension in Kristeva's thought. Rather than suggesting an ethics of alterity, as solicited by the infant's vulnerability displayed in the Leonardo painting, Bellini's Virgins are shown to be "intent on something else that draws their gaze to the side, up above, or nowhere in particular but never centers it in the baby" (*DL*, 247). The space of maternal unrepresentability is not that of alterity, of ethical appeal, but of "a peculiar serene joy" (*DL*, 248), a private economy of interiorized ecstasy. In entering this space of unrepresentability, Bellini does not reject but transfigures the bodily passion of the father, the desire intrinsic to paternity. In identifying with the unrepresentable mother, the painter reaches "the threshold where maternal *jouissance*, alone impassable, is arrayed" (*DL*, 249).

Ecstaticism requires, not temporal difference and deferral, but a reinstatement of the very present that postmodernism has rejected. Yet, in repudiating both classical and modern metaphysics to which they attribute a logic of presence, Deleuze, Kristeva, and other French postmodernists posit difference *en principe*. This conflict can come to the surface in the work of Sloterdijk, for example, because, by refusing to reject totally the intellectual aims of the Enlightenment, he is less embarrassed by signs of the logic of presence in his work than are most postmodernists. Thus in the last sentence of *The Critique of Cynical Reason*, he concludes: "courage can suddenly make itself felt as a euphoric clarity or a seriousness that is wonderfully tranquil within itself. It awakens the present within us. In the present, all at once, awareness climbs to the heights of being. . . . No history makes you old" (*CCR*, 547). To gain the pleromatic fullness of ecstasy requires a present that forgets history, because who in the century of man-made mass death could attain ecstasy without amnesia?[11]

The Problem of Saintly Individuation

The discourse of postmodernity is a language of desire, its economy a libidinal economy, its ethic often bound up with a conatus toward satisfaction. In considering postmodern "metaphysics," differential forces, quanta of power or desire, are stipulated, but there is considerable variation in the ways these forces have been interpreted by postmodern thinkers. Desire may be described in terms of difference and yet may function as a hypostatic plane of libidinal satisfaction, not seamless yet without alterity. I have argued that the reverse Platonism of Deleuze attempts to maintain difference while sublating the other. Where lack or negation appears to be mandated, phantasmatic being is made to take its place in order to maintain the differential character of discourse. If postmodernism is to be differential, then it must think alterity in terms of lack, absence, and negation. But, it could be asked, is alterity nothing but negation and lack, a nonplace from which a certain speech, the speech of the other, issues? And, depending on the answer, how does lack bear on the altruism of saints?

The question for saintly life is not only "Can there be difference without lack?" but also "How is the object of saintly life and action to be described in terms of lack?" Must there not be a positivity bound up with living for the other? And if differential postmodernism, in contrast to pleromatic postmodernism—one that is totalizing—allows the nonconceptualizable Other to be the object of saintly work, must there not also be a "subject" of saintly life? If saint and Other are segregated by the radical character of alterity itself, how can the saint come into relation with the Other?

For there to be a saint who initiates action, who relieves suffering, who experiences compassion, there must in some sense be singular beings who are saints. Yet both ecstatic and differential postmodernisms are fairly well agreed that an account of the subject as an originary consciousness fails to grasp the "infrastructures" that fissure metaphysical conceptions of consciousness. The conditions for saintly life as something singular must be stipulated and the kind of ideality deconstructive analysis undermines must be detached from the term *singularity* by bringing to light the difficulties connected with individuation.

Much of this critical work has already been done in examinations of reference and exemplarity. It remains only to suggest how positive singularity can avoid the logocentric implications so penetratingly exposed by postmodernist critics. To distinguish naively construed individuality from saintly singularity, it is convenient to apply the term *particularity* to the received notion and the term *singularity* to saintly existence.

The concept of particularity is bound up with the problem of reference. To see this, it may be useful to consider that, for recent analytic and phenomenological philosophies of language, the question of how propositions represent the world poses difficulties that can be resolved only at the price both of neutralizing the world's otherness and of introducing mediating notions that explain and stipulate the connections between language and the world. Phenomenological philosophy posits a consciousness that provides access to phenomena whereas analytic philosophies of language specify conditions of intralinguistic coherence. What is to count as a particular is established within the constitutive frameworks of consciousness, on the one hand, and propositional truth conditions, on the other.

For phenomenology, particulars are constituted as such by a consciousness that is intentional. They acquire signification through their relation to a generic universal, an essence, an *eidos*, a form of unity constituted by a consciousness that bestows meaning on them by creating assemblages, a unity that conjoins both material and ideal objects. Particulars are what is presided over by the eidos.[12] Because the eidos is something purely conceptual, it extends over an infinity of possible particulars, which "fall under it as its 'particular exemplifications.'"[13] For Quine's linguistic philosophy, particulars conform to the pattern established in his famous dictum "To be is to be the value of a variable." One meaning that can be ascribed to particulars, then, is that they are whatever can be substituted for a variable in a proposition. Like Husserl, Quine envisions particulars as multiplying ad infinitum, a problem that arises when one thinks of counterfactuals or unrealized particulars, those that did not and could not come into being. Both Quine and Husserl have a horror of the infinite—of the runaway flow of particulars—and so have recourse to universals.[14] For both, particulars derive their meaning from the constructs that regiment them and are homogeneous with respect to the properties stipulated by the ordering construct. Particulars are monadic in a double sense: first, as part of what is heuristically united by the construct (e.g., for Husserl, the relation of the eidos of red to the assemblage of red objects brought together by it), and second, as freestanding wholes themselves—at least when they are time-tied particulars—in the sense of being numerically distinct from one another (for Quine).

In either view of particularity, saints could be interpreted as particulars, as living specimens of the virtues of compassion, generosity, and courage. The notions of exemplarity they presuppose have already been subjected to extended criticism. In the present context, it suffices only to notice that, were the relation between universal and particular, however liberally construed, to determine the character of saintly acts, saintly behavior could be thought of as a series of acts, if not homogeneous, at least commensurable with one another, regimented by the essence of saintliness, and saints themselves could be thought of as members of an ideal social whole: a tribe, a militia, or a club.

How is saintly singularity to be described if we are not to fall back into some premodern or modern notion of particularity? How is the other to be construed if we are not to resort to the notion of a larger whole characterized by suffering and privation? How, then, is the singularity of the other to be preserved, if it can be? Can the other simply be without further elaboration the One who I am not?

Negativity Is Not Transcendence

I have repeatedly stressed the extirpation of lack in ecstatic postmodernism, in a sense I shall explicate.[15] The reason for this insistence is not to show that the other is what I am not, for this only reinstates the other as another myself, as the obverse of my fullness and positivity. In such a relationship, I would be interchangeable with the other, so that the arena of social transactions would be flattened into a single terrain of homogeneous parts. When this situation is pushed to the extreme, as it is in Blanchot's novel *Aminadab*, as Levinas shows, it becomes absurd:

> Between the persons circulating in the strange house where the action takes place, where there is no work to pursue, where they only abide—that is, exist—this social relationship becomes total reciprocity. These beings are not interchangeable but reciprocal, or rather they are interchangeable because they are reciprocal. And then the relationship with the Other becomes impossible.[16]

If neither I nor the other is *constituted* as lack, the other *manifests* negativity as a destitution that is "parasitic" upon lack. For the saint, need is expressed in the other's very existence, as well as in concrete manifestations of suffering in war or natural catastrophe, in poverty, illness, or psychic injury. Every other is different from a "self," seen as a hollowed-out interiority (Levinas), excessive expenditure (Bataille), desiring production (Deleuze), or textual marginality, the result of spatial deflection and temporal delay (Derrida). The negativity of destitution is not a secondary "phenomenon" of lack but something primordial, the always already riven character of suffering, and displays itself as such to the saint. This mode of negation is to be distinguished from the negation that belongs within the totality of a system such as the negation of labor that overcomes the resistance of material being and is dependent upon anterior material existence. Nothing whatsoever precedes the destitution of the other.

If the other manifests herself/himself through destitution yet does not gain identity through being an alter ego or what I am not, is there some alternative way in which the other can be distinguished and that will, at the same time, display the other's singularity? This brings to the fore the question of the other's positivity, her/his *supra-ontological* or *me-ontic* being, in that the other is always already the object of a desire that exceeds any expectation of fulfillment. The saintly desire for the other is excessive and wild. In traditional Christian theological language, the saint desires not only the welfare of the other, the cessation of another's suffering, but also the other's beatitude: not only to sit at the right hand of God oneself but to desire the elevation of the other.

Recall, too, that saintly struggle on behalf of the other is a wrestling with time, the mode of temporalization called "the time that is left." If saintly action is to be effective, suffering must cease before the saint's life and the life of the other come to an end, in Jewish and Christian hagiographic language, the time of earthly life when change is still possible before the fixity of eternal life begins. The problem of an ever-diminishing time span bears directly on saintly singularity in that this singularity can in part be defined as the complex of occurrences that come to pass between the beginning and the end of the saint's activity. The time of a saintly life as expressed in hagiographic narrative is the time-before-it-is-too-late that is, as Kierkegaard claims, lived forward but remembered backward. Each telling of the saint's story, so long as the tradition in which the narrative is embedded remains vital, is an ever-renewed soliciting of the narrative's addressees. To those situated within this tradition, hagiography hammers home its own mode of temporalization, the time-before-it-is-too-late.

Nowhere is this time scheme more forcefully interpreted than in Kierkegaard's tale of the subjection of choice to the compression of time. Imagine, he declares, that a child is offered the alternative of buying a book or a toy. The choice is open so long as the child is still deliberating, but once he selects the toy and the money is spent, he cannot go back to the beginning before the choice was made and buy the book. Similarly the knight errant who throws in his destiny on the side of one army over another and then loses cannot, in good conscience, turn around and offer his services to the winner. The victor can only say, "My friend, you are now my prisoner; there was indeed a time when you could have chosen differently, but now everything is changed" (*PF*, 20 n.). The saintly future is the time-that-is-left in which to alleviate suffering before it is too late.

To return to the problem of singularity, the suffering of the other is, *from the standpoint of the saint*, always greater than the intention that strives to relieve it. The singularity of the other speaks from the nonplace of the difference between the saint's desire and the other's own suffering, so that the other's singularity is always an excess, more than can be encompassed by saintly intention. What is absolutely other gives itself to the saint as this excess. The other, then, as seen by the saint, is the one whose suffering exceeds any saintly effort at amelioration. This is neither a factual description, since saintly effort is often effective, nor an expression of psychological pessimism, which could only paralyze action, but rather a depiction of the infrastructure of saintly experience.

Saintly singularity *as seen from the standpoint of the saint's "flock" and addressees* takes as its starting point the visible manifestations of saintly desire for the Other, the saint's acts of generosity and compassion. From this perspective, saintly singularity is desire released from the bonds of a unifying consciousness, a desire that is unconstrained and excessive yet guided by the suffering of the other. Despite the pain of saintly existence, the addressees of saintly discourse (if not always the saint) see the other not as a weight or burden but as light, to borrow the oxymoron of Milan Kundera, with the unbearable lightness of being.[17] In actuality, no saint can always carry such generosity through to the end.

I have also maintained that postmodern saintliness is not premodern saintliness, because inscribed in postmodern saintly life is the weight of recent history. Hagiography, when written in the idiolect of the postmodern saint, bears the trace of the rational and egalitarian suppositions of the Enlightenment as well as the force of the Kantian moral law and the criticisms and appropriations of it in utilitarian and pragmatic ethics. If liberal theories of justice (John Rawls), phenomenological ethics (Max Scheler), and contemporary Kantianism (Alan Gewirth) fail to persuade, it will not do to return nostalgically and uncritically to an older ethos. Nostalgia is amnesia, a wiping out of both the sea changes brought about by recent history and the sins of older communities, such as slavery in ancient Greece and the persecution of Jews, Moslems, and heretics by medieval Christianity. This backward thrust is an example of the myth of the tabula rasa that leads to impossible dreams, such as Alasdair MacIntyre's hope for the restoration of a monastic ethic or a return to an Aristotelian version of the good life as one governed by the classical virtues.

The postmodern saintly life as a new path in ethics is not a proposal to revert to an older hagiographic discourse, least of all to hide behind its metaphysical presuppositions. It is instead a plea for boldness and risk, for an effort to develop a new altruism in an age grown cynical and hardened to catastrophe: war, genocide, the threat of worldwide ecological collapse, sporadic and unpredictable eruptions of urban violence, the use of torture, the emergence of new diseases. In an epoch grown weary not only of its calamities but of its ecstasies, of its collective political fantasies that destroyed millions of lives, and of its chemically induced stupors and joys, the postmodern saint shows the traces of these disasters. Just as postmodern art forswears the aesthetic purity of modernism, just as postmodern philosophers are only now beginning to forge the instruments for bringing vastly different philosophical languages into discursive contiguity, so postmodern saints derive their modes of action from their immediate modernist predecessors as well as from traditional hagiography.

Borrowing from the compassionate strands of the world's religious traditions, the absurdist gestures of recent modernist art and literature, and modern technologies, saints try to fashion lives of compassion and generosity. They may remain uncanonized, for postmodernism does not encourage institutional canonization, but this does not mean that they need to go unrecognized or unappreciated. The names of saints, revealed under the "rotten sun" (Bataille) of postmodern existence, are written *sous rature*, under erasure (Derrida), and appear as faint traces of alterity (Levinas) beneath the catena of altruistic actions that constitute postmodern hagiography.

4

Levinas and Hillel's Questions

"Philosophy is in crisis," says the postmodern thinker. "Yet," she continues, "we are forced to comport ourselves within its ambit, forced to dance its dance, to use its concepts and to unsay them even before they are said." But what is meant by "philosophy," and how are we to unsay it if we have at our disposal only *its* notions? Can philosophy provide its own critique without lapsing into self-referentiality? Is there an exteriority, an outside of philosophy that speaks otherwise than philosophically, that can call into question philosophy's hierarchy of constructs? And if there is, what boots it if this exteriority must enter into *conversation* with philosophy, so that it is once again trapped by philosophy?

Levinas treats these questions in terms of a relation of languages, by which he means discursive practices: "Greek," the language of philosophy, is the nexus of concepts that constitutes Western thought; "Hebrew," with its square script, *les lettres carrées*, is the vehicle for the interpretive approaches deployed by the sages of Jewish tradition, strategies that speak without speaking and are the language of an ethics that is prior to philosophy. This claim is not meant to imply that ethics is an apophatics, a language of silence, but rather that ethics is spoken otherwise than ontologically. Philosophy for Levinas is an ontology, a thinking of the meaning of being. It is self-enclosed, offering only an internal *point d'appui* for ethical reflection, that of a subject that is construed either as a consciousness in the manner of German idealism and Husserlian phenomenology or as Heideggerian being-in-the-world. To be sure, Heidegger criticizes a material ethic and the positing of conscience as bound up with taking action, but he fails, from Levinas's perspective, to contest the subject as a freedom and thus to check the violence endemic to political and economic life. Rather than proclaiming the demise of ethics, Levinas sees ethics (freshly interpreted) as a challenge to ontology and to a philosophy of the subject. "Philosophy is an egology," says Levinas, in a terse formulation; it must be called to order from outside itself. Judaism will provide postmodernity's thorn in philosophy's side, perpetually remonstrating with philosophy, accusing it not because of any specific infraction but simply for being what it is, the arena at best of cognition and at worst of politics.

But the matter does not end here. If Judaism is to do its job, it must be understood; it must somehow enter into this universal language that it cannot do without; philosophy, in turn, must become Judaized. Each is, as it were, both contaminated and rescued by the other. Although early interpretations of Levinas's philosophical thought often cordoned off his Jewish writings, their essential reciprocal relations have recently come under close scrutiny.[1] In what follows I presuppose the bond between philosophy and Judaism without attempting to develop this line of analysis in detail. Nor do I wish to consider any particular Talmudic text as the inspiration for some aspect of Levinas's thought (for example, the Talmudic invocation to supreme obedience, to do before hearing), as it bears upon his own account of alterity. Instead, I hope to expose a deep and unmanifest connection between a specific rabbinic text and the structure of *Totality and Infinity*, such that the former provides a homologue of the latter as an exposition of egology and alterity. The rabbinic text will be seen as a miniature (in a sense yet to be specified) of Levinas's work. The apothegm to which I refer is one of the most celebrated sayings, virtually a commonplace, of Jewish Talmudic wisdom, from Tractate *Aboth*, 1:14, of the *Mishnah*. *Aboth* is a compilation of contemplative and folkloric sayings, or *Agadah*, which contrast with the legal writings or *Halakhah* of the *Mishnah* as a whole. The chapters of *Aboth* were set aside and ultimately published under the title *Pirke Aboth*. The term *Pirke* simply means chapters, not ethics, and the title has been misleadingly translated as *Ethics of the Fathers*.[2] The saying in question reads, "He [Hillel] used to say: — If I am not for myself who is for me? and when I am for myself what am I? And if not now, when?"[3]

I shall turn first to the meaning of miniaturization, then to some traditional interpretations of Hillel's seminal maxim that are widely separated in time: that of Rabbi Nathan, possibly dating to the third century, and that of the nineteenth-century rabbi Samson Raphael Hirsch. Finally, I shall consider the way in which the structural articulation of *Totality and Infinity* both conceals and reveals its homologue, Hillel's saying and the commentaries upon it in *Pirke Aboth*. Because Hillel's words are known to anyone with even a rudimentary knowledge of rabbinics, it can be assumed that it was not only conceptually available but subliminally operative in Levinas's thought. It is also highly likely that he was acquainted with the famous commentary of Rabbi Nathan on *Pirke Aboth* but less certain that he was conversant with Samson Raphael Hirsch's neo-Kantian gloss on *Pirke Aboth*. However, Levinas's familiarity with the more famous Hermann Cohen's neo-Kantian Judaism would render the philosophical underpinnings of Hirsch's interpretation familiar.[4]

The World of the Very Small

The cultural understanding of the small has been dominated by the view of the infinitesimally minuscule: the atom, the gene, and, more recently, the bytes and pixels of the information culture. Whether envisioned as visible when enlarged by optical instruments or as transportable fragments that can be expanded into actual language and images, the small is understood as a part of a larger whole.

A miniature, however, is not a part but a homologue of a whole. Although little has been written recently on this subject, the miniature was a matter of considerable interest to earlier structuralist and phenomenological thinkers. Thus Lévi-Strauss contends:

> To understand a real object in its totality we always tend to work from its parts. The resistance it offers us is overcome by dividing it. Reduction in scale reverses this situation. Being smaller, the object as a whole seems less formidable. By being quantitatively diminished, it seems to us qualitatively simplified. . . . this quantitative transposition extends and diversifies our power over a homologue of the thing, and by means of it the latter can be grasped, assessed, and apprehended at a glance. (*SM*, 23)

One could object that Levinas has clearly stated his view of rabbinic hermeneutics, that is, that, as gloss, a rabbinic passage entails an expansion of text in a lengthening chain of signifiers, one that is justified by the polysemy of Hebrew words. "Words co-exist rather than being immediately co-ordinated or subordinated to one another,"[5] thus opening associative rather than logical sequences. The quest for meaning goes beyond the putatively plain (*pshat*) sense of the text, so that Levinas is led to conclude, in what might seem like a Derridean gesture of dissemination, that "There is not one verse, not one word of the Old Testament— . . . read by way of Revelation—that does not half-open onto an entire world."[6]

This manner of interpretation cannot be imported into a philosophical work, however. All too often the term *midrash*, now become fashionable, is used to describe the expansion of texts of vaguely rabbinic inspiration. But a midrash is a rabbinic commentary upon Scripture, often narrative but also legal, a description that fails to depict Levinas's philosophical work, even in a stretched sense. Nor can the genre of Levinas's philosophical writings be identified with *Gemara*, the Talmudic commentary upon the *Mishnah* (rather than upon Scripture), for the *Gemara* is a corpus of largely juridical texts. What is more, the associative character of rabbinic interpretation veers radically from any given text that prompts it, whereas Levinas hammers away insistently upon the originary themes of self and other, which guide his analysis in *Totality and Infinity* and which, I argue, are those of Hillel's apothegm.

Miniatures are neither diagrams nor blueprints. They are not, as Lévi-Strauss contends, "passive homologues" of objects, but rather they "constitute a real experiment with the object" (*SM*, 24). The miniature is seen as a solution to a particular problem, one in which the interpreter is not a passive observer; instead, her act of contemplation is, even if only subliminally, already one in which possible permutations are envisaged. A greater richness of the miniature's intelligible dimensions supplants its diminished sensible dimensions.

Yet, it can be objected, the relation of text to miniature is contrived in that what is to be miniaturized is something palpable or visualizable, whereas what is modeled by a miniature of a Levinasian text are an-iconic *echt* Levinasian tropes: pure exteriority, the infinite, diachrony, and temporal transcendence. This objection is valid only if the miniature is construed to be the result of a simple process of mechanical shrinkage or a representation, in an undeconstructed sense of the term. But Gaston Bachelard, who was originally a philosopher of science but came to envision a poetics of space, claims that imagination enters into miniaturization, that: "Values become condensed and enriched in miniature. Platonic dialectics of large and small do not suffice for us to become cognizant of the dynamic values of miniature thinking. One must go beyond logic to experience what is large in what is small."[7]

In support of his account, Bachelard offers this citation from Rostand's *Cyrano de Bergerac*, one that would be difficult to surpass as an analogue for the relation of Hillel's maxim to Levinas's text: "This apple is a little universe in itself, the seed of which being hotter than the other parts, gives out the conserving heat of its globe; and this germ . . . is the little sun of this little world, that warms and feeds the vegetative salt of this little mass."[8] Pointing to the seed's concentrated heat as moving from a visual to a lived image, Bachelard sees it as the ultimate progenitor of the apple, which shelters its generative properties. It is not, however, the apple, the visible fruit, that is the aim of the process, "the principal thing. . . . [but] paradoxically . . . the seed that creates the apple to which it transmits its aromatic saps and conserving strengths."[9]

Bachelard contends that the planetary image of Cyrano's apple is not one that is derived through rational inference. It has nothing in common with, for example, the model of the atom as conceived by Niels Bohr, "a pure synthetic construct of mathematical thoughts."[10] The process that generates miniatures is an oneiric process, one that is ultimately reciprocal: "Values become engulfed in miniature and miniature causes men to dream."[11] Bachelard concludes that the unfettered imagination that generates miniatures is the inverse of the observation that results in a diagram. Rather than summarizing, the oneiric process multiplies images.

Could it not be argued that the world created by oneiric imagination dissolves before the persuasive power of hard fact or, more ominously, the converse, that the oneiric realm of dreams threatens to undo the world of fact, of truths derived from empirical observation? This objection fails to take account of the extraordinary generative power of images. "An absolute image that is self-accomplishing," that of the apple seed, for example, contrasts sharply with "a post-ideated image that is content to summarize existing thoughts." The difference is condensed in a remark of Bachelard that can itself be construed as a miniature: "In Bohr's planetary atom, the little central sun *is not hot*."[12] Imagination, which both gives rise to and is nourished by the miniature, is not bound by a theory of verification according to which truth is arrived at through a confrontation with reality.

Thus freed from the constraint of truth as verification through an encounter with the real, Bachelard can maintain that the imagination cannot be wrong. For him, "the miniscule, a narrow gate, opens up an entire world. The detail of a thing can be the sign of a new world which, like all worlds, contains the attributes of greatness. Miniature is one of the refuges of greatness."[13]

One could also argue against the view that Hillel's adage is a miniature, that miniatures are the products of *technē* (or making), and that texts are not material artifacts with spatial dimensions. But Levinas refers to revealed texts as "living spaces" and to reading as a mode of inhabiting these spaces. The book, for Levinas, is the habitation of Israel as a people of the Book.[14]

Finally, one might object that to think of Hillel's adage as a miniature is to conceive of it as a plan. Like an architect's model or a computer simulation, it would then anticipate a work that remained to be constructed. But, as we have seen in Bachelard, the miniature is not stable but rather shifts with each interpretive move, so that it is as much an afterthought as a forethought. Not only do texts interact but for the traditional interpreter the text, as Levinas reminds his readers, is "lost in signs . . . illuminated by the thought that comes to it from outside or from the other end of the canon, revealing its possibilities which were awaiting its exegesis, immobilized in some way in the letters."[15]

Hillel's Adage: Some Expatiations

It is impossible to grasp the way in which Hillel's maxim functions within Judaic tradition without seeing it in the context of the study of Torah—as the effort to grasp what is divinely revealed in the sacred texts of Scripture and Talmud. To render vivid to Christians the affective register in which such study is conducted, R. Travers Herford speaks of it as "the Pharasaic form of the Beatific vision" and (citing Kepler) as "the effort to think God's thoughts after him."[16] Levinas's account of Torah study takes this paradigm for granted. He writes:

> The statement commented upon exceeds what it originally wants to say; . . . contains more than it contains; perhaps . . . an inexhaustible surplus of meaning [is] locked . . . in its actual words, phonemes and letters. . . . Exegesis would come to free . . . a bewitched significance that smoulders beneath the characters or coils up in all this literature of letters.[17]

Aboth de Rabbi Nathan, The Fathers According to Rabbi Nathan, the oldest commentary on *Pirke Aboth*,[18] based upon an earlier version of the text, presupposes this framework. In Rabbi Nathan's text, the saying that begins "If I am not for myself" is placed in conjunction with two other logia attributed to Hillel, both of which can be read as "seeds" of *echt* Levinasian themes, peace and the critiques of polity and egology.

A detailed excursus into Rabbi Nathan's elaboration of Hillel's logia would extend beyond my concern with the ground plan of *Totality and Infinity*. It is, nevertheless, significant that an ancillary passage in the chapter that contains Hillel's saying reads: "Be of the disciples of Aaron, loving peace and pursuing peace, loving mankind and drawing them to the Torah" (*ARN*, 63). Rabbi Nathan interprets the figure of Aaron as the peacemaker who encourages forgiveness. An additional gloss reads: "[Aaron] would sit with [a man] until he had removed all rancor from his heart. And when the two men met each other, they would embrace and kiss each other." Aaron reconciles them by enacting a remarkable ruse. When two men quarreled, Aaron would come to each and recount how the other had repented, an event that had not yet occurred but that, when envisioned by the angry parties, would generate forgiveness. Thus Aaron would say to each: "My son, mark what thy fellow is saying! He beats his breast and tears his clothing, saying 'Woe unto me! How shall I lift my eyes and look upon my fellow! . . . I am ashamed . . . for I it is who have treated him foully'" (*ARN*, 64). The theme of peace already announced in Levinas's Preface is, of course, a key theme in the conceptual repertoire even if it is not in the structure of *Totality and Infinity*.

The next saying in Rabbi Nathan's work that is contiguous with the passage that is the focal point of my thesis reads: "A name made great is a name destroyed. And he that does not increase, ceases. And he that does not learn, deserves to die. And he that puts the crown to his own use shall perish" (*ARN*, 63). Rabbi Nathan's gloss suggests: first, that one should avoid the attention of government, a thieving institution; second, that not adding to the study of Torah means one will lose what has already been learned; and, finally, that using the crown, which here refers to the tetragrammaton (the unpronounceable name of God), for one's own ends assures that one will perish utterly (i.e., have no place in the world to come).

Consider, now, Rabbi Nathan's gloss on the passage that I have suggested is a homologue for *Totality and Infinity*: "If not I for myself, who then is for me. And being for myself, what am I" (*ARN*, 69). This passage is interpreted not in terms of the dyad self/other, which reflects the duality of the modern subject and the other as an other self, but rather in the context of laying up merit. Thus, the self is one who is under the mandate of Torah, both in terms of *who* is to obey it, only I myself, and *when* such obedience is demanded, only in the here and now. Merit can only be laid up in this lifetime, for, as Scripture asserts, "A living dog is better than a dead lion" (Eccles. 9:4). This life and this life only is the venue for repentance; even the righteous cannot store up merit when they are dead. One may infer that the living process of gaining merit rather than the product, merit itself, is the higher good.

Yet how is one to explain that *merit* is bound up with profit for *myself*? Rabbi Nathan's gloss does not cordon off an egology in the manner of Levinas because, in the absence of the modern subject, there can be no egology. This gloss would seem, therefore, to offer an unpromising homologue for a Levinasian account of the self. Yet the text is open to another interpretation, to which I shall recur: the self of Rabbi Nathan is already fissured by Torah, by merit as the fostering of peace and as repentance both in one's heart and in one's deeds. Moreover, "if not now, when?" conveys the sense of urgency reinforced by the comparison of a dead lion with a live dog.

It is no surprise that *Pirke Aboth* should have proved a lure and a seduction for Samson Raphael Hirsch (1808–88), a leading figure of German Orthodox Jewry. Influenced by the *Aufklarung* and especially by Kant, Hirsch wrote a commentary on the work replete, with the language of duty and of the fellowman. Hirsch's gloss of *Aboth* 1:14 reads:

> It is only through his own efforts that a man can attain spiritual fitness and moral worth, which are the most essential attributes to which he can aspire. Similarly it is primarily upon himself, his own efforts . . . that man must depend in the process of acquiring and . . . preserving the worldly goods he needs. . . . But a man must never say "Since it is solely by my own efforts that I have become what I am, I will use my attainments for myself alone." For it is only in selfless devotion, [when] he actively works to create, . . . and to increase the prosperity and happiness of his fellowman that a man begins to become truly human in the image of God. . . . To this task every moment of your life should be devoted. Do you know whether indeed you will still have another moment to do this work?[19]

On the face of it, this reading would appear to offer rough-and-ready analogies to Levinas's text: the necessity for a self and the total dedication of the self to the other. This is indeed the "plain sense" that may be attributed to the ground plan of *Totality and Infinity*. But I shall argue instead that the plain sense is challenged by the more recondite reading of Rabbi Nathan, in which alterity shadows egology from the outset, and in which the two remain in a deliberate and unresolved tension, one that persists in the Levinasian scheme.

Totality and Infinity: Some Readings

One of the received views of *Totality and Infinity* interprets Levinas as the critic of Heidegger's subsumption of alterity by ontology but as himself following many of the phenomenological leads suggested by *Being and Time*. On the one hand, Levinas concedes that philosophy cannot escape ontology; on the other, despite Heidegger's account of the difference between Being and beings and his critique of the modern subject, Levinas contends that Heidegger does not transcend the totalizing and egological impulses of Western thought. Heidegger's account of the *es gibt* as evidence for Being's generosity is overturned to become the *il y a* in Levinas's thought, a trope for the indeterminate, the murky, the heaviness of being without form. More importantly, for Levinas, Heidegger's treatment of the *Mitsein*, the sphere of being-with-others, regards the Other merely as one who is alongside myself but whose existence does not weigh upon me as a moral force. For Heidegger, ethics, as dominated by modern ontology, treats the being of the subject as will. But this, for Levinas, is a misunderstanding of ethics, which must be an Ethics of ethics, Ethics as first philosophy, prior to ontology. This reading of Levinas generally concedes that the mark or trace of rabbinism must be incised across the history of philosophy as critique, but maintains that *Totality and Infinity* remains principally a conversation with Heidegger's thought.[20]

The genealogical relation of Levinas to Franz Rosenzweig does not challenge the received view just described but rather provides another reading, an account of how Rosenzweig furnished the resources for undermining both Heideggerian ontology and the Hegelian conception of the state. Rosenzweig's quarrel with German idealism is replicated in Levinas's encounter with Heidegger's fundamental ontology. Whereas for Rosenzweig it is the unique self that breaks into the globalizing tendencies of the Fichtean ego and the Hegelian polity, for Levinas it is *autrui*, the other person, who disrupts Heideggerian ontology.[21] Levinas's double indebtedness is summed up by John Llewelyn: "If *Totality and Infinity* is a section-by-section dissection of *Being and Time*, it is also a running commentary and critique of infinite totality that is meant to be replaced by the idea of a finite wholeness," a strategy for which Rosenzweig is responsible.[22]

Robert Bernasconi's analysis of the relationship between empiricism and transcendence offers yet another reading of *Totality and Infinity*. For Levinas, he argues, the face-to-face relation is both a concrete experience and a transcendental precondition for ethics. But if experience is a *prior* condition for ethics, does it not disrupt the possibility of a *transcendental* condition? What is more, Levinas thinks that the beyond of the totality must be reflected within it, so that totality and infinity are not opposed in such a way as to mean "totality versus infinity," both because they could be reintegrated in a Hegelian synthesis and because transcendence must be *enacted* and therefore requires the world. Thus, "the conditions for the possibility of the experience of totality are the conditions for its impossibility."[23] The relation with alterity unfolds within the historical conditions of economic and political existence. Only through this anterior/posterior strategy can a way be negotiated between the discourses of both experience and transcendence. On this reading, "the rupture with the totality shows that there never was a totality."[24]

From Hillel to Levinas

To see the complex relation between the apothegms of Hillel and Levinas, four preconditions, which I have tried to adumbrate in the preceding sections, must be presupposed: first, if Hillel's saying is to be seen as a miniature, the process of miniaturization itself must be understood as dynamic; a miniature is neither a blueprint nor a copy. Second, the saying of Hillel must be discerned not only in the context of other rabbinic sayings in *Pirke Aboth* but as it is appropriated in certain later traditional interpretations. Third, although Heidegger and Rosenzweig provide indispensable languages for the development of the argument of *Totality and Infinity*, the relation between self and Other must also be seen otherwise than in the terms provided by these philosophical predecessors. For Levinas, experience and transcendence perpetually reinstate and undo one another,[25] so that egology is interrupted by alterity, and alterity requires an egology. There is, to be sure, a linear, phenomenological progression from self to

Other in the unfolding of *Totality and Infinity*, but each is infiltrated, virtually sabotaged, by its other.

For Levinas, a key question is "Who must the I be if it is to be affected by the Other while resisting subsuming or being subsumed by that Other?" Does Hillel's question "If I am not for myself, who is for me?" allow for an adumbration of this doubleness? Levinas contends that the I is not a static identity but a being whose very existence consists in reidentifying itself through the happenings of its life (*TI*, 36). Lived as a sequence of such returns to itself, this I is called into question by the Other, a process that Levinas calls Ethics (*TI*, 43). But such a calling into question presupposes a separate self, one who is a cognitive subject (although not only such) and who reduces the otherness of the object to what Levinas calls "the same" by representing it. In fact, the other person cannot be rendered as an object because she or he is the Other, always already given as uncontainable in thought, as an excess refractory to representation, or, in Levinasian terms, as the Cartesian *infinite*, whose ideatum exceeds any idea we can have of it. The Other is not another "myself for myself" (*TI*, 33), perhaps a reference not only to Levinas's negative view of Husserl's contention that the self can be given empathically and thus as another me, but also as a covert reference to Hillel's text.

After the ground plan, the forecourt, as it were, of *Totality and Infinity* as a whole, is laid out in Section 1, Section 2 provides a phenomenological account of the separate self that is opposed both to the Kantian subject and to Heideggerian *Dasein*. This separateness is produced as inner life or psychism arising through thought in its opposition to totality: "The original role of psychism . . . is already a way of being . . . resistance to the totality. Thought or the psychism opens the dimension this way requires," Levinas writes (*TI*, 54). As separate, the self breaks with Being and lives outside of God, in a manner Levinas designates as atheism—a position that is not a negation of God but rather one that defines a being who, without existing as its own cause, nevertheless exists as an independent will.

But before it can exist as a subject of will or cognition, it must exist in a more primordial relation to the world, as enjoyment, as a *zoōn* or vital being who "lives on" the world, relishes and finds satisfaction in it. Such a being is immersed in the density of a medium; a formless space, the elemental (e.g., earth, air, street, and the like). At the same time, a vantage point, a site that is one's own, one's home, is needed as a point of entry, return, and security. The world thus understood is not, as for Heidegger, a nexus of things as objects of utility. "To enjoy without utility, in pure loss, gratuitously . . . in pure expenditure—this is the human," Levinas contends (*TI*, 133). Life thus understood is existence not as cognition but as sensibility. Although Levinas does not hesitate to celebrate the love of life, one might object that need thwarts such simple happiness. Yet for Levinas, without indigence or need there would be no satisfaction (*TI*, 146). But need and satisfaction exact a price: one who has needs is concerned for the future, a worry that can only be overcome through human labor. In sum, for Levinas the lived modalities of self, "egoism, enjoyment, sensibility and the whole dimension of interiority— the articulations of separation—are necessary for the idea of *Infinity*, the relation with the other which opens forth from the separated and finite being" (*TI*, 148). The separated self prior to the advent of the Other signals a break with the epistemological and moral subject of German idealism and would seem to preclude any connection with Samson Raphael Hirsch's neo-Kantian gloss on Hillel's words "If I am not for myself who is for me?" For Hirsch, ethics arises through human action as the result of human effort, so that ethics is, as it were, a labor. Yet Hillel's apothegm reins in Hirsch's Kantianism, in that the "for myself" cannot mean the Kantian self, which is universalizable as a moral agent. Hirsch sees that there must be a self of economy, "acquiring and preserving the worldly goods [that humans] need,"[26] if there is to be a functioning ethical self, a self that, in his terms, can assist the fellowman. For Hirsch, as for Levinas, generosity presupposes an acquisitive self that can, by dint of its labor, satisfy its needs.

Hillel's second question, "If I am for myself only, what am I?," implies a challenge to the view that I see the telos of my life as being the satisfaction of my needs and interests without regard for others. For Levinas, the advent of the Other is in and of itself a critique of the I: "The Other—the absolutely other—paralyzes possession, which he contests by his epiphany in the face" (*TI*, 171). As an insistent and commanding presence, not only does the Other proscribe violence, but the Other comes to me as from a height, contests what I possess, mandates donation, self-divestiture, decrees that I become hostage for her or him. The face as an ethical datum is given not visually but discursively: the face addresses me. In a dense passage, Levinas writes: "Absolute difference, inconceivable in formal logic, is established only by language. Language accomplishes a relation between terms that breaks up the unity of a genus. . . . [and] is perhaps to be defined as the very power to break the continuity of being or of history" (*TI*, 195). In sum, the Other's relation to the self is interlocutory, contesting her or his absorption in discursive content, yet it remains bound to language.

The relation to the Other renders secure the singularity of each and every other but in no way addresses the question of all the others. The assurance of singularity is contrary to the notion of each subject as the fellowman who always already exists as a universal subject. Thus, for Samson Raphael Hirsch, eccentricity in the etymological sense is to be avoided. The *imago dei* is actualized only through "increasing the happiness and prosperity of one's fellowmen." But for Levinas, the totality, the domain of economy, polity, and history, cannot remain untransformed by alterity. Thus, Levinas insists, "Everything that takes place here between us concerns everyone. . . . The face places itself in the full light of the public order" (*TI*, 212), a concern that Levinas calls justice. "The epiphany of the face qua face opens humanity," he maintains (*TI*, 213).

The "correction" supplied by a Levinasian approach (i.e., an insistence upon singularity) to Hirsch's neo-Kantian gloss on Hillel's saying precludes any easy identification of Hirsch and Levinas. Yet the developmental account of *Totality and Infinity* as a progression from self to Other reenacts the movement from man to fellowman, a movement that, for Levinas, must pass through a chain of experiences from enjoyment, labor, and cognition to the disruption of the self by the face of the Other. Yet an alternative view, suggested by the gloss of Rabbi Nathan, unsays this progression and suggests a more profound connectedness between Levinas and Hillel.

Recall that Rabbi Nathan speaks of Hillel's being for oneself in terms of acquiring merit. "If I do not lay up merit in my lifetime, who will lay it up for me?" Even as a separated self, therefore, one is already bound up in a relation with transcendence in that merit consists in obedience to God's commands. Levinas, too, insists upon the primordiality of the relation with infinity: "The idea of infinity (which is not a representation of infinity) sustains activity itself. Theoretical thought, knowledge, and critique, to which activity has been opposed, have the same foundation. The idea of infinity, which is not in its turn a representation of infinity, is the common source of activity and theory" (*TI*, 27).

In addition to mentioning merit, Rabbi Nathan adds the words "in my lifetime," a phrase that would seem to be appropriate only after the coda or concluding phrase of Hillel's apothegm, that is, after the sentence "If not now, when?" But Rabbi Nathan leaps ahead and deploys "in my lifetime" as an adumbration of the sentence about laying up merit for oneself. His gloss continues: "'For a living dog is better than a dead lion' (Eccles. 9:4) better even than Abraham, Isaac and Jacob: for they dwell in the dust" (*ARN*, 69). This astonishing claim does not reflect an atheological hedonism but rather points to life as the deferring of death, the time span in which repentance is still possible. For Rabbi Nathan, the words "living dog" may refer to the sinner who is alive: "If he repents, the Holy One, blessed be He, receives him; but the righteous, once he dies, can no longer lay up additional merit." Even the righteous can no longer acquire merit once dead. Paradoxically, Rabbi Nathan speaks in praise of life but says also that it is precisely in the interest of the world to come that prayer and study are undertaken.

For Levinas, the temporalization opened up by death converges remarkably with Rabbi Nathan's interpretation. Death, says Levinas, is imminent but not yet, and as such, it is postponed or delayed. Unlike Heidegger, for whom existence is an ec-stasis toward death, for Levinas (as for Sartre), death puts an end to my possibilities. But death is also, for Levinas, feared as a hostile other. What is crucial is that death opens an aperture, an interval that is temporalization: on one's way to death, "one has time to be for the Other" (*TI*, 236). As long as there is time, one can stand away from the present, maintain a distance from it, change one's thoughts and actions, repent, and do otherwise. By switching to Rabbi Nathan's trope, one can store up merit, not for an afterlife but for the instantiation of Goodness.

In/conclusions

It is by now widely attested that Levinas's appeal to Jewish sources derives largely from a desire to avoid the pitfalls of what he regards as a unitary tradition in Western philosophy in which Ethics is subordinated to ontology. If Ethics is to be first philosophy, as Levinas argues, it must proceed otherwise than ontologically. Recent interpreters of Levinas's Jewish writings have paid careful attention to the manner in which they provide inspiration for this new articulation of Ethics. The independence of the discursive arenas of philosophical and Jewish thought, maintained by Levinas himself, has been broken by his interpreters, a "contamination" that has yielded fruitful results. It now behooves Levinas's readers to look beyond his explications of specific Talmudic passages to the conceptual and structural affinities between his major works and certain rabbinic texts, affinities that offer yet another perspective on writings that have heretofore (and with good reason) been examined as meditations, principally upon Husserl, Heidegger, or Rosenzweig.

The relation between one of Levinas's major works, *Totality and Infinity*, and Hillel's apothegm about being for oneself exclusively is not merely one of historical influence but, more significantly, of homology, in the sense that one is a miniature of the other, "a little universe in itself." A long hermeneutical tradition has already endowed the apothegm of Hillel with numerous meanings. The ancient and well-known reading of Rabbi Nathan and the less familiar neo-Kantian gloss of Samson Raphael Hirsch have become part of a catena of interpretations that enter into the construction of the miniature I have attempted to sketch and constitute, as Bachelard would have it, "a real experiment with the object." Levinas's conception of the separated self and its disruption by alterity must be seen in the light of this chain of transmission. Hillel's saying together with Hirsch's gloss, is homologous, in part, with the diachronic unfolding of *Totality and Infinity*, its phenomenological trajectory, which proceeds from self to Other. Yet for Levinas, the Other disrupts the antecedent life of a satisfied self, a self that cannot, as Hirsch would have it, simply pass from man to fellowman.

The dimension of alterity is more subtly revealed in Rabbi Nathan's account of Hillel's saying: for Rabbi Nathan, the self is always already imbricated in a transcendence that transforms life into a matter of extreme urgency, an absent presence that is solicited and that solicits. Does not God say, Rabbi Nathan asks: "If thou wilt come to my house, I shall come to thy house; to the place my heart loves, my feet lead me?" (*ARN*, 69). This question is interpreted by Rabbi Nathan to mean that those who go to meet God by attending the house of study, the synagogue, or who, in earlier times, went up to the Temple in Jerusalem, leaving gold and silver behind, are blessed by Him (*ARN*, 69–70). Real time becomes for Rabbi Nathan the alloted span of human life, in which transcendence comes to pass, because in that interval alone merit can be acquired and repentance undertaken. What is miniaturized in this complex of texts, especially that of Rabbi Nathan, is the urgency of the phrase "in my lifetime," an interval that in Levinas's elaboration of time is the period during which good deeds may be done. Death is the enemy not because it terminates my activities as such but because it puts an end to my being for the Other, to the postponement that is one's life as the interval during which Goodness can come to pass.

5

Recontextualizing the Ontological Argument: A Lacanian Analysis

I read Lacan. I ask myself: What is this good for? It is good for nothing. If so, can this be proved? I will try. I will not know, you will not know, if I am successful. In Lacanian terms, if I have succeeded, I have failed; if I fail, I have succeeded. *Doch*, I shall apply Lacanian techniques to one of Western theology's most frequently and strenuously examined texts, Anselm's ontological argument. By remapping the proof, I hope, with Lacanian audacity, to bring forth unforeseen significations and a new approach to the psychoanalytic interpretation of religious texts.

One difficulty in developing a psychoanalytic discourse appropriate to theological texts arises because unconscious content has largely been viewed nondiscursively, in terms of force fields, images, and archetypes, and so could not be read in the same way as theological language. It is just here that Lacan opens up the possibility for linking the unconscious to theological discourse. Arguing that "the unconscious is structured . . . like a language," that a material operates in it according to certain laws, which are the same laws as those discovered in the study of actual languages, Lacan attributes a linguistic and textual character to the unconscious itself. In this view, theological texts and manifestations of the unconscious are homologous and open to common interpretive strategies. Because they are now commensurable, theological texts can be treated like the subject of a psychoanalysis, as manifesting multiple strands of meaning, which become intelligible through the analytic process.

This application of Lacanian method is entirely one of my own devising. In fact, Lacan criticizes the proofs for God's existence as ways "in which, over the centuries, he has been killed off" (*Écrits*, 317). Contrary to this assessment, I shall interpret the argument as Anselm's expression of the Christian's love of God. It is not my aim to come to a decision about the proof's soundness or to decide whether the existence of God or Anselm's conception of Him has been established, but to show how these ends have been achieved to Anselm's satisfaction. Because I shall treat the text like an analysand, I shall often be forced to speak of it in a queer way, as having desires, displaying resistances, and the like.

The success of Anselm's analysis will be measured by the extent to which the full signification of the concept of God is revealed. Successive layers of false meaning are bared through a process Anselm calls "conceiving" (*cogitare*) when it is existentially incomplete but conceptually full and "understanding" (*intelligere*) when it culminates in existential or factual signification. A similar distinction is to be found in Lacan's conception of the analyst's hearing (*entendre*) and understanding what is heard (*comprendre*). Although no psychoanalysis is ever definitively closed, the proof is brought to an end when, through the refining of conceptualization, God's name is seen to be nondifferent from the way He reveals Himself to be. I shall explicate the proof by interweaving logical and psychological elements, just as an analysand mingles conscious and unconscious strands in telling his or her story. But I shall distinguish them when necessary, bearing in mind Lacan's warning about the requirements of the double discourse, conscious and unconscious language, "hieroglyphs inscribed simultaneously on both sides of an obelisk, and whose meaning changes completely from one side to the other."[1]

A Lacanian analysis unfolds in accordance with its own lines of force, which Lacan thinks of as truth, the truth of the patient's desire. The patient cannot grasp the meaning of the symbols in which his desire has become alienated. Interpretation consists in restoring to each significant language fragment the chain of meanings from which it has slipped, so that step by step, through the course of the analysis, a complex but coherent associative fabric of unconscious thoughts is woven together. Anselm's proof also unfolds as a coming to consciousness of desire, the conatus toward a God who is named at the outset against the "voices" that obstruct the realization of desire. The proof aims to know what is already believed as darkly present, that God exists, and that the God whom we have named is such that He is as we have named Him: "a-being-such-that-a-greater-cannot-be-conceived,"[2] who cannot be conceived as otherwise when we have thus conceived him.[3] For the sake of brevity, I shall use such phrases as *God's name*, *the divine name*, or *Anselm's key phrase* to denote Anselm's formulation, rather than the terms *supreme being* or *highest being*, because of conceptual difficulties connected with them that will be considered in the final section of this chapter.

Before embarking on a Lacanian reading proper, it may be useful to notice that some presuppositions I mentioned have already become familiar through Karl Barth's reading of the argument. Barth claims that Anselm's concept of God breaks with the sphere of human thought. Barth thinks of this concept as God's revealed name.[4] My Lacanian reading will also attribute Anselm's key phrase to the sphere outside of conscious language, as the self-revelation of the unconscious, which speaks the language of desire (in this case, God's self-revealing desire) against the text's opposing positions (the Fool's, Gaunilo's). Second, for Barth, the revealed name of God is present from the start—the argument's presupposition and not its conclusion.[5] For Lacan, the language of desire is present from the beginning of the analytic work but must be given the opportunity to come to expression.[6] This means it must transcend empty speech (speech that is alienated from desire) to become full speech (speech from which the mirages of the subject have been cleared away through a recollecting of the past, in the case of the proof, the detritus of "false" images and speech). A third point of convergence lies in the future-directedness of Barth's interpretation and of Lacan's notion of full speech. For Barth, Anselm's concept of a highest being provides us with an ongoing norm for acts of thinking,[7] so that it stretches out toward the future.[8] Because, for Lacan, "the effect of full speech is to reorder past contingencies by conferring on them the effect of necessities to come,"[9] a Lacanian reading must similarly conclude that Anselm's key phrase, when fully expressive of the language of desire, conveys normative force for future thought and action.

The Fool and the Divine Name: *Proslogion* II

Applied to theological texts, a Lacanian psychoanalytic interpretation has a twofold structure. First, there is the obvious level of analysis, that of the contemporary critic of the text—for example, my own role in the present essay. Second (and far less evident) is the therapeutic structure internal to the theological text itself, a *Zweifaltigkeit* inherent in the dialogical character of the argument as such. On the one hand, there is the text's truth strand, the thread of desire that must be made to stand out and be supported against countervalent influences; on the other, there is the level of the resistances, the positions that again and again assert themselves against the text's truth. In this section I hope to describe from a Lacanian perspective the argument's major strands and the linguistic strategies that are used to implement their development.

The structure of the argument's strands or subtexts reflects Lacan's division of psychic life into the objectifications of the subject, his alienated being as disclosed in his assumption of various roles, and the "true subject" or the unconscious, which enters into language through representation by receiving a name (the son of John) or through pronominal reference. This substitution of a name for the true subject reflects a primal alienation that takes place when the subject, an absence or lack, is represented by a linguistic surrogate.

The process of alienation manifests itself in an individual's life history in what Lacan calls the mirror stage. Between the age of six months and about a year and a half the child will identify with the specular image of himself, first with another child, later with his own mirror image. The mirror stage "manifests the affective dynamism by which the subject originally identifies himself with the visual Gestalt of his own body: in relation to the still very profound lack of coordination of his own motility, it represents an ideal unity" (*Écrits*, 18–19). This identification of self with bodily *Gestalt* "situates the agency of the ego, before its social determination, in an ideal direction" (ibid., 18). If the mirror stage is successfully concluded, the infant's feeling of body fragmentation is over-come and a sense of corporeal unity achieved.

But spatiotemporal wholeness is secured at the price of a narcissistic and alienated identification with an iconic or imaginary self, the ego, which henceforth will obstruct the desires of the unconscious. Unlike American ego psychologists, who endorse a strengthening of the ego, Lacan believes the ego is infralinguistic and inhibits the full expression of unconscious desires through false and alienating identifications. Just as the strategies of Anselm's argument will recur over and over again, for Lacan, "this narcissistic moment in the subject is to be found, in all the genetic phases of the individual, in all the degrees of human accomplishment in the person, in a before in which it must assume a libidinal frustration and an after in which it is transcended in a normative sublimation" (ibid., 24).

Before proceeding to the argument proper, I shall divide it into voices or strands to facilitate a psychoanalytic account: Anselm's or the therapeutic strand represents the voice of desire through the language of God's self-revelation; the strands of the Fool and Gaunilo represent the resistances, ego ideals, and mirages of the subject; and the Painter's strand, a weak subtext of Anselm's strand, represents an early effort to extend and amplify it.

In his opening prayer Anselm asks God to help him grasp the full meaning of the divine name, "something-than-which-nothing-greater-can-be-conceived," and not, in Lacanian terms, something imaginary, an expression of the ego. Lacan calls such full understanding symbolic expression. Symbols are taken in their structuralist meaning, not as images but as signifiers, "differential elements in themselves without meaning, which acquire value only in their mutual relations" (*Écrits*, ix). Anselm's prayer is, in part, an appeal for a proof for God's existence, but mainly it pleads for the ability to express discursively the love of God that is Anselm's deepest desire. "But can there be any such Nature," since "the Fool says in his heart, 'God is not'?" Either the Fool speaks nonsense or his denial refers to Anselm's conception of God, which he takes to be mistaken. If the latter, what belief does he offer in its stead? The full content of the Fool's foolishness emerges later, only after Anselm considers the implications of trying to imagine God as a contingent being in *Proslogion* III. In the present context we know only that God is not: there is no Other of the Fool, himself the *imago* that at this stage substitutes for the voice of Anselm's desire. The Fool, a specular image thrown forth by the unconscious to negate the language of desire that declares God to be a being such that no greater can be conceived, will now constitute in various guises an impediment to full divine self-revelation. This first discourse of the self's suppression of desire is the text's expression of the mirror stage.

A more detailed example of theological mirror-stage narcissism, one that may (retrospectively) shed light on Anselm's theological framework, is found in Descartes' account of the attributes he would confer upon himself had he the power to do so: "Now if I had existence from myself, I should have no doubts or wants, and in general nothing would be lacking in me; I should have endowed myself with all the perfections of which I have any idea—in fact I should myself be a God."[10] Sartre thinks of such a being as an "impossible synthesis," but, once posited, such a being, in Lacanian terms, can be abandoned only after the therapy has been completed. In the next step of the argument, Anselm must show that God exists not only intra- but extramentally as well. Anselm introduces a new voice, that of the Painter, which now will be made to speak the language of Anselm's desire. At first, imagining what he is about to paint, the Painter has the painting only in relation to his understanding, because he has not yet painted it. Once the picture has been executed, he has it in relation to his understanding, and he also understands that it exists. The Painter now substitutes for Anselm in the argument; and the painting, for the divine name.

In his effort to put meaning in place of the Fool's nonsense, Anselm resorts to metaphor, a rhetorical strategy crucial to the creation of signification. It is worth noting that for Lacan "metaphor emerges at the precise point where sense emerges from nonsense" (*Écrits*, 158). Metaphor is seen by linguists such as George Lakoff as substituting a concrete reality for an abstract notion. For structural linguistics, metaphor is the emergence of a new meaning when one signifier, related through similarity to another, substitutes for it. By adding a psychoanalytic dimension to the structuralist view, Lacan gives metaphoricity a dynamic thrust: one of these signifiers, the one that is substituted for, falls out of the chain of signifiers, becomes latent, and leaves a space onto which a new signifying chain can be grafted.[11] The name of God has disappeared for the moment, but what has been learned from the trope of the painting may later be grafted into the interval in the signifying chain opened up by the name of God.

The purpose of the digression of the Painter is to establish that there is a disturbance in the Fool's relation to the Other, in this case, to the extramental alterity of God. Anselm begins to illuminate the Fool's pathology by introducing the painting as a metaphor for the divine name. A Lacanian elaboration of the Oedipus story should shed light both on the difficulties of the Fool's position and on Anselm's effort to clarify them. In the Oedipal phase of psychosexual development, the child wishes to be everything to the mother, to substitute for what she is lacking, the phallus. The child now identifies with the symbol of this maternal desire, the phallus, which, for Lacan, is not an organic referent but "the privileged signifier of that mark in which the role of the logos is joined with the advent of desire" (*Écrits*, 287). Should the child persist in this identification with the mother, he would fail to gain entry to the symbolic realm and would become a simple extension of the mother's being.

This stage of the Oedipal phase establishes the ground plan both archetypally and in actuality for the subject's future relations with alterity. The account of the connection of the intramental painting to its actualization manifests a point-for-point structural correspondence with Lacan's description of the fusion phase of the Oedipal stage. The painting as object of the Painter's desire is experienced as different from the understanding whose object it is. Still, so long as it has merely intramental existence, it is not a painting but a lack, the substitute for another lack, the subject's desire for the extramental painting.

In his next move Anselm turns from the imagined to the actual painting, from a mental image to a fully executed object. This transition, in Lacanian terms, moves from the nonsymbolized imaginary to the symbolic realm, here, the fully realized painting. (For Lacan, the symbolic as expression, or *Auspruch*, is, like Anselm's painting, a material signifier.) This transformation of the object of desire into the truth of language first comes about through the resolution of the Oedipal conflict, when the child first encounters proscription in the form of the Law of the Father. The Father proscribes the child's identification with the phallus, which is desired by the mother, while prohibiting the mother from reappropriating her product or returning the child to the womb. The child must give up the phallus that he is in order to have a phallus. In so doing he enters the symbolic order. The presence of the Father is attested through his Law, which is speech. This Law must first be recognized by the mother, since, if the father's position is placed in doubt, the child remains subjected to the mother. Recognition of the Law of the Father gives the child access to the Name of the Father (Lacan plays on the homonym *nom de père* as both name and no-saying of the Father) and with it into the world of human culture (*Écrits*, 196–98). Because for Freud the Father who establishes the Law is the Father of the primal horde slain by his sons, "the symbolic Father is, insofar as he signifies this Law, [also] the dead Father" (ibid., 198). This process, the recognition that the self and the object of desire are autonomous wholes, has been concluded successfully by the Painter, although he is far from giving full discursive expression to the ultimate object of desire, the divine name.

The text goes on to examine the progress made through this excursus by the Fool. Now God's name stands at least in relation to the

Fool's understanding, so that he has come part of the way toward recognizing the alterity of the object (it is present to the understanding). But he has not yet understood it as actual. The Fool, still ignorant of the symbolic register in which the divine name is encoded, is trapped in incomplete alterity. Because he is unable to recognize the conceptual significance of the divine name, the object of his desire cannot be released into independent existence. Using Lacan's metaphor, the Fool refuses entry into the Name-of-the-Father because his desire is snared in the maternal womb of his own understanding. In Anselm's formulation, "even the Fool is convinced that 'something than which nothing greater can be conceived' at least stands in relation to his understanding."

In logical terms, the difficulty connected with the use of the metaphor of the painting is that it substitutes something for something else that can have no substitute, a unique name, a class term whose only member is itself. Stipulating the logical conditions for the use of a unique name by supplying an example can only be misleading. The Fool has an inkling of this problem, which will later be seen to provide the occasion for Gaunilo's attempted refutation of the argument.

Necessary and Contingent Existence: *Proslogion* III

Proslogion II concludes with a summary: when one thinks of a being such that a greater cannot be conceived, one cannot think of this being as existing in thought alone but must think Him as existing also in reality, since this is greater. It is by now a commonplace that the presupposition of this part of the proof, existence is a perfection, has been challenged by Kant's claim that existence adds nothing to the concept of the subject. (There is no more money in one hundred real dollars than there is in one hundred imaginary dollars.) But the version of the argument in *Proslogion* III does not depend upon holding that existence is a property of God (on which the Kantian refutation hangs) but that *necessary* existence is such a property. In Lacanian terms neither the mirror stage nor the first phase of the Oedipal stage has been fully transcended. This is expressed theologically in *Proslogion* II when the Fool ascribes merely conceptual existence to the divine name and failed to attribute otherness (extramental existence) to God. By identifying the understanding with its divine object, he remains snared in the maternal womb. In *Proslogion* III, the psychological impasse of *Proslogion* II is overcome in the context of a discussion of the highest being's necessary existence, as contrasted with what is entailed by attributing contingent existence to Him. In this section I hope to relate the difference between necessary and contingent existence to the required condition for accession to the Name of the Father: the child's acceptance of lack in the form of symbolic castration as the price of admission into language and culture.

A preliminary sketch of this particularly dense part of Anselm's argument and its psychological corollaries may be useful. The argument falls into two parts.[12] First, Anselm posits the hypothesis that, if God exists, he exists as a contingent being. This hypothesis leads to the conclusion that the existence of God is impossible. The psychological outcome can, in Lacanian terms, be expressed as despair and anguish when the deepest desires of the unconscious—in the present instance, Anselm's desire for God—are thwarted. The second part of *Proslogion* III considers the hypothesis that God exists necessarily. If it is true, Anselm's desires are realized, and the "true" subject can enter unreservedly into pure joy and bliss. Such a psychological outcome cannot be fully realized, but this will become apparent only later in the dialogue with Gaunilo.

In the first part of the present section of the argument, its full implications (following Norman Malcolm) are best grasped by considering first what follows from positively affirming God's nonexistence. If God, a being than which none greater can be conceived, does not exist, then He cannot come into existence. If He did, He would merely have happened to come into existence (an impossible contention), or his existence would have been caused by some other thing. In either case, He would be a limited being. In Anselm's terms, "the creature would rise above the Creator." Instead of being an autonomous being, God would be dependent upon another for his existence. But, by our conception of Him, this is clearly impossible. The crucial point for a psychoanalytic development of the argument follows from this: since He cannot come into existence for the reasons given, and if He does not exist, his existence is impossible.

A Lacanian investigation of this possibility is parasitic on one of the most complex articles in *Écrits*, "The Subversion of the Subject and the Dialectic of Desire in the Freudian Unconscious" (*Écrits*, 292–325). We saw earlier that the relationship between the subject and the unconscious is mediated by the Law of the Father and the failure to transcend the identification with maternal desire that ensues when the process that orders these relations remains incomplete.

If the child remains bound to the mother as the source of fulfillment, he is doomed to disappointment, for even if the mother tries to satisfy all his needs, she cannot hope to fulfill his absolute demand for absolute love. Demand transcends the capacity to satisfy need. It is in this gap (*béance*) between need and demand that desire is born. Lacan distinguishes need, a biological force; lack, an irreversible incompleteness; and desire, a conatus "which begins to take shape in the margin in which demand [a request for love] becomes separated from need" (*Écrits*, 311). But because demand is always demand of the Other, it remains at the mercy of the Other's whim, giving rise to the phantom of the Other's omnipotence.

But man does not know his own desire, because the unconscious is the discourse of the Other. Lacan means this in two senses: first, "the *de* is to be understood in the sense of the Latin *de* (objective determination)," discourse from the Other; and second, "the *de* provides what grammarians call the 'subjective determination,' namely that it is *qua* Other that he desires, which is what provides the true compass of human passion" (ibid., 312). This is why the analyst does not try to meet the analysand's demands but speaks in the voice of the Other and asks, "What do you want [*che vuoi*]?" (ibid.) The double meaning attributed to the Other is tied to the inevitability of human frustration and anguish. Just as the maternal Other cannot hope to realize the child's absolute demands for perfection, so too access is barred to the fullness of the Other that is the object of unconscious desires. (This Other is written as Ø, barred O). If the Other as the "locus of truth" and the "treasure of the signifier" is, as Lacan claims, grounded in lack, relations to alterity can only end in despair. The "signifier of a lack in the Other," what Lacan calls the signifier of the barred Other, S(Ø), is inherent in the Other's function as "the treasure of the signifier" (ibid., 316).

This account of the Other provides an entering wedge for understanding the opening section of *Proslogion* III in Lacanian terms. We saw that the Other is "the treasure of the signifier" but cannot itself enter into plenary presence. At the same time, "the Other is required (*che vuoi*) to respond to the value of this treasure" (ibid.) from its own place, that is, it must say what it wants by entering the chain of signification. It can do so either from a buried chain of signifiers or by breaching another (upper) chain of signifiers. The Other is required to respond because, in a point of cardinal importance for Anselm's argument, Lacan insists *"There is no Other than the Other"* (ibid.). Lacan intends this reply in a psychoanalytic and not a theological sense. But in the context of the ontological argument, Lacan's point that "there is no Other than the Other" should be taken at face value. It is now possible to picture in Lacanian terms the psychoanalytic equivalent of hypothesizing God's nonexistence (as based on the contradictory conception of Him as a contingent being): the Other exists only as a lack.

The anguish of this position can be understood in terms of the relation among signifiers. A signifier is defined as that which represents the subject for another signifier. As such this signifier is "the signifier for which all the other signifiers represent the subject: that is to say in the absence of this signifier, all the other signifiers represent nothing" (ibid.). The subject is an absence in the set of signifiers and, as such, inexpressible. (It can be represented as a negative number $[-I]$ and its utterances, whose form is derived through a complex process that need not be replicated here, expressed as v-1, an irrational number; ibid., 317.) In sum, the statements of the unconscious are never directly accessible. It can therefore be argued that the Fool's earlier formulation, "God is not," is the unfortunate result of trying to transcribe unconscious content, God's plenary presence, directly, a procedure that has just been shown to be impossible. In the present context (examining the hypothesized nonexistence of God), anguish is experienced as the result of recognizing: first, that the subject is founded on a nullity; second, that there is no Other of this nullity; and finally, that the individual, thrown into the abyss of his own nonbeing, can only think the existence of God as impossible.

The next step in Anselm's argument considers the alternative hypothesis of God's necessary existence. If God does exist, nothing can have caused his existence, nor can He "just happen to cease to exist. So if He exists, His existence is necessary." Lacan reaches this conclusion by an altogether different route. After speculating on the signifier as founded in lack, Lacan's comments take a remarkably Christian turn. Explicitly rejecting the possibility of rational proof for the existence of God, Lacan suggests the solution that the Christian kerygma proclaims for establishing the existence of the Other: loving him (ibid.).

An alternative account for expressing the subject is also given in a dark Lacanian utterance. To the question "What am I?" Lacan replies: "I am in the place from which a voice is heard clamoring, 'The universe is a defect in the purity of Non-Being' "(ibid.). This oracular pronouncement can be taken to mean that the subject "fades" or withdraws from his discourse. Once outside of language, he cannot know whether he is alive or dead and thus can be said to undergo a kind of death. "This place is called *jouissance* [a term linked to rights and to sexual enjoyment, in this context, to boundless and impossible bliss], and it is the absence of this that makes the universe vain" (ibid.). The gap opened by this analysis parallels in point-for-point fashion the situation explicated in *Proslogion* III. When the I is seen as grounded in lack, a nullity in a chain of signifiers that must, but cannot, be brought into language because these signifiers represent nothing, then God is impossible. But if we begin with the fact that there is speech, even if the chain of signifiers is grounded in nullity, this nullity may be ontologically understood in some alternative fashion. When the I retreats—in theological language, "dies to itself"—or when, in Lacanian terms, "the subject fades," the Non-Being of the Other, which can be discursively formulated only in negative terms, may actually be something boundless, inexpressible, *jouissance* without limit. But if it is necessary that some such fathomless ground exist, still, as Lacan shows, access to it is barred.

This may be why, at the end of *Proslogion* III, the Fool continues to say in his heart: "God is not," although it has been established that "God exists supremely above all things." After the entire argument concerning God's necessary extramental existence has been traversed, the foolishness of the Fool persists. Even if it is *necessary* that there be *jouissance*, he knows he cannot experience it. The diagnosis offered in Anselm's theological terms was already stipulated in *Proslogion* II: a thing is conceived in one way when the word signifying it is thought and in another way when the very thing itself is understood. When hearing the word *God*, it is possible to give the word no meaning or an alien meaning. While some difficulties have been overcome, access to the divine name is barred and merely verbal signification attributed to it.

The Fool's Last Stand: The Most Perfect Island

The resistances of the Fool have crystallized in the argument anticipated in the metaphor of the painting. Gaunilo, a monk of Marmoutier speaking on behalf of the Fool, contends that the distinction between merely verbal conception and genuine understanding, which guarantees the existence of the thing conceived, is an artificial one. They are in fact the same: both are verbal, and verbal existence cannot be translated into actual existence.

To show this, Gaunilo, said to be a monk of Marmoutiers, objects that the earlier analogy of the painting is misleading because the painting is an object created in time: "The picture exists first in the mind of the painter, and afterward in his work."[13] The analogy is stretched to the breaking point if it is argued (as Anselm would be forced to do if the analogy were to hold point-for-point) that, as in the case of God, the nonexistence of the painting is inconceivable. In sum, Gaunilo contends in chapter 4, "I can conceive [of some object such as a painting] according to a fact that is real and familiar to me: but of God or a being greater than all others, I could not conceive at all, except merely according to the word." This formulation will turn out to be a fatal admission for Gaunilo and will enable Anselm, in both Lacanian and conventional theological terms, to bring the argument to the desired conclusion.

In his initial reply Gaunilo does not deny that a being such that a greater cannot be conceived can exist in the understanding, but rather that from this it follows that such a being exists in reality. In chapter 6 he offers a new analogy, that of a most perfect island, a better comparison than the painting because, as the best of its kind, it can claim greater structural affinity to a highest being. But the island's existence in actuality still cannot be proved from its assumption in hypothesis.

> [Because of] the impossibility of discovering what does not exist [it] is called the lost island. . . . Now if someone should tell me that there is such an island, I should easily understand his words, in which there is no difficulty. But, suppose that he went on to say, as if by a logical inference: . . . [This island exists in the understanding but] it is more excellent not to be in the understanding alone, but to exist both in the understanding and in reality, for this reason it must exist. For if it does not exist, any land which really exists is more excellent than it; and so the island already understood by you to be more excellent will not be more excellent. (*Écrits*, 11)

Gaunilo contends such a proof must be a jest, since unreal objects are conceivable without necessarily existing in reality. But in Lacanian terms, Gaunilo makes real progress when the fantasy object, a most perfect island, substitutes for the divine name and thereby advances beyond the limitations of the painting. The success of the therapy will depend upon full recognition of the difference between all other objects and the divine name, to which alone the logic of his argument pertains.

A distinction must be made before the argument's final step and the therapy can be successfully concluded: the difference between conceiving and understanding. For Anselm, understanding is the faculty that grasps factual existence, whereas the faculty of conceiving comprehends whatever is intelligible. Were the existence of God a matter for the understanding, Gaunilo could argue that any existing thing cannot be understood not to exist once it is known that the object *in fact* exists. In the case of conceiving, we can conceive of many things that exist as nonexisting, even when we know that factually they exist. So, objects other than God cannot be understood as nonexisting when they are known to exist, because they can, in fact, be imagined not to exist. But it is self-contradictory to say that a being such that a greater cannot be conceived can be conceived not to exist.

While from a Lacanian perspective both conceiving and understanding would be interpreted as conscious processes, manifestations of the unconscious slip into conceiving, since understanding purports to deal with factual existents rather than the facts of desire. Lacan grants that the perception of factual existents (roughly equivalent to Anselm's "understanding") can be allocated to the ego as "the seat of perceptions . . . [and that it] reflects the essence of the objects it perceives" (ibid., 134). But in doing so it fails to reflect its own unconscious affectations. There are objects—the ego itself, for example—that can become "a means of the speech addressed to you from the unconscious, a weapon to resist its recognition . . . fragmented in that it bears speech, and whole in that it helps in not hearing it" (ibid., 137). Such an object both brings symptoms clearly to view and turns the subject away from them. It is this contact with the "signifying material of his symptoms" that becomes possible at the level Anselm calls "conceiving" and that we are to search for in the meaning of the signifier *most perfect island*.

Access to this signifying material can be gained through a fundamental concept of Lacan's psychoanalytical epistemology, the *objet petit a* (the *a* standing for *autre*). Earlier I suggested that the unconscious is structured as a nexus of signifiers, which successively alienate and channel primordial desire. This path of "lures and alienation" is marked by changing objects, until at last desire becomes reflexive and ends up as the desire for another desire. This process of substitution is interpreted narrowly in terms of its genesis in individual life history and broadly as a law of psychic life. In the first and narrower sense, the lost object is what the subject wishes to be in its initial split from the mother, the phallus for the mother. The narrow sense also includes part objects (such as the breast) substituted by the instincts to fill in the fissure that now separates the child from his desired object. Second, in a broader sense the *objet petit a* designates any signifier or representative of the object of lack when it is deprived of its symbolic referent, the phallus.[14] But as Anika Lemaire points out, "Every object of desire, every object of alienating identification will reveal itself to be ephemeral and destined to be supplanted because it is incapable of stopping up the lack inscribed in the subject from the start by the very fact of his being eclipsed in the signifier."[15]

The most perfect island described by Gaunilo is a signifier that structurally replicates the object that has fallen from the significative chain and, as such, is an *objet petit a*. It cannot fill the fissure between the primordial object of desire and present demand, but it carries out a secondary function, one already envisioned by Lacan in another connection: the island serves (as Lacan says in a moment of theological reflection when speaking of religious icons or images) "as a go-between with the divinity."[16]

A single step remains for Anselm to reveal fully the ontic status of the island as an *objet petit a*. The relation between the Law of the Father and *jouissance* provides the psychological underpinning for Anselm's response to the most perfect island thesis. Anselm's rebuttal is based on a key distinction referred to earlier, that between a being greater than all others and a being than which no greater can be conceived. In Lacanian terms, *jouissance* is encoded in the divine name, which is, for Anselm, throughout the course of the argument "a being such that a greater cannot be conceived." This name is not to be confused with another, "a being greater than all other beings." Anselm's entire therapy, which only now can expose their distinctiveness, depended upon this difference all along. The two concepts, although not alike, are easy to confuse and lead to the unconscious misprisions of the Fool and Gaunilo. Now Anselm shows that a being greater than all other beings is a misleading verbal representation of God and leads to false conclusions about His nature. It is a designation founded on a lack: a greater being than the deficient highest being can be imagined, one than which a greater cannot even be conceived. Unlike Anselm's God, "greatest being" lacks conceptual and ontic fullness.

May it then be assumed that, once this difference is grasped, one can gain admission to a plenum without lack, symbolized by the correct name of God? By no means. The previous analysis has shown that conceptualization of the divine name rests on *difference*: the difference between a highest being and a being such that a greater cannot be conceived, and difference is itself grounded in negation and lack. Does the hope for reaching into the ground of *jouissance* inevitably lead to the lure and seduction of miragelike substitutions? Lacan shows that, although direct access to *jouissance* is barred, it can, through the phallic signifier, be reached in a restricted way. The elusiveness of *jouissance* is not the result of "a bad arrangement of society" or of some lack in the Other (as if the Other existed), or of "original sin," a myth used to explain this exclusion (*Écrits*, 317). Instead, it is to be accounted for by the necessity of the subject's entry into language and culture. But in the economy of desire such accession to symbolization demands a price: sacrificial castration. Because its castration can be imaged, the phallus as image is a natural locus for prohibition, for the curtailment of *jouissance* (ibid., 319). Only by excision of the imaginary phallus, barring it from the plenitude of *jouissance*, can the phallus as signifier or symbol come into being.

When this interpretation is applied to Anselm's argument, Gaunilo's therapy and that of the Fool are brought to closure. Both have come to understand that, if the paternal law has been interiorized, then the fulfillment of primordial desire is barred. Denied direct access to *jouissance*, they can only hear the divine name in its conceptual fullness as a master signifier. In a succinct formula strikingly pertinent to the phase of Anselm's argument just considered, Lacan writes: "Indeed, the law appears to be giving the order, '*Jouis* [have *jouissance*]!,' to which the subject can only reply, '*J'ouis* [I hear],' the jouissance being no more than understood" (ibid.).

PART II

Training Bodies: Pedagogies of Pain

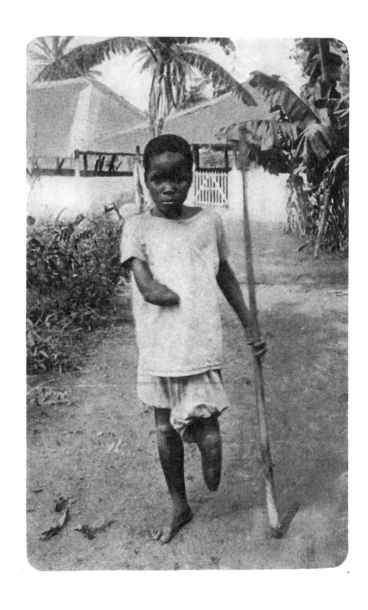

Even though the body has been all quite ground to powder by some severe accident, or by the ruthlessness of enemies, and though it has been so diligently scattered to the winds, or into the water, that there is no trace of it left . . . no, not a hair of its head shall perish. The flesh shall then be spiritual and subject to the spirit, but still flesh, not spirit.

—**Augustine,** *The City of God*

Viewed from a phenomenological perspective, the perspective of what has become known as the "lived body," the body establishes a context for a wide range of inquiries. Thus understood, it can become the object of self-mortification in the interest of religious or aesthetic ends. In addition, suffering may be interpreted as a pedagogy of pain in which self-sacrifice becomes an entering wedge for an ethics of compassion for the other, whose capacity to endure pain is experienced as a solicitation to relieve the other's suffering. Ethics is thus inextricably bound up with corporeal vulnerability.

Illustration: Impongi, a boy of Illnega mutilated by state soldiers. In *Red Rubber: The Story of the Robber Slave Trade Flourishing in the Congo in the Year of Grace 1906*, introd. Sir Harry H. Johnston. General Research and Reference Division, Schomberg Center for Research in Black Culture, The New York Public Library, Astor, Lenox, and Tilden Foundations.

Asceticism as Willed Corporeality
Body in Foucault and Heidegger

Heidegger and Foucault can be envisioned as thinkers of emancipatory askeses, disciplines of liberation in which each may be seen as engaged in freeing knowledge and truth from embedding contexts of repressive epistemological constraints and their ancillary ethical implications, a freeing through which a certain release is attained.[1] Techniques in which historical accretions are not merely jettisoned but reenvisioned are deployed by Heidegger to deliver the relation of Being and beings in what he calls a concealing-revealing and by Foucault to uncover the disguises truth wears by bringing to light the strategic power relations that generate the practices of knowledge, politics, and culture.

Foucault insists that philosophy was and continues to be an " 'ascesis,' *askēsis*," that thinking is a self-transformative exercise (*UP*, 9). He distinguishes *askēsis* from asceticism, understood as the renunciation of pleasure, and interprets it as a mode of self-transformative freedom. In Heidegger, *askēsis* can be seen as a disciplined questioning of the meaning of Being, language, and truth; in Foucault, it consists in a probing of strategies for the formation and reinvention of a self. In a succinct statement of the direction such a project might take, in which issues of sex and gender figure, Foucault proclaims:

> The *askēsis* is a work one performs upon oneself in order to transform oneself or make the self appear that happily one

never attains. Can that be our problem today? We've rid ourselves of asceticism. Yet it's up to us to advance into a homosex-
ual *askēsis* that would make us work on ourselves and invent, I
do not say discover, a manner of being that is still improbable.
(*FL*, 206)

Although the perspective of this statement seems to veer drastically
from that of Heidegger's thought, insofar as Foucault is engaged in
a Nietzschean reversal, he remains comprehensible in Heideggerian
terms: he inverts the meaning of Being experienced as Spirit to see
Being as corporeality. As Otto Pöggeler notes, for Heidegger "this
metaphysical interpretation [of Being as Spirit] is upended when (in
Nietzsche) the body becomes the guiding thread."[2]

Foucault considers repressive self-formation to be an expression
of what he calls "technologies of the self," modes of imposing confor-
mations of thought upon corporeality, especially its sexual expressions. Though Foucault concedes that there are preferable modes of
configuring, he sees no egress from the necessity for an askesis or
discipline of self-formations.[3] Similarly, for Heidegger thought cannot escape the thinking of Being, even when Being is manifested in
calculative representation, its current mode of disclosure, one that
constitutes a clear and present danger—in which, however, there resides a saving power. Heidegger's questioning of the essence of technology is a questioning that is already *unterwegs* (under way) to
deliverance. Through a discipline of silence and listening, presaged
in his earliest work and elaborated in his later descriptions of the essence of technology and the shaping of the artwork, we may encounter the incalculable, which cannot be represented.

I shall, in my analysis, pursue these lines of inquiry by envisioning
each thinker as a questioner of the other. Rather than engage in an
exercise in intellectual history, I shall mention influences upon and
shifts within their thought when these are relevant to the larger narrative.[4] I shall first discuss the meaning of questioning as a point of
orientation, a questioning that includes both existential involvement
and distancing from the question.[5] Then I shall turn to Heidegger's
interrogation of Western philosophy's articulation of Being and truth
and to Foucault's approaches to philosophical discourse, archaeological in the sense of exhuming the rules of conceptual and social practices and genealogical as a tracking of regulations and protocols that
govern the modern subject's self-transformations. Neither approach
will be conceived as a method (a term already tainted by virtue of its

relation to the being of the modern subject), but rather as a purifying activity, an emancipatory askesis.

I shall then consider several modes of askesis as pathways: the paths of thinking, of the appropriation of death and sexuality, and of shaping the body through the practices of medicine and art. In each case, work and thought are not severed, but rather *melete* (Latin *meditatio*) and *gymnasia* (to train oneself) can be seen to interact, to work in tandem as dynamic aspects of self-formation.[6]

Exhibiting an Askesis as the Askesis of Exhibiting

Despite the dearth of extended commentary about Heidegger by Foucault, it is no secret that he considered Heidegger's thought significant for the formation of his own. As early as his 1955 comments on Ludwig Binswanger, Foucault proclaims the advantages of Binswanger's appropriation of Heidegger for psychoanalysis over a purely Freudian description of psychic life. More importantly, Foucault discovers in the later Heidegger the view that human beings are constituted by historical practices, thereby linking Heidegger's depiction of the oblivion of Being to his own archaeological method as an exhuming of the epistemic, social, and political practices that enable a given science or discipline to be seen as true.[7]

Conceding both indebtedness and suspicion, Foucault contrasts his own work, "[t]he precise domain of [which] is what I should call technologies . . . discourses about the subject," with Heidegger's interest in the formation of the object. For Heidegger, it is as "an increasing obsession with *technē* as the only way to arrive at an understanding of objects that the West lost touch with Being." Identifying his own enterprise as a reversal of Heidegger's, Foucault proclaims: "Let's turn the question around and ask which techniques and practices form the Western concept of the subject, giving it its characteristic split of truth and error, freedom and constraint" (*RC*, 161 n. 4). Yet Foucault's allegation that Heidegger is inattentive to the subject neglects the focus in *Being and Time* upon uncovering the obscuring of the being we ourselves are.[8] Foucault's point, however, is not to discover a more primordial ground concealed by the cognitive subject but to bring to the fore the political implications of self-formation.

In something like the manner in which Vedic religions speak of wiping away mind-obscuring karma, Heidegger hopes to illuminate the ways in which truth has been covered over and encrypted.

Speaking of his inquiry as "build[ing] a way, a way of thinking" (*QCT*, 5) that is to bring about an experience of the essence of technology, he warns that we are caught up in what is merely instrumental, technology's effort to take hold of itself in an act of willful mastery (*QCT*, 5). The undoing or *Destruktion* of the notion of instrumentality demands an understanding of the means-end relation, of cause and effect, which Heidegger, in a Nietzschean move, unmasks as a relation of indebtedness, one that is not to be interpreted in moral terms but rather as a thinking of what has heretofore remained unthought in the essence of technology. Indebtedness and responsibility are given new meaning as a letting come forth into presence. Thus, significations that have piggybacked onto one another are peeled away, and the bringing-forth of that which presences into appearance is brought to light. Neither an askesis of repristinization nor a nostalgic willing back, the process Heidegger describes is an undoing of technology as mastery that is at once deconstructive and salvific. Such questioning elicits the meaning of bringing-forth, which is a "moving freely in revealing [*das Entbergen*]," a term derived from *bergen*, "to rescue," and leads back to the much commented upon term *aletheia*, "unconcealment." In the present context, bringing-forth may be read (boldly) as an askesis of cognitive liberation.

Foucault questions, not the ontological conditions that make it possible for there to be philosophical practices at all, but rather how and why at any given time something can be said but not some other thing. He proceeds by interrogating what he calls an archive, "the mass of things spoken in a culture, conserved, valorized, reused, repeated and transformed." He goes on to say that "[t]he 'archive' appears then as a kind of great practice of discourse, a practice which has its rules, its conditions, its functioning and its effects" (*FL*, 58). In proceeding archaeologically, Foucault attempts to understand the rules of formation governing the human sciences, not in a quest for origins, but rather in an effort to uncover a site where he hopes to find the rules and protocols that render possible the existence of the matrix from which thought emerges—in short, of the archive.

Without abandoning archaeology when dealing with the subject as a locus of corporeal activities, Foucault initiates inquiry with a current social or political question, thereby introducing genealogical concerns. Such an analysis is located at the point where an archaeology of problematizations and a genealogy of practices intersect (*UP*,

12–13). This strategy yields an account that shifts from the rule-governed care of the self in the Greco-Roman world to later Christian practices of confession and penitential ritual, a history of progressive etiolation that moves from a disciplined corporeal erotics to a discourse of chastity.

On the face of it, Foucault might ask, is Heidegger's quest not also genealogical, but in the pejorative sense of seeking to return to origins, as his own does not? Does Heidegger not use such phrases as "that which endures primally out of the earliest beginning"? One might reply, however, that, when Heidegger interrogates the essence of technology, he does not intend to reveal a ground or primordium, but rather to heed what has been said and is now no longer said by philosophy. To bring to the fore what cannot now be said, one must first grasp the current mode of Being's revelation, a mode Heidegger calls enframing (*Gestell*). In the mode of enframing, beings manifest themselves as standing-reserve, and Being reveals itself as a storehouse of energy, which is stockpiled in order to be managed. Heidegger states repeatedly that he is not a Romantic seeking to revive the pretechnological past, but rather that he hopes to free thought from the ontological entrapment of the *Gestell* (*QCT*, 22). In Foucauldian terms, enframing expresses power. Like Foucault, Heidegger recognizes in the contemporary will to truth a will to control whose very essence is unfreedom. Thus an emancipatory askesis must somehow be will-less, insofar as "the essence of freedom cannot originally be connected with the will or even with the causality of human willing." Instead, it is as "the happening of revealing, i.e., of truth, that freedom stands in the closest and most intimate kinship" (*QCT*, 25).

Thought's Way: How Thinking Exculpates

Heidegger is careful to maintain that thought's way is not the knowledge of philosophy's history as an account of conceptual change, that the meaning of concepts continues to withdraw from us unless we first know who we ourselves are (*FCM*, 4). Philosophizing "is a questioning in which we inquire into beings as a whole and inquire in such a way that in so doing we ourselves, the questioners, are thereby also included in the question, placed into question" (*FCM*, 9). Unlike the inquiries of the special sciences, such questioning involves the repertoire of all the self's comportments in its world relations, a questioning that itself constitutes a discipline.

For Heidegger, thinking is a transformative art, one that radically changes the way in which the meaning of Being is understood. Metaphysics, or philosophizing that takes the meaning of Being to be self-evident presencing, must be overcome, not bypassed or leapt over. Thinking must engage in the arduous task of passing through the history of metaphysics by thinking what is unthought in it, its concealed ground, Being, or *Seyn* (Heidegger's occasional archaism), as distinguished from the truth of beings. This task is not an academic exercise, but an intense struggle, a recasting of thinking so as to free thinking to experience the truth of Being. Thus, Heidegger insists, even if metaphysical questioning is comprehensive, "No matter how extensively we are concerned *about it*, everything remains a misunderstanding unless we are *gripped* by such questioning. . . . Although we have spoken of philosophy, we have not yet spoken *from out of it*" (*FCM*, 57).

Genuine questioning is not to be confused with an inquiry into phenomena as an interrogation of present being, but is rather a questioning "without why." Contrasting the "why" of aetiological inquiry to the questioning that seeks the "because" of an abyssal ground, Heidegger alludes to the mystical tradition of Angelus Silesius, for whom the rose *is* simply because it *is*. Thus Heidegger writes: "The because which wards off every accounting for and every why, names the simple plain lying before that is without why, upon which everything depends, everything rests."[9]

An askesis, and especially one of questioning, it could be argued, would self-destruct without rules for combatting errancy. But if Heidegger implies that erring consists in making the why the origin of thought, does he not thereby put forward a rule for erring? The why cannot be interpreted in this way, however, for were this the case thought would be trapped by the self-reflexive paradox of the why itself, by the presumption that an explanatory why can be given for rejecting the why. Such an account would already reflect the view that truth is correctness, the possibility of a correspondence between question and answer, that statements mirror states of affairs just as they are.

In his account of truth as correspondence, Heidegger maintains that, as a condition of presentness, there is that which stands in contrast to the present being, that is, in contrast to the thing, and is placed over and against us. The appearing of the thing can be seen as traversing this opposition. The thing's appearing, or crossing over into presence, occurs within an opening whose openness is not created by presenting itself but is prior to it, an openness that is free to take on the strictures of presenting. Thus, "Freedom is setting oneself free for what is manifest in the open, as letting the being be."[10]

If the thinking of Being is without why, "a highly errant . . . matter," may we then conclude that thought is an askesis of nihilism, of the "lawless caprice" pinpointed by Nietzsche, from which the true has vanished (*PLT*, 186)? In a statement whose mood suggests an impassioned quietism, Heidegger, in a 1950 letter to a student, writes: "To think Being means to respond to the appeal of its presencing, an appeal both revealed and veiled" (*PLT*, 185). In a passage reminiscent of the voices of Silesius and Eckhart so familiar to the early Heidegger, thinking is said to demand "long concentration and constant testing of its hearing" if the respondent to the appeal of Being is not to go astray. What must also be thought in this context is the absence of God and the divinities whose fullness now exists in the manner of not being, a "no longer" that is itself "a not-yet" (*PLT*, 184). Heidegger's response is not one of despair but rather can be envisioned as an askesis for what he calls a destitute time: "learning the craft of thinking, unswerving, yet erring" (*PLT*, 186).

For Foucault, philosophy in the positive sense is a stepping back in order to detach oneself from received views of truth. Being an activity directed toward transforming conceptual frameworks and accepted values, to philosophize is both to "think otherwise" and "to do something else."[11] Whereas for Heidegger thinking-questioning interrogates the history of metaphysics, Foucault turns instead to "a history of 'ethics,'" understood as an account of the rules of self-formation "that enable an individual to fashion himself into a subject of ethical conduct" (*UP*, 251). Yet, in a move reminiscent of Heideggerian questioning, Foucault disavows the history of mentalities and of ideas as constituting thought. As distinguished from representations that accompany behavior and from attitudes that ground it, to inquire is to problematize, to step back from modes of acting and place them in question: "Thought is freedom in relation to what one does, the motion by which one detaches oneself from it, establishes it as an object and reflects on it as a problem" (*E*, 17). Problematization defamiliarizes its object by eliciting the conditions that render a political, social, or cultural object possible, to which those engaged in its practices are likely to be oblivious.

Foucault does not hesitate to name such philosophizing thought's critical inspection of itself, an askesis, a getting free of oneself: "The living substance of philosophy" was and continues to be "an 'ascesis,' *askēsis*, an exercise of oneself in the activity of thought" (*UP*, 9). In it, the "truth games" played out in specific technologies of the self are exposed. It is not the manipulation of things and signs that principally concerns Foucault, but the technology of self he identifies as conduct-regulating, a technology of power that determines individual behavior and makes possible the individual's submission to domination. Eschewing straightforward determinism, Foucault acknowledges those technologies of the self that enable individuals alone or with the aid of others to alter themselves, to effect radical changes "upon their own bodies, and souls, thought, conduct, and way of being, so as to transform themselves in order to attain a certain state of happiness, purity, wisdom, perfection or immortality" (*TS*, 18).

Ars Erotica, Artes Moriendi: The Ways of Sex and Death

Before they can consider the thought formations in which sex and death are configured as human constructs, it is crucial for Heidegger and Foucault to disentangle them from the view that they are natural processes. What is meant by nature must be thematized, because a category mistake in this regard might convey the misleading view that the purpose of a liberating askesis is a return to nature.

Although inferences about human sexuality as a natural process might be drawn by attending to what Heidegger means by "world," there is no specific discussion of sexual being in his major works, as there is, for example, of motility.[12] It could be surmised that one among many possible explanations for such reticence stems from a worry about reviving the suppositions of an Aristotelian biology, according to which human sexuality is linked to animal nature, a position that Heidegger would unequivocally reject.

In depicting the being of animals, Heidegger focuses on the distinction between having a world and the privation of world: the animal is "poor in world," whereas human beings are world forming. Disavowing any hierarchical assessment of the difference, Heidegger offers this graphic example: "When we say the lizard is lying on a rock, we ought to cross out the word rock . . . whatever the lizard is lying on is given *in some way* for the lizard and yet is not known to the lizard as rock" (*FCM*, 197). Heidegger contrasts *behavior*, a term applied to animals as "captivated," as impelled by drives (*Trieben*), with *comportment*, a term that refers to the human way of being as inhabiting a world. Animals live in an environment in which they struggle to maintain themselves against a "disinhibiting ring," an environmental encircling that triggers behavior (*FCM*, 253–54). Described privatively, animal being is lived as a withholding of the ability to take something as something. To explicate the meaning of human being, Heidegger does not, however, turn to a contrast between animal disinhibition (*Enthemmung*) and human life as existence in a meaning-laden world or between animal reproduction and human sexuality, but rather to human mortality. "Because captivation belongs to the essence of the animal, the animal cannot die in the sense in which dying is ascribed to human beings but can only come to an end" (*FCM*, 267).

Were one to view Heidegger's account of mortality in *Being and Time* through the lens of Foucault, it might be seen as an exhumation of Dasein's finitude as a fundamental possibility of its existence that Dasein must take upon itself as an askesis in the interest of liberating itself from socially constructed views. Dasein, the being that one is, is an entity distinguished by the fact that Being is an issue for it. For Foucault, the modern subject must be released from the conceptual and institutional practices, the sexual politics that form it, whereas for Heidegger the self is "liberated" when it transforms everyday existence into clarified existence to become the Dasein it is by exposing its death as its ownmost potentiality for Being. Each Dasein must take on this possibility for itself: no one can die for me. What is at stake is the very Being-in-the-world of Dasein. Its death is the possibility of no longer being able to be there. Because death is its ownmost possibility, "Dasein cannot outstrip the possibility of death. Death is the possibility of the absolute impossibility of Dasein," revealed to it not cognitively but through anxiety (*BT*, 294). Such anxiety is not a failing of Dasein but a basic mood grounded in a fundamental comportment, that of care (*Sorge*).

To uncover one's mortality is not yet to grasp the manner in which it is camouflaged in everyday existence. Just as, for Foucault, the sexual discourses entrenched in Western thought exhibit modes of flight from the intensities of pleasure, so, for Heidegger, the public interpretation of death or the They-self, *Das Man*, tranquillizes Dasein in the face of death. Does not everyone, after all, die? But the fact that death occurs is only empirically certain and not yet existentially decisive. Heidegger designates that which brings Dasein out of its evasiveness a call (*Ruf*) of conscience (*des Gewissens*), a summoning of Dasein from its lostness in the They-self. Dasein must respond by gathering itself together so that it can assume its own death. First, a primordial being-guilty, which prepares one for anxiety, must be dislodged from the sense of moral guilt bound up with the Kantian view of conscience. Heidegger calls this new state of mind "resoluteness," "a reticent self-projection upon one's 'ownmost being-guilty,' in which one is ready for anxiety" (*BT*, 343). Resoluteness is not an act of abstract willing but determines what is possible at a specifiable moment.

Yet to grasp becoming ready for anxiety is no simple matter. Just as Dasein must distinguish the interpretation of death by the They-self, which lulls it into tranquillity, from the resolute appropriation of its own death, so, too, it must be alert to the difference between the affect of fear, an awaiting or a feeling threatened in the face of something, and anxiety. The latter is not concerned with anything definite but is a mood that disengages one from the world and renders impossible projecting oneself upon some potentiality for Being that depends on some specific object of concern. The disclosure of this impossibility is intended not to lead to despair but rather to reveal what is already there, the one for whom one is anxious, namely, Dasein itself (*BT*, 393).

Unlike the drifting of fear from one worldly possibility to another, lived as a present that one can neither hold onto nor repeat, anxiety has its own mode of temporality. It brings one up against one's thrownness as a *repeatable* possibility. "The character of having-been is constitutive for . . . anxiety; and bringing one face to face with repeatability is the specific ecstatical mode of this character" (*BT*, 394). Although anxiety is grounded in the pastness of its repeatability, it is resoluteness that makes anxiety possible, and the mode of temporalization of resoluteness is future in that resoluteness is lived as an anticipation of Dasein's death. Thus temporal complexity is intrinsic to an askesis driven by mortality: in the pastness of anxiety Dasein repeats, reappropriates its future mortality in resoluteness. As in the lives of saints in late antiquity who free themselves from worldliness by withdrawal and meditation upon death, anxiety liberates Dasein from concern with the world.[13] Heidegger explicitly states that he perceives anxiety thus understood to be liberating: "Anxiety liberates [Dasein] *from* possibilities that count for nothing" (*BT*, 395).

As with death for Heidegger, for Foucault the truth of sexuality cannot be liberated by understanding sexuality as a "natural" process. "It is not through sexuality that we communicate with the orderly and pleasingly profane world of animals; rather sexuality is a fissure . . . which marks the limit within us and designates us as a limit" (*RC*, 58). Instead (glossing the thought of Bataille), Foucault argues that what gives sexuality its unique character is its power to profane in a world from which, paradoxically, the sacred has already been evacuated. The sacred is reconstructed as an empty form, one that does not revert to natural being but rather proclaims the death of God.[14] What may be disguised as a discourse of natural animality is unmasked as a theological discourse expressing the absence of God.

Transgression thus understood involves limit, a line it crosses ever so briefly, the "narrow zone where it displays the flash of its passage" (*RC*, 60). Without a limit to breach, transgression would not exist, and if the limit were illusory, transgression would have nothing to violate. Limit as limit must return to the uncrossable, to a prohibitive force that invites breaching. It would be "a reductive exercise," as Jeremy R. Carrette believes, to subsume Foucault's efforts to grasp the complexities of his own gay sexuality in terms of "limit experience" (*RC*, 19). Instead, the value of limit experience lies in its enabling the subject to think itself without entrapment (*RC*, 23). Transgression is neither a dialectical overcoming nor a triumph over limits but a nonpositive affirmation that propels being to its limit. The circular path in which it moves leads to the claim that we are becoming more Greek. Yet this circular return to what Foucault calls a homeland (*RC*, 62) cannot be identified with Heidegger's valorization of home, which is embedded in an autochthony that would resolve oppositions.

Linked to the imbrication of sacred and profane, to a limit that is exposed in the ontological void left by the death of God, sexuality is tamed by a language that has become a juridical discourse without a divine lawgiver. Foucault's efforts to unmake this change indicate a step toward inventing forward-looking contemporary social practices that would intensify pleasure. Freedom today, he insists, is not a matter of unleashing desire, which, in any case, is always already expressed in sexual practices, but of escaping deceptively emancipatory strategies, formulaic views of sexuality such as that of the pure sexual encounter. Thus when Foucault speaks of homosexuality as liberating, his remarks are not directed toward establishing a new gay profile, but rather are a move toward defining a new way of life, as "an historic occasion to reopen affective and relational virtualities not so much through the [homosexual's] intrinsic qualities but due to the biases against the position that he occupies" (*FL*, 207). The problem is not that of enhancing self-knowledge but rather that of establishing a new nexus of relations, which Foucault prefers to call friendship (*FL*, 204). Xenophon's account of *philia* as conversing, confiding, rejoicing, or commiserating together into old age can be said to capture this view (*UP*, 201).

Shaping the Body: From Medicine to Artwork

In accordance with the regimen of studying the "arts of oneself, the aesthetics of existence," Foucault maintains that the self is not only a work of conceptual formation but can be shaped as a work of art (*E*, 207). The expression "technology of the self" is to be understood in relation to the term *techne*'s primordial Greek meaning as a "practice," a knowing how or *savoir faire* in the sense of an art (*UP*, 62). But is there not a difficulty in conflating philosophical thought with art in the process of self-formation? Had Heidegger not warned against identifying art and religion with philosophy?

To understand Heidegger's reservations, it is important to see that he contests, not the necessity of encountering art and religion along the way in the quest for revealing the true, but rather their exploitation, their interpretation as tools in the interest of philosophizing (*FCM*, 2–3). Thus Heidegger (like Foucault) does not hesitate to invoke the Greek use of *techne* in depicting the crossing over from truth to the work, proclaiming, "There was a time when the bringing-forth of the true into the beautiful was called *techne*. And the *poēisis* of the fine arts was also called *techne*" (*QCT*, 34).

Lest the difference between philosophy and art be mistakenly imagined as reflecting the distinction between thought as somehow passive and the effort that creates an object as active, it is worth noting that only in speaking *about* philosophy do we remain quiescent. "What is decisive, however, is that we emerge from this dealing with . . . *and take action within metaphysics itself*" (ellipsis in original; *FCM*, 57). Philosophy as a listening-questioning is not a sinking into lethargy but an activity of a special kind, a fundamental attunement as a presupposition for thinking and acting. Heidegger speaks not of affective or cognitive ascertaining but rather of "letting whatever is sleeping *become wakeful*" (*FCM*, 60). Reminiscent of the words of Bach's cantata, "Wachet auf ruft uns die Stimme," conscience issues a wake-up call. In a perhaps unguarded Heideggerian moment, Foucault concludes that critical thinking must "bring an idea to life . . .

light fires, watch the grass grow, listen to the wind, catch the sea-foam in the breeze and scatter it. It would multiply not judgments, but signs of existence; it would summon them, drag them from their sleep."[15]

If art, like philosophy, is to constitute an awakening, Foucault believes that the artistic shaping of the self must issue in new forms of conduct (*UP*, 13). In tracking the history of this shaping, he describes the body in the classical period as the locus of pleasure and the truth of the body as constructed by medical practices. Conceived not only as a fund of knowledge designed for the cure of disease, medicine was also envisaged as a collection of rules specifying dietary and gymnastic regimens that determined how one was to live. The discourse of medicine was intended to forestall death by creating the body as a work that would be immortal, yet constrained by the corruptible matter that nature uses.[16] Although Foucault does not make the connection, such a conception of the body bears comparison with the received view of the artwork as a passport to immortality. Foucault notes that the Greek physician Galen's account of sexuality situates sexuality in the context of death and immortality. To overcome the corruptibility of the body, "nature had to place the principle of a force, an extraordinary dynamis in the body and soul of the living creature" (*CS*, 106). Galen concludes that pleasure is not incidental to sexual acts but is imprinted in the body in a way that is irresistible and that the circulation of fluids and pneuma generated by sexual activity involves the entire body.

Foucault continually wrestles with the question of why Western thought aims to determine the truth about sex rather than to invent ways to intensify sexual pleasure. How, he asks, is an *ars erotica* in this culture to be released from its embedding in a *scientia sexualis*? In reaching for this desideratum he notices that Eastern societies define "an art which would be an art of producing, through sexual relations or with the sexual organ, the type of pleasure that one seeks to make the most intense, the strongest, or as long-lasting as possible" (*RC*, 119). At the same time, he maintains that his analyses are not aimed at excoriating historical practices or reverting to a previously selected default position, but rather attempt to track the ways in which the control of pleasure shapes the subject in the hope of inventing an askesis, at once disciplined and transgressive, that maximizes rather than represses pleasure.[17]

Foucault's diachronic narrative of sexual practices can be seen as moving from care of the self as self-knowledge, from the classical *gnōthi seauton* ("know yourself"), to the era of early Christianity, when the self was interpreted in terms of renunciation of the world and sex. What is crucial in this trajectory is the intervening step of transformation from an erotics that recognizes the freedom of the other to a philosophical askesis as a quest for truth, an "asceticism" that "was not a means of disqualifying the love of boys" but "a means of . . . giving it shape and form, of valorizing it" (*UP*, 245). Corporeality is configured as a progressive etiolation of the body when ancient rules for care of the self give way to later configurations.

Thus, in *Alcibiades I* Socrates persuades Alcibiades to submit to him in a relationship that is essentially pedagogical and in which concern for the self is still bound up with erotic and political practices. Care of the self is envisaged as tendence of the soul, construed not as substance but as activity, and as requiring attention to the divine element in itself. In the second century, attention was still paid to older medical accounts of corporeality, but at the same time a shift from the Platonic culture of dialogue to one of listening to truth and to oneself could be discerned, an attentiveness to self that was designed to uncover failures of strategy rather than moral flaws (*TS*, 34; *RC*, 128). In mining the texts of this period, Foucault finds a new apprehensiveness concerning the effects of the abuse of pleasure on body and soul, a stress on conjugal relations and wariness with regard to the love of boys (*CS*, 39).

The link of self-formation to faith in early Christianity necessitated more abstemious protocols of self-purification.[18] Foucault refers to *exomologēsis*, a term whose Christian meanings include a complex of penitential exercises, such as fasting and sexual abstinence. Unlike the Stoic view that truth about the self is learned by memorizing rules, Christian *exomologēsis* is a dramatic, not a verbal behavior: "Penance is not nominal but theatrical. . . . It rubs out the sin yet reveals the sinner" (*E*, 244). By contrast, *exagoreusis* is the self-renunciatory analysis and disclosure of one's thoughts to another, so that the pedagogical relations of the ancient world become in monastic life a rule of total obedience to one's director (*E*, 246).

Foucault discovers in John Cassian's complex theory of vices, according to which all vices are connected, the special importance of fornication. Even the defeat of a vice may not reflect a spiritual victory if its fall generates a presumptuousness that allows a new vice to erupt. In a structure of paired vices, fornication is tied to greed in that both involve the body. Fornication as a sin of the body must be fought not only mentally but by "mortifying the flesh by vigils, fast and back-breaking labor" (*RC*, 190). Unlike the appetite for food, the sexual appetite is not needed to maintain life and thus can be resisted. Yet, far from discussing actual sexual relations, Cassian describes the fight for chastity as an askesis whose success is measured in terms of the monk's unresponsiveness to various forms of temptation. What is to be fought is a concupiscent volition that may even infiltrate dreams and whose exercise leads to pollution. It is no longer a question of bodily restraint but rather of expunging images from the mind. Foucault notes in Augustine an obsession with the involuntary acts of the body, with libido or the autonomous movements of the sexual organs, organs that do not obey the will's commands (*E*, 182–83).

It should be clear that Foucault writes no ordinary history. In conformity with his stress on modes of stylization, he is less interested in determining the *reason* for the escalation of sexual prohibitions than the *manner* in which sex is given up and the body shaped. Thus it is not merely the transfer from actual to internalized prohibition, from outside to inside, but the development of new techniques, the birth of a desexualized technology of self, that concerns Foucault (*RC*, 195–97).

Circumspect as Heidegger remains about sexuality, it is worth noting that some "conceptual threads" in his religion courses of 1920–21 can be seen as premonitory of Foucault's more open and robust discussion of various forms of Christian asceticism. To be sure, Heidegger does not attend to the minutiae of ritual practices, but in elaborating Christian themes he attempts even in these early lectures to offer as the starting point of inquiry descriptions of factical transactions with the circumambient world, the world in which Christians found themselves.[19] In this context, the fissuring of self by sexuality makes a brief appearance. In his comments on Augustine's description of the self, Heidegger maintains that the despair that would engulf Augustine is mitigated by hope grounded in divine mercy. He notes, however, that the trade-off for this gift is continence. Thus Heidegger: "The righteous man must therefore be examined, tested and proven in his private parts, in his secrets, that is in his heart (inner reflection) and in his loins."[20]

To uncover the meaning of shaping for Heidegger, one must turn not to sexuality but to what may seem far removed, his analysis of the origin of the artwork (*Kunstwerk*). Heidegger notes that the inquiry into the origin of the work already begs the question, since to interrogate art by turning to the artwork presupposes that we know what art is. It is useful, he suggests, to begin with the thingly nature of the work, given that the artwork is in some sense a thing. But the thing must be released from received views of it, especially from the view that thingliness is a fusion of matter and form, a view that is often misleadingly applied to the artwork as a composite of inert material substructure and specific shape. Instead, the work is an event, a happening, one in which, through the work's disclosure of what and how a thing is, a world opens and is made to abide. It is important for the issue of self-formation to grasp the meaning of world, in that world and human existence cannot be thought separately. Thus Heidegger writes:

> World is never an object . . . [but] the ever non-objective to which we are subject as long as the paths of birth and death, blessing and curse keep us transported into Being. Wherever those decisions of our history that relate to our very being are made, taken up and abandoned by us, go unrecognized, and are rediscovered by new inquiry, there the world worlds. (*PLT*, 44–45)

In another seemingly paradoxical claim, Heidegger insists that the artist is not showcased in the artwork but is a passageway for the work. Yet Heidegger also holds that the work does not merely happen but is created or brought forth through the *technē* that is art by the *technitēs*, the artist. He attempts to resolve this difficulty by maintaining that creation is "causing something to emerge as a thing that has been brought forth" (*PLT*, 60). Not the artist but Art is the origin of the work.

A further disclosure of art's ambiguity manifests itself in its truth as preservation. Far from reflecting a merely static persistence, preservation is active as the setting forth of truth. Creation of the artwork entails "the fixing in place of a self-establishing truth in the figure bringing forth the unconcealedness of what is," but the work has an ongoing life. The setting-to-work of truth also means the bringing of "work-being into movement and happening as preservation" (*PLT*, 71). Art, then, is the becoming and happening of truth as creation and preservation. Far from merely reproducing a visible entity, art is a fixing in place of the becoming and happening of truth (*PLT*, 36). Even if beings dissemble, this deception is also a condition for bringing to the fore the opposition of concealing and revealing in the occurring of truth in the artwork (*PLT*, 54–55).

In defiance of what a Heideggerian reading of the body might allow, can these doublings themselves not be set to work to expose the body in all of its thingliness and the work of the self as a bringing of this corporeality cogently into the open? If the art hidden in nature can be brought forth in the artwork, as Heidegger alleges, can the body not be thought anew as a unique work shaped by a *technē* in which artist and artwork constitute a single site, a body that is both one's ownmost and a being for the other, inside and outside itself, a eucharistic body, as it were, that exhibits and shrinks from its sacrality, one in which the history of corporeality is encrypted? Heidegger is hardly likely to view such an askesis with favor. Yet does one not, in making the body one's own by acts of creation and preservation, uncover pointers that, for those who understand, provide direction for bringing about a transformation of oneself?

Blind Man Seeing
From Chiasm to Hyperreality

Once in a great while a play opens that should have irresistible appeal to afficionados of Maurice Merleau-Ponty. Such a play is *Molly Sweeney*, Irish playwright Brian Friel's extraordinary drama about the crisis in the sensory and affective life of a woman born blind who, through surgery, supplants a world of darkness with one of limited sight. Where does sensory richness lie, the play inquires, in the mingled conformation of sound, feeling, taste, and smell in which language and percept are commingled, or in the ability to experience the world as spectacle? Consider the preliminary account of Molly's predicament as interpreted by her husband Frank, a Gaelic hippy, an autodidact of fluctuating enthusiasms. He explains that, bereft of touch and smell, Molly "wouldn't know a flower from a football." He goes on succinctly to summarize the history of the question:

> This problem was debated three hundred years ago by two philosophers, William Molyneux and his friend John Locke. I came across this discussion in a do-it-yourself magazine of all places! Fascinating stuff philosophy. If you are blind . . . said Molyneux . . . you can learn to distinguish between a cube and a sphere just by touching them, by feeling them. Right? . . . Now supposing your vision is suddenly restored, will you be able to tell which object is the cube and which the sphere? Sorry, friend, said Locke . . . you will not be able to tell which is which.

Then who comes along [seventeen years later] to join in the debate but another philosopher, George Berkeley, with his essay entitled "An Essay towards a New Theory of Vision." . . . When the problem was put to the Lord Bishop he came to the same conclusion as his friends. But he went even further. He said there was no necessary connection *at all* between the tactile world . . . and the world of sight . . . that any connection between the two could be established only by experience.[1]

Molly's surgeon corroborates this claim: the world built up by vision is not pregiven but constructed by memory and by the creation of categories and relations.

The Siting of the Sightless

The surgeon has got it right, if by seeing he means a specific mode of world-habitation. For Merleau-Ponty in *The Phenomenology of Perception*, the world is both preconstituted and made. To be sure, nowhere in this work does he mention Molyneux or even Locke. Let us nevertheless follow his recasting of their legacy in his general account of sensation and in his interpretation of blindness and later becoming sighted to see whether we can learn from him and from Molly Sweeney something about the experience of blindness that can provide an entering wedge into the hyperreal and the world of virtual reality.

As described by Merleau-Ponty, sensation inundates; it is total and overwhelming, comparable to the experience of the sacrament of Communion for a believer. The communicant, he tells us, expects and apprehends not a symbol but the real presence of God, which has come to be localized in bread and wine, so that "sensation, is literally a form of communion." For Molly, astonishingly, blindness provides the open sesame of sensation. Speaking of swimming, she reflects: "Just offering yourself to the experience every pore open and eager for that world of pure sensation, of sensation alone— sensation that could not have been enhanced by sight—experience that existed only by touch and feel; and moving swiftly and rhythmically through that enfolding world . . . such liberation, such concordance with it."[2]

Molly has provided a description of sensory experience that dispenses with what Merleau-Ponty calls the standpoint of "intellectualism," from which there are only determinate objects that present themselves through a series of possible experiences, objects that exist for a subject that recognizes them. Contrary to intellectualism, he states that individual colors are experiences that are incommunicable and that become my own when I coincide with color. I do not "lay siege" to impressions by means of thought, so that, for the sake of turning them into knowledge, I cease to be a living being immersed in a world but am changed into a subject of cognition. For the knower, expressions such as "I see with my eyes" are rendered meaningless, for the eye ceases to be me, an instrument of bodily excitation, and can only be viewed as another object in the world (*PP*, 212). Had he been able to foresee the Derridean double genitive, Merleau-Ponty might have attributed a twofold meaning to the expression "sensation of blue": for intellectualism, blue belongs to the *subject* of sensation; in actual experience it is blue itself that takes over and "owns" sensation. Merleau-Ponty intends the latter meaning when he writes: "As I contemplate the blue of the sky, I am not *set over against* it as an acosmic subject. . . . I abandon myself to it and plunge into this mystery, it 'thinks itself within me,' I am the sky itself as it is drawn together and unified, and as it begins to exist for itself; my consciousness is saturated with this limitless blue" (*PP*, 214).

Lest we depict Merleau-Ponty as a phenomenological Schleiermacher or Novalis, or, to update this genealogy, a Timothy Leary, he does not think of ordinary sensation as a drugged trance; we are not as a matter of course awash in sensation. This return to the richness of the sensed is qualified by my body's participation: "my gaze pairs off with color, and my hand with hardness and softness" (*PP*, 214). I am, after all, my body, the prepersonal "system of anonymous 'functions' which draw every particular focus into a general project" that is the delineation of my place in the world (*PP*, 254). This subtle interaction of sentient and sensible fits easily into a Madhyamika Buddhist perspective, which claims that there is no self as an ego or independent consciousness apart from our positing of continuity; there are only the fleeting dhammas, events that arise, persist for a moment, and pass away in endless succession.

If we are left merely with the thought that sensory experience consists in discrete sectors of being that succeed one another and, moreover, exist as unrelated sensory fields, we have not gone beyond the statue described by Condillac, an inert mannequin who receives each of the senses one by one, like successive layers of a costume, and who is finally ventriloquized into speech. But Merleau-Ponty has no such sorry view of corporeality. Nor does he posit a *sensus communis* as a master coordinator of the individual senses, in the manner of Aristotle. Instead, he constructs a view of space in which space is no longer a form of sensory intuition, as Kant believed, or a container that holds things that are laid out *partes extra partes*, but a kind of universal power that allows them to be linked. This is not a distinction without a difference, in that now the unity of space both comes to be and is discovered in the interplay of contingent sensory interactions. Neither a priori nor a posteriori, each sense is endowed with its own mode of world exploration, but it is only as a modality of spatial configuring that the coexistence of things becomes possible. Here, Merleau-Ponty's interrogation of the experience of blindness followed by sight becomes significant both for his theory and for our theme, the hyperreal. The blind person is constantly challenged to imagine what sight must be like, to attach significations to descriptions of shape and color as they must appear to the sighted. These indications are, however, intellectual constructs, so that if sight is later acquired the seen world differs radically from the one anticipated. But intelligence cannot achieve the synthesis of touch, the blind person's way of encountering the world, with sight, a synthesis that is only possible in the realm of the sensory itself.

The removal of cataracts from the eyes of those blind from birth may unlock the experience of sight but not that of space, which already inheres in tactility, Merleau-Ponty contends. If the patient denies the spatiality of the tactile experience, that is only because it appears impoverished when compared with that of visual space. True, the newly sighted patient fails to identify objects and may speak, for example, of the hand as a white patch. Her eye may follow the contours of the object in the way that the hand palpates, but the very gestures of reaching and feeling presuppose spatiality, a site. The patient must learn what it is to see, what it is that makes seeing distinct from the exploration of a haptic field. Yet despite this difference between touch and sight, there is a connectedness, even a unity to our world encounters. In showing this, Merleau-Ponty would seem to have entered terrain where poststructuralists fear to tread: the quest for the origin, the place where both things and ideas come into being out of a more primordial oneness. But the world that analysis uncovers, even if it is a world that is always already there, is "an open totality the synthesis of which is inexhaustible" and of an I that is "demolished and remade by the course of time" (*PP*, 219). A world that reposits itself in this way is "masked" in Nietzsche's sense of the term, not as camouflage for a concealed foundation but rather as attesting to undecidability, the ambiguity of phenomena that deconstruct and refigure themselves and thus are fissured by primordial difference.

The relation of tactility and sight in Merleau-Ponty works in the manner described in Husserl's famous example of apprehending a cube: tactility entails a circumnavigation of an object to obtain a sense of the whole, whereas vision supplies the whole on the basis of the aspect it sees. At the same time, vision is also panoptical, encompassing a field determined by a horizon, whereas the tactile sense can explore the world only as far as the body's mobility allows. Merleau-Ponty does not fail to bring out the difference in experienced temporalization: the successiveness of tactility, one touch after another, and the simultaneity, the panoramic expansiveness, of vision. Thus undecidability is built into temporalization, being and becoming are perspectives intrinsic to sensory world apprehension, for which, it could be argued, Derrida's later account of undecidability and difference, a present that is always already ruptured by delay, provides an elaborate adumbration.

Never hesitating to cull rich phenomenological deposits from the physiological research of the day, though without cosseting the materialists, Merleau-Ponty would probably have engaged Daniel Dennett, Patricia Churchland, and Roger Penrose with interest, perhaps even conceding that consciousness does not exist, since he had already expressed the view that "experience" is a better term for the complex of activities attributed to consciousness (*PP*, 258 n. 1). If forced to take sides, he might have found himself in accord with Penrose, who builds temporal undecidability into the deepest level of neuronal activity:

> Indeed it would be unwise to make too strong an identification between the phenomenon of conscious awareness, with its seeming "flowing" of time and the physicist's use of a real number parameter to denote what would be referred to as a "time coordinate." . . . Can we be specific about the relation between conscious experience and the [real number] parameter that physicists use as the "time" in their physical descriptions? Can there really be any experimental way to test "when" a subjective experience "actually" takes place in relation to this physical parameter? Does it even mean anything in an objective sense to say that a conscious event takes place at any particular time?[3]

Penrose's account depends on an as yet unexplained difference between the quantum level of neural activity and that accessible to classical physics, one that disturbs the standard picture of such activity so that a self-dividing difference is replicated at the level of brain processes. There is no way of pinpointing the "when" of a neural process in its coinciding with experience. Writing in the same vein, Merleau-Ponty insists that, considering the experience of depth, there is in the brain "a functional structure homologous with" it, but the experience itself cannot be correlated with retinal images (*PP*, 258). This impossibility is registered in Molly Sweeney's frustrated outcry when psychologists attempt to correlate neural activity with her visual experience: "Tests, tests, tests . . . Those damned tests with photographs and lights and objects . . . endless tricks and illusions and distortions?"[4]

Merleau-Ponty takes for granted that "visual experience is truer than tactile" (*PP*, 234 n. 1) without worrying about ancient skepticism's account of the deceptions of sight ("Does not a straight stick appear bent in water?") or Berkeley's claim that the moon looks small but touch more truly reveals its immensity. Far outweighing these considerations, for him, is the fact that sight provides a plethora of detail absent from touch. A further advantage is that difference in size marks off difference in distance: the smaller the object is in relation to its actual size, the further away it is. Thus richness and complexity characterize the findings of sight. For the sighted person who becomes blind, we may think of the process described by Merleau-Ponty as a kind of etiolation, a thinning of the visual field, a regress from sense experience to pure being: colors lose their saturation; the spectrum is simplified, so that fewer and fewer colors remain until at last a gray, monochrome stage is reached (*PP*, 9).

Conversely, for a blind person who acquires sight, the richness of the newly acquired spectacle would seem to afford great affective dividends. Merleau-Ponty contends that the patient marvels joyously at the experience of space that has been acquired. Yet when the first exhilaration wears off, Molly Sweeney laments that the familiar is gone and that the immense effort required to recompose the world is too much for her. She reaches a point where she can absorb no more sensation and is forced to shut her eyes in order to recapture darkness. Sensation was holding her in thrall, impinging upon her freedom. The visual is there for her, but she prefers it as an absence. Merleau-Ponty finds in such an absence a blind boy's characterization of vision as enveloping him from a distance, yet penetrating him and holding him in subjection (*PP*, 224).

The Chiasm

In *The Visible and the Invisible*, a subtle shift occurs from the privileging of vision to a greater focus upon tactility and from the relative independence of each sense's world apprehension to their reciprocal imbrication. When one stresses tactility, it is as if sense experience refracts that of blindness: vision looms as an absence. In this view, the world is palpable not only when touched but when seen: "What is this prepossession of the visible . . . ? We would perhaps find the answer in the tactile palpation where the questioner and the questioned are closer, and of which, after all, the palpation of the eye is a remarkable variant. . . . vision is a palpation with the look" (*VI*, 133–34). In the *Phenomenology of Perception*, the tactile is concentrated in manual activity, into the hand that feels and does, agile, prehensile, busy with the world. But in *The Visible and the Invisible*, another concept, one frequently discussed, that of the flesh, emerges: "The flesh is not matter, in the sense of corpuscles of being which would add up or continue on one another to form beings. . . . To designate it, we should need the old term 'element,' in the sense it was used to speak of water, air, earth, and fire, that is, in the sense of a *general thing*" (*VI*, 139). Neither a spatiotemporal individual nor an idea, flesh is something between the two. Just as one hand touching the other suggests the reversibility of sensation, so too the world is not only touched by us but, as flesh, touches and loops around us. Not the Word, as in Christian doctrine, but the world has been made flesh, as if, in a gesture of pantheism, Spinoza's substance had become animated and its modes converted into individual expressions or styles. No longer is it possible to construe blindness as though it were a form of Husserlian bracketing that put the visual out of play in order to illuminate a certain essential relation of the world to the senses but rather, in accordance with Merleau-Ponty's own best insights, existent and world are disclosed *in situ*, so that sensory experience materializes in all of its plenitude.

Still, there is something missing even in this later view of the senses. Although Merleau-Ponty is not unaware of the affect that permeates sensation, emotion does not play a prominent role in his interpretation of sensory fields. It is Derrida who carries us *un pas au-delà* (to borrow Blanchot's phrase), a step beyond yet not beyond the visible. In the catalogue for an exhibit that Derrida organized at the Louvre (October 26, 1990–January 1, 1991), *Memoirs of the Blind: The Self-Portrait and Other Ruins*,[5] he demonstrates that sight enters into an economy of exchange: a sacred mission is bestowed upon the blind in return for their having relinquished sight, an exchange rendered vivid in the tales of the lives of Homer, Tiresias, and Oedipus. Of the blind poet Milton, Derrida writes: "the blind man . . . recoups, and compensates for what his eyes of flesh have to renounce with a spiritual or inner light."[6] It is worth noting that when Molly's newly acquired sight begins to fail and the world becomes hazy, she enters into a medical condition called gnosis, which her husband identifies with mystical knowledge.

The exchange of outer for inner light brings to the fore what transcends sight and cognition, the act of weeping, a point upon which one would have welcomed comment from Merleau-Ponty. The joy and mourning attendant upon the revelation given to the blind seer are, Derrida maintains, veiled by tears. Whereas animals can see and sleep, only human beings can weep. Derrida cites Andrew Marvell's wonderful lines from "Eyes and Tears": "How wisely Nature did decree / With the same eyes to weep and see! . . . Thus let your streams o'erflow your springs, / Till eyes and tears be the same things: / And each the other's difference bears; / These weeping eyes, those seeing tears."[7]

The Hyperreal and the Virtual

What, then, can be gleaned from the experience of blindness—more specifically, from the blind who are newly sighted—that might be of use in an age of the hyperreal and the virtual? Perhaps it is the manner in which flesh is coiled around flesh, not in a unifying synthesis but in an interpenetration in which world and self have become something other than they were, something as yet undetermined and perhaps inherently indeterminable.

With the information revolution, something extraordinary has happened, something that has reduced the visible world to codes, with the genetic code becoming the prototype of coding and constituting, in that sense, a drying up of sensation. What Guy Debord refers to as the culture of spectacle has, according to Jean Baudrillard, disappeared: "We are witnessing the end of perspective," what Merleau-Ponty thought of as the depth of the world, as well as the disappearance of panoptic space, its breadth and range. Instead, images, like language, are reduced to binary formulations so that they "circulate not, any longer, in our memories, but in the luminous, electronic memory of the computers."[8] In what might be thought of as a remarkable parallel, Merleau-Ponty cites a case of "number blindness," the pathology of a man who has memorized a sequence of numbers and can perform certain operations with them but for whom number "has no meaning as a fixed quantity, as a group or a determinate measure" (*PP*, 133). A proponent of strong Artificial Intelligence (AI) might sneer, "But that's all there is: number is operational; the only thing that is missing is a more complex retrieval system." Without entering into intricate AI debates, I want to suggest that Merleau-Ponty's point is that what has been lost in number blindness is the power of "physiognomic perception," the fluid, ever-changing relation with the world in which number is encoded.

This sensory blindness occurs as a decoupling of image and information. What makes the transmission of information possible is the conversion of a signal into numerical atomic constituents or bits, each bit having, for practical purposes, the numerical value of 1 or 0. Rather than encoding information analogically, in which case there is some resemblance between code and the phenomenon encoded, information has been digitized, breaking with any physically discernible relation between object and percept. "A bit has no color, size, or weight, and it can travel at the speed of light."[9] Digitization's advantage is that it achieves high levels of data compression, thereby increasing the amount of data that can be transmitted. With the increased bandwidth, the "number of bits that can be moved through a given circuit in a second" of fiber optic (glass or plastic) cable, the transmission of information is expected to expand even further.[10]

The world of digitization that is depicted in Baudrillard's critique can be said to resemble the physiological condition known as blindsight as it afflicted Molly Sweeney. Claiming that she could see nothing, Molly nevertheless responded to visual cues, reaching for objects as seen rather than touched. But she could not process received signals in the usual way: information was indeed received and somehow used, but without the intervention of a conscious image.

What is missing in Baudrillard's account of information is the sense in which images "televised, computer simulated, or auditory" are generally the *raison d'être*, the final product, of the shipping of information. "Digitizing a signal is to take samples of it, which if closely spaced, can be used to play back a seemingly perfect replica."[11] What is more, the interface, the point of interaction between user and computer, relies increasingly upon images, upon iconic or graphical rather than character-based commands.

Baudrillard seems to concede the point when he depicts the triumph of the information culture as a transformation of the real into the hyperreal, the duplication of the real through some medium of reproduction that results in a hallucinatory doubling of a real that resembles itself. To be sure, there is a volatilizing of events as if the Pythagorean claim that the world is actually made of number had at last been realized. But far from remaining static, a world of formal mathematical relations as Pythagoras envisioned it, modernity's speeding up of all aspects of existence has "propelled us to 'escape velocity,' with the result that we have flown free of the referential sphere of the real,"[12] releasing a plethora of images.

We may still ask to what does the real that the hyperreal has dissipated refer? Has meaning not been leached from the term *reality* by philosophers from Derrida to Donald Davidson? Here we may appeal to the antifoundationalist account of Merleau-Ponty: "Reality is not a crucial appearance underlying the rest, it is the framework of relations with which all appearances tally" (*PP*, 300). It is this framework in its temporal and spatial density that speed has destroyed.

Are there any psychic gains that accrue in the world of the hyperreal? In Milan Kundera's novel *Slowness* ecstasy is the spillover of speed. The cost, however, is high: the loss of the pleasure of slowness. But what is to count as slowness? If we are to avoid falling into quantification, let us think, with Merleau-Ponty, of tactility as succession, which is always already slowly paced: one touch after another cannot be accelerated beyond a certain point. Perhaps evolutionists would say that the slowness of tactility, in which the whole body is the sensorium, is the heritage of one-celled animals. By contrast, vision is simultaneity. Speed is the effort to simulate this all-at-onceness, a kind of regulative ideal, approached but never attained, for once complete coexistence is achieved, motion and, with it, the ecstasy of speed, would vanish.

Accelerated movement has yet another affective consequence: speed turns tragedy into farce so that the eye ceases to be the organ of tears. Thus, for example, in Chaplin's film *Modern Times* the plight of the assembly-line worker, when seen as the inability of lived time to keep up with the speed of the machine, becomes comical. More recently, in Oliver Stone's *Natural Born Killers*, the murder spree of its Bonnie and Clyde protagonists is marked by accelerated filmic images, a fast forwarding that parodies the successive murders they commit. Whatever social commentary may have been intended is offset by the destruction of the affective ranges of sadness and mourning "the tears of which Derrida spoke" now supplanted by in-difference to suffering expressed in derisive laughter and hard-edged ecstasy.

In expanding his narrative of the information culture as an unsaying of the real, Baudrillard proclaims that the individual is no longer the progenitor of another, but clones him or herself, metastasizes the genetic code. "Cloning is the last stage of the history of modeling the body, the stage at which the individual, having been reduced to his abstract and genetic formula, is destined for serial propagation."[13] Such procreation, he thinks, is an act of incest minus the tragedy. What is more, in the industrial age, extensions of the body were mechanical, rebounded upon the body image, and modified in a way that allowed the image to be internalized. But today, Baudrillard continues, there is a point of no return in simulation; prostheses invade the micromolecular core of the body, so that it is not the prosthesis that replicates the body but rather the body that reproduces the prosthesis, just as in the age of the hyperreal the map determines the territory rather than the converse. Consider a *New York Times Magazine* report of the woman who asked for cosmetic surgery that would replicate the face of a Barbie doll.[14]

Virtual Worlds

Virtual reality (VR) is an effort to reproduce actual experience in all of its *Leibhaftigkeit*. It would therefore be a mistake to regard it as a subset of the hyperreal in which the notion of mimesis has disappeared. Just as the newly sighted Molly Sweeney tried to regain the world of touch, VR is an effort to recapture the world as it had once been known by replicating it in order to reinstate the old epistemology of representation. VR can be thought of as a move of epistemic fundamentalism, so that the virtualized subject can say: "This is what sights and sounds, feels and smells really are." Software is programmed to create what is seen and to respond to new information; instruments are developed for the transmission of this information as sensory input. Headphones, adjusted to locate the direction of sound, convey auditory stimuli. Visual simulation is achieved through the use of goggles whose lenses are adjusted to a computer display for each eye. Movements of the head are tracked by a sensor that adjusts what is seen in conformity with those movements so that the computer can synthesize the visual field. It has been theorized that body-suits with sensors could reproduce tactile sensations.[15] When VR is regarded as a simple phenomenon of bilocation, so that we are in two places at the same time, Merleau-Ponty's account of the chiasmatic provides a useful description.

We have seen that the flesh, for him, is not matter, a formless substratum of the real but rather a commingling of world and sense and of the senses with one another. The body is always already in several places at the same time: "It is the coiling over of the visible upon the seeing body, of the tangible upon the touching body, which is attested in particular when the body sees itself, touches itself seeing and touching the things, such that, simultaneously, *as* tangible it descends among them . . . and draws this relationship and even this double relationship from itself, by dehiscence or fission of its own mass" (*VI*, 146). The body does not divide in the manner of one-celled life but, in its experience of itself, bilocates, splits and resynthesizes itself in every perceptual act.

Yet VR is not *simply* a phenomenon of bilocation but is entrapped in the simulations of the hyperreal, which it tries unsuccessfully to escape, an elsewhere that shifts in conformity with one's actions — which, in turn, are determined by the parameters of software programming and instrumentation. The effect of this technology is not to destroy bilocation but rather to virtualize the "actual" spatiotemporal locale of the viewer so that there is no stationary point of reference. Science fiction envisages programming that would overcome this doubleness by becoming part of an individual's neurophysiological processes. Although such programming is highly unlikely, new technologies reflect an effort to create simulations in which there would be no fissure between simulation and the real, no "there" as Heidegger conceives it other than the spatiotemporal coordinates of virtual reality.

With virtualization, the epistemic difficulties connected with knowledge as representation are rendered far more complex and require fundamental reconceptualization that is only now beginning. Paul Virilio observes: "From now on everything will happen without our even moving, without our even having to set out."[16] Although VR is parasitic upon the transposition of the visual into information, the illusion of reality is contingent upon replicating not only the body's sensory capacities but also its kinesthetic experiences. Merleau-Ponty's discussion of the kinestheses or body movements points proleptically to their ultimate virtualization. Although not regarded as a sense, the kinestheses determine the horizon of perception. I move my body from one place to another without looking for it; it is always already there, he contends. The decision to move and the felt movement itself are inseparable. Once movement and the will to move are simultaneous or, to make an even stronger claim, once the conatus to move follows upon the activity of moving, as William James declares, we are only a step away from proclaiming that all the accoutrements of movement, "sensations in the limbs, altered horizons," can simply be the dehiscence of a body that remains at a standstill. Presence and absence, until now discriminable by location—when I am here, I am not there—cannot be told apart, not only at the level of neurophysiology but phenomenologically. Can the world of VR not then be summed up in Molly's account of her post-surgical life?

> My borderline country is where I live now. I'm at home there. . . . It certainly doesn't worry me anymore that what I think I see may be fantasy or indeed what I take to be imagined may very well be real . . . external reality. Real imagined "fact" "fiction" "fantasy" "reality" there it seems to be all right. And why should I question any of it anymore?[17]

The Howl of Oedipus, the Cry of Héloïse
From Asceticism to Postmodern Ethics

Asceticism is a complex of widely varying practices, beliefs, and motives that have appeared in particular historical and cultural contexts. It is, to use the language of art criticism, site-specific. If the historical and phenomenological integrity of asceticism's many manifestations is to be preserved, it is beyond dispute that ascetic phenomena must be allowed to emerge in discrete material and psychosocial meaning constellations.[1]

Yet, I want to argue, there is also for every psycho-social practice an episteme, a cluster of often invisible ideas, that is both the conceptual backdrop and the enabling mechanism for the emergence of ascetic life in situ. Thus, I shall allow myself to speak in more sweeping terms of Western asceticism and a Western episteme, with the understanding that neither term implies theoretical or practical unity but that both point toward a loosely linked, open-ended chain of mythemes and philosophemes. These are narrative and conceptual units that acquire meaning through their relation with one another and, taken together, constitute a tradition. I sometimes refer to the linkage of these units as a chain of signifiers. Concrete practices do not lie outside a tradition but feed back into it in a loop that may overturn a formation or render it more supple. Within this episteme, there are discernible discursive formations—lesser patterns of signification. Thus, no essence of asceticism will be specified. I shall argue that the discursive formations within the episteme of asceticism are bound up with the self-imposition of corporeal and psychic pain or privation; but I shall also argue that not all pain and privation, even when self-generated, is ascetic.

In what follows, four interrelated claims are considered. First, in order to understand the cluster of notions that enter into asceticism as an episteme, two prior and competing discourses, that of *erōs* ("love") and of *dikē* ("justice"), especially as Plato interprets them, must be distinguished. The concepts of body associated with each need to be sorted out, as well as the way in which these views of body are taken up or rejected in ascetic discourse. Second, Western asceticism demands the devaluing of the world, the turning of the world into vanity. In order to see this, the type of negation involved in world negation will be analyzed. Third, within the structure of asceticism, gaps or fissures appear in its understanding of love, pleasure, and pain in the form of an eroticism that asserts and denies itself. This is especially evident in the correspondence of Héloïse and Abelard. The view of the body that emerges presages a new, postmodern understanding of asceticism and its relation to ethics. Finally, this new conception of body will allow asceticism, love, and justice to intersect without integrating them heuristically or dialectically.

The Howl of Oedipus

In one of Greek tragedy's most powerful passages, a messenger recounts the cry of Oedipus upon discovering Jocasta hanged, a cry that gathers into itself the cumulative pain of incest and patricide.

> And with a dread shriek, as though someone beckoned him on, he sprang at the double doors, and from their sockets forced the bending bolts and rushed into the room.
>
> There beheld we the woman hanging by the neck in a twisted noose of swinging cords. But he, when he saw her, with a dread deep cry of misery, loosed the halter whereby she hung . . . Then was the sequel dread to see. For he tore from her raiment the golden brooches wherewith she was decked and lifted them, and smote full on his own eye-balls.[2]

The howl of Oedipus is followed by a remarkable act of automutilation: Oedipus tears out his eyes. Why, it might be asked, is it so unthinkable, so counterintuitive to consider this self-infliction of pain and deprivation an ascetic practice? Perhaps Oedipus's cry of pain is simply the spontaneous response to powerful emotions, whereas asceticism involves a nexus of beliefs and practices that must be consciously set in place and should have a specific aim. I want to argue that the cry of Oedipus, far from being akin to a scream uttered in response to physical injury, a biological reflex, as it were, is a distillate of a certain *telos* ("purpose") and of a complex discursive formation, one that is different from asceticism.

A clue may be derived from Claude Lévi-Strauss's interpretation, not of the Oedipus story itself, upon which he has commented copiously, but of the incest taboo. The incest prohibition, he contends, occurs at the intersection of culture and nature and provides the link between them: "Before it, culture is still non-existent, with it nature's sovereignty over man is ended."[3] Although its universality has been contested by anthropologists, what is crucial for Lévi-Strauss and germane to my argument is his contention that "The *fact of being a rule*, completely independent of its modalities, is indeed the very essence of the incest prohibition."[4] To be sure, nature already operates lawfully in that living things reproduce their own kind and not some other. Nevertheless, it is culture and not nature that regulates allowable degrees of consanguinity in human societies. The aberrations of nature recorded in Sophocles' *Oedipus*, the inability of animals and humans to bring forth their young, are responses by nature to the violation of a social prohibition. What I want to focus on is the regulative character of the taboo, in order to bring to the fore the episteme from which it arises. By "regulative" I mean the establishment of culture's suzerainty over nature as reflecting a reapportionment of power, a reallocation that is essentially a juridical process belonging to a classical episteme, that of justice.

Missing in Lévi-Strauss's explanation is a grasp of the juridical character of the discursive formation to which the Oedipus myth belongs. Early Greek philosophy's understanding of nature as cosmos and cosmos as a juridical *topos* ("theme") belong to this conceptual formation. Beginning with the biologism of Aristotle, the cosmological genealogy of justice, in which the ideals of retributive and distributive justice and of punishment and equity can be traced, has been obscured. It is not at the level of genera and species, or even at the plane of the laws of motion as Aristotle formulates them, that nature is first understood, but rather as a moral field. Plato and Aristotle fabricate a new context for the interpretation of justice, subordinating its cosmic character to a psychological and political discourse. The terms of this discourse are those of the internal relations of the soul's constituent parts and of citizens' relations to one another and to their rulers. When the cosmological dimension of justice is reinstated in Stoicism, it is too late: the political subreption of the cosmic model is now a fait accompli.

Cosmic justice, the episteme in which the order of things is perceived in terms of apportionment or measure, is first brought to the fore in the pre-Socratic fragment of Anaximander: "The Unlimited is the first-principle of things that are. It is that from which the coming-to-be of things and qualities take place and it is that into which they return when they perish by moral necessity, giving satisfaction to one another and making reparation for their injustice, according to the order of time."[5] The *apeiron* ("boundless") is an "ontological storehouse,"[6] the venue of physical change, out of which things come to be and into which they pass away. I want, however, to resist Heidegger's rejection of the axiological or moral dimension of this text: his view that the fragment points to an overcoming of negativity in the coming-to-be or "presencing" of things. Instead, the text describes a moral balance sheet: things make reparations for their injustice. The *apeiron* is always already configured as a moral topos against which wrongs are redressed by reimbursing it for the gift of being. Things and qualities "know" the order of time; they cannot not know when and how to make restitution.

Reparation is also an issue in establishing the boundary between nature and culture. The misreadings of consanguinity that characterize Oedipus's relation to his mother and father is a failure of knowledge about the social order, which requires the intervention of nature's power if equilibrium is to be restored. Divine punishment is meted out for Oedipus's inability to recognize not the precept— Oedipus knows the incest and patricide proscriptions well enough— but the placeholders to whom the proscriptions apply. Thus Oedipus cries out that he has "failed in knowledge of those whom [he] yearned to know [and that] henceforth [he] would be dark."[7] Oedipus's transgression (whatever Freud may have made of it later) does not belong within the framework of a classical definition of erotics but within one of justice, transgression, and punishment. (Much the same case could be made for King Lear, with madness substituting for blindness in the chain of signifiers, and consanguine daughterly obligation for primal sexual transgression.)

What is the function of Oedipus's physical pain within the terrain I have mapped out, the terrain of deficit and expenditure governed by the episteme of justice? (I shall defer for the moment the question of how this pain differs from that of asceticism.) In the realm of justice, pain becomes both the instrument and the sign for power's redistribution. When in classical philosophy justice becomes apolitical discourse, pain is the agent of a punishment that is both pedagogic and retributive. Knowing how much pain is required, no more and no less, demands knowledge of both fact and value: knowledge of justice, the ideal, and of the angle of declination from that ideal reflected in particular cases. Methods for entering the storehouse of truths and applying them form the nub of the Platonic and Aristotelian discourses of justice.

Within the episteme of justice, Oedipus's failure to know his mother lies at the dividing line between nature and culture. The incest taboo is a crossover signifier, belonging to two intertwined chains of meaning: the cosmic and the political dimensions of justice. Violating the rule that is always already in place if any other rule is to follow, he "makes reparation for [this] injustice according to the order of time" through an act of ocular self-mutilation.

The Body of the Just

In praise of the past, first-century Stoic Seneca writes: "In that age which was called golden, Poseidonius maintains that rule was in the hands of the wise. They restrained aggression, protected the weaker from the stronger, advised and dissuaded and indicated what was advantageous and what was not. Their prudence saw to it that their people lacked for nothing, their courage averted dangers and their generosity enabled their subjects to . . . flourish."[8] This Stoic distillate of the classical view of the philosopher depicts the just man as having knowledge, being prudent enough to apply this knowledge, and sufficiently courageous to act upon it.

In considering this account of the Stoic sage, the question is not simply how justice is reflected in the conception of the wise man or of the things done in the body, but what that body must be in order for there to be wisdom. Plato's radical answer is that the body is a disturbance. Thus, for example, in *Phaedo*, the most negative of the discourses on body, Socrates maintains: "The body is a source of endless trouble to us by reason of the mere requirement of food; and is liable also to diseases; . . . it fills us full of loves and lusts and fears and fancies of all kinds . . . even if we are at leisure and betake ourselves to some speculation, the body is always breaking in on us."[9]

The body as a whole, with its auxiliary organs of sensation, obstructs the knowledge of an absolute justice attainable by the rational soul.

For the Socratic just man, no genuine decontamination of the body is possible short of the complete "separation of the soul from the body," a separation achieved in death. Only then is "the release of the soul from the chains of the body" fully consummated.[10] Because the soul alone has access to the world of ideal forms, when the body is severed from the soul, it is cut off from that which is "in the likeness of the divine."[11] Whereas other material things imitate the forms, the disengaged body is not just another thing but a thing bereft of soul. Denied access to forms, it can only imitate an absence. Thus the wise man's body is an imitation of the presence of an absence, of a formless form: death. This imitation cannot have suicide for its object, because for Socrates (if not for the Stoics) man is the property of the gods and as such cannot dispose of his own life. If Socratic discourse is to remain coherent, the wise man can only continue to exist in a deathlike suspension of pain and pleasure.

This view is consistent with the irrelevance attributed to gender in allocating guardianship in the ideal state: "The same education which makes a man a good guardian will make a woman a good guardian for their original nature is the same."[12] In theory, at least, the body of the just is genderless, unhindered by pain or pleasure, the distractions of sensation or the stirrings of desire. With the "biologism" of Aristotle, this view of body and soul would seem to collapse. For Aristotle, after all, soul is the principle of life in the animal body and as such is inseparable from the body. Yet it is not in mere life that the relation of the human soul to its body is determined but, as with Plato, in rational life. Even when this claim is reconfigured by the Stoics, so that reason, along with impression and impulse, becomes a faculty, there is no question as to pride of place. Thus Epictetus:

> What then is a philosopher's matter? Not a ragged coat surely? No it is reason. What is his end? Surely it is not wearing a ragged coat? No it is keeping his reason right. What kind of theorems? Surely not ones with how to grow a large beard or long hair? No, but rather what Zeno says: to understand the elements of reason, what sort of thing each of them is, how they fit together and what their consequences are.[13]

The sage attends not only to the order of state and cosmos but to the examination of reason itself. Although it belongs to the same moral topos, the same episteme of justice as the howl of Oedipus, classical philosophy transposes the death of the body into the body of death, indifferent to the pain of Oedipus because it is indifferent to death.

In sum, within the episteme of justice, reason alone can determine what counts as "reparation for injustice." Traces of the older notion of cosmic justice persist in later classical discourse, so that justice does not assume the *dryly* computational form that the idea of reparation appears to imply. Pain remains an expression of compensatory power or, as in the case of Oedipus, the ideogram or sign of crime and its aftermath, while pleasure inheres in the ratiocinative process itself. By contrast, in the discursive formations of Western asceticism, pain will become a driving force, both instrument and end.

Three discursive strands will enter into the meaning constellation of Western asceticism: first, an erotics, a term defined by Foucault as "the purposeful art of love" (*UP*, 229), which constitutes the focus of the *Symposium* and the first section of the *Phaedrus* and is linked to several fragments of Heraclitus; second, a cosmic heuristics, the subject of the *Timaeus*; and third, an axiology implicit in the biblical text of Ecclesiastes.

The Fire of Eros

> This universe which is the same for all, has not been made by any god or man, but it always has been, is, and will be — an ever-living fire, kindling itself by regular measures and going out by regular measures.[14]

Heraclitus does not envisage fire as an element like the water or air of Miletian physics. It is not a material substratum of the world, for Heraclitus writes, "The phases of fire are craving and satiety."[15] Cosmic fire burns with an erotic glow, which "throws apart and then brings together."[16] The cosmos as a topos of desire will recur in Plato's cosmology, but Heraclitean fire will be downgraded to one among several elements even if it burns, as Plato claims, with the brightness and beauty of the divine form.

Fire as an explicitly erotic motif is absent in the *Symposium* and *Phaedrus*, perhaps because of fire's frequent association in classical discourse not with lust but, honorifically, with light. For an understanding of this terrain, we need only examine Foucault's admirable treatment of these dialogues. He argues as follows: The groundwork for the Socratic discussion of *eros* is laid in culturally accepted views of love that are retained in radically transformed fashion by Socrates. The *Symposium* sets forth the uses and abuses of pleasure, especially with regard to the love of boys, with an eye to explaining the relation of pleasure to truth (*UP*, 229). Its early speeches, like those of the *Phaedrus*, are psychological set pieces about the dishonorable games lovers play and are largely concerned with how to distinguish noble from base love. Aristophanes' speech posits the bisecting of primal human beings, who will continue to seek their lost counterparts. Being halves of a symmetrical whole, they are equals, but this parity of the lovers does not change the basic character of their bond. No issue of proper relations within the erotic can be resolved until love's essential nature is uncovered (ibid., 232–33).

Through the discourse on love of the crone Diotima, Socrates shows that love is by nature an intermediate state born of deficiency and plenty, of ignorance and knowledge. The genuine lover lacks that which he desires, not the beloved's body but truth or beauty itself. For Socrates "it is not exclusion of the body that . . . is fundamental [but] rather that, beyond the appearances of the object, love is a relation to truth," Foucault writes (ibid., 240). The one who has access to truth is the master of love, indifferent to seduction and to the fires of lust. Unlike the other speakers, Socrates does not produce an etiquette of sexual reticence but an account of the soul's resistance to its appetites through the knowledge of its relation to its own desires and to their objects.

This resistance, Foucault alleges, is important for "the transformation of ethics into a morality of renunciation and for the constitution of a hermeneutics of Desire" (ibid., 230), in short, into asceticism. I shall not enter here into the matter of Foucault's much-disputed account of asceticism's relation to the Greco-Roman understanding of the self in his late work.[17] In the present context I take Foucault to be partly right when he suggests that Western asceticism is an outcome of indifference to the body's appetites. Yet this indifference cannot, as Foucault claims, be a transformation of ethics, as he understands this term, for it belongs within the episteme of justice, in which body and soul are severed. By contrast, the body of classical erotics cannot be cordoned off. Love cannot escape the bodily because, insofar as it is lack, it cannot be taken up into the rational soul. Even when love's objects are truth and beauty, love will continue to bear the imprint of a body it cannot jettison. When the transcendent becomes love's object, love will continue to be marked by an ineradicable corporeality that will necessitate a transfiguring *askēsis*. Just this persistence of the body, I shall argue, allows for ethics, in the postmodern sense, to be transferred from the terrain of classical *dikē* to that of *erōs*.

It is not surprising that the two-tiered ontology of ideal forms and physical objects that governs Plato's account of human love also dominates his cosmology. In the great cosmogonic drama of the *Timaeus*, "that which always is and never becomes" is distinguished from "that which is always becoming but never is."[18] It is also not surprising that, because the creator is benevolent and wants all things to be as like himself as possible, the divine craftsman transforms a preexistent chaos in accordance with ideal goodness and beauty. What *is* striking is that the resulting artifact is a living thing, so that the body comes to function as a heuristic device for understanding the cosmos. Because the intelligent is superior to the nonintelligent and intelligence is impossible without soul, Timaeus argues, the creator "implanted reason in soul and soul in body . . . [so that] this world came to be, through God's providence, a living being with soul and intelligence."[19] Thus cosmos and body mirror one another.

Plotinus, eager to protect the beauty of the cosmos against its gnostic depreciation (*Ennead* 2.9.1–18, in *Enneads*, 132–52), refuses to link bodily *eros*, the earthly Aphrodite, with cosmos. Thus, he asks, when "love is represented as homeless, bedless, and bare-footed: would not that be a shabby description of the Cosmos and quite out of the truth?"(*Ennead* 3.5.5, in ibid., 195–96). By contrast, the cosmos of the *Timaeus* might be read as longing for its eternal counterpart. Such a cosmos must be stilled just as bodily desire must be stilled if the soul is to turn toward beauty and truth. Thus, speaking of Valentinian *gnosis*, Peter Brown refers to the calming of human sexual agitation as "the outward visible sign of a mighty subsidence that takes place in the spiritual reaches of the universe."[20]

Hebbel: The Nothingness of the All

> I the Preacher have been king over Israel in Jerusalem . . . I have seen everything that is done under the sun; and behold all is vanity and a striving after wind.[21]

The discursive formations of Western asceticism cannot fall into place until the world is reduced to vanity, to *hebbel*, a mere breath of air. The devaluing of all that is in Ecclesiastes is a far more profound depreciation of the world than Stoic detachment. The Stoic sage classifies things as good or indifferent, can distinguish vice from virtue.

By contrast, the narrator of Ecclesiastes declares, "I applied my mind to know wisdom and to know madness and folly. I perceive that this also is a striving after wind. For in much wisdom is much vexation, and he who increases knowledge increases sorrow."[22] When all is vanity, the all that is *hebhel* refers both to the totality of the world and to the maximum intensity of the worthlessness attributed to the world.

Hebhel, mere wind, can be viewed as the obverse of *ruah*, wind or breath in the honorific sense of spirit. Thus, it is said "you do not know how the spirit [*ruah*] comes to the bones in the womb of a woman with child."[23] This infusion of *ruah* or vital breath into the child is compared in the same verse to the mysterious work of God: "so [too] you do not know the work of God who makes everything."[24]

Here the site of vanity must be distinguished from both the moral topos of justice and the lack that characterizes classical erotics as I have described them: all that is devalued as vanity is God's creation. In his brilliant account of vanity, Jean-Luc Marion suggests that two possible standpoints can be taken toward this totality. The first is the ontological standpoint, the view from inside that posits the world as the sum of beings. From this perspective, the difference between being and not being, suffering and enjoying, knowing and not knowing, looms large. But there is another standpoint from outside the world, such that the world appears "stricken with vanity."[25]

I would, however, take issue with Marion's Heideggerian reading of the inner-worldly perspective as the domain of Being and beings. Despite what has been seen as a veneer of classical philosophy, Ecclesiastes stands under the aegis of the biblical doctrine of creation, of the world as God's work. Missing from Marion's otherwise extraordinary account is a hermeneutic of work. The word for "work" in Ecclesiastes, as in the "work of God" mentioned earlier, is *maaseh*, the same root as the word for story or narrative. The account of creation in the *Timaeus* is one in which the eternal patterns are generated from the *khōra*, or void, so that when the account is referred to as "merely probable" the truth of the account is measured by the forms. By contrast, God's creation or work is plotted, is narrated. Thus, to strike the world with vanity is to cease to be one of the characters in the story and to assume the standpoint of narrator. The demiurge of the *Timaeus* is the fashioner of a divine artifact; the God of Ecclesiastes is the artisan of history, the controller of event-filled time. Sheer temporal passing must end in worldweariness: "All things are full of weariness; a man cannot utter it."[26] When everything that has been repeats itself, when there is nothing new under the sun, as Marion observes, something like the French *ennui* permeates earthly existence.

Vanity is not simply another discursive formation alongside classical erotics. Rather, it denegates Plato's psychology and cosmology, in a denial that denies itself.[27] By denying the world, vanity institutes a negativity, but at the same time it brings the world that is being denied to the fore. It can be argued that classical erotics already reflects an effort to negate at least the corporeality of the world. But vanity, in denying the "all," also denies the denial of the classical world. The body that is negated in classical erotics, a body from which nevertheless there is no dispensation, is transformed in asceticism into the body of temptation. In the new episteme of asceticism, vanity's denegation of classical erotics is reflected in one of asceticism's most powerful opening moves, Paul's declaration: "Creation was subjected to vanity (*mataiotēti*)."[28]

Classical erotics and its denegation as vanity merge into a single topos, that of an asceticism that tries to manage the eruption of materiality into the chain of signifiers, a materiality that manifests itself in the body's unsurpassability. Across cultural and historical lines, ascetics force pain and pleasure into new meaning constellations, so that through practices of self-mortification and deprivation the body is made transparent, a conduit for transcendence. At the same time, the transformed body also becomes an ideogram for this process. Thus, when after twenty years of "pursuing the ascetic life" St. Anthony emerged from his fortress, his friends "were amazed to see that his body maintained its former condition, neither fat from lack of exercise, nor emaciated from fasting and combat with demons, but was just as they had known him prior to his withdrawal."[29] The flesh is shown to be polysemic: resplendent with higher meaning when disciplined, but always ready to erupt into temptation.

Héloïse's Cry

It is now time to revisit the meaning constellations considered earlier, classical erotics and justice, in order to determine how they emerge in postmodernity and to inquire into the prospects for a postmodern retrieval of asceticism. The classical discourse of justice, with its attendant notions of reason, might seem to provide a conceptual site for postmodern moral deliberation. It could also be assumed that classical erotics, with its linking of sexual desire to truth, might be superseded by the pansexuality of contemporary Western culture. Divested of its previous presuppositions, classical erotics could now be reshaped into new conceptual and corporeal practices.

With respect to the Platonic *eros*, Foucault contends that, far from liberating a new sphere of pleasure, contemporary psychology has converted sex into discourse. The ruses that modernity has used to turn sex into a language of power, "to make us love sex, to make the knowledge of it desirable and everything said about it precious,"[30] are comparable to the strategies Christianity once employed to render the body suspect. If sex is discourse, what has become of the ineradicable corporeality of classical erotics? Where are the spoors or traces of a body whose putrescence has been refined away in Christian asceticism by a self-imposed regimen of pain, so that it may become the pure receptacle of transcendence?

Let us pursue these questions by considering Anders Nygren's famous account of the distinction between *eros* and *agapē*. Nygren argues that Platonic eros is "acquisitive desire and longing" and expresses the lover's drive to satisfy a need. Although it may be determined by the worth and beauty of its object, eros remains egocentric. By contrast, Christian agape is unselfish, a love originating in plenitude. Patterned on divine love, "*agapē* loves and creates value in its object."[31] What is more, Nygren attributes a Platonic-erotic thrust to many early Christian accounts of Pauline *agapē*, such that love of the other subserves a beatitude that remains personal.

Despite difficulties both scholarly and philosophical that I shall not rehearse here,[32] Nygren's account is useful from a postmodern perspective in that it captures the powerful sense of need and the penumbra of sensuality that cling to *eros*. When directed toward an object to which value is attributed, need—what the body requires to remain alive—turns into desire, and desires spawn one another. "Desire for something different [becomes] a different desire,"[33] George Simmel affirms. An *eros* expressing need and desire attests to human destitution, a bodily indigence that asceticism will cast into high relief by corporeally mimicking it: hunger by fasting; sexual desire by chastity; bodily ease by self-mortification. Asceticism denegates corporeality: pain and privation deny the visceral body, but at the same time bring it to the fore, in that only the nonidealized body that ascetic practice hopes to perfect can become the terrain of the physical suffering necessary to purify it. It is this version of corporeality, the tenacious residue of the classical *eros*, that postmodernity will reconfigure in a new asceticism that will join the *eros* of need to the terrain of ethics.

Before this new asceticism can become evident, we must show the relation of the classical *eros* to generosity and compassion—to the *Other*. In a response to Nygren, A. Hilary Armstrong contends that, although the primary meaning of *eros* in ancient Greek society was sexual passion from its heights to animal lust, Nygren has failed to see that *eros* is also a god. For Armstrong, love is a desire not only for possession but also for a union of lover and beloved in order to create beauty.[34] Thus, it can be argued, within the same *eros* the element of generosity is always already present in that a gift—beauty—is created in the interest of another.

The corporeal content of the classical *eros* (the body reminding itself of itself endlessly) and the theme of generosity are nowhere more closely intertwined than in the twelfth-century reconfiguration of these philosophemes in the letters of Héloïse to Abelard, a text that, even if spurious, remains a locus classicus for bringing these themes to light.[35] A penumbra of sensuality shadows her renunciation of its physical expression: "The pleasures of lovers which we shared have been too sweet. . . . Wherever I turn they are always before my eyes, bringing with them awakened longings and fantasies which will not even let me sleep. Even during the celebration of the Mass . . . my thoughts are on their wantonness instead of on prayers."[36] The giving of self at first concentrated in her love for Abelard becomes disseminated, distributed, as it were, to the nuns under her care, for whose weaknesses she pleads: "Certainly those who laid down rules for monks were not only completely silent about women but also prescribed regulations which they know to be quite unsuitable for them."[37]

It could be asserted that, both in Abelard's *Historia calamitatum* and in the exchange of letters between Abelard and Héloïse, romantic motifs have infiltrated the discourse of a more traditional asceticism.[38] Thus Abelard writes, "We were united first under one roof, then in heart . . . with our books open before us, more words of love than of our reading passed between us, and more kissing than teaching."[39] In the present context we need only note that in Héloïse is concentrated not merely the motif of generosity but also that of a pain that fissures the discursive formations of asceticism with a cry of desire and longing that presages the postmodern body of ethics.

Héloïse's desire is articulated not only in terms of the recognized vices—greed, anger, pride, and the like—but as a cry for help issuing from a sensual nature only half disowned. Héloïse's love is doomed not because Abelard "was deprived of those organs with which he practiced [his lechery],"[40] nor even because the life of a religious person had been foisted upon her, but because, within the discursive formation of asceticism, no rule of distributive justice could compensate her for a desire that sought not an object but another desire. This is not to say that issues of gender bound up with the reallocation of ecclesial power are lacking. Far from it. Yet, unlike the howl of Oedipus, the primordial cry of the juridical person whose pain is weighed on the scales of justice, the discourse of Héloïse, "like nails that cannot touch wounds gently, but only pierce through them"[41] enters the chain of signifiers as insatiable need. Thus she entreats: "Do not suppose me healthy and so withdraw the grace of your healing. Do not believe I want for nothing and delay helping me in my hour of need. Do not think me strong, lest I fall before you can sustain me."[42]

The Postmodern Body of Ethics

The pain expressed in Héloïse's lament opens the discursive space of a postmodern ethic in which corporeality emerges as a fundamental datum. Consider, first, the way in which postmodernism reconfigures corporeality as a focus of interpretation. On the one hand, the body is seen as a text; on the other, the pain and death to which bodies are subject remain an *hors texte*, an insurpassable negation that slips both inside and outside the field of textuality. The body as text, as a chain of signifiers that convey multiple messages decodable by the astute reader, is a narrative body. Such a body tells its story, one of gender, social position, physical appearance, and the like. When actual or potential pain and death break into this sphere of narration, they introduce proscriptive and prescriptive meaning. No longer does the *body* serve the purpose of self-description; instead, its vulnerability to pain calls the observer to responsibility. When seen in this way, the body is not the body of an other but of the Other. Its vulnerability is not made explicit but is given prereflectively, instantaneously, as it were, in an act of immediate awareness. The lament of Héloïse gives verbal utterance to this prereflective aperçu.

What must bodies be if the Other can disturb one's world, come crashing into one's self-satisfaction? Or, put otherwise, how is the body's vulnerability expressed within the discursive sphere of ethics? Recognition of the body's vulnerability comes from an unlikely quarter. In *The Ego and the Id*, Freud interrupts his account of ego structure with a crucial aside:

A person's own body, and above all its surface, is a place from which both external and internal perceptions may spring. It is seen like any other object, but to the touch it yields two differ-ent kinds of sensations, one of which may be equivalent to an internal perception. . . . Pain too seems to play a part in the process, and the way in which we gain new knowledge of our organs during painful illnesses is perhaps the model of the way by which, in general, we arrive at the idea of our body.

The ego is first and foremost a bodily ego; it is not merely a surface entity but is itself the projection of a surface.[43]

In a note for the English edition, Freud adds: "The ego is ultimately derived from bodily sensations, chiefly from those springing from the surface of the body. It may thus be regarded as a mental projection of the surface of the body."[44]

The new and fruitful notions Freud introduces here are the re-ceptive character of the body, the pedagogy of pain through which the body comes to know itself as vulnerability, and, finally, the dis-persion that enables primordial meanings to arise as differences be-tween the *quanta* and *qualia* of local sensation. These discoveries are nevertheless harnessed by Freud to the notion of a unitary subject. Such a subject is consciousness insofar as it reduces what is specifi-cally Other about other persons to a content of consciousness. Viewed in terms of corporeality, the Other slips back into the chain of signifiers that constitute the narrative body. To use the language of Emmanuel Levinas's philosophy of the otherness, the Other is re-duced to the same.

To avoid such reduction and to conform to the spirit of Maurice Blanchot's remark that one should learn to think with pain, Levinas goes on to envisage pain as the "non-ground" of thought. The inter-twining of thinking and pain follows from his interpretation of sensa-tion as dependent upon two distinct functions of bodily existence: first, vulnerability and susceptibility, sensation's passive side; and, second, aesthetic (in the etymological sense) articulation, its active dimension. On the one hand, sensation leads into language and thought; on the other, it is lived as a field of receptivity. The body of ethics is identified with the passivity of sensation, with the body's defenselessness (*OB*, 53).

Why, it might be asked, is ethics linked to receptivity and to the passivity of corporeality? Is ethics not regularly identified with moral action and the deliberation that precedes it? In terms of my earlier analysis, does ethics not fall within the episteme of justice, the plane of discourse reflected in the howl of Oedipus? Levinas's analysis must be taken a step further: "Corporeality is susceptible to pain . . . exposed to outrage and wounding, to sickness and aging" (*OB*, 56). he maintains. Pain penetrates to the heart of the self that wills and thinks and calls it to order. Thus the body of ethics is a brake or restraint upon the active self prior to action, even to deliberation. Pain challenges self-righteousness. The sphere of moral deliberation, the possibility for the discourse of justice, supervenes upon the primordial level of sheer exposure to the Other, where neither reciprocity nor deliberation is possible. Moral rules and juridical principles are necessary, following from the fact that there is a social order (internalized if not actually in evidence) requiring the allocation of material and nonmaterial goods. But before there can be justice there must be an other.

It is now possible to discern the topos of postmodern asceticism. The fragility of the other may lead not only to refraining from harmful action but to undertaking meliorative action on behalf of the other, to placing the other higher than the self. When such deeds occur repeatedly, they begin to form a pattern of altruistic behavior. Such a pattern begins to take shape when the vulnerability of the other shatters one's ego, turning it into vanity, thus giving vanity a new meaning. Preparation for this new social space requires a new askesis, one that will respond to the cry of Héloïse.

From the Death of the Word to the Rise of the Image in the Choreography of Merce Cunningham

When one of the key figures in the world of dance, who is generally envisaged as an exemplar of high modernism, Merce Cunningham, appeals to the power of images rather than to a semiology of movements as the basis for his new work, then a shift that must be interrogated has occurred. As Wittgenstein demonstrated to philosophers the kinetic force of language in his apothegm "The meaning is in the use," so Cunningham showed the world of modern dance that the meaning is in the action or movement. Along with Martha Graham, Paul Taylor, Murray Louis, and later Twyla Tharp, Phyllis Lamhut, and Pina Bausch, to name only a few, Cunningham helped to transform the balletic character of dance in the twentieth century into a nonreferential, gestural idiom. Movements are often robust, sharp and percussive rather than fluid, while the standardized motions of ballet disappear or are parodied. To be sure, ballet itself had been "modernized," as the work of George Balanchine and Peter Martin, among others, attests. When abetted by ragtime, jazz, the popular tunes of the American musical and Tin Pan Alley, and by such avant-garde composers as John Cage and Meredith Monk, or by no music at all, the melodic musical line accompanying dance is lost.

My purpose is not to chronicle the transformations in modern dance history but rather to demonstrate that an art in which the materiality of the body and the localizability of space are critical is now engaged in a struggle between the visceral and the virtual, between site-specific spatiality and cyberspace. To grasp the character of this tension, it is necessary to explore not only visible changes in the art of dance but also the metaphysical presuppositions of a postmodernist culture of images.

Because the terms *modernism* and *postmodernism* are polysemic, I shall use them with caution. Instead, I shall stress the distinction between *concept*—a term that in the context of dance will be taken to mean a shape generated by forms connected in time—and images, a plethora of pictures without formal relation, as a sorting principle in differentiating dance movements.[1] Postmodernism in dance differs from the significations of the term in other arts. In postmodern architecture, the commitment to modernism's functionality is joined to elements with recognizable historical reference. Within the development of dance, the application of the term *postmodern* undergoes striking shifts. In the early 1970s, postmodern dance was construed as deriving from concepts rather than from the character of movements as such, thus exhibiting what might be seen as modernist tendencies in painting or literature: abstraction, minimalism, and the elimination of the formal subject. Non-Western movements and themes, political commentary and a change of performance venues from the theater to lofts, galleries, and churches altered the dance repertoire at about the same time. In the 1980s, film and videotape came into use to insure the survival of what hitherto had been seen as an ephemeral art.[2]

Merce Cunningham, Sally Banes writes in the 1980s, stands midway between postmodern and modern dance:

> His vertical, vigorous movement style and his use of chance (which segments not only such elements as stage space, timing, and body parts, but also meaning in the dance) seem to create a bodily image of a modern intellect. In . . . the separation of . . . décor and music from the dancing, and the body as the sensuous medium of the art form, [his] practice is modernist; his work and the theories of John Cage, his collaborator, formed an important base from which many of the ideas and actions of the post-modern choreographers sprang.[3]

Today Cunningham speaks of working with a camera, of seeing images, and of using the computer to observe what he has never seen before. Vision construed in this way, Meredith Monk says in her *New York Times* dialogue with Cunningham, is "like seeing between the cracks of reality."[4]

In what follows, I shall consider the shifts in Cunningham's choreographic forms in the context of changing notions of corporeality, from the lived body of phenomenological analysis to the virtual body of cyberspace, from the semiotics of early postmodernism to the culture of images that is likely to constitute a dominant strand of choreographic art in the twenty-first century. In so doing, I shall attend to the philosophical backdrop against which these shifts arise.

Dancing the Concept of an Affect

Although the bodily miming of affect characterized the choreography of such venerable innovators as Martha Graham and Isadora Duncan, Cunningham broke with the conviction that art is an *Äußerung*, or expression, of the subject's inner feeling, a feature that dated to an early phase of modern dance. Despite their differences, Duncan and Graham rejected the balletic view of the fixed torso and the motionless head as the reflective subject or spectator of the body's movements, thereby liberating both head and pelvis, so that inner affects could now be articulated.[5] Although Cunningham studied with Graham, feeling enters into his work not as itself the object of representation or the concept of an affect but rather as the intensity brought by his company's dancers to their rendering of a movement. Even in one of his earliest solos, "Root of an Unfocus," the dance is less about fear, about "how not to be frightened but [rather] how, with fear, to continue."[6]

Cunningham's early work was to have no conceptual or narrative referent. Far from purifying the world of appearances through a species of formalism in which ideas are represented by specific movements, instead movements are linked as a system of signs. Each sign is serendipitously generated, its meaning arising relationally through the differences among signs that, in choreographic semiology, reflect differences in time and space. In a 1952 statement anticipating Derrida's by now familiar notion of *différance*, Cunningham announces, "The fortunate thing in dancing is that space and time cannot be disconnected."[7] Arguing that this view frees dance from a restrictive formalism, Cunningham claims:

> More freeing than [thematic manipulation] would be a formal structure based on time. Now time can be an awful lot of bother with the ordinary penny-pinching counting that has to go on with it, but if one can think of the structure as a space of time

in which anything can happen in any sequence of movement event, and any length of stillness can take place, then the counting is an aid towards freedom rather than discipline towards mechanization.[8]

In the same vein, Carolyn Brown, Cunningham's principal dancer for over two decades, attests to the nonreferential character of movement: "Each movement is given its full value, its own unique meaning—the movement is expressive of itself."[9] She goes on to say: "No talk about meaning or quality. No images given. . . . The dances are treated more as puzzles than works of art: the pieces are space and time, shape and rhythm. The rest is up to us. We put the puzzle together, making of it what we can."[10]

The sets for Cunningham's productions were designed by such luminaries of modern art as Robert Rauschenberg and Jasper Johns, who, in the late 1950s, shared a studio in New York, where they worked with Cunningham and John Cage. To be sure, Rauschenberg and Johns had departed from the rigors of cubism and from abstract expressionism, by which the visual arts sought to represent inner affect. Rauschenberg, in his constructions of this period, turns to the flotsam and jetsam extruded by industrial civilization, disarticulating and reassembling *objets trouvés* so that they become puzzles whose meanings await interpretation. Meanings are dislodged, as it were, from constructions that are intended to reflect the whole of culture seen as impersonal information.[11] In a 1963 statement written for *Pop Art Redefined*, Rauschenberg constructs a statement whose prose dislocates and dizzies in the manner of his visual artifacts:

> I find it nearly impossible to write about Jeepaxle my work. The concept I planetarium struggle to deal with ketchup is opposed to the logical community lift tab inherent in language horses and communication. My fascination with images open 24 hrs. is based on the complex interlocking if disparate visual facts heated pool that have no respect for grammar. . . . The work then has a chance to electric service become its own cliche.[12]

Steve Paxton, a dancer who was trained by Cunningham and who developed a new dance form, "Contact Improvisation," that incorporates movements as varied as martial arts and child's play, notes that Cunningham takes the most mundane activities, such as "brushing one's teeth or riding a bicycle," and incorporates them into an abstract pattern of movements.[13] Such movements can be said to become a chain of signifiers whose sheer mundaneness or familiarity allows meaning to emerge.

Cunningham's anecdote about his collaboration with Rauschenberg in the 1964 dance piece "Winterbranch" illustrates how the familiar can be semiotically reinforced by costume and stage set. In an effort to show what falling down means, Cunningham assumed that one need only fall, get up, or be dragged away. Rauschenberg, however, augmented these motions by introducing new visual supports. Cunningham reminisces: "All I told Rauschenberg was that it was falls, and he thought that tights and leotards [the uniform, as it were, of modern dance] wouldn't be strong enough. In rehearsal I was using towels to drag people off; he replaced those with old pieces of canvas and put us all in sweatpants and white tennis shoes and put black under our eyes like skiers or football players."[14] It is interesting to note that a revival of "Winterbranch," now seen as a modem "classic," was well received, by contrast to "Rondo," a piece that was interpreted by one critic as "bear[ing] the too visible mark of his current work with computerized figures on a screen," when both works were performed at the Brooklyn Academy of Music on October 14, 1997.[15]

To see how a transitional figure, Jasper Johns, affected Cunningham's work, consider Mark C. Taylor's comment about Johns's own deviation from early modernism. He interprets it as a "turn from the subject of abstract expressionism to the object prefigured in Duchamp's ready-mades and Rauschenberg's combines. In an unusually revealing remark, Johns explains, 'I'm interested in things which suggest the world rather than things that suggest personality, things which are rather than in judgments.'"[16] What is important in the present context is Taylor's conclusion that in Johns's use of artificial rather than natural objects, "Johns is a sign painter. His objects are signs. . . . the most common, quotidian, banal signs one can imagine."[17] Perhaps it is because objects can lose their independent significations that Johns resisted designing sets and delegated their creation to other artists. Instead, he focused on costume in order to differentiate one dance from another. When he finally agreed to construct a set for Cunningham's "Walkaround Time," he based it upon a work of Marcel Duchamp.

If we can assume that both Rauschenberg and Johns are artists of the sign, that images are used in signlike fashion in their work, the image is still reined in by the word. The primacy of the sign and its role in high modernist art are illustrated in Kierkegaard's anecdote about a man who passes by a store displaying a sign that reads "Pants pressed here." In due course, he fetches his trousers and brings them in to be ironed, only to be told that the store does not press pants but sells signs.

Signs and Signifiers: The Body as Signification

Yet, it must be asked, can the most conceptual of dances ever be merely a chain of signs? In a philosophical account of dance written from an Anglo-American analytic standpoint, Francis Sparshott asks whether a dance can be "a tissue of signs, of pure meaning-bearers abstracted from the actual dancers who embody the signs? . . . If that is all we see it makes sense to say that we do not see the dance at all."[18]

What emerges in modem dance is a tension between the significations it means to convey, its conceptuality, and its sheer corporeality. In this regard Cunningham does not differ from earlier founding figures, who move epistemically, as it were, from dance as representation to dance as sheer embodiment. It may be recalled that classical ballet often employed the representational resources of mime, such as folding the hands upon the heart to indicate love, raising one hand and placing the other upon the heart to signify swearing an oath. The value of these gestures lay in their self-evidence. The dominant tradition was at first affected only occasionally and piecemeal. As early as the eighteenth century, Jean Georges Noverre advocated narrative unity, a return to natural movement, and an abandonment of the hooped and panniered costumes of the age. Later, François Delsarte developed a taxonomy of dance movements, and at the turn of the century Michel Fokine replaced facial expression and hand movements as sign systems with the deployment of the whole body as an instrument of expression. These premonitory stirrings can be viewed as protesting a choreographic version of a simple correspondence theory of truth, the agreement of word and object — in dance, the gestural mirroring of a prior meaning.

It is Martha Graham, far from a nonconceptual choreographer, who perhaps best enunciates the dancer's sense of embodiment, a corporeality that cannot be expressed only as a chain of signifiers. Her memoir, *Blood Memory*, opens with a hymnlike praise of embodiment:

I am a dancer. I believe that we learn by practice. Whether it means we learn to dance by practicing dancing or to learn to live by practicing living, the principles are the same. In each it is the performance of a dedicated precise set of acts, physical or intellectual, from which comes shape of achievement, a sense of one's being, a satisfaction of spirit. One becomes in some area an athlete of God. . . . The instrument through which the dance speaks is also the instrument through which life is lived—the human body.[19]

To see how Graham views this theocratic athleticism and this emptying of meaning into movement in which body and signification are indissoluble, a theological analogy may be useful. The Patripassian position, first enunciated in the second century by Noetus, reported by Hippolytus and Epaphanius, and later declared heretical, stated that there is only one God, who emptied himself into Christ and thus underwent Christ's human experiences.[20] Transcendence disappears in this kenotic movement, so that there is only the Father totally contained in Christ: transcendence has become immanent.

Cunningham, to this extent the pupil of Graham that he had in fact been, is also committed to dance as expressing the body's physical energy and, as such, becoming "a moving image of life,"[21] even if he considers dance as movement for its own sake rather than as an expression of feeling. This gesture on the part of Graham and Cunningham reflects the stance of Nietzsche's Zarathustra in "The Other Dancing Song," where he cries out: "Oh life. . . . At my foot frantic to dance you cast a glance. . . . My heels twitched and my toes hearkened to understand you . . . ; for the dancer has his ear in his toes."[22] Nietzsche's point is that life (in this context instinct and a feeling of power) cannot be spoken but must be corporealized as dance. Along similar lines, Cunningham writes, "Our ecstasy in dance comes from the possible gift of freedom, the exhilarating moment that this exposing of the bare energy can give us. What is meant is not license, but freedom, that is, a complete awareness of the world and at the same time detachment from it."[23] The modernist revolution brought the premonitory semiotic efforts of Noverre and Delsarte and later of Fokine and others to fruition, but at the price of an uneasy pairing of meaning-bearing sign and dancing body. In the most compelling philosophical articulation of this pairing, Merleau-Ponty argues, in the context of his critique of the mind-body distinction, that the gap between signification and corporeality is bridged because the body is the thought or intention that the body signifies for us (*PP*, 174–79). A spoken word is always already a gesture and its meaning a world. It is not surprising that this materialization of language culminates, if only indirectly, in Derrida's account of an archē-writing whose materiality inhabits language prior to speech.

For Merleau-Ponty, it is not introspection that enables one to read the other's gestures of emotion in acts of empathy. One does not apprehend anger or a threatening attitude as the result of a psychic cause that is concealed behind the carnal gesture, but rather reads anger directly from the gesture itself. Thus one does not think of anger as an essence apart from itself; anger is, as it were, a *carnal* essence. The meaning of a gesture thus understood is not a shadowy thought that lies behind it, but is bound up with the structure of the world embodied in the gesture. The words in different languages that putatively refer to a common concept are not alternative means for expressing the same idea but rather denote "several ways for the human body to sing the world's praises and in the last resort to live it"(ibid., 187).

The social world is one of bodily communication. "It is through my body that I understand other people, just as it is through my body that I perceive 'things,'" Merleau-Ponty insists (ibid., 186). Furthermore, he contends, "communication or comprehension of gestures comes about through the reciprocity of my intentions and the gestures of others. . . . It is as if the other person's intention inhabited my body and mine his" (ibid., 185). This account of the permeability that allows the dancer to transmit affect corporeally may provide an account of the role of the spectator in early modern dance.[24]

In sum, there is perhaps no better description of what modernists among postmodern dancers are after than Merleau-Ponty's comment:

> The body's animation is not the assemblage or juxtaposition of its parts. Nor is it a question of a mind or spirit coming down from somewhere else into an automaton; this would still suppose that the body itself is without an inside and without a "self." There is a human body when, between the seeing and the seen, between touching and the touched, between one eye and the other, between hand and hand, a blending of some sort takes place.[25]

Yet it would be misleading to think of Cunningham's most recent work as explicable in terms of a phenomenology of the lived body.

"Scenario," a work that premiered in October 1997, is a case in point precisely because its aesthetic suggests (misleadingly) a return to the phenomenological body. The dance was performed in a white space illuminated by fluorescent lights. Its costumes, conceived by the high-fashion designer Rei Kawakubo, were stuffed with pillowlike forms to create exaggerated bellies, bosoms, and backsides, calling attention to flesh as protuberance. These bloated shapes suggested tumors, the distensions of disease, their vaguely threatening character mitigated by a sense that they were merely reflections in a distorting mirror or, more to the point, computer-generated variations. Far from being a chiasmatic blending of sensibility and sensed, the lived body was here mocked, deconstructed, by this ambiguity of signification and corporeality.[26]

Dissonance and Dance

Cunningham was originally encouraged to depart from the Graham perspective in the 1940s by the controversial composer John Cage. Not only did he divorce himself from myth and narrative but, together with Cage, he developed an aesthetic that separated dance from the constraints of music, of rhythm and melody. Although music continued to accompany the dance, its experimental dissonances moved on an independent track. Both artists chose to rely on chance, for Cunningham, the toss of a coin in the determination of movement, for Cage, the *I Ching*, in calculating sound arrangement. Thus Cunningham writes:

> When I choreograph a piece by tossing pennies—by chance, that is—I am finding resources in that play, which is not the product of my will, but which is energy and a law which I obey. . . . When I compose in this way . . . I am in touch with a natural resource far greater than my personal inventiveness could ever be . . . and organically rising out of common pools of motor impulses.[27]

It would seem that Cunningham departs both from blind mechanism and from Kant's account of the organism as "an organized natural product, one in which every part is reciprocally both end and means, in which nothing is in vain . . . to be ascribed to a blind mechanism of nature."[28] Yet Cunningham's principle that the grouping of elements does not matter loosens but does not radically alter the

Kantian framework in that, for Cunningham, the freeplay occasioned by chance occurs within "a very strict arrangement."[29]

There is, to be sure, no collaboration among set designer, composer, and choreographer, a dissociative gesture that, in the end, is a lure for such artists as Johns, Rauschenberg, and Frank Stella, the latter being adjured merely to create a set that the dancers could move in.[30] Related to the notion of nondeliberative selection is the development of Cunningham's "Events," an intermissionless performance that consisted of excerpting sections out of a miscellany of movements. One could argue that the principle of this work is rather like that of structural linguistics, in which individual speech, *parole*, is an excision, depending upon need, from the larger pool of lexical and semiotic resources, *langue*. Cunningham is, in this regard, indebted to the music of Earle Brown and Morton Feldman, whose compositions were written in a definitive form but whose individual components were performed serendipitously. Today, improvisation does not occur during the well-rehearsed final performance of Cunningham's works.[31]

Simulacra Dancing

While retaining some features of the earlier semiotic standpoint, the culture of images introduces a new conception of dance, which can only be understood by grasping both an altered view of corporeality as stored information and the ontology of images. Consider first, by contrast to Merleau-Ponty's description of the body as a blending of sensing and sensed, touching and touched, the new view of corporeality described by Mark C. Taylor. The body, he contends, is an intrinsically divided entity. Using autoimmune disease as an entering wedge into understanding the body as dematerialized, as the body that touches and is touched, he argues that the body is always other to itself: "There is mounting evidence that autoimmunity is our 'primal' condition and so-called health is secondary to, and dependent upon, the suppression of an autoimmune response. If this is so, then the self is never at one with others, the world, or even itself."[32]

Consider again Cunningham's distortion of the phenomenological body in one of his most recent works, "Scenario," in which the body materializes as if some weird in utero alteration had taken place, one manifest as a distension of the body's soft parts. That the aesthetic of this work is difficult for more traditional modernists to accept is evinced in the comment by dance critic Anna Kisselgoff: "with performers who look like a cross between Munchkins and the huge round Nanas of the sculptor Niki de Saint Phalle, the choreography looks downright eccentric."[33] When corporeality is envisaged as information, it can only find its expression in the etiolated materiality, the insubstantiality of the image, an insubstantiality that, paradoxically, can express itself as inflated or obese—for example, in the worlds of Disney or Pixar. In contemplating the rise of the image, it is useful to ponder Guy Debord's coinage "the culture of the spectacle," which is intended to suggest not an endless cortege of images but rather a culture in which "capital becomes image." Thus the image is not the product of technology but an ontological thinning out in the arena of economy, the vaporization of capital, as capital had been understood in industrial society. The real dissolves into the hyperreal, by which is meant that all that once had been directly lived has now become representation.[34]

Yet what is there to be represented? Perhaps the most influential postmodern response to this query is to be found in Baudrillard's account of the image. His by now familiar quip "The territory no longer precedes the map. . . . it is the map that precedes the territory— *precession of simulacra*—"[35] suggests that it has become impossible to discover the real and thus impossible to stage an illusion. There is nothing to be represented, no way to represent it. To simulate in the absence of an original is to take negativity, the not, into the simulation itself. For Baudrillard, it is no longer a matter of feigning what is real, of counterfeiting what is not the true state of affairs in the knowledge that the true state is not ontologically precluded— simulation dissolves the very difference between real and imaginary.[36] Simulation challenges the claim to referentiality: truth, having absorbed all the energy of the false, and the real, having internalized the force of the negative, have been transformed into the hyperreal, more real than the real.

Oddly, an account of the current relation of dance to image that is contingent upon the dissolution of the logic of representation was presaged in the 1940s in an essay about mimesis and image by a relatively obscure dancer, mime, painter, and literary figure, Angna Enters. Turning to mime, on the face of it the most representational of arts, she rejects the view that the mime imitates what is anteriorly real. Instead, "it is as though images, either in the creator's memory or in flashes of vision, acting as catalytic agents in relation to aspects of man's life in the world suddenly decide to have a being of their own. Then the creator or performer has to release these images to take their own form."[37] Equally surprising is Enters's claim that the mime should be concerned with what is trivial, in that the trivial may conceal what is most significant in a life—thereby pointing ahead to Derrida's account of margins, of a text that is no longer a finished work but a writing that overruns its boundaries in endless acts of disclosure.

Before returning to Cunningham, let us consider briefly the work of a younger choreographer for whom the new information culture provides inspiration, that of Stephan Koplowitz. Allying himself with site-specific choreography, in the 1980s Koplowitz moved to the use of the Web in shaping a new kind of dance. Departing from theatrical settings, his venues included the fourth-story Vanderbilt Avenue windows of New York City's Grand Central Terminal ("Fenestration," 1987) and the city's Bryant Park, a small stretch of green behind the New York Public Library on Forty-Second Street ("Bytes of Bryant Park," 1997). By inviting responses to Internet solicitations from him, Koplowitz uses the Web to democratize the choreography and staging of his work. Thus "Bytes of Bryant Park" incorporated multiple suggestions he received on his Web page. Outlining his concept of the work on the Web, he provided a map with sites that Web surfers could visit in order to contribute dialogue or to suggest movements. The more than fifty thousand people who visited his Web site, 180 of them having contributed ideas, can continue to access his so-called Webbed Feats Website. What is significant in Koplowitz's relation to a postmodern culture of images is that his interest lies in "the history, architecture, and use of the site" in order to "amplify" the "design and rhythm" of that site. Thus, despite his technological know-how and his extraordinary effort radically to increase participation in the creation of the dance work, Koplowitz remains bound to the notion that the site is actual and thus to a mode of phenomenological realism.

Cunningham, by contrast, although his use of the Web is in all likelihood less polished, may nevertheless have more radically entered into the culture of images. Precisely because his earlier conception of movement derives from the view that movement is autonomous, that it is nonreferential, images enter into his work in a different fashion. Thus, when Meredith Monk inquires, "How has the Life-Forms dance computer extended your vision?" he replies, "With the computer you can make the pictures go very fast or very slow, and you'll find something you never saw before." Thus novel images, speeding up and slowing down, characteristic of the culture of images, is the effect attained. The computer shows Cunningham how "to have the technical possibility of speed and clarity with the legs coupled with activity in the torso and the arms." What is more, the computer does not mechanize motion. In relation to the designing of spatial patterns, he goes on to say, "It was not difficult for me because I've so long used space in a four-facing-four pattern. The computer doesn't mechanize it [space] because it's actually doing it in another dimension."[38]

Although the lived body does not entirely disappear, Cunningham no longer perceives it as a center of orientation. On one occasion, he derived a movement-phrase from the computer, marking it in the studio in the form of a circle. When he realized that he did not have to face in any particular direction, he proceeded to create a system for cutting up the phrase in a variety of ways and to determine the sequence of each segment in vintage Cunningham fashion, by chance. At one point, encouraging the dancers to curve more, he concluded that "for a millimeter of a second, I really understood what Einstein meant about curvature of space."[39]

Yet a desire to put an end to the speed and noise of the culture of images affects the work of Cunningham as much as it does Baudrillard's analyses of contemporary culture. "But also, against the acceleration of networks and circuits," Baudrillard insists, "we will seek slowness; not the nostalgic slowness of the mind, but an insurmountable immobility, that is slower than the slow: inertia and silence."[40] When Meredith Monk suggests that the hyperstimulation of today's culture makes it "easy to lose touch with silence and stillness" and that some of Cunningham's pieces in which these features persist can no longer be understood, Cunningham replies that there is "a whole other area to explore."[41]

PART III

Bodies: Subject or Code?

The world to come will not consist of eating, drinking or human relations but rather the righteous will sit with adorned heads enjoying the radiance of the *Shekhinah* [divine presence].
—**Babylonian Talmud,** *Berakhot* 17a

Interpretations of the body as flesh and sensorium have been challenged by recent genetic accounts of the body envisioned as code. Governed by an intricate system of mathematized information that determines its forms, appetites, capacities, and behaviors, the dematerialized body-subject can be seen as no longer principally the subject of pain and suffering. The view of the body as code can be linked to the identification of dematerializition or abstraction with truth, a perspective whose underpinnings can be traced to the constitutive role attributed to mathematics as a locus of truth in Greek philosophy. The gene's eye view of the body will be considered independently of and in relation to the work of biologists whose research remains within the parameters of phenomenology.

Illustration: *Grave Matters*. Mark C. Taylor and Christian Dietrich Lammerts. Courtesy of the artists.

10

Empathy and Sympathy as Tactile Encounter

Empathy and sympathy are feeling-acts that open unique modes of access to other persons. While they differ from one another in object and intentional structure, both bring other persons into proximity to the experiencing subject. This "bringing near" suggests that empathy and sympathy are misunderstood if they are interpreted as mental acts whose objects yield their meanings only when they are taken as traversing an intervening space, as originating at a remove from the act of apprehension. Sight and hearing are the paradigmatic senses for grasping objects that are given as coming from elsewhere. Visual objects are apprehended as coming into prominence across an illumined space, while auditory sensation, though impinging directly upon the hearer, emanates from a source that the hearer takes to be at some distance from himself. Only touch requires contact, the proximity of feeling to what is felt. It would appear that structural affinities might be found between tactility and the feeling-acts of empathy and sympathy.

While tactility has often been recognized as presenting unique features, so long as it was taken to be one sense among the others, subject to the same categories of interpretation as sight, hearing, and the rest, its idiosyncracies remained unexplained. For the most part, theories of sense based on the localization of sense experience only functionally differentiate the senses in order to provide a formal structure that would account for all sense acts. But tactility subverts this unitary structure, since the body as a whole is the tactile field. The body, with its sensitivity to pressure, temperature, and surface qualities, together with its kinestheses, its felt respiratory movements, its pulse, its hand's capacity for manipulative endeavor, its motility, is the primordial ground of existence as incarnate. This view of the tactile body frees tactility from the "separate but equal" hypothesis that underlies all-encompassing theories of sense. Yet we cannot bypass the history of the problems encountered by these theories, since this history brings to light precisely those aspects of touch that remain refractory to general schema. I shall consider several theories of sense that are brought up short by the peculiarities of touch and reveal features of tactility that are of importance for a phenomenological understanding of empathy and sympathy, and then shall argue that the tactile subject—the subject that can touch and be touched by the other—is the experiencing subject of these feeling-acts.

In the course of this discussion I shall also consider the affinities and overlappings that, though loose, unite empathy and sympathy, while taking into account their differences and particularities. In addition, I shall touch upon the consequences of ignoring the primordiality of tactile experience by considering the *ressentiment* view of pity, which unites empathy to vision rather than placing it in its proper, haptic field.

Empathy, Sympathy, Other Minds

In affirming the possibility of feeling-acts whose referents are other persons, do I not already assume that there are existents like myself? How can I justify this claim in a manner that also opens the possibility of apprehending the other through empathy and sympathy? The existence of a self is given as soon as awareness of experience occurs. This link is manifest in the immediacy of experiencing and permits me to assume that *wherever* there is awareness of experience there must also be an individual self.[1] On these grounds I can acknowledge the possibility that other selves exist, but I do not yet know that a particular "something" that confronts me is a self. For that to be so, I must know that this "something" occurring "there" is occurring as experience. What I perceive is a physical body, but I know that I am witnessing an occurrence of experience when I recognize the "something" I see as an expressive phenomenon. Thus, when I see weeping, an act of a physical body, I also perceive sadness within the unity of a single apprehension. This sadness is included in my grasp of the other's gestures, his wringing hands, tears, and so on.[2] Perhaps, it might be argued, I know the other's sadness by analogy with my own. When I cry I feel sad, so when I see someone else cry, I believe he or she must also be sad. This account, however, distinguishes my sadness from the other's sadness only in terms of the bodies in which the feeling happens. It is a single feeling in two different bodies, my own feeling and not the other's that I apprehend, a doubling up, as it were, of my own affect.[3] The same argument holds against the view that I know how the other feels by imitation. This is, in fact, the position of William James and Nietzsche, who hold that we reproduce "the expression of the other's eyes, his voice, his gait, his posture" so that "a similar feeling originates in us as a consequence of an old association of movement which is drilled to run forward and backward."[4] It is my feeling, and not the other's, that I reproduce. But if I can apprehend the other's feeling in a single act, and if empathy and sympathy are primordial modes of access to the other, they take place without my first having recourse to myself. Instead, access to the other comes about when I concur in the meaning of the other's gesture. Merleau-Ponty writes: "The gesture which I witness outlines an intentional object. This object is genuinely present and fully comprehended when the powers of my body adjust themselves to it and overlap it. The gesture presents itself to me as a question, bringing certain imperceptible bits of the world to my notice, and inviting my concurrence in them" (PP, 185).

While sympathy and empathy are structures of intersubjective encounter, they differ in their aims and intended objects. I take empathy to be the feeling-act through which a self grasps the affective act of another through an affective act of its own. The other's emotion may be occasioned by a concrete object, or it may be free-floating. Thus I may empathize with another's joy over the birth of a child, or I may vicariously feel the other's objectless malaise expressed in his purposeless gaze and gestures. Even if the other's affect is occasioned by some object, my empathy does not depend upon knowledge of the object, although such knowledge may increase or diminish the intensity of empathized affect. I may empathize with X's pain, for example, when I observe his distorted face, but the intensity of my response is less when I know that he only has a toothache rather than Bell's palsy. Sympathy is a feeling-act in which I and x^n others affectively apprehend a common object while experiencing one another as immersed in similar feeling-acts occasioned by mutual participation in the common object. The feeling-act is generally one of sorrow or some other troubling emotion, although it may shade off into a more diffuse affect, a sense of shared value, and so on. Thus, I am in sympathy with my sister over the loss of our father, but I can also be in sympathy with members of my religious community in regard to our shared belief in a transcendent being. Both empathy and sympathy presuppose that the selves that participate in intersubjective feeling-acts are roughly of the same type.[5] I therefore can be said to empathize largely with persons and only rarely with animals, while it is even more difficult to imagine a community of feeling with animals over some shared object. Thus, although my dog is different from me, I can still empathize with his pain when I see him limp, but I should be thought to make a mockery of their situation if I suggested that, united in fellow feeling, my dog and I sympathized with the plight of Cambodian refugees. Not only are certain less-than-human ranges of subjectivity inappropriate for inclusion in sympathetic encounter, but some objects are also ruled out. A person of broad sympathies is thought to bring into proximity a wide variety of feeling-acts but nevertheless to withhold participation in feelings of malice, spite, envy, cruelty, and so on.

Both empathy and sympathy may generate action or find their terminus in feeling alone. If I empathize with the victims of torture, for example, I may take action by uniting with others to bring this condition to public attention, or my empathy might dissipate, shading off from distress to disinterested neutrality. If I unite with others to oppose torture, empathy is supplanted by sympathy: I join others in fellow-feeling in relation to a common object, the suppression of torture. Both empathy and sympathy lie along the same gradient of feeling-acts so that one may occlude or "run into" the other.

Pity and Ressentiment

Pity is, according to Aristotle, "occasioned by undeserved misfortune."[6] To the extent that I pity the other, I must perceive him or her as blameless, so that the suffering of the other canot be conceived as retribution for a mistake or a moral failing.[7] Even when I say, "I pity X for losing his friends, but he has brought it all on himself," I do not mean "X has got his just deserts," but only "X deserves the consequences of lying, welching on his debts, and so on, but I pity him to the extent that he has suffered in excess of what he deserves." There is, however, a well-known view that suggests that pity is a less straightforward feeling-act than this description allows. This is Nietzsche's view that pity is the emotion we feel when a desire for revenge is suppressed. If someone injures me, I may strike back directly, or I may delay my response. Should I strike back, I spontaneously discharge my vengeful feeling, so that it no longer acts upon my psychological life. By contrast, should weakness or fear prevent this, my frustrated rage turns into *ressentiment*. Pity is the fruit of this emotion.[8] So long as I cannot avenge myself against the stronger, I have an interest in supporting the weaker so that I can maintain the object of pity. In order to justify this support, I turn pity into a value.

This interpretation has acquired considerable prestige, in no small measure because psychoanalytic theory claims that empirical support can be mustered for the phenomenon of repression upon which it is based. Yet there is a religious and philosophical tradition that suggests that pity and compassion are valuable in themselves, and that they are, in fact, the source of many of our moral acts. In response to this conflict, it has been argued (by Max Scheler and others) that there is a difference between the spurious emotion that springs from *ressentiment* and genuine pity. We tend to confuse them only because we observe no difference in the actions they motivate. The difference between them is, rather, in their psychological origin: genuine pity derives from a position of strength and superior power, while the other emotion (its nameless double) springs from repressed rage.[9]

This latter position is easier to dispose of than classical *ressentiment* theory itself. While it may be true that an identical act x (contributing to charity) might spring from different motives (love of one's neighbor or flaunting one's wealth), it is unlikely that different motives would produce an identical *chain of acts*. The difference in motive could be expected to derive from a difference in disposition, which would not become manifest in one act but would show itself in x^n acts. If X strikes Y, I would not think of X as hostile and aggressive by disposition unless this sort of behavior was characteristic of him. It is unlikely that, over the long run, the degenerate form of pity would produce a behavioral pattern similar to that produced by a magnanimous disposition.

But even if we dispose of Scheler's revisionist *ressentiment* theory, we have yet to show that the original version is acceptable. We can only arrive at this conclusion through an excursus into its underlying claims. This digression is of interest, for I believe it can be shown that the original *ressentiment* theory is based upon a misunderstanding of corporeality, which, when set right, may help us to see the relationship between touch, empathy, and sympathy.

Nietzsche's *ressentiment* theory is based upon the assumption that passions are the expression of a struggle of forces, particularly those that constitute the organic process of life: "Life would be defined as an enduring form of processes of the establishment of force, in which the different contenders grow unequally."[10] Or, we may think of "The will to life rejoicing in its own inexhaustibility . . . not in order to get rid of terror and pity, not in order to purge oneself of a dangerous affect by its vehement discharge—Aristotle misunderstood it that way—but in order to be oneself the eternal joy of becoming, beyond all terror and pity—that joy which includes even joy in destroying."[11] In this interpretation, the will to life is inexhaustible, although of course individuals die. Furthermore, this will to life expresses itself not in the preservation of the species but in the "sheer joy of becoming." Despite the death of the individual, the process continues.

According to this view, a person is not a consciousness but a body. If this is so, however, Nietzschean vitalism has given to this body too narrow an interpretation, for it cordons off a feature of the body that is intrinsic to corporeal existence, the body's vulnerability. To be as embodied existence, as flesh, is to be fragile. While Nietzsche acknowledges and even celebrates death, he segregates phenomena of vulnerability—sensitivity to temperature, fatigue, exhaustion, sleep, and so on—from death itself. These phenomena are treated metaphysically in the manner of nonbeing. When interpreted in this way, they appear in the vitalist framework as manifestations of decaying life. Their role in the body's everyday corporeal existence is overlooked, as if to manifest them at all is to express an excessively low threshold of sensibility. Nietzschean vitalism interprets the living body as the body awake, as an existence that never lets down its guard, in order to avoid acknowledging the body as vulnerability. What does it mean to exist as an awake body? How does the condition of being awake contrast with that of sleep?

Being awake is the unnoticed foundation of ordinary existence, the standpoint from which the otherness of the world is grasped. Descartes begins to doubt when he finds no criterion to distinguish between the sensations of sleep and waking existence. However, the discovery of the *cogito* through which this uncertainty is dispelled already presupposes the standpoint of being awake, because it is only from this perspective that dreaming and waking life can be distinguished. Erwin Straus writes: "We do not owe the experience of being awake to a judgment; we are, rather, able to judge because we are awake. The possibility of ordering precedes the fact of order."[12] Wakefulness is the ground for the body's motility and sensory confrontations with the other, the precondition of there being a world for me, a world that is suspended in sleep. The most obvious sign of wakefulness is the fact that when I am awake my eyes are open. I can shut out the visible world by closing my lids, yet remain awake. In unusual circumstances, my eyes might remain open while my consciousness is suspended. But the usual state of waking life is being able to see. To "enter a situation with my eyes open" means that I do not delude myself about it but confront it with the alertness of waking life.

For Nietzschean vitalism, human existence is a perpetual self-overcoming, an activity "that neither sleeps nor slumbers." Thus, manifestations of vital somatic life, of its ascending tendency, preclude fatigue and exhaustion. But life thus interpreted is based on a paradigm of one of its pathological conditions, unceasing wakefulness, or insomnia. In insomnia, Levinas writes:

> the ego is swept away by the fatality of being. There is no longer any outside or any inside. Vigilance is quite devoid of objects. That does not come down to saying that it is an experience of nothingness, but that it is as anonymous as the night itself. Attention presupposes the freedom of the ego which directs it: the vigilance of insomnia which keeps our eyes open has no subject. . . . The consciousness of a thinking subject, with its capacity for evanescence, sleep and unconsciousness, is precisely the breakup of the insomnia of anonymous being, the possibility to "suspend," to escape from this corybantic necessity, to take refuge in oneself so as to withdraw from being, to, like Penelope, have a night to oneself to undo the work looked after and supervised during the day. (*EE*, 65)

The body of Nietzschean vitalism lives in ceaseless oscillation between the sensory inundation of forms that characterizes existence in the visible world and the anonymous wakefulness of a subject that cannot suspend consciousness but nevertheless abandons the object structure of the visible field. Since vitalism is characterized by a refusal to relinquish visual consciousness, it is based on a one-sided interpretation of the living body. No adequate account of empathy and sympathy can rest on these foundations, for empathy and sympathy depend upon the body's vulnerability, which vitalism refuses to admit. Since empathy and sympathy are phenomena of proximity, they can only be understood as feeling-acts of a tactile rather than a visual subject.

Touch and Some Theories of Sense

In the history of philosophical theories of sensation,[13] only rarely has touch been highly regarded. But those who thought it worthwhile to single out tactility have discovered that analysis founders when categories applicable to the other senses are applied to touch. By briefly examining some key theories of touch (those of Aristotle, Berkeley, and Condillac), we can bring to light the points at which touch fails to fit into a general analysis of sensation. If we read these difficulties as "breaks" or "ruptures" within an interpretive scheme, we see disclosed phenomena that lie beyond it, "sticking points," as it were, that are keys to the unique spatiotemporal structure of the haptic field, from which empathy and sympathy emerge.

Having remained an enigma in the classical philosophical tradition, touch has fared no better in contemporary physiological theories, in which it is interpreted as a nexus of relationships between afferent receptors of pressure and temperature (with the skin being the primary locus of these receptors) and kinesthetic acts.[14] Important questions still remain unanswered: What is the sense organ of touch? The skin? The body as a whole? When I see or hear, the sense organs of sight and hearing are constituted after the fact, as it were, since I do not see these organs as they see and hear but come to know them from the outside, as if they were the organs of another person. Can this be true of touch? Do I not see my body when I touch? Is not touching always also being touched?

Classical philosophy at least acknowledges the discrepancy between phenomenon and theory. For Aristotle, sensation requires a sense organ, a medium, and an object (*DA*, 424a). Touch is no exception. Yet Aristotle is troubled by the absence of a specialized organ "capable of receiving into itself the sensible form of things without the matter." In the case of touch, we might consider the flesh the sense organ, but Aristotle assigns it a different role. The flesh, like air in the case of light and sound, acts as the medium, but "one whose powers of refraction are imperfect" (ibid.). What, then, is the sense organ? Something still deeper in the body must play this role. The power of perceiving the tangible, the sense organ, is inside the body and connate with the heart. The view that flesh is not a sense is suggested to Aristotle by the fact that contact with the sense organ by an object precludes perception of the object: when I place a white object on my eye I do not perceive it, but if I place something upon my flesh I do perceive it. Thus the flesh cannot be the organ of touch (ibid., 43a). Because Aristotle has determined in advance that touch is a sense, the medium cannot be eliminated. But he notices that touch and taste require contact with their objects, while the other senses do not. This proximity to the object accounts for the difference between touch and taste and the other senses, while misleading us into thinking a medium is absent in touch (ibid., 43b). The matter of proximity proves so troublesome that Aristotle is compelled to add what is, from our point of view, an important break with the main thrust of his account: He posits the vulnerability of flesh. Because of his general theory of sense, however, he is forced to attribute this vulnerability to the medium:

> But there remains this difference between what can be touched and what can be seen or can sound, in the latter two cases we perceive because the medium produces a certain effect upon us, whereas in the perception of objects of touch we are affected not by but along with the medium; it is as though a man were struck through his shield where the shock is not first given to the shield and passed onto the man, but the concussion to both is simultaneous. (Ibid.)

In an attempt to account for the refractory phenomena, Aristotle breaks with his general theory and reveals features of touch that are important for understanding empathy and sympathy: Touch is the most inward sense (even if this view is based upon the erroneous conclusion that the heart is its organ); moreover, it depends upon the proximity of the object. Flesh, even if mistakenly interpreted as the medium, is lived as vulnerability in tactile encounter.

A radically new interpretation is given to touch in the eighteenth century. This new point of view arises in relation to philosophical problems connected with blindness. Before turning to Berkeley's theory, let us consider the question around which this discussion moved: "Whether a man born blind, on recovering the use of his eyes, would be able to name correctly a cube and a sphere on the basis of his tactile experience with these objects."[15] It came to be known (after its propounder) as Molyneux's question and constituted an important issue not only in Berkeley's *Essay towards a New*

Theory of Vision but also in the problematics of Locke's *Essay concerning Human Understanding*. Locke (and Molyneux) answer the question negatively, as might be expected: while the blind man may have obtained experience of a cube and a sphere through touch, he does not have an experience of how these objects which affect touch actually affect sight.[16] Locke thinks that the man would be able to see upon recovery of sight, but he would be unable to name what he saw since to do so would require recourse to an idea that could not have been obtained from experience. Since Locke denies the existence of such ideas, his response to Molyneux's question is more or less predictable, as an outgrowth of his attack on innate ideas.

But Locke leaves important difficulties unresolved. One such difficulty stems from his distinction between primary qualities — the shape, size, and motion of bodies, which were thought to inhere in the bodies themselves — and secondary qualities, the qualities that result from the way we apprehend things. If primary qualities inhere in objects, why, then, should touch and sight give us such different pictures of these objects?[17] Why should these senses remain as insular as they do?

This question could be said to form the nub of Berkeley's *Essay towards a New Theory of Vision*. While Berkeley answers Molyneux's puzzle in the same way as Locke, his examination of the difference between sight and touch moves the argument forward in a manner of interest to us. Berkeley notices that the perception of distance by vision is a consequence of an alteration in the magnitude of objects. He explains this perceived difference mechanistically, in terms of a widening and narrowing of the pupil of the eye together with their associated sensations. But if vision is to teach us distance, we are left without a standard for the perception of magnitudes. This difficulty can be resolved only if we imagine things as tangible objects, so that we can then correct for the discrepancies of sight: "The judgment we make of the magnitude of objects by sight are altogether in reference to their tangible extension. Whenever we say an object is great or small, of this or that determinate measure, I say it must be meant of the tangible, and not the visible extension which though immediately perceived is nevertheless taken little notice of."[18] But, Berkeley is quick to add, the magnitudes of tangible objects cannot always be perceived directly and must be inferred from visible magnitudes. (How, for instance, could we hope to touch the moon?) The ideas of sight are symbols or signs for tangible ideas, with which they are connected from the time of our earliest experience. These signs are items of a divine language that, like the signs of human language, are connected to their objects by means of habit. What is of importance for us in this analysis is that the perspectivalism of vision is seen to distort the character of the object, while touch "tells the truth" about its magnitude. (It is better to *imagine* touching the moon than really seeing it.) Berkeley argues for the primacy of touch in our apprehension of space. Thus, tactile sensation is presupposed when, for example, Berkeley solves the problem of why we do not see upside down when our retinal images are given in this way by suggesting that (in modern terms) we do not see images as projected in the camera, but in terms of the tactile orientation in space provided by our body schema.[19] While still interpreting the data of sense mechanistically, Berkeley understands the relationship between touch and lived space as one of the body's active engagement in the world, though he falls back upon the notion of sense data to account for it.

The philosophical problems of blindness are also of considerable interest to the French Enlightenment, which draws upon interrogation of the blind and evidence from case histories of those born blind and subsequently sighted by means of the surgical removal of their cataracts. Inquiry proceeded within the context of the then current epistemological issues dividing empiricists from one another and from rationalists. The most important contribution of this body of work to the understanding of touch, for our purposes, is to be found in the *Treatise on Sensations* of Condillac. Propelled by Berkeleyan idealism to seek an answer to the question of how we come by our belief in the existence of an external world, Condillac hits upon the device of imagining a statue devoid of sense and motility in order to reflect upon the functions that accrue when each sense, in turn, is bestowed upon it. One of the first discoveries the statue makes after it has been given smell, hearing, and sight and is about to receive touch is that it has a body: "Nature would appear to have only one way of making the child know its body, and this is to make it perceive its sensations not as modifications of its mind, but as modifications of the organs that are their occasioning causes. In this way the ego, instead of being concentrated in the mind, becomes extended and somehow repeated in all parts of the body."[20]

Condillac recognizes that the localization of sensations poses a problem, since we experience these dispersed sensations both as local and as belonging to a single individual. We shall see this vexing question arise again in our investigation of the living body as a tactile subject. For Condillac, these localized sensations teach the body to recognize itself and to distinguish between itself and others. He suggests that the statue's hands will quite naturally pass over its body as well as foreign objects: "Placing its hands upon itself, it will discover that it has a body, but only when it has distinguished the different parts of it and recognized the same sentient being in each. It will discover other bodies when it touches things in which it does not recognize itself."[21] The statue can no longer confuse itself with its local sensations: "As it continues to touch itself . . . everywhere the same sentient being will reply . . . 'This is myself, this is still myself.'"[22] So long as auscultation is confined to itself alone, it does not know that there are others. But if it happens upon another object, "the 'I' which feels itself modified in the hand, does not feel itself modified in the foreign body. The 'I' does not receive the response from the foreign body which it receives from the hand."[23]

In addition, Condillac, who accords a maximum role to sensation in knowledge, confirms Berkeley's attribution of activity to sense. We must recognize the difference between seeing and looking; the eyes themselves analyze the given: "I do not say then . . . that our eyes have to learn to see, for they necessarily see everything that makes an impression upon us; but since seeing is not sufficient for cognition, I say that we have to learn to observe for it is not enough to see in order to have ideas."[24] In his analysis of tactility as the sense that enables us to attain the feeling of a unified self, to distinguish alterity, and to recognize in the body schema the foundation of oriented space, Condillac has, within the framework of a mechanistic psychology, uncovered fundamental features of the tactile body.

The Body of Tactility

While Condillac's insights into the role of touch are instructive, the vitalists were correct in perceiving the body as living and thus inexplicable in terms of sense data. It stands to reason that Condillac's ingenious figure of the progressively animated statue would receive its capacities in the manner of a machine, which acquires a series of successive attachments, since Condillac treats the sensomotorium as though its functions were not themselves already dependent upon the context of the world. Sensations are interpreted as though we could build up from their accumulation a sense of space and a world of material objects. But, for Condillac, the view of sense as active constitutes a "break" in this mechanistic theme. If a sense is active, what propels it to seek its objects? Another sense? This would lead to a meaningless regress. Pleasure and pain? These already depend upon sense. The contemporary mechanists of physiological psychology rely upon the selective character of afferent nerve systems—but these account only for the differentiation of sense input, not for the discrimination of meaning. This differentiation means only that sense organs function in the manner of specialized grids, rather than of maps determining the limits of what can be sensed. But grids are no more active than maps and so cannot account for the difference between looking and seeing.

How, then, do objects come to be what they are for us? What is the indispensible condition for this coming to be, for the manner of givenness of objects? Merleau-Ponty writes: "The fact is that if we want to describe it, we must say that my experience breaks forth into things and transcends itself in them, because it always comes into being within the framework of a certain setting in relation to the world which is the definition of my body" (PP, 303).

The body is that which, though always obstinately "here," places what is other than itself always, and with equal obstinacy, "there."[25]

The body through which objects arise for me is not just any body but *my* body. How does this sense of a particular body as mine come about? If I examine my experience for what cannot be canceled in it, I find that sensation is given in this manner, that is, as mine. Yet it is given to me as localized, "at a remove" from my experience of myself as the subject of mental acts such as judging, thinking, and so on. But if sensation is given to me as though at some distance from myself, where is the "I" from which it is distanced? Edith Stein writes:

> Since sensation is always spatially localized "somewhere" at a distance from the "I" (perhaps very near it but never in it), I can never find the "I" in it by reflection. And this "somewhere" is not an empty point in space, but something filling up all space. All these entities from which my sensations arise are amalgamated into a unity, the unity of my living body, and they are themselves places in the living body.[26]

This articulation of the body and the self as "distance" cannot, of course, physically be measured. (How would I go about measuring the distance of my hand from my self?) Yet some parts of myself feel closer to me than others. (My shoulder feels closer than my hand, unless my hand happens to hurt.) This point from which the parts of my body are distanced is the orienting point of my body, of my incarnate being as a spatial existent. It is a mobile center (my head for vision, my mid-body for touch, etc.). I can, of course, measure the distance of external objects from one another or from my physical body, but, just as I cannot measure the distance of my body parts from their orienting point, "I cannot measure the distance of physical objects from this orienting point, I could never say that the stone I hold in my hand is the same distance or 'only a tiny bit farther' from the zero point than the hand itself."[27] The unbroken unity of the body can be attributed to this structure of articulation around an endlessly mobile center. It enables us to break with the view that regards each sense as a pathway providing information about the world, which is then subsequently synthesized. "The experiencing subject is, by way of each sense, directed to the same 'what.' "[28]

Once the body is understood in this manner (not as an inert subject but as an origin of activity as an ever-changing but unified whole), we can think of the living body as a tactile body. The body as a whole is a potential haptic field. What is more, touch is not merely an epicritic-perceptive system but rather a mode of object manipulation, of spatial orientation (as Berkeley and Condillac understood). While all sensing depends upon the kinestheses, this universal element of sensing is always apprehensible to touch since touch is not only cutaneous receptivity of heat and cold, pressure, surface quality, and so on, but inseparable from the kinestheses as such. It is the sense through which the kinestheses can at one and the same time become active and aware of themselves. While many body movements are not at the center of attention, they become focal through tactile sensations. If we are right, if the primordial manner of being of the lived body is to be understood as tactile, then tactility cannot be included under a generic theory of sense but provides its ground. Thus the manner in which touch yields the world is the most primordial manner of our apprehension of it.

How does touch apprehend the given? If we examine the data of touch, we see that they occur successively rather than simultaneously, since, by and large, one feels only one thing at a time. As a result, the yield of objects is small when compared with sight. But, like sight, touch can give the phenomena of constancy. We can feel the weight of an object as being identical whether lifted by hand, head, foot, or teeth (*PP*, 313). What is important for us is that touch requires proximity to the object as well as commitment, for a change in object is possible only successively. Touch, engaged in palpation, is capable of altering its objects; it is an active intercourse with things, a necessary interaction with the world.[29] Since touch includes the body's ability to move, it provides the sense of "I can," the ability to do, to push, pull, carry, move, and so on (*PP*, 314). In intersubjective encounter it is involved in caress and sexual arousal, as well as in expressions of aggression, slapping, punching, and so on. Touch never lets me forget that I am my body: "The unity and identity of the tactile phenomenon do not come about through any synthesis of recognition in the concept, they are founded upon the unity and identity of the body as a synergic totality. . . . The body is borne towards tactile experience by all its surfaces and all its organs simultaneously, and carries with it a certain typical structure of the tactile world" (*PP*, 316).

Touch and the Other

Ordinary language attests this account of the tactile body and provides a link between touch, empathy, and sympathy. When we say, colloquially, "*X* is touchy," we mean that *X* is hypersensitive, vulnerable to injury. When "I am touched by *Y*'s kindness," I mean that *Y* has compelled me to let down my guard, has drawn close so that I cannot remain indifferent to him. To remain untouched by another is to refuse to engage in a feeling-act that brings to light the other's plight, to refuse to empathize with the other. The active deployment of tactility is expressed in such colloquialisms as "I feel for you," by which we mean my body substitutes for yours, I take on your pain. In empathy I do not merge with the others but retrace the lines of the other's affect. Thus Martin Buber writes:

> Empathy means to glide with one's own feeling into the dynamic structure of an object, a pillar or a crystal or the branch of a tree or even of an animal or a man and as it were to trace it from within, understanding the formation and motoriality of the object with the perception of one's own muscles. Thus it means the exclusion of one's own concreteness, the extinguishing of the actual situation of life, the absorption in pure aestheticism of the reality in which one participates.[30]

This interpretation is in conformity with the view already suggested: empathy touches the consciousness of the other but may be oblivious to the object of the other.

In sympathy, as we have seen, I apprehend the other person as sharing my feeling toward the same object. Thus sympathy includes not only the other but something we hold in common. The feeling of the other must lie along the same gradient as my own but is independent of it. The relationship between myself and other(s) and to the shared object, event, or value are equiprimordial and experienced simultaneously. (Even if I sympathize with a historical character, I do so as though "there.") Thus sympathy is not a relation of dialogue: it is not a Thou that confronts me in a reciprocally experienced event but rather myself in solidarity with the other in relation to something we feel in common. Intensity of affect varies: The object may press lightly upon me or weigh heavily, I may feel intimately connected or only superficially tangential to it. But empathy and sympathy cannot be distinguished in terms of this intensity since degree of feeling is highly variable in both. Sympathy tends to be more enduring, being mediated by a common object, while empathy may be transient. (When empathy lasts we may suspect that it shades off into identification with the other and loss of personal boundary.)

While empathy and sympathy are ordinary feeling-acts that structurally resemble tactile encounters (bringing the other close, tracing his or her affective states, moving or reaching towards the other, etc.), not all tactile contact resembles empathy and sympathy. The sculptor encounters the world as tactile but deploys touch for aesthetic ends. The physician palpates the patient's body to diagnose disease, and so on. In these cases, tactility is deployed in the manner of seeing rather than the converse. When tactility is used in this way, for the creation of pleasurable surfaces or for its cognitive yield, its paradigmatic value for empathy and sympathy may be reduced.[31] This is not to suggest that empathy and sympathy are conscious imitations of tactile encounter, but that tactile encounter when lived at a prereflective level, is vulnerability to the other. Significant data may be provided by touch, which, despite sophisticated diagnostic apparatus, is still useful to the physician in determining a clinical picture of disease. But this mode of tactile apprehension of the other cannot found for us what it means to be as a tactile body, or to apprehend the other as incarnate existence.

11

Levinas's Other and the Culture of the Copy

To an ever-increasing degree, the work of art reproduced becomes the reproduction of a work of art designed for reproducibility. From a photographic negative, for example, one can make any number of prints; to ask for the "authentic" print makes no sense.
— **Walter Benjamin, "The Work of Art in the Age of Its Technical Reproducibility"**

The consciousness of representation lies in knowing that the object is not there. The perceived elements are not the object but are like its "old garments." . . . in the absence of the object they do not force its presence, but by their presence insist on its absence. . . . They . . . mark its removal, as though the represented object . . . were disincarnated in its own reflection.
— **Emmanuel Levinas, "Reality and Its Shadow"**

The movie [*The Matrix*] portrays a Baudrillardian future in which tyrannical, hyper-intelligent machines have enslaved the human race and connected all the humans by cables to a computer matrix where they live in a virtual reality. . . . The "real world" . . . appears almost not at all.
— **Brent Staples, *The New York Times*, May 24, 2002**

When objects of perception or cognition are said to be the same, what is generally meant is that a trait or traits of an object can be found in one or more other objects. A resemblance between or among them is predicated with respect to traits that are repeated despite otherwise diverse attributes. That by virtue of which an object is said to resemble another can be interpreted either as a preexistent form or as an essence inferred from observed qualitative or quantitative properties. Not only may forms or essences be thought to express what is exemplified in objects that are envisaged as their instantiations, but they may be viewed as the origin of that sameness, as imbued with generative power, even if this origin is constituted as such only after the fact. Otherness is determined as the absence of a common trait, essence, or form.

More recently, these accounts of same and other encrypted in the history of metaphysics have been reinscribed in linguistic terms. Language is seen not as representing what is prior to itself but as a code embodying conventions that render repeatability possible, conventions of iterability that enable one to say the same. Or, if we fast forward to a recent description of what is meant by organization in biological life, we find the logic of iterability thus described replicated in the claim that, for such organization to be possible, sameness is intrinsic to "those relations that must exist among the components of a system for it to be a member of a specific class."[1]

The meaning of the same can also be understood in accordance with Husserl's phenomenological principle that objects are disclosed as objects for a consciousness that reaches out to or intends them. Not only are objects subject to the conditions of their disclosure—in that regard in accordance with Kant's transcendental account of cognition—but the being of what is disclosed, of the phenomenon, is subordinate to an intentional consciousness that reasserts itself in all cognitive and perceptual acts. When exteriority is attributed to objects, it is an exteriority determined by the interiority that reveals it, an outside that cannot be other than an outside that is inside. There is no *Ding an sich* apart from the phenomenon as brought to light by a self-identical consciousness.

For Levinas, this epistemological account poses an ethical question. Even in the absence of a reflective awareness of its operations as coercive, the intentionality of consciousness can be perceived as a mechanism of control that subverts otherness, specifically, the otherness of other persons, and, as such, is always already guilty of a certain violence. If the sublation of what is other is to be circumvented, there must be that which cannot become content and which transcends the capacity of consciousness to contain it, an excess that cannot become the aim of an intending act. Such an excess would provide a disconnect, as it were, a disempowering of the consciousness seeking to encompass it. Does the inapprehensibility of this excess, its resistance to description, render it meaningless, or can it be argued that the descriptive and logical properties of language fail to exhaust the uses of language, that in its performative capacity language solicits and commands? Is language not always already an address to and from another who cannot be contained within a common genus, an essence of the "human"? The other as absolute exteriority contests the power of consciousness to reduce it to the same.

I hope to put Levinas's notions of same and other to the test by considering their possible destabilization in a culture of the copy in which the distinction between original and replica is undermined. Can his account of the same as that which is contested by an other whose descriptor is simply that it is otherwise than being be sustained, and, if not, must the other, the condition of ethics, not also be affected? I shall turn first to the Levinasian subject, for whom repetition is lived as re-identification and re-creation of the self, of an ipseity that is a precondition for cognition. I shall then examine some widely disseminated views of gene replication and a theory of artificial life that undermine his description of ipseity, before considering Levinas's view of fecundity as the reproduction of oneself in one's progeny and Kierkegaard's analysis of repetition in relation to the time of ipseity. Finally, I will suggest how Chilean biologists Humberto R. Maturana and Francisco Varela, who interpret replication in terms of recursiveness within autonomous living systems, can be seen to offer some surprising prospects for effecting an accommodation with the Levinasian account of the subject.

Some Preliminaries: Consciousness and the Corporeal I

What can be meant by Levinas's astonishing claim that "alterity is possible only starting from *me*" (*TI*, 40)? Does he not insist that the absolute exteriority of the other cannot be brought into a relation of correlation with the consciousness that intends it without impairing its alterity? Even if *ex hypothesi* the relation of correlation is one in which the self and the other are not reciprocal terms, he cautions that the relata might still be incorporated into a system open to an observer outside itself. More important, even if an unbridgeable distance or exteriority determines the meaning of otherness, Levinas concedes that alterity cannot be hermetically sealed, cordoned off from that which renders it other. Thus otherness is, in a crucial sense, dependent upon the same.

The reduction of exteriority by consciousness is contingent upon what is prior to it, the same produced as an egoism that enters into a relation with the other (*TI*, 38). Levinas avers: "The alterity, the radical heterogeneity of the Other, is possible only if the Other is other with respect to a term whose essence is to remain at the point of departure, to serve as *entry* into the relation, to be the Same not relatively but absolutely. *A term can remain absolutely at the point of departure of the relation only as I*" (*TI*, 36, emphasis in original). To be I is neither to be a sequence of alterations reborn at every instant nor an unchanging essence, but rather that which reidentifies itself in embracing the heterogeneous content it thinks and represents. What is more, and in conformity with Husserl's phenomenological account, the I bends back upon itself and, in this self-apprehension, overcomes its first naïveté.

Yet, in accord with Heidegger's account of the Dasein of *Being and Time*, the Levinasian subject is not a thought-monad, an I that merely represents itself to itself, but an I that is embedded in a concrete system of world relations. For Levinas, world is not a hostile environment but the place in which one can be at home with oneself. Home (primordially, if not in fact) is an enabling site in which one dwells and which allows for the freedom of work and possession. The otherness intrinsic to world relations should not be confused with the relation to the other person, who, unlike the nexus of objects among which one lives, is not simply exterior to oneself. The other cannot be located at a site. Yet even if the "*sway* [pouvoir] of the I will not cross the distance marked by the alterity of the other" (*TI*, 38), must we not ask whether the distance and height that separate me from the other can be envisaged otherwise than spatially? Even if the relation of same and other is enacted as language, still "the Same gathered up in its ipseity as an 'I,' as a particular existent unique and autochthonous" (*TI*, 39), must go out of itself toward the other. If the command of the other is to refrain from harming her/him, the other cannot be a gnostic subject but must be a body that exists in a world, even if this location cannot be pinpointed across an inviolable space.

In elaborating upon what is meant by life as bodily existence, Levinas asserts: "Life is a body, not only a lived body where its self-sufficiency emerges, but a crossroads of physical forces, a body-effect." Yet, he continues, "there is no duality between lived body and physical body. The world life acquires . . . is also the physical world." The relation of life with that which it inhabits is lived as a freedom that is "a by-product of life" (*TI*, 164–65). Bodily existence exhibits both self-mastery and dependence upon what is not itself, the environment in which it dwells and works. Through dwelling and work, the self experiences a sense of security over and against its awareness of the death that is to come, a doubleness lived as a postponement of death and, as such, as the dimension of time. It is this rift at the heart of corporeal existence that is consciousness. For Levinas, consciousness is life's temporality, disincarnate, lived as postponement or having time, as attempting to ward off what threatens one's existence.

To exist as forestalling danger is to will. The body's actions do not, however, follow a preordained goal but are corporeal engagements involved in a process of self-modification. For Levinas, the active self recreates itself along the way, both "seeking and *catching hold* of the goal, with all the contingencies this involves" (*TI*, 167). What is more, the being that acts is one that consciously represents itself as acting. Yet representation is disingenuous, "claim[ing] to substitute itself *after the fact* for this life in reality, so as to constitute this very reality" (*TI*, 169). Representation itself is not merely a negation derived dialectically from relations of the living being to its environment, but an absolutely new event. It is a withdrawal that is lived as entering into relation with another human being encountered as a human face. The face that calls the I into question, Levinas insists, is language (*TI*, 171). It is as a relation to the other that language is first an ethical event that makes possible the offering of a world to another. But "language, far from presupposing universality and generality, first makes them possible. Language presupposes interlocutors, a plurality" (*TI*, 73).

Cloning Ipseity

It can be argued that the body that acts, that is a point of world orientation or exists as a sensate subject, has been undercut by the claims of evolutionary biologists who redesign the body of ordinary experience to become, quintessentially, coded information. In the most radical accounts, such as that of Richard Dawkins, the manifest form of the organism presupposed by the phenomenological body is engaged in ever more tenuous relations with the germ-line, a powerfully active biological entity that is both an agent and a recipient of the body's actions. Dawkins does not deny that the phenotype (an organism's manifest characteristics) is the result of the interaction of genetic makeup and environment. But for Dawkins, phenotype and genes are not inseparable, in that the outcomes of gene activity may lie outside the bodies in which the genes are lodged. Thus, an entity made up exclusively of genes is extended beyond the organism that the genes inhabit to constitute a new individual. The gene's eye view of evolution sees evolution as taking place not on behalf of the organism as an indivisible living unit but rather in the interest of the gene, that "little bit of chromosome which potentially lasts for many generations."[2] Now, modes of inheritance heretofore ascribed to organisms are attributed to genes.

To make sense of this contention, it is crucial to see the centrality of replication in Dawkins's account of the gene's operations.[3] It is in the interest of reproducing itself, the gene, rather than the phenotype that natural selection takes place. For Dawkins, a replicator is anything of which copies can be made. Information-bearing DNA molecules, gene strings, are replicators, active when their effects lead to their being copied, passive when they die out. For Dawkins, the gene is the "unit of heredity" that is retained in the evolutionary process. Only those likely to be copied survive, while passive replicators become extinct (*EP*, 82–85). This account is complicit with Dawkins's famous claim that "a predominant quality to be expected in a successful gene is ruthless selfishness. This gene selfishness will usually give rise to selfishness in individual behavior" (*SG*, 2). What remains clear is that, while the phenotype continues to be an "instrument of replicator preservation," it is not itself preserved but "works as a unit for the preservation and propagation of . . . replicators" (*EP*, 114); or, as he states more graphically, "A body is the genes' way of preserving the genes unaltered" (*SG*, 25). Dawkins maintains that his radical stance is not taken to support the truth of particular factual propositions but rather to open a way of looking at new facts and ideas (*SG*, 1).

Levinas does not, so far as I know, discuss the meaning of genes as replicators. Surprisingly, however, in the essay "Reality and Its Shadow," he develops a notion of resemblance operative in generating images in art that may lend itself to reinscription in the context of gene replication. In contrast to signs or words, which are transparent toward their objects, images refer to objects by way of resemblance. Yet resemblance is not, as Plato would have it, a relation of original to copy, but rather the very movement that engenders the image.

"Reality would not be only what it is, what it is disclosed to be in truth, but also its double, its shadow, its image. Being is not only itself, it escapes itself" (*CPP*, 6). Because a being does not coincide with itself, there is that which remains behind the being, something that withdraws from it. Thus, there is a duality in a being, which is both what it is and also something estranged from itself. It is this relationship between a being and its image that is resemblance (*CPP*, 6).

To be sure, unlike genes, images are visible. Yet Dawkins's interpretation of gene string and phenotype repeats in its context the ontological relation of reality and image, in that for Levinas "by the simple fact of becoming an image, [the represented object] is converted into a non-object; the image as such enters into categories proper to it. . . . The disincarnation of reality by the image is not equivalent to a simple diminution in degree" (*CPP*, 5). The ontology of images provides an unintentional blueprint for the relation of gene string to phenotype in that, like the Levinasian image, genes occupy the place of the object "as though the represented object died, were degraded, were disincarnated in its own reflection" (*CPP*, 7).

The Progeny Who Is and Is Not Me

It is not surprising to find that evolutionary biology is focused upon the modus operandi of reproduction. It is, however, startling to see that, for Levinas, intrinsic to the self that is open to the other is a conatus to replicate itself, a movement in which the self relates itself to its future through a relation to the beloved, a relation he calls fecundity. Thus Levinas writes: "Infinite being, that is, ever recommencing being—which could not bypass subjectivity, for it could not recommence without it—is produced in the guise of fecundity" (*TI*, 268). The birth of a child seen as the outcome of an erotic encounter is not a continuation of one's own possibilities, but a link with a future that one does not control. In the relations of consciousness and world, the I reiterates itself. One's child is, however, a duality within that which is identical rather than a falling back into or reiterating of oneself. The child is not an extension of an I who would ensure its identity in reembodiments, "avatars" of oneself, yet the child is one's own future despite its discontinuity with oneself (*TI*, 268).

That, for Levinas, the child is the son and woman the biological agent of the reproductive process is open to (and has received) warranted criticism. What is more, new reproductive technologies call into question the scenario of eros that Levinas depicts. But it is the telos or goal of reproduction that is most deeply challenged by Dawkins's version of neo-Darwinism. Replication is not in the service of another who is and is not oneself, nor even undertaken in the interest of perpetuating the species or the individual organism as the unit of natural selection. Replication seeks to conserve the active germ replicator, which is, for Dawkins, "the ancestor of an indefinitely long line of descendant replicators" (*EP*, 83). Replicants expand power, that of the germ line, by virtue of a sheer increase in the number of copies. Although some germ lines may die out, "any germ-line replicator is *potentially* immortal" *(EP*, 83).

The interpretation of the gene as code lends itself readily to the modeling of artificial life, life that is humanly contrived, through the use of computational prototypes. Richard Dawkins approvingly cites D'Arcy Thompson's claim that "any animal form can be turned into a related form by a mathematical transformation, although it is not obvious that the transformation will be a simple one" (*EP*, 2). In present-day continuity with this prototype, Stephen Wolfram writes: "thinking in terms of programs is . . . even more obvious for biological systems than for physical ones. For in a physical system the rules of a program must normally be deduced indirectly from the laws of physics. But in a biological organism there is genetic material which can be thought of quite directly as providing a program for the development of the organism."[4]

In turning to computational paradigms not merely to comprehend but to create life, artificial life theorist Christopher Langton asserts that life is not a property of matter but rather of its organization, for which computational models are eminently suited. Now research can be directed "from the *mechanics* of life to the *logic* of life."[5] Langton contends that more can be learned from the "creation of life *in silico*" than could be learned by relying on the organic chemicals of carbon-chain chemistry, in that computational models open up the "space of *possible* life."[6] In effect, what is being sought is to generate behavior through the creation of computational automata.

It has been thought that computers can only do what their programs enable them to do but cannot generate mutations or novel animal behavior. It is now claimed, however, that, if sufficiently powerful, computers can transcend their programs, that they are inherently unpredictable. Langton contends that "it is impossible in the general case to determine *any* non-trivial property of the future behavior of a sufficiently powerful computer from a mere inspection of its program and its initial state alone . . . the only way to find out anything . . . is to start the system up and watch what happens."[7] For Stephen Wolfram, nature itself may be thought of as a universal computer, which generates complexity from simple programs, a claim that can be supported by allowing the programs to keep on running.

Answering Back I: Destabilizing the I

Can Levinas's account of representation as "a determination of the Other by the Same without the Same being determined by the Other" (*TI*, 170) and his description of ipseity as a passive unitary self accommodate some of the conceptual moves embedded in theories of germ-line replication and artificial life? It could be argued that Heidegger's critique of calculative thinking as revealing the meaning of being and his account of enframing as the manifestation of being as will could in effect discredit the ontological underpinnings of artificial life theorists. Had Heidegger not already referred to cybernetics as the metaphysics of the atomic age? It could, however, be countered that Heidegger's critique of cybernetics could not be applied to Darwin's depiction of evolution as involving living systems. But Heidegger contends that Darwin's model of nature is itself one of instrumentality. As Keith Ansell Pearson points out, for Darwin "artifice [is] the common factor in the technical evolution of both nature and human breeding . . . [a view] conditioned by considerations of utility."[8] Utility governs the process. For Heidegger, by contrast and in conformity with biologist Jacob van Uexküll's claims, the animal from whom we are said to evolve inhabits a phenomenal world, an *Umwelt*, but unlike humans is "poor in world."[9]

The picture of evolution criticized by Heidegger presupposes a closed universe, one that could not have taken into account Langton's and Wolfram's newly conceived views of artificial life (commonly referred to as A-life). Could A-life's "bottom-up processes of spontaneous self-organization,"[10] an open universe in which conditions of uncertainty prevail, provide a toehold for the Levinasian same? In consonance with this view, Pearson, citing biologist Gilbert Simondon, notes that the becoming of a biological system must be seen as a metastable equilibrium: "A being does not possess a 'unity in its identity,' which would be that of a stable state in which transformation is not possible, but rather it enjoys a '*transductive unity*,' meaning that it is able to pass out of phase with itself."[11] Becoming as a temporal process does not simply fall upon a pre-existing, stable entity. Instead, time is invented in accordance with this process of ontogenetic change.

Can the Levinasian notion of ipseity open the way for establishing a certain compatibility between Simondon's "metastable equilibrium" and the repetition intrinsic to ipseity? In his crucial essay "Substitution," Levinas maintains: "The identity of ipseity is not due to any kind of distinguishing characteristic . . . like fingerprints, and which as a principle of individuation would win for this identity a proper name. . . . The identity of the 'oneself' is not the inertia of an individuated quiddity. . . . The identity of the *oneself* is not equivalent to the identity of identification" (*BPW*, 84). A separated being that reidentifies itself in this way is not one who is in a stable state but a being that remembers, one whose mode of temporalization is recursive. In consonance with this view of ipseity, Levinas writes in a key passage of *Totality and Infinity*: "The cause of being is thought or known by its effect *as though* it were posterior to its effect. . . . The posteriority of the anterior—an inversion logically absurd—is produced . . . only by memory or by thought . . . the *After* or the *Effect* conditions the *Before* or the *Cause*" (*TI*, 54). The affirmation that memory reverses the ongoingness of the historical order of time is especially significant in that the post hoc constitution of the origin destabilizes the self as identical with itself. If this claim is accepted, how is the self that recreates itself to be understood?

I cannot hope briefly to engage the complex relation of Levinas to Kierkegaard but rather, in a brief excursus, shall consider some crucial configurations of recursiveness in Kierkegaard that wend their way errantly through Levinas's account of the self-repetition of ipseity.[12] In Kierkegaard's work *Repetition* (not mentioned by Levinas in this context), recollection and repetition are seen from the vantage point of the problematic figure of Kierkegaard's pseudonymous author.[13] It is Constantin Constantius who declares that, whereas the Greeks saw knowledge as recollection, modern philosophy sees it as repetition. "Repetition and recollection are the same movement, only in opposite directions; for what is recollected has been, is repeated backwards, whereas repetition properly so-called is recollected forwards."[14] If repetition is possible, he declares, happiness is its psychological outcome, whereas the outcome of recollection is unhappiness. Repetition does not demand novelty, "but it requires courage to will repetition."[15] Is the time of repetition thus understood not the lived time of Levinas's separated self at home with itself? The happy individual, according to Kierkegaard, is one for whom "repetition is a task for freedom . . . [and] signifies freedom itself."[16] One who wills repetition seeks neither perpetual novelty nor the mere preservation of the past. Could it perhaps be argued, without unduly stretching the point, that recollecting forward is an apt figure for determining the future behavior of a computational system not from an inspection of a program's initial state but by running the program?

Answering Back II: The Recursiveness of the Observer

Is it possible to find in the culture of the copy, in which life is configured as code, the reflexivity of consciousness as it is usually understood by phenomenology? Jean-Pierre Dupuy asks whether representation and the transcendental dimension of cognition have been altogether eliminated from meaningful discourse by epistemologies grounded in computation and physical laws.[17] Is it possible to reinscribe the reflexivity of phenomenological consciousness in new terms? Can the role of the observer in self-regulating living systems go proxy, as it were, for that of consciousness?

If phenomenology's account of intentionality can be naturalized, perhaps the best prospects for its reinscription lie in the study of closed autonomous and dynamic living systems as developed in the Chilean school of autopoiesis. According to this group of biologists, changes in a living system (such as that of neural networks) are the result of the system's own activity. External events occur as perturbations of the system, which acquire meaning only as a result of the network's own activity. Humberto R. Maturana and Francisco Varela, founders of the school, maintain that thought does not emanate from a Cartesian *cogito* that guarantees its truth but emerges from the organization of living systems as self-making or self-producing. Maturana (upon whose thought I shall focus) is concerned not with the promise of meaning and truth but rather with the mechanisms or processes that enable living systems to operate successfully.[18]

In Maturana's work "Cognition," the observer is not seen as extrinsic to the operation of living systems but is built into its explanation, defined as the modeling of the system by a "beholder."[19] The designation of a thing as a unity depends upon the observer's stipulation of a distinction between an entity, which may be simple or complex, and its background. It is only complex entities that exhibit both structure, the components that constitute an entity as of a type or class, and organization, the relation among components that generates the dynamics of complex entities. As unities, entities belong to a domain or space in which they can be distinguished. The autonomy of unities as autopoietic systems is what Maturana calls "structure-specified" in that other entities merely trigger changes that are essentially determined by their intrinsic structure (C, 32/6). In sum, for Maturana, living systems belong to "a class of systems each member of which is defined as a composite unity (system), as a network of productions of components which . . . through their interactions recursively constitute and realize the network of productions that produced them" (C, 33/8).

In Levinas's view, the self, which is at first immersed in an environment he calls the elemental, closes off a part of that environment, from which it then distinguishes itself so that it exists as a separated being. The space it inhabits, what Maturana would call its domain, is for Levinas the dwelling or the home. To be sure, the I, the self or ipseity, which is prior to the self at home with itself, is, as we have seen, the accusatory self of responsibility, which renders the self answerable for "everything and everyone." Yet this self is also a unity that is "its own content," a unity out of phase with the rhythms of life that lie outside it (*BPW*, 85–86). The reflexivity of this ipseity, which passively folds back upon itself, which makes possible the self's relations to exteriority, the reduction of the other to the same, is reflected in Maturana's account of the reflexive unity of self-maintaining living systems as they respond to external perturbations. For Levinas, the recursiveness of the same emerges in all of its reflexivity as "the return of being to itself as knowledge" and is produced at the "fulcrum" of an ipseity that "is" as a nonessence or nonquiddity that cannot yet be encapsulated in language (*BPW*, 85).

It is significant that, for Maturana, even if living systems are independent, they are not alone. Systems are structurally coupled with others of a similar type or class, a coupling that is a precondition for establishing what he calls a "consensual domain," in which linguistic distinctions proliferate, piggy-backing, as it were, upon one another. In Maturana's arcane formulation: "When this recursive consensual domain is established an observer sees a generative linguistic domain in which metadescriptions take place. A linguistic domain with such characteristics is a *language*" (C, 43/22). Although, for Levinas, the other does not first appear to the self in the language of concepts but is experienced as the pressure of responsibility, nevertheless self and other are not coinhabitants of a space but share a world. It is as and through language that the world is designated to another: "The generality of the word institutes a common world . . . Language does not exteriorize a representation preexisting in me: it puts in common a world hitherto mine. Language *effectuates* the entry of things into a new ether in which they receive a name and become concepts" (*TI*, 173–74).

But the question remains: who or what performs the function of the observer for Maturana and how is this observer related to phenomenological consciousness as understood by Levinas? For Maturana, behaviors are themselves already descriptions, and recursions are metadescriptions. "When a metadomain of descriptions (or distinctions) is generated in a linguistic domain, the observer is generated. Or, in other words, to operate in a metalinguistic domain . . . is to be an observer" (C, 44/23). An infinite regress is precluded by the built-in limitations of a structure that allows the observer to define her position and to operate as if outside that structure.

To be sure, for Levinas, being determines its modes of being-given, thereby ordering the forms of knowledge that comprehend it. It is as the correlation of that which is and the consciousness that intends it, of the noema, the intentional object, and the noesis or intending act (in Husserl's terms), that being assures the possibility of a certain order of truth. What is crucial is that this relation requires a distinction between beings and the consciousness that brings them to light in accordance with its own laws (*OG*, 100–101). Thus, in addition to the rationality relative to the knowledge of beings, the rationality of evidence, there must be what Levinas calls a change in level or deepening, which is obtained by turning to the subject that intends. "it is a question of awaking a life that evidence absorbed and made us forget, or rendered anonymous. . . . it is a question of descending from the entity illuminated in evidence toward the subject" (*OG*, 18). As ontological objects vary, different modes of consciousness are called into play. Levinas notes that, in the first edition of Husserl's *Logical Investigations*, it is conceded that, even in the realm of pure logic, the so-called "pure law," whose apodicticity is assured, can be filtered through "fluctuating verbal significations" (*OG*, 19) and that therefore an analysis of the psychic acts that intend them is required. "It is only through reflection upon the experience of consciousness that objective terms are maintained in an evidence that . . . awakens to itself only in reflection" (*OG*, 20).

Since Maturana speaks not of reflective consciousness but of observers who are living systems, are we not fully determined by the built-in limitations of these systems as autopoietic unities and by the pre-established parameters of their structural couplings? It must not be forgotten that the world of the observer is one of language. *"Everything that is said is said by an observer to another observer that could be himself"* (C, 30/4, emphasis in original). We as observers can escape from the ways in which structural couplings determine our actions in that "our operation in a linguistic domain . . . allows us to generate a metadomain of descriptions" (C, 48/28). Maturana speaks of thinking, a recursive circling within neurophysiological processes, and of linguistic metadomains, rather than of the emergence of consciousness. What is crucial, however, is that we can arrive from thinking to what functions as self-consciousness through language. As Katherine Hayles notes: "The observer generates self-consciousness . . . when he endlessly describes himself describing himself."[20] Does the reflexivity of the observer as self-generated metadescription not reinscribe what phenomenological inquiry claims to derive as an achievement of the transcendental reduction, the being of consciousness?

The ethical as well as the epistemic implications of this reduction are what is significant for Levinas. In consonance with the received view, he notes that, in *Ideas I*, Husserl questions the trustworthiness of naive evidence and, without repudiating the data of consciousness, initiates a suspension of belief in the existence of the world so that a phenomenon can emerge for consciousness in its essential nature. For Levinas, this account highlights an ambiguity in Husserl's thought that provides an entering wedge for his own new way of configuring the other. Husserl's aim, the preservation of the claims of intuition as the guarantor of certainty, is perpetually placed in question by the transcendental reduction. Yet this placing in question is, for Levinas, not a loss but a liberation from the ideal of adequation and from the hegemony of being.

In *Cartesian Meditations*, Husserl is seen to move further in the direction of a break with the ideal of apodicticity as grounded in adequation, for even if the *cogito sum* is given as indubitable, Levinas notes that transcendental experience itself is submitted to criticism (*OG*, 21–23).[21] The transcendental reduction, for Levinas, is to be interpreted as "a reflection upon reflection . . . a process without completion of the criticism of criticism." Thus, Levinas continues, criticism engenders an awakening of the subject to the "living presence of the I to itself" (*OG*, 22–23).[22] It is this reflexivity that opens the possibility for expanding the Levinasian account of the same to encompass Maturana's version of the recursiveness of living systems without endorsing the model of computational automata.

Maturana contends that, as inhabitants of consensual domains, we are not locked into "the closure of our individual autopoiesis" (C, 48/29). Because we are affected by and affect the lives of others, our conduct is inescapably ethical. What is more, Maturana warns, interactions that develop through structural couplings might enable totalitarian political systems to totally specify "the experiences of the human beings under [their] sway" (C, 48/28). At the same time, loving relations with others are possible. "Love," he contends, "is not blind because it does not negate, love accepts, and, therefore, is visionary" (C, 49/29). Similarly, for Levinas, individuals can become the bearers of forces that command them so that they derive their meaning from a social and historical totality. For Levinas, however, the ethical relation cannot be one of a love that is visionary in that vision reduces otherness to the same. Moreover, for Maturana, the ethical relation is one of mirroring in that we learn to see ourselves and others as reciprocal reflections. For Levinas, meaning arises from the "diachronic foreignness of the other in my responsibility for him, [from] this 'difference among indiscernibles'—I and the other—without common genus . . . [from] a non-indifference in me for the other" (OG, 167). The ethical relation demands a radical diachrony of time that could resist the synchronic mode of structural coupling. The self, for Levinas, is opened to a meaning that is beyond what "each one's internal representation signifies" and "beyond my perseverance in being" (OG, 166–67), a reflexivity that is drawn to but cannot internalize the other.

Is the Levinasian account of the same, understood as the reduction of exteriority by a consciousness that apprehends it, subverted by the culture of the copy as manifested in recent accounts of the activity of genes? And if so, is an ethics based on the radical alterity of the other person not also undermined? Or does the Levinasian view of an ipseity that is prior to, and the condition for, ethics as well as for rational consciousness offer grounds that both challenge and accommodate the culture of the copy? For Levinas, the starting point for thinking the same is bound up with the thinking of essence, a term that can be standardly understood as the guarantor of the sameness of its instantiations and as imbued with generative power. Thinking cannot occur apart from its relation to being but must think what Levinas calls the essance of being, insisting that "we write 'essance' with an 'a' . . . to give a name to the verbal aspect of the word 'being.'" He goes on to say that "the experience of nameable beings and of *esse* itself is the result of . . . an experience of the fundamental . . . an ontological experience of the firmness of the earth." This fundament grounds his claim that *"experience of identity* or *experience of being qua being* are tautological" (*OG*, 112).

Levinas's account can hardly be rendered compatible with those of hard-line gene determinists or of theorists for whom the self is an artifact of computational processes. In the former view, a gene-line is seen as having no rigid boundaries, as potentially immortal, and the purpose of natural selection is the preservation of the gene-line. Although Levinas does not comment specifically on such claims, there are surprising affinities between his description of the connection between reality and image and the relation of genes to visible bodies. Thus, his critique of the image may provide an entering wedge for a critical analysis of gene-line determinism.

The recursiveness of Levinasian ipseity is presaged in Kierkegaard's account of repetition and displayed in the temporalization of change in organisms that are described by some biologists as expressing "meta-stable equilibrium." More significant is the possibility for the "naturalization" of the Levinasian subject when his notion of self is seen as refracted through the lens of the autopoietic school of biology. According to its founders, Maturana and Varela, the observer who exists in and through language emerges as a result of the recursiveness of living systems. Self-consciousness is an outcome of the activity of the internal structures of unities that break through their isolation by means of language, relations that are seen as opening the way for a visionary ethics of love. In Levinas's account, the passive, preoriginary self of ipseity is a living system, one for which not love but a preoriginary openness to the other who cannot be conceptualized is the condition of ethics.

From Neo-Platonism to Souls in Silico
Quests for Immortality

"Sie haben alle müde Münde / Und helle Seelen ohne Saum [they all have weary mouths / pure souls without a seam]," wrote Rilke longingly.[1] Humans in their mortality could not hope to attain the enviable purity of the awe-inspiring and mysterious angelic soul. The yearning for soul has become far more complex in postmodernity, in that "soul" has been rendered moot in modernity's various accounts of mind-body dualism. In its Cartesian version, mind as the ground of certainty came to occupy the void left by the evacuation of soul. With the demise of the modern subject, famously described as the ghost in the machine, we may now ask who comes after the subject. According to Jean-Luc Nancy, the question is about "the deconstruction of interiority, of self-presence, of consciousness, of mastery."[2]

With the emergence of a new conceptual landscape of dematerialization, unlike Nancy, many contemporary philosophers turn, not to a plural subject, a we, but to the subject is envisioned as an etiolated, mathematized body, a string of genes that have become the bearers of immortality. Consider these words in a popular account of the gene as the agent of natural selection: "The genetic material in organisms today traces back generation by generation through an unbroken chain of descent (with modification) of ancestral molecules that have copied and replaced themselves ever since the origin of life on earth about 4 billion years ago. . . . Only germline genes are potentially immortal; somatic entities (ourselves included) are merely ephemeral vessels that evolved as a means of perpetuating DNA."[3]

I hope to show that Neoplatonic configurations of soul arise transgressively in genetic transfiguration. In what might be seen as acts of biological prestidigitation, we are brought back in and as our genes or, in Derridean terms, we re-arise spectrally: "For there to be ghost, there must be a return to the body, but to a body that is more abstract than ever. The spectrogenic process corresponds to a paradoxical *incorporation*." One returns not to the old body but as "an incarnation in *another artifactual body*, a ghost,"[4] which haunts what I call the "Pythagorean body." Has Darwin's "dangerous idea," to borrow Daniel C. Dennett's phrase, drawn the specter of soul into the apocalyptic events of our world, or can Pythagorean bodies be read otherwise?

In what follows, I point first to some manifestations of the depersonalized subject. Next I examine the accounts of soul in the Neoplatonist philosophies of Plotinus and Iamblichus, in order to show that the gene-self of evolutionary biology, surprisingly, evokes the Pythagorean soul of Neoplatonic speculation. I go on to describe the recent conceptual shift from the materiality of a visible and tangible body to the soul *in silico*. Finally, I consider whether identity, as constructed through invisible gene-links rather than through bodily resemblance, offers an opportunity to break with the twentieth century's nefarious uses of evolutionary biology, or whether it perpetuates the danger.

The Flight of the Subject

By contrast with the ghostly self of postmodernity, the modern self is often posited as an individual entity, a body and the perceptual experiences it causes. Such an individual is born, persists in existence for a time, and dies. Consider analytic philosopher P. F. Strawson's by now canonical mid-century description of the idea of the person as "the concept of a type of entity such that both predicates ascribing states of consciousness and predicates ascribing corporeal characteristics . . . are equally applicable to a single individual of that single type."[5]

Modernist notions of mind-body continuity, whether materially or linguistically construed, are challenged by depictions of contemporary socio-cultural upheavals. Jean Baudrillard sees a radical shift in the transformation of the play of appearances of the body into genetic code, blurring the boundary between the human and the inhuman. "At the level of genes, the genome and the genotype, the signs distinctive of humanity are fading . . . immortality [of the soul] has passed into the (biological, genetic) code, the only immortal token which remains."[6] He goes on to ask whether we have not returned to "a (clonal, metastatic) de facto eternity," not in a beyond but in our world.[7] At the same time, and paradoxically, Baudrillard notes a "galloping acceleration, a dizzying whirl of mobility," a hastening of events, a turbulence that does not bring history to a close but results in the swallowing up of events in a "retroversion of history."[8] These retroversions may have swallowed up entitative notions of self, but, unnoticed by Baudrillard, the soul remains as an absent presence in a culture in which its meanings have expanded from music to food, as well as in the gene bodies we are thought to be.

In his account of personal identity, analytic philosopher Derek Parfit is more likely to see himself as the heir of Strawson than the friend of Baudrillard. It can, however, be argued that his puzzle cases and the hyperbolic tropes of Baudrillard are not altogether dissimilar. Would a teletransported replica of me still be me? Parfit asks. If certain things happened to me, would I become a different me or would I actually cease to exist? By now a shibboleth for many philosophers is Parfit's claim that, although we ordinarily ascribe thought to thinkers, we cannot conclude from the content of our experiences that a thinker is a separately existing entity. To be sure, there is no demarcating a person apart from a brain, a body, and a chain of physical and mental events. But what matters for Parfit's reductionist view, a phrase he understands honorifically, is that persons are defined by what he calls Relation R, a psychological connectedness/continuity that may be ascribed to any number of causes, for example, brain states.[9] Our thoughts and experiences can be fully described without claiming that they belong to a thinker or to a subject of experiences, and they are better accounted for by "an *impersonal* description."[10]

That the ongoingness of psychological states can be depicted in an impersonal way leads Parfit to envisage a conception of the person that Baudrillard might see as "the simulation of an infinite trajectory."[11] Parfit takes cognizance of Thomas Nagel's term *series person*, by which is meant an r-related series of embodied brains, such as might be created by a scanning replicator that annually destroys and then reproduces a person's brain and body, and of which blueprints can be made just in case an individual happens to be destroyed.[12] This sci-fi scenario may well be otiose for Parfit, since the "I" that I am is always already a series-person in that intrinsic to the criterion of identity is the connectedness of my multiple psychic states, which may be ascribed to any cause.

If my continuous experiences constitute who I am, death is a mere break with these experiences, so that, for Parfit, the possibility of my death as tragic in any classical sense is precluded. Baudrillard becomes Parfit's odd bedfellow when he asserts that a celebratory death too must be ruled out. Yet for both there is solace for the demise of the subject: the appeal to imaginative creation, a surprisingly modernist solution. Baudrillard does not, as might be expected, counterpose the impersonal play of illusions and phantasms, of simulacra that refer to nothing other than themselves or to "electronic encephalization" as having consoling power.[13] Instead he urges transposing language games onto social and historical phenomena, "the heteroclite tropes which are the delight of a vulgar imagination."[14] Despite the reductionist view of self that Parfit espouses, like Baudrillard he proclaims: "We may want our lives to have greater unity in the way that an artist can create a unified work." It is up to us, he contends, "to express or fulfill our particular values or beliefs."[15]

Such reversions to modernist accounts reflect a flight from the Pythagorean body, a body that in its postmodern genetic guise can be viewed as a re/disfiguring of Neoplatonic descriptions of the soul's nonmateriality, rationality, control of behavior, and immortality. I shall argue, first, that soul enters into the mathematical algorithms used by evolutionary biologists and artifical life theorists not as a gesture of nostalgia but as the object of a quest for what Neoplatonists claimed to have found in the Pythagorean conception of soul as number, a standing against death that must remain, as for Heidegger, the unthought standard of the measure of that which cannot be fathomed.

I shall treat the story of the gene not as the grand narrative of evolutionary biology but as a tale fissured transgressively by another tale, that of the soul. I shall argue that, far from reflecting a will to enumerate, to calculate, in the mathematized models of soul in antiquity soul is itself conceived as divine number. As such, soul enters errantly into postmodern accounts of the gene as the agent of replication. In considering the relation of soul to number, I shall attempt to follow Heidegger's path of thinking:[16] attending to what was thought as presaging the thinking that is to come.

The Soul in Pagan Neoplatonism

Speaking of early and later thinking, Heidegger says of Anaximander's philosophy of nature and Nietzsche's will to power that they "bring the Same to language, but what they say is not identical. . . . [When] we can speak of the Same in terms of things that are not identical, the fundamental condition of a thoughtful dialogue between recent and early times is automatically fulfilled."[17] While it must be conceded that quantitative thinking has eventuated in planning and ordering, so long as we do not lose sight of the *Seinsfrage* there can be, for Heidegger, a "historic dialogue between thinkers." One need not speak only of degeneracy, but of being "adrift in errancy" toward that which is Greek, and of this errancy as the "space in which history unfolds."[18]

To be sure, Heidegger decries the principle of *nihil est sine ratione* ("nothing is without reason"), which expresses the being of calculation. In this view, a thing can be said to exist "when and only when it has been established as a calculable object for cognition."[19] Although being and reason are primordially inseparable, being has become *ratio*: "The differentiation into being and ground/reason remains concealed."[20] Heidegger sees ratio as a forked growth, like a bifurcated tree (in old German known as *Zwiesel*), such that ratio and that upon which it rests are not severed.[21]

When ratio is seen, however, as numeration and as being, it cannot exhibit the requisite mode of togetherness. As in Aristotle, reason is unmoored because number is envisaged as bound up with time as the now, such that "The now is number, not limit, not *peras* but *arithmos*." Limit must be one with the being that it limits, whereas "Number is not bound to what it numbers. Number can determine something without itself being dependent . . . on the content and mode of being of what is counted."[22]

The accounts of soul to which I shall turn elude this difficulty. In the belonging-together of number and soul, number is no longer a measure applied to an entity or to a motion but is itself both measure and the being that is measured. Thus (to borrow Heidegger's distinction), soul is the same as but not identical to number, an identity in difference not unlike the bifurcated tree, the *Zwiesel*.

It goes without saying that there is a sea of commentary about the nature of soul in Neoplatonic philosophies. Nevertheless, to track the lineage of the Pythagorean body, some remarks about what is revealed and concealed by the proper names *Plotinus* and *Iamblichus* are required. For Plotinus, ultimate reality, "the one," is seen as a hierarchy of degrees of unity. Three hypostases—the one, intellect (*nous*, or mind), and soul—are organized in order of dependence, each being a diminution of the power of the preceding level and requiring additional faculties for its support. This descent is depicted as the participation of a lower stratum in a higher and, in a manner distinctive to Plotinus, as emanation, a flowing or streaming forth.[23]

The emanation doctrine implies that entities disseminate their perfections, thus helping to explain how spiritual principles exercise causality. The energy or power of agency is not reduced by the activity of the divine hypostases, which must be envisaged not as creative agents but rather as imbricated in a process that is always already fully determined. The self-dissemination of the one is sometimes interpreted as governed by the principle of plenitude, the need to exemplify every kind of being. Evolutionary biologists, however, reject this principle in that not a plethora of types of genetic material but rather appropriately adaptive forms of DNA are needed for the creation of new species.[24]

For Plotinus, receiving a shape is the result not of creative agency but of a being's imitation of its source. Beings have a desire to rise, to return to their causes. In its unrealizable striving to attain a perfect vision of that which is higher, intellect, the first hypostasis, is compelled to splinter its vision into a world of individual forms,[25] a path that ends in materialization. Just as the gene may be seen as coded instruction, in contrast to its apparent expression as phenotype, for Plotinus the visible manifestation of an entity, its image, requires correction and dematerialization accompanied by despatialization.[26]

It is crucial to recall that, beyond individual souls, soul as such is a hypostatic plane that flows from the intelligible or divine mind, which contains it. As one and without distinction, soul lends itself to division, a division that is manifested as entry into a body. At the hypostatic level, soul possesses the vision of a superior condition and, thus understood, is not the soul either of any particular existent or even of the cosmos (*Enneads*, 4.1.1, 255). Plotinus's account is worth citing at length:

> The nature which is at once visible and indivisible, which we affirm to be soul, has not the unity of an extended thing: it does not consist of separate sections; its divisibility lies in its presence at every point of the recipient, but it is indivisible as dwelling entire in the total and entire in any part. . . .

Itself devoid of mass, it is present to all mass . . . it has never known partition . . . but remains a self-gathered integral, and is parted among bodies [in that] bodies cannot receive it except in some partitive mode; the partition, in other words, is an occurrence in body, not in soul. (*Enneads*, 4.1.1, 257)

The types of soul must be distinguished: the soul that remains in the intelligible-realm but is somehow different from it; the world-soul, which rules the cosmos as cosmic agency that initiates change while itself remaining unchanged; and individual souls. In a dense analysis in the manner of Deleuze, Eric Alliez attributes the fall of the soul not to its intrinsic nature or as dependent upon intelligence, from which it derives in the manner of the cosmic hypostases, but to its own initiative, which he calls the soul's audacity, its move from "undivided multiplicity" to real division. "Henceforth the lower potentiality ceases to tend toward the higher."[27] The move is one from a cosmic to a temporal image, disconnecting time from the quantifiable order of the cosmos and connecting it to that of soul. In a less subjectivized reading, Eyjolfur Kjalar Emilsson holds: "As immanent in the cosmos, soul is a set of instructions," and, in that regard, like a genetic code or computer program.[28] I make a stronger and essentially different claim: that codes and programs can be seen as transgressive expressions of soul in the culture of postmodernity.

Plotinus's odd view of the relation of soul and body is pertinent to the analysis of the computational modeling of the gene, which I shall consider shortly. Unlike Aristotle, for whom the soul is the actuality of the body, inseparable from it, Plotinus sees the connection as that of a compound, as both conceptually and actually separable. Still, Plotinus maintains that soul cannot be in body or in space as in a container, since such claims presuppose that the soul is itself a body (*Enneads*, 4.3.20, 277). Nor is the soul present as form in matter, given that these are inseparable. We imagine the soul to be in the body because the body is visibly animate, and from this we infer that it is ensouled (ibid.). Rejecting the analogy of helmsman to ship or even of the skill of the helmsman to the steering of the ship, Plotinus finds a more satisfactory analogy in the relation of light to air: "The light is the stable thing, the air flows in and out; when the air passes beyond the lit area it is dark; under the light it is lit" (ibid., 4.3.22, 278).

Plotinus comes to the astonishing conclusion that he has found a genuine parallel to the body-soul relation in the claim that "the air is in the light rather than the light in the air" (ibid.). Plotinus thus confirms Plato's view of the all, in that Plato puts the body in the soul and not the soul in the body (*Timaeus* 34B).[29] That the body is in the soul as the air flows in and out of the light can be seen spectrally in the claim of evolutionary biologists that the visible body is, *in nuce*, in the genes, the latter outlasting observable corporeality, a ghost or *Spuk* of the soul's incorporation of body.[30]

The nature of the soul as deathless is wedded to Plotinus's view of the good such that, as in Plato's *Republic*, the good "exist[s] beyond and above Being . . . beyond and above the intellectual principle and all Intellection" (*Enneads*, 1.7.1, 65). If soul is turned toward the intellectual principle, it may come to possess the good. What is more, soul possesses life, and "life is the Good to the living" (ibid., 1.7.2, 65). Not unaware of the worm in the apple, Plotinus contends: "If life is a good, is there good for all that lives? No: in the vile, life limps: it is like the eye to the dim-sighted; it fails of its task" (ibid., 1.7.3, 65). Yet even if mingled with evil, life is still a good. Is death then an evil? No, for in what is by now a familiar apothegm of Platonism, if the soul can continue to attend to its proper functions after death, "then death will be no evil but a good" (ibid., 1.7.3, 66). The notion that life in the body can be considered an evil, and that even in this life the soul must separate itself from evil and pursue the good (ibid.), re-arises spectrally in the envisaging of genes. Traits that enable individuals of a given species to act for the good of others, thus to pursue a good, are borne by genes.

The Numbers Game

In his analysis of mathematics in Neoplatonism, Dominic O'Meara argues that, to see the soul as number, one must turn from Plotinus to Iamblichus, who sought to lay down an older and more authentic Platonism that reflected Pythagorean notions.[31] In conformity with Aristotle, Plotinus had identified number with the category of quantity. At the same time, he saw numbers themselves as substances distinguishable from quantitative measure applied by the soul to sensible things. Plotinus could not see how numbers in themselves could be substances, while numbers inhering in objects did not exist, but were measures (*Enneads*, 6.1.4, 445–46).

This sticking point is pondered by Iamblichus. By positing a multilayered participational doctrine of forms, he is able to transcend a purely quantitative view of number. In his account, there is a transcendent form, a universal form or form that is immanent in objects, and, finally, the formed material particular. He designates these levels unparticipated, participated, and participant forms.[32] Similarly, mathematical objects are arranged hierarchically as physical numbers, intelligible numbers, and divine numbers, which transcend the intelligible.[33] Rejecting the suggestion that numbers are merely incidental to the things that they measure, Iamblichus is home free: numbers exist in things like other immanent forms and are not merely accompanying attributes.

Mathematical objects are not the result of abstracting from matter but are self-existent, superior in being to sensible things—ontological algorithms, as it were. Iamblichus calls the number in which sensible things participate "physical number" and makes the striking claim that number includes all other principles responsible for the structure of sensible things. Thus O'Meara comments:

> What is the difference between physical number and the other principles responsible for the physical structuration of sensible things? In the treatise on Pythagoreanism, Iamblichus does not seem to envisage such a distinction. Physical number includes all the principles of sensible things. Or rather, the objects studied by the mathematician contain in a paradigmatic way whatever is responsible for the organization of sensible objects. Iamblichus has a tendency to lead back all the constitutive principles of the world to mathematical principles.[34]

In considering the inseparability of soul and number, it should be noted that letters, characters, and numbers are used by some Neoplatonists in formulating a thaumaturgical theory of soul premonitory of later kabbalistic speculation. Theodorus of Asine appeals to letters, characters, and numbers to account for the nature of the soul. Although Iamblichus insists that the soul is number, he rebukes Theodorus on the grounds that, even if the soul were number, this idea and other metaphysical principles cannot be derived through arbitrary numerological manipulation.[35]

What, then, is the precise relation of individual souls to number for Iamblichus? Recall that for Plotinus, even an embodied soul remains purely in itself, but when the soul acts it goes outside itself and undergoes change. Although subject to alteration, the soul does not become totally transitory, in that it must persist through many lives. Thus, the soul is intermediate between permanence and change.[36] In his commentary on Neoplatonic doctrines of soul, Carlos Steel maintains that its intermediate status forces the soul to create its own order of reason, "mathematical forms that at the same time are intelligible forms and models of sensible things."[37] Mathematical discourse is precisely this plenitude or fullness of the rational.[38]

Iamblichus considers the soul to be the intertwining of geometric figure, number, and a harmony bringing disconnected things into proportion. In his treatise *On General Mathematical Science*, he attributes extraordinary generative power to the mathematicals:

> The soul exists in ratios common with all mathematicals, possessing on the one hand the power of discerning them, and on the other hand the power of generating and producing the incorporeal measures themselves, and with these measures the soul has the capacity to fit together the generation and completion of forms in matter by means of images, proceeding from the invisible to the visible, and joining together the things outside with those inside. . . . In brief the definition of the soul contains in itself the sum total of mathematical reality.[39]

This description is cut to fit the gene, allowing for significant terminological changes. Although evolutionary biologists and artificial life theorists may not believe that genes contain the whole of mathematical reality, they would be likely to endorse the generative power of calculative models. Could the genome, as the collection of an organism's genes, not be seen as a writing under erasure of "that actuality of [soul]" described by Iamblichus, to which "the power of reason belongs?"[40] Can we say, then, that both soul and gene are codes of iterability, of repeatable traces engaged in a Derridean play of difference?

This play is discernible yet again in the mode of temporalization of each. Consider first Plotinus's claim that, in the divine realm, all is eternal presence. "Life—instantaneously entire, complete, at no point broken into period or part—which belongs to the authentic existent by its very existence . . . this is eternity," he maintains (*Enneads*, 3.7.3, 225). By contrast, generated things exist in time and can expect "the annulment of [their] futurity" (ibid., 3.7.4, 225). For Plotinus, there was a time when time was other than transiency, when it was at rest within the authentic existent, until stirred by an active principle, the all-soul (ibid., 3.7.11, 234).

But how could time have been at rest? For Plotinus, eternity is not itself repose but merely a participant in repose, and therefore eternity can be fissured by difference, by time: eternity is "something in the nature of unity, yet compact of diversity. Where we see life we think of it as movement, where all is unvaried self-identity we call it Repose; and we know it as, at once, Difference and Identity when we recognize that all is unity with variety" (ibid., 3.7.3, 224). What is more: "Soul put[s] forth its energy in act after act in a constant progress of novelty . . . while the ceaseless forward movement of Life brings with it unending Time," an endless futurity that is inconceivable apart from soul (ibid., 3.7.11, 234).

Must we not acknowledge that there is in soul and in Darwin's dangerous idea (the forward movement of life) the same efferent play of difference? Is this "constant progress of novelty," this "ceaseless forward movement of life," not borne by replicant genes, by the *Spuk*, or ghost, of soul?

Whose Life Is It, Anyway?

When evolutionary biology considers the body as code, what is envisaged is not the dissolution of the body as phenotype, the bodily expression of genes in interaction with the environment, but rather the demotion of the body's privileged status. The organism's form is severed from what counts as the individual biological entity, the gene, which is said to be the "real" agent and recipient of heritable action. Thus Richard Dawkins, who famously refers to the selfishness of genes, offers no disclaimer to the view that "any animal form can be transformed into a related form by a mathematical transformation although . . . the translation may not be a simple one."[41] The gene's eye view sees evolution as taking place not on behalf of the organism as the indivisible unit of biological individuality, in accordance with older accounts, but rather in the interest of the gene, "that little bit of chromosome that lasts for many generations" (*SG*, 33).

Dawkins's endorsement of the self-organizing propensities of genes and his denial that higher purposiveness governs the process are effectively expressed in Daniel Dennett's metaphor of cranes and skyhooks. Mindlike accounts of evolutionary change are referred to as skyhooks, which function like the *deus ex machina* of classical drama, while cranes do the actual everyday work of lifting, without appeal to mental causes. Thus:

> A skyhook is a mind-first force or power or process, an exception to the principle that all design and apparent design is ultimately the result of mindless, motiveless mechanicity. A crane

. . . is a subprocessor special feature of a design process that can be demonstrated to speed up the basic, slow process of natural selection . . . and is demonstrably a product of the process.[42]

For Dennett there are only cranes and no skyhooks. To be sure, neither Dennett nor Dawkins denies the significance of organisms. What is perceived as radical in Dawkins's description of the phenotype is his expansion of standard accounts to include not only the organism's perceptible attributes but outcomes of gene activity that lie outside the bodies in which the genes are lodged (*EP*, 292).

To make sense of the contention that gene activity can be outside the body, it is crucial to see the centrality of replication in Dawkins's account. For Dawkins, a replicator is anything of which copies can be made. Information-bearing DNA molecules, gene strings, are replicators, active when their effects lead to their being copied, passive when they die out. The gene is the "unit of heredity" that is to be retained in the evolutionary process. Only those likely to be copied survive, while passive replicators become extinct (ibid., 83–85). Difference does not disappear, since each gene is defined in relation to alternative forms of the gene, alleles, a difference within the same. It is still genes that are the units that labor in the interest of self-replication, genes all the way down.

Although the phenotype continues to be "the all important instrument of preservation" (ibid., 47), it is not what is preserved, or, as Dawkins avers more graphically: "A body is the gene's way of preserving the genes unaltered" (*SG*, 22). To be sure, Dawkins concedes, genes are strung together along chromosomes, which, in turn, enter into more complex forms and finally into organisms. Yet he insists upon an "atomistic" account of the gene as the unit of selection that actually survives, a Pythagorean entity, a soul-like vehicle of its own immortality.

In his Gifford lectures, Holmes Rolston, III, departing from Dawkins, insists that the organism is more than an aggregate of selfish genes. It is far better to begin with the whole organism as a synthesis that "codes its morphologies and behaviors in the genes which are analytic units of that synthesis, each gene, a cybernetic bit of the program that codes the specific form of life."[43] Although this claim is embedded in his larger theological program, it is possible to consider Rolston's claim for the organism apart from this framework. Appealing to the language of computer science, he asserts that "the integrated knowledge of the whole organism is 'discharged' level by level as one goes down through the organ, cell, organelle, enzyme, protein molecule, DNA coding,"[44] replicating Iamblichus in top-down or descending order of forms as well as numbers.

Just as the soul, for Iamblichus, is seen as the bearer of value, the gene is viewed by some evolutionary biologists as a carrier of ethical norms. It must be recalled, however, that even if genes provide the means for the emergence of self-sacrificial acts on the part of individual animals, such altruistic acts are undertaken in the ultimate interest of gene replication. Genes may be value-coded, but the realization of value is measured in terms of reproductive success. In a by now classical formulation, E. O. Wilson defines evolutionary altruism as "enhancing the personal genetic fitness of others at the cost of genetic fitness on the part of the altruist; either reduc[ing] its own survival capacity or curtail[ing] its own reproduction or both."[45] Evolutionary biologists largely agree that altruistic traits are acquired in the interest of self-preservation and that genetically anchored rules are rules of prudence. Plotinus's narrative of the relation of the soul's desire for the good is re/disfigured as gene activity that allows for the replication of a particular good, so that this good is not lost.

A New Heaven on a New Earth?

The interpretation of the body as code lends itself readily to the modeling of life that is humanly contrived through the use of computational prototypes, thus advancing the pervasiveness of Pythagorean design. In turning to computational paradigms for the understanding of biological life, Christopher Langton asserts that life is a property not of matter but rather of its organization, for which computational models are eminently suited, so that now research can be directed away from "the mechanics of life to the logic of life."[46]

It could be argued that the creation of artificial life would be served most effectively by relying upon the organic chemicals of carbon-chain chemistry. Apart from the practical difficulties inherent in such an effort, Langton contends that more can be learned from the "creation of life *in silico*," in that it opens up the "space of *possible* life."[47]

Dennett makes a more modest claim for artificial life. The development of genetic algorithms indeed enables us to simulate and manipulate evolutionary processes, but, despite the flexibility of the program, its parameters are set. Nevertheless, such programs afford an opportunity to "'rewind the tape of life' and replay it again and again in many variations."[48] What is mimed is the genotype as "a bag of instructions," a procreative artifice that specifies behaviors or modifies structures. In essence, what Langton seeks is to generate behavior through the creation of computational automata.[49] Now the human agent steps out of the picture as breeder and allows the computer to engage in the process of selection.

In some recent simulation systems, even the earlier proxies for the human agent, the algorithmic breeding agents, are eliminated. The computer programs themselves compete for computer processing unit (CPU) time and memory space. Langton maintains: "The programs reproduce themselves and the ones that are better at this task take over the population."[50] In Baudrillardian fashion, Thomas S. Ray, the developer of one such program, the Tierra, contends: "There is no connection between the Tierran world and the real physical world. I have created a virtual universe that is self-contained."[51] Computers are now seen to transcend the instructions of their programs and to generate mutations, or novel behavior. If sufficiently powerful, they are unpredictable. Langton declares: "It is impossible to determine any non-trivial property of the future behavior of a sufficiently powerful computer from a mere inspection of its program and its initial state."[52] The only way to determine changes is to run the program.

Who Are We, after All?

Dawkins's account of gene evolution is not archeologically but eschatologically driven: the tape does not run backward, but forward. The purpose of reproduction is the perpetuation neither of the species nor of the individual organism as the unit of natural selection, but rather the conservation of the active germ replicator, the "ancestor of an indefinitely long line of descendents." Although some germ lines may die out, "any germ line replicator is potentially immortal" (*EP*, 83).

From these claims, it is possible to infer that the germ line poses a challenge to the identity of the individual as phenotype and, as such, to the *genos* or *ethnos* to which she or he belongs. But what is meant by appearance, by resemblance? In analyzing the concept of resemblance, Derrida considers the resemblance of Socrates to the tribe of poets, contending that if Socrates resembles them, it does not mean he is their fellow. Yet he is also like them, both speaking and not speaking from the place from which they speak, and playing on the spatiality of place as "a political place and a habitation."[53] Is Socrates the one he seems, the same, speaking from the same place as the others, or is he other than the others?

Consider now another text, another place: the Levitical consecration of Aaron and his sons as priests for all generations: "And you shall command the people of Israel that they bring to you pure beaten oil for the light, that a lamp may be set up to burn continually. In the tent of meeting outside the veil which is before the testimony, Aaron and his sons shall tend it from evening to morning before the Lord. It shall be a statute forever to be observed through their generations."[54]

For traditional Judaism, this command wends its way forward in postexilic form. Those who now claim patrilineal descent from the priestly caste as determined through oral transmission may, upon the occasion of the pilgrim festivals, engage in the practice of blessing the congregation. Standing before the assembled congregants, they drape their prayer shawls around head and body. With outspread fingers, their hands having earlier been washed by those who claim descent from the Levites, the "descendents of Aaron," they then turn to the congregation and recite a blessing. Because the divine presence is now said to rest upon them, the congregation must avert its eyes from the performers.

How does the "fact" of priestly descent re-arise in a postmodern culture of virtualized multiple identities? Those claiming priestly origin and belonging to groups historically identified as of Israelite descent have been seen as providing an interesting gene pool for scientific inquiry. After genetic testing, an identical gene borne on the y, or male, chromosome was found to be present in 10 percent of those claiming such descent, and absent in other members of the larger group. Recently it came to media attention that the Lemba people of southern Africa claim that they are Israelites and that approximately the same proportion of the male population have the requisite gene, a claim borne out by genetic testing. The phenotypical bodies of the heretofore recognized groups and of the Lemba are now bearers of a newly minted gene-borne identity, an identity determined not by virtue of manifest characteristics but by genetic similarity in a new-old relation of same and other, identity and difference.

Are narratives of genetic likeness simply descriptions of a technologically contrived functional immortality, as Baudrillard would have it, or might they be entering wedges into reconstructing accounts of authochthony as based upon physical resemblances? Is the description of the gene-self a narrative of continuity that can be told and untold in the Plotinian language of soul as that which is "devoid of all mass . . . a self-gathered integral, . . . parted among bodies [in that] bodies cannot receive it except in some partitive mode; the partition, in other words, is an occurrence in body, not in soul" (*Enneads*, 5.4, 318)?

Do body and soul, gene and visible body, each remain other to the other, or does what is other re-arise spectrally? Speaking of *Geist*, Derrida warns that "the entirely other announces itself in the path of the most rigorous repetition. And this repetition is also the most vertiginous and the most abyssal."[55] Did not soul, as an absent presence unmentioned in the narrative of natural selection, give rise in the last century to apocalyptic political consummations? Is the gene as that which is computationally modeled, a *Spuk* or specter of soul, likely to undergo the previous fate of Darwin's dangerous idea? Or can genes wander errantly through bodies that differ, underlining invidious distinctions to become nomads of a differentiated same—in Plotinus's words, like soul, "a choral dance under the rule of number" (*Enneads*, 5.4, 318)?

PART IV

Nihilation and the Ethics of Alterity

[One who is after the truth] sets out to be a man of learning. . . . One who wants to give free play to his subjectivity sets out, perhaps, to be a writer. But what is a man to do who is after something that lies between? And yet such examples of lying "between" are provided by every moral maxim, for instance . . . thou shalt not kill. . . . It is neither a verity not a subjective statement. . . . In many respects we keep to it strictly; in other respects . . . precisely defined exceptions are admitted. But in . . . cases of a third kind, as . . . in the imagination, in our desires, in the drama, or in newspaper reports . . . we roam in a quite unregulated manner between abhorrence and allurement. Something that is neither a verity nor a subjective statement is sometimes called a requirement. . . . that has been firmly attached to the dogmas of religion and . . . the law, and has thus been given the character of a truth arrived at by a process of deduction.

— Robert Musil, *The Man without Qualities*

From the perspective of an ethics of the other, negation can be construed as nihilatory force exerted against another or others. In the context of individuals, another as other is seen as breaking into the self-containment of the subject, so that the presence of that other is experienced as proscribing violence against her/him. More radically, the ethical can be manifested as a willingness to substitute oneself for the other when she/he is in mortal danger. Recent accounts of altruism as biologically determined may be thought to undermine this view of self-negation. What is more, an ethics of alterity fails to account for the moral status of harms inflicted on oneself. The violence exerted against multiple others in acts of mass extermination requires new accounts of the global languages of technology and information, as well as of the "logics" that may ground extermination, so that the interpreter is compelled to plot a course between and among them.

Illustration: Nineteenth-century gouache, Japan. Collection of the author.

The Semantic Spaces of Terror
A Theological Response

The future is always unpredictable. Ideals . . . must themselves be
framed out of the possibilities of existing conditions, even if these be
the conditions that constitute a corporate and industrial age. The ideals take shape and gain a content as they operate in remaking
conditions. . . . A program of ends and ideals if kept apart from sensible and flexible method becomes an encumbrance. . . . For its hard
and rigid character assumes a fixed world and a static individual; and
neither of these things exists.
 — **John Dewey,** *Individualism Old and New*

Information at one and the same time means the appraisal that as
quickly, comprehensively, and unequivocally and profitably as possible acquaints contemporary humanity with the securing of its necessities, its requirements and their satisfaction. . . . Information is also the
arrangement that places all objects and stuffs in a form for humans
that suffices to securely establish human domination over the whole
earth and even over what lies beyond this planet.
 — **Martin Heidegger,** *The Principle of Reason*

Modern business organizations are *emergent* — they reside in a state of
continual process of change. Globalization, deregulation, increased
competition, mergers and acquisitions, and the like all reveal organizations in transition. . . . Agile development emphasizes the human or

crafted aspects of software development over the engineering aspects — individuals and interactions over processing and tools . . . responding to change over following a plan.

Mark Lycett, Robert D. Macredie, Chaitali Patel,
and Ray J. Paul, Computer, June 2003

It would seem that Terror and violence stand together, inhabiting the same semantic space.[1] The extraordinary ambiguities that attach to the term *Terror* require multiple approaches, interpretations both deconstructive and additive, which constitute a space whose boundaries are in constant and uneasy flux. Here, I shall successively undertake readings of Heidegger, Levinas, Derrida, Dominique Janicaud, and software developers, the proponents of so-called agile thought. Each will be seen as a critic who both undermines and supports specific positions of the preceding thinker. Thus, my interest is in creating a conversation, a semantic space in which both convergence and dissension constitute an ever-expanding, provocative discourse of Terror. Does the difficulty in finding and identifying the terrorist and in assessing the extent of the danger she or he poses point to a radically new mode of violence? How do war and the violence intrinsic to existing political, social, and economic relations differ from the violence of Terror? What role do the beliefs and practices of the world's religions play in configuring this space?

Heidegger and the Violence of Reason

Does the term *Terror* refer to a fundamentally new species of violence, or does it derive from ontotheological thought, thought for which the meaning of Being is grounded in the principle of reason? Is Terror a consequence of thought's failure to take account of the contingency and facticity presupposed by thinking? Is the culprit as Heidegger thinks, the principle of reason, *nihil est sine ratione* ("nothing is without reason"), an assertion that culminates in the way in which modern science interrogates that which is? In sum, if at this moment the language of the being of beings is that of the principle of reason, as Heidegger maintains, is Terror (whose most recent manifestations were, of course, unknown to him) the inevitable outcome?

Heidegger invokes the principle of reason not as an explanatory principle — to do so would be to endorse the efficacy of explanation itself — but rather as grounding the meaning of being in the present epoch. The principle functions as a demand requiring that the knowledge of objects be self-grounded so that the object itself is securely founded. The omnipresence of the demand to give reasons is taken for granted, rendering one oblivious to the meaning of being intrinsic to the language of the demand itself. For Heidegger, the modus operandi of the principle lies in the discernment and elimination of contradictions among competing facts and theories. Information provided by technological instruments under the sway of the principle is heeded, but no attention is paid to the demand itself. The primrose path down which the principle of reason leads terminates in the atomic age: "Its historical spiritual existence [is characterized as] the rapacity for and availability of natural energy," in sum, "an epoch molded by the atom."[2]

In the light of this rapacity, Heidegger sees modern technology as belonging to a mode of revealing that is "a setting-in-order" so that the energy locked in nature is transformed and distributed and everything thus "stockpiled" is turned into what he famously calls "standing reserve" (*QCT*, 15–17). When it penetrates everyday consciousness, the principle of reason emerges as information, the media spin that enters ordinary life in a manner reminiscent of his earlier depiction of the idle chatter (*Gerede*) of Everyman (*das Mann*). Theology itself is under the domination of this principle, for if efficacy accrues to the supreme principle of reason, as Leibniz maintains, then efficacy requires a cause, God. "The principle holds only insofar as God exists. But God exists only insofar as the principle of reason holds."[3]

Is it possible that, in freeing God from the ways in which he has been traditionally identified, as first cause or highest value, Heidegger has pulled off a Kierkegaardian move, thereby opening the way for a living faith? Yet even if Heidegger undoes the fetters of ontotheology, does he not subordinate theology to the primacy of the primordiality claims of his own thought, to Dasein's authentic modes of being in the world? Thus, for example, it is not sin that is primordial but guilt, the prior disposition that renders sin possible.[4]

What then, we may ask, is to be done? Heidegger would see this question as falling under the domination of the very principle that is being questioned. With Goethe, he avers, one should stick to the antifoundationalism of a "because" that is "without why," a why that is "without ground" but is itself ground. This "because" is "an abiding" that allows the composite word *ground/reason* to speak without demand. But in light of the epoch in which we live, Heidegger is forced to concede:

Nevertheless we must ask why? For we cannot leap out of the present age that is held in the sway of the fundamental principle of rendering sufficient reasons. But we may not desist from holding to the because. . . . We must do one thing: follow the force of the fundamental principle for all cognition . . . ; and something else: pondering what is all-powerful in the word of being.[5]

Has Heidegger not reverted to the rationality of modernity as the default position by urging that one simply resign oneself to that which is in any case foreordained, the *Geschick* or destining of the history of being as reason? In responding to the violence of modernity by reflecting upon the ontological ground of the structure of the demand inherent in the principle of reason, does he not thereby surrender to an inactive quietism that carries over to the time of Terror?

There is, however, a way of being that eludes the violence of technology's rule. In his account of the meaning of building (*bauen*), Heidegger describes an intimacy with earth, an intimacy that resists the domination of technology and that is lived as dwelling in the primal oneness of the fourfold—earth, sky, the divinities, and mortals. To dwell is the positive act of "sparing and preserving" the earth, a saving that is a setting free of the earth's own being: "Saving the earth does not master the earth and does not subjugate it, which is merely one step from spoliation."[6] It would seem that the relation to earth is free of "the historial," free of the manner in which being is sent forth in a given epoch. Through their relation to earth, human beings are living beings.[7] While insisting that, for Heidegger, the nonhistorial is not a return to the state of nature, Michel Haar maintains that the background structures of human existence remain constant from one epoch to another. Haar further points out that local rootedness, an expression of the nonhistorial dimension of existence, has an extraordinary hold upon Heidegger.[8] Attunement to his place of origin is attested in this autobiographical remark: "The inner relationship of my own work to the Black Forest and its people comes from a centuries-long and irreplaceable rootedness in the Alemannian Swabian soil."[9] Still, Heidegger maintains, "We can gain access to the Earth only through world."[10]

A vast literature has accumulated concerning the relation of Heidegger's view of rootedness to that of National Socialism.[11] What is relevant in the present context are the questions germane to the matter of Terror that his analysis generates. Is the violence of the stateless terrorist, the terrorist who is everywhere and nowhere, an expression of the rootlessness that Heidegger finds in the world of omnipresent technology, or is Terror in fact the expression of an ineradicable autochthony? Is the relative simplicity of the lethal weapons used by stateless terrorists dictated by concerns of efficiency, or is this simplicity a semi-conscious effort to return to a primordial pretechnological violence?

Moving beyond Ontology with Levinas

If autochthony spawns violence and if disentangling from ontotheology does not suffice to liberate a discourse with which to confront the violence of Terror, must we not look elsewhere, beyond the primordial comportments of human existence described in *Being and Time* or the revealing/concealing of *aletheia* in Heidegger's later work? For Levinas, it is the sheer otherness of the other human being that commands nonviolence. Although invoking the other may, by now, have a familiar ring, a defamiliarization becomes possible when the nonviolence of ethics focuses upon a self that "is on the hither side of all willing." Is such a letting go of volition not reminiscent of Heidegger's quest for a will-less release from tutelage to the principle of reason? But it is not Dasein, being-in-the-world, that emerges from Levinas's ethical purgation of Heidegger's ontological analysis but rather "being-in-question." Levinas rewrites the meaning of questioning not in terms of ground but as a questioning that is "put in question, being put before the question, having to answer" (*AT*, 22–23). The issue is "whether the Da of my Dasein is not already the usurpation of someone else's place" (ibid., 23).

For Levinas, one should have as one's primary concern the violence that reaches its acme with the destruction of the other, whereas for Heidegger it is my death as my ownmost possibility, "the possibility of impossibility," that concerns me (ibid., 155). My humanity is expressed not in envisaging my death but in opening myself to the death of the other. There is in the other "a being face-to-face precisely as if he were exposed to some threat at point blank range as if he were about to be delivered to his death." Levinas, continuing, graphically comments: "The human being in his face is the most naked; nakedness itself," a face that calls out to and requires me (ibid., 162–63). Even if my presence is in fact useless, it remains an attestation of my availability.

Must we not ask whether the terrorist who is an absent presence has a face? For Levinas, such a question cannot be answered without introducing the notion of justice as a struggle with evil. Speaking of the executioner, a figure of violence for whom I shall hereafter substitute the terrorist, he contends that "the executioner threatens my neighbor and in this sense calls for violence, and no longer has a face" (*EN*, 104). Although I may be responsible for the other, there must also be a concern for what he calls "the third," a sphere of other others or of justice. Were this not the case, my responsibility for the other would be interminable. Levinas concludes that "a certain measure of violence [is] necessary in terms of justice": judges, institutions, and the state cannot be eliminated. In sum, one must live in "a world of citizens, and not only in the order of the Face to Face" (ibid., 105). The state's legitimacy remains contingent, however, upon the prior relation to the face. State power does not liberate me from responsibility in that if someone is harmed by a third party this harm remains my concern. One can think of the Levinasian face as a synecdoche: "All the others are present in the face of the other." Citing Dostoyevsky, he holds that "All are responsible for one another and I more than anyone else" (*EN*, 107).

For Levinas, what is primordial, the precondition of otherness, does not suffice to bring an end to violence. The third must be protected, and protection requires force so that passivity in relation to the face of the other is insufficient as the sole condition for ethics. What is more, in relation to the executioner (or terrorist) the other cannot be the primordial requirement for ethics as prior to thought in that one must first determine through a cognitive and evaluative process whether another is the other of ethics or the executioner, whether another requires my placing myself at her/his disposal or whether that other is actually the object of justified violence. Thus judgment can be prior to the presumably immediate command of alterity.

Deconstructing Terror: Derrida

For Levinas, the sublation of otherness can take the form of knowing the other and thereby reducing the other to a possession of consciousness. The other is transformed into the same, an outside becomes an interiorized other. In this regard, Derrida, in his depiction of Terror, both expands and deconstructs the Levinasian account. Focusing especially on the September 11 attack on the World Trade Center, he sees the suicidal impulse of those who hijacked the planes and crashed into the twin towers as a desire to appropriate the techno-scientific and military power of the perceived enemy and to destroy it. The discourse of those currently in power is "exposed to aggression . . . but the aggression of which it is the object comes as [if] from the inside." Derrida perceives in September 11 two suicides in a single act: the suicide of the terrorist as attacker, and the suicide of an internalized other who is at the same time the source of the terrorist's original empowerment. In analyzing the impact of Terror, it is noteworthy that Derrida, in Levinasian fashion, resorts to its facelessness, "the anonymous invisibility of the enemy because of the undetermined origin of the terror, because we cannot put a face on such terror (individual or state)."[12]

Derrida maintains further that Terror is traumatic and resists incorporation into an explanatory scheme. It is a happening whose mode of temporalization is not that of the present or past but of a future that could be *worse than anything that has ever taken place*," a biological, chemical, or nuclear attack whose source, unlike that of the Cold War, must remain unknown and whose outcome remains unpredictable: "Traumatism is produced by the future, . . . rather than by an aggression that is over and done with."[13] Does this claim not reach back to Heidegger's view that "so long as we do not through thinking experience what is [the essence of technology] we can never belong to what will be"?[14]

Even if September 11 is unknowable, is it not, after all, an event? In his conception of "event" Derrida acknowledges indebtedness to Heidegger's account of *Ereignis* as the belonging together of man and being such that man is delivered over to the other in what Heidegger calls the event of appropriation. For Heidegger, Being now gives itself as Enframing, the setting-upon that which is so that beings morph into standing-reserve, commodities to be used and manipulated. Any effort to master the being of technology that inheres in the order of Enframing would be futile, since human being cannot subordinate Being to itself.[15]

What is needed is a thinking that enters into the event of appropriation, into "the calculation of what is calculable," the being of the world as technology and information.[16] Derrida might be said to appropriate this analysis by standing it on its head. For him, the "event" is an undergoing that remains incomprehensible, that both opens itself up to and resists experience. The event character of the event is for him a proliferation of incomprehensibles: "I do not comprehend my own incomprehension."[17]

Linked to the incomprehensibility of Terror is the unsettling semantic instability of the language used to describe it. In contrast to the setting-to-order that Heidegger attributes to the language of technology, Derrida depicts the disorder, the conceptual chaos, the impossibility of determining the borders between concepts and a questioning of the concept of border itself. [18]

Still, in consonance with Heidegger, he detects in technoscientific discourse relations of force and, in further conformity with Heidegger, argues that "'state terrorism' is no longer a question of occupying a territory but of securing some technoeconomic power or political control that has but minimal need for territory." Even in the case of oil reserves, "one can simply secure the rights to lay down a pipeline."[19]

In light of Terror's indefinability, what accounts for the usual characterization of September 11 as a "major event?" One must first disinter the ways in which information is channeled to see how the designation has been shaped. On the one hand, Derrida maintains, there is the "brute fact," as understood in standard empirical terms, that opens the way to compassion for the victims, a sympathy he endorses; on the other, there is the grid of beliefs through which September 11 is assessed as being "a major event." For Derrida, if that which occurs is to count as an event, it must be unpredictable, incomprehensible, a surprise, and, quintessentially, unforeseeable. Moreover, an event is always traumatic, inflicting a wound on the anticipated course of experience and history.[20] It is precisely in this regard that September 11 is not an event. Derrida reminds us that the attack was predictable in that it was presaged by other episodes of violence, especially by a previous assault on the same target. Yet what might be regarded as a penumbra of mystery continues to haunt September 11, something that remains impervious to representation and that allows for its interpretation as a major event.

What response can be made to the semantic instability of Terror, for which September 11 has come to stand? On the one hand, Derrida speaks of responsibility in a time of a risk that must nonetheless be assumed (in the absence of knowledge) as a wager rather than as a decision that relies on prediction. At the same time, he seems to yearn for a certain stability, for a transformation that would bring about a new international law whose force would be marshalled in the service of international institutions. Such changes would demand a new conception of sovereignty. Since such radical transformation is unlikely, he affirms the importance of the juridical sphere in its existing shape.[21]

But far from simply affirming a juridical status quo, Derrida formulates a conception of a new and unprecedented form of sovereignty that would go beyond what had been envisioned by Kant and, more recently, by Hannah Arendt. Sovereignty would not accrue to a supra-national entity but would, rather, consist in a "de-stateification" whose power would be allied not only with law but also with justice.[22] Like the messiah described in what can be construed as his theological work, such a state does not arrive but is always to come. The democracy he envisages that will never arrive is not to be confused with the fixity of a Kantian regulative ideal. Because of "the aporia of the demos," the fact that the demos is at once an incalculable singularity that can undo the social bond and a universality of calculation, of the citizen before the law, democracy can only exist in a fervor of anticipation. He concedes, however, that even the flawed traditional concept of democracy has the virtue of self-criticism and the possibility of improvement.[23]

Though democracy may be yet to come, globalization as a totalizing gesture appears to be firmly in place. Those favoring globalization describe its virtues: new modes of communication, the opening of markets and the equalization of opportunity. Derrida, however, denies that anything like globalization as democratizing has occurred in light of the glaring inequities that persist worldwide. "Globalization," he contends, "is a simulacrum, a rhetorical artifice, or weapon that dissimulates a growing imbalance." As soon as this deterritorialized structure appears to be manageable, "it escapes into the hands of international non-state structures . . . terrorism of the 'September 11' sort (wealthy, hypersophisticated, telecommunicative, anonymous and without an assignable state)."[24]

Both Derrida and Heidegger associate American interests with the culture of technology and information. Thus, Heidegger maintains, contemporary life that manifests itself as information "must be heard with an American-English pronunciation."[25] In a similar vein, Derrida alleges that, whether one approves of American policy or not, an American discourse whose norms are derived from "the discourse of violence" is now pervasive.[26] Does Heidegger's account of the destining of Being not imply that the rule of Enframing cannot be surmounted, thereby precluding the ascription of blame for acting in conformity with its dictates? Or does he hold that the creators of techno-scientific discourse are, after all, responsible for such actions, as .his critique of "Americanization" suggests? If the former, it would seem that there is no exit from the hegemony of the language of technology. One must ask of Derrida whether the terrorist whose loyalties may not be determined by specifiable boundaries reflects the chaotic conceptuality of Terror or whether Terror is an expansion of Heideggerian Enframing, a subtle refinement of existing technology that reflects a "skill in means." The state embodies the double coding of Derrida's celebrated *pharmakon*, the drug that is both remedy and poison. Does Derrida, then, not swerve between the protective role of the state in regard to international violence and the limitations of a state burdened, with regard to sovereignty, by a hardened theological legacy?[27]

I shall not enter into Derrida's complex etymological analysis of the term *religion*. What is significant for present purposes is his claim that in the course of Roman and Christian history *religion* acquired a double meaning: on the one hand, that of sacrality; on the other, that of obligation, "the experience of *belief* . . . (. . . the fiduciary or the trustworthy in the act of faith, . . . the testimonial that is always beyond proof . . .); and the experience of . . . *sacredness* or of *holiness*."[28] However, in the course of the expansion of Christianity, sacrality is subordinated to obligation construed as indebtedness so that theological discourse comes to be reframed in economic terms. This duality does not disappear but wends its way errantly into the contemporary situation of the world's religions. On the one hand, the Enlightenment posture of tele-techno-scientific reason requires trustworthiness, a faith in the social bond and "a promise to tell the truth" that binds not only the juridical but also the scientific community.[29] Yet on the other, there is a reaction to this complex, a fear of the self that has internalized this discourse and of deracination. Thus Derrida writes: "Religion today allies itself with tele-technoscience to which it reacts with all its forces. It is on *the one hand* globalization . . . exploiting tele-mediatization. But on *the other hand* it reacts immediately, *simultaneously* declaring war on what gives it this new power."[30]

But the living spontaneity that contests tele-technoscience is haunted by what he characterizes as "autoimmunity," the suicide of the defenses that were to protect the organism from external forces, thereby immunizing the organism against its own immune system. Derrida concludes: "In our 'wars of religion,' violence has two ages. The one . . . appears contemporary . . . in sync with . . . military tele-technology, . . . and cyberspaced culture. The other is a new archaic violence. It counters the first and everything it represents. Revenge.

Resorting to the same resources, it reverts . . . to the premachinal living being."[31] Archaic violence is itself fissured: on the one hand, there is the violent uprooting from the putatively authentic and sacred, from "family, nation, blood and soil," as Heidegger understood them. Yet, in response to the question I raised earlier—Is Terror simply a subtle form of technoscience?—Derrida perceives a more complex connection. Terror is a repristinization of the machine itself, "an animist relation to the teletechnic machine," know-how rather than knowledge, so that tele-technoscience "is to be both used and exorcised."[32] Thus it would seem, paradoxically, that the terrorist as described by Derrida sees in the teletechnic machine what Heidegger finds in the crafted thing: earth rather than utility.

What then happens to the sacred dimension of religion? "Ontotheology encrypts faith and destines it to the condition of a Spanish Marrano," the Spanish Jew who, in response to the Inquisition, worships as a Christian but secretly holds onto his heritage. Such faith exhibits the "emblem of a still life, an open pomegranate one Passover evening on a tray."[33]

Reason's Share: The *Partage* of Janicaud

Can the probing insights in Heidegger's account of the event of global technology be loosened from the grip of the *Geschick*, the destining of being? In congruity with Heidegger's view, Janicaud depicts an all-encompassing global language, which he terms techno-discourse, a world of rational rules and a meta-rationality that is the rationality of reason itself. Its language, techno-discourse, transcends the operational practices of specific technical discourses to become the lingua franca of an all-embracing audio-visual information culture, which constitutes and disseminates meaning. Janicaud writes: "Techno-discourse . . . is a parasitic language inextricably woven into technology, contributing to its diffusion . . . making almost impossible any radical analysis or any questioning of contemporary technological phenomena. Every technology has its vocabulary, its codes . . . its operative scenarios. Such is not the case with techno-discourse; it is neither strictly scientific, nor philosophic, [nor] poetic."[34]

In successfully realizing predetermined ends within a plurality of specific domains, rationality "runs wild" and becomes the subject of a will to totalize or, as Heidegger had observed, transforms thinking into calculation. In its social, political, economic and cultural manifestations, rationality is globalized as power. Janicaud concludes that "the scientific and technological revolution is only the most recent manifestation of a process that is much older, more fundamental: the *potentialization* of knowledge as power."[35] Although Heidegger has struggled admirably with the *Ereignis* of global technology, Janicaud maintains that his thought risks remaining merely "formal, rhetorical or edifying if . . . not confronted with the specificities of techno-scientific evolution."[36] Can one enter thoughtfully into the meaning of power in the present epoch, Janicaud asks, without being acquainted with actual techno-scientific possibilities?

In consonance with Hegel, Janicaud contends that reason is inescapable; it is what he calls *partage*, our share or allotment. Arguing for a mode of reason that is not the consequence of fate or destiny in the manner of Heidegger, *partage* is a self-reversal of an omnipresent rationality that does not descend into irrationality. Our *partage*, or lot, is not an abstract structure that stifles singularities, "life's fragility and changeability." He continues, "It is no longer a matter of defining a universal space for the progress of knowledge [but] more a matter of giving back to thinking its biting critique [one that lies between] an ineliminable destinal element and our human all too human portion."[37] Janicaud contends that his interest is not in the rational as an abstraction but rather in its expression as power, and thus, following Heidegger, in the incalculable postulates that are the "invisible shadow" of the calculable.[38]

Janicaud maintains that, having successfully achieved goals identifiable within scientific domains, rationality "runs wild" and transforms thinking into calculation. Still, no sharp boundary can be drawn between calculative reason and Being in any historically penetrating genealogical analysis. Instead, contemporary rationality should be seen as an encounter with the incalculable, with what Heidegger calls the *Unberechenbare*, in that it is not possible to determine calculatively what is presupposed by the global organization of techno-scientific development. The scale and magnitude of what appears to be calculable, the gigantic, morphs into the incalculable, which now haunts the logic of modernity. Mobilizing for unlimited development and expansion without an ultimate or highest aim, the incalculable is simply the unrestricted advancement of power.

As manifested in the logic of Terror, incalculability may be the outcome of the rationality of development. Unlike its expression in mass exterminations, however, a catastrophe whose extent is revealed in the language of number, the magnitude of Terror, I would argue, is that of size as symbol and of affective intensity. Thus the physical height of the World Trade Center embodied the economic significance of the transactions that occurred behind its walls. Borrowing Janicaud's terms for the incalculable, Terror can be seen as "the dark side of total mastery and the terrifying 'logic of a surplus of power.'"[39]

Is there any egress from the entrapment in techno-discourse, an acknowledgment of its own limits, an outside that remains refractory to incorporation within a limited whole? Janicaud notes that Nietzsche provides some premonitory insights into such rationality when he asserts that "a superior civilization must give man a double brain . . . one to experience science, the other to experience non-science. Lying next to one another without confusion, separable, self-contained. Our health demands this."[40] Nietzsche's claim may seem less than helpful in that he offers no account of how the domains are to be segregated, no description of a gatekeeping mechanism. There is, however, in Nietzsche's *aperçu* an implied paradigm of what constitutes health: the parceling out of discourses and the solidification of difference itself in what we have already seen designated as *partage*, with its connotations of share, allotment.[41] As escape hatch, *partage* not only provides a way out of entrapment in techno-discourse but also dodges a retreat from rationality intrinsic to Heidegger's solution. One need not, as with Heidegger, think an unthought that is other, apart from rationality. Instead, we must recognize rationality as inescapable, as our lot. Difference then must be inscribed within the rational itself.

Even if the will to objectivity must be understood in light of its history as power, we must not, Janicaud contends, effect a break with rationality but rather must recognize that the rational can face "its destiny of power" and, in so doing, need not return to its claims of self-sufficiency. In pondering the enigma of rationality—and this is the crucial point—"there is released the possibility of an 'examination of the *conscience*' of the rational facing its destiny of power" (my emphasis). It is this reserve of open possibility that challenges the evil of rationality. We can envisage this *partage* or limiting of power because "the possible is held in reserve at the foundation of the power of the rational."[42] What opens this fissure in rationality is its confrontation with its power, with the evil inherent in it.

A totally rational, self-enclosed system must implode or reverse itself, just as production and efficiency, when maximized, may implode and manifest themselves in individual atomization and insecurity. In this view, could one not argue that Terror is such an implosion prior to "the conscience of the rational," the conscience that generates dread and anxiety in the face of the Terror whose whence and whither could not be predicted? Are there not affinities between Janicaud's conscience and Derrida's logic of the supplement, of that which is added to a discourse that in actuality shapes it and the effect of the margin, of what is at the limit of a discourse but whose power configures its center? Is Terror not the violent manifestation of an outside that threatens to topple the structure of the whole?

Developing Software: Monkeys and Elephants

Is Janicaud not compelled to ask how the resources of a thinking that is searching for itself after its postmodern dissolution is to be apportioned? One must see, he maintains, that: "Planning is not enough to succeed. Practice reinvents itself with each instant."[43] Is it possible that the tension described by Janicaud between goal-based rationality and what he terms *partage* is replicated in the world of infoculture itself in the tension between plan-driven programs and what is now called an agile approach to software development? In the "Manifesto for Agile Software Development," agility is defined as a commitment to "individuals and interactions over processes and tools, working software over comprehensive documentation, customer collaboration over contract negotiation," and, especially significant, "responding to change over following a plan."[44] Unlike engineering processes that run through to completion by following a preset pattern strictly defined, plans for developing software are unlikely to succeed by trying to regulate things in advance. It is argued that "inspect-and-adapt cycles" are better adapted to unpredictability.[45]

The advantages of agility may not, however, offset the claim that constancy of practice breeds reliability. Moreover, with agility the power structure of organizations may be subject to frequent change. Decision-making authority is democratized, sometimes empowering managers and at other times programmers. In an Aesopian fable told by software engineer Barry Boehm, the conflict is depicted as a conflict between an elephant and a monkey. The elephant is strong and self-sufficient, while the monkey is agile and swift. Unlike the plodding elephant, the nimble monkey can climb trees to procure fruit, but when the supply gives out, the heavy elephant is able to carry the monkey on its back across a swift river whose current could bear the monkey away. The moral is obvious: both are needed.[46] Agility thrives in an atmosphere in which people see themselves as having considerable freedom, whereas plan-driven projects flourish in a culture where roles are defined by specific policies and procedures.

Without straining the analogy, can one discern in agility a replica of the semantic instability, the conceptual chaos, the impossibility of determining the border between concepts, as well as the questioning of the concept of border itself, that Derrida links to Terror? By contrast, do plan-driven approaches not repeat the setting-to-order that Heidegger ascribes to Enframing and the language of technology? Do the ties between agility and plan-driven methods not repeat Janicaud's account of the parceling out of discourses, the solidification of difference designated as *partage*, with its connotations of share, allotment? Are the software developers who do not abandon planning but who insist that "no decision is ideal for all time," who are continually absorbed in the agile practice of rethinking that they term *reflection*, not engaged in the parceling out of *partage*?[47] Does Terror not inhabit the interstices within and among these discourses? Consider again Nietzsche's claim, cited earlier, that we have a "double brain to experience science and non-science," that each part is self-contained, and that "our health demands this."[48]

The Warring Logics of Genocide

The very mention of genocide usually elicits a shudder, a *frisson* of horror, of psychological revulsion and moral outrage. Images of mass annihilation, of the dead and dying that the term evokes are especially troubling, since genocidal killing, now endemic to the world of postmodernity, is envisioned as a slaughter of innocents. It is understood that those earmarked for destruction are selected on the basis of criteria that lie outside the standard rules of conduct in war, even if genocidal events occur in the context of what is designated conventionally as war. Genocidal killing is often justified by its perpetrators not principally on the grounds of what the dead are presumed to have done but rather as required by an ontological flaw, as it were, attributed to the victims.

The significations conveyed in ordinary usage pass into the criteria of what counts as genocide as defined by international law. Imbricated in its juridical phraseology is a visceral aversion to what the term evokes, the destruction wreaked upon countless numbers of individuals because of who they are or who they are alleged to be, individuals whose "crime" is an identity to which negative value is ascribed and which can be eliminated only through the extermination of its bearers. The legal definition takes cognizance both of the magnitude of the exterminations and of the fact that groups targeted are deliberately rather than randomly chosen. In addition to the parameters established by the legal definition of genocide, I shall also consider meanings ascribed to the term *ethnic cleansing* as starting points for a discussion of the warring logics intrinsic to events of mass extermination.

I shall then turn to Janicaud's insightful account of the way in which rationality is currently configured as it bears upon, even if (as I believe) it fails fully to capture, the character of the warring logics at work in genocide. I interpret "logic" as referring not to rules of inference deployed to determine the status of arguments or to a mode of reasoning invoked to justify moral norms but rather to a complex of interpretive indicators or perspectives that arise within the sphere of events. In the case of genocidal acts, these "logics" are exhibited as the modus operandi of the acts themselves. The first of these warring logics is best described as the rationality of unencumbered replicability, the sensed multiplication of individuals so that vast numbers are seen as indistinguishable from one another. This absence of distinctiveness gives rise to a second logic, the logic of indiscernibles, so that individuals lacking difference meld into an undifferentiated sameness, a solidary yet formless being from which individuation is absent, which I shall explicate in terms of Levinas's concept of the *il y a*.

In so doing, I do not wish to offer an account of the psychology of the perpetrators. Instead, I shall proceed somewhat in the phenomenologically minimalist manner Janicaud attributes to Merleau-Ponty: "the visible dimension of Invisibility . . . a search for source-forms [*formes-mères*], an investigation of bodily encroachments and social rumblings" that are cultural in appearance.[1] I shall take for granted the cultural, political specificity of individual events but cannot, in the present context, undertake an analysis of each. However, I shall presume that the logics of techno-science are imbricated in widely divergent social and cultural situations, even when the means of extermination differ. What is more, I shall argue that this logic is involved in movements of resistance to it.[2]

Genocide or Ethnic Cleansing: Juridical Perspectives

Before turning to the warring logics of genocide, consider first its international legal definition as found in Articles II and III of the 1948 "Convention on the Prevention and Punishment of Genocide." Identifying genocide's mental and physical aspects, the document states:

The mental, "the intent to destroy in whole or in part, a national, ethnical or racial group as such," and the physical, which includes five acts: "killing members of the group, causing serious bodily or mental harm to members of the group . . . deliberately inflicting conditions of life calculated to bring about its destruction in whole or in part, imposing measures intended to prevent births within the group, forcibly transferring children of the group to another group."[3]

Acts constituting part of a *policy* to destroy a group's existence are seen as genocidal and as warranting punishment. The document goes on to declare that targeted groups fall into categories: those that are national, politically constituted; those that are ethnically and culturally determined; those that are racial, identified by their physical characteristics; and those that are religious, defined by beliefs, doctrines, and practices. Crucial for my subsequent discussion is the claim that "group identity is often imposed by the perpetrators."[4] Equally significant for my account is this document's ascription of the term *genocide* to the prevention of births within a targeted group.

Who, it may be asked, is the referent of the "we" who are incensed by genocide? The aversiveness to genocide reflected in the legal text that defines it is grounded in the assumption of a humanity that shares a moral perspective, one that presupposes a sense of outrage. Thus the Preamble to the "Rome Statute of the International Criminal Court" explicitly states that the states who are parties to the statute are: "*Mindful* that during this century millions of children, women and men have been victims of unimaginable atrocities that deeply shock the conscience of humanity" and that "this delicate mosaic of a common humanity may be shattered at any time" (italics in original).[5] Without endorsing the ground upon which this sense of abomination is predicated, that is, the notion of a universal humanity, I shall nevertheless concur in the claim that our responses are dependent upon the "vocabulary of our culture and its sustaining archetypes," an agreement that does not preclude critical self-awareness of the ways in which memories are transmitted.[6] With this caveat in mind, I shall accept as a premise the claim that genocide usually engenders this visceral antipathy.

In its difference from genocide, ethnic cleansing is alleged to fall under the rubric of "war crimes" or "crimes against humanity." A report of the Human Rights Watch notes: "'Ethnic cleansing' is not formally defined under international law," but "a UN Commission of

Experts has defined the term as a 'purposeful policy designed by one ethnic or religious group to remove by violent and terror-inspiring means the civilian population of another ethnic group or religious group from certain geographical areas to the exclusion of the purged group or groups.'"[7]

Thus, Human Rights Watch categorizes as ethnic cleansing the effort of the government of the Sudan "to remove the Masalit and Fur populations from large parts of Darfur [the western region of the Sudan] by violent means," moving them to government-controlled towns.[8] In addition, the document notes that these areas, in accordance with the definition, have been occupied by Janjaweed and other ethnic Arab groups.

That the line between genocide and ethnic cleansing cannot easily be drawn is attested by the difficulty that the Bush administration reportedly experienced in attempting to classify the situation in Darfur. According to an account in *The New York Times*, thousands of people in Darfur have been killed and more than a million driven from their homes by invading militias. Colin Powell commented that he was not prepared to select the correct legal term: "All I know is that there are at least a million people who are desperately in need and many of them will die if we don't get the international community mobilized. . . . And it won't make a whole lot of difference after the fact what you've called it."[9] In a follow-up op-ed, Nicholas Kristof maintains that the 320,000 deaths in the Darfur region, in which "the world has acquiesced shamefully" by ignoring the event, more than justifies applying the term *genocide*. In describing an attack by the Janjaweed against the local Zaghawa tribespeople he writes that, using ethnic and racial language, the invaders shouted "We will not let Zaghawa here." The attack, Kristoff claims, "was part of a deliberate strategy to ensure that the village would be forever uninhabitable, that the Zaghawa would never live there again. The Janjaweed poisoned wells by stuffing them with the corpses of people and donkeys . . . blew up a dam, burned all the homes . . . a school, a clinic and a mosque."[10] In regard to their operative logics, both genocide and ethnic cleansing invite scrutiny in that mass extermination plays a crucial role (whether as means or end) in each.

Yet the question plaguing the interpreter remains: How can she or he ascertain that what is alleged to have happened actually did happen? I shall assume that, even if understandably cautious theories of truth presume that there is no purely transparent language that could render events just as they transpired, nevertheless, the observer works within the parameters of what can and cannot have been. Thus we may say "It could have been *x* or *y* but it could not have been *z*" where *z* constitutes a denial of both *x* and *y*.[11] In the present instance, the interpreter may not be sure that events occur exactly as recounted, but she or he cannot dismiss the claim that extermination has occurred, its significance, and the responsibility to make known what is happening in Darfur.

Rules and Power, the Power of Rules

Is there a discernible mode of rationality that governs the economy and technology of postmodernity? Janicaud describes an all-encompassing global language, which he terms techno-discourse, a world of rational rules, a meta-rationality that is the rationality inhering in the rational itself. In its social, political, economic, and cultural manifestations, this rationality is expressed as power. He argues further for the possibility of a self-reversal of this omnipresent rationality that nevertheless will not descend into irrationality, but will open into the alternative exercise of reason that he calls *partage*. Janicaud, in consonance with Hegel, maintains that reason is inescapable: *partage* means reason is our share or allotment. I shall not enter into difficulties bound up with the claims for this reversal but shall focus on the operation of techno-discourse as a point of departure for understanding one of the logics of genocide.

Techno-discourse does not refer to the practices of specific operational technical discourses but instead becomes the language of an all-embracing audio-visual information culture that constitutes and disseminates meaning. Thus, as we have seen, Janicaud writes: "Every technology has its vocabulary, its codes . . . its operative scenarios. Such is not the case with techno-discourse; it is neither strictly scientific, nor philosophic, [nor] poetic."[12] However—and this is Janicaud's point—"the scientific and technological revolution is only the most recent manifestation of a process that is much older, more fundamental: the *potentialization* of knowledge as power."[13] We are now compelled "to think techno-science" to confront the "possibilities and the dynamics of a process without precedent."[14]

Janicaud maintains that, in successfully realizing predetermined ends within a plurality of specific domains in which they are operative, rationality "runs wild" and becomes the subject of a will to totalize or, as Heidegger would have it, transforms thinking into calculation. For Janicaud, however, a historically penetrating genealogical analysis precludes drawing a sharp boundary between calculative reason and Being. Instead, he depicts contemporary rationality as an encounter with the incalculable: the question of what is presupposed by development, by the "postulates of power," cannot be answered calculatively. The sheer scale and magnitude of what seems calculable, the gigantic, resists quantitative reduction and morphs into the incalculable. As the shadow haunting the logic of modernity, "the Incalculable is nothing other than the unconditioned advancement of power, which is continually remeasured and reevaluated." Respecting only scientific technical success, the incalculable mobilizes "for unlimited development and expansion without any definitive highest aim." Reason is delivered to its "destiny of power," a destiny that mandates that we confront the enigmas of power by considering a phenomenology of its effects.[15]

The rationality of development manifested as the incalculable unleashes "the dark side of total mastery and the terrifying 'logic' of a surplus of power," a logic that expresses itself in the "unbearable scourge" of the mass exterminations endemic to the present age.[16] The language of these catastrophic events is that of number, a language that conceals while revealing the incalculability of their magnitude: "First World War 8.7 million dead; Second World War 40 million, Hitler's camps 7 million, Stalin's camps 30 million. Solzhenitsyn's figures."[17]

What role, it may be asked, does techno-discourse play in racial and ethnic genocides? I argue that the imagined replicability of individuals is intrinsic to the logic of techno-discourse and that the replicability principle is then applied to living peoples. Janicaud does not discuss the role of replicability, however, and for him the explanation for mass extermination lies elsewhere. He argues that initial observations of differences in power harden into the exercise of power as domination so that a mystique of hierarchy is created. To be sure, hierarchy plays a significant role in forming constellations of power. The testimony of Rudolf Hoess, the ex-commandant of Auschwitz, at his trial in Nuremberg speaks in hierarchical terms of "strict orders as transmitted by Reichsfuehrer SS, Himmler."[18] Ultimately appealing to the *Fuehrerprinzip*, to Hitler as the final authority in all matters, he states, "Being a member of the SS and [obedient to its discipline] all orders issued by its leader and by Hitler were right."[19] Similarly, Albert Speer, who, in disdain of traditional bureaucracy, developed new, looser lines of organization and was distrusted by old-line officials, overcame objections to his strategies in that none of his critics could have invoked the nimbus of Hitler. "The backing of the Fuehrer counted for everything," Speer asserted.[20]

Janicaud contends that Nazism attempted to justify the manner in which it exercised power by grounding itself in what it saw as biological science and in an alleged instinct of aggression. He argues further that Nazism may "find an unexpected reprieve in techno-scientism . . . an appeal to power supported by material ameliorations." Thus, the spirit of Nazism was a social mirror of aspects of the power of techno-science.[21] I argue, however, that the "soothing effect" relied upon by the Nazis derived from the efficiency and speed of new technologies and, as such, did not reflect their relation to the deeper logics of techno-discourse. To be sure, Rudolf Hoess, speaking of the use of the gas Cyclon B, states: "It had a soothing effect on me. . . . We had shortly to begin a mass killing of the Jews. . . . Now we [Hoess and Eichmann] had discovered the gas and the means."[22] But rather than offering a reprieve from the demands of techno-science, his remark is a response to the deeper threatening aspect of its logic: the power to produce an infinite number of copies of entities as found in a variety of domains. A model is thus in place for one of Nazism's more profound fears, that of the unending replication of the despised other. The perceived uncontrollable multiplication of those who were the subject of loathing elicited the turn to strategies that would be taken as foolproof, those that insured total extermination of the other.

The possibility of unending reproduction is anticipated in Hegel's account of the wrong or bad infinite. For Hegel, every "something" others itself to become yet another "something" in a never-ending procession. Infinity thus understood "is only a negation of the finite; but the finite rises again, the same as ever, and is never got rid of and absorbed."[23] Hegel's wrong infinite can be read as an eerie, premonitory expression of a mode of genocidal logic, the fear of number "gone wild." In light of this logic, consider the following entry in the *Stroop Report*, a collection of thirty-two teletypes prepared by Major General Juergen (nee Josef) Stroop for SS Chief Heinrich Himmler reporting the daily operations of the SS in the Warsaw Ghetto and written in the idiom of statistics. Stroop reports that, having received little training,

> the men of the Waffen-SS . . . must be given special recognition
> for their daring, courage and devotion to duty. . . . Wehrmacht

Engineers also executed their tasks of blowing up bunkers, sewers and concrete houses with tireless devotion.

Only the continuous and tireless commitment of all forces made it possible to apprehend and/or destroy 56,065 Jews.[24]

He asserted that still others whose numbers could not be ascertained were eliminated by other means.

The Nazi use of technologies, gas chambers to kill and crematoria to dispose of the dead, is by now a matter of common knowledge. What must be noted is that various modes of incineration were seen not only as efficient and as rituals of "purification" but as preventing further replication. A dispatch from the Central Management of the Building Section in Auschwitz reports that corpses from the gas chambers in nearby Birkenau were burnt in four crematoria at the rate of 4,416 within twenty-four hours.[25] In addition, fire was used as a method both of killing and of generating terror. The Stroop report notes that the SS started fires in the ghetto, forcing Jews to emerge from their hiding places so that they were burned when attempting to escape. In addition, "measures had been taken to liquidate them as the other Jews, immediately." Five thousand three hundred Jews were apprehended for transfer in this way.[26] On May 16, 1943, it was reported that all 56,065 Jews were "apprehended and destroyed," and that the SS suffered no losses. "The Jewish quarter of Warsaw is no more."[27]

It should also be noted that, in the early phases of the deportations to Auschwitz, women and children were sent directly to the gas chambers upon arrival. No doubt they were seen as useless, but it must be added that they could also be perceived as providing links to an interminable future. This fear is discernible in the Nazi effort to curtail the numbers of the Slavic population, even if this population was not destined for total extermination. To this end, medical experiments were conducted that would enable a surgeon and a properly equipped staff "to sterilize several hundred or even a thousand in one day."[28]

In a memoir concerning an earlier genocidal event, what has been referred to as the Turkish Armenocide of 1915–22, Aram Andonian cites one Zeki Bey, who does not hesitate to kill a child by dashing it to the ground. Bey asserts:

Don't think that I have killed an innocent being. Even the newborn babes of this people are criminals for they will carry the seeds of vengeance in themselves. If you wish to spare tomorrow, kill even their children.

And they spared none.[29]

Formless Being

Is there a genocidal logic other than that of unstoppable proliferation to be found in the context of mass extermination? I have maintained that the vast numbers of those targeted are no longer seen as individuals but, in accordance with the logic of replication, as identical units. In conformity with Leibniz's principle of the identity of indiscernibles, if *a* has the properties of *b* and only those of *b*, and *b* has only the properties of *a*, then *a* and *b* are identical. Thus, in contrast to genocide's innumerable individual victims, this nondifference can also be viewed as the converging of these individuals to constitute a vast, formless mass, a mass that is simply there. The absence of discernible difference is anticipated in the Pre-Socratic philosopher Anaximander's *apeiron*, the unlimited, and in the *khōra* depicted in Derrida's analysis of Plato's *Timaeus*. The *apeiron* is an ontological storehouse of that which will come into being, however, and the *khōra* gives place to *mythos* and *logos*. By contrast, the formlessness that arises in the logic of genocide is one of irreparable loss, the disintegration of individuals into a mound of indistinguishable units.

I have suggested elsewhere that "what must be brought to the fore is the indeterminateness of Being that would ensue if one imagined not what is prior to beings but the disappearance of all beings . . . an impersonal anonymous residue."[30] Levinas designates this being that wells up in the absence of beings as the *il y a*. In his account, it preexists the emergence of individuals and is disclosed through horror. A medium "not reducible to a system of operational references," it is a "nocturnal space" into which things can disappear but which cannot itself withdraw.[31] The *il y a* is not to be identified with Heidegger's nonbeing as that toward which anguish is directed, but rather with Being itself. For Levinas, it is not the coming to an end of one's individual existence that is the ground of anguished care but rather the endless continuity of being.[32] He speaks of insomnia or wakefulness as the inability to suspend the primordial affective encounter with the *il y a* through sleep. Because one's own being or subjectivity is lost in the formlessness of the *il y a*, however, insomnia cannot be an existential deportment of the individual but must be attributed to the *il y a* itself.[33]

Nevertheless, the *il y a* should be interpreted not as a despairing retreat from the possibility of ethical existence but rather as a move toward an ethics of otherness. In its doubleness, the *il y a* refers both to the elemental, a terrain that lies escheat prior to the emergence of individuation and the structures of human existence, and also, as we have seen, to Being as that into which the already-existing individual can sink. It is crucial to note that this immersion undoes egoity and de-nucleates the self, an undoing that "strike[s] with absurdity the active transcendental ego."[34] This surrender of egoity allows for the advent of the Other, whose very emergence is to be read as proscribing violence and who is the primal source of the moral life. In confronting the face of the Other, one is in the presence of a proscription against harming the Other, who is understood not primordially as a visible phenomenon but as an imperative, as discourse rather than percept, language rather than image.

Is it possible to render the inundation by media images of extermination, of formless mounds of corpses and vast numbers of the living herded together awaiting death, in terms of the menace and destruction of the *il y a*? An eerie parallel can be discerned in Primo Levi's depiction of arrival at the concentration camp Auschwitz: "The world into which one was precipitated was terrible, yes, but also indecipherable. It did not conform to any model; the enemy was all around but also inside, the we lost its limits."[35] What is more, the logic of the *il y a* is further attested in efforts to conceal genocide. As that which seemingly was already defined by formless expansion, genocide may beget further genocides. Thus Philip Gourevich speculates that a new war could spark a bloody regional conflict involving multiple African states. It "would be a war *about* the genocide in that Hutu power attempts to see itself as in a continuum with earlier Rwandan violence while depending on genocide to justify its rule."[36] Thus genocides would continue to breed while seeking meta-level justification by appealing to previous genocides.

In sum, the proliferation of individuals whose observable differences have been obliterated has led to an identity of indiscernibles so that individuality disappears. Instead, a new logic supervenes, that of individuals melded into a formless mass. Does the camp, Primo Levi's *Lager*, a world that is "indecipherable," that "conforms to no model," not provide an existential referent for the Levinasian *il y a*? Are the logics manifested within a given genocidal event not operative in a universe of expanding genocides?

Explaining the Shiver of Horror

Neither Janicaud's account of techno-discourse nor Levinas's description of immersion in the formlessness of the *il y a* need be seen as entrapments from which there is no egress. Consider that the *il y a* itself is not an insuperable obstacle to ethics in that it undermines an egoity that hampers self-giving. What is more, in its conceptual inapprehensibility and ego-destroying character, the *il y a* can be read as the obverse of the infinite, the transcendent locus of Good. As such, it is locked into a structural pairing with the Good, as it were. For Levinas, thought must be penetrated by an infinite transcendence, which shatters the thought that thinks it. Like the *il y a*, the infinite exceeds any idea we can have of it. The infinite is not merely unimaginable magnitude but the object of a desire for a Good beyond being. God, who remains transcendent, is beyond conceptual grasp yet enters existence by way of the Other.[37] The obligation to the Other is itself infinitized so that one becomes one-for-the-other. In so doing, one does not use signs to communicate this self-abandonment. Instead, one makes oneself into a sign, a process Levinas calls "sincerity." The referent of this sincerity is termed "glory," the glory of the infinite. Rather than being immersed in the *il y a*, the subject that is expelled from itself places itself at another's disposal. If glory is a proclaiming of peace and a proscription of violence, as Levinas claims, glory can be called the dynamism of the infinite and can be contrasted with the insomnia, or wakefulness, discernible as the dynamism of the *il y a*.

It is clear that resistance to genocide at the risk of one's life can be considered a prime expression of an ethics of otherness. But what requires explanation is the far lesser claim to goodness evinced in the widespread response of revulsion to genocide, the frisson of horror that is neither heroic resistance on the one hand, nor the self-serving exculpatory professions of revulsion by perpetrators, on the other. Although Levinas does not consider the matter, this common response of horror can be linked to the idea of the infinite in relation to the *il y a*, an infinite that is expressed in and as the revulsion that wells up in confronting dead others, even at a remove from proximity to the event. Neither a psychological law based on observation nor a universal moral law, the frisson of horror, I would maintain, inhabits a discursive space between the command of alterity to refrain from violence, a command that is a precondition of actual language, and the shudder itself, a gesture that is a sign epitomizing that which seeks but cannot find further articulation.

This revulsion can also be interpreted as arising in Janicaud's resolution of the dilemma posed by the rationality of techno-discourse. Rather than abandoning rationality, he develops, as we have seen, an alternative view of reason. Simply put, "to think is to enter into relation,"[38] but there is a limit within the relational, a *partage*, a multivalent term that carries connotations of share, allotment. We need not, as Heidegger does, think that which is unthought, that is other apart from rationality. Instead we are to acknowledge that rationality is inescapable, that it is our lot. Difference must be inscribed within the rational itself.

To be sure, when rationality is expressed as the will to objectivity, it is to be understood as power, its history as the history of power. However we must not, Janicaud contends, effect a break with rationality but rather see that the rational can face "its destiny of power." In so doing, rationality need not return to its claims of self-sufficiency. Denying that *partage* is a destiny that, in the manner of Heidegger, has been "plotted in the obscure heart of Being, . . . it is enacted *between* us and Being." Our *partage* is not abstract but is played out historically. In what is perhaps the most cogent formulation of this perspective, he maintains that "one must take possession of the legacy of modern reason such that it ceaselessly analyzes and recovers itself . . . there is no formula offering a conciliatory universality." He goes on to say, "Rationality does not guarantee understanding: it ignores or stifles singularities and nuance, life's fragility and changeability. Destiny become *partage* is reason made more reasonable."[39]

In pondering the enigma of rationality, that which it cannot think—and this is the crucial point—"there is released the possibility of an 'examination of the *conscience*' of the rational facing its destiny of power" (my emphasis). It is this reserve of open possibility that challenges the evil of rationality. We can envisage this *partage* or limiting of power because "the possible is held in reserve at the foundation of the power of the rational."[40] What opens this fissure in rationality is its confrontation with its power, with the evil inherent in it. A totally rational, self-enclosed system must implode upon or reverse itself, just as production and efficiency, when maximized, may implode and manifest themselves in individual atomization and insecurity. Although there can be no "conciliatory universality," there is a reserve in rationality itself that confronts the evil intrinsic to it and renders possible an examination of the conscience of the rational that opens the way to the shudder of horror, the gesture of repudiation.

■ ■ ■

The response to genocide understood as the extermination of peoples is, I have maintained, most frequently one of revulsion and horror, a reaction that can be attributed to a radical overturning and reversal of the warring logics intrinsic to genocide. As exhibited within a genocidal event itself, the first of these logics is manifested as the rationality of unencumbered replicability. When it is applied to groups of peoples, they are seen as potentially capable of multiplying endlesslesly. What is more, in targeted groups individuals are viewed as indistinguishable from one another.

The logic of replicability is embedded in techno-discourse, an all-encompassing global language enacted as a complex of rational rules operative in various domains of contemporary existence: economy, polity, technology, and culture. As depicted by Janicaud, techno-discourse is expressed as power. When the rule of replicability is applied by the perpetrators of genocide to a despised or feared people, unstoppable multiplication is seen as requiring their total extermination. At the same time, the absence of individual distinctiveness gives rise to a second logic, the logic of indiscernibles. Identical and seemingly isolated monads meld into an undifferentiated sameness, a solidary formlessness that is best described in terms of Levinas's concept of the *il y a*, indeterminate being.

Both the logic of infinite replication as imbricated in techno-discourse and the logic of formless being are subject to movements of reversal. According to Janicaud, as techno-discourse reaches its limits, it undoes itself and thereby liberates the possibility of *conscience*. The rational, when faced with its nature as power, repudiates the terrifying logic of the surplus of power that eventuates in genocidal killing and, in this undoing, arrives at a *partage*, an allotment or limiting of power. It is this emergence of conscience as a dislodging of techno-discourse that, I argue, releases the horror one confronts in the face of genocide.

The "reversal" of the second mode of genocidal logic, the suppression of individuality in the *il y a*, is brought about by the effort to think that which is unencompassible by thought, the infinite. To be sure, like the *il y a*, the infinite in its excessiveness precludes conceptual grasp. Not, however, to be confused with the formlessness of being, the infinite is the object of a desire for what is beyond being, for a Good that mandates responsibility for the Other. As the expression of divine transcendence, the infinite releases the moral revulsion that is the common response to genocide.

In a 1991 work that sparked considerable debate in French philosophical circles, Janicaud rejects what he conceives to be a theologizing tendency, a phenomenology of the invisible that he attributes at least in part to the influence of Levinas.[41] Arguing against foundationalist perspectives that "overburden immanence with transcendence," Janicaud insists that he has resolved the principal issues of the debate in his account of a minimalist phenomenology that would undo its speculative unity. Heretofore seen as an ideal, phenomenology should now be an inspiration that nourishes multiple practices.[42] It is my aim not to wade into the murky waters of this dispute but rather to exploit the tension between the thought of Levinas and that of Janicaud in order to illuminate the warring logics of genocide and the reversal of these logics that issues in the *frisson* of horror, the visceral response to the mass exterminations of the present age.

15

Incursions of Alterity
The Double Bind of Obligation

What, we might ask, could Gregory Bateson's description of the double bind have to do with the question of evil? I hope to show that the double bind, the claim that no matter what one does one cannot win, not only plays a role in determining the development of schizophrenia, as Bateson maintains, but is intrinsic to the emergence of the moral life.[1] I view the double bind as a prior condition for deciding that a contemplated act is evil and for the sense of obligation that enters into the avoidance or pursuit of ends that are deemed to be evil. I argue further that double binds arise not only in individual but also in sociohistorical contexts in which otherness is in conflict with collective rules. The route taken in support of these claims will, of necessity, be circuitous.

I shall begin with Levinas's premise that ethics originates in alterity, in the otherness of the other person, whose very existence, as it impinges upon the self, is experienced as a proscription against exerting violence against that other. But I maintain that the understanding of evil that can be inferred from this account requires expansion. There are not only harms one does to another but harms that one inflicts upon oneself, the evils of physically injurious and psychologically debilitating acts committed against oneself. I examine such acts in light of George Ainslie's discussion of how temporal distance affects the ways in which we make choices, preferring present satisfactions over remote gains. Next, I consider evils that are inherent in the very modes of rationality that govern contemporary collective life and form the context for evils that can be termed radical war and widespread poverty. To this end, I shall continue to appeal to Janicaud's analysis of techno-discourse, a mode of rationality underlying radical evils. These disparate modes of evil are linked by virtue of the double binds that come into play in the self's relation to itself and within a sociocultural whole.

Levinas's Philosophy and the Double Bind of Alterity

Levinas maintains that moral awareness begins when the other person is disclosed, in her immediacy, not as another myself but as absolutely other. Perceived in this way, the other is grasped not as a composite of sense data but as an ethical imperative that is not prescriptive but proscriptive: the other acts upon the self as a directive to refrain from harming or doing violence to that other. That another individual may be given as an object of perception or cognition is not in question in contexts of everyday existence. But when disclosed as an object in the world, otherness disintegrates, and the other enters consciousness as one of its possessions or as part of a totalizing nexus of sociohistorical relations. In thus reducing the other to a content of one's own consciousness, one is always already guilty before the other. In Levinas's radical view of otherness, the face of the other is revealed primordially not as a phenomenon but as a command to refrain from doing violence to the other.[2]

It is not hard to see in this account features of the double bind, a situation that, according to Bateson, involves two or more persons one of whom repeatedly experiences negative injunctions from the other. Such injunctions can enjoin one either to act or to refrain from acting in a given way and may entail punishment if disobeyed. A secondary injunction to undertake or fail to undertake an action may be in direct conflict with a primary prohibition according to which the other (the putatively benevolent parent) is not to be seen as punitive. The pattern of conflicting demands that comes into play in the double bind may enter into all of one's interpersonal situations and, for the recipient, remains inescapable.

It should be noted that the double bind does not go unnoticed in the work of Derrida. It functions most effectively in the context of the problem of translation, a problem that he finds instantiated in the biblical account of the tower of Babel. God's resentment at the "pretensions of men to make a name for themselves" or, as Derrida would have it, the preemption of the power to name, results in God's dispersion of languages and the imposition of his name, the name of the Father, upon men. At the same time, God demands that humans speak a name they must but dare not translate, the name of God. These conflicting injunctions constitute the double bind that Derrida renders as "translate my name, but whatever you do, do not translate my name."[3] The dilemma for Derrida is one of semiotic permeability, of the simultaneous possibility and impossibility of transporting meaning across linguistic boundaries. By contrast, the double bind of Levinas is expressed in the difficulties generated by an other-regarding ethic, one of repeated negative injunctions issued by the alterity or otherness of the other person. Such an ethic may designate as evil self-regarding claims, as well as those imposed by a social field that operates in disregard of the demands of the other. The pain arising from the double bind of these conflicting claims is unmistakable.

The basic question for Levinas can be construed as a weighing of epistemic against moral claims. Is meaning, he asks, derived from what is revealed to one's consciousness, thought as revealing the truth of being? Or is meaning primordially ethical, showing itself in and through one's relation to the other? In his words, is meaning not "the consciousness of that inassimilable strangeness of the other, the bad conscience of my responsibility, the bad conscience of that difference of the non-additive other . . . ? In it there can be heard the demand that keeps me in question and elicits my response or responsibility."[4]

If the proscription against violence is to be effective, it enters into one's relations with another as an ever-present meta-rule that proscribes doing harm to the other. Even more radically, Levinas advocates placing the other before the self, so that one is willing to substitute oneself for the other, even when she or he is in a life-threatening situation. It is apparent that this rule is in conflict both with the juridical rules of most societies, which allow for at least retaliatory violence, and with the desire for self-preservation. When alterity precipitates a conflict of rules, we are caught in the double bind of obligation that inaugurates moral existence.

The Evils of Techno-discourse

In his description of the etiology of schizophrenia, Bateson attributes this "mental condition" to a double bind understood both epistemically as a confusion of logical types played out against one another and interpersonally as difficulty in communication between self and other. Appealing to the theory of logical types, according to which the members of a class and the class of which they are members operate at different levels of abstraction, Bateson concludes that the difficulty in distinguishing these logical levels is reflected in situations of actual communication. Errors are made in the classification of messages, a process determined by contextual cues.[5] Yet for Bateson, the schizophrenic's response is somehow experienced as defining the context of her life, so that the result of repeated primary negative injunctions "enforced by punishment or signals which threaten survival" traps the individual. There is no exit from the field of prohibitory restrictions.[6]

Just such a conflict of rules is inherent at a macrolevel in the evil of an all-encompassing discourse, the globalization of rule-bound thinking, what Janicaud calls techno-discourse. In a world of rational rules, any violation of these rules is bound to induce psychological dissonance, an inability to function within the ambit of the logical and social constraints of that world. Moreover, if we want to comprehend the constraints themselves, the "rationality of the rational," as Janicaud calls it, the conditions for understanding this meta-rationality already presuppose the rules they are to explain. Must we not move from a formal to a merely operational definition, Janicaud asks, to rules that enable us to distinguish true from false statements or, borrowing Quine's terms, to "an exposition of truth functions"?[7] We are constrained to think of rationality as arising in the process of its determination through the formation of operational rules or, referring to French philosopher Jean Ladrière, through the enactment of constitutive and transformational procedures, "the constitution of a network of mutual connections."[8]

However—and this is Janicaud's point—in successfully realizing predetermined ends within a plurality of specific domains, rationality "runs wild" and becomes the subject of a will to totalize, or, as Heidegger had observed, transforms thinking into calculation. In its social, political, economic, and cultural manifestations, rationality is globalized as power. Its language, techno-discourse, transcends the operational practices of specific technical discourses to become the lingua franca of an all-embracing audio-visual information culture, which constitutes and disseminates meaning. Thus, says Janicaud:

> Techno-discourse . . . is a parasitic language inextricably woven
> into technology, contributing to its diffusion . . . making almost

impossible any radical analysis or any questioning of contemporary technological phenomena. Every technology has its vocabulary, its codes . . . its operative scenarios. Such is not the case with techno-discourse; it is neither strictly scientific, nor philosophic, [nor] poetic.[9]

Janicaud concludes that "the scientific and technological revolution is only the most recent manifestation of a process that is much older, more fundamental: the *potentialization* of knowledge as power."[10]

Is there any egress from the entrapment in techno-discourse? Can rationality thus understood acknowledge its own limits, an outside that remains refractory to incorporation within a limited whole? Janicaud notes that Nietzsche already provides some premonitory insights into such rationality when he asserts that "a superior civilization must give man a double brain . . . one to experience science, the other to experience non-science. Lying next to one another without confusion, separable, self-contained. Our health demands this."[11] Nietzsche's claim may seem less than helpful in that he offers no account of how the domains are to be segregated, no description of a gatekeeping mechanism. Yet there is in Nietzsche's *aperçu* an implied paradigm of what constitutes health: the parceling out of discourses and the solidification of difference itself.

Continuing along this Nietzschean road of parceling out, Janicaud points to the dilemma posed by rationality: "To think is to enter into relation."[12] But there is a limit within the relational that he calls *partage,* a multivalent term that carries connotations of share, allotment. One need not, as with Heidegger, think an unthought that is other, apart from rationality. Instead, we must recognize rationality as inescapable, as our lot. Difference, then, must be inscribed within the rational itself.

As I stated earlier, when rationality is expressed as the will to objectivity, it must be understood as power, its history as the history of power. One does not, Janicaud contends, effect a break with rationality, but one must instead recognize that the rational can face "its destiny of power." Consider again Janicaud's words: "there is released the possibility of an 'examination of the *conscience*' of the rational facing its destiny of power" (my emphasis), a reserve of open possibility that challenges the evil of rationality. "The possible is held in reserve at the foundation of the power of the rational."[13] A self-enclosed system that is totally rational must implode or reverse itself, just as production and efficiency, when they reach an extreme of development, implode and result in individual atomization and insecurity.

Reversal is not to be understood as a dialectical movement of negation. Rather, reversal is that which "rationalization cannot or does not wish to think."[14] But if one clings both to the reversal of thinking and to thinking, can one renounce the power of the rational nonirrationally? Janicaud's query expresses a classical double bind. When the effects of power become sufficiently great, we are compelled to think about rationality. At the same time, we try to escape rationality by thinking what cannot be formalized, that is, "the constitutive limits of the power of the rational," so that the rational will somehow fall outside itself.[15] The demands of rationality thus construed remain consistent with Bateson's principle: whether you do or whether you don't, you will still be punished.

Yet it is at this point that a barrier seems to be broken, releasing one into a freedom that is beyond power, for the purity of this outside "has the value of a sign transcending all instrumentalizations. It calls the rational to its vocation of freedom and to an absolute autonomy. . . . It connects with a possible that does not seem mortgaged by the will to power; under the starry sky, a mark of the Enigma."[16] The joyful possibility of an open future unconstrained by the rules of techno-discourse is a gift bestowed by rationality as it undoes itself.

But Janicaud does not consider a crucial question: Does possibility, when presenting itself as the outside of rationality, not dissemble? In Bateson's terms, does this open possibility not aspire to appear otherwise than as the agent of an inescapable rationality? Yet without the evil of the rationality that has expelled it, possibility could not impinge upon rationality, a rationality that is and is not *partage.* May we not infer from Janicaud's account the impossibility of overcoming the aporias of rationality, a double bind that arises within rationality as a pathological process, the pathos (in an etymological sense) of ethics? In sum, although "Operative reality has passed the point of no return," it may have "outside itself or within *itself* the resources that would permit it to master the mastery, or better still: to open itself to the reserved but still closed dimensions of language and the Enigma."[17] How, we may ask, are we to "master the mastery" if rationality is the prerequisite of the move that condemns it? Just as the child, in condemning the mother who has caused her to see something that is not there, is condemning herself, so the painful double bind of alterity arises as the self-condemnation of rationality itself.

Evil as Harming Oneself

I have argued that Levinas's description of an alterity-driven ethics can be expanded to include an account of what drives the rationality of a techno-discourse "run wild" to undo itself. The relation of ethical existence and otherness can also be extended by considering the self as riven by difference. Although conceding that the self is multifunctional—a thinking, feeling, and laboring self—Levinas maintains that it remains at bottom a unitary self and that ethical imperatives arise solely through incursions of another outside the self. But the self often inflicts harms upon itself that do not directly involve others. In self-defeating or self-harming behavior, the agent and the one acted upon are in a relation of internal partition, so that the self is always already multiple. The claim of intrapsychic multiplicity has generated widely differing responses: hermeneutical, Paul Ricoeur; historico-political, Jon Elster; economic, George Loewenstein; and psychological, George Ainslie, upon whose work I shall focus because his account of self-defeating behavior can be read as an illuminating example of a double bind.

Ainslie begins by asking whether doing something we later repent can be satisfactorily explained by Aristotle's account of *akrasia*, or weakness of will. Even if, for Aristotle, the self is partitioned into rational and passionate elements and the passions can get in the way of reason, it is still possible for the rational part to overcome them. But Aristotle fails to explain reason's inability to control self-harming behaviors. What is more, the role of time in decision making is absent from his account.

Utility theorists, who consider the maximization of satisfaction to be what motivates action, represent an advance over cognitivist analyses such as that of Aristotle. Hume, an early representative of the utility view, astutely grasps the nature of intrapsychic conflict as modeled on our relations with others, arguing that our reactions to our own pleasures and pains can be compared to our responses to the pleasures and pains of others. Moreover, our reactions occur over a period of time. Thus, says Hume:

> The direct survey of another's pleasure naturally gives us plea-
> sure, and therefore produces pain when compared to our own.

His pain, considered in itself, is painful to us but augments the idea of our own happiness and gives us pleasure. The prospect of past pain is agreeable, when we are satisfied with our present condition; as our past pleasures on the other hand give us uneasiness, when we enjoy nothing at present equal to them. The comparison, being the same as when we reflect upon the sentiment of others, must be attended by the same effects.[18]

Ainslie contends that Freud goes further. In describing acts of choosing as reflecting a conflict between the reality and pleasure principles, Freud takes time into account. The reality principle does not eliminate but "safeguards" the pleasure principle: "A momentary pleasure, uncertain in its results, is given up, but only in order to gain along the new path, an assured pleasure at a later time."[19] Surprisingly absent from Ainslie's historical tracking of the effect of time on moral choice is attention to Heidegger's depiction of life as lived in anticipation of one's own death, thereby drawing attention to the primacy of future time. For Ainslie, these earlier thinkers failed to see the self as a population of bargaining agents, a "free for all" forum in which competing promises of reward vie for selection. More graphically, "the mind bears less resemblance to a fact-gathering or puzzle-solving apparatus than to a population of foraging organisms."[20] Also lacking in past accounts was a nuanced comprehension of the self's relation to its future or, to borrow Jon Elster's term, its "time preference," by which is meant "an expression of the relative importance that at one point of time one accords to various later times."[21]

To understand self-harming behavior, Ainslie maintains, we must grasp the self's irrational relation to time, its valuing of "future events in inverse proportion to their expected delays," so that value is discounted in relation to temporal distance.[22] Choices affecting the future that are made in the present can be expressed in two ways, as exponential and as hyperbolic discounting. In exponential discounting, it is assumed that the discounting of value for the passage of time occurs at a constant rate, whereas in hyperbolic discounting, the temporal proximity of a goal affects which goal is chosen, so that choice is tilted to the poorer but earlier alternative. In order to comprehend how exponential discounting works, consider Ainslie's example: I purchase a new car for $10,000 today, and it is discounted (or loses value) at 20 percent a year. Now if we suppose that I had ordered the same car a year ago, to be delivered not then (a year ago) but today, it would have been worth $8,000 to me; if ordered two years ago, it would have been worth $6,400. In the exponential view, temporal distance diminishes the car's value at a constant rate.[23]

Still, it is one thing to discount time in regard to marketplace ventures but another to discount future time in relation to self-harming activities, such as excessive drinking or drug taking, which may cause subsequent damage or regret. In the effort to attain satisfaction, people's preferences veer between gratifying a habit (drinking, binge eating, and the like) and giving it up, oscillations that are determined by how near in time an opportunity for indulgence may be. In such instances, "people devalue future goods not at a constant rate but proportionally to their delay, so that their discount curve will be hyperbolic."[24] In effect, Ainslie's hyperbolic discounter can be envisaged as saying: "The sooner the better, even if what I get soon is actually less desirable than what I might have later on."

If, as Ainslie maintains, the self is a mélange of conflicting preferences, a population, the regularities of exponential discounting give way to the warring alternatives of hyperbolic discounting. Differing satisfactions become dominant at different points *because* of their timing. Thus for Ainslie, an option must not only promise more than competing options but also must act so that the rival options waiting in the wings do not sabotage a given choice. Not only must multiple competing rewards subvert present contenders, but they must also ward off future dangers.[25] That decisions can be arrived at is explained as the result of transactions resembling those that foster agreement in the larger social world.[26]

The preference for short-range harmful satisfactions is complicated by the tendency for harmful behavior to become repetitive. Choices may be grouped into series that, when taken together, appear to constitute a personal rule, each choice setting a precedent for succeeding choices and thereby undermining other reward-getting tactics.[27] Often enough, harmful short-range satisfactions, such as having a drink, are interpreted as exceptions and not as intended to set precedents.[28]

Ainslie contends that these exceptions may, even unconsciously, constitute rules that (in Bateson's terms) could be experienced as paradoxical commands. Ainslie writes:

> There is an inevitable clash between two kinds of reward-getting strategies: Belief in the importance of external tasks — amassing wealth . . . discovering knowledge — leads to

behaviors itself that rush to completion: but a tacit realization of the importance of appetite motivates a search for obstacles to solution or for gambles that will intermittently undo [these behaviors]. Consciousness of the second task spoils the very belief in the first task that makes the first task strict enough to be an optimal pacer of reward.[29]

Might one allege, arguably to be sure, that Heidegger's view of inauthentic existence can be understood as a hyperbolic discounting of death's inevitability?

We may ask: Is the evil of time-bound self-defeating behavior as described by Ainslie is the inevitable outcome of every double bind? In an amendment to the older, catch-22 version of his theory, Bateson considers the possibility of an indeterminate outcome when rules conflict, an indeterminacy that depends upon a widening of the context in which the rules are operative. The original double-bind theory dealt with what Bateson later calls *transforms*—we might think of them as inner content—as if transforms were actual objects driven by physical forces. He now maintains that the double bind is the result of a tangling of the rules involved in making and in acquiring the transforms. The point of his revision is that a situation from which schizophrenia would seem to emerge necessarily might generate positive consequences, for example, the creation of art or humor. A double bind can arise in an experiential nexus from which it can either enrich or impoverish, engender "gifts" or "confusions."[30] Bateson maintains that such open possibilities are "experienced breaches in the weave of contextual structures [and] are in fact double binds" that manifest an ambiguity of what he terms *transcontextuality*.[31]

Not all transcontextual situations have positive outcomes that can be measured by enhanced creativity. Applying his amended double-bind theory to alcoholism, a complex alternation of sobriety and intoxication, Bateson argues that the self is in conflict with a real or fictitious intrapsychic other. When this behavior is symmetrical, the actions of two individuals are similar, the behavior of the first prompting more of the same behavior in the second. When the behaviors are complementary, each behaves differently from the other, yet the first stimulates alternative but somehow fitting behavior in the second.[32] In what Bateson designates "alcoholic pride," an intrapsychic symmetrical relationship is established, grounded in the alcoholic's claim that she can will to overcome her addiction by asserting, "I can do it. Drink will not do me in," though she ultimately gives way. This outcome of the double bind is in remarkable conformity with Ainslie's model: the long-range higher interest goal is subverted by the cumulative power of repeated harmful short-range choices.

Alcoholics Anonymous and others argue, however, that a positive outcome is possible for the alcoholic if she can establish a connection with an other that is greater than the self. The symmetrical relations that issue in self-harming behavior might in that case be reversed and a new, complementary relation established. Although switching to relations of complementarity may lead to behavioral changes, Bateson maintains that the new configuration may not be preferable to intrapsychic relations of symmetry. Moreover, one could ask: What if the alcoholic believed that the relation to a greater power were not itself complementary but symmetrical and emulative?[33] Even in situations of transcontextuality, Bateson implies, there are some circumstances in which the negative side of the double bind prevails.

■ ■ ■

According to Levinas, ethics begins with the advent of the other person, who is apprehended not as a phenomenon, an object of perception or cognition, but as an injunction to refrain from doing violence to the other. Resistance to this moral mandate is the defining characteristic of evil. Using Levinas's account of otherness as an entering wedge, I try to show that otherness can take on new ethical significations, that the term *other* can acquire a polysemy absent from his analysis.

Janicaud applies the term in the context of an all-encompassing social and linguistic framework in which otherness can be construed as an implosion of a sociocultural rationality "run wild," a techno-discourse that eventuates in the evils of a global society. Hegel's notion of history, politics, and economy ordered as a totality, as well as Heidegger's description of the relation between Being and beings, are freshly configured to take account of the logic of techno-science not as an epistemological construct but as a logic of power. Janicaud's innovation lies in showing that alterity works not at the level of self and other but within the totalizing context of techno-discourse, undoing it and thereby unlocking an ethical domain of open possibility that evades the discourses of power.

What is more, Levinas provides no account of harms inflicted by the self against itself, evils that can be helpfully explained by turning to the temporal context in which self-harming moral choices are made. Ainslie sees self-harming behaviors in the light of hyperbolic discounting, choosing temporally proximate but less desirable rewards in preference to long-term, more worthwhile goals, thus discounting value with the passing of time. Such evils arise intrapsychically, without the commanding presence of the other.

These dissimilar evils are linked by their dependence upon conflicting injunctions, the double bind invoked by Bateson to explain pathological psychic states or (rarely) acts of creative imagination. But the double bind has yet another role that has gone unnoticed, that of a necessary (if not yet sufficient) condition for the emergence of a moral field such that, in its absence, the ascription of evil could not arise.

16

Memory, History, Revelation
Writing the Dead Other

A piece of historical writing is often thought of as a narrative inter-preting the times of those who can themselves no longer depict the epoch in which they lived and moved and had their being. The sub-jects of this story are no longer here to attest to their era's culture, economy, institutions, politics, and way of life, whether to praise or to excoriate them. The historian is challenged to configure for the living the lives and times of dead others, making inferences from the clues that are trusted by the profession: archives, artifacts, and trans-mitted traditions. What remains unstated in this account is the man-ner in which the narrator speaks about, but not for, the past.

To see how and why this is so, it may be useful further to develop an everyday belief about history: it is a commonplace that history is a recounting of the remembered events of a community's past. This contention brings out history's relation to time, social existence, lan-guage, and truth and provides a good starting point for inquiring into the relations among history, memory, and revelation. In this view, history deals with events once but no longer present, events that are stored up, made conscious in the manner of that which is no more, in short, remembered. These occurrences are given linguistic shape, organized into a coherent narrative, interpreted. The recounting is attentive to the sequences of the events that provide historical con-tent, to their diachronicity, although the historian may choose to schematize them synchronically. Event and story generally unfold in the manner of "earlier" and "later" as seen from the perspective of "now," the present of the narrator. Although the fissure or distance between events in their individuality, their *Eigentlichkeit*, and the historical telling is acknowledged in this commonsense view, the later account of what occurred is believed to mirror what actually happened. Standard historical discourse is also understood to be about narrated events that are communal, so that, for example, the personal memoir becomes history insofar as it bears upon a collectively shared past.

This everyday view of history presupposes that the narrated material of history aims at a truth that is understood as a matching of event and narration. The standard of judging history is veracity: to issue a historical statement is to promise that one's assertions are true in the sense that what is alleged to have happened did happen, that one's claims are as accurate as one's proximity to one's sources can make them. This sense of veracity is embodied in Aristotle's famous distinction between historian and poet: the historian "describes the thing that has been," the poet "a kind of thing that might be."[1]

Implicit also in the everyday view is the supposition that the "original," the remembered, and the narrated event are homologous. Each layer is transparent toward a more primordial one, until the original events themselves are brought to the fore. What if, however, event and story are not homologous? How, then, do memory and story reflect the event? Is the relation of story to event to be grasped as a transposition of codes, a decoding into narrative language of what is encoded as a chronicle of sequential particulars?[2] The difficulty of relating event to narrative has been widely interpreted by metahistorians as the failure to take the metaphoricity of historical writing into account. Hayden White's description of the connection between event and narrative, for example, rightly rejects the myth of the given, the view that events are a field of lambent facts, merely "there," awaiting subsequent narrative articulation. Instead, White suggests, historical narratives achieve their explanatory effect not through the reproduction of events, themselves already encoded in tropes, but through the development of metaphorically articulated correspondences between events and conventional story types. Thus, for White, historical narrative lies between the events described in the historical record and the icon or story type that will render them accessible: "The narrative mediates between the events reported in it and the generic plot structures conventionally used in our culture to endow unfamiliar events and situations with meaning."[3]

This view of history rightly breaks with accounts of historical writing as the representation of factlike events. However, it fails to thematize the structure of time and memory generally presupposed by narrative form. In fact, memory is not mentioned at all, as if narrative (and not only historical narrative) were not parasitic upon remembering and forgetting. With the introduction of memory, formidable new questions arise. If history is contingent upon the memory of individuals, as the commonsense view presupposes, is historical writing merely a narrative decoding of fragmented personal memories, memory writ large? And, furthermore, what is the value of either memory or history if, as Nietzsche sometimes seems to argue, life is better served by forgetting than remembering? Is human existence not torn between the impetus to get on with it, to be rid of the ball and chain of *Nachträglichkeit*, of what comes later, as Nietzsche advises, on the one hand and, on the other, the desire to speak for the dead, who cannot speak for themselves?

Some historical narratives contain breaks in structure that I shall call their discursive space of authorization. Such spaces are often signaled by specific formulae, such as the announcement in Exodus "I am that I am." The formula is a warning that there is a blank in the narrative that points to the governance of the events it recounts by that which is altogether outside the narrative. These blank spaces are the placeholders of revelation, a kind of white light that, unlike the formulae that announce them, illuminate the events recounted without ever becoming the focus of visibility. What is more, narratives so authorized are *eo ipso* historical in that they appeal to the veridical character of the remembered material. Like the canonical documents of the historical world religions, mythical narratives derive their force from their discursive space of authorization. The suspension of time within the world of myth and ritual, the *in illo tempore* property of myth described by Mircea Eliade, is in actuality an appeal to the uprightness of memory, an effort by a community, in Aristotle's terms, "to recapture the thing that has been." Even those myths most susceptible to synchronic articulation are promissory notes redeemable on stipulated occasions by recitation or reenactment, attesting: "Thus it was with the god(s) or ancestors."

In what follows I shall inquire first into the meaning of past time and the writing of history. Next, I shall consider the question of memory, especially the materialist challenge to traditional accounts with, perhaps, some surprising outcomes. Finally, I shall discuss the relation of revelation to memory and history.

Past Time

From the everyday perspective, what once existed but exists no longer (or at least not in the same way) belongs to the past, a past that is irrecoverable and, a fortiori, unchangeable. Events cannot be lived in the manner of firstness, in their *Leibhaftigkeit*, but only as gray replicas of what they once were. At best, they can be relived in memory. Like the reconstruction of old cities ravaged by war or time and recreated by urban plastic surgery, memories might be regarded as plaster casts of the past. Conventional wisdom suggests that one may remember and restore the past or forget and deny it, but one concedes that what was has passed away. The conventional view is sufficiently pragmatic to recognize the hopelessness of nostalgia by conceding the past's irretrievability. But both the yearning for *Wiederholen*, bringing back what was, and the realization that the past is gone are grounded in the same view of time: the past is imagined, on the one hand, as an entity, *en bloc*, as everything that was, and, on the other hand, as made up of measurable and articulated "now-points" that nest, as it were, in time.

Heidegger describes this everyday standpoint as parasitic upon a more fundamental understanding of temporality. Challenging this view of the past in his by now familiar critique of hypostatized time, he shows that human existence is lived not as a series of discrete now-points that pass by but rather as an *ecstasis*, a reaching forward out of itself toward the existent's own nonbeing. Life is lived in anticipation of death: not as something not yet present, for death will never be present to someone, but rather as not being able to be anywhere. Hegel already notices the importance of human mortality in deriving other expressions of nonbeing, for example, logical negation. But if for Hegel the negative is ultimately transcended, for Heidegger the human being is "thrown," suspended over the abyss of its own nonexistence, oriented by its own projected nonbeing. The critical point I want to note is that, because death orients human existence in time, for Heidegger the most primordial mode of time is the future (*BT*, 377).

What, then, of the past? It cannot remain unaffected by a life that is configured toward the future. The past, too, must be governed by this structure in that the "I" who existed before is the being who *even then* looked ahead, *even then* was always already thrown over the abyss of its own nonexistence (ibid., 376). For Heidegger, the future, with its structure of anticipation and possibility, prevailed in one's past thoughts and acts just as it does now (ibid., 437). Thus the past is not the temporal modification of some static content. To overstate the case (but only by a hair), it is as if the content of the past is merely incidental to displaying the past's relation to the future: the past *für uns* (for us) is what is behind us but the past *für sich* (of itself) is, as it were, always already ahead of itself.

Heidegger is right to insist that the everyday view of time is blind to its grounding in existence as a giving oneself over to time, right to conclude that nonbeing is encountered in death. But what has been passed over in his thought is the primacy of the past in determining the structure of time. The significance of the past has likewise remained hidden in both Bergson's and Husserl's accounts of time. Despite the importance of Bergson's discovery of *durée* ("lived time," the time of human experience over and against measurable or clock time) and Husserl's uncovering of the stretched character of the present moment—of its retentions, what is preserved of past moments, and protentions, or forward-stretching anticipations that cling to the instant—the role of the past in configuring temporality has been covered over.

I want to argue that the past first comes to the fore as a split, a scission, a fissure in the world as a spatially organized assemblage. The spatial world as a material nexus is what, at least hypothetically, can be made visible by stationing oneself so that access is gained to a place or object that is currently out of sight. The world also offers itself as resistance that can be materially overcome. A rock that is too heavy can be moved with a lever. But that which has gone by cannot be brought back materially: no, not, never. *"It was" is the unsurpassable negation that breaks into the materiality of the world*. That which opens up through this negation, the past, appears to offer itself to my grasp, appears to be *entitative*, but it can only return as word or image. The "no, not, never" is not merely a mode of time's disclosure, one of time's *ecstases*, to use Heidegger's term, but is time as the break thrown open by the world between itself and itself in the mode of "It was before but cannot be again."

Still, all this is not yet as strange as I think it needs to become if the relation of memory and history is to be explicated. If the claims for the primordiality of the past are such that time and the "not" are practically commutable, or interchangeable, terms, how is the future to be interpreted? Is not the future also a mode of temporality? On the face of it, the future would seem to be as primordial as the past because it, too, is bound up with the "not" in the form of "not yet."

But the "not yet" rests upon, requires, what went before. This is not to preclude the emergence of novelty but rather to suggest that the "before" is a necessary but not a sufficient condition for emergent being. That the future requires the past is obvious, but how is the past to be taken up into the future?

The past, the "not" expressed as the irrecoverability of what has gone by, I have suggested, is experienced as retained, as imprinted or stored, metaphors, kept as image and word. Memory is not something apart from the ongoing experience of retrieval but is the process of bringing back what was previously encoded. Even if, *per hypothesi*, some original "scene" could be replicated, the gap that opens between first and second occasions creates an unsurpassable difference between them. It would be meaningless to speak of origins here because access to the past is constituted after the fact. Firstness is conferred in the very act of remembering. Thus the statement "I was at the Grand Canyon last summer" means I am now conferring at a remove the first flush of that experience. Upon analysis, language about the past is second-order discourse but without any first-order level to which definitive appeal can be made. If this is so, there is something truly artful in ordinary memory: just as Proust or Joyce work to "disentangle" or "reembody" past events, "setting up a resonance between two objects [to produce] an epiphany,"[4] so too memory works post hoc to body forth the past.

It could be argued against the claim for the primordiality of the past that existence is lived as an annihilation of possibles, and that the future rather than the past is the field of possibility. Yet are not acts of memory selective interpretations generated by negating possible articulations of the past based on criteria of relevance for the present? The past does not give itself all at once as spectacle before an absolute subject, but is disclosed by the "not" that is imprinted, in Derrida's phrase, *sous rature*, under erasure, in what is actually imaged and told. Memory holds before itself what will take shape as the remembered past. *To remember is to grasp occurrences in the manner of holding in front of oneself not only that which was but that which could have been.* It is this double disclosiveness of memory, its inclusion of paths not taken, that places possibility within the conspectus of the past.

The proposition "I stayed home last summer" is not merely a statement of fact but suggests many rejected possibles: my staying home may reflect a decision to avoid preparation for a camping trip or turning down an opportunity to see Eastern Europe once again, along with numerous other rejected options. Remembering is a hermeneutical act whose grammatical structure, the indicative "it was," is, as it were, the limiting case of the counterfactual conditional "It could have been but was not," which circumscribes it. In sum, possibility's connection to the future is parasitic upon its relation to the past: what is held before memory is experienced as that which occurred, surrounded by a penumbra of negated possibles, which are expressed in the grammatical form of the counterfactual conditional.

Memory's retrieval of the past as a selection of negated possibles is governed by a desire to recover the past *wie es eigentlich gewesen war*, to retrieve the truth of the past as it really was. If, in the commonsense view, memory cannot replicate the past, it can at least strive for an accurate approximation of past events. But better and worse approximations depend upon prior standards of exactitude, which already presuppose the transparency of language toward the being of the past. If the past is to be retrieved, the "not of that which can never be made present," the past's ungroundedness, must be intrinsic to that which is recovered. If remembering that which was is delimited by what could not have been, not even on the broadest interpretation, then retrieval must proceed by way of exclusion. Thus, for example, the Grand Canyon might be remembered either as an example of early geological stratification resulting from glacial melting or as the way the world must have looked when it issued from the hand of God, but never as an island in the middle of the Pacific. "It was thus and so" is, as it were, memory's reaching for the limiting case, for that which is not ruled out by "It could not have been thus."

But there is further significance in attributing the establishment of "veridical" memory to acts of exclusion. To assert that which could not have been as that which was or is is self-deception or deception of the other, even if unintended. Deception — and this is the point — is an ethical matter, so that the discursive space of memory is always already an ethical space. But if, as I argued earlier, neither word nor image render the past transparent, represent it, truth-telling is undermined from the start. To be sure, intersubjective communication is possible at a pragmatic level as an encoding and decoding of signs. But the truthfulness of one to another is always already traduced, so that guilt toward another is always already incurred by virtue of the original sin of language: the impossibility of a purely transparent language that would render discursive rectitude possible. The historian will be caught by the imperative to tell the truth and the impossibility of conveying it.[5] On the face of it, this would appear to eliminate historical accountability. Not so. The historian is bound by the negative grounding of historical narrative: "It could not have been thus."

Before adumbrating this issue, a consideration of some recent materialist interpretations of memory, which may at first appear to bear little resemblance to my treatment of memory thus far, should prove important both for their suggestiveness and for their surprising convergence with my textual/hermeneutical account in some significant respects.

Remembering

I should like to sketch briefly two quite different materialist views of memory that bear on the problem of memory's relation to history. The first is a materialistic monism posited in the interest of what can be thought of as a unified field theory of the real, one that is consistent with the ontology of modern physics and from which consciousness is not excluded. By naturalizing consciousness it purports to demystify and liberate conscious phenomena such as remembering from an oppressive metaphysical matrix. The second is a materialism grounded in social philosophy that tries to show how the products of a materially construed mind can be commodified.

According to the more radical versions of the first view of memory, conscious phenomena are nothing more than the effects of the brain's activities, just as material objects are nothing more than the nuclear particles that go to make them up. Much of the effort to render this position plausible consists in decoding the language of sensations, thoughts, and memories and encoding it into brain process language. Because there are numerous difficulties in positing a straightforward identity of brain state and mental state, some radical materialists argue it is better to examine the conditions that justify ascribing mental states to people but insist that the conditions of ascription themselves be observable material conditions. Thus, what is observable is not likely to be simple behavior, for example, withdrawing one's hand from the fire, screaming, and so on as justifying the imputing of the term "burning sensation." Rather, to clinch matters, it is thought better to examine complex neurophysiological data to justify the ascription of pain.

Radical materialists reject the Cartesian view that there is some switching station where mind and body communicate and that a single consciousness masterminds the process. Instead, it is argued that mind is nothing more than a multiplicity of information-processing bits, that consciousness is not a special faculty but a qualitative enhancement of bits that are already there.[6] Daniel Dennett, a leading exponent of this position, contends that what is there are memes, complex ideas that form themselves into memorable units, ideas such as wheel, wearing clothes, a sonata, chess, or calculus. "Borne by language . . . 'images' and other data structures, take up residence in an individual brain . . . thereby turning it into a mind."[7] Their evolutionary utility explains the endurance of some memes rather than others.

It could be objected that higher mental processes, such as remembering, are not like the "ouch" of a burning sensation, which can be reduced to neurological mechanisms. Dennett argues, to the contrary, that the increased complexity of a mental process requires no special explanation. "There is no single definitive 'stream of consciousness,' because there is no central headquarters . . . where it all comes together. . . . Instead of such a single stream there are multiple channels in which specialist circuits try . . . to do various things, creating Multiple Drafts as they go. Most . . . are short lived . . . but some get promoted to further functional roles," which accord with higher-order mental processes.[8] But what explains the experience of consciousness? This, Dennett thinks, can be explained in terms of "memory-loading" and "broadcasting," which bring previous learning to bear upon current problems. That these features seem to be the effect of an occult consciousness is, he argues, a magical trick or illusion created by nature.[9]

In the case of memory, there is a special relationship to time: the content is inseparable from its pastness. What physical descriptions could cover the before and after, the sequentiality of experience? For the radical materialist the question dissolves. There are only changes in movement and location in various parts of the brain, changes that do not converge anywhere. At some point, Dennett contends, "the corner is turned from the timing of representations to the representation of timing."[10]

According to a second materialist view, the neo-Marxism of Jean-François Lyotard—to oversimplify the matter somewhat— information is knowledge, and knowledge is capital. What is more, if brains or their electronic memory surrogates are knowledge-producing technologies, they too must be construed as commodities. For Lyotard, the last phase of the historical process eventuates in the stockpiling of information and an ever-increasing reliance on technologies of data processing. Unlike Dennett, for whom the multiple channels of computer models provide analogies for brain activities, what is crucial for Lyotard is the potential of these technologies to *supplant* brain processes. By controlling memorizing, the new technologies eliminate time-bound difference by compressing temporally separate events into a single time, a detemporalization that need not depend on brain conditions.[11] In short, by creating autonomous systems unconstrained by brain activity, by human corporeality, the contemporary economy creates memory borne by hardware, memory without a body. Lyotard writes:

> Among the material complexes we know, the human brain is the most capable of producing complexity . . . as the production of the new technologies proves. . . .
>
> And yet its own survival requires that it be fed by a body, which . . . can survive only in the conditions of life on earth. . . . one of the essential objectives of research today is to overcome the obstacle that the body places in the way of the development of communicational technologies, i.e. the new extended memory.[12]

In the past, Lyotard contends, "ethnocultures" conserved information by gathering up dispersed local memories into historical narrative, so that narrative itself became a technical apparatus for converting the emotional charge of events into meaning and information.[13] Far from considering the new technologies a sign of progress, Lyotard decries "the barbarism, illiteracy and impoverishment of language [and] . . . remodelling of opinion" he believes they have created. The electronic global information network, Lyotard claims, will dispose of the memories of culturally borne narratives so "that in the last analysis it [global memory] is nobody's memory,"[14] just as Dennett's memes are, in the end, nobody's memes but simply information that takes up residence in a mind. Lyotard's materialism, unlike that of Dennett; is shot through with pessimism. The Hegelian subject is regenerated in materialist guise as a repressive "cosmic memory . . . of which Leibniz could have said . . . it is on the way to producing a monad much more complete than humanity itself was ever able to be."[15]

Memory, Text, and Revelation

Two models of memory familiar in the history of philosophy, first invoked in Plato's *Theaetetus*, undergird the contemporary materialisms I have considered, that of memory as a kind of pictographic writing or imprint (the memes and multiple drafts of Dennett's analysis) and that of memory as a storehouse, in Lyotard's account. According to the imprint paradigm, a block of wax is imagined as implanted in the mind of each human being such that the wax tablet is held before a thought or perception that is to be recalled. The wax receives the impression "as from the seal of a ring" and retains it. If the imprint is effaced, the perception or thought is lost or forgotten; if incoming data is identified with an imprint with which it does not coincide, this mismatching counts as error.[16] In the second paradigm, the mind is an aviary that warehouses birds, while the birds themselves represent kinds of knowledge. One sort of knowledge is that which is learned in order to be stored for future use, knowledge that is "prior to possession," and the other knowledge that is possessed already and can be fetched up at will.[17]

Consider first Lyotard's account of the storehouse model as an ever-expanding memory bank that stores information to be retrieved in the interest of attaining a purchase upon time by neutralizing events, stopping that flow of time, gathering and conserving what is extended in time as a single, temporally flattened stock of information. Lyotard writes: "What is already known cannot . . . be experienced as an event. Consequently, if one wants to control a process, the best way of so doing is to subordinate the present to what is (still) called the 'future' since in these conditions the 'future' will be completely predetermined."[18]

Lyotard's description can be viewed as providing a postmodern context for envisaging what Levinas calls "totality"—the sociopolitical whole dominated by war and violence, in which individuals, unknown to themselves, are reduced to being the bearers of forces that command them and from which they derive their meaning (*TI*, 21). His version of the storehouse view brings to the fore what enables the totality to continue in postmodernity, the *memory* of totality, one in which historical narratives are encoded in structures that pre-empt their diversity. Highlighted in Lyotard's description is a cosmic memory that produces its own meta-narratives, suppressing, in Dennett's terms, multiple drafts, the multitrack interpretations of sensory input.

Narratives generated by the totality attempt to acquire the sort of consensus sought by science.[19] Thus, they do not gain their truth from what I have described as history's mode of negation: the constraint imposed upon historical narrative by the condition "It could have been w, x, or y, but it could not have been z." Instead, the meta-narratives I have identified with the concept of totality become necessary narratives written in the mode of "it could only have been thus."

Whereas Lyotard's account is helpful in grasping the linguistic turn in the process of totalization, my earlier remarks about experience as time-bound and about the primordiality of past time would seem to preclude finding any utility in Dennett's model of memory. In fact, his account of time is seriously flawed in that he can be shown to assume one of the central claims he is challenging, the claim that experience presupposes temporal comprehension. If everything can be explained in terms of change in movement and location in various parts of the brain and the "corner is somehow turned" from sequentiality to the representation of time as Dennett alleges, movement and location suggest that time is something actual, like material objects that existed earlier but are understood later. But if time is not like material objects, as Dennett acknowledges, the predication of sequentiality that enables the corner "somehow" to be turned trades on some sort of ongoing awareness of time all along.

What stands fast in Dennett's account is, first, his assertion that there is no "central headquarters" where everything comes together in consciousness and, second, that multiple channels produce multiple drafts of what is remembered. The past does not manifest itself all at once as spectacle before a subject but is imprinted, in Derrida's phrase, *sous rature*, in that which is actually imaged and told. What is ineliminable and right in Dennett's modeling of memory is its scriptic character, a point he explicitly acknowledges: "The Multiple Drafts model makes 'writing it down' in memory criterial for consciousness; that is *what it is* for the 'given' to be 'taken'—to be taken one way rather than another."[20]

But if memory is scriptic, it can be reinscribed in another interpretive framework, that of writing and text. In a brief aside, Dennett astonishingly appropriates the tongue-in-cheek version of Derrida's position described in David Lodge's novel *Nice Work* as simply a more outré version of his own, suggesting that the Derridean character in the novel and he think alike: "There is no 'Self' . . . a finite or unique soul or essence that constitutes a person's identity . . . there are no origins, there is only production, we produce ourselves in language."[21] Dennett refers to this position as "semiotic materialism."[22] There is no reason why, from history's metonymic perspective, the subject position of the historical narrator cannot be seen as dispersed in an infinite web of memes. My point is that not only can the materialist reading of consciousness not escape the hermeneutical issues raised by the linguisticality of mind but that, without this built-in textual or scriptic character, its account of mind would exclude all but a description of electro-magnetic impulses.[23]

What happens when the text of memory is recorded in the narrative exegetics of the historian? Is there a simple doubling of the exegetical field, or does something outside the text command the historian's rememoration? And if so, does this *hors texte*, history's outside, the discursive space of authorization, have any bearing on the relation of history to revelation? I suggested earlier that the blank space in historical narratives that points to the governance of the events they recount by that which is altogether exterior to the narrative is the discursive space of revelation. In the case of what I have called "concentrated revelation," the entire narrative is tendered as standing under the authority of what transcends it. In such narratives, as Franz Rosenzweig wrote in a letter to Martin Buber, "The primary content of revelation is revelation itself." The falling into language of revelation, even the language of the first person proclamation of transcendent presence, the "I am" of Exodus, is always already "the beginning of interpretation."[24]

I want, however, to insist that not only historical narratives that profess revelatory status but historical narratives generally should be construed as revelatory texts. Being the narrator for the dead others who cannot be made present, who belong to an irrecoverable past, the historian becomes accountable for them. She or he works at both being and not being the others, enters into the texture of their age but at the same time remains cognizant not only of their temporal distance but of their otherness, which resists narrative encapsulation.

To see how the resistance of the other is bound up with revelation, it may be useful to inquire first into the practice of history. How does the historian *qua* historian, whose task is descriptive yet who stands commanded by absent others, go about practicing her or his professional task? In considering these questions it may be useful to think of the historian as governed by something like the method proposed in Jorge Luis Borges's tale about re-creating Cervantes's *Don Quixote*. According to "Pierre Menard, Author of the Quixote," the contemporary writer first "essays variations of a formal or psychological type," or what I earlier described as the metonymic dimension of history, a free, speculative variation in the form "It could have been *w*, *x*, or *y*." Second, the writer "sacrifice[s] these variations to the 'original' text and reason[s] out this annihilation in an irrefutable manner,"[25] what I should like to call the moment of historical elenchus: "it could not have been thus." The first is history's metonymic, the second its deictic moment, each indispensable. Metonymy operates in accordance with the Derridean logic of the supplement: the moment of difference, narrative ambiguity, addition, improvisation, and the subliminal. Without it, historical memory would assume the perspective of the totality, in Lyotard's terms, mere atemporal retrieval of facts. Deprived of the deictic moment, the historian, unrestricted by the laws of discourse, would enter a realm of fantasy, become deaf to the command of the dead to show that "It could not have been thus."

Still, it may be asked, ought the other's sheer externality be taken as tantamount to transcendence as understood in the documents of concentrated revelation? What could justify such an audacious comparison? It can only be justified by beginning with the premise that the historian, as the one who recounts that which was, stands under judgment. Entrusted by her or his calling to become custodian of the past, the historian is judged not only by the standards of what is thought of as historical scholarship, immersion in place and period, but in turn by what sanctions them: the demand of the absent dead that the historian avoid deception by honoring the limit condition of historical writing, the "not" of the past: "It could not have been thus." The concept "the judgment of history" is altogether different from the concept "historical narrative that stands under judgment." The first reflects a verdict of history's winners in the struggle of historical forces. The second assumes that history is judged in accordance with the claims of dead others. Although I am far from endorsing Nietzsche's position in his account of the uses and abuses of history, his caution is worth noting: "Who compels you to judge? If it is your wish—you must prove first that you are capable of justice. As judges you must stand higher than that which is to be judged; as it is you only have come later."[26]

How does this standing under judgment manifest itself in the writing of history? Not in the metonymic aspect of history, through which history can become fantasy, nor in its deictic side, the moment of reasoned calculation that would return history to a standard of truth based on the transparency of language and to a naturalistic ontology. But the deictic aspect of history, in honoring the "not" of the past by effecting the historical elenchus, "It could not have been thus," situates itself by reference to that which cannot be incorporated into the narrative, the command of dead others that transcends narrative intention, is in excess of it, exterior. This is not simple exteriority—the dead other cannot be incorporated into my interpretive framework or into any system of signs—but rather an excess that opens the dimension of the more, of an unincorporable infinite. In Levinas's terms, "judgment is the act of situating by reference to infinity" (*TI*, 240). The invisible dead undo or unwrite the predicative and iterative historical narrative in the blank space that is the placeholder, in historical writing, of an infinite transcendence.

17

Exemplary Individuals
Toward a Phenomenological Ethics

Efforts to develop a phenomenological ethics have until now begun from two altogether different starting points. The first, a tack taken by Max Scheler, Nicolai Hartmann, and others, assumes that values are instantiated in the world and have properties that open them to intuitive grasp. Values are independent in being and accessible to us without being attached to things.[1] The second starts with the embodied existent's actual encounters with other persons and finds in these transactions an empirical locus for what is prescribed or forbidden in the moral realm. Levinas turns to the experience of the other to develop a phenomenology of social existence in which concrete interactions with others disclose a sphere of responsibility prior to ethical language or action (*TI*, 194–216). The first approach pre-supposes that values, like classes or kinds, are real, even if they are never actualized in particular objects or situations. Values may be simultaneously disclosed as universal and essential or as possibly but not necessarily inhering in specific phenomenologically revealed experiences. But once values are separable from concrete phenomena and can be intuited apart from context, they function as metaphysical constructs accounting for perceived identities. By contrast, the second phenomenological approach uncovers concrete social phenomena and precludes hypostatized values, a course that necessitates a language that disarticulates, "vibrates and disjoins" in conformity with what it manifests (*VI*, 10). The problem of generality is not avoided, but a new mode of generality, which precedes the reification of universals—goodness, justice, and the like—is exhibited. I shall call this type of generality *carnal generality*, a conception developed *nolens volens*, as it were, in the work of Levinas and Merleau-Ponty, and I will call the phenomena that exhibit it *carnal generals*. Because carnal generality is rarely thematized in post-Husserlian phenomenology, it must be tracked down in the contexts in which it occurs, a process not unlike that through which carnal generality originally emerges.

In what follows, I address three problems: first, using the phenomenological strategies of Merleau-Ponty and Levinas, I describe how the conditions of embodied existence make carnal generality possible. Second, I turn to paradigmatic lives both within and outside of recognized religious traditions and show how such lives function as carnal generals. Finally, I examine some competing claims that my own might mistakenly be thought to resemble—Nelson Goodman's view that an account of samples can serve to show how conduct is exemplary, and Alasdair MacIntyre's contention that a community's consensus about what moral properties are to be prized, what are to count as virtues, can serve as the ground for resolving ethical disputes—and suggest reasons for preferring a phenomenological account of exemplary lives.

Transcendental Structures of the Moral Life

The notion of carnal generality arises in the work of both Merleau-Ponty and Levinas in connection with the search for access to meaning that cannot be incorporated in concepts because concepts presuppose a logos "more fundamental than the logos of objective thought endowing the latter with its relative validity" (*PP*, 365). For Merleau-Ponty, generality is inscribed in the incarnate subject, an ensemble of self-transcending acts and lingual capacities. By contrast, Levinas focuses on the alterity of other persons and its impact upon the self, an alterity that cannot be brought into conceptual focus by language. Both agree that the psycho-physiological primordium that is the incarnate subject expresses a generality of which universals and essences are derivative types.

This distinctive mode of generality, carnal generality, is exhibited by context-specific complexes, carnal generals. It is important to distinguish the latter term from two others that influenced both Levinas and Merleau-Ponty, with which it might therefore be confused: Hegel's concrete universals and Husserl's material essences.[2] Levinas provides a full account of Husserl's philosophy of essences in *The Theory of Intuition in Husserl's Phenomenology*.[3]

Carnal generality is not exhibited by concrete universals, self-particularizing or self-specifying universals, because these express the self-development of the whole, the Absolute, and as such do not require human corporeality as an unsurpassable condition for thought and language. Similarly, the term *carnal general* is not an equivalent for material essence, a designation for the structural limits of an object, which, when surpassed, entail the object's destruction. The term *material essence* can apply only to the body as object, not to the body as incarnate subject (*PP*, 203ff.).

In his analyses of social existence, Merleau-Ponty speaks of essences and occasionally of carnal essences, intelligible structures whose meaning comes to light through successive exfoliations of the context in which they are embedded. He attributes positive significance to the term *essence*, preferring it to *universal* because, for him, universals derive from a spectator theory of knowledge, a gaze without a body. What universals gain in comprehensiveness they lose in complexity, the capacity to express lived experience. The term *carnal generality* is almost never used. It occurs, so far as I know, in a manner relevant for the present context only once, in connection with his account of living conversation. Dialogue, he argues, introduces a new dimension into language, the encounter with other persons as the precondition of communication. The other with whom I speak is another myself: "Language is founded upon the phenomenon of the mirror, ego, alter-ego, or of the echo, in other words of a *carnal generality*" (my emphasis).[4] This generality is constituted by the power of the self to inhabit the body of the other. Language is the "magic machine" that effects this mobility, makes carnal generality possible, and is its expression. Together the other and I form an ensemble of significations, a single flesh that is traversed by and expresses meaning.

The blurring of the distinction between self and other is parasitic upon a more primordial relation, that of visible and invisible. The elements of this dyad are inseparable from the start and constitute the field where carnal generality arises. This field is a primordium of sensibility prior to the subject/object distinction. The difference between perceiver and perceived, subject and other, loosens and shifts. There is an overlap between the body sensing and the body sensed, looking and being looked at. Body and world intersect in a "chiasmatic," a crossing. But there is also a difference within this unity of the visible field that bypasses the mind/matter and substance/property distinctions:

> To designate it we should need the old term "element" in the sense it was used to speak of water, air, earth, and fire, that is, in the sense of a *general thing*, midway between the spatiotemporal individual and the idea, a sort of incarnate principle that brings a style of being wherever there is a fragment of being. The flesh is in this sense an "element" of being. (*VI*, 139)

For Levinas, while the difference between subject and object is overcome in cognition, the breach between self and other is unsurpassable. This difference, rather than the resemblance between self and other and the ontic parity of the two that it presupposes, is what opens discourse. While Merleau-Ponty grasps the significance of prediscursive corporeality for the emergence of generality, he suppresses the condition of difference between self and other, which, for reasons that will become clear later, makes the ethical relation possible.

Levinas, like Merleau-Ponty, uses the term *universal* to denote a derivative form of generality, the unity of classes or kinds. Still, for him authentic generality depends not on shared properties but on other persons, who open up the possibility for generality: "The relation with the other does not only stimulate, provoke generalization, does not only supply it with the pretext and the occasion . . . but is this generalization itself. Generalization is a universalization—but universalization is not the entry of a sensible thing into a no-man's land of the ideal" (*TI*, 173–74). The ideality of genus is parasitic upon concrete relations with others rather than the converse. Intersubjective encounter, together with its conditions of emergence, constitutes the space in which carnal generals are manifested. In what follows, I shall treat carnal generality both eidetically, as the structure of some material condition, and genetically, as an expression of its emergence in some specific context.

The Face

Carnal generals are meaning complexes that require material conditions for their emergence but express more than is revealed in their sensible content. The human face is a carnal general, a premier instance of a corporeal complex whose meaning is wider than its sensible form. Rilke, Max Picard, and Sartre already mark off the face as a unique bodily locus for expressing exemplification.[5]

While the face is rarely thematized in Merleau-Ponty's work, he comments on its meaning in an arresting passage that occurs in the context of defending significant wholes as basic units of meaning:

> The human signification is given before the alleged sensible sign. A face is a center of human expression, the transparent envelope of the attitudes and desires of others, the place of manifestation, the barely material support for a multitude of intentions. That is why it is impossible for us to treat a face or a body, even a dead body, like a thing. They are sacred entities, not the "givens of sight."[6]

The face is not an ensemble of its elements—eyes, mouth, nose and so on—but exists first as expression. Only afterward do the elements fall into place as elements tending toward this expressive end. It is also given as being different from things, so much so that there is something sacred about faces. The "sacrality" of the face consists in its being the "transparent envelope" of the inner life of the other, the locale where interior and exterior horizons meet.

For Levinas, the face introduces a radically new dimension into the field of phenomena. The primary meaning of the face is not its transparency toward the ensemble of meanings that constitute the other's inner life but "as resisting possession of one's own power" (*TI*, 197ff.). The face of the other person addresses one, solicits a relation with it that is ethical. It is given "in its nudity" both from a height as a "magisterial" presence, a presence that teaches, and in nearness as need soliciting caritas. The face is itself nondiscursive but provides a warranty for discourse; the latter is defined structurally as a system of signs. For Levinas, Merleau-Ponty understands the unity of thinking and speaking but not the origin of discourse in the ethical: "Merleau-Ponty among others and better than others, showed that disincarnate thought thinking speech before speaking it . . . was a myth. Already thought consists in foraging in the system of signs in the particular tongue of a people" (*TI*, 206). Despite important differences between them concerning the character of intersubjectivity, Levinas commends Merleau-Ponty for his attentive reading of the fifth of Husserl's *Cartesian Meditations* because Levinas sees in this text, despite Husserl's egocentric frame of reference, a break with the egological constitution of other persons. Thus for Merleau-Ponty thought is the extension of the "I can" of the body.[7]

Levinas contrasts Merleau-Ponty's account of signs with his own view: "It is not the mediation of the sign that forms signification, but signification (whose primordial event is the face-to-face) that makes the sign function possible" (*TI*, 206). The face is the warranty for language: it means more than can be discursively given and lies beyond discourse. It is the incarnation of a generality that is supra rather than infra discursive. The face expresses generality not by suppressing individuation but by stressing singularity and differentiation: each and every face is a discrete term that proscribes the killing of the other. This proscription cannot be stated in the form of a categorical imperative because it is not a formal principle that can function in the absence of faces. Such a proscription can offer no criteria for deciding conflicts of interest that must be settled by jurisprudence, for Levinas the most significant of human discourses. Primordial generality expressed in the basic proscription opened up by the sensible configuration of the human countenance links up with other acts, such as gift-giving, that exhibit a derivative but authentic generality. Such linkage is possible because the face of the other challenges one's inalienable right to property and to enjoyment of the world and propels one toward generosity. Private satisfaction is subordinated to the other's need.

Levinas goes so far as to derive the possibility of general terms from the imperative imposed by faces to relinquish one's own individual satisfaction. He argues that, when we desire something, the object of desire is singular. Even if it is quantitiatively plural, it is, when desired, construed as something unitary, in conformity with the desire whose satisfaction is sought. Objects become general only when seen as possible objects of satisfaction for others. "The generality of the object is correlative with the generosity of the subject" (*TI*, 76). The apprehension of general meanings is primordially an ethical and only secondarily a cognitive act.

The temporal structure of the manner in which the face is apprehended differs from the time scheme of presence that characterizes consciousness. The face is a datum that comes from elsewhere and whose origin is irrecoverable, a completed past in the trace of transcendence, "the breaking point but also the binding place" (*OB*, 12). It exhibits the track or spoor of an archaic transcendence or, alternatively, from my point of view but not that of Levinas, the track of the totality of humankind or of all sentient beings, past, present, and future, none of which can be brought into plenary presence. In some religious traditions—to an extent in Franciscan piety, in some forms of Judaism, and in Buddhism, among others, the trace is of the latter type.

Hagiography and Phenomenology of Saints' Lives

Levinas describes the transcendental structure of ethical existence, the primordial features of social transactions that make moral life possible, but his account does not address the question of why some persons violate the claims of alterity, while some make such claims central. Why do those whose lives are structured responses to the needs of others react as they do when encountering the claims of alterity? What role do such persons play in the lives of those to whom they respond and in social existence generally?

Some unique features of saintly lives may be brought to light with the help of an unlikely analogy. The psychologist Oliver Sacks recounts how a pair of idiot savant twins, "undersized with disproportionately large hands, monotonous squeaky voices, a variety of peculiar ticks and mannerisms, and a very high degenerative myopia," would engage in a "singular and purely numerical conversation,"[8] a mathematical game in which they exceeded the competence of the most sophisticated mathematicians. Astounded, Sacks watched as one uttered a prime number and waited for the other to respond with the next prime number until they were exchanging twenty figure primes. He concluded that the twins did not form abstract notions of numbers but experienced them in some sensuous and immediate way. Even if they depended upon algorithms, these too were envisioned spatially rather than algebraically: "They . . . dwell among strange scenes of numbers they create dramaturgically, a whole world made of numbers. They have . . . a most singular imagination—and not the least of its singularities is that it can imagine only numbers. . . . They see them as a vast natural scene."[9]

Saints are not unlike this: they are idiot savants of the ethical, although, in contrast to the twins, they often possess considerable psychological acuity, as well as remarkable powers of political and social organization. The English word *saint*, as well as Romance language equivalents, derives from the Latin *sanctum*, dedicated or set apart for the worship of deity. Thus, in the Western Christian tradition a linguistic link connects saints with theistic belief. I shall, however, define the saint as one whose adult life in its entirety is devoted to the alleviation of sorrow (psychological suffering) and pain (physical suffering) that afflict other persons without distinction of rank or group or, alternatively, that afflict sentient beings, whatever the cost in pain or sorrow to him or herself. In this view, theistic belief may, but need not be, a component of the saint's belief system.

Mysticism in its multiple expressions has also been of the greatest historical importance in providing the conceptual language for the moral vision I have described. I argue, however, that, despite the claims of many saints to have had unmediated experiences of some divine power or source, not all saints are mystics nor are all mystics saints. In fact, it is central to my thesis that, though many who lead or have led selfless lives are or were mystics and theists, and some (such as Dorothy Day or Mother Theresa) were or are at least theists, Buddhists as well as contemporary post-Christian nonbelievers perform or have performed selfless acts in prisons, slave labor and concentration camps, epidemics, and wars that meet the criteria I propose. Moreover, I also believe it is possible to develop a conception of saintliness that can survive modern and postmodern criticism, such as that of Feuerbach, Marx, Nietzsche, and Freud. Here I can address such criticism only tangentially. I hope instead to uncover the singularities, the landscapes of saintly imagination by, as Sacks said of the idiot savant twins, "observing them with a full and sympathetic phenomenological openness, as they think and interact . . . pursuing their own lives spontaneously in their own singular way."[10]

With several noteworthy exceptions, few recent theologians have examined the relevance of saints' lives for moral philosophy.[11] In part, this is the result of the modern psychological and sociological criticisms of altruism alluded to earlier, but it is also a consequence of contemporary text-critical sophistication. The lives of saints transmitted by religious traditions as idealized biography or autobiography are constructed artifacts, the social products of already well-developed institutional and theological frameworks. Because these texts are, in the Western Jewish and Christian traditions, so often bound up with mystical doctrines, it is worth noting some interpretive strictures that have been proposed in connection with the comparative study of mystical texts in order to determine whether they affect any consideration of saints' lives. Arguing against an older generation of theorists, such as W. T. Stace, R. C. Zaehner, and William James, who endorse a common core of mystical experience that cuts across cultural and theological lines, these investigations support a difference in experience as well as in doctrinal claims. Thus Carl A. Keller suggests an analysis of literary genres to pinpoint thematic and stylistic differences in accounts of mystical experience, while Steven Katz argues that specific religious traditions influence not only post-experiential reports of the mystic but also define in advance what the mystic will hear, see, or feel.[12]

A seeming uniformity of expression may conceal differences in experience and underlying doctrine, so that such terms as *God, being, union,* or *nothingness* become vacuous in the absence of supporting context. These caveats provide an important corrective to earlier studies, which presume a common core of experiences, such as merging with an absolute center of power and goodness, a claim not always present in reports of experiences that match in other respects. Still, if experiences are defined only intrareligiously, any effort at comparison is foreclosed. While the warnings I have cited remain pertinent in considering mystical texts, they are less crucial in analyzing saints' lives and utterances. Once the distinction between mystic and saint is drawn, the saint's experience can be considered in terms of his or her actual or envisioned acts. These are, of course, incorporated into a conceptual framework, but, more important, they are articulated within a context anchored in human need, and therefore one that remains relatively constant. The description of saintly life suggested earlier—self-sacrifice for the alleviation of the suffering of persons and/or sentient beings in disregard of the cost to the saint's own life—is also distinct from the criteria for canonization within the Roman Catholic Church, although many whose cults are institutionally sanctioned fulfill the proposed criteria. For this reason, attention to the hagiographic literature of several religious traditions, despite its formulaic and idealizing tendencies, may be rewarding.

In the Christian tradition, two strands in the literature describing the experiences of saints are often intertwined. These must be distinguished in order to see what is distinctive to saintly life in contrast to other theological considerations. One strand is concerned with truth or knowledge of the divine, knowledge generally arrived at by interior contemplation, the other, with ethical matters in which love, charity, and compassion figure. In the former, a language of considerable semantic density, together with attestations of the experience's ineffability, must be penetrated. St. Teresa of Avila focuses largely on the truth aspect of her experience and says little about the ethical. But a close reading shows that, in describing the third stage of prayer, St. Teresa differentiates the soul's union with God from the soul's other faculties, which remain intact:

> It happens that when the will is in union, the soul realizes that the will is captive and rejoicing, and that it alone is experiencing great quiet, while on the other hand understanding and memory are so free that they can attend to business and do works of charity . . . The soul is both Mary and Martha. Thus the soul is as it were occupied in the active and in the contemplative life. It is doing works of charity and the business pertaining to its life.[13]

On the face of it, the fourth stage of prayer, described as an elevation of the soul, rapture, is distinguishable from union and entirely free of ethical concerns. It is irresistible: "I felt as if I were being ground to powder," St. Teresa writes.[14] But careful reading of her report shows that even in rapture the ethical can be distinguished from the contemplative and remains distinct, however bound up with it. Thus, in actually describing the fourth stage, she insists that the soul rejoices "in some good thing, in which are comprised all good things at once, but it cannot comprehend this good thing."[15] What can the fruits of this incomprehensible good thing be? Not the bliss of divine proximity, which is mixed with intense bodily pain. Rather, it is the detachment this "good thing" provides to do God's work. The soul now gives scant weight to earthly values such as honors and money, which are singled out as particularly worthless. Instead, these special favors granted by God are interpreted as proofs that God wants to use her "in order to help a great many people."[16]

In the Franciscan religiosity of St. Catherine of Siena, truth subserves the piety of the heart. Truth is required "to show her the world's need and how storm-tossed and offensive this is to God,"[17] so that truth is in the service of the other's suffering. In the life of St. Catherine, the soul's transformation occurs in a three-phase process: first, immersion in the divine life; then, self-castigation, a result of the first step; and finally, an opening out of the soul into the spirit of charity. She speaks of communion with God "when the soul is in God and God is in the soul as the fish is in the sea and the sea is in the fish."[18] She goes on to say that from her new self-knowledge "a holy justice gave birth to hatred and displeasure against herself . . . her imperfection . . . which seems to be the cause of all the evils of the world."[19] Thus before she can address the world's need she must undergo acute suffering.

It is worth noting a paradox in the *imitatio Christi* aspect of Christian saintly life: on the one hand the saint alleviates suffering, but on the other imposes it on him or herself. Is it not the obligation of another, if not the saint's own, to alleviate her or his own suffering? This paradox is not directly addressed in the work of St. Catherine. But she nevertheless remarks that "in this life guilt is not atoned for by suffering as suffering but rather by suffering borne with desire, love and contrition of heart. The value is not in the suffering but in the soul's desire."[20] This text also foreshadows a possible response to modern psychological criticisms of saintly asceticism by disclaiming any independent value for suffering. St. Catherine's response disposes of the argument that if saints suffer they must attribute value to suffering, that suffering thus is undertaken for its own sake, but it fails to blunt the power of Nietzsche's criticism which interprets asceticism as a reorientation of wills to power and of ascetic suffering as enhancing and reinforcing desire.[21] A response to this argument lies outside the scope of the present analysis. But even if Nietzsche's conclusion that suffering enhances desire is true, it does not vitiate the claim that saints see and respond to human need or that their lives exhibit carnal generality.

Earlier I spoke not only of the clarity of the saint's moral vision but also of the absence of rational mediation in arriving at it, of the idiot savant character of saintly moral vision. The analogy to the idiot savant is intended in an only slightly stretched sense. Consider St. Teresa's protests about her poor memory: "Over and over again I have proved my mind has to be spoon-fed to retain anything."[22] But when she describes the content of her vision she declares: "It is like one who without having taken the slightest trouble in order to learn to read or even having studied, finds himself in possession of all existing knowledge; he has no idea of how or whence it has come, since he has never done any work, even so much as was necessary for the learning of the alphabet."[23] Thus far I have distinguished the difference between saintly vision *tout court* from the mystical elements that frequently accompany it. This is the problem of the psychology of the saintly imagination. I have yet to address the relation of saintly consciousness to the problem of carnal generality.

I suggested earlier, in conformity with Levinas's analysis, that faces exhibit the track or spoor of transcendence or, alternatively, the trace of the totality of humankind or of all sentient beings. What the saint apprehends in a direct and immediate fashion is the trace of transcendence in the other. One way in which the religious imagination envisions the saint's relation to the trace is illustrated in an eighteenth-century Jewish Hasidic tale in which the human countenance serves as an an-iconic sign of transcendence. The Baal Shem Tob, a holy sage, summons up Samael, the lord of demons, about an important matter. Infuriated, Samael reminds the holy man that he has been summoned in this way only three times before: at the fall of man, when the golden calf was made, and when Jerusalem was destroyed. "The Baal Shem Tob ordered the disciples to bare their foreheads and, on every forehead, Samael saw the sign of the image in which God creates man. He did what was asked of him but before leaving he said, 'Sons of the living God, permit me to stay here a little longer and look at your foreheads.'"[24] The saint brings into reflective consciousness the trace of transcendence, which overcomes the power that opposes it.

I suggested earlier that the ethical claim of the face may be in the trace of all humankind rather than in the track of a theistically interpreted transcendence. In an antinomian Buddhist tale inserted in a text of Buddhist orthodoxy, *The Milindapanha*, a prostitute is praised for indiscriminate practice of saintliness. A king, Soka, asks whether there is anyone who can make the Ganges flow backward. All concede this is impossible except the courtesan Bidumati. She invites the king to witness an act of truth performed through the practice of the scorned profession of prostitution. Successfully reversing the water's flow, she claims this miraculous act has been achieved by a sinful woman because, in performing her services, she gives herself to all without distinguishing brahman from servant. "I regard them all alike . . . free . . . from fawning and from dislike, do I do service to him who has bought me."[25]

It is worth noting that some antinomian writers who create fictional universes in which sainthood plays a role retain the distinctive marks of sainthood I have described. In Genet's world of theft, rape, murder, and betrayal, selflessness sets the saint apart, even if the suffering he hopes to alleviate breaks with categories sanctioned by Christian orthodoxies. Thus, in the reformatory of Metray, as shown by Genet in *Miracle of the Rose*, to become the catamite of some powerful figure is cynically referred to as "relieving suffering humanity," but, transformed through the vision of one of the novel's characters, it is seen as "the sign of a charity so potent it even seeped into my vice."[26] Similarly, Michel Tournier, in *The Ogre*, a reworking of the St. Christopher legend, depicts a peeping Tom and pornographer, a man otherwise completely ordinary, who takes on the burden of carrying the Christ child in the person of a small Jewish boy who is in hiding during the Second World War.[27]

Saints as Carnal Generals

Saints not only see carnal generality in such privileged nodes as faces; they also are carnal generals. To grasp the manner in which saintly lives "signify" requires an account first of the way the meaning of sanctity is communicated, how the vision of the saint acquires external and visible shape, then of the way moral responses to the saint's language, rituals, images, and social behavior, his or her *acta sanctae*, are activated.

In *Otherwise than Being or Beyond Essence*, Levinas offers a description of the moral self that provides a groundwork for answering these questions. The work is an effort to show the conditions that make possible the existence of a self that sacrifices itself. Such a self cannot be beyond being, transcending the material conditions of existence, nor can it lack being in the sense of being nonexistent. Yet it cannot be "in" being, either, because being's mode of manifesting itself involves the coming-to-presence of something to a consciousness that represents. The representational function of consciousness allows no egress from consciousness. The alterity of the other is reduced to a content of consciousness. If all three alternatives are exhausted, what account can we give of the moral self? It must show itself in a way that is otherwise than being, a way that bypasses representation. Its self-manifestation cannot do without corporeal existence, but at the same time the moral self must be revealed in a manner spatially and temporally different from representation.

Levinas argues that ethical existence is directly related to a psycho-physiological primordium, that the structures of the self that make self-sacrifice possible depend upon properties of the body's sensibility. His account is (roughly speaking) an epiphenomenalist description of the moral self. Epiphenomenalism can be defined as "a dualistic theory that asserts the occurrence of peculiarly mental events but makes their occurrence completely dependent on physical events."[28]

Just as classical epiphenomenalism insists on the existence of the brain and brain states for cognition, Levinas asserts that the body's capacity for sensation, the structure of sensibility, opens the possibility for the emergence of a self that sacrifices itself, has the capacity to be "hollowed out" through the existence of the other (*OB*, 14–15). To grasp the character of this self, he considers the double nature of sensibility: on the one hand, sensibility opens into representation; on the other, it exhibits a "being affected" prior to the bending of sensibility toward cognitive structure. In considering representation, Levinas suggests that the datum sensed and the act of sensing are functionally distinct but that both lie within sensation. In the context of representation, sensation consists in a putting out of phase of sensing and sensed and a recovery of itself across the breach of time. This is the mode of being's temporalization. Coming-to-presence occurs as the continuous pulsing of sensation, as a movement of loss and recovery. The very same structure opens up the other aspect of sensibility, the capacity to be affected, to be exposed, wounded, or outraged. In this context, the other person can impinge on the self as on a raw nerve (*OB*, 61–98). Egoity, the self that enjoys and represents, is displaced. Thus the precondition for the effective reception of the impact of the other is created.

It is my claim that this structure is the transcendental condition for ethical life and a fortiori a necessary presupposition for the life of the saint. In most lives this structure occasionally takes precedence over the claims of egoity, but in the lives of saints sensibility is totally exposed, at least for a time. This explains in part the acute despair rendered vividly present in accounts of saints' lives.

The same "mechanism," the structure of sensibility, also makes possible the reception of the "message" of the saint. The saint acts on the pure sensibility, the capacity to be wounded or pained, of those to whom she or he appeals. In order to affect this capacity in the other, the saint will not rely on rational discourse, even when language is the medium of communication. What is kerygmatic in such discourse is not the information conveyed but the proximity between the persons addressed and the saintly interlocutor. Genuine discourse is contact and presupposes a relation with the one addressed apart from the message communicated. This notion of proximity does not diminish the physical distance between beings but attests to the immediacy of the other's presence. Proximity is thus a relation with the other without conceptual mediation. The nearness of the saint is immediately meaningful as soliciting the one who is near to join in encountering and alleviating suffering. The saint acts not only by mitigating suffering *tout court* but also by arousing and disturbing consciousness so that cognition and representation are disrupted and the urgency of a moral plea requiring a response is conveyed. The appeal of miracles and of various excesses connected with the traditional behavior of saints can in part be accounted for by the necessity of bringing the divine or human other near through nondiscursive means. The danger of irrational excess cannot be overlooked, but I believe the structures I have described are at least in part self-correcting. I will consider this claim in detail when I take up a view different from my own, that moral problems are best resolved against a background of consensus about the virtues.

The Problem of Exemplification

I have argued that sensibility is the corporeal structure that enables saints to respond to suffering and for others who witness the saint's work to be inspired by it. One account of the saint's power to engender imitation, on the face of it promising, seems to me to fall wide of the mark. This is the view that, in taking the saint to be an exemplary figure, we mean that the saint's acts are samples of ethical behavior and the saint's life as a whole a sample of compassion, generosity, and love. The idea of samples, originally invoked by Wittgenstein to show what cannot otherwise be pictured or said, is employed by Nelson Goodman to show how values function. Although Goodman focuses on aesthetic values, the notion of samples is easily transferred to the context of ethical values. The utility of samples lies in their enabling us to learn the character of the whole of which they are samples. Thus, in the case I am considering, one would watch the saint's behavior in order to learn what goodness, compassion, and love are like.

One pitfall in considering things as samples is already discussed by Goodman himself. If a sample is taken to learn what the whole of which it is a sample is like, how can we tell if the sample is helpful? Goodman counters this objection by showing that samples are useful if they are fair samples, those which have been produced in conformity with finely tuned inductive techniques. Thus, while we can never test all the air in Los Angeles, we can get a good idea of what it is like by taking a fair sample.

But applying this notion of exemplification to an ethical context presents unique difficulties. If we consider the life of the saint as a sample, what is the saint's life to be a fair sample of? Perhaps, as I noted earlier, of compassion or love, but surely also of justice and fairness. If so, there is something circular about the method of fair sampling, which cannot be gotten round by the pragmatic argument

Goodman uses: in practice, the use of inductive technique enables us to know the whole when we know a part. The saint's life is, among other things, a fair sample of fairness. To take a fair sample involves a prior notion of fairness. But, it could be countered, the term *fair* applied to samples does not mean fairness in the sense of equity or justice, notions we appeal to when we speak of the saint, but refers instead to proportionality, context relevance, and the like. It is just here that phenomenological analysis points up the weakness of the sample paradigm in this amended form. The idea of fairness in the context of inductive technique is parasitic upon more primordial conditions of equity found in interpersonal relations such as sharing and returning what is not one's own. A fair sample is one in which the part represents the quality in question so that it does not misrepresent or mislead about the whole. This necessary recourse to concepts of equity arising in interpersonal relations shows that inductive technique is already bound to a prior order of interpersonal transactions. Fairness and equity arise from concrete social transactions rather than the converse.

It is worth noting that, despite its phenomenological grounding, a related difficulty besets the conception of the paradigmatic individual in Max Scheler's account. Scheler argues that good and bad factual models are instances of the pure types of value-persons, the pure models for factual models, of which the saint is the highest type. Thus the historical model, the actually existing individual, originates in the exemplar:

> It is certain that factual models originate for man *in* . . . other factual men as objects of some kind of experience. Yet these men, as they are experienced, are not the exemplars themselves. Although we frequently say, "This *X* is my model," what we mean by "model" is not at all this factual man in his flesh and blood. We mean that this *X* is an *exemplification* of our model proper—perhaps the only one, perhaps evidentially the uniquely possible one. But even in this case he functions merely as exemplar. The model itself is seen in men who function as exemplars. . . . But the model is not extracted or abstracted from the empirically contingent natures of such men, nor is it found as a real or abstract part of the exemplars.[29]

Like Goodman, Scheler thinks of the paradigmatic individual as exemplifying an ideal type, although he does not have recourse to statistical or other scientifically binding norms in his description of exemplification. Thus he does not turn to a notion of fairness traceable to prior conceptions of equity and justice that, in turn, depend on interpersonal transactions. But he fails to grasp the primordiality of these transactions, from which values are subsequently derived. Because the order of experience precedes the order of abstract reflection, the proscriptive character of the human face precedes the concept of fairness or justice, and the saint's healing actions the concept of compassion. Were the converse true, there would be no alleviation of physical or psychological suffering without prior conceptual values by means of which they could be justified, or saints without prior exemplary types. The saint opens the possibility for value types by providing the warranty for the values that are then brought to light.

Saintliness and the Virtues

The account I have given of the saint's role in ethical existence is in part a response to a general attitude of pessimism about the failure of recent moral theories to settle moral questions. I believe that this failure can be attributed to the heterogeneous background claims that govern attempts to resolve disputed questions. In this regard, my position is in conformity with that of Alasdair MacIntyre in his by now celebrated *After Virtue*. MacIntyre argues that moral claims are incommensurable because they lack a common account of the virtues, "dispositions not only to act but to feel in particular ways. . . . Moral education is an *education sentimentale*."[30] Aristotle, he believes, offers such an account. MacIntyre's response to the incommensurability of the principles used to resolve moral questions—the development of moral communities in which intellectual and moral life can be sustained—is not, I believe, persuasive.

While many criticisms of his position have appeared, I shall take up three of my own that are pertinent to my argument in that I believe my position avoids these difficulties. These criticisms therefore provide indirect support for my position. First, MacIntyre acknowledges that agreement must be secured about what are to count as virtues if we wish to establish small communities that will live in accordance with such Aristotelean values as *sophrosyne* or *phronēsis*. Thus MacIntyre's view already depends on well-honed traditions. But these are precisely what are lacking, because they are in dispute. Second, the consensus arrived at by homogeneous communities has been shown historically to be untrustworthy. Nazi Germany and

South Africa under apartheid are examples of such communities. Third, Aristotle's criterion of rationality, without which the theory of virtues founders, is linked to his doctrine of an unmoved mover, a hierarchy of nature, and a metaphysics of substance, all of which have been subjected to penetrating modern criticisms.[31] Without this anchorage, recourse to the virtues loses plausibility and leads to an appeal to the incommensurable principles criticized by MacIntyre from the start.

Turning to the saint's life, while not without difficulties, avoids some of the problems that plague MacIntyre's account. First, while my starting point, like MacIntyre's, is arbitrary, it does not depend upon communal sanction. Instead I begin with a phenomenology of saintly acts and their precipitating conditions that is relatively constant across cultural differences. I also suggest universal primordial structures that make the saint's experience communicable and the saint's language effective. Second, it must be conceded that saints have sometimes generated emotional and behavioral excesses and themselves displayed extreme behavior such as radical ascetic practices. In the Western Christian tradition, they have endorsed policies that have harmed Jews, Moslems, and heretics. While such harm cannot be dismissed, it was often the result of an institutional framework that encouraged deviation from the content of saintly vision: the alleviation of suffering. The universal application of the alleviation-of-suffering principle offers at least the possibility for self-correction of saintly behavior. Third, my description of the exemplary individual is compatible with a number of traditional Western metaphysical positions, with Buddhism, as well as with postmodern attacks on traditional metaphysics. While the latter still remains to be demonstrated in detail, at least a plurality of conceptual structures can accommodate my account. The saint's metaphysical baggage is, as I argued earlier, light. The saint hopes to ease pain and sorrow and to communicate with imperative force the suffering of the afflicted to others so that such alleviation is seen as the primary task of human life.

PART Ⅴ

Conversations

Talk, in its dictionary definition, "may be one-sided, the mere utterance of words with little thought. Communication may be uninvited or unreciprocated." Conversation, by contrast, is "a speak[ing] together informally and alternately [in] an interchange of thoughts."

18

Interview with Emmanuel Levinas

Edith Wyschogrod: Is there a turning (*Kehre*), a change in your work, such that instead of finding moral significations by way of phenomenology, through what is inscribed in the face of the Other, you find it in language? If there is such a change, I would like to know why you now rely on the Logos more than previously.

Emmanuel Levinas: I am quite surprised that [you assert] there is a change and that there is no longer phenomenology. [In fact] there is not at all an analysis of language. It is a certain manner of speaking, of finding in language what was always signified phenomenologically. I don't at all proceed like Heidegger, who attributes a special wisdom to language. I use the word *disinterestedness*. It is grounded in the phenomenon of disinterestedness in which can be found the trace of two words, *interest* and *disinterest*. It is only a way of suggesting. I do not attribute, I do not lend, to language this revelatory power. What is more, I now strongly insist on the element of taking, of grasping, both in our concepts as perception and as comprehension. But there are grounds for this. The emergence of the hand in comprehension is extremely old. It is also very Husserlian. In any case, I was never aware of a transition from a logical phenomenology to the Logos, to wisdom. That there is a wisdom in language is possible. I would be very happy to find it, but it is not at all something definitive for me. The word *Kehre* is Heideggerian. He is a very great philosopher whom one cannot imitate.

EW: It seems to me that *Otherwise than Being* is a work of the greatest importance, more radical, if I may say so, than *Totality and Infinity*, and that people have hardly begun to understand it. I would like to consider three subjects you develop in this work: the question of God, the theological problematic, the question of language—that is, the difference between Saying [*le Dire*] and the said [*le dit*]—and the question of skepticism. To begin with the question of language, to which you attribute so much importance: you distinguish between the Saying and the said. Now, on principle, it is absolutely necessary to have the said once you have posited the Saying. Haven't you then really returned to the roots of Western philosophy? How can you avoid entangling ethics in ontology?

EL: The Saying and the said . . . The ethical moment is the Saying. But one can't dispense with the said. I am going to respond to you in a very general way about this. There is, in *Otherwise than Being*, the necessary return to ontology, starting with the section on the advent of the third—the return to ontology, not ontology as such, but to theory in general or, if you wish, justice, which must be added to charity. For the word *charity*, I always think of the Hebrew *chesed*. I use the word *beauty*, which in my mind is always the Hebrew word *yefed*. [*Yefed* in Hebrew means both "beauty" and "Greek." The point appears to be that beauty, the aesthetic dimension, figures in Greek rather than in Judaic thought.] I would even say there is an insistence toward the end of *Otherwise than Being* on the fact that there cannot be [moral] existence as a couple *à deux*). There is not existence as a couple because existents are numerous [more than two] and the whole theme of multiplicity, of plurality, is very much present in *Totality and Infinity*. Also, it is an attempt to think plurality otherwise than it has been thought by the Neo-Platonists. For the Neo-Platonist, plurality was always a privation (*privatio*) of actuality, of the soul. Discourse was always less than the unity of the One. The One could not even have consciousness of self because then it would be two. On the contrary, there was the [Neo-Platonic] idea of plurality and plurality as I always think of it, the "for you" [*pour vous*]. One of the blessings of multiplicity is that there are many more relations of love in the world when there is plurality. But in that case, [when there is plurality] it is absolutely necessary to compare the incomparable, and, in consequence, to think in language. In speech, alongside of Saying there absolutely must be a said. The latter is what unifies the one who speaks. It is that in which multiplicity is reflected in a meaning, and in this sense the said is important. It is not, after all, adversity that matters. It is never to forget that justice comes from *chesed* [Hebrew for "favor, goodness, lovingkindness"]. I am thinking especially of Hobbes. He says that justice, that polity itself comes from the fact that animality has been limited. There are certainly more concrete analyses to show how [justice comes about] in language. I am in the process of reading a work about Lacan, a thesis, a maddening work, but with a pretension to extreme rigor. In it there is also the idea of the work, which is outside the unconscious and which has its place, one that is precisely the order of the said. I was very struck that the order of the said is the world. And for me too the order of the said is, finally, civil society, the state. If you know the last pages of *Otherwise than Being*, there is the insistence on the state, institutions, judges, and justice; one could not be a Jew and speak otherwise. All this is vague as an answer.

EW: You spoke of Neo-Platonism. If one wants to describe the difference between your efforts and Western theology, that is to say, Christian theology, I think one could explain it somewhat like this. At the beginning of Western philosophy, Parmenides showed that the fundamental question is that of being. There are essential links between being, language, and thought. The One and thinking belong to being, but in Jewish tradition God, who is also One, is indigent like the poor that you describe. The One of Parmenides lacks nothing. Appearance and multiplicity come into being so that being can manifest itself, but the biblical God is, on the contrary, a hidden God. Multiplicity was commanded not because God wanted to show Himself but because he needed the world in order for there to be justice. If one begins with the biblical God and not with being, ethics is primary and metaphysics secondary. That is to say, the world's reason for being is the possibility of justice. Have I grasped the intention of your theological thinking when I characterize it as the reverse of the Parmenidean understanding of being?

EL: That's quite right. Justice, I call it responsibility for the other, right? There is, even in *Totality and Infinity*, the evocation of the *zim-zum* [the idea in Kabbalistic writings of the self-contraction of God in order to create the void in which creation can take place], but I won't venture into that. I am thinking, in effect, of a God who is bored [*s'ennuie*] to be alone. It is Christian, too. I do not say that it is uniquely Jewish. It is a God whose grandeur, whose justice and *rachamim* ["mercy"] you see everywhere. You see his humility; it is a

God who comes down. I would say to you I find in Descartes the importance that I attached to the idea of the infinite. It is a God who has not negated the finite and who has entered into the finite. It is a made idea in itself. But in concrete phenomenological terms this means it is a God who has sent you the other human being. Remember that is theology; there is also philosophy of religion, right? It is concretely this rending of the finite; it is the constitution of society. It is the fact that there is a human being sent toward the other human being. That is my central thesis and consequently it is this structure that is divinity. It never appears. There is only His word in the face of the Other. All this bears out that the essential thing is not to appear, not to show itself, not to be thought, to be witnessed. It is to go toward the other human being, who is God's divinity. I would willingly accept this as being something systematic, but finally it is, in the end, most appropriate that the essential thing is not to appear. He never appears when He reads the finite. I think that phenomenology is staging [*mise en scène*]. The essential thing is not at all to verify whether the concept has lost its meaning. It is to know what is the concrete conjuncture [*conjoncture*] in which this concept has a meaning. And, as a result, for me the idea of the infinite, that is to say, the idea that holds more than it can hold, a thought that thinks more than it can think, is concretely the social relation with the Other. In that sense, [it is] phenomenological. One thinks it as a construction, what I would call staging, a way of thinking that does not at all resemble it [discursive thinking]; it is neither deduction nor dialectic. One reconstitutes [a play] exactly as the stage director who is confronted with the play and who says what it is concretely, the circumstances. I would willingly accept that. I think also that Descartes' proof for the existence of God [from the idea of the infinite] is much more a description of God's existence, the fact that he comes down in the idea.

EW: In an article about your work, I suggested that the staging of religion is the same as the staging of ethics, that there is no difference between the two. Is that how you think of their relation?

EL: That's right, it is the same thing. But the fact that it is staging, that is phenomenology. Husserl calls it recovery of the concrete horizon, as it originates. It is not a question of moving from the noema to the noesis. That is not really anything, for when you move from the noema to the noesis you find in the noesis [merely] all that it has forgotten. In the noema you don't see it, but you see in the noesis the concrete concatenation in which the idea has its meaning. It is absolutely clear, you recover the meaning of the word, the meaning of being, the meaning of the philosophical, what is one. It is not to be the neighbor of the one, it is not the proximity of the one. Proximity is always understood in Western philosophy as a crash, a sudden bursting, as a loss. But now then, how much better it is to be two than to be alone. I think the essential thing for philosophy is to affirm the excellence proper to society.

EW: You mean, then, that your philosophy is a social philosophy.

EL: There is an excellence intrinsic to the social "we" that is better than God. [*Nous, c'est mieux que le Dieu.*] God is alone with men; men are in fellowship with God. [*Dieu il est seul avec les hommes, les hommes sont en société avec le Dieu.*]

EW: In your recent work—and I am thinking now of *Of God Who Comes to Mind*—you give up philosophical theology as well as a theology of faith in that you see both as speaking the language of ontology. You replace this way of speaking with such phenomena as the relation with the Other, the recognition of the Other's height. These are now theologically significant. Why, then, should it be necessary for Jews to obey the Law or for Christians to perform the sacraments?

EL: That religion knows more of this [the significance of alterity] than philosophy is possible, in Jewish religion much more so than in the sacramental. There is, by contrast [to the sacramental], this impression of an elevated ethic. It is the response of an average Jew that I am making. I am going to tell you what I have said elsewhere about the events of Sabra and Shatilla [the names of Palestinian refugee camps in Lebanon raided by Israel in 1981]. I then cited a text of the *Gemara* [the part of the Talmud that expands upon the Law—transmitted orally and codified as the Mishnah]. I will recount it to you. It is the scene of the *meraglim* [Hebrew for "spies"] who are sent to spy out the land. The *Gemara* says that this test shows that the negative report [of the spies] is always a serious fault because in effect these men have spoken ill of the land and have been punished because they spoke ill of the land. Well, the *Gemara* says it is perhaps for another reason they were punished. It is because they said, "He is stronger than we." "He" can refer to the enemy or to God. The text [of the *Gemara*] says they were not punished because they spoke ill of the land, for the land is only stone and wood; the Holy Land is only stone and wood, and they were punished for a stronger reason.

[The reference is to Numbers 31: "But the men that went up with him (Caleb) said, 'We are not able to go up against the people (the Canaanites) for they are stronger than we.'" But the Hebrew word *mimenu* can mean either "he" or "we," an ambiguity giving rise to the gloss of R. Haninah. In the *Gemara*, "A grievous statement did they (the spies) make at that moment, viz.: 'For they are stronger than we,' read not 'than we' but 'than He.' . . . Even the master of the house cannot remove His furniture from there" (*Sotah* 35a). The gloss says that the spies sin, not because they overestimate the strength of the enemy, but for a deeper reason, because they doubt that God could remove the Canaanites from the land. [The implication Levinas draws is that in the case of Sabra and Shatillah the defense of the Holy Land, of stones and trees, as it were, can be outweighed by other, perhaps humane, considerations bound up with the sanctity of the Other.] That is how one goes beyond the sacraments. In that text [*Sotah* 35a] I read the order of things. No doubt there are many Jews who penetrate into the interiority of the sacraments. No doubt there are all the levels but in the end there is the priority of *hesed* ["lovingkindness"], of *chesed* and *rachamim* ["mercy"], the law of nonreciprocity. [Judaism] sharpens nonreciprocity, what I call asymmetry, the relation with the Other. And even in Maimonides, in the last chapter of the *Guide for the Perplexed*, he insists on this nonreciprocity. [Lovingkindness, righteousness, and judgment are stressed in Book III, chap. 54 of Maimonides' *Guide for the Perplexed*.] I do not support, I do not prohibit, but I must tell you that in Judaism there are also sacraments; people live it as a sacrament.

EW: The idea of the infinite is a pivotal point in your thought. You explain it as something that is not finite and that is interior to the human person. But you have also repudiated the mystical as something questionable. One nevertheless finds some mystics, Meister Eckhart, for example, who develop a phenomenology of the inner life that resembles what you describe, an interior space devoid of will ready to receive the Holy Spirit and to be filled by the will of God. How is one to distinguish, if we pursue the phenomenological method, the idea of the infinite in me from mysticism of the Eckhart type?

EL: Listen, I must tell you, mysticism, mysticism of the good kind, cannot be rejected, only cheap mysticism. I haven't read much Eckhart, but, in any case, that is not at all what I mean by the idea of the infinite in me and what must be developed phenomenologically. It is not at all an interior piety. Interior piety is always subordinated to its social form. One is always three, never two, as with Buber. And I always cite Chapter 58 of Isaiah. There were some very shrewd people [then] who sought *Krevah hashem*, the proximity of God. Isaiah tells them it is necessary to free the slaves, feed the hungry, clothe the naked, and not flee the flesh of the other, not the face, but the very flesh. ["Is it not to deal thy bread to the hungry, / And that thou bring the poor that are cast out to thy house? / When thou seest the naked, that thou cover him, / And that thou hid not thyself from thine own flesh?" Isaiah 58:7.] It is very important because it is there that everything is played out, and it is not at all a diminishing. There is something suspicious about the interior life. In *Ethics and Infinity*, there is also the relation with the book in European civilization. When one says, "It is in the book [*dans le livre*]," one says it is "bookish [*livresque*]." "You have written in the book and you are pleased." But in reality we have a relation with the book. Things are not played out in the depths of my consciousness. They are played out in the book for the Jew. He does not introspect but searches the book. And the book is the Bible. I believe that the Bible prefigures the world's literature. The novel recounts the same narratives as the Bible. [The claim is intended to demonstrate the power of narrative and is further explicated below.] And consequently I reject the depths of self as a point of reference. The depths of self are not possible without the book.

EW: So writing [*l'écriture*] is the most important thing?

EL: God's command comes to pass the moment you have spoken [a verse] and heard what you said: the *pasuk* [Hebrew word for "verse"] is as if it has come from one's own mouth. The prophet receives the message; he is the one who reads it. And that, too, is a response to your question about mysticism. It is not the last word.

EW: Yet Eckhart's mysticism seems to be self-emptying.

EL: But it is very much a matter of personal salvation there.

EW: Perhaps we can return to the question of Heidegger. He distinguishes between *reden* and *sprechen*. The latter is concerned with the existential constitution of language and the former with empirical language. With respect to *reden*, he distinguishes two moments: *hören* ["hearing"] and *schweigen* ["keeping silent"]. Is there any relation between your account of Saying and the said and Heidegger's distinctions?

EL: That I can't tell you exactly. Surely the Saying and the said are also *Zeuge* [belong to the nexus of things, in Heidegger's sense]. When I buy a metro ticket, there is an exchange of remarks. All administrative language is like that.

It is not in administrative language, where there is an exchange of information, that language operates. In contemporary linguistics and philosophy, one takes the exchange of information to be the meaning of language. In my opinion, this is the inversion of what the word is. Saying [*le dire*] reaches down even there, although it cannot reach down completely because when I ask for my ticket I still say, "Would you please [*s'il vous plait*]," I say "Thank you [*merci*]." "There is a utilitarian language, but I distinguish utilitarian language, where the said is very important, where the information that is relayed is the main issue and not at all the fact that I stand before the Other. I say that there is in all administrative language a part of language and in all language a part that is administrative. It is perfectly obvious. I have not built much on this distinction. To make a long story short, I want to summarize. When I again leaf through *Otherwise than Being*, I say at bottom that I have not at all done this intentionally. I convey, I bear in mind the familiar Jewish distinction. The man who does what God says because he wishes to, *chenu ha mitzuveh* ["the one who is not commanded"], is less great than the one who does so because he is commanded, *ha mitzuveh* ["the one who is commanded"]. The Jew who fulfills the Sabbath—this action is more important than the one who says, in effect, one should relax once in a while, or who spontaneously does some good action. This is paradoxical because we think, as Europeans, that when one does something spontaneously, it is worth much more than when it is commanded. In reality, in *Otherwise than Being* it turns out that free action for the Other is not at all a pure choice, that it is commanded, that it begins with an obligation, that it begins with obsession. It is phenomenologically the attempt to say what it means when one has been commanded because if you say, "It is necessary when I have been commanded that I freely consent," there is only spontaneous action.

EW: You have written "doing before hearing." The implication is that Israel is willing to do what is commanded even before hearing what the specific commandments are.

EL: That's right. Exactly. To do before being commanded is to prophesy; it is inspiration. The prophet agrees to this [transmitting God's message] in advance [before knowing its content]. This is, in the end, the great theme of *Otherwise than Being*, the obsession with the Other before my freedom, after I act.

EW: You have developed the role of skepticism that "unsays" the said of philosophy. Has your thinking been rightly understood as a dialectical theology in that skepticism remains a perpetual moment in philosophy? Do you think that theology today requires such a moment and cannot be expressed through affirmation and denial? A Hegelian moment, perhaps?

EL: I am going to tell you that skepticism is the problem of how one can contest theory within theoretical language. In *Of God Who Comes to Mind*, in the end, there is a text that is called "Manner of Speaking [*façon de parler*]." It concerns the theme of skepticism, as if language were able to speak without leaving its trace in the said. The Heideggerian idea is that the whole of language bears the ultimate secret of the absolute. For him, the absolute is being. By invoking the fact that skepticism always comes back, one can affirm skeptical being while affirming being.

EW: Even so, in Hegel's *Phenomenology* the moment of skepticism is also a perpetual moment in that in one way or another it keeps coming back.

EL: But not in the end. It is that which moves the dialectic. It is precisely because of this bad consciousness that one has to say theory is the fundamental, the primary attitude.

EW: But there is a modern dialectic, not Hegelian, the dialectic of Sartre, for example, that recommences, that is perpetual.

EL: That has always been foreign to me. I have neither an idea of a progression toward the truth, that is, the Hegelian idea that there is a progression toward truth . . .

EW: Nor that of Sartre.

EL: That there is the impossibility of remaining somewhere, that is strange, not remaining somewhere, not remaining in itself. It [remaining somewhere] is everything I affirm philosophically. Skepticism is evoked solely in order to say that one thinks philosophically even when one states the skeptical position. It [philosophy] leaves traces.

EW: The possibility of philosophy is also the possibility of skepticism?

EL: Yes, certainly.

EW: The next question is about biblical language. If the language of the Bible is, so to speak, a translation of divine language, it belongs to the said. How are we to distinguish between sacred and everyday language? Is sacred language subject to linguistic rules? How can something that belongs to the Said exact obedience?

EL: What I said to you earlier about the relativity of these distinctions answers or perhaps does not answer this question you ask. In the end, we live in a world where we compare things, where we think, where we posit general things, where there is justice. In *Otherwise than Being*, objectivity is founded on justice. So, I do not scorn the said. To the contrary, there is a said that is inspired, the Bible, and, by contrast, what I said to you earlier concerning the relationship of all writing to the national literatures that one learns in school, Molière or Shakespeare or Dostoyevsky or Pushkin. These are not absolutely separate from sacred language. There is, as a result, the problem of the kinship of artistic inspiration, literary, in any case, and inspiration as such. I would go that far. In a little text that I will give you [*Ethics and Infinity*], I was asked what were my earliest influences. I said the Bible and Pushkin. I even included all of Russian literature. Profane language is everyday language, administrative language. Prophecy is not only in the Bible for me.

EW: Do you then distinguish everyday language, sacred language, and poetic language from one another?

EL: In any case, I do not look for wisdom in Hölderlin, who is foreign to me.

EW: I have a further question about poetry.

EL: But Pushkin, I assure you, is holy. I must tell you that one day I received a visit of someone from Israel. As he came in, he noticed Pushkin in my home. He said, "Ich bin awngekumen in a yiddish hoiz." [Yiddish for "I have entered a Jewish home." It is a standard joke among those of Levinas's background and generation

that, because Pushkin was so widely admired in Jewish circles, finding his works in someone's home could be posited as a sign that its
owner was Jewish rather than that would naturally be expected, that
is, Russian.]

EW: In some recent observations on the subject of poetry, you
said that poetry belongs to Saying rather than the said. Do you think
that art, especially contemporary art, places ontology in question? If
I read you rightly, you distinguish between art that embodies the *il y
a*, infra-discursive or pagan being, and art works in which morality
is expressed. Do you think that art can undialectically express the
culture and rules of a society? After all, Kant says in the *Third Critique* that beauty like morality can be something disinterested.

EL: Notice, I said this but I have some reservations about it because I claim that, in extending the Bible, [narrative] art both serves
and profanes it. For me profanation is also part of the sacred attitude.
I do not much like the sacred. But it is also inspired.

EW: Your work has been seen as a critique of the sacred.

EL: Yes, to the extent that there is a kind of conformation of the
form itself with what has been said. [If art reflected the Good] one
would have to see all the forms at the outset, and then one would
have to say that behind the beautiful there is the Good. The beautiful
must be distinguished from the Good, but the beautiful is also inspired. That's an easy answer, but all the same . . . There is goodness
in beauty, and there is certainly an idolatrous moment in art, I think.
The idolatrous moment is very strong. Of, if you will, in the end the
good that is in it is absorbed by the form. I wrote something some
time ago, "Reality and Its Shadow," where this is very clear. One
experiences the accommodation in resemblance, in form. It remains
a moment, but at the same time it is necessary to complete it [the
form].

EW: One can go beyond it?

EL: Go beyond it? Not go beyond it so much as see that it is a
part of the truth. One can't make prayer out of Pushkin, but he is,
after all, quite lofty.

EW: But you don't find this kind of loftiness in German poetry?
In Rilke, perhaps? Isn't Rilke something else again?

EL: In Goethe.

EW: That's not like Hölderlin?

EL: But Hölderlin lacks gravity [*n'est pas sérieux*]. Perhaps this is an antipathy that arises from the fact that Heidegger makes Hölderlin more important than the Bible. For Heidegger, Hölderlin is more important than anything else. All this Germanic world that is magnified there, the gods that have fled, that is absolutely foreign to me.

EW: How do you interpret all the interest that has been shown in Nietzsche here in France? Why is there such interest?

EL: Nietzsche speaks in a unique way.

EW: Prophetically?

EL: Prophetically. It is for this reason that they do not at all see that it is the prophetism of Nietzsche that is unique. And then I think that one cannot fight Nietzsche by showing that he contradicts himself because it is you who are made ridiculous in so doing, not Nietzsche. The language Nietzsche speaks has no time to turn against itself. As with skepticism, one can't refute it because the distance you always have to recross in connection with what you have just said does not exist before [the skeptical utterance]. That is the power inspired by this man.

EW: I want to ask you some questions about recent French philosophy. Do you think there is a tendency in French thought today to contrast itself with German Romanticism, even though it is indebted to this philosophy? That is to say, perhaps one could distinguish two moments in German philosophy, the Kantian moment and the Romantic moment, represented today in Heidegger. Derrida, despite certain poetic tendencies in his thought, is opposed to the Greek spirit and stresses writing, perhaps a Jewish moment in thinking, Kabbalistic maybe, but Jewish nonetheless. Lévi-Strauss in his studies of kinship structure also finds the *imago dei*, if one can put it thus in relation to him, in "primitive" societies. Your thought especially comes to fruition in awareness of this tendency. My question: Do you think such a tendency exists and if you think it does, how does your work relate to it?

EL: Now for Derrida. That he knows Kabbalah!

EW: Didn't he write an essay in *Dissemination* on Phillipe Sollers in which the Kabbalah figures in an important way?

EL: And as to your question, I find that what I said could seem to lump all these people together with all that talk of God. There are people together with all that talk of God. There are people who turn toward this, but in the end it is foreign to our epoch. There is a return of interest in epistemology in France, reflections on modern science by people like Michel Serres. Then there is Foucault. Scientific thought, that is the main tendency in France. There is a certain return to the ideas of Brunschvicg. With Derrida, who does not at all do a critique of science, there is probably also the idea that metaphysical language is a deconstructed language . . .

EW: People in the United States are interested in Derrida, literary critics more than philosophers.

EL: Is he communicable because so much is tied to the French language? *Dissemination* is all French speech. But, I will tell you, when someone presents me with a surrealist painter, I always ask whether he is able also to make a likeness. Does it resemble what it is meant to resemble? When I am told that he knows how to make a likeness, then perhaps it is worth seeing what else he is doing. Derrida knows how to make a likeness. If you consider Derrida's *Speech and Phenomena*, it's a masterpiece, this little book of 120 pages where there is nothing in excess, where one moves forward through the most rigorous steps. The same with *The Introduction to the Origin of Geometry* and his work on Rousseau, the very remarkable *Of Grammatology*. Then there are things like *The Postcard*, a dreamlike work, and credit is due in my opinion to the first [type].

EW: This position is often taken in America. Derrida wrote something in response to John Searle, *Limited Inc*, responding to Searle about an interpretation of J. L. Austin's philosophy.

EL: He [Austin] was a master philosopher.

EW: I suggested there were affinities between your work and his in an article. But to return. Derrida was criticized because of this piece; because of the sharpness and also the circuitousness of his retorts.

EL: His playful irony?

EW: Yes. But this is not done in the same way in Anglo-American philosophy.

EL: There is still another question. We have spoken of your interest in my past as well as my present thinking, the question that is most important to you and that you want to develop. Perhaps I am finished with what I have to say. But what I would like [to still consider] is the economy of time. I would like to develop that. You understand I am saying what I think about this in a very crude way. I think that this relation that is not knowledge, not something grasped, not intentionality is the diachrony of time. It is, if you will, what can be called the relation with God who is in excess of the relation with the Other but is, however, in the relation with the Other. There is not a thematization of God. This relation, this orientation that is not thematization, is time. Saying is not negative, not thematization, not objectivation. Positively, it is time that cannot then be interpreted as Husserl interprets it. Husserl thinks that time is presence, it is the present, that the past is the time that one retains and the future, what is to come. What is to come [*l'avenir*] is my term for the future [*le futur*] because what is to come is something that must come [*venir*], a time that one anticipates. In reality, the final human mystery is simultaneity. I think that the formula I already use in *Of God Who Comes to Mind*, is *adieu*. When you say *adieu*, you use the preposition *à*, which still remains an orientation within simultaneity and in space. But there is no preposition that can better mark this orientation than time itself.

EW: You mean that there is no way to mark time except through space?

EL: Yes, but there are the prepositions *avant*, *après*.

EW: But what about *à*?

EL: *À* is almost spatial; *à* is toward [*vers*]. In this regard, the important philosopher is Bergson.

EW: His view of duration?

EL: Duration, yes, the relation with the absolutely unknown, if you will. Except that with Bergson this relation becomes a conformation to something that is known. Whereas what there is in time is that it is always future [*futur*], that the relation with the future [*le futur*] is not less but in excess of what it can contain.

EW: Than can be contained in the present?

EL: When one is European, one is platonist; when the European says "cannot contain," what is meant is romantic love. Now, I think that not being able to contain means a surplus, an excellence proper to something, a social excellence. In the Plotinian tradition, society is less good than being alone. My next to last article is "Bad Conscience and the Inexorable." I was very surprised to find traces of this already in *Totality and Infinity*. I didn't know it was already there. I did several lectures about this, which take place every two years. There was a session on Neo-Platonism where I presented a paper about Neo-Platonism. This was a first attempt at a temporality that is not afraid of the present, [time] as a function of the relation with another, that is to say, past time, the past that can never be made present, the past of the other for whom you are responsible. And [there is] a future [*avenir*] that is precisely this prophetic inspiration that is a relation with the Other but that belongs to the future. Do you understand? As for me, I still do not entirely understand this.

December 31, 1982

19

Postmodernism and the Desire for God
An E-mail Exchange

EDITH WYSCHOGROD AND
JOHN D. CAPUTO

John D. Caputo: In just the past year [1998] we have seen two books edited by English theologians—one entitled *The Postmodern God*, the other *Post-Secular Philosophy*—that have pressed the claim that "postmodern" must be understood to mean or at least to include "postsecular," that the delimitation of the claims of Enlightenment rationalism must also involve the delimitation of Enlightenment secularism.[1] A critical stance toward modernism goes hand in hand with a critical stance toward secularism. In France, Jacques Derrida's most recent work has taken a turn toward what he calls "religion without religion," that is, toward a thinking that involves a certain repetition of basic religious structures, most notably the "messianic." Derrida now analyzes in detail notions like the gift, hospitality, testimony—and most recently, forgiveness—that have always belonged to classical religious discourse. As you well know, on the continent this renewal is very much the effect of the impact Levinas's work has had. This is especially true of Derrida himself and also of Jean-Luc Marion, who speaks of a God "without being," without the "idols" of what Heidegger calls "onto-theo-logic." As these thinkers have been arguing, it seems that God is making a comeback.

This is a fascinating development, and one that sends shock waves through certain American "postmodernist" writers who, however avant-garde they might be in their own work on the question of God and religion, remain deeply and intractably modernist in protecting the rear guard of modernist critiques of religion. Religion is one "other" that these thinkers, who are otherwise deeply persuaded about the power of the "other," do not want to hear about. I have many friends who love to talk about exposing philosophy to the "other," still better to the "unconditionally" or "wholly" other, but when I mention religion, they turn pale. It turns out that by "other" they mean literature. So their unconditional, wholly other is constrained by several conditions, and religion is just too, too other for them, too *tout autre*, if I may say so.

This development raises many questions. What does "God" mean if one speaks of a "postmodern God"? What do "reason" and "philosophy" mean? What can we say today of the most ancient religious motif of all, the desire for God?

What do you make of these developments?

Edith Wyschogrod: Much of the process of rediscovery hangs, I think, on the way in which immanence and transcendence are now being construed in the postsecular conversation. The problem in the present context has been, at least in part, framed by the way in which Levinas has been drawn into the God question. For Levinas, the Other is the other person, whose very existence places a demand of noninjury upon me, an ethical demand that I read in the face-to-face relation with the Other. But it has not gone unnoticed that the Other is in the track or trace of transcendence, which, for Levinas, is construed in terms of a God who has always already passed by, who cannot be made present. This allows for a transcendence that, for him, is seen in conformity with rabbinic tradition. Ethics is first philosophy, and the Old One, the Ancient of Days, is, as it were, cordoned off. But the *imago dei* (to be construed an-iconically, in conformity with Jewish tradition) is not a representation of God but an invisible writing that more than hints at an immanentist theology. Our postsecular friends, like Philip Blond, maintain that Levinas's thought is deeply dualistic in that the otherness of the Other and the otherness of God—or, to use Levinas's term, of illeity (the He)— cannot be maintained. Levinas's Otherness, it is argued, has sustained an interest in ethics as a means to eradicate a world that is debased. Now Blond (and John Milbank) want to save the appearances by an appeal to God, not by rereading the appearances as redeemed, but as a therapeutic gesture in the direction of philosophy, making the world safe for philosophy by showing that God's infinite distance does not destroy but proves to be the ground for the realization of human possibility. It is I think a misreading of Levinas to see him as world-denying or at least world-castigating in the manner of early Buddhism. But what has been correctly perceived is that Levinas has opened the need for thinking through the paradox of the Other as being in the track of transcendence, but of transcendence as also being (somehow) in the track or trace of the Other.

JC: I quite agree with you about the line Blond takes on Levinas. Blond says, in effect, that for Levinas the Good is otherwise than being because being is evil. It is a shocking misrepresentation, almost a denunciation of a thinker who is no doubt the single most important figure in putting the question of God back on the table for philosophical discussion, who has opened the eyes of a highly secular philosophical world to the question of God. It is, furthermore, an ironic denunciation, inasmuch as for Levinas the whole force of the name of God, of the Ancient of Days, of the past that was never present, is spent in the name of earthly peace and social justice—spent, I am tempted to say, "without remainder." That is why I would like to hear more about what you mean when you say, as I understand it, that today we experience the need not only to think the other person as a trace of God but also to think God as the trace of the Other. Is that what you mean by an "immanentist theology"? Is that the direction a "postmodern" theology or religion would take for you? Or even a "religion without religion," to use Derrida's expression?

EW: To answer your question about my position with regard to immanence, if it can be answered, let me rehearse some commonplaces attributable to the Enlightenment: the historical myth of progress, the myth of theological projection, and the myth of psychological maturity. The first has been demolished by our genocidal century; the second, by recent criticisms of how projection was thought to be anchored—whose projection, what standard of rationality?—and the third, by the claim that psychological maturity is a social construction, a cultural artifact. God was seen as an obstruction in many versions of these myths, but the demythologization of all three has left a space, as it were, for God.

Meanwhile a non-Freudian account of desire has been developed by some recent thinkers who focus on social factors and others who stress responsibility over unconscious motivation—a desire that carries with it all the intensity of Freud's description of sexuality. But some who have assimilated accounts of desire as overwhelming intensity lacking an object have sought to find this intensity in an inner-worldly source transcending the individual. The death-of-God theologians, Thomas Altizer and others, saw God as emptying himself into the world. Let us rejoice, they proclaimed, in our Nietzschean legacy. Levinas, by contrast, proclaimed a radical transcendence that, as I hinted earlier, could not be sustained. A historical precedent for the death of God is the old Patripassian heresy, the idea that the Father emptied himself into the Son. Today the problem is to avoid the immanentism characteristic of extreme radical and national ideologies, the violence of immanentism run amok. Here Levinas helps. The Other in her or his singularity precludes such sacralization. It is here—in the area of social justice—that the Other restrains the claims of transcendence.

What do you think? How does this fit in with your view, in *Against Ethics*, that obligation, scandalously, cannot be fulfilled?

JC: I would certainly defend an idea of transcendence, but I would begin with a more fragile and undecidable sense of transcendence. The world is filled with the divine, but the markings of the divine are undecidable. The Other lays claim to us irresistibly, by which, of course, I do not mean that we are coerced, for we are always free to walk away from the Other. But even when we do walk away, which we do with great regularity, the claim remains standing, testified to by our negligence, testified to privately, so that it rises up in glory vis-à-vis the misery of our own self-love. That, of course, is what we learn from Levinas, and how can we thank him enough for that lesson? But for me, this claim is clouded by a certain indeterminacy. It is real, it is irresistible, but still for me the claim that the neighbor lays upon me flickers in a twilight, so that in the end I do not know what lays claims to me. I know that I am laid claim to by the neighbor or the stranger, and I know that I am debased in not responding. But I also lack the wherewithal to answer the "genealogical" critic who says that I am historically constituted to respond and even to feel debased in not responding, and that I could be constituted otherwise. True enough, I think, that may be so, but I am not excused and the claim is irresistible. That is why the claim is "desertified," as Derrida would say, comes to me like a voice in the desert, with a certain desertlike dryness or indeterminacy. Levinas, I think, will not settle for this undecidability. He wants to back it up, as it were, by rooting it in a desire for the Good, a desire for God, Who deflects this desire from itself—Himself, Herself?—and orders us to the neighbor, almost as if this were a certain divine command theory. That is a more robust sense of transcendence than phenomenology allows. (I would not be as quick to leave phenomenology as Levinas. I seek protection in phenomenology.) That is perhaps what you mean when you refer to a sense of transcendence in Levinas that cannot be sustained.

I think we must be content to say that this claim arises from the fragility of the face of the neighbor, which is a phenomenological matter, an ethical phenomenology, not in the sense of the intuition of pure ethical values or essences, but in the sense of the concrete experience of the approach of the neighbor. I would describe this experience as a faith, to be sure, since I do not know what is going on here. I am overtaken by a claim that I do not comprehend in advance, but it is what Kant might call a practical faith, a pragmatics. That is how and where transcendence first presents itself, first shows its face, if I may say so. But in a properly religious faith, for which the name of God is indispensable, this indeterminacy is specified by being lodged in a concrete historical religious tradition—Christian, or Jewish, or other. That tradition gives us texts to read, stories to savor and remember, communities to support us, prophets to chasten us, and generally puts a fine point on this more opaque and dark phenomenology of the approach of the neighbor. A concrete faith tradition fills in the lines, determines what is otherwise a more "desert"-like experience, as it is for Derrida and his "religion without religion."

The disciples say, "Lord when did we see you hungry and give you to eat?" That is the great story of transcendence for me. The important thing is that it is a question, which is a sign of undecidability here, for at the time of giving the gift the disciples did not know that this was the Lord. I am laid claim to by the Other who is hungry, and that is all. It is just a gift. Now, the story comes along and shapes this phenomenological approach by adding later on, whenever you did this to the least of mine, you did this to me. Now the name of God is introduced. That also is faith. These two senses of transcendence are both matters of faith, two senses of faith. They do not differ as "reason" and "faith," but the second faith is more determinate, more specified, the faith of what Derrida would call a "concrete messianism," rather than his more desertified "messianic." Both are faith, and both are a risk, but the more determinate the faith, the bigger the risk. And for Kierkegaard, the greater the risk, the greater the passion and subjective intensity that is required.

Is this at all like thinking God as the trace of the Other or an "immanentist theology" for you?

EW: From the opening question of our conversation, "Why God? Why now?" we have shifted, and rightly so, to: "What can be said about a God that lays claim upon us by way of *Spuren*, the track or trace of transcendence inscribed in the face of the other?" And, with you, I acknowledge that we confide ourselves to narratives in the twilight—perhaps in the twilight of what Nietzsche called idols—in which the demand of the neighbor is always already clouded by the suspicion of religion as socio-cultural construct or, more ominously, a conspiracy against our corporeal and aesthetic sensibilities. I agree, we must attribute undecidability to transcendence while assenting to Levinas's claim that transcendence cannot be separated from ethical responsibility. We are indeed indebted to Levinas for refiguring the traditional aspects of God, divine mercy, and justice, as an ethic of alterity.

Yet I cannot wholeheartedly endorse an immanentism of traces, for that is a theology of fear. By detaching God from the ethical claim of the Other, Levinas acknowledges that one can have religious experience but points out, rightly, that the mystic disengaged from the epiphany of the face lives in isolation. Religious wars, he asserts, may result in the absence of the constraints of alterity. I share these worries, but I shall argue for a theology of both risk and intensity. In the case of Levinas, his fear stems in part from his being steeped in a tradition that is an outgrowth of a nineteenth-century quarrel between Lithuanian Hasidic Judaism and Mithnagdic Judaism, which is geared to the study of texts rather than to prayer. The primary representative of Mithnagdic (non-Hasidic) Judaism was an extraordinary figure, the Gaon of Vilna, whose follower, Haim of Volozhin, played an important role in Levinas's spiritual formation. What drove the Mithnagdic practitioners of Judaism wild was precisely the Hasidic stress upon prayer rather than upon immersion in rabbinic learning. They were deeply suspicious of Hasidism's emphasis upon religious fervor, the white heat of religious emotion.

I share Levinas's suspicion of the frenzy, religious and secular, that has fired the cataclysms of the twentieth century, but I cannot identify entirely either with an immanentism of the trace or with Buber's Romantic version of Hasidism. I would appeal to an ineradicable desire, which is indeed a desire for the Other, but also a desire for desire, a desire that intensifies as it falls back into itself. Described by Diotima in Plato's *Symposium* and reinscribed in recent French thought (e.g., in Derrida's essay "Plato's Pharmakon"), this desire is an ineluctable yearning that knows nevertheless that it yearns for that which may burn and destroy, a risk caught in the story of Moses that remains determinative for the rabbis and so captivated Augustine, who yearned to speak with God face to face. I call what is lacking in Levinas the erotics of transcendence. Both adopting and distancing myself from Levinas, I suggest that the desire for transcendence reflects the hubris of asking and the humility of knowing that what is asked for cannot be granted.

JC: Levinas calls the desire for God, for the Good, "nonerotic par excellence." But you want this desire to be somehow touched with erotic desire, and to include a desire for desire. Now, if I understand you correctly, Levinas would object that this would lead desire back to the self. When Augustine says he is in love with love, he means that he is not only in love with the beloved, but also in love with the joy of love, with the *jouissance* that love brings. Levinas does not condemn that, by any means, but he says that the ethical relation to the neighbor and the stranger does not involve this *jouissance*, is nonerotic, since we do not always like the neighbor or the stranger. But you want to invoke a non-Freudian eros, after Freud—or even before Freud, in Plato—whom you cite, where eros, taken in a wider sense, incites a desire for the Forms, first of all for the Beautiful, but eventually for the Good. In that sense, the desire for God has an erotic component.

Without using the language of eros, either in Freud or in Plato, I would say that the "desire for God" is indeed a passion. If it is not a passion then it does not interest us, does not carry us off and hold us captive, and it has no subjective intensity. Then we would not care. This desire transfixes us, concerns us "all the way down," so to speak; otherwise we would be lukewarm or indifferent. That is as it should be for beings made of "flesh." Kant's "pure practical reason," which masters its "pathological impulses," is a philosopher's creation, a fiction of a dualist philosophical anthropology. It lacks not only biblical but also phenomenological credentials. Desire arises from beings made of flesh, and it is directed toward flesh, toward the fate of the flesh of the other. This may take the form of joy, *jouissance*, the rejoicing of flesh and flesh, love and eros. But sometimes this passion is compassion, suffering with the flesh of the other, with flesh laid low.

Who would say that we can do without overarching desire, a deep desire, desire beyond desire? That for me is in no small part a desire for the future, a passion for the future. We are made up of such desire, and we are at bottom very affirmative, affirming this future, desiring it, hoping and having faith. The name of God is tied up with this desire for the future. The passion for God is a passion for this future. Although his critics do not recognize it, what I am saying here is what Derrida says, what he calls a passion for the impossible, which he also calls a desire for God. But then, at this point, Derrida inserts Augustine's question: *Quid ergo amo cum deum meum amo?* "What then do I love when I love my God?" I love this question because it assumes that, of course, one loves God. Who could deny that? Who would be so hard of heart as not to love God? That would contradict our very make-up, which is to be a passion, a desire, a love of God, of the future. But this love has the indeterminacy that I spoke of and the problem is to determine it, if we can, to ask: What or who are we loving when we love God? Our Maker or our Mommy? Justice and the Trace of God in the Other—or an illusion? I do not know. That is why I am asking the question. But this nonknowing does not stop me, does not stop the passion, or the love, or the desire; the nonknowing even intensifies the desire. So I keep on the move, by a certain faith.

EW: Perhaps one way to approach the erotics of transcendence is to entertain as a hypothesis the idea that the desire for pleasure is natural. Indeed, Levinas does not deny the claims of pleasure, such as those of eating or living in a house, pleasures that are both licit and necessary. Unlike Kant, who concedes that the wish for happiness is natural but that the entitlement to it must be earned and that we require the afterlife in order to gain enough time to do so, Levinas does not think we must deserve these simple joys. At a more complex level, Levinas speaks movingly of the eros of flesh, the pleasures of the caress, which involves one with the other, the near one, but not as the Other of ethics (as you observed). The proximity of eros is not the proximity of ethics. What Levinas fears is the transfer of the intensities of eros to transcendence because the braking power of another's flesh is absent and sheer intensity is unleashed. No matter how close bodies may be, one is distinguishable from the other, but with the transcendent, boundaries disappear. As Levinas avers, with Buber in mind, the mystic speaks to himself in the second person, as if he has entered into God, as if the moth were circled by the fire and burned by it.

The desire I want to talk about is one that is inherently unfulfillable (akin to but not identical with Derrida's passion for the impossible). It is a desire that is always already (messianically) ahead of itself but also remains a desire for the archaic (Augustine's yearning to speak with God as Moses did). It is a desire for the eternal return of the same (the past by way of the future, the future always already in the past), but is not a desire for a static eternity. The messianic is in the trace of a past that cannot be made present. This time scheme avoids what has come to be called by continental philosophers "the logic of presence," which, as Levinas and Derrida have shown, belies time's passing and the otherness of what can never be made present. The yearning for originary presence turns time as presence into static being. It is just this difficulty that besets Buber's admirable effort to encounter the other. Buber's philosophy of dialogue is halfway there, but the yearning for originary presence sets the encounter in a between that is a kind of freeze-frame, white-hot, to be sure, but in which time stops.

Perhaps Teresa of Avila's account of the interior castle in which she wanders freely — that most nomadic of women — seeking but not finding, moving from despair to *jouissance* and back, describes what I am getting at. To be sure, she speaks in the language of interiority, yet God is an inside that is forever outside, the proximate One. The desire for God ignites a *jouissance* that does not impede responsibility for others. Yes, desire is excess and, as Levinas fears, can be expressed in fanaticism.

JC: Then by the "erotics of transcendence" we are to understand the desire for God, *amor dei, le désir de Dieu*. Is that a fair translation for you? I am prepared to say that this desire is a fundamental feature of our make-up. *Inquietum est cor nostrum*: that is the law of our heart. Our hearts are structurally restless, with the restlessness of this desire, which is, as you say, "inherently unfulfillable" and not a desire for "static eternity," which is part of its so-called "postmodernity," and does not expect rest. That is what interests me, the way this most classical, most biblical, desire, this most Augustinian aspiration, has been rediscovered, refashioned — "repeated," as Derrida says — in what is popularly called "postmodernism," or at least a certain version or voice of postmodernism. You, in your book *Saints and Postmodernism*, and I, in *Against Ethics*, both sought to identify a voice in postmodernism that is inspired by this aspiration, that draws its breath from this desire, because until recently, that voice has been almost lost in most of what is popularly consumed under the name *postmodernism*.

Clearly, in its postmodern articulation this desire has been repeated with a difference. For one thing, it does not enjoy a metaphysical status; it does not describe an essence. We would have to concede that such desire has been historically constituted, that it is an effect of texts and traditions, biblical but also nonbiblical, belonging to the historical legacy not only of Jerusalem but also of Athens. We have lost our innocence that this desire is something ahistorical, that we could not be constituted otherwise. For another, this desire is beset by undecidability, on which I have been insisting. We today cannot avoid Augustine's question, What do I love and desire when I love and desire God? But the structure of this desire, the repetition of this structure, is found today among thinkers who are, by conventional standards, "atheists"—like Derrida, the late Jean-François Lyotard, and others. I would also insist, as you do, that this postmodern desire is deeply ethical and political, associating itself with the most disadvantaged and the outcast. So I would agree with you that this desire for God must never be dissociated from the neighbor, lest it become a mystical or religious narcissism.

In a certain way, the most important feature of this postmodern desire for God is, for me, that it throws the very distinction between theism and atheism into undecidability. Take Derrida's work on "hospitality," that most ancient virtue of nomadic peoples. Derrida says that this must be translated into a politics of hospitality for the nomads of our own times, the immigrants and displaced peoples who search for a home today. Now, by the standards of religious orthodoxy—and this is what Derrida says about himself—he "rightly passes as an atheist."[2] But given what he says about hospitality and the passion for justice, which is for him the passion for God, the desire for God, I understand less and less each day what such atheism would mean. And given what you say about Teresa of Avila and her nomadism, about her God Who is not only inside but also outside, I can even see a point of contact between her mystical castle and a deconstructive desire, the passion for the impossible. Does that go too far?

EW: Perhaps the French *le désir de Dieu* approaches what I mean by the eros of transcendence. The expression entails a strange ambiguity: desire belonging to God, God's own desire, and our desire for God. We desire that God's desire be directed toward us, what the tradition called seeking God's love. We are entangled in a legacy of multiple religious narratives, but this should not mean that, having criticized Enlightenment rationality, postmoderns are free to return to a premodern religiosity. I am in accord with your description of the "restless heart," a condition I would describe as the nerve ends of desire, which desire God. I worry, however, about a certain essentialism that this account implies.

Undecidability is indeed a key issue, not only with regard to the indistinguishability of atheism from belief but in connection with related matters, especially that of semblance. It is a truism to note that Western philosophy has focused on the issue of the difference between appearance and reality. Whether the real was thought to be an idea or an object reached by the senses, the real could, after all, be ascertained. Thus, however much the word had varied, the melody remained the same: philosophers claimed to know the real.

In the postmodern culture of images, so-called virtual reality raises the problem to a new level. Consider, for example, the violence of virtuality and, conversely, the virtualization of violence. Nothing is more common in the postmodern world than the replication of the violence of interactive video games and Internet images. In a world of semblances, people die by violence, but their deaths are and are not understood as being real. Violence is envisaged as simultaneously actualizing and de-realizing death. If all is semblance, a game, death's finality is fictive, undecidable. The question of atheism's undecidability can be construed as though the ethics of the atheist were a thinned-out version of theological ethics, a position to which Nietzsche alerted us. Both belief and atheism have become, to use our language, virtualized, thus less and less distinguishable from one another. What is more, if transcendence and immanence are inextricable, the atheist could see *le désir de Dieu* not only as our desire for God but also as God's desire. The atheist can acknowledge that the one who places herself at the disposal of the other bears witness to more than the sheer fact that the self must subject itself to another. The other's vulnerable flesh breaks into semblances not to attest cognitive certainty but to make an ethical claim that transcends the presentation of face and body as phenomena.

JC: I think it is important to remember that the idea behind undecidability has never been to leave us adrift in indecision but to raise the intensity of the decision, the "responsibility" for the decision. The more decidable things are, the more rule governed they are and the more easily we can excuse ourselves for what we have done by saying, "This is really not my doing, it's the rule." The idea is that, at a certain point, one needs to act, so the resolution of the undecidability is carried out in the pragmatic order. As a "cognitive" matter, the debate goes on and can last forever. The quest for what you call "cognitive certainty" always fails. That is what happens, in my view, with respect to God, a word that, I believe, has primarily a pragmatic rather than a semantic force. God, as Kierkegaard—or "Johannes Climacus"—said, is primarily a deed not a thought. As a thought, "God" is the thought of what we cannot think, of what is too much, or too high, for thought, and if we wait for clarification we will wait forever. But God, without the scare quotes, means something to do— hospitality, for example. That is why I do not know what it means to say that one who affirms unconditional hospitality, if there is such a thing, can rightly pass for an atheist, not if God is the God of hospitality. The name of God is very powerful, full of force, of pragmatic effect, ordering us to the neighbor, directing our desire, *le désir de Dieu*, to the neighbor, as Levinas says. So the name of God is not to be used lightly, not to be used in vain, because it is a proclamation of peace and commits the one who uses it to peace.

Now, as you say, there is anything but peace in the world of virtual reality, which is a world of violence, of violence compounded with violence, filled with virtual death. When schoolchildren kill their teachers and classmates, we are convinced that they have been overcome by the images in which they are immersed, that they reenact the virtual murders they witness hour after hour on video and TV monitors. How real for them is the difference between pulling a trigger on a gun and clicking a mouse? They learn afterward—in the flesh, so to speak, and always too late—that these dead and wounded bodies are not only images, that the images are surfaces of vulnerable flesh. But I would say that the godlessness of the virtual world is not to be found in the image, but in the violence, and, if in the image, then in the extent to which it facilitates violence. The first question many people have about Mark Taylor's recent work on Las Vegas as the emblem of the postmodern world has to do with violence.[3] How does such an image establish critical leverage on murder, on racial injustice, on poverty, or at least provide the possibility for a critique?

But I do not think that it is simply a question of establishing an adequate theory of the difference between image and reality, as if we had to mount a defense of a new realism. That is the reaction, a reactionary reaction, of certain "religious realists" who are frightened by contemporary theories of interpretation, textuality, and imagology, who "resist theory." I think it is, rather, a question of a critical appreciation of the pragmatic difference between images that spill blood and images that spell peace. I would agree that we have no access to an image-free reality, that there is no flesh that is not clothed in images. We always have to do with a world that is constantly being imaged, today more than ever, when the power of representation has been multiplied to infinity. The "real" will always be saturated with image, or it will not appear at all. It is a question of pragmatics, of the deed. Godlessness is not the image, or the undecidability between image and reality, and it is not a question of breaking up images with a new realism. After all, what is older, more biblical, and more beautiful than to be an image? Is not the whole biblical form of life organized around the idea of becoming, of making ourselves, the image of God, which means the image of peace and hospitality? Where have there been greater expenditures of imaging and imagination than in religious discourse? The issue is to meet image with image, to interrupt the "virtualization of violence and the violence of virtualization," as you so strikingly put it, with God's image and God's power, with the power of a divine imagination and a divine imagology.

So the *amor dei*, *le désir de Dieu*, in this culture of images, is to be the *imago dei*, to let the images of God fly up like sparks, and to affirm a certain holy undecidability between the "image" and "God."

EW: We must indeed act in the absence of a cognitive certainty that is, in any case, unattainable. Still, I want to hold that ethical responsibility cannot be cordoned off from cognitive undecidability. The field in which decisions are enacted, the everyday world and, if I may be forgiven a cumbersome expression, the discursive space of authorization, the space of Ethics, are intertwined. By the latter I mean the space in my world that is seized by the Other who "burglarizes" the comfortable house, which constitutes for many of us our ordinary existence, with the force of her or his claims. Yet I want to say, with Levinas, that I remain an empiricist: the need of the other is my opportunity for action in a world I cannot but must know, if only in the sense of anticipating the consequences of my actions. My being for the other is contingent upon the way in which the world engages me. Thus the problem of virtuality, or, as the French prefer, of simulacra, is intrinsic to the way in which we encounter the Other in the culture of images.

Are we not beings whose encounter with the world remains governed by the limits of our particular perspectives? Perhaps nowhere has cognitive uncertainty been paired more intimately with radical nonviolence than in the tradition of the Jains of the Gujarat province of India. In a highly complex orchestration of this uncertainty, Jain logicians argue that every possible assertion—for example, that a thing is, that it is not—must be prefaced by the term *perhaps* or *maybe*. We can never be sure about what we assert, but what stands fast for us is the proscription against violence, against doing harm to living beings. I cite this non-Western tradition to suggest that metaphysical uncertainty can be acknowledged at the same time as the wrongness of violence is attested.

To return to the problem of images, you suggest that the problem is that of violence and not of images as such. But can violence be segregated from the image? Just as motive cannot be segregated from the act, violence and its aim are inseparable. Did not William James argue that act and intent are inseparable, that in fact the body acts before the intention comes to cognitive awareness? Violence becomes what it is by virtue of its object. Unlike desire, which may be objectless, violence is aimed at what can be specified. Violence inhabits the image that solicits it.

My worry about the culture of images is that, just as alterity steals in as a thief in the night, so too do images. The world's religions are replete with temptation stories, the "evil one" that tempts Hasidic masters, the demons that assault St. Anthony, the armies of Mara that attack Gautama the Buddha. Awareness of this infiltration by the other that is other than ethical otherness has generated rituals of purification. In a post-Freudian postmodern world, "Forgive them, for they know not what they do" has become "Forgive them, for although they do not, cannot know what they do, they are responsible."

It must be pointed out that the issue of images is a thorny question in Judaic tradition. To be sure, the Hebrew Bible is rich in epiphanies. Yet Aaron's fashioning and Moses' smashing of the golden calf remain paradigmatic. Without rehearsing a complex history, it can be said that the fear of idolatry is central to Jewish belief. As a religion of the text, Judaism is compatible with the intertextuality of hermeneutical and poststructuralist interpretation. Nevertheless, is not the power of the narrative about smashing images itself contingent upon the extraordinary images it evokes—the golden figures, the dancing virgins, the ire of Moses? Like Maimonides, Levinas is concerned with the idolatry of the image and turns to the primordial language of saying or command that precedes what is said in actual speech. What are we to think? Does the plethora of images in our culture preclude the sacralization of specific images? Is idolatry a political rather than a theological issue? Can the virtual be marshaled so as to make a joyful noise unto the Lord?

JC: I would say that idolatry is both theological and ethico-political, because whatever form it takes, it means that I have constructed an image of myself and I have excluded the other: That is a danger for both politics and theology. The idol threatens to subvert the desire for God and turn it into an act of self-love, even as it makes hospitality a way to pursue our own interests. So, as a concluding remark in our conversation about God, let me say something about idolatry.

I begin by expressing my admiration for what you say about the Jains; they sound very "postmodern," as you describe them. I too think we must attach a coefficient of uncertainty to our positive claims, our "positions," all the while unflinchingly facing up to our responsibility to the neighbor and the stranger. That responsibility runs on its own, as it were, and does not wait for philosophers or theologians or anyone else to validate it. We are overtaken by it, "burglarized"—to use the Levinasian expression you cite. It steals past the guard of cognitive scrutiny, whether we like it or not, whether or not it meets certain cognitive standards. That is why Kant thought that, if Newtonian physics invalidates ethical responsibility, then so much the worse for Newtonian physics, whose cognitive status must now be redescribed to allow for ethics. Ethics works in the dark, without the light of cognitive validation. The voice of conscience is a voice sounding in the dark.

But it is interesting to me that the voice of conscience has been reinterpreted in postmodernism as the voice of the Other, as the Other in me, as the call addressed to me by the Other, rather than my own inner voice, the inner soliloquy the ego has with itself. I cannot ascertain or determine who calls when the other calls—is it God, my unconscious, a linguistic or a cultural constellation, or simply the other one, the neighbor or the stranger? That is undecidable, but it is no less urgent or inescapable, and I am no less accused. The specifically religious gesture, at least in the case of biblical religion, is to determine this voice as the voice of God, who says that whatever you do to these least ones of mine, these little nobodies, for good or for ill, you do to me. That determines, fixes the call with the name of God, raises the stakes, takes the risk of faith. But it is still a risk we take in the dark, and it does not relieve us of the need to ask: "What do I love when I love my God?"

Now, whatever their differences, I am inclined to see a continuity between textualists and imagologists, between the textualist insistence on the undecidability between signifier and signified, which typifies post-structuralism, and the imagological insistence on the undecidability between image and reality, which typifies postmodernism. There is nothing outside the text and there is nothing outside the image, not in the sense that there is nothing real but in the sense that nothing comes naked and unmediated, untouched by text or image. There is no uninterpreted fact of the matter that relieves us of our responsibility to read, sort through, and interpret the texts and images in which we are immersed. As to how things are without text and image, we are utterly in the dark.

But that is not a wail of despair for me. I do not lament these aporias and difficulties and curse the day the text or image was born. I take this undecidability to be the phenomenology of our times, the best description available of the difficulty of our life amidst what David Tracy calls "plurality and ambiguity." Undecidability is, I think, the setting in which a very ancient desire, the *amor dei, le désir de Dieu*, is enacted, reenacted, repeated—the site of our religion, even if this be what Derrida calls a religion without religion. That is what interests me today, the desire for God, a postcritical, poststructural, postmodern desire. That is the form this desire takes now, at the end of the Enlightenment's failure to reduce that desire to something less than it is, a fin-de-siècle desire coming at the end of the millennium and of a century of horrors.

The threat of the idol, which is the image fashioned by our own narcissism, is countered not by absolute invisibility, which asks too much of beings made of flesh, but by the icon. The icon is the visible image that draws us beyond ourselves because we cannot consume it whole with our vision. The icon gives form and body to our desire, to a self-transcending desire to think what we cannot comprehend, to love what we cannot have, to give without return. The icon incarnates the eros of transcendence, the desire for God, which is made flesh in the neighbor and the stranger, above all in the least of these little ones. Beyond the dispassionate God of classical metaphysical theology, beyond the deiform Ego of modernity, the God takes flesh in what St. Paul calls *ta me onta*, the nonbeings and nobodies of this world, not as a *prima causa* but as a command: whatsoever you do unto these little ones you do to Me. This command can only be heard in the dark. One task for thinking now, after metaphysics, would be to describe the various icons of our desire for God.

EW: Our path has led from "Why God? Why now?" to the question of how we are to think God. If negation is postmodernity's conceptual legacy, let us invoke it. Consider first the ancient skeptics who claimed that we cannot know the way things are. Postmoderns, following Nietzsche, contend that our knowledge is perspectival, that our assertions about what is are prefaced by a perhaps, a maybe, and that what we claim to know, whether we realize it or not, is enmeshed in moral claims. Many medieval mystics negated the possibility of making affirmative statements about God and asserted that we can only say what God is not. But, as Derrida has pointed out, behind such talk is the assumption that there is a fully present, omniscient, and omnipotent being. Postmoderns whose thinking runs along the lines of recent French thought envisage instead a God of excess, restless—one who is more than can be encompassed by thought. To be in the image of God, in this context, means to express this superabundance as hospitality and as gift, a hospitality such as Abraham is described as having extended to the angels—a gift that transcends what Aristotle called magnanimity in that it entails not the disbursal of one's goods but the willingness to suffer in the place of the other. In Hegel's philosophy, it is the negative that moves the historical process along. The slips and glitches, the disasters of history, are seen by Hegel as necessary, as fueling historical progress. The process is seen as rational and is realized at history's end in an immanent and self-reflective Absolute, Hegel's God. That history is not rational has been shown by Nietzsche and Kierkegaard, among others. The postmodern thinker recognizes that the progress promised by the Enlightenment and German Idealism has eluded us. Yet in his account of history Hegel has also argued that we can look back at the images of history—wind the film backward, as it were. In the age of virtuality, where a plethora of images confuses and startles, this looking backward initiates a responsibility to dead others. We cannot say for sure "Thus it was," but we remain responsible for the dead others.

The risks entailed by postmodern ethics are significant. Perhaps we have preempted the other's narrative. No longer can we fill in the blanks with the assurance that God wants this or that. In the light of this dismantling of conceptual structures, what remains? We are left with a desire that has no specifiable object, a desire that desires the desire of the Other, whose desire is infinite. Yet God's desire is also a command. So I would insist on a twofold perspective. There is the desire of God's desire, our yearning for it, our effort to lure God. I have called the exaltation and joy of this desire the erotics of transcendence, known to Hasidic masters and Christian saints. Levinas is right to be wary of this enthusiasm whose religious and secular versions have been implicated in the horrors of the twentieth century. We cannot evade the ecstatic, but we can in flesh and bone feel the constraint of alterity. The second perspective is not a vision of alterity but the pressure of the other, who commands us in her or his vulnerability. How can we know we have been commanded? We cannot say for sure. Perhaps, perhaps . . . And yet we are constrained.

20

Heterological History
A Conversation

EDITH WYSCHOGROD AND CARL RASCHKE

In *The Ethics of Remembering*, Edith Wyschogrod applies the familiar postmodernist concept of "heterology"—the study of Otherness or "alterity"—to the philosophy of history. The following conversation with Carl Raschke explores the notion of "heterological history," as Wyschogrod delineates it, in relationship to a variety of contemporary philosophical and theological themes.

Carl Raschke: In *The Ethics of Remembering*, you challenge the post-structuralist (and hence postmodernist) deployment of the "trace" as it pertains to the reading, and the writing, of history. Whereas in such writers as Derrida, Taylor, and even to a certain extent Levinas the trace implies an unrecoverable presence, you seem to be arguing that the "ethical" demands of historiography, in which the other is both engaged and "named," lead us toward a new understanding of "heterology." This understanding differs from how the word has been used by many philosophers to date. Do I misread you?

Edith Wyschogrod: Your question raises fundamental issues of absent presence. I argue that the past itself is inscrutable and thus always already an unsurpassable negation. It would seem that only an apophatics of history would be possible. Yet here the model—I invoke it with fear and trembling—of a broken natural theology may help. Just as Levinasian ethics is contingent upon the face not in its phenomenological *Leibhaftigkeit* but as trace, so that there both is and is not flesh, so too the artifacts and images of the past both are and are not signifiers. Here Kierkegaard helps. We make the motions of faith (religiosity A)—but B, faith itself, is a secret, the secret of a command imposed upon us, not by, but as, the vulnerability of the other, whose givenness is not infra-phenomenal but supra-phenomenonal.

In what sense are we to construe alterity, the subject of the hetero-logical historian? Whose alterity? What narrative? Two directions occur to me. First, there is the character of the past itself. I claim that the past is "an unsurpassable negation" that can never be brought back materially, so that there is an apophasis belonging to the past that cannot be overcome. Yet second, the past is transmitted via lan-guage and image. So the past is a secret in the Derridean sense. But this secret begs to be revealed.

CR: The problem you raise in the book, so far as I read it, is an inextricably critical one, so far as "postmodern" philosophy of his-tory, or at least a "historical" reading of the textuality of the past, is concerned. Though I know you have little in common with the theo-logical movement known as "Radical Orthodoxy"—and would not want even to be associated in such a way—you are responding to the same kind of perceived dissymmetry in the Derridean wing of postmodernism. Can we call them "the Branch Derrideans"? That dissymmetry consists in the refusal of presence. Radical Orthodoxy, of course, indulges in a Romantic reading of Augustinianism and Chalcedonianism in what amounts at the same time to a curious "the-ologization" of Heidegger, the utterance of Being as presence in the Christian incarnation. Radical orthodoxy wants to go beyond "onto-theology," which it claims was invented by Scotus, to recover what it seems to suggest is a divine presence that has been overhistoricized by modern and, hence, postmodern thought. This overhistoriciza-tion, following the argument of Michael Gillespie, in their view is what has led to nihilism.

The overhistoricization of the divine derives from the overdeter-mination of the sign of divinity, Derrida's "transcendental signified." Ironically, you too appear to be aware of the perils of this overdeter-mination, particularly to the degree that you talk about the "com-modification" of alterity and the loss of mediation within "specular culture." Baudrillard's strange sort of horizontal eschatology does not seem to suit you. In fact, you suggest a strategy, which you don't develop very far, of out-Augustining Augustine through something you call "semiological memory."

In the final chapter, you point toward a remembering (in the Heideggerian sense) of fractured memory through an ethic of community. Is it possible—and I hesitate to say it—you are on the same track as the Radical Orthodoxy movement, but with a far more sophisticated hermeneutic? The power of the Levinasian, rather than the Derridean, critique of Heidegger looms large here for me and seems to be an overshadowing "presence" in your own argument.

EW: You speak about my worries with regard to the perils of the overdetermination of the sign of divinity, especially with the commodification of alterity and Baudrillard's, shall we say, eschatology of the simulacra. Are my fears, you ask, reminiscent of Radical Orthodoxy's concerns with postmodernism?

I should like to point to some fundamental differences: First, there is what I call the discursive space of authorization, which, for me, is the alterity of a transcendent other in her/his corporeal vulnerability, whose traces are found in the discursive and artifactual "mud" of history. The docetism of Milbank, his emphasis upon a resurrection body that feasts ghostlike at an eschatological banquet, remains ethically problematic—feasting while others fast, as it were. Thus, what authorizes his discourse is a future that willy-nilly has lost contact with the vicissitudes of time. (At least Nietzsche's eternal recurrence takes account of willing the same, with all of its pains as well as pleasures). Moreover, Milbank uses his conceptual repertoire, the social sciences, in order to criticize, first, the bad boys of modernity, but second a supervening postmodernism that both criticizes and endorses Enlightenment suppositions.

It then becomes possible to say, as Milbank does, that theology is the queen of the social sciences. As far as Catherine Pickstock is concerned, and, mutatis mutandis, Marion, after the depradations of modernity's heritage of nominalism are cleared away, there is recourse to liturgy as the default position. Pickstock is astonishingly nonbiblical: her return to the Latin rite is, as you note, a Romantic reading of Chalcedon and Augustine, a criticism to which Marion is not vulnerable, as his brilliant use of Ecclesiastes in *God beyond Being* attests.

To return to Milbank: he has suggested that an ethics of alterity (such as the one that can be found in my work) based on self-sacrifice is masochistic, an odd appeal to psychoanalytic categories, and overlooks the ways in which the ascetic tradition has used pain. There is a problem, however, in a purely Levinasian account of alterity: finding ways to pleasure once one has abandoned Aristotelian and Kantian orthodoxies and nineteenth-century visions of progress. Is it possible to develop a poetics of history, one in which an aesthesis of the past could open intense registers of pleasure? There are, of course, dangers, such as reading the past in a re-platonizing mode by identifying the beautiful and the good, as in Whitehead and Harteshorne, or by aestheticizing the blood and gore of history, as in epic traditions, or via a transgressive ascetic of indulgence. I need to think more about the possibility of finding hedonic byways to engage the heterological historian.

CR: What you say about historical aesthesis, and the possibilities as well as the perils of the hedonicity of the "mud" of history, is extremely provocative, to say the least. It is clear that Radical Orthodoxy has no sense of concrete history, a pure semiotic history, a history that is in many ways anterior to the writing of history, which is what we usually mean by history, as Michel de Certeau reminds us. I would argue that Milbank is in actuality an Anglican sort of old Hegelian, one who affirms the *principium theologicum* of "incarnation" without acceding to the transdialectic of grave and resurrection that makes Christian eschatology possible in the first place. Radical Orthodoxy in this sense is far less biblical, and hence less "orthodox," than neo-orthodoxy ever was. A truly "radical" form of orthodoxy would take up the challenge of what you would call "aestheticization," because the faith of Calvary, as opposed to some kind of pseudo-Johannine *conjunctio oppositorum*, requires it.

I don't want to sound like I am doing "Christian theology" here, but it seems that heterological history by necessity involves us in the pain and pleasure of history, implied in the dramaturgy of Christian narrative, not to mention the very iconicity of the Cross. Such a hedonics of history can never really be written; it can only be simulated, which renders it a portion of the "spectacle of history." But heterological history also demands the deconstruction of all "spectacular" narratives of history. If I read you in the manner I believe you seek to be read, then can we urge that the heterological historian is doing something much bolder than reconstituting certain "voices" from the past that have been barred from recitation within the royal theater of discourse? Is the heterological historian not going beyond the writing of history to the "aesthetic" demonstration of sign-charged *revelata*—*revelata* that quiver not just in the violence of the mud and blood, but in the still, small passions of the nameless ones, *revelata* that are not yet nameable because they bear the trace of the name beyond names?

They are *revelata* that confound the master narratives of all history making, including the theological or the sort of "liturgical" that, in true Augustinian fashion, can't distinguish between *signum* and *res*. I guess my question, therefore, is (ironically speaking): Isn't heterological history the truest sort of "radical doxy" (not an "ortho-doxy," but a "hetero-doxy," if by *heteros* we mean the trace of the divine glory and by *doxa* we mean the "glory, or presence, that can only be named in its incalculable, and often radically humble, trace")? A radical orthodoxy seeks to put on Pilate's robes. A radical heterology takes up its cross.

EW: I would agree about Milbank, who identifies Hegel's enterprise with his own. Milbank's theological critique, one that is nevertheless a critique through practice of "all historical human community," is not Hegelian to the core. The Christian story is not over and done with, superseded by philosophy, although, for him, Hegel succeeds in overcoming the individual subject of modernity. It is here that Pickstock becomes interesting in her claim for the Christian liturgical consummation of philosophy, the Latin rite. I cannot endorse this sanitization of philosophy, one that also precludes pluralism, but I can understand the aesthestic pull to which she is subject. I too am, I confess, a swooner before the discursive and material constructions of the past. But here one must appeal to a deconstructed *aesthesis*, to the *aesthesis* of ruins, as it were, for even the artifacts of the past that are intact bear the scars of time's passing.

Whether we gaze at the ruins of Ankhor or the relatively sound Sainte Chapelle, each is always already fissured by time. Even restoration, the plastic surgery of the Sistine Chapel's ceiling, attests to the depredations of time, perhaps even more so. Each of these instances becomes a simulation of itself in Benjamin's sense of the reproduction, but now one that lacks an original. Yet it is time's power negated and the negation of this negation, or denegation, as Derrida calls it, that opens the way for an aesthetics of recovery of a past that is present and absent.

But aesthetic power is always (and already) fissured by the mortuary power of the past, the pain of past suffering, from which there is no dispensation. Still, you may ask, can the heterological historian continue to keep the promise to focus upon the suffering other in this context? A hedonics of history, you say, cannot be written but only simulated. Narration is, as Ricoeur noticed, wedged between description and prescription. Have I fallen into a Platonic trap of binding the good and the beautiful? Your phrase *"revelata* that quiver" suggests another passion, however, one that is both attested and evaded by Levinas. I am glad that you mentioned glory, in that I have thought and written about glory, tracking its flashing from Aquinas to Levinas.

Thus I would appeal to a revivified notion of glory, one attested in the broken body of the other, both that of the victim and that of the one who is willing to substitute her/himself for the other. One is compelled to surround this claim with caveats: Look out for the creation of suffering in order to suffer, for pride in one's strength to withstand vicissitude. But the language of glory can be used to describe the suspension of the *conatus* to know or to do, as becoming pure passivity before the need of the other. The one who does so says in effect, *"Me voici,* here I am," bears witness to and is chastened by the glory of the infinite and in so doing is glorified.

CR: What you say about "glory" raises some interesting questions regarding a kind of "biblical" thinking about history versus the "sacramental" historicism that seems to dominate most of the Radical Orthodox writers. It would seem to me that Pickstock, in particular, forces a kind of "aesthetic eschatology" of the historical, which others such as Milbank try to adapt to the political sphere. Aesthetic politics with an eschatological drive, of course, can be a disturbing sign, as your work on totalization, and that of other thinkers such as Eric Voegelin, have pointed out. The term *orthodoxy,* of course, could be rendered from the Greek as "right glory." It is the very nature of "orthodoxy" to have solved in its peculiar kind of theological aesthesis the problem of the brokenness of history. That brokenness, and even history's madness, is "redesigned" in terms of an architecture of "glorious" simulacra for the sake of a vicarious divine kingdom. That was the point of Dostoyevsky's Grand Inquisitor. Biblical "theology" draws glory from brokenness, not from the simulacra of the "religious."

I think that was always the fundamental argument of neo-orthodoxy, as opposed to Radical Orthodoxy. I am wondering if you could talk more about ruins and monuments in this vein. I guess my question comes down to this: can a heterological history go beyond the "aesthetic" and move toward the "prophetic" (particularly in Levinas's sense of "prophetic," that is, an ontology that transcends all forms of Hellenic *aesthesis*).

EW: I think we may be picking up some special meanings of a polysemic term, that is, *history*, and in so doing we have lost sight of its diachronicity. To be sure, we have focused on framework issues, history under the aegis of "aesthetic eschatology" (Pickstock) or of a "political eschatology" (Milbank). I would like to turn our conversation from radical orthodoxy's spin on the future to another perspective on the question of communities to come.

To begin with, the historian bestows the narrative of the past as a gift to the future, a future we must think of in terms of possibility. As Blanchot points out, possibility is excess, always (and already) something more, "to be plus the power to be." The challenge is to convert the plethora of images and information, which rapidly disintegrate into the detritus of culture, into artifactual existents. It is not the Heideggerian nostalgia for *Dinge* (handmade objects fraught with human meaning) that provides the model but rather *bricolage*, in Lévi-Strauss's sense. What I am getting at is the construction of community as an artwork. If there is an eschatological vision here, it is community as the gratuitous production for and of nothing, which, as I tried to say in my book, "unwrites the predicative and iterative schema" that provided its conditions. Neither didactic in the sense of the moral work of art nor sentimental in a Romantic sense, such a community would be a "workless work," one that depends upon the desire and the *conatus* both to archive and to undo.

As for the question of ruins, which you raised and which in part led to these reflections, I see ruins as artifactual existents and artifactual existents as discursive. Thus the temples of Ankhor Wat, the Arch of Titus, and the Lukasa memory board (a royal genealogical record of the Luba people of Africa) are linguistic, and, conversely, linguistic records written and oral conjure up material worlds. My point: we must think through the ethics of alterity as applied to history as both an unsaying and a desire for the possible, the desire for a future community. I will risk this: the work of the historian, whether her/his medium is the written word or the visual image, is the creation of a vast Web site that is not totalizing but disseminated, hypertextual, like and unlike the *khōra* of the *Timaeus* as glossed by Derrida.

CR: I take it you are saying, then, that the heterological historian opens up what we might call an ontology of the never-before-spoken, a speaking not of the "unspoken" in the more general, Heideggerian sense, but of that which prior to its historicization was not deemed (perhaps because it signifies what was hitherto the "unredeemed" of history) but of the unspeakable and speechless. Because this kind of "diachronic" heterology reaches beyond the "ethical" horizons of texts that generate discourses of redemption, it also offers a prospectus for an "ethos," and hence an "architectonic," of community, that is, neither a content/architecture nor a "frame" (*parergon*) in Derrida's sense. It is interesting that you are going this way, because lately I have wished to speak about "red narratives" (the "religious" in the semiotic sense), as opposed to Derrida's "white mythologies" (the "metaphysical" texture of all our historicizing). The problem of the red narrative arises from the way in which we historicize about the "native"—particularly the "Native American"—who demands to be more than the ethico-political construct of victim, the hetero-voice that speaks "indigenously" in a deeper way than the dialectic of repression and recovery can allow and therefore requires a new kind of "historical thinking."

Here I am taking Vine Deloria to a more philosophical level. Can the heterological historian deal with narratives that are rich and real, that in a strange way can even be considered "Western," but are not "white" or "Euro-linguistic," that do not permit of stereotypical sorts of discursive dichotomizations ("religious" versus "scientific," "literacy" versus "morality," etc.), which in fact dismiss them and render them silent in the name of "recovering" them? I am not asking you to respond to this particular thesis (i.e., the "red" and the "white"), but I am asking, in effect, whether the possibility of community in heterological history truly signifies that our "common" discourse must change as we become "interested" (in Levinas's peculiar meaning of the word) in the alterity of what has not yet been signified as history.

Is it possible for a heterological historian to continue to speak as a historian at all? I am reminded, by way of analogy, of the anthropologist who "goes native." Even that trope is ill advised, for we are talking not so much about the deconstruction of the narratives of history as about their death and reinscription. Certainly this kind of death and reinscription is happening on an ad hoc basis in contemporary literature. What about history, or the history of philosophy and theology?

EW: In thinking about the very interesting issue of the historian's relation to death and reinscription, I want to consider a new context suggested by your comments: the heterological historian as situated at the interface of community and economy. The historian cannot ignore the process of globalization, that of the making and distribution of goods, including information and services, for which new power constellations have been created. One tires of hearing this point reiterated, yet still, this is the world the hetero-voice (your term) must address.

I should like to treat the matter genealogically and resort (like Heidegger) to the pre-Socratics as the default position for contextualizing the global economy. Let's appeal to Anaximander's notion of the *apeiron*, the unlimited, "the first principle of things that are, a 'that' from which the coming-to-be of things and qualities takes place and to which they return making reparation according to the order of time."

The *apeiron* can be seen as an ontological storehouse but, contra Heidegger, also as a moral topos, one whose very existence places a demand upon us: things must make reparation for their injustice according to the order of time. This, I would argue, is the topos out of which the Greek *dikē*, justice, emanates as a demand for reparation, one that is always already unrealized in that reparation is impossible because of the diachronicity of historical time. The task of the heterological historian, then, is to insert her/himself into this topos, to affect it with alterity, not only in the sense of introducing the voice of the other but by shifting from cyclical to vertical or linear time. The narrative is a call for community issued by the historian through the very act of narration, a call for the redistribution of narrative space.

Such a historian is the practitioner of an *askesis*: she/he follows Blanchot's injunction that one should learn to think with pain. All of this may be placing too great an onus upon the historian. But let me risk the following. The historian is engaged in transmitting the texts of the past (visual, artifactual, oral, and written) in the manner Foucault attributes to the Stoic practice of writing: identity is constituted through the recollection of things said, along with the interplay of readings and assimilative writing that, taken together, constitute an identity through which a history can be read.[1] The aim of the historian may not be to attain Stoic harmony but may still be one in which a disseminated commonality is discernible, one in which the "we" is constituted as an unformed "formation" of others.

CR: It strikes me that the hetero-historians truly have their work cut out for them. You raise the question of historical writing as a form of historical justice. But in drawing on Heidegger, and, ultimately, Anaximander you raise a profound and to a certain extent disquieting question — to what extent does a disseminated commonality, which can in the last analysis only be metaphorized, run the risk of pushing the writing of history toward some latter-day grand narrative of divine default, an epic of "revenge against time," in Nietzsche's sense? I recognize that heterological history is a two-edged sword, so to speak. The thinking of history, like all thinking, requires a profound anamnesis. And the sign of the heterological invariably speaks for this anamnesis.

Yet Nietzsche, in his warning about the "abuse" of history, urges us to forget as well. I acknowledge that even this caveat poses the equal danger of denying history, which is what most historicizing amounts to, if we follow de Certeau's discussion about the writing of history. The genius of the heterological historian, as you frame it, is her or his ability to remake de Certeau's "theater of history" into a theater of cruelty, a deconstitution of the representations that forge the regime of historical writing by carrying them from stage to street, by ringing down the curtain on specular culture (your term) and instantiating a "participatory" play of justice. Where do we end up: the day of Yahweh, or Thermidor? It seems to me that the beauty of a "heterological" community is not its endless iterability but its unidentified "electability." Is the question of justice ultimately global, or providential? You have written extensively about saints. In terms of heterological history, who might they be? That is where the question of community, it seems to me, arises.

EW: The transformation of a particular narrative into a grand narrative is a danger intrinsic to narrative, as is the construing of narrative as a script for action. The alternative is silence. But narratives can build into the text the conditions of their own permeability, the narrative of the other Other. There is also help in Lyotard's understanding of the differend: restoring to the plaintifs of history the means to argue. When the idiom of one of several parties to a dispute becomes the language of litigation, the wrong suffered by the other cannot be heard. This position also, at least in part, takes care of the Nietzschean injunction to let memory go in that, as Lyotard points out, the option to speak also entails the option not to speak. Thus "It is possible that p" is true means we can also say "It is possible that not p." He says that "the opposite of speaking is possible does not mean the necessity of keeping quiet. To be able not to speak is not the same as not to be able to speak."[2]

What he is getting at is the difference between imposed silence and the power to withhold speech. To release the speech of the victim into the arena of public language gives the historian, whether she/he wants this power or not, the power to remain silent and thus to censor. The historian speaks from a juridical terrain. Without naming any specific group, let us say Group *A* has been both the victim and the perpetrator of historical mayhem. The historian judges how to present the "case of *A*." Whether the historian acknowledges this power or not, historical language conceals an operational dimension, even if its subject is a remote historical event. Thus, for example, the relation of imperial Rome to its colonies has been taken to resemble and to differ from modern colonialism: the historian works from the order of the same and the different, from the contemporary horizon to that of the past (to invoke Gadamer). Historians themselves cannot avoid being appropriators and despoilers, which is why the primordial stationing of the historian in the terrain of *dikē*, justice, attentive to the imperative of the other, is crucial.

CR: That clears things up immensely. Yet I would raise, in summation, the issue of what might be called the heterology of justice itself.

Empowering the victim of history with the option to speak or to remain silent may in the final word be what the writing of history is all about. No matter what option the victim selects, she or he is disestablishing, or deconstituting, the juridical narratives that have given audibility to former cries of injustice or the uncovering of censored accounts. We do not have to be at all arcane here. The history of slavery, its critique, and its abolition, for example — not to mention the emergence in the late twentieth century of feminist reading and writing of herstory — is a series of reciprocally inscribed layers of moral judicial texts that can be sequenced as progressive "heterological" interventions into some prior narrative of the right and the good. Not to speak is simply to refuse to inscribe a new layer. Thus, heterological history may be the instrument of historical transformation in its own right. I am wondering if you could comment, finally, on the relationship between historical dialectics in the classic Marxist sense and the writing of heterological history.

EW: Thanks for putting the matter of justice so well. You ask about the Marxist view in relation to heterological history. One could argue that Marx reads metaphysics as economy and economy as metaphysics. This claim does not open the way to interpreting

Marx as a monistic materialist. To be sure, the conflict between bourgeoisie and proletariat is about distribution of commodities, but commodities circulate as discourse, that is, as a relation of meaning constellations. The discovery of the link between power and discourse is not a discovery of Foucault but rather is reflected in Marx's view of fetishization: one could alternatively argue, as Ernst Bloch does, that the production process is like the Hegelian idea. Of course, to interpretations of Marx there is no end. But what is pertinent in all of this is that the saga of production is, as has often been noted, teleological and totalizing. As Nancy claims, human beings, in this interpretation, produce their own essence as production.

The preoriginary condition of the community of the heterological historian is exteriority, the commanding presence of the other. I argue that what remains outside of the production process is a welcoming of the other, hospitality and peace. All this may have a polyannaish ring, as long as one does not recognize that such a community must be watchful, attentive to the ever-present possibility of violence. After all, the other plays a proscriptive role that may invite what it is hoped she/he will prevent. Law transforms the primordial relation with the other into specific rules, but law requires vigilance. Yet the historian offers hope, hope for what may be possible (if improbable), in part through her gift of inscription. Citing Nietzsche, she may say that when the past speaks, it speaks as an oracle to the future.

PART VI

The Art in Ethics

Pa Ubu: By our green candle . . . let us consult our Conscience. There he is in the suitcase, all covered with cobwebs. As you can see, we don't overwork him. . . . And we should like to know how you have the insolence to appear before us in your shirt tails.

Conscience: Conscience like truth usually goes without a shirt.

—**Alfred Jarry**, *Ubu Roi*

There is an artistry in ethics, that of alterity, an artistry that may be manifested in works of literature, music, and the visual arts. Such works may allow the sensory inundation of what is reflected upon to enter into reflection itself, or absence may inscribe its traces on the surface of the work. Unlike didactic art that attempts to teach right and wrong in what is ultimately propositional form, such works may elicit the white noise or chaos of an unheard unsayability in the transgressive language of the said.

Illustration: S. Augustinus. Music Division, New York Public Library for the Performing Arts, Astor, Lenox, and Tilden Foundations.

Diogenes. Print Collection, Miriam and Ira D. Wallach Division of Art, Prints, and Photographs, The New York Public Library, Astor, Lenox, and Tilden Foundations.

Between Swooners and Cynics
The Art of Envisioning God

The semiotic possibilities of the Hebrew of Genesis 1:31, "Viyar Elohim et kol asher asa vehinei tov meod [God saw everything that he had made and indeed it was very good]," include cognitive, moral, and aesthetic dimensions. Some traditional interpretations see the text as asserting that the world is well-wrought, that nature's means, cunningly adapted to its ends, are indications of divine purposiveness, and that obedience to divine ordinances is a manifestation of human goodness. Other accounts focus upon the created order as a vast spectacle that attests nature's power to arouse awe and rapture, a perspective reflected in the Romantic coupling of art and nature. Thus F. W. J. Schelling, in a lecture of 1804, declares: "The universe is formed in God as an absolute work of art and in eternal beauty . . . beauty in which infinite intention interpenetrates infinite necessity."[1]

Does the Romantic rapture of this Schellingian pronouncement not wend its way into postmodernity in the gaze of the tourist who inwardly cordons off the admiring hordes to proclaim the beauty of that primordial beginning as rendered by Michelangelo or Giovanni di Paolo? Is there a connection between God envisaged as creator and the ascription of beauty? Is the link understood as one of direct agency? These questions presuppose a way of seeing hidden in our manner of questioning, in our comportments toward what is viewed as beautiful. Thus the wide-eyed ecstatic, whom I shall hereafter refer to as the "swooner," asks, "*Ah, what is beauty really*," while the doubting protester, whom, in conformity with an ancient philosophical tradition, I shall call the "cynic," inquires disparagingly, "What is beauty *anyway*?"

I shall not try to determine why some things rather than others may be called beautiful or to weigh received accounts of beauty. Instead, I shall focus on the world orientations or dispositions of the questioner, the "Ah" of the swooner and the "anyway" of the cynic, as each encounters the referent of the term *beauty*. By tracking the philosophical matrices from which these perspectives derive, I hope to show that swooners and cynics cannot do without one another if the extremes of naïveté and nihilism are to be avoided and that each must be taken into account in speaking about God. I shall consider how the disruption of the cynic erupts into the beautiful, disfigures it, but in so doing helps to transfigure it, and I shall conclude by describing some ways in which theological thinking is bound up with both.

Swooning and the Sublime

It might be thought that swooning before the artwork or the phenomena of nature can be traced to *thaūmazein*, the Greek term for wonder or amazement referred to in the philosophies of Plato and Aristotle. But the view that swooning is allied to wonder is, in part, the result of an often-unacknowledged redescription of the Greek *thaūmazein* in a nineteenth-century Romantic aesthetic. Considered to be a devaluing of the world and a plunging into an inner world, the Romantic aesthetic, as depicted by its adversaries, is the very opposite of the serenity of the ancients. Thus, Schelling discerns in the aesthetics of his contemporaries characteristics the ancients had censured: "audacious fire, and violent, shrieking, fleeting antitheses." Or, as Johann Joachim Winckelmann declares: "One finds oneself as if at a party where everyone wants to talk at once."[2]

It goes without saying that accounts of beauty abound in Plato, Aristotle, and their immediate successors. But, as Schelling had already noticed, the claim that for classical thought the beholder dissolves into ecstasy before that which is beautiful must be dismantled. Accordingly, the notion that swooning began in Athens requires revision. To be sure, Plato describes an eager young man, Theatetus in the dialogue of that name, as "astonished." It is not, however, beauty but "the ridiculous and wonderful contradictions" of ordinary speech that became grist for the mill of the Sophists that are the sources of his astonishment. Theatetus exclaims, "I am amazed . . . my head quite swims with the contemplation" of their questions. For Socrates, the young man's amazement proves that he is a true philosopher and leads Socrates to announce: "For wonder [*thaūmazein*] is the feeling of a philosopher, and philosophy begins in wonder."[3] Lest we identify wonder with affect, with what the swooner feels, recall that the *thaūmazein* of Theatetus is bound up with intellect, with attempting to settle the logical disputes of the sophists.

Socrates is not, however, insensitive to the ambiguities inherent in his own account, conceding that beauty crosses the line between the world of the senses and physical pleasures and that of mind. Consider Socrates' quandary in *Philebus* 66: "Has mind a greater share of beauty than pleasure, and is mind or pleasure the fairer of the two?" His respondent, Protarchus, admits that certain pleasures make us ashamed, so "we put them out of sight, consign them to darkness," and turn instead to "the eternal nature of measure and the mean." Socrates is forced to acknowledge that "there are pleasures that accompany the sciences and those that accompany the senses, and that both pleasure and mind are wanting in self-sufficiency."[4] Is there, in the admission that mind is not self-sufficient, a certain return of the repressed, a pleasure of the senses that cannot be eliminated? Unsurprisingly, Socrates concludes that mind is far ahead.

Continuing Plato's line of thought, Aristotle, in what is by now a truism, declares: "It is owing to their wonder that men both now begin and at first began to philosophize. They wondered originally at the obvious difficulties . . . then advanced to difficulties about greater matters, the phenomena of the moon and those of the sun and of the stars and about the genesis of the universe."[5] Stunned by the mystery and sheer magnitude of what they saw, even the lovers of myth sought to flee their ignorance. Aristotle insists that he does not mean to reinstate the naïveté of those who wonder about "self-moving marionettes, or the solstices, or the incommensurability of the diagonal of a square with the side."[6] Rather, he contends, in order to escape from ignorance one should seek to know the *causes* of things.

If not in the world of ancient Athens, where then, and when, are the voices of the swooners first heard, the "Ah" that persists in the aesthetic predilections of postmodern times? I shall not enter into the question of the cultural determinants that may have generated a gasp before the Gothic cathedral or the water lilies of Monet, the fjords of Norway or the peaks of the Himalayas. Nor shall I ask how the beauty of a fragment isolated in a moment of emotion, of pristine aesthesis, may be inwardized and saved. Needless to say, the *thaūmaz-ein* of the classical world passed through a long and troubled history before wonder became awe in the face of "beauty without limit." In response to the veneration of the plastic arts and poetry of the Greeks, one nineteenth-century critic, Paul Friedrich Richter, dismisses the ineluctable nostalgia for what is irretrievable. Realizing that we can no more reexperience the classical past in its own being than we can repeat fleeting natural phenomena, Richter maintains: "Duplication of a whole people would be a greater wonder than a fantastic sky of clouds completely matching some former sky. Not even in Greece could antiquity be resurrected."[7]

The limitless beauty rhapsodized by Richter's contemporaries is seen by him as "the romantic, the undulant hum of a vibrating string or bell whose sound waves fade away into ever greater distances and is finally lost in ourselves."[8] While he acknowledges a Romantic impulse in other times and places, he finds its quintessential expression in Christianity, especially in the Marian piety of southern Europe. Thus Richter states: "The peerless Mary endows all women with Romantic nobility; a Venus is merely beautiful, but a madonna is Romantic. This higher love is . . . the very blossom or flower of Christianity, which with its ardent zeal in opposing the earthly dissolves the beautiful body into the beautiful soul in order to love the body in the soul, the beautiful in the infinite."[9]

To understand the onset of the great wash of feeling in the presence of the beautiful in modernity, we must look to the philosophy of Kant. How, it might be asked, could the sober Kant, so opposed to what he called *Schwärmerei*, to the *Sturm und Drang* mindset exhibited by some of his contemporaries, have furthered the interest of the swooners? Was he not so practical as to have said, "What a pity that the lilies do not spin?"[10] and so work-obsessed that he changed his lodgings when a neighbor refused to do away with the noisy rooster that disturbed his philosophical speculations?[11] I shall not delve into the details of Kant's life for fear of drifting into ad hominem arguments and shall turn instead to his *Third Critique*, a work whose purpose can be seen as bridging the gulf between theoretical and practical reason, between the knowledge of nature and the moral life.

What Kant calls the understanding provides us with a grid prior to experience through which we acquire a knowledge of nature as an object of sense.[12] By contrast, practical or moral reason is "the supersensible in the subject" (*CJ*, 32). Prior to all experience, practical reason legislates in the moral realm and has pride of place in that it can prescribe limits to the understanding. The gulf between what we tend to call fact and value may seem unbridgeable, but Kant thinks nature has a purpose and that we can find in the understanding of nature a way of bringing the two together. The purposiveness of nature can be grasped in a twofold way: first, as having to exist in conformity with the concept of freedom, and second, as a certain possibility presupposed in nature, namely, the nature of the human being as a sensible being (*CJ*, 32). What is important for my argument is Kant's claim that there is a special pleasure in the apprehension of nature as having a purpose, even if we cannot know this purpose.

When judged subjectively prior to any concept, purposiveness is the subject of aesthetic judgments; when judged objectively as the harmony of a thing's concept with its form, it is the subject of what Kant calls teleological judgments (*CJ*, 29). In aesthetic judgments, we judge the object to be purposive but are unable to explain its purpose, so that we experience a purposiveness without purpose, as in apprehending the beauty of a tree, a bird of paradise, or, as he disconcertingly suggests, the beauty of foliage in wallpaper (*CJ*, 66). In the case of teleological judgment, we actually know what the object's purpose is.

This distinction between types of judgment provides the ground for Kant's account of beauty. When the form of an object is merely reflected upon without reference to a concept and is judged as the ground of pleasure, it is called "beautiful," and the faculty of judging such an object, "taste" (*CJ*, 28). But the pleasure I experience when seeing a beautiful object is necessarily private. If a judgment of taste is based on private experience, is it possible to secure agreement about judgments of taste? Yet such judgments are valid for all, according to Kant, because there is a subjective yet common ground for them, a sense common to all (*sensus communis*). Still, agreement about what is beautiful secured through a judgment, albeit a judgment of taste, can hardly be expected to give rise to swooning.

Not only must the reception of the artwork be considered, but also the role of the artist. The creation of an artwork that is not merely pleasant but purposive in itself calls for greatness in the artist. Such a work requires "genius . . . the innate mental disposition (*ingenium*) through which nature gives the rule to art" (*CJ*, 150). Because artistic talent is itself a natural faculty, genius must be seen as a natural gift. Although in the realm of morality Kant appeals to the universality of law, he insists that no rule can be given for creating a work of genius: "Hence originality must be its first property" (*CJ*, 150). Artistic skill cannot be transmitted but dies with the artist. Even if the work of the artist is not one of unfettered imagination but rather of imagination constrained by understanding (*CJ*, 152), Kant nevertheless makes extraordinary claims for the power of imagination: as the productive faculty of cognition, imagination "is very powerful in creating another nature, as it were, out of the material that actual nature gives it. We entertain ourselves with it when experience becomes too commonplace and by it we remold experience . . . working up [this material] into something that surpasses nature" (*CJ*, 157). Nietzsche remains Kant's successor when he proclaims, "Artists should see nothing as it is, but fuller, simpler, stronger: to that end, their lives must contain a kind of youth and spring, a kind of habitual intoxication."[13] Thus, despite Nietzsche's critique of what he saw as residual Christian belief in Kant's view of the moral law and his contention that Kant remained untouched by the beauty of antiquity, praise for the imagination of the genius enters in scarcely altered form into his own thought.

But the genius of the artist does not of itself suffice to account for the emergence of the swoon of the viewer. Kant must first explain the difference between the beautiful and what he calls the sublime. Beauty inheres in the form of the object and is discovered through quiet contemplation, whereas the sublime, by contrast, is formless, exhibits no purpose, and is apprehended in a state of excitation, "a momentary checking of the vital powers and a consequent stronger outflow of them" (*CJ*, 83). Judgments of sublimity are universally valid, disinterested, and necessary. They exhibit subjective purposiveness and are perplexing in that the object of such judgments is formless and the state of the subject is one of excitation. The claim of universality can, however, be accounted for as depending upon the supersensible, upon moral feeling.

Kant goes on to distinguish between the mathematical sublime, that of magnitude, and the dynamical sublime, that of power. With regard to the former, we try to think that which is not merely great but absolutely great. Because we perceive that sensible standards cannot measure infinite magnitude, we are left with a feeling of pain but, at the same time, the sheer attempt to think the sublime excites in us the "feeling of a supersensible faculty" (*CJ*, 88). Kant explains: "The mind feels itself moved in the representation of the sublime in nature, while in aesthetic judgments about the beautiful it is in *restful* contemplation. This movement may . . . be compared to a vibration, an alternating attraction towards and repulsion from the same object" (*CJ*, 97).

When nature is interpreted as might, as power that arouses fear but nevertheless has no dominion over us, it is understood as dynamically sublime (*CJ*, 99). Consider Kant's example:

> Bold, overhanging, and as it were threatening rocks; clouds piled up in the sky, moving with lightning flashes and thunder peals; volcanoes in all their violence of destruction; hurricanes with their track of devastation, the boundless ocean in a state of tumult; the lofty waterfall of a mighty river . . . these exhibit our faculty of resistance as insignificantly small in comparison with their might. But the sight of them is the more attractive, the more fearful it is, provided only that we are in security. (*CJ*, 100)

I can think of no better illustration of Kant's account than the well-known painting *Man Viewing Storm at Sea*, by Caspar David Friedrich. A figure is standing on a cliff, his back toward the viewer, and from the relative safety of this vantage point looks out at an infinite expanse of raging sea, which seems to retreat into the depths of the painting. It could be argued that Friedrich's work exhibits a form of Romanticism denigrated by Nietzsche when he wrote: "A romantic is an artist whose great dissatisfaction with himself makes him creative—who looks away, looks back from himself and from his world."[14]

There is, however, a more troubling example of the sublime adduced by Kant—its concrete historical embodiment in war. Kant, an admirer of the French Revolution but also a defender of peace, remarks: "War, if it is carried on with order and with a sacred respect for the rights of citizens, has something sublime in it" (*CJ*, 102).[15] Such Kantian niceties as the rights of the citizen vanish in Nietzsche's praise for the sheer exhilaration of war. "In times of painful tension and vulnerability," Nietzsche urges, "choose war: it hardens, it produces muscle,"[16] an outcome whose desirability would hardly have been sanctioned by Kant.

After Ecstasy: Cynicism as Critique

Having traced the route of the swooner to the threshold of postmodernity, I can now turn to the path of the cynic. Is cynicism a necessary moment that disrupts the swoon, thereby casting a pall over ecstasy, or can ecstasy reassert itself? It might be thought that the spoilers of swooning would be found not among the cynics but rather among the ancient skeptics, such as Carneades (214–129 B.C.E.), who held that there is no way to distinguish fantastic from allegedly true representations and, when forced to respond to those who said that this view would paralyze action, proposed a doctrine of probability.[17] The physician and skeptic Sextus Empiricus (ca. 250 C.E.) argued that skeptics lay out conflicting accounts of opposing appearances or ideas, with each account being equally convincing. This strategy leads to a suspension of judgment, so that, in any opposed pair of accounts, neither alternative is accepted or rejected. Skeptics may assent to the feelings forced upon them by appearances, feelings that are passive and unwilled, but will make no claims about the relation of these appearances to external objects. Judgment is also suspended in moral matters, given that those who hold that some things are good and others bad are perpetually distressed and fail to attain the serenity thought to be desirable.[18] What troubled the ancient skeptics, some scholars argue, were not perceived contradictions but rather the claims made for the basic assumptions or the framework within which dogmatic philosophers work. Rather than demolishing all claims to knowledge, the skeptics refine them, paring away misleading affirmations by suspending judgment about the trustworthiness of our knowledge beyond that which appears.[19]

To track the genealogy of later critiques of swooning, we must look not to the skeptics but to the ancient cynics, those wild men who are said to have lived vagrant lives, assaulted established values, and called attention to themselves through imaginative gestures of protest. They stressed acts rather than discourses, although recent scholarship suggests that their imaginative improvisations generated new literary forms, that is, burlesques and parodies.[20] Consider first the crafty cynic Diogenes of Sinope (413–323 B.C.E.) as a conceptual persona, a phrase coined by Gilles Deleuze to refer to the specific nexus of concepts laid out by a thinker as generally signaled by her or his proper name, rather than the thinker as an existing individual.[21]

According to legend, Diogenes lived in the Greek-speaking town of Sinope on the Turkish coast of the Black Sea, where his father, Hicesius, was in charge of issuing the city's currency. Diogenes was charged with altering the legal tender of Sinope, either by counterfeiting or in some way defacing it, and was forced into exile. His gesture was confirmed by the oracle at Delphi, who told him, "Falsify," a command that led him to reorient his life, so that he tested the mores of his society as one tests coins to see whether they are genuine. By defacing the values of his day, Diogenes acquired the title "The Dog," because it is known that dogs recognize friends, who, for Diogenes, are those suited to philosophy, and enemies, those whom dogs drive away.[22] Philosophy is not equated with Plato's account of ideal forms but rather with a concern for the concrete particulars of life. In fact, Diogenes is alleged to have said, "Plato is a waste of time."[23]

Yet, as commentators insist, Diogenes was a *parhesiast*, that is, one committed to speaking the truth.[24] According to ancient sources, he regarded money as the source of evil, endured a life of poverty, committed indecent acts that can be discreetly referred to as those people do not perform in public, went barefoot, and slept in tubs, a style that has been described as a return to nature. He is reputed to have ordered Alexander the Great not to stand between him and the sun, thereby displaying a quality of soul that Alexander admitted to having envied.[25] Contemptuous of laws and lawgivers, Diogenes polemicized against rulers and even in Hades continued to make a pest of himself by mocking dead kings. When asked where he was from, he is reputed to have replied, "I am a citizen of the world," a cosmopolitan, thus envisioning a single social space.[26]

According to contemporary German culture critic Peter Sloterdijk, author of *The Critique of Cynical Reason*, Diogenes was the Urhippie and proto-Bohemian of the ancient world. When Diogenes is portrayed in ancient sources as one who is virtuous and rational, what is meant is that he illuminates the sham of law and custom,[27] a description that gave rise to the famous image of his holding up a lamp to search for an honest man. Yet another tale reports his capture by pirates in the Aegean Sea, who sold him as a slave, a status he promptly reversed by becoming the tutor of his master's sons, training them in endurance. His life may be summed up by the epitaph carved on the pillar that, along with a statue of a dog in Parian marble, stands over his grave: "Tell me, Oh Dog! Who is the man whose monument thou art guarding? He is no one but the Dog himself? Diogenes indeed! . . . He was a man from Sinope. He who used to live in a tub? Yes, indeed, he himself! But now in his death, he lives among the stars!"[28]

For Nietzsche, the life of Diogenes is exemplary in that the lives of cynics "recognize the animal, the commonplace, the rule in themselves . . . that itch which makes them talk of themselves and their like before witnesses,—sometimes they even wallow in books as in their own dung."[29] Because cynicism replicates the behavior of ordinary folk, whom he often belittles, Diogenes goes on to say that "cynicism is the only form in which base souls approach honesty and the higher man must listen closely then to every coarse or subtle cynicism."[30]

The image of Diogenes may figure in Nietzsche's famed depiction of the madman who lights a lantern in the bright morning hours, crying out in the marketplace "Where is God?" and answering his own question with the claim "God is dead." This image was first placed in a theological perspective by Tertullian, who valorized the metaphor of light and praised Diogenes' search with a lamp in broad daylight in contrast to the heretic Marcion, who lost the light of faith. For Nietzsche, the lantern uncovers what he sees as the pointlessness of the quest for transcendence.[31] The anecdote can be read as a cynical parody of a parody, the madman displacing Diogenes of Sinope, who, in turn, refers to himself as Socrates gone mad.[32]

May we not ask whether Nietzsche's cynicism undoes itself to become a new swooning, a cynicism that protests rationality in the name of a new ecstasy? Inspired by Nietzsche, Sloterdijk argues that the present age is characterized by a diffuse but pervasive suspicion of social and political institutions. The distrustfulness of today's cynic does not express itself in the visibly eccentric but morally purposive gestures of Diogenes, whom Sloterdijk admires. Instead, he argues, the contemporary cynic is simply attuned to society's mores: "Cynicism is the universally widespread way in which enlightened people see to it that they are not taken for suckers." Thus, the enlightened or wised-up cynic understands the emptiness of his position but sees himself as merely complying with circumstances, so that, for him, "cynicism is enlightened false consciousness" (*CCR*, 5). Contemporary cynicism succeeds in outfoxing moral ideologies, as well as the critique of such ideologies, because it is aware of its falsity. The cynicism of the present merely reappropriates the rationality of the Enlightenment, which Sloterdijk sees as doomed: "To continue enlightenment means to be prepared for the fact that everything that in consciousness is mere morality will lose out against the unavoidable amoralism of the real" (ibid., 82). For Sloterdijk, the joylessness of this false cynicism must be replaced by the higher kynicism of the ancients, by the world-affirming cynicism of Nietzsche, by the swoon of ecstasy.[33] His stance can be interpreted as the affirming of a negation, the negation of contemporary cynicism by way of another cynicism, one whose strategy is that of disruption. It is this notion of cynicism that enters into postmodern artworks as commentary and critique, thus as a kind of disfiguring of what the artwork represents. The swooning of the Romantic is broken by a cynical consciousness now built into the artwork itself. Must all of this, one might ask, lead to philosophical nihilism and psychological despair?

Swooning Cynics and the Work of Art

Can the gasp of the swooner before the beauty of the artwork be recovered in an age of suspicion? Or does the challenge of the cynic call the swooner's vision of art to order by recalling the world "outside," that of the iniquities and atrocities of the present age? But if art is to be schooled by moral concerns, can art avoid falling into the contemporary didacticism of Socialist Realism or into the pseudo-heroics of Fascist kitsch? Can the beauty of the artwork be brought into question by a good that transcends it, incorporate that good, perhaps even that which is ugly, without ceasing to be a work of art?

Consider, first, that the artwork is a presentation of images and that images are a substitute for the being of a thing. As such, the image is a doubling of reality. In ordinary recollection, I am aware of an object in its absence, but in art I am confronted with a substitute, a tableau, even when the artwork is abstract and does not purport to represent the real directly. Both artist and viewer under the sway of the image are inundated by pure sensation, which promotes a forgetting of the world itself. Does the "Ah" of the swooner then require the prose of criticism, the language of the cynic, to call attention to the world?

Consider Baudrillard's caustic analysis of the historico-cultural nexus from which the artwork emerges, a world he perceives to be the flotsam and jetsam of the past. History, he protests, refuses to come to an end but resurfaces as a waste product. He writes: "We have to come to terms with the idea that everything that was not bio-degradable or exterminable is today recyclable. . . . We shall not be spared the worst—that is, History will not come to an end—since the leftovers . . . communism, ethnic groups, conflicts, ideologies, are indefinitely recyclable. What is stupendous is that nothing has really disappeared."[34]

Can there be artworks that do not require an accompanying cynical explanation such as that of Baudrillard, works that are self-explanatory, cynical in the manner of Diogenes? Can the artist as cynic not create assemblages of found objects, of the detritus of the past, as exemplified in the art of Robert Rauschenberg, or culture-collages, as it were, that unsay one another, as depicted in the works of Anselm Kiefer? Or consider artist C. F. G. Boggs's replicas of British and American paper money, which he claimed to find beautiful. Like Diogenes, who defaced the currency of Sinope, Boggs was accused of counterfeiting while the counterfeit notes, Boggs's bills, soared in value in the art market.[35] Such art requires no cynical prose supplement for the discursive elaboration of the tension between protest and artistic expression.

It can be argued further that the creation of innumerable copies of a work constitutes a cynical gesture. Benjamin, in an essay written in 1936 (thus antedating the advent of computer-generated images), maintained that in the age of mechanical reproduction copies of artworks jeopardized the authority of the original. The passing of time between its creation and the present that determines whether an artwork is original, what Benjamin called its "aura," cannot be transmitted by a copy. Although reproduction has long been possible through other techniques, such as engraving or wood-cutting, new technologies allow for the production of reproductions in unprecedented quantities.[36] But the fact of reproduction itself, in the culture of the replica, can be integrated into the artwork as a critique of reproduction by introducing multiple identical images for which there is no original into the work's visual surface. Consider Andy Warhol's copies of familiar objects, from soup cans to likenesses of the Mona Lisa, which remind the viewer of the role of the replica in the commodification of the world. The cloned objects of the world enter the artwork as an outside that is inside and an inside that extends outward in a stream of objects. While remanding critique to the artwork itself, the viewer is still drawn into an overwhelming field of color and shape.

Theologies of Rapture, Theologies of Protest

Can theological thinking overwrite or reinscribe in its own language(s) the conversation between Diogenes the cynic and the Romantic artist? Recall that the visual artwork consists of images and images may be obliterated, but that an image may be dislodged without being destroyed by a process of erasure through which it remains as an absent presence in the work. Such an artwork is not simply a palimpsest, in which a new work is physically painted over an older one, rendering previous images invisible, but rather one in which images are overlaid in another way. To understand how erasure works, it must be seen in the context of the trace, a concept that has been explicated in what is by now a tradition from Heidegger to Derrida. Traces are not signs. Signs are transparent in that they reveal their objects, whereas traces cannot be integrated into the order of the world. Instead, traces are not visible as such but mark a transcendence that is present in absence. The effort to coerce an absent image into appearing assures its loss; it can only be glimpsed in and through the images that are present. The images that are there may not dislodge the absent or hidden images but rather help to continue their influence.

To see this, consider again Caspar David Friedrich's painting of the man poised on the cliff, with his back toward the viewer, gazing at the infinite expanse of sea "formless, exhibiting no purpose," which we may interpret as an attempt to represent what cannot be represented, the sublime in Kant's sense. Were an artist of today to paint in the manner of Friedrich, we would be likely to dismiss such work as sentimental. However, a 1961 painting by Michaelangelo Pistoletto, *Man Seen from the Back: The Present*,[37] seems to imprint a postmodern mark upon Friedrich's painting. Pistoletto's figure, his back to the viewer, is dressed in a business suit, hands in his trouser pockets. In place of storm and sea, the man stares into a dark void. Shadowy figures, ghostlike white and red patches of light, emerge from this black background, which functions like the tain of a mirror, its dark, unreflective surface making its reflecting surface possible. Pistoletto writes: "Man has always attempted to double himself as a means of attempting to know himself. And part of man's mind has always remained attached to the reproduction of himself."[38] Yet the spots of light are not pictorial replicas of the man but vague, incandescent shapes.

Suspended between representation and abstraction, the painting oscillates between the concrete and the conceptual. Pistoletto writes: "These two presences of myself were the two lives that were at one and the same time tearing me in two and calling me to the task of their unification."[39] Have we, then, with Pistoletto's man seen from the back, returned to Romantic inwardization, to a pristine immersion in feeling? Does Pistoletto's statement not reinscribe a form of Romanticism criticized by Nietzsche when he says: "A romantic is an artist whose great dissatisfaction with himself makes him creative—who looks away, looks back from himself and from his world"?[40] Or does the art of Pistoletto both express and transcend this dissatisfaction? Is not "every critique [a] pioneering work on the pain of the times [*Zeitschmerz*] and a piece of exemplary healing?" as Sloterdijk asks (*CCR*, xxxvi).

What has theology to gain from the depiction of an artwork as a system of traces, of images that are nested inside one another? Theologically understood, the trace is the mark of the sacred that has disrupted or passed through the beautiful. One must know how to read or, rather, not to read traces, how to remain attentive to them. There is in the trace the suggestion of a "more," of something uncontainable in language.

Consider once more the position of the interpreter who holds that Genesis 1:31 attests the purposiveness in the order of creation and that of the interpreter who is struck by its pristine beauty. The latter might be moved to adopt Nietzsche's words: "Play, the useless — as the ideal of him who is overfull of strength, as 'childlike.' The childlikeness of God *pais paizon* [a child playing]."[41] Could such a world not be "a work of art that gives birth to itself," as Nietzsche thought? Yet is there not an Augustinian text, a text under erasure, nested in this excessiveness? It reads: "Since then Thou fillest heaven and earth, do they contain thee? Or as they contain thee not, dost thou fill them and yet there remains something over? . . . Is it that Thou art wholly everywhere while nothing contains thee?"[42]

The beauty of the artwork solicits this excessiveness by directing attention away from itself:

> By the very beauty of his work, the artist somehow beckons the spectator, instead of fixing his eyes wholly on the beauty of the work he has made, to pass over this beauty and to look in fondness at him who made it . . . as one who hears the [words but loses] what is most important, [must pass to] the meaning of which the words are merely the signs.[43]

Yet how does one know when one has found that of which the word "gives sign"? Are the interpreters of Genesis 1:31 not poised before a swirl of traces: Nietzsche in Augustine, Augustine in Nietzsche, cynics and swooners in endless conversation?

Facts, Fiction, *Ficciones*
Truth in the Study of Religion

What is it that we ask for when we ask for truth in the study of religion? Before trying to link the two key terms of this inquiry, truth and religion, let me tell you a story, a tale about truth in which the idea of fact but not yet of religion figures prominently.

Absent in the narrative I am about to recount is the romance of the story. What must be repressed in the telling is that facts are objects of our desire, of a certain *Sehnsucht*, not because by nature we want to know, as Aristotle maintained, but because we long for presence and certainty. We have a yearning for the *viva vox* of events both recent and long past, the recovery of the texture of things in all of their *Leib-haftigkeit*, their living presence, even as they drift away. The pathos of the past is its irrecoverability, the pathos of the present, the slip-page, the always already pastness of the present. We seek an immediacy inherently unattainable, an imagined plenary presence, one whose real pleasure is generated by the aura of melancholy that clings to the impossibility of repossessing the past. "You fill up my senses," John Denver's popular song exults—time held at bay in a moment of sensory inundation.

Getting at the facts is the Enlightenment's way of living the myth of immediacy. The Enlightenment account of time promises a full re-covery of events by stationing the observer outside of time or placing the observer in control of time by making time part of her computa-tional scheme. In this view, time is made up of homogeneous units, so that it does not matter where the observer stands. The price is immediacy. The direct apprehension of a luminous object of contemplation or the sensory flooding of conscious awareness gives way to accuracy, the manner of being of the represented object.

The study of religion is involved in this romance of facts in a special way. The object of attention, religion, the linguistic and ritual articulations of communities in their concern with the sacred, gives the study of religion, when seen as the quest for facts about religion, its ineluctuable pathos. The student of religion must inquire of the artifactual, literary, and oral archives of religious communities, "What luminous object or what dark and terrifying thing did the worshippers see when they saw it?" but know that, qua observer, she stands at an unbreachable distance from these arcana. I can think of no one who has expressed this better than the poet John Ashberry, when he writes:

> And when these immense structures go down, no one hears:
> a flash and then it's gone
> leaving behind a feeling that something happened there once,
> like wind tearing at the current,
> but no memory and no crying either.
> There was no one to tell us what it meant
> when it meant what it did.[1]

The Facts

To return to the tale about facts after this brief excursus into romance, I invite you, to use Umberto Eco's phrase, to take an "inferential walk," to ask some leading questions about facts and truth. In demanding the truth about something, are we not asking for a description of the object just as it is, of the facts, whatever these are? But what do we mean by "the facts"? Facts are what settle matters. Each day's heat and clammy dampness, for example, is a fact that, taken together with numerous successive and similar meteorological phenomena, supports the generalization that one lives in a tropical climate. Facts, in this reading, are the atomic constituents of our beliefs, the elementary bits that no reasonable person could dispute, what brooks no disagreement. This view of facts works from the bottom up, as it were, from part to whole.

Using the same ontological presuppositions, we could proceed from whole to part. In that view, facts are the sediment that remains after the whole that is to be studied is subjected to scrutiny in the light of some stipulated end. We want to know, for example, why the forests of Europe are vanishing. Eliminate numerous co-present phenomena—temperature changes, the appearance of certain plant diseases, and the like—and take note of what is left: only with the advent of acid rain do we see the forests disappear. In the vanishing forest example, facts become facts by way of a process of selection, of paring down a wider phenomenological field by applying criteria of relevance to rein in a portion of it.

Still missing from this account of fact and truth is a version of how the phenomenological field can be restricted with greater stringency through the application of finer-grained methods of control. By positing hypotheses that purport to explain natural phenomena and by regulating the conditions of observation, modern science tries to arrive at the truth about them. Observations conducted in this narrower framework may be limited either exclusively by the conditions of the hypothesis (as in many geological or astronomical observations) or by both the hypothesis and the special circumstances of the laboratory (as in experiments in chemistry) so that occurrences irrelevant to the anticipated outcome stipulated by the hypothesis are screened out.

This sketch of facts takes truth and fact to be for most purposes interchangeable terms. Thus both parts of the statement "What is true is a fact, and what is false is contrary to fact" can be construed as saying the same thing. The understanding of truth that is presupposed by the factuality blueprint I have drawn takes for granted: first, that our beliefs are so related to things and events that true beliefs can be distinguished from false ones; second, that certain strategies of justification linking the way things are to our statements about them will convert our statements into warranted beliefs; and, finally, that inquiry should be undertaken from a standpoint of studied neutrality, be disinterested, reflect, in Leibniz's famous dictum, the view from nowhere.

But it was not always so with truth. The concept of truth I have just discussed, factual truth, was proferred as a correction to the older view that the word *true* does not primarily describe the relation of things to our convictions about them. Instead, *true* refers to what exists in a realm apart, a realm of etiolated ideas or forms characterized by the properties of generality and nonmateriality. Forms or ideas are objects that mortals disciplined in the appropriate way can grasp, the *archai*, of which everyday objects are pale reflections. This is, of course, the Platonic view of truth, which has endured as a strand in Jewish, Christian, and Islamic thought through the Middle Ages and into the present. It was undermined first by Aristotle's claim that the forms do not exist in isolation but inhere in existing things and later by the various versions of factuality that I have sketched. What Platonism has in common with the realist account of truth as fact is that, as in some versions of realism, it appeals to occult entities that require special means of access. Atoms and waves are like Platonic ideas or forms in that they are not available to ordinary experience.

In both the realist and idealist truth narratives, language is seen as transparent, a glass placed over the world that brings the world into plenary presence. Both the facts of philosophical realism and the forms of Platonic rationalism have the same psychological outcome: they confer the longed-for certainty that I described earlier, that is, they are experienced as true in the sense that, once apprehended, their force cannot be countermanded. Thus there is a covert affinity, a co-dependence between idealism and realism in this regard.

The force of fact as modernity has construed it has not gone uncontested. In recent times, the existentialist has argued that the appeal of facts cannot decide issues of meaning in our lives; the pragmatist claims that the fluidity and richness of context and the social outcomes of a putative truth are ignored in the realist's description of facts; the cultural historian or sociologist of knowledge holds that the realist notion of facts reflects prior social accords about how fact and truth are to be reckoned rather than the relation of neutral observer and world; the ordinary language philosopher believes that realism is just another language game; and the deconstructionist sees linguistic, psychological, and political bad faith in the claims made for the primacy of speech, present time, and representation in the history of Western thought.

In the light of this narrative, how, then, are we to interpret the factual perspective in the study of religion? Let us reflect for a moment on the object of study, religion. What is it that is brought into focus when religion becomes the subject of critical analysis? The facts about the beliefs and practices that articulate a community's encounter with the sacred? The facts about the origins of religious experience? The facts about doctrine, worship, and ritual in comparative perspective? The facts about the founding and the transmission of a tradition? The facts about the relation of religion to society, economy, and polity?

Consider, for example, these statements explaining the origin of religion, selected at random from among its most distinguished modern interpreters. Vico: "Each people naturally created by itself its own gods through a certain natural instinct man has for divinity."[2] Freud: religion arises "as a childhood neurosis . . . that mankind will surmount."[3] Durkheim: for the primitive, religion begins with "the coming together of a number of men associated in the same life . . . which transforms each of them. All that [the primitive] knows is that he is raised above himself and that he sees a life different from the one he ordinarily leads."[4] These remarks show that the perspective of modern realism, the hegemony of "the facts," already infiltrates the understanding of the object of inquiry, religion, in that it entails a belief about the real: the object of inquiry can be explained by analyzing the facts about it. Although the assertions cited from Vico, Freud, and Durkheim are far from reflecting a narrow scientism, the reductive ontology of philosophical realism governs the quest for an explanation of religion in biological, psychological, and social terms.

Why, we may ask, *should* the study of religion still be configured as factual? Why should the student of religion bracket her own beliefs and practices to assume the disinterested standpoint of the observer rather than that of the participant? Or if she starts from the perspective of an atheological postmodernity in one or several of its many versions, why should she cling to the conditions of a factuality that has been unmasked in what is by now itself a tradition of criticism, beginning with Kierkegaard and Nietzsche and continuing with Heidegger, Foucault, and Derrida, to name a few? And if the ideal of factuality is still to be retained in the study of religion, how should it be retained, how reconfigured?

If factuality is to remain useful in the study of religion, does the student of religion not need to see what has been forgotten or effaced in the historical and cultural production of the factual attitude? Does she not need to bring to light its linguistic rules and its criteria of rationality? One (by no means the only) way of achieving this has been suggested by Foucault, who speaks not about objects of study but about discursive formations. These are ordered constellations of statements that point not to " 'things,' 'facts,' 'realities,' or 'beings,' " but to the "law of possibility, rules of existence for the objects that are . . . described within it."[5] Statements, as he defines the term, do not describe the world but rather reveal the conditions of emergence of the object of study. The meaning of a statement is limited not by its grammatical structure or what it refers to but by the historical pattern of significations it inhabits. Just as "the affirmation that the earth is round or that species evolve does not constitute the same statement before and after Copernicus, before and after Darwin,"[6] so too the idea "these are the facts" does not mean the same thing before and after, for example, the birth of modern science.

Derrida makes us attentive to still other features of truth. Western thought is structured as a system of binary oppositions, terms that are not antonyms in the dictionary sense but metaphysical constructs that sustain philosophical thinking. Each pair of opposites is made up of a dominant and a repressed term. By reversing the order of the terms—for instance, of speech and writing—we can discern in what ways the repressed term sustains the coherence of the text, how writing actually inheres unnoticed in our notions of language. At the same time, it becomes possible to graft new meanings onto traditional concepts, meanings that are released through the gesture of reversal itself.

The result of the neo-historicist and deconstructive analyses I have described—and I could have cited existential or pragmatic criticisms of factuality—may alter the study of religion in fundamental ways. Foucault, in one of his more melodramatic moments, warns:

> At the end of such an enterprise one may not recover those unities that, out of methodological rigour, one initially held in suspense: one may be compelled to . . . ignore influences and traditions, abandon definitively the question of origin, allow the commanding presence of authors to fade into the background; and thus everything that was thought to be proper to the history of ideas may disappear from view.[7]

Fiction

If the notion of fact reflects the effort to say what is, fiction attempts to imagine what is not, to bring absence into presence, to construct a world that does not exist. We need not go all the way with George Steiner's account of fiction in order to endorse his comment that fiction "is a way to unsay the world, to image and speak it otherwise":[8] If we reverse the binary oppositions fact/fiction, presence/absence, myth/logos, the liberation of the fictive may generate new possibilities for the study of religion.

We must be careful, however: the binary opposites themselves are the product of a long tradition so that we cannot simply sign away to fiction the object of our study or our access routes to it. Instead, we must remain attentive to the way in which the opposition fact/fiction is constructed as a co-dependence of the opposites upon one another, to the way fictional narratives are formed, to the social forces they reflect, to the continuities and differences between the narratives told by religious communities themselves and the meta-narratives we construct about them.

From the inception of the Western tradition, "the speaking otherwise" that fiction is could not be dissociated from its opposite, truth. We must remind ourselves, however, that the co-implication of speaking what is and what is not is earlier articulated not as fact and fiction but, in Greek thought, as the opposition of *mythos* and *logos*. Myth in the Greek sense is fictive but not yet fiction, precisely because logos, and not fact, is its co-determinant. For Plato, logos is bound up with an eternal realm of forms, the source of being and truth, with re-memoration or anamnesis as the access route to truth, and with a special askesis, the practices of the philosopher, as the mode of human cultivation that assures entry to the realm of truth.

In Plato's *Phaedrus*, Socrates speaks of myth as proto-philosophy, as allegory, which can be cashed out only in terms of probability rather than certainty, a sheer waste of time. Does that not remind us of modernity's frequent disdain for fiction and preference for fact? Philosophy speaks clearly, whereas myth stammers in images. Thus Socrates says:

> These allegories are very nice, but he is not to be envied who has to invent them; much labour and ingenuity will be required of him . . . he must go on and rehabilitate Hippocentaurs and chimeras dire . . . And if he is skeptical about them and would reduce them . . . to rules of probability, this sort of crude philosophy will take up a great deal of time.[9]

Worst of all, myths lie. They depict the crimes of the gods when in fact gods commit no crimes, cannot fall from virtue.[10]

Yet, in the *Republic*'s famous myth of autochthonous origin, does Socrates not endorse the noble life? Does he not devise the "audacious fiction" that citizens of the ideal state are earth-born, thus insuring absolute fidelity to the soil from which they spring?[11] It would seem that Socrates rejects myths preserving ancient traditions about the exploits of the gods while endorsing pedagogically useful myths, myths that exhibit personal and political virtue. This distinction produces a break in the idea of myth itself, an entering wedge for the discursive space of fiction. Traditional myths are presented as handed down, as acquiring their force from their antiquity, whereas constructed myths are made out of whole cloth or of avowedly found elements malleable enough so that they can be stretched to suit didactic purposes.

The genre of the constructed myth cannot be decided: as didactic it is "within the true," a proto-philosophical work; on its narrative side, it is myth; as a conscious construction of the imagination that recounts events in largely nondialogical prose, it opens the space of fiction. More important, as fiction, it is a lie, not blind error but intentional falsity. As George Steiner puts the matter: "Language is centrally fictive because the enemy is 'reality'": because we will not "abide with the 'Thing which is.'"[12]

In the turn from myth to fiction, the theme of the lie persists. Rousseau's account of fiction in *Reveries of a Solitary Walker* begins with a discussion of lying, an apologetics for his own questionable practices. "What surprised me most," he writes, "was that when I recalled these fabrications I felt no real repentance. I whose horror of falsehood outweighs all my other feelings . . . by what strange inconsistency could I lie so cheerfully without compulsion or profit?"[13]

To answer this question, he takes up the difference between withholding the truth and deliberate deception. In this context he makes the astonishing claim that, while in the abstract truth is precious, "in the particular or individual sense, truth is not always such a good thing; sometimes it is a bad thing and very often it is a matter of indifference."[14] The principal criterion that determines whether counterfactual statements are blameworthy or innocent is utility. That which has value is property, whose value is, in turn, "founded solely on usefulness." From this, Rousseau, long before postmoderns like Foucault identified language as a commodity, deduces: "Truth without any possible usefulness can never be something we owe to one another; it follows therefore that anyone who conceals or disguises it is not telling a lie."[15]

Rousseau's second criterion for ascertaining the guilt or innocence of a statement contrary to fact is the bearing it has upon another. If one injures no one by it, a statement is not a lie. But it is often hard to determine whether a statement is useful or injurious. How should one judge? "It is better," says Rousseau, "to be guided by the voice of conscience than by the light of reason."[16] He concludes, and this is the point: "To lie to one's own advantage is an imposture, to lie to the advantage of others is a fraud, and to lie to the detriment of others is a slander . . . To lie without advantage or disadvantage to oneself or others is not to lie; it is not falsehood but fiction."[17] Here it should be evident that we have departed from the terrain of Platonic myth and logos and entered that of the modern subject.

The moral trappings Rousseau affixes to his account fall, as it were, like lead balloons, for it is clear that the space of fiction has been opened as a neutral space, where the disinterested modern subject is free to say what is not. It can become, as it does for Rousseau and the Romantic subject, a space of uninhibited pleasure, from which the constraints of both logic and concrete actuality have been ejected and where the imagination is free to wander. "Thinking," Rousseau writes, in contrast to reverie, "has always been for me a disagreeable and thankless occupation. During these wanderings my soul roams and soars through the universe on the wings of imagination, in ecstasies which surpass all other pleasures."[18] But, unlike the mythical world, the spaces of fiction are largely devoid of a transcendent sacred.

In sum, what this brief genealogical sampling reveals is the persistence of the fictive imagination in describing the world as other than it is. Myth as saying what is not acquires its measure from the logos, the divine reason common to cosmos and human intellect. Fiction says that it says what is not and thereby subjects itself to the standard posed by modernity, *fact as utility*.

Fiction as understood in the modern West has lost its moorings in transcendence, though they still form the boundaries of the mythical imagination. From within their self-stipulated horizons, the Bible, the Koran, the sutras of Hinduism and Buddhism, not to speak of the traditions that generated the *Popol Vuh* or the *Black Bagre*—are neither the counterpart of fact nor the phantasmagoric creations of reverie, hence, in no way fiction from a modernist perspective. Nor could the concept of fiction become serviceable as a hermeneutical instrument so that explanation itself could be viewed as fiction. From the standpoint of the binary opposites fact/fiction as construed by modernity, the pejorative meaning of fiction with regard to truth is determined by the meaning of fact. If the purpose of interpretation is the truth about its object, only the facts are true. The discursive space of fact is the truth, of fiction the lie.

If we were to suppose for a moment that the idea of fiction ruled the study of religion—and this is the point toward which I have been heading—the study of religion still would be governed by modernity's ideal of factuality, factualness turned on its head—and it is the ideal of factuality that has ruled accounts of religion from Vico to Feuerbach, from Durkheim to the present era. The modernist's view of interpretation is perhaps best condensed in the by now infamous quip attributed to Gershom Scholem, scholar of Jewish mysticism, "Mysticism is nonsense, the study of mysticism is science."

Nietzsche and Narrative

If fiction as I have described it fails as an interpretive instrument, must we abandon narrative as a resource in the study of religion? And if not, what must narrative become if it is to serve us? With Nietzsche's genealogical analysis of factuality, it becomes possible to construe narrative not only as an object of study but as a hermeneutical instrument. I shall consider Nietzsche not as a resting place for the study of religion but as a deconstructive moment necessary to clear the way for a new look at fiction, a fiction that is not the opposite of facts but has become (borrowing a term from Jorge Luis Borges) what I call *ficciones*.

Consider Nietzsche's contribution to the fall of fact in the modernist's sense. Fundamental to Nietzsche's position is the continuity of our concepts of truth with our acts of valuing. For Nietzsche, moral judgments, as they have been interpreted in a tradition that passes through Socrates, the Biblical prophets, Christianity, and modern philosophy, involve self-discipline, the subjugation of instinct through a renunciation of the senses. But moral judgments require truth as their support, so much so that truth and goodness become indistinguishable. "The true world—attainable for the sage, the pious, the virtuous man; he lives in it, he is it," says Nietzsche.[19]

The vision that sustains morality segregates the true world attainable by reason from the apparent world: "The true world has been constructed out of contradiction to the actual world . . . [an] apparent world [that is] merely a moral-optical illusion," Nietzsche writes.[20] Could Nietzsche mean to endorse a transvaluation of values such that the true world would be abolished in favor of the apparent world? Substituting the apparent world for the true world would not alter the conceptual landscape one whit, as Nietzsche recognizes: "The true world—we have abolished. What world has remained? The apparent one perhaps? But no! With the true world we have also abolished the apparent one."[21]

It is worth focusing a moment on this last point. The fact/fiction polarities I have been describing are much like Nietzsche's true and apparent worlds. Both take for granted the empirical strain that runs through modern thought. But Nietzsche shows that the world of appearances is encumbered with heavy baggage. The destruction of the true world does not leave factuality intact because the true world and the world of facts are interrelated constructs: they rise and fall together.

But there is more. I have insisted all along that fiction is a negation of the real through the creation of a counterworld, that fiction, when viewed against the background of factuality, is a kind of lie. Against what concept of truth could a lie be measured in Nietzsche's terms if both the true world and the appearances are demolished? Yet there are lies in Nietzsche's world. "By lie," Nietzsche says, "I mean wishing *not* to see something that one does see; wishing not to see something *as* one sees it."[22] To lie, in this view, is not to refuse to see it as it is—modernity's ideal of factuality—but rather to refuse to see what one sees.

To be sure, this assertion reflects what is by now a truism: Nietzsche's view of truth is a version of sophistic relativism. What is perhaps less apparent is that Nietzschean perspectivalism contains some interesting suggestions for the study of religion. First, what is alleged to be true reflects the convictions and concerns of the speaker: truth is not disinterested. This statement involves us in a reflexive paradox that only reinforces the claim: the statement that truth is not disinterested is itself not a disinterested statement. For the study of religion, the question "Says who?" enters the process of interpretation. Did St. Simeon reek of filth and decay during his brief stay in the monastery? Check the interests of Theodosius, who tells the story. Did St. Anthony challenge or reinforce the claims of the church? Ferret out the agendas of Athanasius, his biographer. Does the *Sundiata* as it has come down to us express the virtues of West African kings, the interests of the griot, or those of the French transmitters of the tale?

Hermeneutical suspicion of this sort is linked to a deeper claim about truth: truth reflects interests in the shape of metaphors that come to seem canonical. Thus, in a by now vintage Nietzscheanism, we find: "What then is truth? A mobile army of metaphors, metonyms and anthropomorphisms—in short, a sum of human relations, which have been enhanced, transposed, and embellished poetically and rhetorically, and which after long use seem canonical and obligatory."[23] It will no longer suffice to say dismissively of narrative "It is only a story," leaning thereby upon the modernist's account of fiction, because, as Nietzsche warns, any truth is enmeshed in "a mobile army of metaphors." By positing the narrative dimension of truth and value, Nietzsche has opened the way for the transformation of fiction into *ficciones*.

Ficciones

What do fictions become when they take up into themselves the story of their own ontological errancy? What happens to fact and fiction when shards of the metaphysical history through which they have passed in a return of the suppressed percolate at the surface of the narrative? How do such fictions bring to the fore, not the old metaphors for truth and certainty, but, as Nietzsche and later Derrida would have it, the fact of their worn-outness, their lack of sensuous power, metaphors that are like "coins which have lost their pictures and now matter only as metal, no longer as coins"?[24]

That narrative is useful in the study of history has been perceived, and rightly—by Hayden White and Louis Mink, for example. But narrative is, in their reading, the bodying forth of an ensemble of relations as a single whole, still bound up with fact as its lexical opposite. What has been missed is the sea change in the conception of fiction in such writers as Borges, Beckett, Blanchot, and a host of lesser-known figures, who not only dissolve narrative but take up the conditions of narrative disclosure, what and how it reveals and conceals, into the narrative itself. Fictions with such characteristics have metamorphosed into *ficciones*, the term Borges, as a spinner of metaphysical conceits, applies to his stories. Their strategy—and this before postmodern criticism had made the move—is, in part, to reconfigure the world as that which is to be read. I shall confine my attention to Borges's *ficciones* in order to spy out some of their tactics and to comment upon them as resources for the student of religion.

Ficciones can become a sinuous form for thematizing the sacred, bringing forth its silences not by forcing them into speech but by devising strategies of encounter that simultaneously attest to and preserve that silence. In Borges's tale "The God's Script," an Aztec priest of the god Qaholom is confined in a vast prison with a jaguar, whom he can, on occasion, glimpse over the wall that separates them. Upon the jaguar's skin is incised an eschatological formula that would prevent a final apocalypse, free the priest from the prison in which the Spaniards have incarcerated him, and make him more powerful than Montezuma. But he maintains silence.

What *ficciones* must the student of religion devise in her encounter with the sacred in the culture, the text, the ritual to which she is devoting her gifts of training, intellectual powers, and affect? With what cautions must she surround herself? Perhaps, like Borges's Aztec priest, she may say: "I devoted long years to learning the order and configuration of the [jaguar's] spots . . . I shall not recite the hardships of my toil. More than once I cried out to the vault that it was impossible to decipher that text. Gradually the concrete enigma I labored at disturbed me less than the generic enigma of a sentence written by a God."[25]

Consider next Borges's tale "Pierre Menard, Author of the *Quixote*." There is much in its details that the student of religion might ponder. This *ficcion* concerns the effort of a French symbolist writer, Pierre Menard, to recompose the *Quixote*, not to transcribe or copy it, but to produce a few pages "which would coincide—word for word and line for line—with those of Miguel de Cervantes."[26] Thinking at first to obtain so commanding a knowledge of the history, religion, and language of the period that he would become Cervantes, he later discards the idea, not only because it is virtually impossible but because it is also uninteresting. Rather than fitting into the skin of Cervantes, then, he "would go on being Pierre Menard and reach the Quixote through the experiences of Pierre Menard."[27]

The few pages Menard produces are identical with those of the earlier work, but the Menard text is a palimpsest through which the traces not only of Menard's many previous drafts but also of what transpired between the now of the text and the "then" of the "original" writing could be seen, a "then" that the poet John Ashberry, in the poem I cited earlier, referred to as a time when the unknowable "it" of some original fact "meant what it did." What is more, Borges adds, Menard has willy-nilly enriched the art of reading in a bold stroke, the technique "of the deliberate anachronism and the erroneous attribution." Applying this principle may lead us into odd errancies: "To go through the *Odyssey* as if it were posterior to the *Aeneid* . . . to fill the most placid works with adventure. . . . To attribute the *Imitatio Christi* to Louis Ferdinand Céline or to James Joyce, is this not a sufficient renovation of its tenuous spiritual indications?"[28]

What can the student of religion derive from Pierre Menard? First, the tale brings to the fore the problem of the fusion of horizons, the merging of one's own historical presuppositions with those of the text, as the aim of interpretation. Far from endorsing such fusion in a straightforward way, the story depicts the gesture of empathy, of *Verstehen*, on the part of the twentieth-century interpreter as a move that must first master the minutiae of the ethos and period to be studied. Such study does not lead to replication but brings to reflective awareness the "lie" that fictions, even in their transmogrified form as *ficciones*, must conceal. *Ficciones* must illuminate difference, that between the present of the text and the past it brings to light, as well as the conditions of its own production. The challenge to the student of religion is to exhibit these conditions not with a heavy-handed laying out of hermeneutical principles but with the "wonderful lightness" of Menard.

The next gesture suggested by Menard is difficult for the student of religion because it takes liberties with well-defined objects of study, unities carefully crafted by the work of many scholars. Even those who, like Foucault, are willing to play fast and loose with constituted disciplines are reluctant to tinker with chronological sequence. Such tinkering is, if one can put it so, the joy-ride through history Borges describes when, to cite his example, the *Aeneid* is interpreted through the eyes of Homer. Though clearly a device to be used with care, might not such tactics suggest fruitful experiments, for example, for feminist scholarship? What would become of Hegel's theory of tragedy if the interpreter stationed herself in the position of Antigone (as some feminist scholars have done), or if the traditions of medieval women's Saivite love poetry became the lens through which the religious erotic poetics of Emily Dickinson were focused? Under what textual circumstances, the interpreter must decide, would such a strategy be productive and at what point would it degenerate into self-parody?

I have yet to consider one of the thornier issues confronting the study of religion, that of interested and disinterested observers. Concealed in the Menard story is a preemptive gesture of the narrator that is intended to warrant his version of the story. The gesture is reflexive. By placing the author in the story, the tales themselves recount the power struggle that reading is: the voice of judgment that is the reader's is also that of the author, who stands both inside and outside the tale. The power/knowledge equation thus rendered within the text itself serves to remind us that texts are controlled by interests. Riding the subway on a recent visit to New York, I had occasion to ponder the point. Lines I could have mistaken for graffiti, but which were not, were printed in an authorized advertising space.

They read "You are tough and I am tough / But who will write whose epitaph?" and their author was not an anonymous rider but an emigré poet from the former Soviet Union, Joseph Brodsky.

Does all that I have said about the relation of truth and fact to power and interest vitiate the possibility of fact? Is the fall of the modern view of factuality the end of fact? The romance of fact, the yearning for certainty that accompanies truth in modernity's sense, is not likely to disappear, nor with it the correlative space of modern fiction. Yet when truth as fact is countered by *ficciones* rather than fiction, fact becomes both suspicious of and transparent to itself.

Because there can be no final death knell for fact and truth, let us ponder this identical sentence of Cervantes and Menard: "History is the mother of truth, . . . exemplar and advisor to the present, and the future's counselor."[29] But let us give the last word to Menard, who, Borges says, is an admirer of William James. Unlike Cervantes, when Menard writes "history is the mother of truth," he defines history not as an inquiry into reality but as its origin. Historical truth for him is not what has happened; it is what we judge to have happened.[30] The phrase "exemplar and adviser to the present, and the future's counselor" has become for Menard—as it might become in the study of religion—in Borges's words "brazenly pragmatic."

Eating the Text, Defiling the Hands
Specters in Arnold Schoenberg's Opera Moses and Aron

"A masterpiece always moves, by definition, in the manner of a ghost," its mode of temporalization, its timing, always out of joint, spectrally disorganizing the "cause" that is called the "original," Derrida tells us (*SoM*, 18). Can there be an "original" describing an event that has already occurred but that rearises spectrally in the gap between theophany and inscription, the space between the golden calf and the tablets of the law (Exodus 32:19–20), between the idol as a physical artifact and writing? These questions are raised in the context of Arnold Schoenberg's opera *Moses and Aron*,[1] a masterpiece that, moving between music and text, purports to explore the relation of the Absolute as idea to the image that is alleged to manifest it. The complex tensions between idea and image are brought forward through an innovative combination of speech, vocal, and instrumental music that I shall call Schoenberg's "theosonics."

In what follows, I consider the relation between Moses, who insists upon the word in its ideality, and Aron, who maintains the necessity for its transposition into phenomenal manifestation, and the reversals their positions undergo. The complex of questions posed and suspended by the Mosaic traditions of phenomenality and ideality, as manifested in the calf and the tablets, I argue, returns in Schoenberg's work as spectral re-enactments of older Jewish and Christian traditions exemplified in the comments on Moses in Maimonides' *Guide for the Perplexed* and in the brief remarks on Moses in

Augustine's *Confessions*. I turn also to the process of semiotic idealization itself, that is, the progressive understanding of textual inwardization first manifested in acts of ingesting the text described in a number of biblical passages. In what can be viewed as a countermove, I then consider a rabbinic tradition that contends that sacred food must be segregated from sacred text and that each confers sacred defilement, a "defiling of the hands." Against this backdrop, Schoenberg's Moses is shown, to borrow Derridean terms, to be "the founder of the spirit of a people, . . . the figure of a revenant-survivant, a Ghost survivor" (*SoM*, 146). I maintain further that the effort to create a transcendent object in phonic and musical sound alters the Maimonidean and Augustinian perspectives that have been brought into Schoenberg's theosonics, so that the feared images return to fissure the word. The unintended preservation of these older traditions rearises spectrally not as an effort to perpetuate the past but, as Adorno might put it, "at the vanguard of the new . . . in the interstices of the new."[2]

I shall forgo the temptation to examine the "ana-chronique" specter of Freud's Moses that haunts many contemporary accounts of Moses. Instead, I shall focus upon the spectral rearising of Jewish and Christian interpretations of Moses as they infiltrate Schoenberg's theosonics.

A God without Images

It is not possible to enter into the complex intellectual and artistic influences on Schoenberg's work, nor to do more than allude to his innovative compositional techniques. It is, however, useful to note that Schoenberg attended closely to Schopenhauer's account of the relation between idea (*Vorstellung*) and representation (*Darstellung*) and to Schopenhauer's view that music reveals the inmost essence of the world as will. While Schopenhauer's perspective remains deeply embedded in Schoenberg's aesthetic, Schoenberg modifies Schopenhauer's assertion about music, arguing for the necessity of mediation, the translation of the Absolute into perceptually available content, even if such translation attenuates the power of the unrepresentable.[3] It is also likely that Schoenberg was aware of Hermann Cohen's widely disseminated view that God is the logical condition of reality and, as such, an idea. Nor could Helena Petrovna Blavatsky's theosophy and Rudolf Steiner's anthroposophy, teachings that stressed the notion of divine unity and influenced high modernist artists such as his friend Wasily Kandinsky, have escaped Schoenberg's notice.[4]

Yet it is important to see that *Moses and Aron*, first conceived as an oratorio in which the chorus played a leading role, alternately reflecting the *vox dei* and the *vox populi*, a work in which numerous didactic exclamatory exchanges between the principals occurred, underwent significant revision as an opera. Moving from the more static oratorio form to the theatricality of opera, the miracles of Aron (Act 1) and the orgy before the golden calf (Act 2) were augmented, and the speech of Aron in the unfinished third act, to which I shall recur, was conceptually modified to acknowledge the power of images.[5]

There is no reason to believe that a link can be forged between the sense-laden aspect of Schoenberg's Moses and the Moses of Numbers 10:1–2, verses in which Moses is commanded by God to make two silver trumpets and given elaborate instructions about their use. It is, rather, the Moses of halting speech and thaumaturgical power that Schoenberg sees as soliciting musical adumbration. His self-proclaimed identification with this Moses became more profound with the rise of Nazism, whose potential he feared early on, a fear reflected in this theological declaration by the Israelites: "We know that we were chosen to think the thought of the one eternal, unimaginable, invisible God through to completion, in short, to keep it alive! And there is nothing that can compare with that mission."[6]

The opera *Moses and Aron* is structured so that each protagonist dominates for a time, only to be undone by the other. Moses and the voice from the burning bush do not sing but resort to a stylized song-speech, *Sprechstimme*, devised by Schoenberg to convey conceptual density and the abstractness of divine speech, whereas Aron's words are sung in fluid musical lines, limited always by Schoenberg's twelve-tone row system, "rows or tones where no tone can recur before its turn comes, and then only subject to permutation."[7] The solo voices articulate a chain of transmission: from the burning bush comes God's voice, heard as the voice of Moses, and Moses' voice, in turn, issues from Aron. But the distinction between the personae of Moses and Aron blurs when, at the end of the last scene of the second act, the opera's original closing, Moses, exhausted, submits to an ineluctable contingency and materiality: "Unimaginable God! / Inexpressible many-sided idea, / Will you let it be so explained? / Shall Aron, my mouth, fashion / this image? / Then I have fashioned an image too, / false, / as an image must be. / Thus am I defeated! / Thus all was but madness that / I believed before, / and can but must not be given voice. / O word, thou word that I lack."[8]

Before Moses' final capitulation to the image, he depicts God as one who "is unseen, cannot be measured, everlasting and eternal because ever-present and almighty" (*MaA*, 44). In this context, Moses appears to replicate the aniconic view of Jewish interpretation, the anathema pronounced upon the sacralization of the image, the elevation of its demonic potential into idolatry. As exemplified in Maimonides, the most serious theological error consists in the imputation of corporeality to God, an error that undergirds idolatry in that idolatry, as he defines it, is the idea that a particular form represents the agent between God and his creatures (*GP*, 228). These errors are precipitated by the unfettering of a figural imagination required by ordinary mortals in order to render theological truths accessible but which disfigures this truth through figuration itself. Maimonides concedes that prophecy requires both the logical and the imaginative faculties, even if the rational faculty is to predominate. Restated in Adorno's terms, "pure" figuration is self-defeating, "for it augments the chaotic moment lurking in all art as its pre-condition."[9]

Another danger of the hypertrophied imagination feared by Maimonides is its power to unleash a mixture of true and imaginary things (*GP*, 228). In prophetic visions the *viva vox* of God is absent; when thought to be heard, it is only imagined to be present. Moses alone is exempt from the mediation of deceptive screening images: "All prophets are prophetically addressed through an angel except Moses our teacher, in reference to whom Scripture says, 'Mouth to mouth I speak to him'" (ibid., 245). This view seems to suggest that the danger of the golden calf lies in its ontological status as image, one in a series of images, an artifactual expression of an excess of imagination. But we shall see that a far more complex picture, one involving a series of idolatrous specters and their reversals, of simulacra restrained and unleashed, begins to emerge, that, far from belonging to a panoply of images, the golden calf reflects a desperate effort to restrict the dissemination of images and the conjurations that give rise to them. At the same time, it is an attempt to substitute itself for the infinite semantic potential of writing, of a particular system of signs that is the law as incised upon tablets that are broken but rearise spectrally.

Consider again Maimonides' worry, his dread of the simulacrum, his fear that there may be no way to distinguish true from imaginary things. The Platonic principle that purports to select the true from the imaginary does not divide forms from appearances but rather reflects a testing of rival claimants within the sphere of appearances themselves, an effort that is, at bottom, not taxonomical but evaluative, as Deleuze has pointed out.[10] He writes: "This problem of distinguishing between things and their simulacra . . . is a question of making the difference, thus of operating in the depths of the immediate. . . . It is a dangerous trial without thread and without net, for according to the ancient custom of myth and epic, false claimants must die."[11] As division that is always already anterior to full presence, the state of difference itself is prior to the determination of the true, prior to the forms that, being a post hoc imposition, are intended to ground what must remain heterological and refractory to grounding.

That the golden calf is not an image but rather stanches the flow of runaway images and is an attestation of fixity is implied by Aron's words, which attribute theonomic properties to it: "These are your gods O Israel who brought you up out of the land of Egypt." This view rearises in Schoenberg's Aron, who mummifies in the form of the calf the god that lives in all things, "unchangeable [*unwandelbar*], even as a Law" (*MaA*, 90). In addition to the specter of animism, the opera depicts a crucial episode of violence, the suicides of four virgins, who cry out "Arouse us to first and last rapture," and the pandemic orgy of sexuality and death that ensues (*MaA*, 102).[12] Can Aron, after all, and not Moses become the redresser of historical grievances, liberator and righter of wrongs, if, as Derrida shows, "One never inherits without coming to terms with some specter, and therefore with more than one specter" (*SoM*, 21)?

In his study of Moses, Martin Buber is not unaware of certain spectral manifestations in the account of the golden calf in Exodus.[13] After the post-Davidian kingdom is divided into north and south, Buber suggests, Jeroboam, the northern king, revives the cultic centers of Dan and Bethel, thereby hoping to circumvent the necessity of making pilgrimages to Jerusalem, which would reinforce loyalty to the Davidian kingship rather than to himself (I Kings 12:26 ff.). In order to clinch the supremacy of these shrines, Jeroboam makes two golden calves and, in a remarkable act of doubling, repeats Aron's words: "Behold your gods O Israel who brought you up out of the land of Egypt." While some scholars hold that the Jeroboam narrative reflects an older tradition, Buber refuses to credit this view, arguing instead that Jeroboam's calves replicate a common motif in Semitic cultures and are intended merely to serve as markers of God's throne. Not Jeroboam, Buber argues, but the people could not distinguish between the bearer of the God and God, a perspective that is then foisted by an editorial hand upon Jeroboam himself. Thus the specter of an "originary" idolatry is revealed and concealed as a proscription against idolatry in "the malediction inscribed in the law itself" (*SoM*, 21).

It has been argued that rivalry exists not only between Israel's God and the idol, as is attested in the prohibition against idols, but also among the idols themselves. A minority view, upheld by some contemporary biblical scholars, suggests that a positive tradition once provided the basis for the subsequently negative account of the calf. Without entering into the scholarly pros and cons of this interpretation, its claims may be worth noting. It is argued that the pejorative term for golden calf as idol (*egel*) is used in Exodus 32, whereas the term for a bovine animal is denoted by the word *re'em* in the Balaam oracles and in Psalms 22:22. In the latter, the Hebrew version of the text reads "Save me from the horns of the wild ox," but the Greek Syrian version reads "Answer me from the horns of the wild ox (*re'em*)," implying that God himself responds to the lament of the psalmist from out of the horns of the *re'em*.[14]

Reason, Magic, and the Magic of Reason

In the theosonics of Schoenberg's *Moses and Aron*, the issue of idol and image can be seen to disclose a Platonic pattern that, in Derridean terms, "associates in a strict fashion image with specter and idol with phantasm, with the phantasma in its phantomatic or errant dimension as living-dead" (*SoM*, 147). In the crucial fifth scene of Act II, the golden calf is interpreted by Aron as belonging to a panoply of living theophanic images, invoked not by him but by Moses himself, images that include the pillar of fire and the burning bush. Moses, however, falls victim to a category mistake when he fails to perceive the difference between phantomatic idol as stancher of images and the ongoing stream of theophanic conjurations. The golden calf is inert, at once an artifact that lies somewhere between artwork and implement, and a commodity having the value of the gold from which it has been fashioned. By contrast, Moses' own works are dynamic but dangerous conjurations: his rod is changed into a serpent, the Red Sea is split, and the like. The competing claimants in this context are not the idol and the stream of theophanic conjurations but the multiple conjured events themselves.

It is possible for a product of conjuration to appear to replicate the function of the calf. Consider the episode of the Israelites' complaints about the lack of food and water as they trek through the desert and the Lord's response, the sending of venomous snakes (Numbers 21:5–9). After Moses intercedes on behalf of the people, the Lord directs him to make a bronze serpent, so that anyone looking at the effigy will recover. But Moses' fashioning of the bronze serpent remains an act of conjuration undertaken in the interest of healing. To be sure, the bronze serpent is later interpreted by the Israelites as a cultic effigy before which burnt offerings are made until it is smashed by King Hezekiah (II Kings 18:4), an act that might be construed as mimetic of the destruction of the golden calf by Moses. It is not unreasonable, however, to infer that the bronze serpent, like the staff of Asclepius in Greek mythology, is revered principally for its ongoing thaumaturgical properties. By contrast, the golden calf is, as it were, proto-scriptic, the stancher of images, the one who is identified by the Israelites as the historical god of Israel who brought them out of the land of Egypt (Exodus 32:7–8).[15]

Derrida has described conjuration as a certain efficacy of voice: "the magical incantation destined to *evoke*, to bring forth with the voice, to *convoke* a charm or a spirit. Conjuration . . . makes come by definition, what is not there at the present moment of the appeal. . . . its words cause something to happen" (*SoM*, 41). In the ancient world, Moses' name was frequently linked to thaumaturgical practices, and tributes to Moses' powers as a magician are described by Pliny and Eusebius, among others. Origen, in his negative depiction of Jews as sorcerers, writes in *Contra Celsus* that Jews derived their power from Moses their teacher.[16]

Nowhere does distinguishing between theophanic phenomena and conjuration cause greater difficulty than in the rationalist theology of Maimonides. In a discourse whose misogyny is striking even for its day, Maimonides defends the harsh prescriptions intended to guard against conjuration as practiced in biblical times, even justifying putting witches to death. The grounds of his critique of witchcraft are both pragmatic and ethical. "No analogy and no reasoning can discover any relation between these performances . . . and the promised result," he insists (*GP*, 332). But witchcraft is also seen as a species of idolatry, and, as such, it promotes false beliefs generally. In support of the latter claim, Maimonides singles out Sabean religious doctrines as intending "criticism and an attack on the evident miracles by which all people learnt that there exists a God who is judge over all people" (ibid., 318).

The aporias of the rationalist position are obvious. If authentication is based upon the relation between practice and result, and if witchcraft succeeds in producing the promised result, what would distinguish it from miracle? Either the question is begged from the start, that is, negative outcomes mean that witchcraft is at work, or the line between witchcraft and miracle cannot be drawn on the grounds proposed.

Earlier it was noted that Schoenberg is able to link the golden calf phenomenologically to Moses' acts of thaumaturgy in that each endeavors to capture divine power in sensuous images. Their connectedness does not preclude Schoenberg's observing that there may be rival claimants to sacred power within the sphere of Israelite conjuration itself. In the single completed scene of a contemplated third act written shortly before Schoenberg's death, Moses attributes acts of conjuration to Aron, for example, forcing water from the rock. Moses remonstrates, "You expose them to strange gods. . . . you do as the people do" (*MaA*, 126). Failing to serve the divine idea (*Gottesdanken*) and engaging instead in thaumaturgical practices results in an inevitable miscegenation of the sensuous images of conjuration. No principle is offered by means of which the genuine and spurious claimants can be distinguished, because no principle applicable to sensual images could possibly determine which acts embody God's power.

Eating One's Words

Perhaps the most astonishing act of conjuration in the golden calf narrative of Exodus is strangely absent from Schoenberg's opera: the ingestion of the ashes of the calf after it is demolished and the pieces burned. Consider the text: "And he [Moses] took the calf which they had made, and burnt it with fire, and ground it to powder, and scattered it upon the water, and made the people of Israel drink it" (Exodus 32:20). Traditional interpretation treats this material as depicting an act of negative conjuration and as a certain archivization of the forbidden idol. Before turning to these interpretations, consider first Derrida's claim that "(repression is an archivization), that is to say, to archive *otherwise* is to repress the archive while archiving the repression; *otherwise* of course . . . than according to the current conscious patent modes of archivization."[17] Israelite consciousness will both repress and remember that which is most feared, idolatry. By ingesting the ash, the people simultaneously conceal and inwardize what has been proscribed but will nevertheless return spectrally. It might be asked, when that which has been ingested is ash, how can ash be transformed into language, into the words of proscription? The material residue must first, to use contemporary terms, be turned into bytes, which will, in turn, be transformed into words, into a system of meaning-bearing signs. Thus the biblical narrative can be interpreted as leading from material residue to virtualization, from virtualization to linguistic expression.

This trajectory may appear to be foisted anachronistically upon the biblical narrative out of postmodern considerations, but it can be shown to be already intrinsic to traditional interpretation. Twelfth-century commentator Rashi (Solomon, son of Isaac) links Exodus 32:20, the ingesting of the ash of the incinerated calf, to the testing of the *Sotah*, a wife suspected of infidelity (Numbers 5:12–31). The wife appears before a priest, who prepares a mixture of holy water and dust taken from the floor of the tabernacle, forces her to swear that she will be cursed if found guilty, and transcribes the curses into a book. The woman is compelled to ingest the ashes of the burned script, together with a burnt cereal offering. If, after drinking this brew, she experiences bitter pain and her body swells, she is deemed guilty and becomes an execration, one who is separated from her people; if these corporeal changes do not occur, she is free. It might be asked why Moses must force the Israelites to ingest the ash, in a test comparable to the trial of the *Sotah*, when their guilt is already clear. Has not the worship of the golden calf been witnessed by all? Neither Midrash nor Mishnah comment on this point, although it could be surmised that, if tested, the innocence of those Israelites who were not idolators in their hearts could be demonstrated.

What is crucial from the present perspective is that the characters written by the priest fall into the water, that the tangible ash must be transformed into text, archived, to re-emerge corporeally in the manner of a Freudian symptom. Rashi's linking of the destruction of the golden calf to the rites connected with the trial of the *Sotah* binds what must be repressed to what must also be archived, what is to be remembered to what must be forgotten. No physical remainder of the calf but only that which is written, the graphematic incarnation of lexical and semiotic elements, can be exhumed. The errancy of the word that demands interpretation will supplant the worship of the idol, but the idol will remain spectrally within the word. No trace of what the priest has written may remain in the world outside the *Sotah* herself: the outside is now inside, the nonspace where the "true," the "authentic," archive abides. The Mishnah goes so far as to note that a priest may not use an instrument that leaves a lasting trace, but must write "only with ink," with what can be blotted out (*Sotah* 2:4). Buber remarks, without considering the aporias suggested by his statement: by "means of writing one can embody in the stone what has been revealed . . . so that it is no longer simply an event, but also word by word, it continues to serve as evidence of a revelation. . . . What Moses says may be clumsy but not what he writes."[18]

We are now prepared to delve into a meaning of writing that could not be gleaned from the episode of the *Sotah* alone. Moses' demolition of the golden calf is hardly surprising; it is more difficult to account for the smashing of the tablets of the law that precedes this act. Were they not the tables of the testimony "written on both sides" whose writing "was the writing of God, graven upon the tables?" Yet "as soon as he came near the camp and saw the calf and the dancing, Moses' anger burned hot, and he threw the tablets out of his hands and broke them at the foot of the mountain" (Exodus 32:19). The traditional explanation, given in Rashi, is that an apostate is forbidden to eat the Paschal lamb, having violated *one* of the commandments; a fortiori, those who violated all the commandments cannot possibly receive the tablets from God. What is bestowed upon the Israelites is a second set of tablets, upon which are written characters identical to the first. Moreover, although God had promised to inscribe the text, it is Moses who now writes these words at God's dictation (Exodus 34:27). Does not the second set unleash the specter of the first? Are the tablets not haunted by a more originary language, language now indistinguishable save for a temporal difference? But earlier and later events themselves cannot be discriminated, for, as Derrida claims:

> Repetition *and* first time: this is perhaps the question of the event as question of the ghost. *What* is a ghost? What is the *effectivity* of the presence of a specter, that is, of what seems to remain as ineffective, virtual, insubstantial as a simulacrum? Is there *there*, between the thing itself and its simulacrum, an opposition that holds up? Repetition *and* first time, but also repetition and last time, since the singularity of any first time makes of it also a last time. (*SoM*, 10)

Are we not, with the second set of tablets, in the presence of a Derridean hauntology, a ghostly revanescence that "produces an automatism of repetition, no less than it finds its principle of reason there" (*SoM*, 173)? Not only would the breaking of the first set prevent the undeserving idolators from receiving the law, as the tradition states, but it would serve the unstated purpose of preventing the idolatrous worship of the physical tablets. It is the writing itself that can be replicated, that has perlocutionary force, and that solicits interpretation.

The act of ingesting the word is not unique to Exodus. Just as the letters of words are swallowed by the worshippers of the calf and by the *Sotah*, so too there are other references to eating God's words. Reversing the negative connotations of ingestion, Jeremiah proclaims: "Thy words were found and I ate them, and thy words became to me a joy and the delight of my heart" (Jeremiah 15:16). In a more elaborate account of ingestion, Ezekiel is instructed by a heavenly voice " 'Open your mouth and eat what I give you.' And when I looked behold a hand was stretched out to me, and lo, a written scroll was in it." Although the scroll contains words of lamentation, when eaten, Ezekiel declares: "It was in my mouth as sweet as honey" (Ezekiel 2:8–3:3).

The intimate connection between sacred food and the written scroll is attested in a rabbinic account of the classification called "defiling the hands." Yet far from perceiving sacred defilement as a step toward inwardization, rabbinic thought is fearful of the reciprocal contamination of scroll and food.

Thus Michael Broyde writes:

> Defiling the hands is a status of ritual purity (or impurity) . . . enacted by the Talmudic sages not to promote ritual purity, but to protect holy works from destruction or desecration. . . . People would store holy food in the ark with holy scrolls, saying both are holy. To prevent this conduct which led to rats, mice, and weasels eating the scrolls as well as the sacred food, the Sages enacted a series of rabbinic decrees to deter this conduct.[19]

Broyde goes on to recount that, despite the sacrality common to both food and writing, the latter must be protected against dangers that normally befall the former. The touching of either sacred food or holy scrolls—a holy scroll is defined as one whose rescue from a fire would be permitted on the Sabbath, when such labors are normally forbidden—defiles, so that touching one when the other has been touched requires purification. We have seen that the text as sacred food has no place in Schoenberg's theosonics. The ideality of the word precludes confusion with the materiality of what can be ingested. Thus Schoenberg's Moses might have endorsed the rabbinic proscriptions that protect the text, sacred writing, from defilement through tactile miscegenation in what can be seen as a ghostly reappearance in Schoenberg of this rabbinic separation of kinds.

Some Faces of Moses

In Augustine's account of Moses, one whose complexity cannot be engaged here, the etiolation or aetherialization of a physical substance that is inwardized is no longer in evidence. It is now the ideality of voice that is identified with truth. The backdrop for Augustine's discussion of Moses is the creation narrative as transmitted by Moses. Longing to see Moses, Augustine laments with characteristic fervor that he can no longer encounter Moses face-to-face, so that he might beseech him to explain God's word. "If he spoke in Hebrew, his words would strike my ears in vain and none of their meaning would reach my mind. If he spoke in Latin, I should know what he said. But how should I know whether what he said was true?" Augustine asks.[20] Yet, it would seem, not Moses' words but rather "truths [that] are deep inside [him], in [his] most intimate thoughts," constitute the ultimate court of appeal.[21] Not only do foreign languages act as screens but even one's own language is, as it were, a foreign language with regard to inner truth. The univocity of truth is assured only because God is *fons et origo* of all truth. It is God who filled Moses with himself, who attests to the goodness of truth, or rather to truth as goodness. As Derrida (speaking of Husserl) has shown: "The determination of being as ideality is properly a valuation, an ethico-theoretical act that revives the decision that founded philosophy in its Platonic form" (*SoM*, 53). Intended to ensure the sameness of the object each time it is repeated, this ideality is contingent upon repetition. Does not the specter of a Platonic Augustine haunt Schoenberg's Moses when he insists that his thoughts repeat the "great thoughts" of the patriarchs?

Yet the aporias of voice are not absent from Augustine's discourse about Moses, in which image, thing, and phonic element are inseparably intertwined with the notion of a simple source or origin of truth. Moses' account of creation as passed on to us is likened by Augustine to a spring whose waters "are carried by a maze of channels over a wider area than could be reached by any single stream drawing its water from the same source and flowing through many different places."[22] Similarly, Augustine avers, from Moses' words "uttered in all brevity . . . there gush clear streams of truth from which each derives her or his own interpretation."[23] How, it must be asked, do the waters of a flowing stream represent their source? "There are things like reflecting pools and images, an infinite reference from one to the other but no longer a source or a spring," Derrida maintains (*G*, 36). What is more, he goes on to say, without a simple origin, "what is reflected is split in itself and not only as an addition to itself of its image. The reflection, the image, the double, splits what it doubles. The origin of the speculation becomes a difference" (ibid.). Does not Augustine abandon truth's univocity when he concedes that numerous meanings could be drawn from Moses' text, that semiotic difference is in fact intrinsic to scripture? Were there not myriad meanings, and had Moses not seen them all? If he were Moses, Augustine speculates, he would prefer to envision multiple significations rather than "impose a single true meaning so explicitly that it would exclude all others."[24]

Are we to imagine, then, that Augustine allows for an increment of textual novelty as a text is interpreted over time? Or are we, to use Augustine's spectral evocation of biblical ingestion, to think that truth resides in the great belly of memory, as if Moses had eaten God's words? Does the text not function so that we may have access to some part of the truth, which was seen as a whole by Moses? Thus, Augustine writes: "Moses was conscious of every truth we can deduce from [Scripture] and others besides that we cannot or cannot yet find in them but are nevertheless to be found."[25] Moses' inmost self is the repository of the entire truth as a collection of theonomic semes, as it were.

Though I cannot enter into the complexities of the context in which Derrida's analysis occurs, his warning against a certain reading of polysemy is crucial here: "Polysemy always puts out its multiplicities and variations within the horizon, at least of some integral reading which contains no absolute rift, no senseless deviation—the horizon of the final parousia of a meaning at last deciphered, revealed, made present in the rich collection of its determinations."[26] Derrida points to a critical difference between "discursive polysemy" and "textual dissemination," a difference that is "precisely 'difference itself,' an implacable difference."[27]

Without difference there can be no meaning, yet when meaning manifests itself in its self-presence, it erases difference. It is thus not the polysemic potential of texts that Augustine fears, for he has conceded that Moses can entertain numerous meanings so long as all are true, but rather the uncontrolled outflow of a textual stream whose interpretations cannot be brought to closure.

It is not surprising that the polysemy of texts also fails to alarm Maimonides and even serves a pedagogic purpose, so that several meanings may be attributed to key words without theological jeopardy. Thus, Maimonides says, Moses teaches that belief in God's existence can be brought about by exhibiting the meaning of the phrase *Ehyeh asher Ehyeh*, the name *Eyeh* deriving from *hayah*, in the sense of existing (*GP*, 94). The sentence is not a tautology in that the first *Eyeh* and the second are not identical. Critical issues might be raised by a post-Heideggerian analysis of the sense in which "existence" is meant, of the semiotic potential of *Eyeh*, but such considerations would divert us from noting the toleration within the tradition of a certain polysemy. Maimonides takes the first *Eyeh* to be a noun, *asher* to be an incomplete noun, which must be completed by the second *Eyeh*, the second being the attribute by which the first is to be described. God is the Being (*Eyeh*) whose existence is posited as absolute (*Eyeh*). It is the second *Eyeh*, posited as a property of the first and without which the first is meaningless, that strives both to maintain unrepresentability and to describe the unrepresentable.[28]

Adorno realizes that the obverse of this process, a striving after a submersion of the concrete in the unrepresentable, is a quest for a spurious and harmful unity. Speaking of the artwork, he contends that its "unity cannot be what it must, i.e., unity of a manifold. By synthesizing the many, unity inflicts damage on them, hence also on itself."[29] If this remark can be taken as a plea for an art of dissemination rather than for multiple meanings that can ultimately be unified, can Schoenberg's *Moses and Aron* be construed as such a work, a theosonics of fissures and gaps?

In commenting on the disarticulation of artworks, Adorno points to the refusal of certain contemporary works to come to closure once the technical and aesthetic conventions involved in their production have been set aside. "Art of the highest caliber pushes beyond totality towards a state of fragmentation," he declares.[30] Hegel's bad infinite has been chosen, as it were, as an aesthetic technique by modernists such as Beckett. What is more, Adorno continues, such a work of art, one that defies convention, cannot die, "no more than can the hunter Gracchus."[31] Does Schoenberg not proclaim the same fragmentation, repetition, and deathlessness when, in the opera version of the single scene in the third act of *Moses and Aron*, Aron falls dead only after Moses utters the words condemning him to eternal repetition: "You were and ever shall be hurled back into the wasteland" (*MaA*, 130)?

Adorno, like Schoenberg, is obsessed with the question of transforming the abstract possibility of art into a concrete possibility. By virtue of a process Adorno calls *metier*, the artist challenges the forces the artwork embodies, so that the work is always already putting itself into question, destroying and resurrecting itself, bringing what is outside itself into itself. Adorno calls this disseminative power "talking back," a radical questioning that, in the case of *Moses and Aron*, can be seen to break into the claims of the Absolute's unrepresentability. Is it not Aron, then, who talks back, who attacks the inviolability of God's word, which Moses believes embodies the Absolute? In Schoenberg's version of Exodus 32:19, Moses proclaims that the tablets of the law set forth his idea, are one with it, but Aron replies scornfully, "They're images also, just part of the whole idea" (ibid., 116). It is only at this point, when the word of God is reduced to a sensuous image, that Moses despairs, proclaiming, "Then I smash to pieces both these tables, / And I shall ask him to withdraw the task given to me" (ibid.).

Is it Aron alone who talks back, whose specter rearises to haunt presumptions of the Absolute's unity with the word? Is it Aron who contests the ghosts of Maimonides and of Augustine, who reappear in the Schopenhauerian idealism of Moses? Or is there a double revenescence, Moses and Aron talking back to the God of both calf and tablet, reminding God of his promises? Consider the oratorio version of the third scene of the third act, in which Moses appoints Eleazer as his successor and consecrates the people into the service of the Eternal. At that moment Moses addresses these words to Aron: "You know why you will not see the Promised Land / Because you did not really need to see it — / You beheld it as you took on God's voice through me and grasped God's way / . . . So you lost God's land but had been already in it."[32] The promised land is not any land, not an original space or time but a there that is not there, a past that has already passed by and cannot be made present, cannot be awaited as such, and yet, impossibly, must be awaited. This is Moses' promise of what cannot arrive, in Derrida's terms, "the impossible itself. . . . this condition of the possibility of the event is also the condition of its impossibility . . . the messianic without messianism that guides us like the blind" (*SoM*, 65). Is this impossibility of messianism itself not Schoenberg's Moses talking back?

Killing the Cat
Sacrifice and Beauty in Genet and Mishima

Genet's heroes are "as at home in infamy as a fish is in water."[1] According to Sartre, the effect produced by Genet's use of crime is not "an ethics of evil" but its metamorphosis into a "black aestheticism."[2] For Mishima, descriptions of blood and gore produce a comparable result: "when blood flows existence as a whole receives its first endorsement."[3] The works I consider, Genet's *Funeral Rites* and Mishima's *Temple of the Golden Pavilion*, include theoretical accounts of beauty and sacrifice that, despite their speculative nature, produce an aesthetic intoxication nearly comparable to that of the novels' transgressive events.

Just this exhilaration, according to Georges Bataille, lies at the basis of both sacrifice and literature, because what compels and excites in sacrificial ritual and fiction is "what uses up our strength and our resources and, if necessary, places our life in danger."[4] It would be something of a truism to suggest that literature is simply a scaled-down version of sacrifice. Bataille's far bolder claim is the converse: not only is sacrifice a legacy that religion bequeaths to literature, but *actual* "sacrifice [is] a novel, a fictional tale illustrated in a bloody manner."[5] This affirmation is based on the view that the victim, human or animal, *plays* at being king or god, so that sacrifice is always already a literary artifact. "Plung[ed] into anguish tied to a feeling of vertiginous, contagious destruction, which fascinate[s] while it appall[s],"[6] the spectator is captive to the sacrificial *fascinans*

375

not merely as an object of horror but as a divine object. "It is the god who agrees to the sacrifice,"[7] so that enactment of the rite means losing oneself in death.

To be sure, Bataille acknowledges, only rarely does literature strive for, much less achieve, the emotional intensity attained in ritual sacrifice. That the idea of this fervid passion as literature's aim extends into Genet's fiction is hardly surprising, given the pervasiveness of Bataille's influence in French literary culture. More striking is Mishima's relation to Bataille, not only because the latter offers an apt hermeneutical strategy for decoding Mishima's works but because Bataille's account of sacrifice is already a textual impulse in Mishima's fiction, as his own remarks attest: "If one misses one's night one will never have another opportunity to achieve a peak of happiness in life. Instrumental in this conviction . . . [was] my reading of Nietzsche during the war and my fellow-feeling for the philosopher Georges Bataille, the 'Nietzsche of eroticism.'"[8] What is more, not only is the idea that fiction is sacrifice a claim about genre, about the kind of thing fiction is, but ritual sacrifice is itself made an explicit theme in both Genet's and Mishima's novels.

The centrality of violence in Bataille's theory should not be overlooked. In his by now "classic" account of sacrifice, René Girard notices that violence is central not only to sacrifice but also to prohibition. He considers this insight Bataille's chief contribution to the understanding of the phenomenon. Girard writes: "Bataille is inclined to treat violence in terms of some rare and precious condiment, the only spice still capable of stimulating the jaded appetite of modern man. Yet Bataille is able to transcend . . . decadent aestheticism . . . [to] explain . . . that 'the prohibition eliminates violence, and our violent impulses destroy our inner calm without which human consciousness cannot exist.'"[9]

Both writers are in important ways Nietzscheans: they see Western "religion, morality and philosophy [as] decaden[t] forms of man."[10] But their art is not one of simple negation in that such art, depending for its effect upon the framework it purports to destroy, creates nothing new. Nihilistic art, for these writers, requires existential transformation in that, for them (as for Nietzsche), art includes not only a metamorphosis of fictional persons through sin and transgression but also the negative self-transfiguring of the artist. By shattering the distinction between maker and product, the artist brings his own reconfigured "life" into his text as a discursive strand. This move is recursive: text and life are reciprocally transforming. Once the strategies of the written text force an expanded textual space and the boundary between art and life is blurred, multiple layers of sacrifice—"autobiographical" and "fictional"—intersect within an indeterminate field of textuality.

The inclusion of an autobiographical element extrinsic to the fictional text is particularly vexing in both Mishima and Genet, since their lives pose serious moral questions for a reader forced to rub her nose in such matters as Genet's thefts and equivocal conduct during the Nazi occupation of France and Mishima's postwar creation of a Fascistic private army, as well as his ritual suicide. In what follows, I refrain from considering these matters and focus on the sacrificial immolation of a cat in Genet's *Funeral Rites* and the killing of a cat in the Zen koan "Nansen Kills a Cat" in Mishima's *Temple of the Golden Pavilion*.[11] The occurrence of the cat killing in both works is fortuitous, but the episodes highlight the importance in both texts of the link between sacred immolation and the theme of beauty. Although the cat killing is an entering wedge into each work's account of negative transcendence, each incident is expanded in terms of widely divergent strategies. Genet's work fastens on totemic cannibalism in such a way that the text itself acquires liturgical force. Mishima, by contrast, uses a traditional Zen koan to propound a nihilistic aesthetic. Beauty is interpreted in terms of Buddhist emptiness (*sunyata*), so that the experience of beauty oscillates between precipitating a Buddhist enlightenment and Western nihilism.

Beauty and Appearances

Genet refuses to identify beauty with beautiful appearances, a rejection that should not be confused with Plato's denigration of appearances on the grounds that they are merely derivative instantiations of a true world of ideal forms. For Plato, appearances are too "low," so that the soul must transcend them by rising to the world of forms, whereas for Genet they are too "high." In Genet's work, the soul, in a reverse movement, plunges into the abyss, where the artist dredges up the most despairing lives and embellishes them with a language of "carnal sumptuousness."[12] The despair of the plunge is camouflaged by a language at the furthest remove from the exalted affective states this language purports to describe. At the same time, wretchedness is not prettified but is simultaneously heightened and parodied, thereby avoiding the abstraction of the Platonic forms while still bypassing beautiful appearances.

Beauty also comes into being when "visible established beauty is destroyed" and a new beauty arises on its shattered ground, one that Genet calls "poetry."[13] Neither a Platonic form nor a visible icon, "poetry is the break (or rather the meeting at the breaking point) between the visible and the invisible."[14] Moreover, Genet stakes a moral claim of sorts for poetry. Appearances deceive not because they hide a noumenal truth but rather because they mask the absence of all grounds. Bringing this masking into view is a kind of "moral" objective of the writer. Even if Genet's negations go so far as to negate the reader herself, even if Genet does not mean to communicate with his readers as Derrida insists,[15] the moral challenge of unmasking is inscribed as a negative ethics on the aesthetic surface of the text.

If poetry is the art that brings nonbeing into view, what is the ontic status of poems themselves? Genet cites a young catamite as an example of a poem. On the face of it, to think of those he calls the pimps and queens of his imagination as poems seems absurd in that poems are linguistic artifacts. Yet Genet's characters are not persons but fantasies of "authorial" consciousness, linguistic icons. Language, he contends, opens up the beauty of remembered catamites or configures new ones; by giving expression to the object, he hopes to purge himself of both name and object. Names are not referring terms in the sense of denoting entities but rather evoke their referents in all of their historical and cultural associations. Names "proliferate and snap me up," Genet writes in *The Thief's Journal*.[16] Words are intended to produce aesthetic effects through their power to shock, a power derived from contrasting the most sordid with the most exalted descriptions. The reader is cast into "foulness [which] lands him in a garden where roses bloom, roses whose beauty is the indiscriminate mixing of the folded petals with insect holes."[17]

Mishima's account of beauty is linked to a life of action. Appealing to the traditional Japanese *Bunburyodo* ideal of combining literature and the martial arts, Mishima affirms the inextricability of the two. So intimate is their relation, Mishima writes, that "I gradually learned from the sun and steel how to pursue words with the body not merely pursue the body with words."[18] Yet the verbal arts cannot attain parity with the arts of action because of a difficulty inherent in language itself. Originally the product of a cohesive social group whose emotions and needs are expressed in epic poetry, language degenerates and acquires an altogether different function: the representation of the individual ego. Thus, paradoxically, the more refined the style, the more the original function of language decays, since refinement only serves to disclose the authorial ego. By contrast, the body is immune to egoistic corruption not because the body is in its very nature already individual—thus, individuality would not be a fall—but rather because stripping muscles of their individuality (through "steel") results in a carnal abstractness, a universality that "suffers no private corrosion."[19] He goes on to say, "Action perishes with the blossom, but literature is an imperishable flower. And an imperishable flower is, of course, an artificial flower."[20]

In the *Temple of the Golden Pavilion*, the work to be considered in what follows, the narrator and chief character, Mizoguchi, is ugly, stunted, a stutterer. Able to rely neither on language nor on the body, he hopes to find beauty through a relationship to beautiful appearances, which he then destroys in a ghastly act of sacrifice.

Killing the Cat and Cannibalistic Sacrifice

Episodes of violence related to the creation or destruction of beauty abound in the works of Genet and Mishima. Mishima's protagonists strike out against the destruction of beauty (*The Sailor Who Fell with Grace from the Sea*) or, conversely, against beauty itself (*Thirst for Love*), or try to create beauty through ritual suicide (the short story "Patriotism" and *Runaway Horses*). In *Temple of the Golden Pavilion*, Mishima explores the paradoxes that arise when an effort is made to destroy beautiful appearances, paradoxes that are explicated through the interpretation of a well-known Zen koan from the *Mumonkan*, "Nansen Kills a Cat." This koan can be contrasted with the brief but pivotal incident of cat killing in Genet's *Funeral Rites*, to which I shall now turn.

This event occurs early in Genet's novel and links the creation of beauty to the novel's central theme of sacrifice. The murder of the cat should be interpreted in conjunction with a fantasy concerning a cannibalistic feast that is the climax of its concluding section. The first episode, the cat killing, occurs during the German occupation of Paris in World War II, a time of scarcity and hunger. Riton, one of the narrator's lovers and a member of the French collaborationist militia, decides to kill a cat to assuage his hunger: "The Tom was big and fat. The murder was ghastly."[21] At first, Riton tries to kill it by hurling his hammer "because the blow does not kill it by . . . continuous participation in the murder by approving it every second."[22] Because in its furious will to live the cat evades his blows, he is forced to apply more direct methods. After attempting to strangle it, in a horrifying coda to the rite, Riton finally hangs the animal.

The point of this account is that, as the cat struggles, Riton notices that it "was living more intensely, its life was exalted by danger."[23] Genet's gory description of this exaltation parallels nearly word for word Bataille's depiction of sacrifice. The cat has become negatively numinous and, when finally ingested, the food of a sacramental meal that is a black mass.

The killing and eating of the cat is consummated only at the end of the novel in an imagined cannibalistic rite:

> On the shore where ferns grow, the savage moonworshippers were dancing around a fire in the forest. The tribe that had been invited to the feast was revelling in the dance and in anticipation of the young body that was cooking in a caldron, I was . . . dancing . . . to the sound of the tom-tom. I was making my body supple. I was preparing to receive the totemic food. I was sure I was the God.[24]

The narrator has become Bataille's divine object in an imagined "primitive" sacrifice. In this totemic feast, the narrator, rejected as thief and pederast, "ingests" the person of a dead hero of the French Resistance who had been his lover and through whom he is now able to find roots in a France from which he has been cast out. The cannibalistic feast resolves the novel's conflict: the author's/narrator's struggle with a dual love, the love for Jean, hero of the Resistance, and the forbidden erotic relation to Jean's obverse, Riton. Through ritual sacrifice, the narrator becomes French once again.

Sacrifice also begets beauty, in two ways. First, betrayal depends upon there having been a prior love, and love is a relation of dependence on the other. Betrayal shatters this dependence and allows the self to free itself: "Indispensable for achieving beauty; love. And cruelty shattering that love."[25] Second, beauty is born when the celebrant in the sacrifice is restored to communal life. But how is beauty created by overcoming alienation, when Genet's aesthetic rests on expressing it in acts of rebellion? The cannibalistic fantasy of the novel's coda demonstrates that rebellion need not be an end in itself but may generate reconciliation through extreme transgression, the consumption of human flesh. This becomes clear when the outcome of the imagined anthropophagy is considered. In a key passage, Genet writes:

Finally Jean appeared from somewhere, dead and naked. Walking on his heels, he brought me his corpse, which was cooked to a turn. He laid it out on the table and disappeared. . . . Alone at the table . . . I sat and ate. I belonged to the tribe. And not in a superficial way by virtue of my being born into it, but by the grace of an adoption in which it was granted to me to take part in a religious feast. . . . Jean D's death thus gave me roots. . . . The beauty of sacrifice for the homeland moves me.[26]

The transgressive sacrifice results in the narrator's becoming an adoptive son of the tribe by sacrificing one of its natural members, thus echoing the familiar passage from Paul's letter to the Romans in which Paul grafts the branch, the gentiles, onto the original olive tree, Israel, joining the gentile to the house of Israel (Romans 9:11). For Genet, the graft or the adoptive son is preferable to the original tree or natural son, since adoption requires an act of the spirit. A second outcome, parasitic upon the first, is the restoration of right relations between the narrator and his homeland at the price of blood: when blood is shed and linked with transgressive ritual, beauty results. Even if beauty is not the goal of the sacrifice, it is its outcome attaching, itself as a phantasm to whatever other significations sacrifice may have.

Just as the first sacrifice, the cat killing that relieves Riton's hunger, can only be "set right," that is, be made beautiful, through a fully realized blood sacrifice, the "false" hero Riton must be superseded by the "true" hero Jean D. Yet if the feast reconciles the narrator, then Riton is not blotted out but brought into a new equation: sacrifice does not result in a permanent sublation of what is negatively numinous but in a temporary overcoming. The refractory object continues to recur and remains a solicitation to endless reenactment.

Nansen Kills a Cat: Preliminary Interpretations

In the *Temple of the Golden Pavilion*, Mishima offers three exegeses of the Zen koan "Nansen Kills a Cat," contained in the *Mumonkan*, a thirteenth-century collection with glosses by Master Mumon. The biblical and hagiographic literature that forms the backdrop of Genet's cat killing recedes in Mishima without entirely disappearing. Instead, that literature remains an absent presence, an undercurrent by way of Bataille and Nietzsche that intersects, overlaps, reinforces, and resists the Zen hermeneutic given in the *teisho*, or comments of the Zen master, through which the text of the koan is mediated. According to a present-day master:

> Koan are Zen Masters' sayings and doings in which they freely and directly express their Zen experience. The primary role of the koan in Zen is to help in the actual training of Zen monks. The philosophical or dogmatic studies of koan are of secondary significance because the standpoint of such studies is fundamentally different from that of true Zen training, in which the only aim is to experience and live the real working spirit of Zen.[27]

The koan is woven into the fabric of Mishima's narrative so that "independent" interpretations of it are often indistinguishable from its function in the narrated lives of the protagonists, thereby reinforcing the role that the koan traditionally plays. Because of the complexity of this interweaving, I shall, in the present section, pick out the koan's interpretations as given in the novel, without which further hermeneutical progress could not be made.

The text of the koan reads:

> Once the monks of the Eastern Hall and the Western Hall were disputing about a cat. Nansen, holding up the cat said, "Monks, if you can say a word of Zen, I will spare the cat. If you cannot, I will kill it!" No monk could answer. Nansen finally killed the cat. In the evening, when Joshu came back, Nansen told him of the incident. Joshu took off his sandal, put it on his head, and walked off. Nansen said, "If you had been there, I could have saved the cat!"[28]

In the novel, the ugly and stuttering Mizoguchi, a young acolyte at the luminously beautiful Kinkakuji temple in Kyoto, is the target of the koan's philosophical interpretations. He will offer his own violent reading of the koan through an act of sacrifice, of sacred arson, by setting fire to the golden temple, an action that is predictable from the novel's start.

Mizoguchi encounters the first gloss on the evening when the Japanese learn of their defeat in World War II. In despair, Mizoguchi hopes for consolation from the temple's Superior, who delivers a sermon on the koan "Nansen Kills a Cat." Never uttering a word about Japan's defeat, the Superior offers a traditional interpretation of it.[29]

Gloss 1. Nansen slays the cat in order to destroy the illusion of self and to empty his mind. By killing the cat, Nansen shows that there is no opposition between self and others. Nansen's act is known as the murdering sword. Joshu's gesture, placing the lowly shoe on his head, is the lifegiving sword and demonstrates the compassionate way of the Boddhisattva who seeks to release human-kind from suffering.

The second exegetical occasion occurs when the handsome but club-footed Kashiwagi, a descendant of a family of Rinzai priests, cruelly taunts Mizoguchi about his stutter in what could be interpreted as a Zen provocation (the use of painful methods). Kashiwagi prefaces his exegesis with the celebrated words about attaining deliverance in the *Rinzairoku*: "When ye meet the Buddha, kill the Buddha!" a saying generally interpreted as a command to slay the ego. Before glossing the text, he relativizes all interpretations, including his own, with the assertion that they are dependent on one's life situation. Kashiwagi's gloss can be thus summarized:

Gloss 2. All the beauty in the world is concentrated in the body of the cat so that, in killing the cat, Nansen kills beauty. But beauty gives itself to all and is no one's private possession. The cat is then likened to a painfully diseased tooth in which beauty inheres as it does in the cat. The tooth may be extracted, but how can the extracted object cause pain? The living tooth must be different from the one held in my hand. Was the beauty in me or in it? If neither, then where? But even if the cat, like the inert tooth, is dead, the problem is unresolved in that the root of beauty may not have been cut. By placing the shoe on his head, Joshu satirizes Nansen's solution. For Joshu, there is no getting around the enduring pain of the tooth.

Kashiwagi states that he identifies with Nansen because of an episode in which he killed a young girl's love for himself, as Nansen killed the cat, and the inept Mizoguchi is Joshu, who envies the flawlessly executed cruelties of Kashiwagi and the exhilaration they generate.

   The third gloss occurs near the end of the novel when Mizoguchi learns that an admired friend whom he had assumed died in an accident actually committed suicide. It is Kashiwagi who reveals this fact and who announces as a general principle that, however disillusioning, it is better to know such things than not to know. Knowledge, he claims, makes life bearable by transforming the world while leaving it just as it is. Kashiwagi's remark is pure Nietzsche: "We could not have our intellect if we did not need to have it . . . if we could live otherwise."[30] The final gloss, like the second, is Kashiwagi's:

> Gloss 3. The priests of the Eastern and Western halls who are fighting for the cat want to convert the animal into knowledge thereby preserving its life. But Nansen, a man of action, kills it. Joshu, on the other hand, knows that beauty is something that sleeps and so must be protected by knowledge.

The glosses, taken together, form a disseminated text in which each both continues and jostles against the others. The reader is forced into the hermeneutical process, to embark on "an inferential walk."[31]

Beauty and Sacrifice: The Speech and Silence of the Koan

I shall now suggest some possible inferential walks by examining the relation of the novel's "actors" to the sacrificial activity described in the koan.

Consider, first, gloss 3 in the preceding section. In Kashiwagi's interpretation, Nansen slays the cat, who is beauty protected by knowledge. Killing the cat and, with it, the anodyne for pain, which is knowledge, turns Nansen into the destroyer of ease, that is, of release from pain. Nansen's sacrifice is, then, fully in accord with Bataille's view that sacrifice intensifies affect. In gloss 2, Nansen hopes by killing the cat, who is like a painful tooth, to annihilate the source of pain. Nansen's role has turned into the opposite of his role in gloss 3, in which his action intensifies pain. In gloss 2, Joshu mocks Nansen's solution, suggesting that pain cannot be killed, but in gloss 3 Joshu becomes the protector of knowledge, which anesthetizes the pain of beauty. The seemingly firm identities of Nansen and Joshu are disseminated, made fluid, each ebbing and flowing eternally in a Nietzschean move that defies a linear solution to the problem posed by the koan.

Koanic "reason" is errant: successive glosses alter the status not only of Nansen and Joshu but of the novel's characters, for whom Nansen and Joshu are masks. Early in the work, Mizoguchi thinks of Joshu as quietly enduring pain (gloss 1) and identifies with him, but, in the novel's coda, Mizoguchi takes action, burns down the golden temple, slays the cat, "kills" beauty. Nor does he become the Joshu of gloss 3, the defender of knowledge, since now Mizoguchi rejects knowledge in favor of direct action. On the face of it, then, he is the Nansen of gloss 2, killer of the cat and with it of pain.

But the koan invites further reflection. Can beauty be killed, after all? If not, Mizoguchi may kill the cat by his incendiary act, but pain will still continue. If so, Mizoguchi is the Nansen of gloss 3. And is Mizoguchi a man of action after all? If an acolyte burns down the temple, perhaps, the text suggests, the only honorable consummation of such an act is ritual suicide. But Mizoguchi refuses to commit *sep-ukku*. In that case, does he become the Joshu of gloss 3, who reflects the way of knowledge? Who and what is sacrificed? The temple? The various ego constellations of Mizoguchi's changing personae? Does the shimmering surface of the novel itself, as Bataille's account of the sacrificial character of fiction suggests, not offer itself as an always already disseminated sacrifice to the creation of beauty?

Fresh paradoxes are endlessly generated by the koan's centrifugal power. Pondering the destruction of beauty, Mizoguchi considers the option of murdering the temple's Superior. But this option is precluded when Mizoguchi sees that persons, unlike things, may appear to be mortal but "a phantasm of immortality emerges from the apparently destructible aspect of human beauty [whereas] the apparently indestructible Golden Temple g[ives] rise to the possibility of destroying it."[32] Mizoguchi concludes, paradoxically, that mortal things cannot be destroyed but immortal things can.

The koan's vibratory power does not finish with the reader. Perhaps through his incendiary sacrifice, Mizoguchi hopes, in Buddhist fashion, to become egoless in accordance with the early gloss of the Superior on the day of Japan's defeat. If so, Mizoguchi's immolation of the temple could imply obedience to the traditional command to slay the self: "When you meet the Buddha, kill the Buddha." What is more, the koan's glosses can be seen to slide away from Mizoguchi so as to apply to Kashiwagi, to the temple's Superior, and to all the others who inhabit Mishima's novel.

Until the final section of the novel, successive glosses leave untouched the meaning of the term *beauty* while attempting to configure its fate in a sequence of altered contexts. The reason for this is that there is no ontic center, no essence: beauty has no semantic core, is void or empty. Thus, the narrator declares:

> Beauty was never completed in any single detail of the temple for each detail adumbrated the beauty of the succeeding detail.
> . . . It dreamed of perfection but knew no completion . . . and

so it was that the various adumbrations of a beauty which did not exist had become the underlying motif of the Golden Temple. . . . Nothingness was the very structure of this beauty.[33]

Although Mishima does not allude to the *Milindapanha*, a dialogue between a Buddhist sage and a Hellenized Bactrian king, his account of beauty reflects this Buddhist text's well-known analysis of names. When asked what a chariot is, the sage, Nagasena, replies that it is not the unity of its parts nor any one part but a name denoting their functional unity.[34] For Mishima, beauty is not a quality independent of the temple's details but a term designating the functional unity of its parts. Thus, the term applies to that which is always already empty. Moreover, it can be inferred that, if each detail adumbrates the beauty of succeeding details and the number of these is indeterminate, the open-ended series can only approach but never attain perfection. Thus, beauty is something like a Kantian regulative ideal in that it exerts a certain force upon the existing details of the temple. This unattainable perfection is the form or idea of an absence: a negative transcendence that "endures" beyond the temple's contingent parts. What is more, if beauty's existence depends upon the temple's succeeding details and each of these can be destroyed, then sacrifice is the destruction not of a whole but of these interlocking elements.

Discursive paradoxes, however, seem to be different from existential choices: decisions embarked upon appear to settle matters. Mizoguchi decides whether beauty can be demolished. When he burns the temple, he declares himself: he is on the side of beauty's frangibility. Yet beauty's negative noumenality continues to rearise in the discursive space opened by the paradox, thereby undoing the finality of choice. Perhaps the cat does not die after all; perhaps the god must be sacrificed ever anew.

In/conclusions

For both Mishima and Genet, beauty invites profanation and transgression in the futile effort to possess it. Both see beauty as the self-manifestation of nonbeing through acts of sacrifice, for which Bataille's account provides a description. It might seem that sacrifice for Genet results in ontic fullness, in the plenary presence of the god. But killing the cat is radically nihilatory. Eating destroys the thing eaten. Thus Genet: "I wanted to swallow myself by opening my mouth very wide and turning it over my head so that it would take in my whole body, and then the universe until all that would remain of me would be a ball of eaten thing which would little by little be annihilated. That is how I see the end of the world."[35]

For Mishima, the novel/koan roars with the roar of enlightenment. Neither existing nor nonexisting, neither belonging to the flux of becoming nor outside it, beauty is empty. This does not mean that the word *beauty* is vacuous but rather that the beauty of beautiful appearances is without ontological ground and manifests itself only by sacrificing itself. In a *teisho* on Mumon's commentary on the koan, the present-day Zen master Zenkei Shibayama sees in Joshu's response to the sacrifice of the cat the koan's endless solicitation: Joshu "tells us to appreciate the wonder of resurrection in the fact of the Great Death. Then the killed cat will bloom in red as a flower; flow in blue as a stream. It is ever alive, not only with Master Joshu, but with you in your hand and in your foot today."[36]

25

The Art in Ethics
Aesthetics, Objectivity, and Alterity in the Philosophy of Levinas

Two objections arise repeatedly in connection with Emmanuel Levinas's philosophy of language. First, it is argued, in the spirit of Jürgen Habermas and K. O. Apel, for whom ethics is grounded in discursive reason, that for Levinas ethics is an unmediated relation to the other and, as such, transcends linguistic and conceptual structure. Ethics is not a matter of moral argument but of solicitation by the other, who by virtue of sheer otherness resists violence. Levinas's access routes to the other are nonlinguistic: they include the human face, an idea of the infinite that exceeds any description of it, and sensation as a noncognitive relation between sensing and sensed. His position is not merely a restatement of the poverty of language with regard to transcendence, one made familiar through negative theology, because for negative theology, even if one cannot say what God is, propositional language is not excluded but is restricted to statements of negation. In sum, the first argument against Levinas is that, if ethics is beyond language, then ethics remains silent, and rationally derived moral norms are meaningless. Language has become a liability, a fall, and ethics an inchoate relation to the other.

A second standard reproach directed at Levinas is that he disparages the aesthetic by relegating art and poetry to a status inferior to that of philosophy and, a fortiori, to ethics. In his early *Existence and Existents* (conceived between 1940 and 1945), for example, art is interpreted as divesting things of their forms so that things cannot be made present, as they are in cognition. Although it may seem para-doxical to sever art from form, Levinas explains that form always arises in a context. In cognition and relations of utility, we experience objects in a network of relations, whereas art lifts entities out of the world to create a field not of forms but of pure sensations (*EE*, 52–57).

In the 1948 "Reality and Its Shadow," Levinas argues that art substitutes images for being. The image is not a transparent sign pointing toward objects, through which objects become intelligible; instead, images are the doubles of objects, resemble them, in the sense that shadows resemble things. This duality of thing and image is born in resemblance. A kind of duplicity or evasion is created in that the image neither yields the object nor replicates it in an ontolog-ical sense. As a nonobject, the image lies outside the world, is not in time. Because images cannot move along naturally in the stream of becoming, they immobilize time, freezing it. This atemporality, un-like the eternity of concepts, distorts the flow of becoming. The image is trapped and cannot free itself for the world of action (*CPP*, 5–12).

Artists are under the sway of images, possessed by them. Insofar as the literary artist is also a purveyor of images, the same criticism applies, mutatis mutandis, to fiction and poetry. This interpretation presupposes Heidegger's view that the true poet is not a creator but a passageway for being, as well as André Breton's and the surrealists' belief that literature is an automatic or spontaneous production, dream rather than work. In sum, Levinas is charged with a Platonic aesthetic: art is infraethical and infracognitive. If art is "legitimate," it is so only as the handmaiden of ethics and requires augmentation by criticism. In this view, Levinas could be seen as endorsing straightforwardly didactic tales or Socialist Realism as the highest types of art; such is far from being the case, however, as Levinas shows in his sympathetic and nuanced analyses of complex contem-porary writers and painters.

I shall argue that the objections I have rehearsed can be countered by a new reading of Levinas's view of the "art" of literature. The two frequently voiced objections I have sketched—first, that ethics is an unmediated relation to the other and, as such, beyond discursive lan-guage, and second, that the language of art is infracognitive and dan-gerously nonethical—are actually linked. When these objections are taken together, the problems that arise in connection with Levinas's view of religious language can be resolved, at least partially, because important clues for the interpretation of ethico-religious expression can be found in the uses of literary language. This claim can be established by turning to Levinas's treatment of contemporary French writers, specifically: Marcel Proust, master of images and the inundation of subjectivity by pure sensibility; Michel Leiris, advocate of total freedom; and Maurice Blanchot, artist of the nocturnal, of the nothing that speaks.

I argue further that it is helpful to think of Levinas's rendering of the aesthetic by relating it to the stratigraphy of Kierkegaard's account of life stages. Kierkegaard criticizes the immediacy of the aesthetic from a higher standpoint while reintroducing immediacy at the still higher level of the religious. For Levinas, aesthetic experience—both as creation and as appreciation of the aesthetic object—is a kind of shamanistic seizure of consciousness by being prior to being's assumption of form. But if being as disclosed in art is formless and ethics (for Levinas, bound up with and often indistinguishable from the religious) is also beyond form, then common strategies for grasping this immediacy may be developed. Art and ethics in Levinas's sense can be thought of as fields in which disclosures of formlessness occur: in art, the amorphous power of being; in ethics, the other who calls me to responsibility. Each—possession in the case of art and revelation in the case of ethics—grips the individual, in the one instance dissolving, in the other singularizing individuality by positing the other in her uniqueness. In the aesthetic of Proust, Leiris, and Blanchot, Levinas finds linguistic strategies of indirection with which to bring out that which, strictly speaking, does not belong to phenomenality but to experiences of formlessness.

Not only is a Kierkegaard-like articulation of the aesthetic and the ethical a structural inference, but Levinas explicitly refers to Kierkegaard's account of faith to shed light on the status of religious language generally. In his brief comments on Kierkegaard in *Proper Names*, Levinas (unsurprisingly), like Buber, faults Kierkegaard, first, for describing Abraham as transcending the ethical and thereby falling into violence, and second, for interpreting the ethical as expressing the universal and thus bypassing the subjectivity of the individual existent. This second point is of greater interest to Levinas in that his own discourse—the entire topos of responsibility and alterity—is based on a contrary premise: that ethics as consciousness of responsibility for the other individuates, "posits you as a singular individual" (*PN*, 113). This difficulty is far from fatal to a comparison of the relation of the aesthetic to higher planes of meaning in both thinkers. Kierkegaard's ethical stage is roughly comparable to what Levinas calls justice, the juridical plane that allows for the settling of actual disputes in social existence, whereas ethics, for Levinas, is more properly equated with religion or faith in Kierkegaard. It is in this light that Levinas's comments about Kierkegaard should be understood.

Levinas and Kierkegaard

Kierkegaard's unique contribution to philosophy, Levinas asserts, is his account of belief (*croyance*). I shall fasten on this point because features of this analysis are repeated in Levinas's description of the literary languages forged by Proust, Leiris, and Blanchot. If there is a *language* of belief, it can then be argued that there is something like a concept of religious language in Levinas and that the specific character of this language can be explicated. We are then justified in turning to the works of literary figures who have developed strategies of indirect communication to convey what is, to use Levinas's formulation, otherwise than being and beyond essence. In a crucial passage on belief, Levinas writes that, for Kierkegaard:

> Belief is not an imperfect knowledge of a truth . . . that is merely uncertain. For in that case belief would be a mere degradation of knowledge. . . .
>
> Belief translates the condition of an existence . . . that is at the same time needy and indigent. . . . *Belief is linked to a truth that suffers.* The truth that *suffers* and is persecuted is very different from a truth improperly approached. . . . it is through suffering truth that one can describe the very manifestation of the divine. . . . A certainty that coexists with an absolute uncertainty to the point that one may wonder . . . whether God's suffering and the lack of recognition of the truth would not reach their highest degree in a total *incognito.* (*PN,* 69, italics in original)

This passage describes the fault lines of transcendence as they are inscribed in language. Transcendence is the subject of belief rather than of knowledge. But Levinas does not appeal to one of two generally accepted positions: either that belief is more certain than knowledge because based on revelation or, by contrast, that belief is a weaker form of knowledge because it is not founded on evidence.

Taking issue with both of the received views, Levinas segregates religious from propositional truth, arguing instead that belief has nothing whatsoever to do with certainty. Religious truth is a function of its mode of self-manifestation, true only if it is not puffed up in presenting itself, "persecuted" rather than "triumphant." Thus religious truths are not warranted beliefs, those resting on evidence showing them to be well founded. Instead, the truth of belief lies in its refusal to put itself forward, "to say [its] name." Religious truth appears incognito, shows itself as "that about which one would say nothing."

In Levinas's reading, Kierkegaard's "glimpse of truth" overturns Heidegger's view of truth as unconcealment and points the way toward a new persecuted language that hides and shelters transcendence. This language is the very language developed through the literary artistry of Proust, Leiris, and Blanchot.

Proust: The Diffractions of Self

Levinas reads Proust as a "master of the differential calculus of souls, a psychologist of the infinitesimal" (*PN*, 99). But, unlike many standard interpreters, who hold that in Proust the relation of the soul to itself is that of primary emotion to emotion reflected upon, he contends that Proustian reflection is itself infected with emotion. Levinas writes: "Proustian reflection, dominated by a separation between the *I* and its state, imparts its own accent to the inner life by a kind of refraction. It is as if I were constantly accompanied by another self, in unparalleled friendship, but also in a cold strangeness that life attempts to overcome. The mystery in Proust is the mystery of the other" (*PN*, 102).

Because consciousness works through scission or doubling in Proust, it would seem that images could be interpreted as the relation of reality to shadow mentioned earlier, in which the shadow replicates objects but lacks independent ontological status. Despite Levinas's stress on the process of doubling, such an account would be misleading. In Proust the doubled self is a stranger to itself because its two components are asymmetrical, cannot be made equal. This inequality is not the result of different intentions of consciousness (to use Husserlian language), the difference between reflection and affect, between reflection and a stratum reflected upon. Instead the emotion of the stratum reflected upon infiltrates reflection: in Freudian terms, reflection belongs to the level of the cathexes. What accounts for this asymmetry—and this is the novelty of Levinas's interpretation—is the other, who can never be reached, the other that penetrates the heart of the self. Thus, Levinas suggests, "The knowledge of what Albertine is doing, what Albertine is seeing and who is seeing Albertine has no intrinsic interest as knowledge, but it is infinitely exciting because of its deep strangeness in Albertine—because of that strangeness that laughs in the face of knowledge" (*PN*, 102).

For Levinas, Proust is the writer who shows the inescapability of the other within solitude, an intrusion of the other distinguishable from the understanding of the other in collective solidarity. Like Buber, Levinas argues that the other who is part of a collectivity cannot be experienced in her alterity. Thus Levinas: "the pathos of socialism crumbles against the eternal Bastille . . . in which we find ourselves when the celebration is over, the torches gone out and the crowd drawn back" (*PN*, 103). "Genuine" alterity is an absence that rends the psyche, worms its way into the self, and prevents the ego from losing track of the other, who, in her absence, fissures the self in its interiority.

Proust's artistry, often seen as the power to depict sensation, would seem to lend weight to Levinas's theory of the image as subverting form and giving rise to an inundation by sensibility, and *À la recherche du temps perdu* would seem to be a premier example of that theory. Instead, Proust is not the depicter of infraontological shadows but—to coin what now seems less and less an oxymoron—an artist of alterity.

If Proustian fiction evokes alterity, is it possible to think of Proust as a didactic writer, an artist of fabular discourse? But there can be no artistry of fables, because they articulate moral principles and these do not lend themselves to successful artistic rendering. Instead, Proust's fiction is a kind of protoethics, a revelation within language of the persecution of self by another. To be sure, in Proust's writing the persecution of alterity is bound up with actual persecution: Albertine as absence and mystery shades off into the Albertine who actually tortures Marcel. The point, however, is that Albertine as other eludes plenary presence, cannot become a datum of consciousness. Proust is the "phenomenologist" of what cannot be recovered, of the other's concealment, not because of the other's artifices of camouflage—although there is artifice aplenty in Albertine, Odette, Monsieur Charlus, and the rest—but because to be other is to remain hidden *en principe*.

Biffures: Levinas and Leiris

Levinas interprets the first volume of Leiris's autobiography, *Biffures*, as depicting alterity by unmasking the pretensions of cognition and thereby suggesting a strategy of indirection for religious language, although Levinas does not specifically articulate this link. For Leiris, thought has two intrinsic characteristics that deflect it from achieving clarity and certainty, ideals that are in any case deceptive. The first, bifurcation (*bifurs*), is the deflection of a line of thought from what appears to be its natural path, so that it heads in a new and unexpected direction (*OS*, 145). The second, erasure (*biffures*), is the alteration or rubbing out of the univocal meaning of an idea at the point of its inception. Leiris, Levinas suggests, rejects free association as the primary law of thought and instead attributes the linkage of ideas to erasure. Ideas connected in this way do not dislodge previous ideas: "thought, at the moment of its '*biffure*' [crossing out], still counts by its crossed out meaning; its different meanings participate in one another" (ibid., 146).

Leiris's notion of erasure creates a space in which ideas nest inside one another rather than a streaming of thought articulated as temporal passage. It is, of course, paradoxical that autobiographical writing should be spatialized, in that it is a depiction of a life as experienced through time. Levinas compares Leiris's spatial conception of ideas to painter Charles Lapicque's "space that is mainly an order of simultaneity," a space where "each object sheds its volume" and in which lines do not form the framework for objects but suggest multiple hookups (ibid.).

It is because thought is conceived as a mode of spatialization that Levinas thinks Leiris's art falls short as a discourse of otherness. Only sound as encapsulated in the heard word of another attests to the presence of the other (ibid., 142). Leiris, he concedes, has brought to light the process that underlies thought's inception, bifurcation, and erasure, but Leiris's insights still presuppose "the primacy of thought in relation to language stated in the classic phrase 'that which is well conceived'" (ibid., 150).

It is surprising that Levinas's analysis does not take into account the many passages in which Leiris stresses violence and wounding, although these are *echt* Levinasian themes. In *Manhood*, for example, Leiris says of the bullfight (*la carrida*), "It is not the spectacle that is essential but the sacrifice,"[1] and again, "Looking back to my earliest childhood, I find memories of *wounded women*."[2] The matter at issue is not this omission but Levinas's retreat from his original insights, his refusal to press the connection between Leiris's account of bifurcation and erasure and the problematic of alterity, in part, at least, because of Levinas's own inner struggle against image making.

Despite Levinas's downplaying of erasure in Leiris, it is possible to relate the use of erasure to the pregnant concept of the trace, a key Levinasian theme. Not a sign, because signs are transparent with respect to their objects, the trace is the marker of the immemorial past of a transcendence that has passed by. Traces are dues, tracks, or trails that cannot be integrated into the order of the world wherever transcendence inscribes and erases itself, preeminently in the human face. The effort to coerce transcendence into appearing assures its loss; it can only be glimpsed in and through another as Other.

Levinas's use of the trace has been linked to Heidegger's account in *Holzwege* of old forest trails that the experienced woodsman knows how to read but that mean nothing to others. Yet missing in Heidegger's description and found in Leiris's view of *biffures* is the idea of the accretion of meaning, the nesting of one idea in another. This cumulative character is intrinsic to Levinas's trace in that transcendence, expunged from the order of the world, "nests" in faces, sensation, the time between heartbeats, and other Levinasian "tropes" for transcendence. Like the idea of the infinite, there is more in them than can be contained by cognition. (One could argue that Derrida's account of the trace, as well as his tactic of placing terms under erasure [*sous rature*], could also be linked to Leiris's *Biffures*.)

But the spatialization of Leiris's art, which makes possible its connection with the trace, renders it mute. It is an art of silence. In this context Levinas contrasts and extols critique, the word, at the expense of the image and thus backs away from the art of Leiris: the use of the word "wrenches experience away from its esthetic self-sufficiency. . . . In this sense . . . critique, the spoken word of a living being speaking to a living being, leads the image, with which art was content, back to fully real being. The language of critique takes us out of our dreams, of which artistic language is an integral part" (*OS*, 148–49). For Levinas, critique is secondarily commentary on the formal aesthetic properties of a work, and primarily the placing of literary discourse within a moral framework.

In sum, although Levinas acknowledges Leiris's breakthrough in seizing the moment of thought as bifurcation and erasure, his suspicion of image making prevents his connecting the former with the trace. Despite Levinas's ambivalence toward Leiris's literary strategies, these find their way into his antiphenomenology of the trace.

Blanchot on Levinas: Tracing the Differences

The influence of Blanchot on Levinas is more complex than that of either Proust or Leiris, in part because it is reciprocal. It may be useful to focus first on Blanchot's *The Writing of the Disaster*, a late work (1980) that takes into account not only the large Levinasian corpus available by that time but also Levinas's 1975 work about Blanchot.[3] In *The Writing of the Disaster* Levinas may be exhibited through the focus of Blanchot's poetics of negation.

In this work, Blanchot tries to think negation both as actual apocalypse, seen through the cataclysmic events of the twentieth century, and as the destruction of traditional metaphysical interpretations of being, time, and history or, more primordially, as their aboriginal *Ur*-absence. Defining disaster, Blanchot writes, "I call disaster that which does not have the ultimate for a limit: it bears the ultimate away in the disaster" (*WoD*, 28). Because the disaster is a sweeping away of all limit, there is neither self nor event to describe, so that "the disaster does not put me into question but annuls the question, makes it disappear—as if along with the question I too disappeared in the disaster which never appears" (ibid.). Lying outside the chain of facts and events, the disaster cannot be said to happen in any straightforward sense. Instead, it is always behind itself, "always takes place after having taken place," so that it lies outside experience (ibid.). It should be noted that Blanchot's earlier fiction articulates this post hoc constitution of events that never existed. The question of how to speak about the disaster should not be confused with the speech about an object that is thought to be indescribable because contradictory attributes are ascribed to it. The disaster is an event, yet as pure negation it falls outside the realm of ontology. As an absence that is extraontological, it is linked to Levinas's problematic: Can there be speech about another who is never present?

Blanchot comments on the problem of ineffability—his own as well as that of Levinas—in his remarks on Levinas. Turning to the question of the relation to the other and the giving of gifts, he argues that, despite their unbreachable differences, the works of Levinas, Bataille, and Heidegger are related in and through the idea of alterity. For Levinas, he claims, alterity means "the transcendence of another person, the infinite relation of the one person to another [that] obligates beyond any obligation" (ibid., 109). This relation opens up the idea of the gift, which for Levinas means "detachment, a disinterestedness which is *suffered*, patient responsibility [for the other] that endures all the way to 'substitution,' 'one for the other'" (ibid.). By contrast, Blanchot contends, for Bataille the gift is an indication of excessive expenditure and plays a transgressive social role. More important, for Heidegger, the gift is implied by the expression *es gibt*, a crucial locution in his account of *Ereignis* (appropriation). The *es gibt* points not to a subject who gives but to the object bestowed: the gift of language (ibid., 110).

Heidegger's interpretation of the gift as the bestowing of language reflects a dangerous sanctification of language, according to Blanchot, one directly opposed by Levinas, for whom language is justified by the speaker who provides the warranty for it. In contrast to the cultic idea of language as *in itself* holy, Levinas, Blanchot says, thinks of language as itself always already skeptical, as a self-questioning that opens the possibility of its own unmaking.

Against the backdrop of language as undoing itself, Blanchot describes writing as a "giving withholding," giving because language tries to bring otherness into speech, and withholding because speech tries to justify itself. If "giving withholding" is the work of writing, what is to be written and how is it to be written? If "the object" of writing is the disaster, Blanchot suggests in a terse formulation, the task of the writer is to show "*in*discretion with respect to the *in*effable" (ibid., 114). The key words of this phrase are governed by the prefix *in*, the same prefix that introduces the word *infinity*, an *in* shot through with Levinasian resonances: infinity is not only the negation of the finite but also the excess or beyond of the finite. This appears to be its meaning in Blanchot's declaration: "the ineffable, the unspeakable would be circumscribed by Speaking raised to infinity" (ibid.). Such an elevation of speaking signifies that what is spoken is not some content that eludes language but unsayability itself, "what escapes all that can be said" (ibid.).

But why is this saying characterized as indiscreet? Blanchot glosses "indiscretion" by appealing to Levinasian "Saying": the unspoken covenant between speaker and hearer promising that his or her language will be marked by alterity. Unsayability, Blanchot suggests, "escapes," becomes indiscreet, only "under the auspices of Saying" (ibid.). But the escape of unsayability, that is, the bursting into language of what cannot be said, is also restrained by Saying, by the Other, which resists linguistic captivity. Thus, for Blanchot, speech paradoxically breaks forth, is unreserved, and is held back, reserved, by the authority of Saying. From these remarks about writing as a relation to Levinasian Saying, it is possible to assert that, for the later Blanchot, writing is an ethics in Levinas's sense.

In Blanchot's comments on unsayability, what comes to the fore is not principally Levinas's contrast between Saying, the warranty for speech, and the said, what actually falls into language, but the *movement* from ineffability to speech. In his fictional works (if for him the distinction between fiction and criticism can be maintained), Blanchot fixes on the *escape route* of unsayability, on how it seeps into language without losing its unsayability, in a world where distinctions such as inside and outside are eroded. Blanchot's own art explicates this loss of foothold as characters glide from one level to another—death and life, sickness and health—in a world in which levels mingle and are intercalated.

Levinas on Blanchot: Before Language

What makes Blanchot perhaps the writer par excellence for Levinas is that in Blanchot's works meaning is before rather than after language, a "situation" that forces language to a breaking point. The assertion that meaning is anterior to language implies that meaning does not belong to the same topos as language, not because meaning inheres in a world that is prior to language and then represented by it but because meaning is (somehow) inimical to language. Thus in his 1966 essay on Blanchot, "The Servant and Her Master," Levinas writes: "Does the meaningful depend upon a certain order of propositions built upon a certain grammar in order for it to constitute a logical discourse? Or does meaning make language explode, and then mean among these broken bits (grammar, in Blanchot, comes out safe and sound!), but already in spirit and in truth without awaiting any later interpretation?" (*PN*, 142–43).

If meaning is prior to language, there is no coming to grips with meaning, no arguments that can be brought to bear for or against it. Thus Blanchot reverses a dictum of literary modernism, that language dissolves established meanings by showing that meaning precedes language, paralyzes language even before it speaks. The alinguisticality of meaning precludes its communication by way of language. "Make it possible for me to speak to you," a Blanchot character says in *Waiting Forgetting*, as Levinas notices (ibid., 142). This citation supports my earlier contention that Blanchot is obsessed with the impassability, the blocking of meaning, which is as close by as the Other yet always out of reach.

To depict this blocking of meaning, Blanchot is compelled to rely on the bleakness of a speech locked into itself, from which the Other is absent and in which, as Levinas says, "Nothing *extra*-ordinary [outside itself] takes place" (ibid., 141). Because language cannot go outside itself, it can only repeat itself, "like a cancerous cell, without producing anything other than repetition and tautology" (ibid., 142). Not only do specific events recur, but the fact of repetition is made thematic. The reflexivity that I earlier alleged to characterize unspeakability also can be attributed to repetition. Levinas cites a crucial passage: "They would always converse there . . . of the instant when they would no longer be there. Even though they knew they would always be there talking about such an instant, they thought there was nothing more worthy of their eternity than to spend it evoking its end" (ibid.).[4]

Anything can become a marker of repetition—persons, rooms, their furnishings—in that all are exiled from any organizing nexus. What is depicted through repetition is the "effort of nothingness and, as it were, the way it labors, strains, and 'happens' and steps aside from its identity of emptiness" (ibid., 144).

Although this comment refers to *Waiting Forgetting*, it is likely that Levinas also has in mind Blanchot's view that writing exhibits language as negation, so that what denies also affirms. For this language speaks as absence. The language of negation therefore does not cease with silence but continues because silence speaks. But if language is the speech of silence, it cannot be heard. The poet then is "he who hears a language that makes nothing heard" (*SL*, 51).

Blanchot's silences, Levinas claims, are not stillness but a rustling. For Blanchot, ordinary language is punctuated by silences because it is purposeful: it communicates meaning and stops when this purpose is fulfilled. But literary language is always already silence, and therefore it cannot cease. Divested of its referential function, this language, for Blanchot, is exiled from itself. A word that designates an immense outside supplants the intimacy of the word spoken to another. Levinas notes that, in Blanchot, language speaks from the other side of walls. Perhaps—for Blanchot it is always perhaps—language merely replicates the enclosed linguistic space of the listener, not an outside but the same over and over again, an echo that does not just repeat aloud what is at first a murmur merging with it. It is now silence become echoing space, so that, in effect, words are now exterior. Consider this memorable passage in Blanchot's novel *When the Time Comes*:

> At night in the South, when I get up, I know that it isn't a question of proximity, or of distance, or of an event belonging to me or of a truth capable of speaking, this is not a scene or the beginning of something. An image, but a futile one, an instant but a sterile one. Someone for whom I am nothing and who is nothing to me—without bonds, without beginning, without end—a point, and outside this point, nothing in the world that is not foreign to me.[5]

One suffocates inside language, for there is no discernable outside, just as Blanchot's characters stifle inside the bleak rooms in which they are locked. Thus he writes in the same work: "I didn't imagine that anyone lived in the room or in any other room in the world, if there were any others. . . . For me, at this moment, for me the world was fully represented by this room with . . . its little piece[s] of furniture. It would have been madness to expect the walls to disappear. Besides, I was not conscious of the world."[6]

It is not hard to equate this locked-in space with the enclosure of Levinas's separated self, the individual within the same, the world of cognition, work, play, and habitation. To be sure, for Levinas, the same is not the joyless terrain of Blanchot's walled-in spaces, but it is still the locus of the absence of meaning. And yet Blanchot's topos of repetition is magnetized by alterity just as the structural articulation of what Levinas calls the same is fissured by its obsession with the Other. Joseph Libertson, in his study of Bataille, Blanchot, and Levinas, sums up this situation when he writes: "Totalization is possible only because identity, relation, comprehension and action are moments of an insatiability in being: the exigency of the Other. . . . The time of the Same . . . is its eternal return and its metamorphosis: a time in which the Same is never entirely the Same, the 'world' is never entirely the 'world,' because Time is the element of the Other's approach."[7]

Blanchot's language cannot speak alterity, Levinas maintains, cannot grasp it in a concept, simply because alterity resists conceptual grasp. But the errant word "gives sign," a giving that is a nonpurposive relation with another. Such signs are not referential, not transparent with respect to a cogent. Instead, what is bestowed on the Other is "the voice that has been imparted and entrusted to you and not what it says." For Blanchot, Levinas writes, "poetry transforms words into unfettered signs," signs let loose that can seep into the enclosed world of immanence, "go from the Same to the other [*Autre*] from Self to Other [*Autrui*], . . . give sign to undo the structure of language."[8]

Still, the poetic word can misfire in its errancy. Blanchot, Levinas contends, catches the word just "before" its fall into the process of totalization and after its "origination" in exteriority. As such, the poetic word, like the idea of the infinite, has no objective content that can fulfill it but instead "preserves the movement located between seeing and saying, that language of pure transcendence without correlative, . . . noesis without noema."[9]

I argued earlier that, in Levinas, the strategies of aesthetic language seemingly abandoned at a higher level find their place in this author's conception of ethics and religious language. Nowhere are aesthetics and ethics more interwoven than in Levinas's comments on Blanchot, comments that exhibit totality as the plane of the always already broken and incomplete infiltration by alterity.

Levinas, Kierkegaard, and the Poetry of the Ethical

Despite Levinas's critique of art and literature, I have argued that Proust, Leiris, and Blanchot are, for Levinas, artists of alterity in different ways and in varying degrees. Each has, in his unique fashion, found out how to release into language the immediacy of the experience of the Other as Other. (In fact, for Levinas their greatness lies in just this discovery.) I have also maintained that the relation of art and literature to ethics in Levinas's sense roughly replicates Kierkegaard's strategy of importing the immediacy of the aesthetic into the religious, despite Kierkegaard's critique of the aesthetic personality. The analogy must be seen against the backdrop of Levinas's linking transcendent meaning with ethics.

Yet Levinas explicitly rejects the idea that the ethical in the Kierkegaardian sense could be countermanded by God's word spoken to the faithful one. Ethics precludes violence, so that a conflict between ethics in the transcendent sense and in the sense of the moral law would not occur. This position is made explicit by Blanchot, in a text that could be mistaken for the work of Levinas. Comparing Kafka with Kierkegaard and siding with Kafka, Blanchot writes: "Kierkegaard can renounce Regine; he can renounce the ethical level. Access to the religious level is not thereby compromised;

rather it is made possible. But Kafka, if he abandons the earthly happiness of a normal life, also abandons the steadiness of a just life. He makes himself an outlaw, deprives himself of the ground . . . he needs in order to be" (SL, 61).

Yet, Blanchot continues, "for Kafka everything is more unclear because he seeks to fuse the work's demand [writing] with the demand which could pertain to his salvation" (SL, 62). In this reading, poetry is not didactic in the narrow sense but a discourse touched by transcendence; it cannot, as such, remain a mere means deployed in the interest of salvation: such poetry becomes an ethics.

PART VII

Comparing Philosophies

"Bhante Nagasena, will you converse with me?"

"Your majesty, if you will converse with me as the wise converse, I will, but if you converse with me as kings converse, I will not."

"Bhante Nagasena, how do the wise converse?"

"Your majesty, when the wise converse, whether they become entangled by their opponents' arguments or extricate themselves, whether they or their opponents are convicted of error, whether their own superiority or that of their opponents is established, nothing in all this can make them angry. Thus, your majesty, do the wise converse."

"And how, bhante, do kings converse?"

"Your majesty, when kings converse, they advance a proposition, and whoever opposes it, they order his punishment saying, 'Punish that fellow.' Thus, your majesty, do kings converse."

—*Questions of King Milinda*

The generative questions and metaphors stretching between and among differing contexts and approaches function as conceptual monorails that allow for comparison without obliterating philosophical difference. Like the tightrope walker of Nietzsche's *Zarathustra*, however, the philosopher, swaying between alternatives, risks falling by confusing similarity and difference, inside and outside, and negation of the other as soon as she or he stations her- or himself at a terminal point of the monorail.

Illustration: Old country bridge. Photograph by Meggie Wyschogrod.

26

The Moral Self
Levinas and Hermann Cohen

The work of Levinas attempts to give an account of the uniqueness of the human person, starting from what he believes to be peculiar to persons, the recognition of others as the source of moral obligation. This criterion had already been proposed in the literature of neo-Kantianism, but the formulation it received there had been found wanting. According to Heidegger, the neo-Kantian sees in the ethical a means for transcending human finitude: "There is something in the categorical imperative which exceeds the finite being."[1] But for Heidegger the concept of the ethical can display itself only in relation to a finite being. Levinas is familiar with the theory of the moral self in neo-Kantianism, particularly in the work of Hermann Cohen, and with Heidegger's criticism of its deficiencies.[2] Nevertheless, I shall argue that Levinas is in significant conversation with Cohen's thinking, that his own construing of the human person reflects a correction of Cohen's view in accordance with lessons learned from Heidegger's phenomenological approach, and that he puts forward a Cohen-like view in order to overcome the deficiencies of Heidegger's account. I shall not attempt to give a systematic exposition of Cohen's theory of the self but shall confine my remarks to what is pertinent in Cohen's thought to Levinas's account of the self. For this reason, I propose to emphasize the last work of Cohen, for only after Cohen had completed his "existential turn"[3] could his work enter into dialogue with what is germane to that of Levinas: Cohen's conception of the human person as a unique individual, an "I."

This is not to say that Levinas's view of the human person is derived from Cohen, a merely corrected version of Cohen's moral subject. Rather, he shares with Cohen the basic assumption that an awareness of the other as a moral datum, as imperative or command, is constitutive of the self.[4]

Cohen and Transcending Ontology

Levinas's work is characterized by a remarkable paucity of reference to Cohen. Two singularly revealing remarks, however, provide clues to the role that Cohen's view of the self plays in his own formulation of the problem. Both are brief and cryptic, and both are made in the context of a broader discussion in which Cohen's work seems merely to exemplify a larger issue.[5] I shall treat each remark separately. In his early thesis on Husserl's theory of intuition, Levinas distinguishes Husserl's work from that of certain German thinkers of the latter half of the nineteenth century.[6] Believing that the sciences exhaust the totality of what can be known about being, these thinkers leave to philosophy the task of investigating the process of knowing itself; philosophy is interpreted as "knowledge about knowledge," as epistemology. Cohen (although not, of course, Husserl) is seen as belonging to this class of thinkers. Levinas's first remark on Cohen reads:

> The naturalist and psychologistic philosophers were identifying philosophy and experimental psychology (Wundt, Erdmann, Sigwart), while the Marburg school (Hermann Cohen, Natorp), Alois Riehl, the school of Windelband, etc., were trying to renew the Kantian critique by interpreting it as a theory of knowledge. *Common to all these philosophers is the identification of philosophy and theory of knowledge, the latter being understood as a reflection on the sciences.*[7]

Here Levinas's view is strictly in accord with Heidegger's interpretation of Cohen: Heidegger thinks that the knowledge of being is relegated to science, whereas to philosophy is assigned the residual task of reflecting upon the character of knowledge. For the neo-Kantian, "there appeared to remain only the knowledge about science, not of that-which-is."[8]

But Levinas's remark also shows that, among those who identify philosophy with theory of knowledge, there are not only some who, like Cohen, wish to renew the Kantian critique but also others who fail to distinguish empirical psychology from philosophy. They (Wundt et al.) assume that an adequate view of the nature of knowledge could be derived by investigating the experiences of mental life. But psychology itself is interpreted by them as a science of nature, whose methods are no different from those of physics and chemistry. This standpoint distinguishes them from Cohen, for whom no theory of knowledge can be based upon induction, since induction can never yield the necessary universal elements of experience. For Cohen, a rationally derived theory of knowledge can be applied to the science of nature but never deduced from it.[9] This difference between Cohen and the psychologizers is not trivial: while both identify philosophy with epistemology, Cohen does not attribute a psychological origin to the laws of logic or to the ethical law. The last is especially significant. Although important differences between Cohen and Levinas remain, Levinas is free to enter into conversation with Cohen's work in the shared assumption that the moral law (whatever the conditions of its discovery) is not psychological in origin and thus that the self of responsibility cannot be explained in accordance with psychological laws.

Levinas's second remark on Cohen serves a positive function. It is inserted into a context in which the issue is a distinction between rhetoric and genuine conversation. Levinas argues that, despite their difference in purpose and content, both are language, and all language reverts to the interlocutor of dialogue. This holds even for Plato, for whom the theory of ideas seems to intervene between the content of a discourse and the persons actually engaging in conversation. Against this background Levinas remarks: "Hermann Cohen (in this a Platonist) maintained that one can love only ideas; but the notion of an Idea is in the last analysis tantamount to the transmutation of the other into the Other [person]" (*TI*, 71). What does this mean? Does the love of the Idea represent a false start if a genuine understanding of language is to be attained? And does Cohen also fall into this difficulty?

If we examine the antecedent passage closely, we find (as we have already noted) that Levinas distinguishes between two kinds of conversation illumined by Plato. This distinction is based not upon the content of discourse but upon the way in which the discoursing persons present themselves: either in terms of social role or as exposed to the interlocutor. Does one approach one's neighbor with ruse (like the sophist in the Platonic dialogues), or does one speak directly to the other? Is the conversation "rhetoric" or is it "philosophical discourse"? Does it attempt to corrupt the freedom of the other, or does it appeal to this freedom?[10] If the former, discourse has become violence, since violence first occurs as false discourse. Taking a stand in conversation with the other not only is aimed at bringing to light the theme of the discourse but is a constitutive act: it enables the self to emerge either as a being of violence, who intends to corrupt the freedom of the other person, or as a self, who recognizes the other as an ethically significant being.[11] In the first type, the other is reduced to the being of objects; in the second, the other, "beyond all *emprise*," is grasped as an ethical datum. This disengagement from all objectivity means positively that the other is presented as a face, as expression, as language. An other has become the Other, the interlocutor. This face-to-face approach is justice.

But is this absolute experience of the "face to face" in Plato one that Levinas believes can be found in Cohen? Is it not enough to say, since Levinas speaks of Cohen as a Platonist and a lover of ideas, that Levinas's account of Plato is sufficient for understanding his affinity for Cohen? We do so at the risk of ignoring Cohen's own remarks on Plato, for Cohen specifically dissociates his view of the love for ideas from the Platonic eros for the forms (*RRSJ*, chap. 9). In fact, Platonic love is, for Cohen, the pivotal point around which an understanding of the difference between Platonic ideality and his own ethical idealism and monotheism turns. It might seem that Plato, by recognizing the true as directed toward beauty, truth, and justice, transcended the view of eros as sexual in character and thereby grounded ethical existence in an erotically grasped apprehension of value. But Cohen specifically denies this, arguing instead that Plato has only shown the "comprehensive significance of eros for culture in general" (ibid., 144). According to Cohen, Plato fails to give full ideality to the forms: Platonic ideality is compromised through the participation of culture in the forms. Thus, when Levinas characterizes Cohen's love for the ideas as Platonic, he means only to show that the convergence between the two thinkers consists in the view that the true eros must be directed toward ideality. But Levinas knows that the character and function of this ideality differ in each.

For Cohen, ideality derives its source from logical necessity: the highest expression of this necessity is the God of monotheism. At no point, however, does the concept of God acquire actuality, for were

God to become actual he would take on the ontological structure appropriate only to phenomenal existents. The concept of actuality for Cohen means relating thought to sensation and must be excluded from the concept of God. God can, in that sense, have no actuality (ibid., 45).

Still, for Cohen, the idea of the unique God whose mode of being differs from that of the universe has a positive content: while the idea is not itself something actual, it is able to achieve something for actuality by functioning as an ethical ideal that becomes fruitful in man's love for God. The power of the idea to actualize itself comes about through love. When asked how it is possible to love an idea, Cohen replies: "How is it possible to love anything but an idea?" (ibid., 160). Since one can love only ideas, it would appear that Cohen means by "love" some form of knowledge. This is, however, strictly speaking not the case. For Cohen, pity, originating in the relations between man and man, in the experience of the poor, the economically deprived, is the primal form of human love. But is not ideality incompatible with pity? For Cohen, ideality is retained as an aspect of pity: poverty is given not only through sense as an item of cognition but as an axiological datum. Once the necessity of God is perceived the poor man and the stranger are apprehended in their universality as fellowmen. Levinas's position converges in this regard with that of Cohen: all men are poor, since all men are subjected to the contingencies of economy. Furthermore, the stranger, one who is different from oneself, is included in this circle of compassion. What for Cohen is an inequity in economy becomes for Levinas a constitutive inequity between self and other.[12] The asymmetry of social space founds a self of responsibility constituted as a difference in "height" between the commanding presence of the other and the percipient. Levinas's affinity for Cohen can now be understood in the light of Cohen's use of the idea: transcending the Platonic doctrine of forms, the unique God of monotheism is the content of the idea and gives rise to compassion for the other.

Totality and the Loss of the I

Despite its primacy, a relational self based only on a moral intuiting of the other ignores the evidence of nonmoral experiences, those based on embodiment, perception, and so on, which are integrated into human existence together with the apprehension of other persons. While Cohen takes little account of an infra-rational self, Levinas (borrowing from Heidegger) holds that nothing can be taken for granted. Even bare individuality, the sheer existence of the existent, must be derived phenomenologically.[13] The emergence of the existent is attested by examining the irreducible experiences of the already-constituted self. The advent of this self is adduced proleptically through the history of culture as a splitting off from a more primordial oneness, from mere being without any appearances, from the *apeiron*, or unboundedness. The moment of separation is also exhibited in the life of the individual (both as a primordial condition and as a permanent possibility of human existence) in such experiences as need, satiety, dwelling, work, and so on.

Once the separated individual has been constituted as the self that dwells and works, it is possible to consider the self from a quite different point of view. Levinas has brought to light the meaning of the act of separation and the various intentional structures that constitute it. The self can be interpreted not only as a system of meaningful intentional structures, however, but also as the sum of the observed behaviors that constitute its cultural acts. This aspect of the life of the self is open to investigation, to third-person description. It is the self of totality (*TI*, 21–30, 176–77, and passim). But far from these behaviors constituting the moral self, the ascription of selfhood to a sum of behaviors distorts the moral self by identifying it with manifest acts. Constituted as a unity by the historian after the fact, the self of totality is its completed series of behaviors.[14] Levinas means that the perspective of the historian confers unity upon a given sequence so that the string of behaviors expresses, in relation to a specifiable set of spatial coordinates, a single if highly ramified meaning.

But does not an observer-constituted self presume (falsely) that an account of the self can be given that attributes to it the ontological structure of what Heidegger calls "objects present-at-hand," that it has the character of something that constantly remains, the extended thing as it is found in nature? (See *BT*, esp. 67–69, 70–71.) Levinas recognizes this difficulty:

> Works have a destiny independent of the I, are integrated in an ensemble of works. . . . Integration in an economic world does not commit the interiority from which works proceed. This inner life does not die away like a straw fire, but does not recognize itself in the existence attributed to it within economy. . . . From the work I am only deduced and am already ill-understood, betrayed rather than expressed. (*TI*, 176)

Despite this acknowledgment, Levinas legitimizes this "falsification" as long as one admits its partiality. It reflects a single aspect of the self in formation, a necessary mode of givenness, which cannot be bypassed. There is no eliminating the self that is the sum total of one's works. Thus, one's works are a sign, and this signifying character serves a necessary function. It conceals and thus protects the privacy of an interiority never expressed in activity:

> The *who* involved in activity is not expressed in the activity, is not present, does not attend his own manifestation, but is simply signified in it by a sign in a system of signs, that is as a being who is manifested precisely as absent from his manifestation: a manifestation in the absence of being—a phenomenon. . . . Here phenomenality does not simply designate a relativity of knowledge, but a mode of being where nothing is ultimate, where everything is a sign. (Ibid., 178)

The self of totality derives from a positivistic interpretation of human existence, but this does not reflect an aberrant understanding of existence, a falling away into a "they-self" constituted by society in terms of what "people do." It represents a possibility of the self at an infra-ethical level. The individual is integrated into a historical order, but in the manner of an object of nature subject to natural laws, into a totality whose creation is the function of history.

Levinas's view of man as a member of totality is not without its antecedents in Cohen's thought: Cohen considers the infra-ethical individual to be part of the "dark blind mass of state and society,"[15] a homogeneous unit that does not yet recognize the social constitution of the self through compassion or pity. Man in his social groupings shows the opposing tendencies of singularity and plurality, but neither of these forms in itself gives rise to the absolute self. Just as, for Levinas, the separated individual is not yet the moral individual but incorporable into the totality, for Cohen singularity presupposes membership in an infra-ethical plurality (*Mehrheit*). The very recognition of individuality implies the existence of other individuals whose likenesses entail unity as a principle. Plurality, too, being a logical class forming a unity of its own, requires something beyond itself. But prior to its merger into a still more inclusive whole, its form of unity must be understood as extending over every member of the group, although the form of this unity is still infra-ethical. The individual is a unit in a series: one man next to other men, just the next man (*Nebensmensch*; *RRSJ*, 133–34).

But is not the next man already the fellowman? Cohen argues that conceptual knowledge is required to achieve the transformation of the next man into the fellowman, since "experience refutes" their identity. By "experience" Cohen means the violence that individuals and states inflict upon one another. This relationship of violence is attested in Cohen's conception of the "opposing man" (*Gegenmensch*), who comes into being as a consequence of the social differentiation that prevails in the plurality, "for the social differentiation does not appear to be organized according to rank and order of coexistence but according to subordination and subjugation" (*RRSJ*, 128). Levinas shares with Cohen the view that, before the recognition of other persons as moral data, social existence *is* violence. But the end of social existence is peace, not as a mere cessation of violence but as a new existential condition, which both Cohen and Levinas refer to as "Messianism." For Cohen, this altered condition of society results in a collectivity of moral individuals, which he designates "totality" (*Allheit*). The meaning given to the term by Cohen runs directly counter to Levinas's usage. For Levinas, "totality" is the sum of observed and comprehensible behaviors constituting the social universe, but for Cohen "totality" designates the highest human goal, an ideal endpoint of the human spirit achieved through the ethical development of man. The full force of the difference in the understanding of the term is brought out in Cohen's description of the individual as a member of the Messianic society: "The moral individual is the *individual of totality*, and therefore not only does he not vanish, but he achieves completion only in historical development, as prescribed by Messianism. The moral concept of the individual could not be realized apart from this development. *The idea of the historical development of the individual represents the total value, the high point of the moral person*" (*RRSJ*, 308; italics in original). It must be remembered that what Levinas calls "totality" corresponds to Cohen's society of the next man, prior to constitution of the individual as an ethical being.

Interiority and the Loss of the World

The self of totality, for Levinas, ultimately falls under criticism through the emergence of the moral self, but penultimately the existence of the totalized self is disrupted by the resistance of interiority to incorporation into a totality. As a historical being, the individual is integrated into a continuum whose ongoingness is irreversible. But the separated individual as interiority breaks into this order, the order of totality.

The structural condition of the disruption of totality depends upon the intentional character of consciousness, which comes to the fore in cognition. Intending acts of consciousness remain impervious to detection and thus cannot be totalized. But while the self that cognizes effects a break with the hypostatized, third-person self constituted in totality, it fails to provide the required conditions for genuine individuality. This failure results from the structure of cognition itself, which yields the object through a movement of prior disclosure. That is to say, objects come to fulfill antecedent indications of them, come into plenary presence as objects intended. Consciousness is dynamic, thrusting toward objects rather than remaining inert before a transcendent content that comes to it from the "outside." Furthermore, consciousness bestows meaning: an object is apprehended as something, as a "this" or a "that." For Levinas, consciousness is the power of consciousness: cognizing entails a foredisclosure of the object, thus forcing the otherness of the object to become (in Levinas's term) the Same.[16] What was at first felt to be different from consciousness, so that cognizing act and content appeared to be discrete, is revealed to be a false bifurcation. The foredisclosing character of consciousness destroys the independence of its objects and thus reveals cognition itself to be a form of violence. The cognitive self is constituted as *homo homini lupus*. There are no bounds to its voracious appetites: the world is swallowed up by self-aggrandizing acts of cognition. Still, the intentional structure of consciousness is not a monolithic egology without self-differentiation. The reduction of otherness by the self is not produced as a tautology, "I am I," but is articulated as the lived structures of this identity. "The I is not being [such that it] remains always the same, but is the being whose existing consists in identifying itself, in recovering its identity throughout all that happens to it" (*TI*, 36). This "becoming other" and yet "remaining the same" can only be transcended by uncovering the primordial structure of the intersubjective self, which allows the meaning of the "I" to become manifest.

The Face and the Moral Self

Levinas's view of the social self as arising in intersubjective encounter relies upon two unrelated modes of inquiry: the first an interrogation of the phenomenological data; the second, a destructuring of language.[17] While the modes of access may differ, they are made to converge upon the object of inquiry, which gives itself in a variety of ways. Thus, for example, the other person reveals himself both linguistically as the speaker of words and in the bodiliness, the *Leibhaftigkeit*, of flesh, that is, as the face. Attentiveness to multiple modes of self-presentation yields not a truer picture in the sense of one that corresponds more adequately to the object given but a richer, more complex account of what the given means.

The difficulty of rendering such an account is particularly acute for Levinas, since the object in question, the other person, remains refractory to usual modes of apprehension. I have already suggested that a cognitive grasp of the other reduces the other's alterity; the boundary between cognizing consciousness and its intended object disappears. Heidegger's understanding of the mode in which other persons are apprehended avoids the distortions of this naturalistic perspective, as Levinas concedes, but in the long run only evades the issue of the other's alterity at a deeper level. For Heidegger, being-in-the-world presumes Being-with-others as existentially constitutive for Dasein, emphasizing that Being-with is not a mere being alongside of in an indifferent relation to the other. Indeed, relation with another is lived as concernful solicitude, "a leap ahead of the other so that the other can become transparent to himself" (*BT*, 157–62). Nonetheless, Levinas argues, Being-with fails to free Dasein from its monadic solitude because Being-with exhausts itself in its initial impulse: once the other has been shown his existence as a being-toward-death, responsibility for the other ceases. Even if Being-with is constitutive of Dasein's existence as concernful solicitude, *the* other remains merely *an* other, an aperture through which the meaning of being can become manifest. The value of the other person is secondary to the primacy of being.

For Levinas, Cohen's account is in one sense "truer" than Heidegger's, since Cohen concludes that the other person is known through pity and compassion (*Mitleid*):

> This is the turning point at which religion, as it were, emerges from ethics. The observation of another man's suffering is not an inert affect to which I surrender myself, particularly not when I observe it not as a natural or empirical phenomenon, but when I make of it a question mark for my whole orientation in the world. . . . In suffering a dazzling light suddenly makes me see the dark spots in the sun of life. It is through the discovery of the thou that the I is liberated. (*RRSJ*, 18)

But, for Levinas, Cohen's analysis is methodologically misguided from the start, since for him conceptual necessity rather than phenomenological "eliciting" determines the character of the moral self. Cohen's view of the other person as fellowman is predicated upon the correlation between man and God, the mutually conditioning divine-human relation from which he deduces that man, God's partner in dialogue, cannot be infra-ethical. The possibility of the dialogue depends upon what can be shared by the participants: ratio as ethical reason.[18] Man in relation to God is a morally rational being only insofar as he has become the fellowman. For Levinas, by contrast, the knowledge of the other as a moral datum that founds the ethical self can never be derived from more fundamental premises such as the correlation between man and God but must be the object of a phenomenological intuition.

The apprehension of the face, for Levinas, provides one such mode of access to the other. The face is not merely perceived, although it is always possible to limit one's apprehension of it so that it is grasped as an object in the world among others. But this requires a distortion of a more primordial apprehension of the face given to moral intuition as value-laden. The face is not arbitrarily assigned axiological significance, but instead this significance derives from the meaning of the face as expressing the body's vulnerability. As such, it appears in the form of a demand to respect this vulnerability by resisting the impulses of violence that inhere in egoity. Thus, the face is given not to cognitive intentionality but to an affective aim: desire. The desire for the other can never be filled; it challenges the contentment and sovereignty of egoity. The mode of access to the face is borrowed from the structure of lived intentionality in infra-cognitive experience to account for the mode in which the other is apprehended as an "epiphany of the ethical" (*TI*, 194–204; *DEHH*, 197–98 and passim). The specific phenomenality of the face precludes any interpretation of it either as a visible object or as a concept: grasped as beyond being, it cannot appear within the limits of a horizon. On the other hand, the face is not a symbol bearing a meaning apart from itself that it brings into discursive clarity. "The face is abstract": by this Levinas means the face is not an object of sense in the usual way, even though it may misleadingly appear to be such an object. The illusion of concreteness that results from its appearance as an object of sense gives rise to an ambiguity that disrupts the expected order of the world.[19] Although the face is given as if it were a spatial object, it is actually a spatialized presentation of temporality. The other is in the "trace" not of a noumenal dimension that operates causally within phenomenality but of an immemorial past impervious to memory. This past cannot be recollected or repeated; it lies beyond historical process, beyond being. The trace opens into a personal order given in the form of the third person: "The profile that the irreversible past takes on through the trace is the profile of the 'He'"(*DEHH*, 199), and again, "The face is the unique opening where the meaning of the Transcendent . . . is maintained as transcendence" (ibid., 198). It is not difficult to see that, for Levinas, the face has become an aniconic *imago dei*.

What are the consequences of this peculiar mode of givenness? We have already seen that Levinas presumes access routes to the presented that bypass cognitive intentionality, since the other is apprehended in desire. The self that results from this mode of apprehension resembles, at a higher level, the separated self of need. Unlike need, desire can never be satisfied; the desiring self remains a perpetual lack. It can never be conceived as a "something," since it has the being of lack, of a nonoriginary emptiness. The other edges up to or "presses" against this emptiness, revealing itself as proximate (ibid., 225). Since the face is only incidentally apprehended as a visual object, this impingement in proximity is experienced as a touching of the self by an other, a tactile incursion upon egoistic individuality through which the other becomes an ethical datum.

The Moral Self: Emergence and Formation

Nowhere are the parallels between Levinas and Cohen more striking than in the understanding of the relational character of the moral self and the process of its formation. For both, the emergence of the moral self transforms lower-level functions. Although it is conceptually grasped only after these lower levels are laid down, it acts teleologically and proleptically in relation to infra-ethical egoity. Once the moral self emerges through the apprehension of the other as one who suffers, egoity is on the way to becoming full individuality.

I have spoken of the face and its meaning in Levinas, particularly its power to transcend visibility and to express a "thou-ought." Apprehended as an axiological datum, the face summons a self that lies beyond egoity. The self that emerges in the wake of the encounter with an other bears no hallmark. It is neither the substratum of qualities nor the functional unity attributed to a succession of experiences. Still, like the self of need it can be "cornered"; it exists as obsession.

The moral self is obsessed with the other in an etymological sense: the other is experienced as a nearness of being (ibid., 230).

Obsession in the sense acquired through destructuring not only reveals the other as "nearness of being" but is also the most primordial manifestation of meaning.[20] Language is founded in obsession. Levinas implies that meaning is a phenomenon that requires explanation, but explanation itself already presumes the possibility of meaning. Therefore, accounting for meaning must be given in terms of an infra-cognitive encounter with alterity. This precognitive awareness of the "I" is also reflected in the grammatical accusative (the French *se*) of reflexive pronouns. The form is passive, pointing to an experience of the self as guilty prior to all activity, guilt through which the self becomes an "I." Levinas uses the term "ownmost self" (*soi-même*) to distinguish the self of obsession and proximity from egoistic individuality. This self is beyond ontology, empty of being. Since it cannot become the source or origin of anything (it is *pré-originaire*),[21] it can only deploy the ego-self for its own purposes. With no interests to defend, it "is" only through the impingement of the other; the interest of the other becomes its interest. The preoriginary self places egoity at the service of the other, substituting for him, and so on. Since to formulate this idea as an imperative would subordinate morality either to an inductively derived general principle or a self-evident moral law, Levinas speaks of obsession as anarchic, without principle.[22]

Is the moral self arising from obsession then nothing? Or, at best, if it is something, must it be negatively defined? Just as in the case of the separated self Levinas resorted to the lived experiences of the already-constituted self as indicative of a more primordial level, he turns to the elementary modes of being of the lived body for his account of the moral self. This self is a living unity that, unlike egoity, knows no moments of respite and is attested in such "experiences"[23] as insomnia, pure wakefulness without consciousness of specific objects, the sense of "living in one's own skin," the dead time between heartbeats, the time between inhalation and exhalation. Each of these "experiences" conveys a sense of contraction in which the fullness of the body's being-present slackens.

The mode of temporalization of these "experiences" reflects this contracted mode of existence. The other intrudes upon the time of egoity, so that the sequential structure of time, its irreversibility and apparent seamlessness, is broken. For egoity, memory brings the past into the present while retaining its character as past. Intersubjective time, by contrast, effects the unmaking of the past. This mode of temporalization is lived as pardon. Functioning retroactively, pardon alters the character of the past, giving it a new meaning, treating it as though it had not occurred: time is now seen as a "spreading" from the other to the self. Pardon affords the possibility of breaking with the ultimacy of continuous time while retaining a connection with what had been broken (*TI*, 282 ff.).

For Cohen, the emergence of the moral self involves a two-stage process: the transformation of the opposing man into the fellowman and of the fellowman into the unique individual. The establishment of the fellowman does not yet bestow individuality upon the self, since in the context of morality the self as fellowman is merely an abstract individual (an individual only insofar as he is an autonomous source of willing). The relation to God is required to transform man into a "living and individual human creature," an "I." Man is not yet "alone," cannot yet "stand up for himself." For Levinas, this distinction is artificial: the relation to God is already established in intersubjective encounter. This follows from Levinas's commitment to phenomenological method: the ethical cannot be separated from what appears. Since there is no reality behind the scenes apart from the world, the ethical is apprehended within the world as the result of a special set of intentions, which bestow a unique meaning upon the given: the ethical meaning that belongs to the face and to language, which function as clues opening up a moral dimension. Since values are not, for Levinas, found as instantiations within the given, they can only be awakened by privileged data. This takes place in a single step: as soon as the face is seen or language experienced as bearing the warranty of the person who speaks, the moral self in the "trace" of transcendence is born as the absolute self.

For Cohen, there is a lag between the ethical individual and the moral self founded upon *religio*. Ethics alone leads inevitably to despair, from which the individual cannot be liberated through ethics. This despair is a consequence of the inability of the juridical sphere (which has competence only over legal culpability) to liberate the individual from guilt. The law can pronounce a man guilty: in society, the judge makes a determination of fact according to the relevant "paragraph of the law," but he cannot make a judgment about human guilt. When the criminal is declared guilty, he must take the burden of guilt upon himself. Still, he cannot exonerate himself: ethics demands the transition to religion. Once guilt reverts to the self and cannot be eradicated by juridical means, it becomes sin (*RRSJ*,

266 ff). It is the individual who takes sin on himself and in so doing makes himself an absolute self. But even here the individual does not do so without reference to the other: the absolute self (the individual I) makes itself in correlation with or before God. Cohen is careful to dissociate the notion of sin from the nature of man: if man were evil by nature, sin would be a cause and belong to the phenomenal realm. But sin is an idea, a necessary first principle, which is tested in experience and whose correctness is pragmatically established. Cohen means that, rather than beginning with the individual, "sin before God" may be used as a hypothesis whose fruitfulness is determined by whether it will yield the individual. It may appear that Cohen (perversely) applies the method of science to sin. But this is a misinterpretation of his intent: in actuality, sin is employed as a transitional concept in the Hegelian sense in order to mediate between social plurality and a higher stage, that of the absolute individual.[24]

The Idea of the Infinite

Who is the absolute individual who emerges after the burden of individual guilt is assumed? For Cohen, this unique "I" is neither a substance bearing qualities nor a functional concept but a regulative idea: the moral self is conceived as an infinite task. The will's efforts at actualization approach asymptotically but never attain the moral perfection of the ideal. For Cohen, the individual's potential for moral development as infinite must be understood as part of a two-sided process, one entailing the concept of formal perfection, the other that of endless continuity. As a moral ideal, the infinite is a measuring rod of ethical perfection. Yet the natural background is necessarily connected to the moral infinite as its accompanying sphere of actualization, with God the logically necessary guarantor of this continuity.[25]

In his last work, Cohen interprets the process Messianically and eschatologically: immortality is the infinite development of the human race toward an ideal endpoint, a Messianic society in which "the individual soul is always only the impetus of the ascent, always the sum total of ascents that come together in the infinite development."[26] Since Cohen ties the implementation of the ideal to a biblically derived Messianism, he stipulates the material condition required for the infinite progress of humanity, "an infinitely ramified heredity to carry the human race forward."[27] The separation of the two types of infinity is required by Cohen's struggle against pantheism:

> The human soul is not the world-soul. Its infinity does not coincide with that of the world, but it has always to remain limited to the specific context of man and his moral infinity. The universe has no morality. Its infinity is a mathematical moral one and is contained in it. It can be thought of as a task only with regard to mathematical insight and inquiry. The human soul, on the contrary, is always an infinite task, which can never be contained in any finite element.[28]

But what of the individual when the body dies, if he is merely a moment in the forward course of human progress, "only the infinite impetus in the infinite task"? What Cohen calls the "empirical prejudice" leads us to believe that the individual is tied to the organism when actually personal identity depends not upon the organism, but upon the relation to God: "The spirit returns to God. . . . The development removes the individual from its seeming identity with its former body, and turns it over to the infinite development of matter, as the negative condition for the infinite task of holiness."[29] The moral infinite is the necessary condition for personal immortality, while the infinite as the ongoingness of the phenomenal sphere is required for the progress of mankind as a whole.

While the infinite appears to have a quite different signification in Levinas's work, upon closer investigation parallels can be seen. Levinas begins by arguing that an examination of our ideas reveals that ideas are related to their content as container to contained, that is, we conceive of our ideas as adequate to their content. Notions of truth and falsity depend upon this presupposition. But, as soon as we think of the infinite, the possibility of adequacy is challenged and we are brought to a point where the process of cognition itself is undermined. We apprehend the inadequacy of cognition when confronted with a content, the infinite, which exceeds any idea we can have of it. The challenge to cognition awakens a moral self, first by disrupting the structure of egoity through presentation of a nonincorporable content, and second by awakening a desire that can never be replete, a desire for the infinite.[30]

The form of Levinas's argument is Cartesian: the idea of the infinite is a thought that could not have been self-produced. If the idea of the infinite is not self-generated, where does it come from? For Levinas, it is produced in the act of being revealed (*TI*, 26). Levinas adapts the form of the Cartesian conclusion on Kantian grounds: existence is not a property that adds something to the concept of God. The idea of the infinite is used to prove neither the existence of God nor that of the self. It quickens a moral self by fostering an encounter with alterity, in a process that bypasses cognition. The moral self in Levinas does not function as a regulative idea, since the moral self is not a necessary object of thought by which the understanding reaches for ever more connecting links in the realm of experience but is given as passive subjectivity simultaneously with the quest for alterity.[31]

Levinas explicitly rejects the Kantian notion of infinity on the grounds that infinity is, for Kant, a demand of reason required for the conceptual completion of finite being. The same objection would hold for Cohen. In relation to Kant, Levinas writes:

> The Kantian notion of infinity figures in an ideal of reason the projection of its existence in a beyond, the ideal completion of what is given incomplete—but without the incomplete being confronted with a privileged experience of infinity, without it drawing the limits of its finitude from such a confrontation. The finite is here no longer conceived by relation to the infinite; quite the contrary, the infinite presupposes the finite which it amplifies infinitely. (*TI*, 106)

Levinas views the Kantian infinite as the most anti-Cartesian moment in Kant. This may be so, but Levinas remains, *malgré lui*, Kantian rather than Cartesian, since he relates the infinite to moral imperatives instead of to the self-perfection of God. In addition, he, like Cohen, attaches special significance to paternity as holding a privileged place in relation to the future of man. The child is at once self and other, guaranteeing one's own continuity through another while accepting the alterity of the other: "My child is a stranger . . . but a stranger who is not only mine for he is me" (ibid., 267). While it is true that he does not ground this mode of biological continuity in conceptual necessity so that it extends the chain of heredity infinitely, as in Cohen, paternity phenomenologically founds the transcendental dimension in time and history. Levinas writes: "In paternity being is produced as multiple and as split into the same and other; this is its ultimate structure. It is society and hence it is time" (ibid., 270). For both Cohen and Levinas, the infinite involves a complex dialectic between transcendence and history expressed as the unfinished character, the openendedness, of the moral realm, which gives the self its meaning. What appears to have been disclosed at every level of the recursive engagement of a phenomenological and neo-Kantian perspective is that the latter has by no means exhausted its power.

27

Autochthony and Welcome
Discourses of Exile in Derrida and Levinas

Is hospitality not a solicitation to its addressee, "*Viens*, all that I have, all that I am, is at your disposal"? Is hospitality, as Levinas writes, "an incessant alienation of the ego . . . by the guest entrusted to it . . . being torn from oneself for another in giving to the other the bread from one's mouth," a one for the other that fissures the ego, hospitality that does not expect reciprocity and withholds nothing from the guest (*OB*, 79)? Or is there, as Derrida observes, an ineliminable tension between an unconditional offer to another and the juridical, political, and economic conditions that actually constitute the offer, without which the extending of hospitality is meaningless? Does this tension inhere in Abraham's proffering of bread and refreshment to the three strangers who arrive after God appears to him at Mamre (Genesis 18:4–5), an offer generally adduced as a paradigmatic instance of biblical hospitality?

Because the invitation to the other, "*Viens*," issues from a corporeal subject to another corporeal subject, who must traverse a space to a site to which that other is invited, it would seem that hospitality is bound up with distance and contiguity. But the awareness of the "to and fro" of this traversal is, for Levinas, a theoretical apprehension of space that is contingent upon a prior relation to the other, not one of perception but of proximity. In Levinas's terms in *Otherwise than Being; or, Beyond Essence*:

As a subject that approaches, I am not in the approach called to play the role of a perceiver that reflects or welcomes. . . . Proximity is not a state, a repose, but a restlessness, null site, outside of the place of rest. It overwhelms the calm of the non-ubiquity of a being which becomes a rest on a site. No site then is ever sufficiently a proximity. (*OB*, 82)

Prior to representation or reflection, the subject who approaches in proximity, the one who is nigh (near), the neighbor, is caught up in the relation to the other, in what Levinas calls fraternity, itself a primordial act of signifying. It would seem that meaning is born in and as hospitality thus understood.

Yet if, as Levinas also concedes, ontological significations cannot be disengaged from their empirical conditions, the relation with the Other may call the world into question but is not produced outside the world. Thus in *Totality and Infinity*, Levinas maintains that human relationships must not remain "a beatific contemplation of the other" which would (in his view) constitute idolatry. In contrast to his later account of hospitality in *Otherwise than Being* as occurring at a "null site," that of a proximity that cannot be measured, the earlier work acknowledges the necessity for habitation. For there to be hospitality there must be a home: "Recollection in a home open to the other [is] hospitality" (*TI*, 172). The home is a site that allows for self-enclosure, the shutting in of oneself that constitutes individuation, yet is also open to the other. To be sure, the home founds possession or ownership but is not itself owned in the same way as are moveable goods; it is possessed because "it already . . . is hospitable for its proprietor"(ibid., 157). Yet the home is "the very opposite of a root. It indicates a disengagement, a wandering that has made it possible" (ibid., 172). Did Abraham, the biblical paradigm of hospitality, not claim, "A wandering Aramean was my father"?

The Problem of Autochthony: Abraham and Lot

The other who can be seen as the neighbor can also, for Levinas, be encountered as a magisterial presence. It is the presence of the other as a human face that binds me in fraternity, another that is encountered as asymmetrical and higher than myself. Does Abraham in Genesis 18:2 not run from the entrance of his tent and "bow down to the ground" in a primal gesture of hospitality as subservience to the other, to the strangers in recognition of their alterity and of the else-where from which they come? Derrida sees this event as an exemplary instance of hospitality in the Abrahamic religions,[1] an account that would support Levinas's contention that "the relation with the other is accomplished as service and hospitality" (*TI*, 300).

The biblical narrative continues with Abraham's intervention on behalf of the righteous in the sinful city of Sodom, Genesis 18:16–23. This plea is followed by Lot's serving as host to the strangers and his effort to protect them from the sexual desires of the citizens of Sodom by offering his virgin daughters in their stead. The alarming implications of the proposed trade with respect to the status of daughters requires extended analysis that cannot be undertaken here. What is relevant in the present context is the sacrifice, the becoming hostage of that which is held dear. For Levinas, the primordial act of expiation is the willingness to substitute for the other.[2] Is this acceptance of being hostage for the other not also the very law of hospitality?

These brief comments on Genesis 18:1–9 and Genesis 19:1–11 lie within the disclosive conditions of a Levinasian biblical hermeneutic, but arguably the aporias of the Abrahamic narrative require further exploration. If one invites another to one's home, is not the precondition of this hospitality a certain agency and a certain belonging to a site on the part of the host? Do these conditions not presuppose that the host is justified in soliciting the other in that the host can lay claim to the site? Thus, the right to invite would seem to be intrinsic to the act of invitation. If, however, the other is absolutely other, descriptively unspecifiable, the host can only offer the other in her or his unspecifiability a nonsite. And if so, has the host not abandoned the power of agency required in order to fulfill the responsibility to offer food and shelter? The difficulty is compounded when we see that the face of the other, which in its vulnerability solicits hospitality, always already relates one to a third party. The other "moves into the form of the We, aspires to a State, institutions, laws, which are the source of a universality. But politics bears a tyranny within itself; it deforms the I and the other who have given rise to it, for it judges them according to universal rules" (*TI*, 300).

Still, it is not enough to define the stranger in terms of ethos, family, civil society, or the state, as did Hegel.[3] Today, as Derrida reminds us, states attempt to regulate the boundaries between public and private, to control the technological channels of communication, thereby altering these boundaries. The state is an outside that is inside so that being at home (*chez soi*) in an inviolable domain is no longer possible.[4] Derrida points to current ethnic, national and religious reactions against anonymous technologies. It must also be added that the rationality of the infoculture, what Janicaud calls technodiscourse, exerts a power of its own.[5]

To be sure, the rationality of technodiscourse can contest the space of the site but the latter does not disappear. If the site persists, the paradox of hospitality—in Derrida's terms, "the unconditional or the hyperbolic, on the one hand, and the juridicopolitical, . . . on the other"—cannot be eliminated.[6] The ethical then extends between the two, the one governed by the absolute gift, the other by the rules of economy, between hospitality of the proper name, "Peter, come," or of the absence of the name, "Whoever you are, you are welcome. As my interlocutor you are absolutely strange to me, the stranger par excellence."[7] If this tension is to be maintained, the nameless subject of ethics must be deterritorialized so that she or he emanates from a null site. Still, it must be recalled that, for Levinas, it is impossible to become detached from empirical conditions, as though significations could be produced from outside the world. Yet is the other as signifying, as the subject of approach and proximity, not decorporealized, dispossessed of its empiricity in the interest of this deterritorialization? Levinas describes the subject as a self in the accusative, passive in its exposure to being, an offering of itself that is a suffering. "The subject is in the accusative, expelled from being, outside of being" (*OB*, 110). If so, must it not be conceded that the one who suffers, who is not a gnostic subject but an incarnate someone, be somewhere?

I cannot enter into the details of Levinas's critique of an autochthony that he sees as grounding Heidegger's philosophy. However, insofar as the relation of hospitality to alterity and to a certain politics of the site is at issue in the present context, it is necessary to consider, however briefly, Heidegger's account of dwelling. For Heidegger, in Levinas's view, being at home is inextricably tied to autochthony: to dwell is to be rooted in the earth. To be, *Ich bin*, is linked to the word *bauen*, to build, so that the manner in which one exists is as one who dwells.[8] For Heidegger, it is poetry both as a measuring of that which cannot be measured, the Godhead, and as a kind of building that opens the possibility of dwelling. Significant in the present context is the claim that authentic poetry exists as long as there is kindness, understood not as a welcoming of the other in her alterity but as "the pure" that comes "to the dwelling being of man . . . as the claim and appeal of the measure to the heart."[9]

In *Totality and Infinity*, the hospitable subject is, as I have already noted, localized, inhabiting a site from which food and shelter are offered and, as such, having the right to invite. The home in its concreteness exists as granted to a subject by a political or an economic entity that is empowered to do so. The home is always already a place of inclusion and exclusion, of friend and enemy, a place in which the stranger may evoke distrust: is she or he friend or enemy? In an exemplary biblical instance of such suspicion, it may be recalled that the men of Sodom say of Lot, "This fellow came here as an alien, and he would play the judge" (Genesis 19:9).

Bending Etymologies

Is the friend/enemy relation not already to be discerned in the etymology of the term *hospitality*? It can be assumed that Indo-European *ghosti* is the root of Latin *hospitalitas* and of old Norse *gestri*, a root that denotes guest and host, someone with whom one has reciprocal duties of hospitality. The term also derives from the Latin *hostis*, enemy or stranger, as in *hostile*.[10]

Does not German *Gastfreundlichkeit*, "hospitality," evoke its root *Geist*, "spirit or ghost," so that one is reminded of the spectral possibility of the enemy in the guest? In what might be seen as a subtle correction of this picture, Carl Schmitt (admittedly a politically problematic thinker, who figures in Derrida's account of hospitality) considers another etymological distinction having important semiotic implications.[11] In order to preserve the Christian injunction to love one's enemies, Schmitt distinguishes personal animus from political enmity, thereby cordoning off a discursive space for the personal, in which Christian love can be expressed. Derrida explains: "In Chapter 3 of *The Concept of the Political*, [Schmitt] emphasizes . . . that *inimicus* is not *hostis* in Latin and *ekhthros* and *polemios* is not *poleimos* in Greek. This allows him to conclude that Christ's teaching concerns the love we must show to our private enemies, to those we might be tempted to hate through personal or subjective passion and not to public enemies."[12]

For Schmitt, the precondition for the possibility of politics is a war that does not presuppose hatred of an enemy (*hostis*). But for Derrida the reciprocal imbrication of public and personal cannot be dismissed. Turning to the text of Matthew 5:43–44, Derrida links the command to love one's enemy to the Levitical command to love one's neighbor. The neighbor, Derrida maintains, is *eo ipso* a member of the same ethnic group (*amith*) as oneself and thus always already belongs to the political in Schmitt's sense. Thus, if one loves the enemy as one loves the neighbor, Derrida concludes, "it would be difficult to keep the potential opposition between one's neighbor and one's enemy." Is the political then not already "within the sphere of the private"?[13] Do the men of Sodom not see Lot as an enemy when he assumes the role of judge because he attempts to usurp an autochthony he does not possess?

The Linguistic Turn and the Political

The etymological difference between *hostis* and *inimicus*, an aporia that brings to light what is ineliminably political in the sphere of the private, can be discerned in Levinas's account of the rhetorical aspect of language. Consider first that, for Levinas, hospitality arises in and as language. The relation with the other not only leads to the generality that language or the word makes possible but *is* this generality, the primordial donation or offering of the world as word. To be sure, Levinas insists that the relation to the other is realized in and as the vocative, the language of interpellation: "The interpellated one is called upon to speak, to come to the assistance of his word" (*TI*, 69). Such speech is essentially a coinciding of teacher and teaching, so that true teaching is not merely drawing out of truths (a recognizably Kierkegaardian point). Instead, "truth is made possible by relation with the other, our master," so that justice crystallizes in recognizing in the other a magisterial presence (ibid., 72). But—and this is the point—Levinas concedes that "rhetoric, taking the position of him who approaches the neighbor with ruse . . . is absent from no discourse" (ibid., 70). As propaganda, diplomacy, and so on, rhetoric solicits the other's agreement and is, as such, violence, injustice. If rhetoric is always already intrinsic to language, must it not also infiltrate hospitality? Referring to Carl Schmitt, Derrida writes, "War has its own rules and perspectives, its strategies and tactics, but they presuppose a political decision . . . naming who is the enemy.[14]

   In addition, it is crucial to note that, for Levinas, the relation to another is not that of two monadic individuals but ineliminably plural. The other is imbricated in social existence, thus already reflecting a third person who opens the possibility for justice. The relation to the other is not one of intimacy, an *a deux*, but one in which "the third party looks [out] at me in the eyes of the Other—language is justice . . . the epiphany of the face qua face opens humanity" (*TI*, 213). The meaning of "third . . . in the eyes of the other" is a matter of considerable complexity. The other is both destitute and an equal. "His equality within this essential poverty consists in referring to the third party . . . whom the other already serves. . . . He comes to join me in service" (ibid.). Once hospitality and justice are linked, the category of the political cannot be bypassed.

In this regard, it is helpful to elaborate further upon Derrida's reading of Schmitt's "polemical use of the concept of the political" and rendering of the friend/enemy relation.[15] For Schmitt, Derrida argues, key concepts are already presupposed in the analyses intended to establish them. Thus, "concepts of the polemical are never implemented . . . except in a polemical field [and] have a strictly polemical use."[16] This question-begging, as it were, is intrinsic to the "logical matrix" of Schmitt's vision of the political. Derrida writes: "The State presupposes the political, to be sure logically distinguished from it; but the analysis of the political . . . its irreducible core, the friend/enemy configuration, can only privilege . . . as its sole guiding thread, the State form of this configuration—the friend or enemy qua citizen."[17]

One must, of course, decide who is to count as the friend. There are, Derrida maintains, three logical possibilities in determining the meaning of this crucial relation. First, there is no friend without the possibility of killing, a possibility that establishes a political or non-natural community that is contingent upon the mortality of all parties, so that the parties are, in a sense, "dead for one another." Second, what is true of the enemy, his mortality, suspends or annuls friendship. The same possibility, mortality, is true of both friend and enemy, yet altogether different in relation to the friend. The interdiction against killing in the case of the friend both expresses and forbids this possibility. Third, Derrida asks whether there may be a politics of friendship beyond that of killing, whether *polis* and *filia* can be associated differently. We are, Derrida says, at the crossroads of an "undecidable triviality." Are we, in pondering this tension, returned to Aristotle's apothegm "My friend, there is no friend"?[18]

Are we, in applying comparable logical strategies to hospitality, compelled to say to a putative host, "There is no hospitality"? Like the bestowing of a gift, hospitality consists in an act of donation, in giving something to someone, as Derrida points out, conditional when the gratitude of the guest is expected but unconditional if no reciprocity is anticipated. When conditional, the mastery of the host is asserted in that it is he who invites, whose house, city, and nation control the relation to the guest. When hospitality is unconditional, no invitation is issued. The other, his coming a pure surprise, simply arrives and is welcomed with no thought given to the possible consequences. "For unconditional hospitality to take place you have to accept the risk of the other coming and destroying the place . . . stealing everything or killing everyone."[19]

Levinasian hospitality can be seen to exhibit a similar tension: one invites another to one's home, thereby implicitly expressing proprietary rights, while the other who arrives exerts an unconditional ethical demand. In response to the other who has come, one must be willing unconditionally to offer oneself as hostage for that other, so that self-donation is, in its pure form, the gift of death. For Derrida, the risk of "wild war and terrible aggression" renders the question of pure hospitality's existence undecidable. Can it then be said that the apothegm "My friend, there is no friend" rearises spectrally in Derrida's claim, with respect to hospitality, "There may be no such thing"?[20]

In/conclusion

The inquiry into the private and the political, into the meaning of friend and enemy, is not an excursus in the analysis of hospitality but exposes the risks and paradoxes built into the discussions of hospitality in the works of Levinas and Derrida. The personal is shown to remain personal yet is at the same time already demonstrably political; autochthony persists while engaging in its own deterritorialization. As Derrida argues, "Absolute hospitality requires that I risk opening my home to the stranger . . . to the absolutely unknown, who remains anonymous" so that the other can "have a place in the place that I offer him."[21] Still, it must be asked, is hospitality not also rendered to one who is named as well as to the nameless subject? If I am host, is there not already a collusion between hospitality and power? Even if, as host, I may be willing to risk inviting the enemy into my home, does not the fact that I speak from a site implicate me in the *polemos* of the political? Private or family law is always already mediated by public or state law, which can be both repressive and protective, in keeping with Schmitt's model of friend and enemy as grounding political power. Is this configuration of power not attested in the failure to extend the privileges of inhabitants to the resident alien, as exemplified in the men of Sodom's questioning of Lot's right to extend hospitality to the stranger?

Although the absence of physical boundaries in the virtual spaces of the new communication technologies radically alters biblical accounts of the home, one does not feed the hungry and shelter the destitute from the nowhere of a Web site. Virtual space is infiltrated by an ethical subject who is always already corporeal. To say this is not to confuse the corporeality of the ethical subject with a state of nature, as it were, but rather to see the subject in her/his bodily vulnerability as contesting political power grounded in the friend/enemy distinction, wherever it is to be found.

28

Time and Nonbeing in Derrida and Quine

Contemporary philosophers may be divided into two classes: those who believe in normative epistemological discourse governed by canons of objectivity and rationality continuous with those of science, and those who think of cognitive discourse as one among many claimants to meaning. Richard Rorty argues that, if there is "no common commensurating ground between them, all we can do is be hermeneutic about the opposition."[1] In this interpretation, it is futile to try to breach the distinctive discursive modes and ontological claims separating the work of Quine and Derrida. Quine belongs in the systematic cognitive camp, since he thinks the criteria of science are superior to any other epistemic "take" on the flux of experience,[2] even if he also believes ontological claims are "cultural posits."[3] Derrida holds that epistemological preferences based on self-evidence or rational justification conceal a linguistic and metaphysical infrastructure that undermines all truth claims. He often supports something verging on epistemological nihilism which he brings to light by means of odd rhetorical strategies: punning, *double entendre*, and so on.

I believe, *per contra*, that we can disclose a "common commensurating ground" deeper than the relativism and conventionalism that characterize both Quine's and Derrida's views of knowing, one that may also help dispose of such disjunctive and prejudicial distinctions as cognitive/hermeneutic, rational/irrational, and so on. This common ground, both commensurating link and entering wedge, is the time pattern each attributes to language. The temporal structure of language is important to Quine's view of stimulus meaning and enters his theory of translation at a critical point: in his account of the relation of class terms to counterfactuality.[4] It is also central to Derrida's deconstruction of speech and presence and to his claims concerning the repressive character of writing. I hope, following Quine, to gain access to the common features of their accounts of the temporal structure of language by resorting to the fiction of an unknown language. Thus Quine's question "How do we translate a hitherto unknown language?" doubles up recursively as both subject matter and method of this paper. I shall not proceed as a bilingual fluent in both languages, since this is, as Quine cautions, self-defeating: even if "it is such bilingual translation that does most justice to the jungle language, reflections upon it reveal least about the nature of meaning: for the bilingual translator works by an intrasubjective communing of a split personality" (MT, 475). Though heeding Quine's warning, I shall nevertheless station myself in Derridean territory, since it offers the familiar topography of the tradition to be dismantled. This decision leaves me free to incorporate both Quine's caveat and Derrida's protocols into my methodological weave. I shall focus on some seminal earlier works where the affinities between them are most apparent.

The Abyss of Meaning

Derrida and Quine agree that verbal expressions do not mirror occult entities that are their meanings. The best we can do is to examine the clues language itself provides. Quine (in the essays on translation) stations himself inside an existing language at the periphery of a hitherto unknown language since any attempt to achieve linguistic neutrality is thwarted by the observer's own linguistic code and the lack of Ur-meanings. Quine warns: "Even historical gradations if somehow traced down the ages and used as clues to translation between separated evolutionary stages would still be gradations only and in no sense clues to fixed ideas beneath the flux of language" (ibid., 459).

But if there are no "fixed ideas beneath the flux of language," Quine sometimes speaks as if there were fixed stimulus meanings, which both trigger and cash out at least those utterances that are reports of observations: "Observation sentences peel nicely; their meanings, stimulus meanings, emerge absolute and free of all resid- ual verbal taint" (ibid., 477). But Quine proposes a caveat that is fatal to the idea of fixity: "The obstacle is . . . that any one intercul- tural correlation of words and phrases and hence of theories will be just one of many empirically admissible correlations, whether it is suggested by historical gradations or by unaided analogy; there is nothing for such a correlation to be right or wrong about" (ibid., 459). I shall return to this point later, since important affinities be- tween Quine and Derrida are obscured if we forget the free play Quine allows to "the intercultural correlation of words and phrases."

It is harder to nail down the claims that make up Derrida's indict- ment of fixed meanings, though they are, in outline, fairly clear. Thinking in the Western metaphysical tradition is understood as the presence of meaning to a primordial intuition of being as presence. Following Heidegger, Derrida believes the shifting metaphors and metonymies of our philosophical language reflect attempts to think through the meaning of what is. A decisive shift occurred with Des- cartes' turn to self-certainty as the ground for establishing the truth concerning what is. It is impossible to think outside this pattern of ontological claims processed by consciousness, which provides the warranty for their truth, unless we are willing to break with the norms governing the traditional relations between thought and that which is. Such a break carries the price of radical perspectivalism and loss of coherence, since coherent discourse is defined by the ca- tegorial parameters that privilege present time and the object struc- ture of reality. Derrida's pessimistic account of our land-locked thinking, though not his antinomian frame of mind, has its counter- part in Quine. Consider:

> When we compare theories, doctrines, points of view, cultures, on the score of what sorts of things there are said to be, we are comparing them in a respect which itself makes sense only provincially. It makes sense only as far afield as our efforts to translate our domestic idioms of identity and quantification bring encouragement in the way of simple and natural-looking correspondences. . . . There is a notion that our provincial ways of positing objects and conceiving nature may be best appreci- ated for what they are by standing off and seeing them against a cosmopolitan background of alien culture; but the notion comes to nothing for there is no *pou stoū*.[5]

But Derrida does not believe that improving our methods of for- malization or refining our scrutiny of the conditions of utterance helps, since the techniques only implicate us more deeply in the concealed commitments of language. Instead, we can disclose this linguistic provincialism and ultimately breach it, at least in part, by turning to thinkers who, conducting bold thought experiments, dismantle this history bit by metaphysical bit. Heidegger, Lévi-Strauss, and Freud are examples. Derrida also turns to the linguistic theories of Saussure and Jakobson, who, by examining the phonemic, lexical, and grammatical structures of languages, see in signs the "simples" of linguistic structure. According to the classical theory signs represent the present in its absence: "When we cannot take hold of the thing we go through the detour of signs" (*SP*, 138). Every sign comprises two elements: a signifier, an acoustical linguistic bit; and a signified, the concept to which it refers. But Saussure, departing from classical theories of signs, acknowledges their arbitrariness. Transposed into the language of signs, meaning is not ontically grounded in the signified but derives instead from the differences among signs in an open-ended system of signs. For Derrida, "signs function not by virtue of the compact force of their cores but by the network of oppositions that distinguish them and relate them to one another" (ibid., 139). Concepts "mean" only intersignificantly and not by virtue of their transparency toward an ontological ground. We are left with "nothing but a field of indefinite substitutions in the closure of a finite ensemble."[6]

The problem of substitution is at the heart of Quine's thought but belongs in the context of his remarks on synonymy. I shall come to this later in some detail. For Quine, the whole fabric of language is the functional equivalent of Derrida's web of signs. ("The unit of empirical significance is the whole of science.") Scientific language depends upon intralinguistic contexts far removed from the impingements of experience. Thus sentences such as "Neutrinos lack mass" are different from observation sentences. For such theory-laden sentences, Quine admits, "no hint of the stimulatory conditions of assent or dissent can be dreamed of that does not include verbal stimulation from within the language" (MT, 477). Isolating stimulus meaning from intralinguistic determination requires a closer look; I shall come to this in due course. At present we need only notice an important similarity: the exclusion of stimulus meaning from the intralinguistic web rests on the same assumptions as those Derrida attributes to the classical theory of signs, that is, empirical meaning depends upon an ontically grounded signified. But since there are many empirically admissible linguistic correlations with stimulus situations, the stability of stimulus meanings is questionable. This drives Quine to appeal to a common human nature to establish the parameters of admissible correlation: "What provides the lexicographer with an entering wedge is the fact there are many basic features of men's way of conceptualizing their environment, of breaking the world down into things common to all cultures" (PML, 30).

For Derrida, the indicative power of signs is unstable from the start. Meaning depends upon differences within signs and among them. *Différance* (with an *a*) is the term Derrida uses to point to these differences. It is an undecidable term, which does not designate anything but describes an absence. Neither a concept, which can be cashed out by some anterior meaning, nor a negative particle, since there is no original to negate, *"différance* is the nonfull, nonsimple, 'origin'; it is the structured and differing origin of differences."[7] *Différance* includes the sense of postponing until later as well as dissimilarity or alterity, as determined by spatial criteria. Both meanings are important, since *différance* embraces economic calculation (with its connotation of delay, deferring, and the like), detour, respite, reserve, and representation. While *différance* produces *differences*, such as those within and among signs, it is prior to phenomenologically accessible difference. It is "the movement by which language or any code, any system of references in general, becomes historically constituted as a fabric of differences" (*SP*, 141).

This analysis poses formidable difficulties. Are we to understand the time scheme of signs by means of an occult Ur-temporality preceding the visible fabric of language? If not, then how? Does Derrida appeal to a hypostatized nonbeing? Perhaps not, since Derrida attributes functional rather than ontic status to *différance* and refrains from regarding *différance* as the transcendental ground of a system. In fact, Derrida turns to existing languages themselves to uncover the tracks or traces of *différance*. Yet what are they the tracks or traces of? The structure of time concealed though not obliterated by the time scheme of the present, by the structure of the subject as source point from which the nows of the present spring. What is the concealing structure and what does it conceal? Each new now seems to be something that is, a being or a produced object. Time appears to be a hypostatized series of instants produced by an autonomous subject. The classical account of time Derrida describes is not exactly circular but (borrowing Quine's metaphor) it is "a closed curve," since the order of experience presupposes this model of time and is then used in explaining time. Actually Derrida thinks the present carries the trace of a more primordial structure reflecting the dependence of time on space, the periodicity of time, which can only be thought of in terms of intervals or spacing. This opens time out, as it were, from its purely subjectively generated now-points to an outside:

> Since the trace is the intimate relation of the living present with its outside, the openness upon exteriority in general, upon the sphere of what is not one's own, etc., *the temporalization of sense is, from the outset, a "spacing."* As soon as we admit spacing both as interval and difference, and as openness upon the outside, there can no longer be an absolute inside, for the "outside" has insinuated itself into the movement by which the inside of the nonspatial, which is called "time," appears. (Ibid., 86; emphasis in original)

Derrida thinks of this spacing of time as a kind of Ur-writing. "This play of traces must be a sort of inscription prior to writing, a proto-writing without a present origin, without an *archē*" (ibid., 146). Not only is actual writing the result of the differential structure of language, but Derrida makes the far bolder claim that "language is a possibility founded upon the general possibility of writing" (*G*, 52). In sum, Derrida claims to have discovered the time scheme of language in writing, since time cannot be cordoned off from the spacing that articulates its periodicity. We find the track of this spacing characteristic of writing in all language.

Différance and the Nominalist Crisis

I have, borrowing Quine's own reservations, already criticized the notion of stable stimulus meanings.[8] I have yet to show that this instability derives from a play of differences in Derrida's sense. Still, one difference has already appeared as the precondition of Quine's analysis of radical translation: the irreducible difference between English and the hitherto unknown language. This difference is obvious but not trivial, since Quine finds meaning not by correlating exact verbal equivalents with some stimulus situation but in the differences that mark off verbal expressions from one another interlinguistically and from their prompting stimulus situations. The stimulus situations are not (in Derrida's terms) "points of presence," which "orient," "balance," or "organize" the structure, "Limiting its free play."[9] Instead, the linguist decides on meanings by "querying combinations of native sentences and stimulus situations so as to narrow down his guesses" (MT, 461). Thus the translator tries to pare down differences, though he cannot, *ex hypothesi*, do away with them altogether:

> The translation of a vast range of native sentences covered by the semantic correlation can never be corroborated or supported at all except cantilever fashion: it is simply what comes out of the analytical hypotheses [conjectural relations of parts of whole observation sentences] when they are applied beyond the zone that supports them. That these unverifiable translations proceed without mishap must not be taken as pragmatic evidence of good lexicography for mishap is impossible. (Ibid., 476)

There is only a system of differences with no constraining center, no core meaning to slip up on.

But the notion that meaning appears as a play of differences is parasitic upon a more far-reaching claim: *différance* opens up the time scheme of language and imprints its trace within and among signs. Can we imagine this claim as underlying Quine's theory of meaning? Could some equivalent term go proxy for *différance*, "the nonfull, nonpresent origin," an origin that may involve even our most primordial meanings, stimulus meanings, in nonbeing? We are forced to answer "yes" to both questions. The functional equivalent for *différance* in Quine's thinking is "counterfactuality," but to see this I must first show what drives Derrida's analysis and then how, despite the apparently incommensurate contexts, Quine's remarks on counterfactuality affirm a (roughly) similar position, even provide a support system, of sorts, for *différance*.

A part of my work is already done, for when we looked into the time scheme of language we saw that Derrida thinks of the present as a web of differences. Deconstructing this web reveals the periodicity of time, its structure as interval and spacing. The spacing of time is marked by its punctiform nature. Were we to live in purely deconstructed time, so to speak, these instants would pulsate without linkage. Derrida's analysis opens up the possibility of deconstructed time, presenting us with the impasse of unbreachable particulars, infinite in number, in which meaning is ruled out. The metaphysical tradition from Parmenides on is an attempt to protect thinking against this diffraction of time and being. This tradition, as Derrida reads it, is a botched effort to overcome what I shall call "the nominalist crisis" by proposing grounding principles, each of which turns out to be merely provisional and must be abandoned in the end because it reinforces the ordinary conception of time, one in which "non-presence is always thought in the form of presence—we might say through *form* as such or as the modalization of presence. The past and future are always determined as past and future presents."[10]

Quine expresses the crisis of nominalism within the framework of science itself, whereas Derrida, following Heidegger, usually interprets the ontology of science as an extreme expression of the metaphysical tradition he is deconstructing. Yet their concurrence is deeper than this difference seems to allow. Both are sensitive to the problem of the transiency of the conditions of utterance, which goes against the grain of the ideality of language. Derrida expresses the nominalist crisis in terms of non-ontic simples: the time pulses brought to light by the analysis of *différance*. Quine's simples are similarly non-ontic. They are the infinite numbers of counterfactuals that would clot our thinking if we were to support stimulus meanings in a rigorously nominalist fashion—without, that is, recourse to universals. I shall describe how Quine goes about this later. The dilemma confronting the radical empirico-nominalist is arriving at sameness of meaning across discrete dated particulars, regimenting our language so that in linking up particulars (a necessary but regrettable condition if we are to speak at all) we do not necessarily obscure what Quine calls the "disreputability of their origin," a "bastardy" that "to the enlightened mind is no disgrace" (SO, 458).

It is easier to see the problem as common to Derrida and Quine if the strategies they use to disclose it bear at least some family resemblances. Derrida rarely turns to stimulus meaning to show the time scheme of *différance*, but, in a gloss on an early theory of Freud's, stimulus meanings play a role in illustrating the play of differences as a difference in quantity of forces. In this context Derrida actually gives an account of Freud's resolution of the nominalist crisis and identifies his own position with Freud's. According to this early neurological theory, Freud shows how particular percepts (what Quine and Freud would call nerve-to-nerve excitations) are linked to form unitary meanings. In this connection Freud brings to light the key notions of resistance and trace. Dividing neurons into functional classes, Freud claims that one set, the perceptual neurons, are sensitive to stimuli but do not retain them. These impressions leave no trace because there is nothing to resist them. But another class of neurons (psi neurons) offer opposition to the incoming impressions and retain the printed trace because the force of incursion of the incoming impression and the force of resistance are unequal. (Were they equal they would, of course, simply cancel each other.) The difference between breaching, the breaking of the neural path, and the resistance of the psi neurons is the origin of memory. In fact, memory is this difference. But memory also depends upon repetition. Since the original impression differs quantitatively from the repetition, still another difference is established between the trace and the repetitions. Yet Freud notices that consciousness gives us not differences of quantity but differences of quality: "Consciousness gives us what are called '*qualities*,' sensations which are different and whose difference is distinguished according to its relations with the external world. Within this difference there are in fact no quantities in it. It may be asked *how* qualities originate and *where* qualities originate."[11] Perhaps, Freud thinks, there is another set of neurons in addition to those already mentioned. But how is qualitative difference to be explained without recourse to quantity? "We have just encountered a permeability and a breaching which proceed from no quantity at all. From what then? From pure time, from temporalization in its conjunction with spacing: from periodicity."[12]

Quine does not think of this problem in psychological terms. Instead of analyzing memory, he gives the crisis of particularity a linguistic turn: how do we arrive at sameness of meaning when sensory input is discrete and tied to time? Quine's solution is to think of "dated particular events" as event *forms* to prevent our being inundated by particulars. Quine's theory of stimulus meaning hangs on this substitution of universals for dated particular events, for without them we would be adrift in a sea not of actual particulars only but of particulars that did not and could not happen. To show this, I must cite Quine at some length:

> The several stimulations which we assemble in classes to form stimulus meanings, must themselves be taken for present purposes not as dated particular events but as repeatable event forms. We are to say not that two stimulations have occurred that were just alike, but that the same stimulus has *re*curred. To see the necessity of this attitude consider again the positive stimulus meaning of an occasion S. It is the class Z of all those stimulations that *would* prompt assent to S. If the stimulations were taken as events rather than event forms, then Z would

have to be a class of events which largely did not happen and could not happen, but which would prompt assent to S if they were to happen. Whenever Z contained one realized or unrealized particular event σ, it would have to contain all other unrealized duplicates of σ; and how many are there of these? Certainly it is hopeless nonsense to talk thus of unrealized particulars and try to assemble them into classes. Unrealized entities have to be construed as universals, simply because there are no places and dates by which to distinguish between those that are in other respects alike.[13]

Quine's first break with radical particularity occurs when he urges us to assemble existing particulars into event forms. (Compare this with Derrida's remark: "When Freud writes in the *Project* that facilitations serve the primary function, . . . he complies with a dual necessity: that of recognizing *différance* as the origin and at the same time crossing out the concept of primariness."[14]) Were Quine, *per contra*, to stick with particulars or classes of particulars come what may, he would be driven to consider all stimulation that *would* prompt assent to S as supports for the meaning of S, and these could be infinite. But since there can be no class names of nonexisting events, he admits we must construe these unrealized entities as universals. Derrida might conclude that Quine has given us a myth of origins to account for the emergence of universals, but, in all fairness, Quine has already thought of this. He remarks: "this vast supplementary force of *could* . . . is perhaps a vestige of Indo-European myth, fossilized in the subjunctive mood" (PML, 54).

Substitutes, Supplements, Synonymy

We cannot think of linguistic substitution without first settling on what we mean by identity and difference. For radically empirico-nominalist thinkers, identity is always suspect, for it suppresses the time scheme of language and hypostatizes occult entities across a fabric of differences. Thus we can dispose of identity *tout court*. Though it may be invoked as a convention to insure parsimony (as in the case of universals going proxy for counterfactual stimulus meanings in Quine), it always conceals difference. Conditions of interchangeability assume considerable importance in this context.

Derrida approaches substitution historically as the chain of metaphysical concepts that regularly replace each other in Western thought and linguistically as a system of signs that go proxy for one another. This does not complicate matters as much as one might think because the mechanism of substitution is, in both cases, surprisingly similar. This is because Derrida thinks linguistic structure mirrors prior metaphysical commitments. Derrida thinks of substitution in a radically nominalist way: substitutes are different from originals; they supplement but cannot replace them, since in a radically relational reading of language as an interlocking system of signs there is no original to replace. The term *supplement* connotes both substitution and addition. Derrida understands supplementarity as "in reality *différance*, the operation of differing which . . . both fissures and retards presence submitting it simultaneously to primordial division and delay. . . . The supplementary difference stands in vicariously for presence due to its primordial deficiency" (*SP*, 88). Or again, "Supplementarity . . . is . . . the play of presence and absence, the opening of this play that no metaphysical or ontological concept can comprehend" (*G*, 244).

The theme of supplementarity is inseparable from that of writing, since linguistic supplements are signs and signs are graphematic. The idea of supplementarity also carries a kind of moral force, which depends on the value we place on nature and culture: the supplement is the debased (cultural) proxy of the (natural) original. Writing is not merely a case in point but the structural condition of substitution itself. In the *Phaedrus*, Plato, like the tradition that will follow, treats writing with suspicion as the cultural remedy for forgetting, because writing aggravates the affliction it promises to cure. The "dead letter" signals forgetting, a loss of the time-derived sinuosities of living speech.[15] At the same time, we also fear the putatively innocent original, what is altogether excluded from language and therefore from writing: "the purity of nature, of animality, primitivism, childhood, madness, divinity," all of those ineffable "phenomena" that Derrida calls "life without *différance*" (*G*, 244). (Think of Quine's remarks on the purity of origins cited earlier: "Bastardy to the enlightened mind is no disgrace." If this "liberal line accords with the Oxford philosophy of ordinary language" (SO, 458), as Quine claims, it accords a fortiori with the Derridean practice of deconstruction.)

Quine treats the problem of significant sequence in much the same way as Derrida by proposing that coherent discourse can be determined in terms of what it excludes. For Quine, the criterion of exclusion is "bizarreness of idiom." Thus Quine tells us: "Concerning the notion of significant sequence. . . . It is describable without appeal to meanings as such, as denoting any sequence which could be uttered in the society under consideration without reactions suggesting bizarreness of idiom" (PML, 54). This criterion comes as close as one could wish to what Derrida means by "madness," "primitivity," and the like as exclusions determining what counts as coherent discourse, as "life without *différance*" and thus without language.

While the conditions of substitution are developed in connection with the supplement of writing in Derrida, for Quine the idea of substitution arises together with his account of synonymy. This is a central issue in Quine, and I can touch only on matters pertinent to the present context. Of cognitive synonymy dependent on truth conditions, we need say very little, only that Quine thinks "that interchangeability *salva veritate* is too weak a condition for synonymy if the language as a whole is *extensional*" and that in other languages "it is an unilluminating condition, involving something like a vicious circle" (ibid., 57). A fortiori synonymy in the sense of complete identity in psychological associations or poetic quality is ruled out. Quine turns instead to sameness of stimulus meaning as a possibly useful criterion of synonymy. To assess its worth, we must test its range of applicability. Stimulus meaning, Quine finds, is limited to occasion sentences, those that command assent or dissent when accompanied by prompting stimulation. But unlike occasion sentences such as "Rabbit," some other sentences depend largely on "collateral information," so that their meanings can never be cashed out by stimulus meanings *simpliciter*. Assent to the sentence "Bachelor," for example, may be prompted by a glimpse of an appropriate face but still requires collateral information to round out the meaning. Moreover, the same stimulus may fail to elicit "Bachelor" if there are two or more speakers. This limitation would seem to be fatal if we mean to establish stimulus meaning as a condition for determining intersubjective synonymy. But this restriction, Quine urges, presents no obstacle. If we first think of "Bachelor" and "Unmarried man" as intrasubjectively synonymous, then they may be synonymous for each and every member of the community, though, of course, the stimulus triggers will vary from person to person. But—and this is the point I have been leading up to—there is no bypassing the single-speaker constraint, since here alone the criterion of the sameness of stimulus-meaning functions unchecked:

> What we find is that, though the concept of stimulus meaning is so very remote from "true meaning" when applied to the observational occasion sentences "Bachelor" and "Unmarried

man," still synonymy is definable as sameness of stimulus meaning just as faithfully for these sentences as for the choicest observation sentences—as long as we stick to one speaker. For each speaker "Bachelor" and "Unmarried man" are . . . alike in stimulus meaning without having the same meaning in any acceptably defined sense of "meaning" (for stimulus meaning in the case of "Bachelor" is nothing of the kind). Very well; let us welcome the synonymy and let the meaning go. (MT, 246)

To relate intrasubjective synonymy to the Derridean supplement, I must digress briefly in order to consider Derrida's views of the role intrasubjective discourse plays in establishing meanings in the context of Husserl's theory of language. In Derrida's reading, the conditions of meaning for Husserl lie outside the empirical conditions of utterance, since Husserl gives primacy to expression (a purely linguistic function tied to the logical power of language) over indication (a movement toward an empirical content not yet present). The model for expression (this means for meaningful discourse *tout court* in Husserl's thought), Derrida thinks, is the interior monologue. Inner conversation preserves signified meaning, though it relies on a medium that is nonempirical, the silent voice of solitary mental life. This is what Derrida calls the "phenomenological" voice, "diaphanous" enough to efface itself while still bringing the signified into presence. Derrida thinks of the action of voice as "an auto-affection" covering up the spacing that, as we have seen, is proper to time. Instead, voice promotes a conception of being as identical with itself, present to itself, forming the substance of a subject. Derrida claims:

> The operation of "hearing oneself speak" is an auto-affection of a unique kind. On the one hand, it operates within the medium of universality; what appears as signified therein must be idealities that are *idealiter* indefinitely repeatable or transmissible as the same. On the other hand, the subject can hear or speak to himself and be affected by the signifier he produces, without passing through an external detour, the world, the sphere of what is not "his own." (*SP*, 78)

But we saw earlier that for Derrida self-presence is actually not identical with itself and carries a retentional trace: "It is always already a trace" (ibid., 85). Once we admit the trace as spacing, as the relation of the living present with something outside itself, there can no longer be any isolated inside, for the outside has insinuated itself into the inside, into the nonspatial, as the pulsation of time.

We are now prepared to return to Quine's remarks on intrasubjective synonymy. Consider his comment: "The concept of stimulus meaning is remote from 'true meaning' when applied to the inobservational sentence 'Bachelor'" (MT, 468). Such inobservational sentences depend upon intralinguistic supplement, a socially derived web of language one has at one's disposal. But this supplement is brought into play, in Derrida's terms, when "the subject can hear or speak to himself . . . , without passing through an external detour, the world" (SP, 78). Still, and this is of cardinal importance, "synonymy is definable as sameness of stimulus meaning just as faithfully for these sentences as for the choicest observation sentence," so long as we retain the single-speaker constraint. Even in observational occasion sentences whose stimulus meaning prompts assent from only one speaker, intrasubjective assent is shot through with difference, the chain of particular stimulus meanings that elicit or would elicit its utterance. Yet because synonymy is standardized only intrasubjectively ("Bachelor" and "Unmarried man" mean the same only under the single-speaker constraint), difference is also repressed. Consider Derrida's earlier remark: "The operation of hearing oneself speak is an auto-affection of a unique kind. . . . what appears as signified therein must be idealities . . . transmissible as the same" (ibid.). This ideality (if sense without reference can be so described) is foreclosed by Quine even in the case of such putatively analytic pairings as "Bachelor" and "Unmarried man." The intrasubjective synonymy of such sentences, in Derrida's terms, forces an external detour, the triggering and cashing out of meaning by way of the world. On these grounds, Derrida could only endorse the deconstructive spirit, if not the letter (in all the senses Derrida gives to the term *letter*) of Quine's remark: "Let us welcome the synonymy and let the meaning go."

■   ■   ■

In conclusion, let me first draw attention to the points of convergence themselves. Second, I shall link up the threads of these convergences in order to show how these affinities support a common central purpose: to develop a new philosophy of experience whose "commensurating ground" is the time design of language. The points of convergence are these:

1. *The impossibility of grounding meaning.* Quine and Derrida reject the view of meaning that construes it as the mental counterpart of some verbal expression. In his essays on translation, Quine tries to

anchor meaning in some empirically stable source and finds this ground in stimulus situations. But there is no way of telling if, let alone how, verbal expressions match these stimulus situations *tout court*, since an indefinite number of linguistic possibilities, some contradictory, may square with the observed data. Derrida's claim is stronger: nothing at all can serve as the foundation for the free play of signs, whose differences rather than ontic anchorage account for meaning. Yet the tendency of language to say what there is conceals something like a biological ground: desire, need, lack, death, negative phenomena that are ineffable. These inchoate desires do not simply disappear. Instead, they are incised in language as a kind of Ur-writing and are carried along lexically and syntactically by the system of signs. This biological ground is unstable and in principle lacks verbal equivalents.

2. *The creation of substitutions for the absent or unstable origin.* Derrida claims that single thread holds the Western metaphysical tradition together: "the production and recollection of beings in presence." We can muster evidence for this by genealogically tracking the terms used to designate first principles—*eidos, archē, ousia*, and so on—which express what there is in the time scheme of the present. Each of these ideal meanings hides the unstable base of metaphysical language while purporting to go proxy for it. At the same time, a putative ground or origin is assigned to this language, proleptically concealing its lack of foundation. What holds for metaphysical language holds, mutatis mutandis, for other languages mirroring this history of substitutions. Quine finds the ideality of language in the analytic-synthetic distinction and assails it on related grounds. He recognizes the totality of at least our warranted beliefs about what there is as "the unit of empirical significance" and gives it the place Derrida assigns to the web of signs.[16] It would be misleading to suppose that Quine supports anything like the claim of a nonpresent origin, since, at least on the face of it, this claim seems "to impute being where we might otherwise be content to recognize that there is nothing."[17] Yet counterfactuality in Quine's description of stimulus meaning is the functional equivalent for the "non-present origin" in Derrida's account. Quine, like Derrida, acknowledges that there can be no talk of unequivocal sameness of meaning. If we wish to preserve sameness of stimulus meaning of a sentence S, we must assemble the required stimulations to cash it out into classes and also take account of all the stimulations that did not and will not occur but that *would* prompt assent to S by substituting universals for them. A *horror*

infiniti drives us to interpret counterfactual stimulus situations in terms of universals rather than as an indeterminate number of particulars.[18]

3. *The quest for the empirical roots of meanings that are established intra-subjectively.* In a gloss on Husserl's distinction between expression and indication (a distinction roughly approximating Frege's sense and reference), Derrida claims that they are not as neatly separable as Husserl supposes. Because Husserl links the structural requirements of expression to solitary mental life, the indicative layer of language is cordoned off and subordinated to expression, thus suppressing its empirical root and giving to expression a spurious independence. Quine's interest in intrasubjective meaning is confined to showing that sentences like "Bachelor" and "Unmarried man," whose stimulus meaning is nonidentical *between* persons, are interchangeable so long as we restrict ourselves to their stimulus meaning for a single speaker. This analysis supports a Derridean claim: by pointing to the single-speaker constraint, Quine shows—without, of course, intending this—how, in Derrida's terms, the "ideality of language" is based on the model of solitary mental life but is shot through with empirical content. Thus, since sameness of stimulus meaning for these sentences is realized only intrasubjectively, we can show, stretching Quine's analysis somewhat, how sameness of meaning might seem to bypass the world, so that sentences like "Bachelor" and "Unmarried man" *appear* to be related independently of matters of fact though *actually* they are not.

Each of these points of convergence is a move against the epistemic difficulties of classical empiricism, an effort to fashion "an empiricism without dogmas." Though Derrida's favorable references to Heidegger's work may seem to plant him squarely in opposition to any ontology linking up with the ontology of science, Derrida never jettisons science *tout court*: "Grammatological practice must go beyond metaphysical positivism and scientism . . . freeing science of its metaphysical bonds."[19] Both Quine and Derrida think of our "so-called knowledge and beliefs" as humanly contrived, "a man-made fabric," a web of signs. Moreover, our knowledge and beliefs are a total *Anschauung*, which gives us our "take" on the flux of experience. The new empiricism is constructivist and holistic.

A corollary of this new view breaks down one of the most cherished tenets of the old empiricism: each statement about the world can be correlated to a limited, specifiable range of sensory events.

For Quine, once this tenet is denied, it follows that we can no longer separate analytic statements—those that hold "come what may"—from synthetic statements, those that are contingent on experience: if we tinker drastically enough with the system of our beliefs, synthetic statements also hold "come what may," just as analytic statements are alleged to do.[20] Similarly, Derrida rejects the notion of a "transcendental signified," something "given," the referent of a statement *simpliciter*, since meaning depends upon the interconnectedness of a chain of signs. Still, the new empiricism retains a bit of umbilical cord linking it with the old. Despite the constructed and holistic character attributed to our knowing, "each of us is also given a continuing barrage of sensory stimulations,"[21] to which we respond (even if for Derrida the *significant* promptings are "inner" biological triggers—needs, desires, and the like). Quine claims that when we adjust our beliefs to these stimulations, we do so on pragmatic grounds. Derrida, wary of the theory/practice distinction, which he sees as linked to an older metaphysical tradition, takes a more occult view of our relation to these stimulations: they write themselves into our language, *malgré nous*, as traces. But—and this is the chief point—once a one-to-one correlation between sensory prompting and linguistic bit is ruled out, the time pattern of language alone marks off the individual events of sensation and reflection. Time works against recovering the event, since time *is* just the event's passing and nothing more. Quine and Derrida think at least one of our difficulties is the muddle we get into when we try to arrest the flux by creating metaphysical substitutes for "dated particular events" when in fact events, to borrow a trope from Anaximander, Socrates' old *bête noir*, "perish by moral necessity," even though reifying ontologies try to "make reparations for the injustice of time" while forgetting "the order of time."[22]

29

The Logic of Artifactual Existents
John Dewey and Claude Lévi-Strauss

Scientific thinking as a model for human inquiry has fallen under criticism, often by those who number themselves among its most ardent admirers. In the case of John Dewey, the romance with science comes to an inconclusive end, since he has no quarrel with the explanatory force of scientific concepts or with the power of science as an organon of theoretical constructs that express the underlying regularities of phenomena. Instead, it is the lackluster record of science in addressing the multi-layered world in which we live—one to which Dewey attributes purpose and passion—that leads him to seek a principle of mediation between the world of experienced quality and that of science, which weighs "like an incubus upon such a wide area of beliefs and aspirations" (*EaN*, 382). Unable to abandon the methods of the particular sciences, whose successes he believes are attested in their fruits, and reluctant to give up the distinctively human cosmos, Dewey turns for his model of inquiry to the world of doers. Shrewd and versatile, everyday mechanics, artisans, inventors, and craftsmen never lose sight of the needs and desires of human society. This aspect of Dewey's thought has been praised or derided by those who regard themselves as tough or tender-minded critics, respectively. But such responses show, I think, that the unique character of his newly discovered method has remained undetected; instead, it has, for the most part, been interpreted as waffling.[1] My thesis here is that Dewey is in fact reaching for a new mode of inquiry, whose outlines are clearly visible in some richly suggestive passages in his later work (especially but by no means exclusively in *Experience and Nature*), but that this method has in fact received full elaboration in the work of anthropologist Claude Lévi-Strauss as a paradigm for understanding the principles of thought operative in the mythological consciousness of nonliterate societies. This particular thought form, *bricolage*, plays the role of negotiator between the competing claims of nature and culture; it is a "science of the concrete," uniting structure and event in a fashion quite different from that of science *simpliciter*. Of course, these categories are developed independently of Dewey's earlier efforts to heal the same breach and, in contrast to Dewey's metaphysical interest, emerge from the context of Lévi-Strauss's empirical investigations. What is more, Dewey's "instrumentalism"[2] contrasts sharply with Lévi-Strauss's view of the primacy of structure.[3] It is all the more striking, therefore, that the concept of bricolage, the "science of the concrete," proves useful in bringing to conceptual clarity the artifactual character of tools or apparatus in Dewey's work, the products of qualitative thinking. The term has, of course, entered literary discourse.

Science and Bricolage

Who is the *bricoleur*? What purposes or ends inform his dealings with the world? The history of the term is instructive:

> In its old sense the verb "bricoler" applied to ball games and billiards, to hunting, shooting, and riding. It was however always used with reference to some extraneous movement: a ball rebounding, a dog straying or a horse swerving from its direct course to avoid an obstacle. And in our own time the "bricoleur" is still someone who works with his hands and uses devious means compared to those of a craftsman. (*SM*, 16 ff.)

It would be misleading to interpret the distinction between craftsman and *bricoleur* in this text as pointing to a difference between Dewey's view of craft and Lévi-Strauss's bricolage since what is stressed here is the quality of inventiveness, a "making do" with limited means, and this is precisely what characterizes Dewey's artisan. For Dewey, "acumen, shrewdness, inventiveness, accumulation and transmission of information are products of the necessity under which man labors," when he converts immediate feeling into ordered interest

(*EaN*, 122). The real contrast to the work of the bricoleur is the construction project of the engineer; the latter begins with a plan, assembles what is needed in order to fulfill it, and builds in conformity with this "blueprint." The bricoleur works with a limited group of materials, which are at hand but bear no intrinsic relation to his project. What he has available is:

> the contingent result of all the occasions there have been to renew or enrich the stock or to maintain it with the remains of previous constructions or destructions. The set of the "bricoleur's" means cannot therefore be defined in terms of a project. . . . It is to be defined only by its potential use or, putting this in another way and in the language of the "bricoleur" himself, because the elements are collected or retained on the principle that "they may always come in handy."(*SM*, 17–18)

These elements are versatile, lending themselves to distinctive use up to a point, but they are at the same time multi-functional. Thus "they each represent a set of actual and possible relations; they are 'operators' but they can be used for any operations of the same type" (ibid., 18).

Three aspects of bricolage emerge from this account:

1. Understood as method, bricolage depends upon versatility, the ability to select from what is only incidentally present in the environment, as well as upon resourcefulness in overcoming obstacles (the horse swerving, the ball rebounding, etc.) not by meeting them head-on but by means of circumambience and cunning.

2. Understood as a mode of cognition, bricolage refuses primacy to a preceding conceptual scheme, which is then used to bring into being an object that will be in conformity with itself, a "something" whose excellence will be judged in terms of its agreement with or deviation from an antecedent plan. Instead, the bricoleur seizes upon what is available and remains in dialogue with an environment, re-forming his intentions as he selects and conserves from funds of cultural experience.

3. Understood as a mode of activity, bricolage chooses what is distinctive in any context. But the bricoleur does not specialize; instead, he "hangs loose" in relation to his materials. Control is slack rather than rigid, yet bricolage is not a mere scrambling of accidentally present elements. This modus operandi is pertinent to the question of ends or purpose in bricolage. Since the procedure involves

recomposing whatever is at hand, the result may be a compromise between a fortuitous arrangement of elements and an original project.

The experiences that drive Lévi-Strauss to bricolage and Dewey to a similar paradigm appear to be based on the familiar discrepancy between the cognitive dimension in "making" and science as an affair of knowledge. This question takes on added pertinence when knowledge ceases to be contemplative, as is the case in scientific thinking. What is it that we do in our practical intercourse with the world? Is this "doing" methodologically distinct from scientific inquiry, or does science shade off into an infra-scientific commerce with things?[4] While there is a family resemblance between bricolage and scientific thinking, our practical dealings with the world exhibit unique aspects that set them apart from scientific thought. For Lévi-Strauss, the fact that the pragmatic sophistication of neolithic man does not proceed in a straight line of steady growth to the methods of modern science is evidence for the independence of our practical relations to the world:

> These are certainly not a function of different stages of development of the human mind but rather of two strategic levels at which nature is accessible to scientific enquiry: one roughly adapted to that of perception and the imagination: the other at a remove from it. It is as if the necessary connections which are the object of all science, neolithic or modern, could be arrived at by two different routes, one very close to, and the other more remote from, sensible intuition. (*SM*, 15)

While Lévi-Strauss begins with an unexplained fact—the perceived complexity of nonliterate societies' dealing with the world—and attempts to create a space for it by enlarging our conception of cognitivity, Dewey's point of departure is an unfulfilled human need. Science has divorced itself from the concerns of life, so its manner of apprehending the world must be supplemented by developing a wider notion of experience.[5] Science has given us a world not merely isolated from experience but in opposition to it: "Etymologically, 'science' may signify tested and authentic instance of knowledge. But knowledge has also a meaning more liberal and more humane. It signifies events understood, events so discriminately penetrated by thought that mind is literally at home in them" (*EaN*, 161). One form of this "supplement" is, for Dewey, applied science. So important has "application" become for him that he thinks of it as "more truly science than what is conventionally called pure science" (ibid.). This preeminence derives from what he sees as its human import; applied science attempts to bring about changes in existence in accordance with human needs and ends. For Dewey, "applied" science is not related to "pure" science as genus to species. Rather, application compels us to perceive the real situation of science and thus forces a reworking of our conception of scientific thinking itself. Dewey denies that application, since it derives from human need, is foreign to the world. Human nature is not extraneous to nature, something lying outside it, but is part of nature itself. It is, in fact, a loss of sensed continuity that Dewey means to highlight.

But when Dewey speaks of applied science as the genuine article, he means not only to stress man's existence in nature but something more primary, which refers to the nature of scientific inquiry itself. This is the requirement that theories terminate in some situation of existential reference, that is, that theory find application. Abstraction from existence is a necessary moment in the process of inquiry, but abstraction that prescinds from context, that terminates in itself, is not the end point of inquiry. It may be necessary to formulate theories as free from particular existential reference, but such theories are meaningless unless they become operational. Thus, for Dewey, "No matter how far physical theory carries its abstractions, it would contradict the very intent of the latter if they went beyond possibility of application to every kind of *observable* existential materials."[6]

Therefore, science is *necessarily* applied, that is, applied in a primary sense. "Science," properly understood, is thus an ellipsis for "applied science." If scientific thinking is itself *intrinsically* a process of application and if, as Dewey believes, human nature is as much part of the referential field of science as any other natural object, a science that fails to become applied in a secondary sense, that is, to take human ends into account, has failed to fulfill its objective: it is science alienated from itself. Thus, the task of Dewey's new method (which I have compared to bricolage) is nothing less than an effort to free science from its alienation (*EaN*, 161). This appears to be what Dewey means when he speaks of "the instrumental objects of science" as being "completely themselves" only when they "direct the changes of nature" toward more fulfilling ends. Application, as direction toward more fulfilling ends, is not something extrinsic to nature but an ingredient within it; if we make this principle our own, we behave in conformity with nature and, in freeing ourselves, engage in freeing nature from its alienated status: "If we free ourselves from preconceptions, application of "science" means application *in*, not application *to*. Application *in* something signifies a more extensive interaction of natural events with one another, an elimination of distance and obstacles; provision of opportunities for interactions that reveal potentialities previously hidden and that bring into existence new histories with new initiations and new endings" (ibid., 162). "Application" in Dewey's sense is by no means strictly speaking "bricolage." It is far more wide-ranging, since application presumes the existence of modern science, of an alienated nature, and of a world rendered lifeless through its transformation into a physico-chemical model, whereas bricolage can be conceived apart from this context.[7] But application restores to science some of the aspects belonging to bricolage that have been prescinded from it as a result of its necessary but alienating extrusion of existential factors.[8] Similarly "application" acquires many of the meanings that Dewey attributes to tools: they may be the work of the bricoleur and are certainly found in both a pre- and postscientific world. Thus in attending to artifactual function, we may learn something of what is wanting in the concept of "application."

Tools and Signs

For Dewey, tools are a means of creating and stabilizing meanings. Abstract in function and concrete in their material existence, tools embody a certain ideality[9] in that they never exist for themselves alone but are always means for some absent end. Thus tools are related to that which does not yet exist; they necessarily carry a transcendent reference (*EaN*, 185). Tools testify to the ability to distinguish immediate existence from future efficacy. Things that merely *are* can become tools when their immediate properties can be usefully deployed. It is use that is discovered and constitutes the thread between the thing in its brute existence and its consequences. Were it not for the human ability to unite thing and effect and, what is especially significant, to recall the connection, the feeling of warmth would cease when the fire goes out, a stick revert to inert existence when it no longer serves as a lever (ibid., 186 ff.). For Dewey, the bits and pieces that become tools may not be the discards of an obvious antecedent use (like the cogwheels of Lévi-Strauss's bricoleur). Still, the *functions* of tools are historically funded; technological culture is cumulative. Dewey stresses improvisation; nevertheless, in the making of tools, tools function within a nexus of existing tools. Tools are not constructed of *objets trouvés*: the new tool may be more complex than its component elements, but these, too, have civilizational meaning, as well as multiple efficacies.

Since human beings are self-oriented, it is easy to interpret tools in a univocal fashion as extensions of the body. But this understanding is false. Since tools are relational, man is only one of the relata and the world the other. Thus, the hammer is not merely an extension of my hand but is related to the nail (ibid.). It is only by virtue of its objective connection that the hammer's utility to man is sustained. A tool is a transactional mediating factor establishing a bond between the aspect of nature that is human and the aspect that is world. (As such, it plays a role similar to the one I have attributed to "application" in the context of science: it is a necessary though not yet sufficient condition for the liberation from alienation.) Tools can play this mediating role because they function as signs. Like the elements collected by the bricoleur, tools represent a set of actual and possible relations and, like them, are "operators," useful for operations of the same type (*SM*, 18).

But signs are ultimately (if not directly) linguistic in character, and just this transposability from material existence to meaning enables tools or the elements of the bricoleur to take on linguistic function. It may be recalled that Lévi-Strauss is interested in bricolage largely for its utility in interpreting the mythological consciousness of nonliterate societies, rather than for its value in understanding the technologies of these groups. (In point of fact, myth, technology, institution, and rite are hardly separable.) Here, however, a caveat is in order. For Lévi-Strauss, what applies to bricolage applies, mutatis mutandis, to myth. But the shift from a material to a discursive formation is not innocuous.[10] The proposed homologies must be tested at every point. What is more, we may not apply what is predicated of myth in Lévi-Strauss mutatis mutandis to Dewey's view of tools, even if we may do so more freely with regard to bricolage *simpliciter*. The first difficulty arises because bricolage proceeds within the framework of immediacy, building up the artifactual product from elements at its disposal. But myth, partly because of its linguistic character, begins with a vision of the cosmos as a whole and derives secondary meaning structures deductively. Myth "attempts to reach by the shortest possible means a general understanding of the universe—and not only a general but a total understanding."[11] It does not work up its material in accordance with inductive constraints, nor does the concrete demand of physical material offer resistance to its requirements (as in the case of bricolage). Instead, myth creates a "block universe." This difference remains unacknowledged in Lévi-Strauss's attribution of homologous structure to myth and bricolage.

While Dewey rejects the totalizing aspects of mythical thought, still the concept of bricolage is useful in understanding the linguistic aspect of tools, once we bear the preceding strictures in mind. For Lévi-Strauss, bricolage itself is already linguistic, since it works by means of signs (*SM*, 20). Similarly, Dewey's tools "signify" and, being significative, have linguistic meaning; therefore, any useful attempt to gloss the meaning of tools must be able to account for this dimension. That the term *sign* is used almost univocally in Lévi-Strauss and in Dewey should become apparent from the remarks that follow.

For Lévi-Strauss, signs are mediating constructs that lie midway between images and concepts. They resemble images in their concreteness but are more like concepts in "their powers of reference. Neither concepts nor signs relate exclusively to themselves; either may be substituted for something else. Concepts, however, have an unlimited capacity in this respect, while signs have not" (ibid., 18).

It may be helpful to imagine the sign as an image in flight toward the concept, though, since the image remains the signifying element in signs, this flight is doomed to fall back upon itself. Images can exist alongside ideational factors and serve as placeholders for future ideational content, but the being of the sign depends upon the back-and-forth oscillation between them. Images are relatively static, while concepts are flexible and have theoretically unlimited relations with other entities of the same sort. Signs have the characteristics of both: they are "permutable," that is, they can enter into successive relations with other entities, but the number of such relations is limited (ibid., 20). These limitations of the sign are its strength, however. (In Dewey's terms, signs might be said to have "existential adhesions," while concepts are "abstractions.") Signs not only refer to the world but are enmeshed in it: "One way indeed in which signs can be opposed to concepts is that whereas concepts aim to be wholly transparent with respect to reality, signs allow and even require the interposing and incorporation of a certain amount of human culture into reality. Signs in Peirce's vigorous phrase 'address somebody.'" (ibid.). The idea that signs are social, that as Lévi-Strauss (citing Peirce) claims, "they 'address somebody,'" is also a central feature of Dewey's theory of signs.[12] For Dewey, all language is social:

sounds may be common to men and animals, but only in the context of social interaction can sound become language.[13] Animals may signal, but signaling acts are infralinguistic. Language is present only when the individual is able to envisage a situation of mutuality, one in which two individuals participate. The requisite for language is thus not its material medium or a merely mechanical response to signals but the ability to project into the standpoint of the other. "To understand," according to Dewey, "is to be able, to participate together. It is to make cross-reference, which, when acted upon, brings about a partaking in a common inclusive undertaking" (*EaN*, 178–79). The result is shared meaning, such that a common signification can be "read" from things. To mutually apprehend a thing is not to grasp its static essence but to understand it in terms of its consequences (ibid., 182). Dewey refers to the terminus of this process as a "percept," but Dewey's "percept" is not an image: it is closer to what Lévi-Strauss means by "signs." Midway between image and concept, it is secure, able to enter relations, but is limited by the concrete image that holds the ideational content together.

That the perceived is analogous to signs in Dewey's thinking can be brought to light by contrasting it with what is fully conceptual, the objects of science, spatiotemporal nodes that lend themselves to mathematical formulation. Such scientific objects can be controlled through a system of substitution, while percepts remain bound to qualitative determinations: "By means of [substitution], a thing which is within grasp is used to stand for another thing which is not immediately had, or which is beyond control. The technique of equations and other functions characteristic of modern science is, taken generically, a method of thoroughgoing substitutions. It is a system of exchange and mutual conversion carried to its limit" (ibid., 142). In effect, Dewey's text could serve to illustrate Lévi-Strauss's contention that concepts have unlimited relations with entities of the same sort.

We have seen that signs are different from concepts, but not yet how tools are different from scientific objects, which are expressed by concepts. Scientific thinking treats the individual thing as a composite of parts: "a large number of elementary independent variables, points, moments, numerical units, particles of mass and energy or more elementary space-times." If we try to convert these elements back into things, Dewey claims, we have not individuals but "instances, cases, specimens of some general relation or law" (ibid., 143). By contrast, tools, despite their instrumental function, remain linked to their thingly properties. This thingliness, which enables us to read their meanings from the face of their "imagy" qualities, is what facilitates their use as signs.[14]

Since the tool is a sign, it is possible to interpret the significance of tools in terms of the wide range of meanings we have ascribed to signs. The "imagy" aspect of signs belongs also to tools. At the same time, the tool finds its place in the human order as an ancillary of work: the tool has meaning in the context of transformations of existence that produce utility. Thus, it is instrumental without being only instrumental. Just as the sign fluctuates between image and percept, the tool lies on a gradient where one fixed pole is the aesthetic object, linked by its materiality to the image, and the other is the abstract object of science, divested of existential adhesions. This does not mean that the tool is a compromise between them, existing now as one, now as the other. On the contrary, to exist as a tool is to have a unique mode of being in which utility and aesthetic satisfaction oscillate so that either may predominate at any given moment. To speak of the tool as an aesthetic object does not mean that aesthetic quality only and necessarily derives from the tool's beauty: the aesthetic dimension *may* arise from the appearance of the tool, but it can also come from the satisfaction to be had in handling it, or the pleasure to be derived from its working well. The last enables Dewey to place the machine on a gradient with the tool, despite the machine's potentially alienated character.[15] Function also marks off the tool from ceremonial objects although the tool may be invested with ceremonial properties. Thus, for Dewey, "spears, snares, gins, traps, utensils, baskets and webs may have their potency enhanced by adherence to ceremonial design, but the design is never a complete substitute for conformity to the efficacious resistances and adaptations of natural materials."[16]

Art and "Savages"

I have considered tools in contrast to scientific objects as resembling in important respects works of bricolage. But I have also maintained that tools have aesthetic quality, that they are in some respects like works of art. If so, how is the artwork to be marked off from the tool? And is the idea of bricolage as pertinent to the understanding of artworks as it is to the understanding of tools? Lévi-Strauss's remarks on the origin of the work of art shed light on these questions since, for him, bricolage figures in the creation of the artwork. What is more, his understanding of aesthetic experience shows interesting convergences with Dewey's account.

Once Lévi-Strauss acknowledges that bricolage plays a role in fashioning the artwork, the function of bricolage must be seen in a new light, as extending beyond the production of assemblages and tools. Although Lévi-Strauss does not acknowledge this new function, it cannot be viewed as merely additive, for meanings that accrue to the artwork emanate from its character as expression and derive only incidentally from the material elements that enter into its formation. An alteration in its sphere of application must mark a change in meaning. Unlike the case of myth, with which bricolage is believed to be homologous, in art bricolage transcends its original role as a permutative rearrangement of elements and is implicated in the creation of new meaning. For Lévi-Strauss, the artwork does not come into being by means of pure bricolage but lies midway between bricolage and the scientific object. In pure bricolage, the elements are defined by two criteria: "They have had a use," that is, "they are not raw materials but wrought products," and "they can be used again"(*SM*, 35 ff.). But the artwork is a new creation.

If the created object, unlike a work of bricolage, is something new, it must be grasped in a unique act of access: we seize the aesthetic object as a whole in an unmediated apprehension of its qualitative existence. (We shall see that, for Dewey, aesthetic experience is similarly conceived.) What is more, for Lévi-Strauss the character of the artwork is determined by the requirement that it be apprehended as a totality. This is literally interpreted as a matter of scale: if we are to grasp it in its entirety and at once, the artwork must be a miniature. All works of art are small-scale models; reducing the size of objects produces a homologue for things on a scale suited to holistic apprehension. (Large-scale works are not, for Lévi-Strauss, counter-instances since, in nearly every case, they can be seen as reductions when compared to the conceptual "size" of their originals: the Sistine Chapel may be larger than life, but it is smaller than the Creation it depicts; ibid., 23.) Miniaturization also enables the perceiver to manipulate the object in imagination and so to participate in its recreation. The aesthetic object, perennially unfinished, awaits the work of the perceiver, who, like the creator, becomes, in part, a bricoleur.

This theory of the aesthetic object, in which bricolage plays a prominent part, may be said to hold, mutatis mutandis, for Dewey's interpretation of aesthetic experience in three respects:

1. The art object is given in an immediate and qualitative apprehension and is given as a whole. (Thus Dewey: "A work of art elicits and accentuates this quality of being a whole and of belonging to the larger, all-inclusive, whole which is the universe in which we live"; *AE*, 195)

2. Aesthetic experience is lived by the perceiver as well as by the creator in an active and participatory fashion, since the act of aesthetic apprehension is defined as an experiment with the possibilities of the artwork through imaginative reconstruction.

3. The material elements of the work, the "instrumental set," are not brute existents but replete with cumulative social meaning.

Dewey's emphasis on the first point—the qualitative aspect of experience—is central to his understanding of the artwork and requires explication. For Dewey, it may be remembered, the world in which we find ourselves is one of situations, of contextual wholes that reveal qualitative characteristics. It is "pervasive quality" that gives to any situation its unity. Experienced qualities are infinite in number; they may be pleasant or painful, red or sad, and so on. But when a situation presents ambiguity or doubt as its pervasive quality (and this not in any merely subjective sense but as belonging properly to the existential situation), thinking or the activity of inquiry is generated.[17] Yet when discord is the pervasive quality, the experienced disharmony may be resolved aesthetically rather than cognitively:

> The discord is the occasion that induces reflection. Desire for restoration of the union converts mere emotion into interest in objects as conditions of realization of harmony. With the realization, material of reflection is incorporated into objects as their meanings. Since the artist cares in a peculiar way for the phase of experience in which union is achieved, he does not shun moments of resistance and tension. [Rather he brings] to living consciousness an experience that is unified and total. (*AE*, 15)

It is in this context that the origin of the work of art is to be understood. For Dewey artworks are exemplary instances of qualitative thinking, since in the work of art a material medium is shaped to express a pervasive quality. And, since art is not segregated from life but is its most refined and intensive aspect, pervasive quality is generated as it is in life, in an interaction of the living creature with its environment.

Of course, the artist also lives in a world of cultural meaning and so seeks more than a simple redress for his biological discomforts. This cultural matrix is conceived in the form of a circle: the artwork must achieve harmonious reintegration of organism and environment in conformity with the social nature of human existence, which, in turn, is bound up with language; and language renders social existence possible. For Dewey, artworks (like tools) are linguistic objects irrespective of medium. Following Peirce, Dewey assumes that language, being social, has a triadic character: every utterance involves a speaker, a thing said, and one spoken to (ibid., 106). The artwork, being an instance of language, mediates between speaker and hearer, even if the artist alone plays the part of speaker and society. A further result of this interpretation of the character of language implicates the percipient as one of the relata. He or she is the "somebody" who is addressed: "For to perceive, a beholder must *create* his own experience. And his creation must include relations comparable to those which the original producer underwent. . . . There is work done on the part of the percipient as there is on the part of the artist" (ibid., 54). What is unique to Dewey's theory is not its linguistic character but the fact that aesthetic experience is not confined to the fine arts alone: "The material of esthetic experience in being human —human in connection with the nature of which it is a part—is social. Aesthetic experience is a manifestation, a record and celebration of the life of a civilization, a means of promoting its development, and is also the ultimate judgment upon the quality of a civilization" (ibid., 326). Every instance of "alert and active commerce with the world" is aesthetic in the broad sense. (Thus there is a mode of transaction common to art and tools.) Such experience involves a sense of heightened vitality as an immediacy of response to environmental challenge.

For Dewey, such initiative and resilience are expressed in the paradigm of the "savage," whose activity reflects animal vigor and creative intelligence. *Savage* is less a descriptive term than an intellectual construct, a homologue for a pretechnological situation, one in which cunning without cruelty, unconstrained bodily awareness without artificial distinction of sense and intellect, may be found.[18] While Dewey suggests that much of the life of the "savage" is "sodden," still:

When the savage is most alive he is most observant of the world around him and most taut with energy. As he watches what is stirred around him, he, too, is stirred. His observation is both action and preparation and foresight of the future. He is active in his whole being when he looks and listens as when he steals his quarry or stealthily retreats from a foe. His senses are sentinels of immediate thought and outposts of action, and not, as they so often are with us, mere pathways along which material is gathered to be stored away for a delayed and remote possibility. (Ibid., 19)

Dewey draws frequently on the "savage's" intercourse with tools to illustrate productive encounters with the environment that break the pattern of dissociation characteristic of modern life and return technology to the qualitative existence from which it springs. What is more, a crucial turning point in Dewey's theory of meaning as it develops in *Experience and Nature* is derived from a context of cultural anthropology: Malinowski's discussion of meaning as it functions in nonliterate societies. In this sense, "savage" speech becomes the model for Dewey's own pragmatic theory of meaning. According to Malinowski, for the "native" the meaning of a word lies in the use of the object for which it stands, just as a tool means something in use but has no meaning unless it can be handled (*EaN*, 205 ff.). Language is in the service of activity.

For Lévi-Strauss, functional anthropology cannot account for culture (and thus a fortiori for language), since functional anthropology interprets culture as a response to basic need.[19] Thus the significance of cognitive categories (which for Lévi-Strauss is the consequence of a predisposition of brain structure to develop particular thought categories in prescribed ways) is missed in a functional interpretation.[20] Lévi-Strauss's "savage" bears no resemblance either "to the creature barely emerged from an animal condition and still a prey to his needs and instincts who has so often been imagined nor to that consciousness governed by emotions and lost in a maze of confusion and participations."[21] Apart from the issue of functionalism, the problem of "savages" occupies a special place in the work of Lévi-Strauss and, in its wider ramifications, falls outside the scope of this paper. I shall therefore confine myself to some remarks pertinent to the relation of "savages" to bricolage. One purpose of the study of "savages" in Lévi-Strauss is to:

Construct a theoretical model of a society which corresponds to none that can be observed in reality but will help us to disentangle [citing Rousseau] "what in the present nature of Man is original and what is artificial." It also helps us [citing Rousseau] "to know closely a state which no longer exists, which may never have existed, which probably never will exist and of which we must, nonetheless have an exact notion if we are to judge our present situation correctly."[22]

For Lévi-Strauss, mankind ought to have kept to a "middle ground," that "original" condition somewhere "between the indolence of the primitive state and the questing activity to which we are prompted by our *amour propre*," as Rousseau suggested.[23] If Western civilization had not taken a turn toward mechanization, the level of technological culture it had achieved, Rousseau's "middle ground," would have accorded with human needs, since that state was in no way primitive. In fact, it "presupposes and tolerates a certain degree of progress . . . even if 'the example of the savages . . . found at this point of development, seems to confirm that mankind was designed to remain at it forever.' "[24]

While Dewey does not envision any such "middle state" as a lost Eden, he imagines a nexus of tools "transacting" our business with the world as potentially altering an otherwise mechanized civilization. Once tools become a problem to be thematized, we can at least envision this possibility. What has been discovered in tools is a mode of access to the "imagy" in experience that appears and is prevented from vanishing through its incorporation into artifactual relation and, by extension, into myth (Lévi-Strauss) and art (Lévi-Strauss and Dewey). For Dewey, tools are the concrete means through which a natural bond to the future is brought into being. In fact, Dewey's encounter with tools constitutes an artifactual mediation between image and concept, nature and culture, structure and event. In having brought tools into reflective awareness as a unique mode of relation, Dewey may well have been the first to take notice of the manner in which knowing proceeds when mediated by tools. A "science of the concrete" has taken shape in Dewey's work and bears many features attributed to bricolage.

30

The Mathematical Model in Plato and Some Surrogates in a Jain Theory of Knowledge

One of the generative questions in Benjamin Nelson's late work was: What accounts for the breakthrough insights that permit the reduction of all quality to quantity, the proclaiming of a mathematical reality behind the experiential immediacies of experience and the affirmation of a homogeneous time and space throughout the universe, insights that characterize Western science? It is a question that exercise both Nelson and Joseph Needham; both consider it from an intercivilizational perspective. To put the matter in Needham's terms: "What was it that happened in Renaissance Europe when mathematics and science joined in a combination qualitatively new and destined to transform the world?"[1]

Nelson first answers these questions by examining Western orientations and institutions of the twelfth and thirteenth centuries. He shows that in a "sacro-magical if sacramentalized" reading of creator and cosmos "there appears a stress upon the need and ability of men to know and explain natural phenomena by the principles of natural philosophy; to offer rational justification of their acts and opinions."[2] In the same context, Nelson speaks of a two-fold commitment to the "concrete individual person" and to an "objective Universal." Armed with Nelson's questions (the subject of fruitful conversations long before the appearance of the article cited) I pondered the issues of whether these factors, already nascent in the epistemic structure of Plato's dialogues concerned with the Ideas, could not be displayed against an Indian system remarkably similar in hierarchical structure and philosophic intent. Only in the light of these similarities, I thought, would the key difference—the existence of an "objective Universal" in one and not the other—emerge.

The same aim governs both Platonic and Jain epistemologies: the overcoming of sense experience in order to attain a more adequate access to truth. But in the former structures of universalization—the ideas of number and geometric form—lead to this overcoming, while in the latter certain ad hoc extensions of sense are made to play this part. I shall not attempt to ground larger claims, such as the existence of an ongoing tradition unbroken from Plato to the twelfth century. Nelson would be the first to puncture so ominously unhistorical a claim. I attempt, rather, to bring out the difference between a system that engages the constructs of a contemporary mathematics and eventuates in an *objective* Universal and one that fails to do so.

Both Plato and a Jain text, *The Tathvārthādhigama Sūtra* of Śri Umāsvāti, with the commentary of Śri Pujyapada,[3] argue that the knowledge of sensibles is merely preliminary to higher forms of knowing and that these in turn culminate in a highest or ultimate form of knowledge. Furthermore, both Jain and Platonic systems concur in claiming necessity, apodicticity, and comprehensiveness or totalizing power for such knowledge. In the light of these common considerations, I argue here that a difference in what are considered possible objects of knowledge by each system accounts for the positing of differently conceived faculties of knowledge. I argue, further, that the faculties alleged to attain higher knowledge in Jain epistemology are compatible with the Jain understanding of the objects of knowledge. Thus, an internally consistent account of knowing is provided in a scheme that (1) assumes the actuality of the material world, but (2) presupposes that knowledge of the world in some sense falls short of ultimate truth, and (3) lacks mathematical paradigms for providing a means of transition between the world of ordinary experience and that of final knowledge.

In order to support these claims, it is important to clarify in advance how the possible objects of knowledge are understood in each system and how the transition from lower to higher knowledge is effected. In the Platonic account, the move from lower to higher epistemological levels is achieved by conferring a unique status upon a class of objects, number and figure, which facilitates a transition between apprehension of the empirical world and the world of Ideas. When applied to practical ends, these objects are still encumbered by visible images, but when divested of their concrete applications, they are themselves Ideas. The assumptions of arithmetic and geometry do not themselves constitute the ultimate ground of certainty, for mathematical hypotheses, which may appear certain to the mathematical sciences, must be subjected to philosophical analysis. Ultimate knowledge involves the systematic relationship and harmony of the world of Forms in their hierarchical nature and as they control the world of experience. Mathematical knowledge is seen both as the model for and the prolegomenon to this ultimate vision.

The *Tattvārthādhigama Sūtra* shares at least this basic assumption with the Platonic view: namely, that there is a duplicity in Being, which generates the appearance of things as multiple and temporal. Multiplicity and temporality themselves, however, are not interpreted as giving rise to the notion of objects as numerable, to the operation of counting as such, leading in turn to a conception of number that can be freed from its empirical context.[4] In consequence, the transcendence of the spatiotemporal order must be achieved in an attempt to acquire transcendent knowledge without recourse to elements and relations other than those immediately given, those the spatiotemporal continuum itself directly presents. The conditions for transcending the spatiotemporal world are seen as lodged within the perimeter of the world. Jain ontology presupposes the materiality of the world (including not only matter but time, space, and motion among its elements).[5] No tertiary class of entities, that is, entities that are neither material (in the broad sense suggested) nor spiritual, is predicated. Thus no object comparable to number and figure, incorporating both the permanence and stability of the ideal realm and the multiplicity of the sensible realm, is introduced. Only the world itself can be predicated as the object of knowing, through which access to higher forms of knowledge can be acquired.

One further point remains to be clarified before pressing the claim that, despite their common supposition that knowledge of sensibles is preliminary to higher knowledge, the ontological status and character ascribed to the objects of knowledge in each system will determine the ground and structure of the faculties needed for the apprehension of these objects. This point relates to the Jain understanding of the ontology of sensibles. In the context of ordinary experience, physical objects are so arranged that they appear to be governed by inviolable rules, such as the rule that it is impossible for an observer to both be and not be in the same place at a given instant.

The Jain system supposes that the laws governing temporal sequentiality and spatial contiguity are viable within the context of ordinary experience, but *relevant only to it*. It presupposes no immutable laws of nature that would militate against the disruption of the perceived order of the world, such as are assumed by Platonic or Aristotelean metaphysics. The spatiotemporal order of nature is seen as applicable within the parameters set by sense experience but is nowhere interpreted as having eternal and necessary status.[6]

Since, as we have already seen, no entities comparable to mathematical objects are posited, the world of sensibles remains the only object of knowledge. Thus, a faculty that could provide the transition from lower to higher knowledge must have the world (of objects, persons, etc.) as its only cognitive sphere. Furthermore, that faculty need not be governed by the laws that sense perception leads one to believe are inherent in the nature of things. Having laid down these premises, it becomes possible to posit "supernormal" powers (clairvoyance and telepathy) as faculties that can mediate the transition from sense perception to the final phase of knowledge, omniscience.[7] These powers function as epistemological alternatives to the mathematical model in Plato's account of knowing in the sense of providing a link between graded levels of knowledge. But rather than multiplying entities (as the ontological status conferred upon Mathematical Ideas compels us to do) the Jain model assumes the permeability of the physical and mental (a quasi-physical concept)[8] worlds to Spirit so that the occult powers predicated enable the adept to penetrate the physical order.

The epistemological course chosen by Plato is to posit objects that are neither entities found in the world nor mental "objects" corresponding to them. Thus existents need not be "penetrated" or rearranged. Plato's account of knowledge seeks to resolve the perplexity arising from "the sea of change" by diverting attention from the world of *aisthesis*, that is, from "the world of sensations and judgments in accordance with them."[9] Arithmetic, being the science of number, has this salutary effect, for its objects lack specific referents: "Arithmetic has a very great and elevating effect, compelling the soul to reason about abstract number, and rebelling against the introduction of visible or tangible objects into the argument."[10] Geometry, while making use of visible forms and reasoning about them, is not thinking about these "but of the ideals which they resemble, not of" the figure geometers draw but of the absolute square and the absolute diameter.[11] The positing of mathematical objects makes it possible for the mind, rather than the eye, to become the percipient.

For *The Tathvārthādhigama Sūtra* and its commentator, the soul's percipience depends not upon the ontological status of the object beheld but upon the elimination of karmic accumulation from the soul. Karma is specific to the various modes of cognition. Thus, to attain supernormal powers the karma appropriate to preceding modes of cognition, in addition to the karma obscuring the power that the knower wishes to achieve, must be eliminated in order to "cut through" the world of perception.[12] Compare Socrates' view of the soul's function:

> But in my opinion, that knowledge only which is of being and of the unseen can make the world look upwards, and whether a man gapes at the heavens or blinks on the ground, seeking to learn some particular of sense, I would deny that he can learn, for nothing of that sort is a matter of science; his soul is looking downwards and not upwards whether his way to knowledge is by water or by land, whether he floats or only lies on his back.[13]

with that of Śri Pujyapada:

> The disciple asks the saint with reverence, "O master, what is good for the soul?" The Saint says, "Liberation." He again asks the saint, "What is the nature of this liberation, and what is the way to attain it?" The saint answers, "Liberation is the attainment of an altogether different state of the soul, on the removal of all the impurities of karmic matter, and the body, characterized by all the inherent qualities of the soul such as knowledge and bliss free from pain and suffering."[14]

It is instructive from the standpoint of our argument (that objects of knowledge determine the character of the faculty that apprehends them) to notice the end or goal toward which knowledge in each case tends. For Plato, the object of genuine knowledge is being and the unseen, for which Mathematical Ideas provide the model. For Jain epistemology the end of knowledge is freedom from attachment to the body and liberation from the variety of standpoints according to which a thing may be viewed. A fundamental doctrine of the Jain system holds that, since contradictory attributes may be predicated of a thing, no affirmation can be regarded as absolutely true or false, the truth or falsity of an affirmation depending upon the standpoint from which the affirmation is made. The liberated soul transcends the relativity of viewpoint provided by modes of knowledge less encompassing than total omniscience.[15] The motive that engenders the quest for knowledge is the desire for release, for the avoidance of pain, for infinite perception, that is, for the knowledge of substance without reference to its shifting conditions or modes.

The notion of standpoints that govern the apprehension of truth at any given level of knowledge is foreign to Plato's conception of truth, since it is precisely the independence of mathematical truths from the standpoint of the thinker and from the conditions of contingency inhering in the sensible world that confers certainty upon the objects of mathematics. While mathematics may be said to "liberate" from the world of sensible objects, the knowledge to which it provides a link is not that of undifferentiated oneness but rather the hierarchically organized world of Forms governing the realm of experience.[16] The role of the Ideas is crucial in this connection, for it is through the Ideas that the many particulars are integrated into a totalizing scheme: the many sensibles may be united through participation in a single Idea. While this doctrine is governed by the notion of "one over many," as Aristotle alleges, it need not be interpreted as presupposing that Plato understands the Ideas in a univocal sense. In fact, a number of interpretations is proferred, each of which can still be subsumed under the conception "one over many." Plato means to include as Ideas: ethical and aesthetic notions such as those of the Good, of Justice, and of Beauty; Ideas of metaphysical notions such as the One and the Many, or Being and Non-Being; Mathematical Ideas such as those of the geometer (the circle, the diameter, etc.) and of the arithmetician (numbers such as two, three, etc.); Ideas of natural kinds such as man or stone; Ideas for kinds of manufactured objects (tables, chairs, beds etc.).[17] In each of these instances, Plato is guided by the notion that many particulars participate in a single Idea.

In Jain epistemology there are no such organizing archetypes enabling the lower to be taken up into the higher through participation (since the lower derives its being from the higher). While Jain epistemology recognizes a number of cognitive modes—sense perception, scriptural knowledge, clairvoyance, and telepathy[18]—no object of these modes serves simultaneously as an object of knowledge and an organizing principle for objects of an ontologically lower level. The indicator for epistemological difference is karma, since each cognitive mode is obscured by its own karmic variant.

Higher forms of cognition presuppose the destruction of karma, so that the knowledge conferred by the higher faculties manifests itself upon the ground of the soul. Such knowledge is termed "direct" (without the intermediation of the sense organs) and eliminates the temporal and spatial sequentiality characteristic of indirect cognitive modes. Direct knowledge is seen to be independent of what we might term "incoming data." The data given to the higher faculties are not different in kind from those of sense experience and its derivatives: rather, they are perceived without relation to events contiguous to the observer and organized without reference to the modes of organizing data characteristic of ordinary experience. It is thus not the character of the data which changes but rather their principles of organization.

It would seem that *the adept* apprehends data in their plenary presence, though *we* take it that two independent series of data are juxtaposed, so that two discrete series are experienced as a single event. Thus event *A* (let us say the death of a man in Bengal) belongs to a series of events (viewed spatially) that are accessible only to those in his immediate vicinity in Bengal. A quite different series of events is accessible to observer *A'* in Gujarat. Two series of events normally unconnected by relations of proximity are now linked through the interest of observer *A'* in the death of the man in Bengal. Clairvoyance enables the adept to implement his "interest" by bringing into contiguity in the mind of a single observer two disparate series. The observer is able to transcend the normal relations of temporal and spatial sequentiality through the development of a power that no longer requires the presence of physical objects in order for perception of these objects to take place.

An analogous case is made for telepathy: one grasps what another is thinking without reference to spoken utterance. While the theoretical suppositions underlying the relations of language to thought are not stated in *The Tathvarthādhigama Sūtra* or in the commentary, it would appear that thinking is an infra-auditory linguistic process, a form of speaking that can be understood by one who possesses the appropriate faculty.

It is instructive to notice how the sūtra regards specific types of clairvoyance and telepathy. Two modes of clairvoyance are posited, one based on birth, the other depending upon merit and produced by the tranquillization and annihilation of karmic matter.[19] There are also two varieties of telepathy: one "straight," the other "curved" or winding. "Straight" telepathy enables the adept to acquire knowledge of "speech, body, and mind" when these are objects in the mind of another. "Curved" telepathy need not have recourse to objects; it attains access to past and future. The temporal extensiveness of the two differs in that the former is alleged to cover only several births; its spatial range is thought to extend from two to eight miles but not beyond. The latter is said to cover from seven to eight births in the past and future of oneself and others and is said to range spatially from eight miles "up to the entire abode of human beings."[20]

The doctrine underlying these examples, namely, that preceding existences can be recalled, ought not to be confused with the Platonic doctrine of recollection. In the *Meno* we notice that recollection is of principles, their application being a matter of deductive inference. Thus, knowledge of the nature of squares and triangles enables one to deduce the relationship between the area of a square and the length of its sides and then to recognize that if one wishes to construct a square whose area will be twice the length of its sides one cannot do so by doubling the length of the sides.[21] For Plato, knowledge derived from recollection yields not information about sense experiences but knowledge of general principles.

Moreover, the primary purpose in introducing the recollection theory, as the *Phaedo* clearly establishes, is to demonstrate the pre-existence of the soul. In the *Phaedo*, Plato presumes archetypal forms and copies that resemble them. An ideal standard must be known before a judgment can be made about sense particulars; all sensible things aim at this standard but fall short of it;[22] and, furthermore, we "acquire this knowledge before we were born, and were born having the use of it." The position is summarized thus:

> Then may we not say . . . that . . . there is an absolute beauty, and goodness, and an absolute essence of all things; and if this which is now discovered to have existed in our former state, we refer all our sensation, and with this compare them finding these ideas to be pre-existent and our inborn possessions—then our soul must have had a prior existence, but if not, there would be no force in the argument.[23]

It is only in the *Republic* that mathematical knowledge provides the same function as clairvoyance and telepathy in the Jain system, since it is here that mathematical knowledge is seen as the stepping stone between the world of appearances and that of intelligible forms. Here a new view of knowledge is put forward, which assumes the central-ity of dialectic, a method of philosophical analysis conducted without reliance upon the data of sense perception and credited with being able to arrive at unquestioned first principles. In the simile of the line, Plato divides the intelligible world into two regions: that of mathe-matics and that of dialectic, each characterized by methodological differences in the attainment of its conclusions. The former may still use visible representations of its constructs, while the latter is occu-pied with purely intelligible forms.[24] Furthermore, both begin from hypotheses, the mathematician treating them as if they were first principles and arriving at conclusions without questioning initial as-sumptions, the dialectician treating hypotheses as hypotheses and nothing more. Dialectic recognizes the tentative character of hypoth-eses and uses them only to arrive at first principles. It is then possible to retrace the steps involved in reverse order and thus, descending, to arrive at conclusions that are solidly founded.[25] Accordingly, the verification of the principles of arithmetic and geometry is not a mat-ter of probable induction starting from particular facts of sense expe-rience but is obtained by logical deduction from self-evident first principles.

The Jain logician also recognizes deduction as a legitimate mode of inference. Thus (to cite a common example) observing smoke on the hill, and knowing the invariable concomitance of smoke and fire, we are led to conclude that there is fire on the hill. But the Jain logi-cian argues that the premises themselves are based on sense experi-ence and therefore deductive inference counts as sense knowledge. The same karma that obstructs sense experience is also alleged to obstruct correct inference. Such knowledge is, in fact, classified as "indirect," in contradistinction to clairvoyance and telepathy. Jain epistemology stresses that "sensory cognition, remembrance, recog-nition, induction and deduction are synonyms,"[26] since the karma ob-structing each is of the same type. In this sense, the Jain view is close to that of simple empiricism in maintaining that (short of omni-science) knowledge is based upon the percepts and their relations.

Despite its inner coherence, a scheme that depends upon the viola-tion of basic physical principles has obvious difficulties. The Jain system manages to maintain a certain economy, however, by avoid-ing the multiplication of entities qualitatively different from those found in the world of appearances.[27] In the Platonic scheme, not only are ideal entities, such as the Mathematical Ideas, posited, but, to make sense of these, other additional entities are required. Aristotle argues that Plato considered it necessary to furnish ideal perfect instances of the Mathematical Ideas and so posited the existence of intermediate ideal objects, Mathematical Numbers, involving the existence of identical units that are multiple like sense particulars but share the mode of being of eidetic entities.[28] Mathematical Numbers thus removed some difficulties in the understanding of mathematical operations engendered by the view that Mathematical Ideas are themselves unique and nonassociable through arithmetic processes such as addition. Aristotle summarizes the case thus: "Some (Plato) say both kinds of numbers exist, that which has a before and after being identical with Ideas and Mathematical Numbers being different from the Ideas and sensible things."[29] Aristotle characterizes the Mathematical Numbers as being made up of ideal units or ones, each of which is identical with every other. "Mathematical Number is counted thus—after 1, 2 (which consists of another 1 besides the former 1), and 3 (which consists of another 1 besides those two), and the other numbers similarly." Comparable geometrical entities are also presumed to have been posited by Plato.[30]

This view of arithmetic structure permits solution of what has been called the "ontological methexis" problem, that is, the question of how each object remaining solidary (monadic) can combine with other objects into groups or assemblages. The solution is suggested by the nature of Ideal and Mathematical Numbers. Existing objects can participate in a genus since the genus exhibits the mode of being of *arithmos*, that is, it exhibits the mode of being of each ideal number, yet its members, like the homogeneous monads in the realm of Mathematical Number (which are themselves outside change and time) can nevertheless be arranged into definite numbers.[31] It is clear that, for Plato, the sense world is transcended by organizing the multiplicity of sensibles into more comprehensive assemblages and by using the objects of arithmetic and geometry to provide a model for the world of Forms. The Jain scheme depends on no such model, for it assumes that, while knowledge of sensibles can become increasingly comprehensive, no objects or relations in that world, and no faculty commensurate with it, however complex, can serve as a paradigm for ultimate knowledge. For Jain epistemology, no mode of cognition will satisfy apart from total omniscience.

31

Soft Nominalism in Quine and the School of Dignāga

Nominalists argue that everything that is must be particular. D. M. Armstrong contends, "Nominalists deny that there is any objective identity in things which are not identical. Realists, on the other hand, hold that the apparent situation is the real situation. There genuinely is, or can be, something identical. Besides particulars there are universals."[1] Quine appreciates the difficulties of this position. Because the "quixotic" nominalist "foreswears quantification over universals, for example, classes, altogether," Quine prefers "conceptualism," a position that acknowledges that there are universals but holds them to be "manmade." "Tactically conceptualism is . . . the strongest position . . . for the tired nominalist can lapse into conceptualism, and still allay his puritanic conscience with the reflection that he has not quite taken to eating lotus with the Platonists."[2] In what follows I shall take Quine to be a tired nominalist.

A school of Yogācāra Buddhist logicians, whose leading figures include Dignāga, Dharmakīrti, and Dharmottara, in works dating from A.D. 450 and after,[3] offers a criticism of universals and an account of particulars that, in a number of significant respects, conforms to Quine's description of "tired" nominalism. Affinities with Quine's work are all the more striking in light of the contrasting frameworks of traditional Indian philosophies, on the one hand, and the theoretical structures of modern science and the logic of quantification that are the underpinning of Quine's analyses, on the other.

Although Quine, more than most recent philosophers, makes use of the link between quantification and existence to develop the implications of ontological claims while the Yogācārins lack the technical resources of predicate calculus, the relations between Buddhist nominalism and Quine's version should not be overlooked. Instead, analysis should focus on Quine's account of sense data, ostension, identity, and hypostasis.[4] I shall consider six distinct but interrelated theses of the Yogācāra logicians that, taken together, describe what there is. If allowances are made for methodological differences, each of these ontological commitments can, when explicated, be viewed as theses to which Quine subscribes entirely or in important respects. The theses are:

1. Point-instants are what there is, and these are inscrutable. Each point-instant is unique, shared by nothing else. It is qualityless, timeless, and indivisible. Point-instants have efficacy, but cognitive acts cannot directly represent them.

2. Percepts, like concepts, are constructs. A moment of pure sensibility signals the presence of objects, but memory and productive imagination build up the percept. Percepts are artificial cuts uniting segments of an uninterrupted flow of sensations.

3. Because knowledge does not directly mirror primordial particulars, the test of valid knowledge is pragmatic rather than the correctness of representation. Knowing an object "secures" it so that it can become the aim of successful human action.

4. Inference, an indirect means of grasping objects, can, along with sense perception, yield genuine knowledge. Like perception, inference delivers the object so that it can become the aim of successful action. By means of inference, absent objects are indirectly cognized through marks or signs. Apprehending an object by means of its mark widens the process of generalization already present *in nuce* in perception because we are forced to imagine an absent object as an object-in-general.

5. Because names cannot directly mirror the point-instants, they cannot affirm anything. Instead, names signify through a system of intralinguistic exclusions that depends upon the fabric of language. Cognitive acts create the illusion that percepts and names reflect ontic entities when in fact spontaneous mental acts forge identity by suppressing several types of difference, including the difference between point-instant and brute sensation, between brute sensations

and the perception of common objects, among percepts that are repeated, and between percept and linguistic expression. The suppression of difference occurs spontaneously at the more primordial levels of cognition, but conscious choice comes into play at more complex cognitive stages. Realists fail to grasp the makeshift character of general terms, a character that results from the origin of such terms in the obliterating of differences. The failure to perceive that identity is imputed across a chain of differences encourages treating terms designating attributes as if they were referring terms.

Particulars, Point-instants, and Sense Impressions

The Buddhist logicians' discussion of what there is centers on the relation between ontic simples and the possibility of knowing them. Because what is posited as ontologically ultimate is not the object experienced in sensation, Buddhist efforts are directed toward showing how trustworthy knowledge can be secured despite the inaccessibility of ontic simples. What there is, is the unique single moment, without extension or temporal duration: "The particular means an entity or an essence which is unique, which is shared by nothing else."[5] Although point-instants are inscrutable, they signal their presence by triggering momentary sensations. In fact, "the essence of reality is just efficiency . . . the capacity to produce something . . . a force."[6] The test for correctly applying the term *real* is: "Does the object so described produce an effect?" Because effects are not mirror images of point-instants, clarifying their relation is a matter of considerable importance in justifying the point-instant doctrine's plausibility.

Just as the sense data, the first effect of point-instants, do not reflect them directly, common objects of experience do not represent sense data. The next step is to construct something distinctly conceived, "a compact chain of moments cognized in a construction" and realized in perception as a "definite cognition."[7] The Buddhist analysis warns against construing sensation in terms of some given sense datum ranging over specifiable point-instants. Similarly, no cluster of definite sensations makes up the specified range of a definite cognition. This supports a claim I consider in detail later, that, far from reflecting the naive term-by-term empiricism Quine criticizes, this analysis of sensation approximates Quine's own view of the matter.[8]

An exact connection between point-instants and sensations cannot be posited because of the inscrutability of point-instants. Buddhist doctrine holds that point-instants *cause* sensations, but a cause is not the influence of one fact upon another. Rather, *cause* is a term that designates the co-presence of two facts, followed by another fact referred to as their result. The Yogācārins take this Hume-like doctrine of causes to hold *ceteris paribus* for sensation: "Because the object and the sensation produced by it are together producing (i.e. are only followed by) one mental sensation, there is no mutual real influence between them."[9]

In the Buddhist account of sensation described thus far, it could be argued that having a sensation is prima facie evidence only for the felt impression itself, because we can never be sure that point instants cause any *given* sensation. How can we know, for example, that a sensation is not caused by an imaginary object? The Buddhists contend that we can detect genuine occurrences of object-determined sensations by the variability of the sensation, its vividness or dimness depending on the proximity of the object. While no measure of the force of the ultimate *ens* is possible, there is a rule of thumb for detecting the presence of ontic simples as against imaginary objects: "When an object of cognition produces a vivid flash of consciousness, if it is near, and a dim one if it is far, although remote but still amenable to the sense, it is a particular."[10]

Brute sensibility manifested as vivid or dim is purely receptive. There are as yet no distinct percepts. Just as point-instants prompt sensations, sensations are "the immediately preceding homogeneous cause" of percepts.[11] The constructed image is linked to the sensed object through a process of coordination: "When . . . a cognition has sprung from an object, this . . . means that this cognition is coordinated to the momentary object, as, e.g., the cognition produced by this patch of blue color is *coordinated* to this blue."[12] The act of coordination is not different from the cognitive result: mental content and mental act, process and product, are distinguishable analytically but not in fact. The moment of brute sensibility and that of the definite percept are neither qualitatively nor temporally distinct.[13]

There is still something woolly about the preceding account in that exactly how coordination pinpoints the blue patch is not explained. Pinpointing cannot be analogous to attaining higher resolution in a photograph because metaphors of this type introduce the rejected representation theory of perception. A strategy for resolving this difficulty is to claim that, in addition to coordination, the object must be rendered definite through contrast with correlative images.[14] When we become aware of the object's likeness to other blue things and its dissimilarity to nonblue things, the percept is established as this blue patch. In forming a determinate percept, the perceptual field as a whole is called into play.

Before turning to Quine's description of perception, it is important to dispose of a notion Quine rejects, Carnap's account of the relation of the physical world to sense data. Carnap's view is nearly identical to one repudiated by the Buddhists but, if carelessly interpreted, might actually be confused with it. Quine recounts that Carnap "explained spatio-temporal point instants as quadruples of real numbers and envisaged assignment of sense qualities to point-instants according to certain canons."[15] Carnap (pace Quine) went on to say: "Quality q is at point-instant 'x; y; z; t.' He assigned truth values to these, which were to be modified with the growth of experience."[16] But Quine finds hopeless efforts to translate statements of this form into the language either of logic or of sense data. By denying that sense data are reflections of point-instants, the Buddhists can be seen to be endorsing Quine's rejection of the view implicit in the verification theory of meaning: "To each statement there is associated a unique range of possible sensory events such that the occurrence of any of them would add to the likelihood of the truth of the statement, and . . . another unique range of possible sensory events whose occurrence would detract from that likelihood."[17]

Although Quine repudiates Carnap's point-instant theory, he does not reject the notion of stimulus meaning *tout court*. One account of stimulus meaning important for the present comparison occurs in the context of criticizing mental entities without sacrificing the function of sense data or of being conscious. Sensing, Quine argues, is tied to receiving stimuli, and these are differently apprehended by different persons experiencing a single event. Consider cutting one's finger. The cut finger cues one's own nervous responses and those of other persons differently. Nerves from one's own afflicted finger and from one's own eyes, as well as nerves from the eyes of others, are all involved, but one is closer to one's own cut finger than are those who merely see it.[18] Once we reject mental entities, there are only the events of the physical world: the cut finger, the neural responses, the varying degree of proximity of stimulus to the organism. "There ceases to be an iron curtain between the private and the public; there remains only a smoke screen, a matter of varying degrees of privacy of events in the physical world."[19]

Quine's view stresses that stimulus meaning is contingent on proximity to the prompting events. For the most part, the more intense the stimulus, the more likely it is to be one's own. Earlier we saw that, for the Buddhist, shifts in vividness of impression depend on localization and enable us to distinguish real from imaginary objects. Quine's account can be read as a special application of this view: the vividness/dimness doctrine is used (in cases like pain) to tell to which organism, mine or another's, sensation belongs without introducing mental entities.

Quine and the Buddhists agree that, in Quine's terms, sense data "stand in the closest possible correspondence to the experimental measurable conditions of physical stimulation of the end organs."[20] Sense data include "variformed and varicolored visual patches, vari-textured, varitemperatured tactual feels, and an assortment of tones, tastes and smells" that we are trained to associate with physicalist language.[21] This agreement should not obscure the fact that for Quine the term *sense data* is theory-laden, the result of a developing empirical psychology,[22] while for the Buddhists sense data is a first-order term descriptive of instances of sensation. For them, sense data *are* mental occurrences, while Quine thinks sense data, physical particles, and commonsense objects enter an inclusive and evolving conceptual scheme, that of natural science. Making allowances for this difference in framework, the Buddhists concur with Quine's claim that all three work together in constituting the conceptual design of experience. For Quine, each is fundamental in a different respect:

> Sense data are *evidentally* fundamental: every man is beholden to his senses for every hint of bodies. The physical particles are *naturally* fundamental . . . : laws of behavior of those particles afford . . . the simplest formulation of a general theory of what happens. Common sense bodies are *conceptually* fundamental: it is by reference to them that the very notions of reality and evidence are acquired, and that the concepts which have to do with physical particles or even with sense data tend to be framed or phrased.[23]

Quine's scheme accounts for how knowledge is built up, but offers no criterion for determining its reliability generally. The Yogācārins, like Quine, seek a test for the trustworthiness of knowledge. For the Buddhists, the criterion is pragmatic: knowledge is credible if it can be followed by successful action. Right knowledge directs our attention to objects such that one can tell that the object is reached when it can become the aim of a possible purposive action. Knowledge of objects does not compel action but is its necessary precondition. Because sentient beings are by nature likely to pursue what they desire, activity is intrinsic to their behavior, and the knowledge they will want is naturally geared to activity.[24] Quine believes the whole of antecedent knowledge to be the tacit backdrop for determining further knowledge and belief. This is his celebrated holism: "Our knowledge is a man-made fabric which impinges on experience only along the edges." Or, to change the figure: "Total science is like a field of force whose boundary conditions are experience. A conflict with experience at the periphery occasions readjustments in the interior of the field."[25] Quine denies that this view commits him to beliefs about truth held by card-carrying pragmatists. To William James's view that the test of what a truth means is both the conduct it inspires and what it predicts about our experience that moves us to such conduct, Quine says, in effect: we ought to welcome the prediction and let the conduct go.[26] In short, when the Buddhists *distinguish* between knowledge and purposive action, their account of pragmatism accords with Quine's, but the Buddhist stress on successful action as the *criterion* for knowledge constitutes a decisive difference.

Universals

Both Quine and the Buddhists hold that the claim "There are attributes," abstract entities that correspond to general names, is false. Their analyses fall into two parts: first, an account of why the assertion is false; and second, if false, why realists believe it to be true. In dealing with the falsity of the realist's claim, they consider broad epistemological and logical issues, while in taking account of the realist's reasons for supporting the claim, they turn to psychological questions about the origin of universals.

There is a remarkable convergence in the descriptions of the rejected realist theory and why it is false. Quine rejects the view that because things have something in common the property they share is a real attribute: "The words 'houses,' 'roses,' and 'sunsets' are true of sundry individual entities which are houses and roses and sunsets, . . . but there is not, in addition, any entity whatever, individual or otherwise, which is named by the word 'redness.' "[27]

Jinendrabuddhi's commentary claims: "[A] (single representation contrives) in some way to represent . . . (a series of things) having different forms, as though they were non-different. . . . The difference of individual form [is effaced] and replace[d] by one general form. [This general form] is projected and dispersed in the external world as if (it were so many real objects)."[28] Despite the psychological thrust of the Yogācāra analysis, Quine and the Yogācārins agree that some terms have a spread that ranges over many individuals. But it does not follow from this that, apart from the individuals described by it, the term denotes a separate entity.

While the independent existence of universals is repudiated, there is in Quine and the Buddhists considerable tolerance for the utility of general terms. The Buddhists argue that inferences from signs to commonsense objects cannot proceed without general term, while Quine shows that general terms serve the interest of parsimony and communicability. I shall turn to each of these concerns in detail.

Earlier we saw the Buddhists acknowledge two modes of teaching objects: sensation and inference. A principle important for inference is already present in sensation: the suppression of difference between different sense data. This suppression is required because percepts result from the coordination of multiple sense data. Generalization, which proceeds by fastening on repetitions and ignoring irrelevant difference, already occurs at the sensory level but is fully realized only in connection with inference. For Dharmakīrti, inference is of two types: for oneself, when cognizing something by recognizing a mark or sign that points to an object, and for others, the formulation in speech of what has been so cognized. Consider the case of smoke and fire. Synthetic imagination constructs an image of fire to which the term *fire* is applied. Because the term does not refer to any specific fire but rather to an imaginary one, it can apply to any fire: it is a general term. How can we be sure no real fire is envisaged? The impression of an imaginary fire remains constant without varying in vividness. (As we saw earlier, only variation of impression can attest the action of some original and rule out imagining.) Dharmottara states: "The universal character of something is that essence which exists owing to generality, i.e. that essence that belongs to an indefinite number of points of reality. Indeed, the fire existing in imagination refers equally to every possible fire. Therefore it represents the universal essence. This essence is grasped by inference."[29] But understanding the general term *fire* does not yet count as a completed act of inference. The final step is imagining the object-in-general as a real fire, which could become the aim of some purposive action. We can conclude from this analysis that general terms arise in the absence of an original referent. Once a general term is settled upon, it can apply to an "indefinite number of points of reality" no matter how many of these there are.

For the Yogācārins, the key issue in this analysis is that general terms fill a cognitive gap resulting from the limits of sensation: failing omnisentience, we are forced to infer the existence of absent objects from signs. That a general name ranges over an indefinite number of particulars is noted by them but remains incidental to the name's capacity to substitute for absent objects. For Quine, general terms are a solution to the nominalist's worry about inundation by successive time-tied particulars. To this end, a language must be devised not only to describe events that do occur but also to apply to events that did not and could not occur. In a lengthy but crucial passage, cited in Chapter 28 but worth repeating in part, Quine comments: "Certainly it is hopeless nonsense to talk thus of unrealized particulars and try to assemble them into classes. Unrealized entities have to be construed as universals, simply because there are no places and dates by which to distinguish between those that are in other respects alike."[30]

The break with radical particularity in this analysis occurs when existing particulars are assembled into event forms. (This step can be compared with the Buddhist's recognizing that general terms range over "an indefinite number of points of reality.") Quine's next step is to construe unrealized entities that are alike as universals because if, *per contra*, we failed to do so, we would be inundated not only by actual particulars but by particulars that did not and could not happen. This step is roughly comparable to the Buddhist view that "the fire existing in imagination refers to every possible fire" in that "possible fire" can range over an indefinite number of fires. But such comparison can be misleading if we think the Buddhists notice counterfactuality because they are prompted by considerations of parsimony. Instead they seek to guard against linking the object-in-general, the imagined fire, to nonfires. The epistemological hope is that no fires will be mistaken for nonfires and no nonfires for fires.

Negative Naming

Dignāga and his followers offer a striking and original account of the negative character of naming: the meaning of a name consists in the repudiation of the discrepant meaning.[31] Rejecting the view that this entails a double meaning of terms—part of the meaning arising from negation and the other from affirmative assertion—he claims: "The 'own' meaning of the word is just the repudiation of the contrary and nothing else. . . . The word expresses *per differentiam* its own meaning."[32] Affirmation without difference conveys nothing at all. But why is pure negation not equally meaningless? For the Yogācārins, the answer is that this is simply what naming words are: "The meaning of a word consists in its being different from other meanings. As soon as it is expressed we feel straight off that the contrary is rejected."[33] This response begs the question unless we think that defining meaning as "being different from other meanings" is an indirect appeal to the whole fabric of language (much like Quine's invoking the totality of science) to account for signification.

We saw earlier that general terms refer to mental images. ("It is just this mental image that constitutes the whole universal.") If universals are negatively and intralinguistically determined, it is hard to see how they can be coordinated with the positive character of images. But the difficulty disappears if we recall that an extralinguistic image is already a universal of sorts in the sense that it effaces individual differences among sensations and replaces them with a general form.[34]

In Vācaspatimiśra's account of the nominalism of the school of Dignāga, suppressing differences is seen as a thread running though the Buddhist analysis of knowledge at every stage. First, the difference between a point-instant and other point-instants, then the difference between image and world are posited. The latter makes possible the phenomenon of projection: an image can be projected upon the world once the distinction between the two is sublated. "Our conceptions which follow on our pure sensations, don't seize the difference between the external object of pure sensation and the internal image of thought construction."[35] Notice that the Yogācārin claims we neglect or overlook a difference between object and image. This view is to be distinguished from the Brahmanical cognition of nondifference, a position that reifies negative entities. But how does the sense of construing something as the same arise? Dignāga thinks that different entities may nevertheless produce similar stimuli: "A unity of result . . . is produced which allows [setting aside] those individuals which do not produce the same result," a unity "which has the form of a universal."[36] The drift of the last remark is also found in Quine's comment "General terms . . . must have appeared at an early stage [in human history] because similar stimuli tend psychologically to induce similar responses."[37]

Three points important for comparison with Quine on the origin of common names stand out in the preceding account. First, in the image stage, dissimilar stimuli are overlooked in order to form an image (e.g., of a cow). The now nondifferentiated image is coordinated with a word (*cow*). Second, at the same time another process occurs: the word attains its meaning by repudiating other words. Finally, we continue to impute identity to repeated images as well as to their causes.

Quine offers an ingenious account of the origin of common names, which shares some of the important features of the Buddhist version. In his description of the progress from singular terms to common names, Quine begins with momentary things and their relations. Imagine a volume of water, a momentary stage of the Hudson. The Hudson River is a process extending through time, but the river stages are its momentary parts. Distinguishing between river stages and the river processes enables us to impute identity to time-extended objects. Thus Quine argues:

> The truth is you *can* bathe in the *river* twice, but not in the same river stage. You can bathe in two river stages which are stages of the same river, and this is what constitutes bathing in the same river twice. A river is a process through time, and the river stages are its momentary parts. Identification of the river bathed in once with the river bathed in again is just what determines our subject matter to be a river process as opposed to a river stage.[38]

We read identity in the place of relating discrete river stages. This part of Quine's description comes as close as could be expected to the Yogācāra account of neglecting difference discussed earlier.

We can also *point* to the river, but pointing is ambiguous because we cannot tell if, when we point, we mean a river stage or the Hudson River. The ambiguity of ostension forces us to impute identity to sample momentary objects like river stages in order to nail down the reference of the ostension.[39] Imputation of identity in Quine's account of singular names does the work of repudiating discrepant meaning in the Buddhist view. In specifying *Hudson* we say, in effect: not a river stage, not a multiplicity of water molecules, not a reference to "any one of an unlimited number of further less natural summations to which [a river stage] belongs."[40] For Quine, what a term is to include is learned inductively by adducing fresh examples, but these too are grasped through ostension, so that the process of repudiating meanings is implicated not only at the start but in further refining the use of singular names.[41]

Quine thinks there is no difference between ostensions that designate stages of time-tied processes and those used to show spatial extensions. Pointing to some red object is like designating a river stage. Just as the Hudson is a summation of river stages, the color red is the sum of all red things: "Red is the largest red thing in the universe—the scattered total thing whose parts are all the red things."[42]

Such general terms offer no difficulties, but some adjectives may not fit the pattern of terms that stand for a summation of spatial or temporal extensions. If so, they may be the source of the realist's difficulty. Quine's view of this problem is succinctly summarized by Gustav Bergmann:

> The explanation takes the form of an anthropological fable. Its hero is misled by a faulty analogy. As it happens, some adjectives may be thought of as standing for a sum of extensions. So he is led to hope this is so for all adjectives. Quine constructs a simple universe [a diagram of squares and triangles] in which the sum of all triangles coincides with the sum of all squares. Negatively this frustrates that hope because the constructed figure leads to an unresolvable contradiction: squares and triangles turn out to be identical. Positively we are told that "in ostensively explaining 'square' . . . we say each time 'This is square' *without* imputing identity of indicated object from one occasion to the next."[43]

In the case of square or triangle, unlike red or Hudson, we arrive at a summation without imputing identity from one occasion of pointing to the next. This leads to interpreting as identical not an object "but an attribute, squareness, which is *shared by* the individual objects."[44]

The example of the paradox provided by Quine's universe of regions where triangles and squares turn out to be identical is foreign to Buddhist analysis. Because shape and, a fortiori, geometrical form are rarely considered in Indian philosophy, assumptions about their treatment must remain speculative. One can only suppose that "square" would be fitted to the model of other extensions like "blue patch" analyzed earlier and explained by the method of overlooking differences in a repeated series.

The range of entities considered to exist in Buddhist ontology is limited in part by tradition but also by entrenched referentialism: the distinction between meaning and reference is absent from Yogācāra accounts of what there is. Quine (following Frege) assumes that names purporting to designate spatiotemporal entities but having no referents nonetheless have meaning. Cerberus is a meaningful term even if it does not name anything. Syncategorematic terms do not name but, like Cerberus, are also meaningful.[45] Even when a word names something, we cannot identify the meaning with the object denoted by the name. *Everest* and *Chomolungma* name the same object, yet the names are not synonymous because they denote an altogether different range of associations in the minds of their users.[46]

Because of their commitment to radical referentialism, the Yogācāra logicians are faced with special difficulties in dealing with entities that cannot possibly exist, as well as things that can but do not exist. This difficulty is confronted in connection with their general treatment of negation. Nominalist constraints prohibit treating negative grammatical particles as quasi-referring terms as some Brahmanical realists do. Instead, a negative statement is considered true only if the empirical conditions for its converse affirmative statement are present. Thus, "There is no jar" is considered true only if the conditions under which the jar could be an object of sensation are present but the jar is not. "Everywhere negation, on analysis, refers to possibilities of sensation."[47] Negating the existence of objects inaccessible to experience is blamed for faulty reasoning.

In considering terms like *Cerberus*, Quine endorses the distinction between meaning and reference, in part because these terms are aesthetically and anthropologically rich. Buddhists derive such significance from a religious context I have deliberately set aside here. Still, Quine's remark that "precise and satisfactory formulation of the notion of meaning is an unsolved problem of semantics" could be construed as referentialist in spirit.[48]

■ ■ ■

That there are differences between Quine's nominalism and that of the Buddhist logicians is hardly surprising. What is striking is the extent to which substantial points of agreement can be found. The six ontological theses held by the Buddhists that I enumerated at the beginning of this paper can now be reduced to four. These are claims Vācaspatimiśra attributes to Dignāga and his followers. I conclude that to each of these claims Quine can offer qualified assent.

1. Ultimate particulars are unique and inscrutable. They trigger sensations but cannot themselves be given linguistic form. Quine

can agree, so long as we recognize that the concept of sense data is a posit of empirical psychology to account for the connection between the physical world and mental content. Sense data and point-instants do not stake out mutually exclusive claims for primordiality. Physical particles are *naturally* fundamental; sense data are *evidentially* fundamental.

2. The judgment "This is that" functions to impute unity to what includes differences in time, place, and quality. Names are a convenient way to designate this unity. Quine can agree about the principle of difference, which is summed up in his maxim concerning the identification of indiscernibles: "Objects indistinguishable from one another within the terms of a given discourse should be construed as identical for that discourse."[49] He would probably stipulate that to understand *how* the principle of difference works in practice we must also grasp the role of ostension in assigning names to temporal and spatial extensions.

3. What a term is to include is the result of arbitrary agreement. Quine can concur. But there are better and worse ways of assigning names: manageable conceptual simplicity leading to maximal simplicity in our total world-picture should be the rule.

4. Names are general terms uniting particulars but are not because of this independent entities. Quine can agree, provided that the restricted context of the present discussion, a physicalist conceptual scheme, which confers some degree of categorial symmetry with Buddhist ontology, is stipulated. There is, Quine thinks, every reason to "rejoice in general terms" because of a gain in communicability and parsimony, but general terms (like *square*) should not commit us to corresponding abstract entities even if, for reasons of convenience, they may be treated as proper names. Still, Quine would probably protest that his view of names is misrepresented if the heart of his doctrine about names is ignored:

> Names are a red herring. The use of alleged names . . . is no commitment to corresponding entities. . . . Names, in fact, can be dispensed with altogether in favor of *un*naming general terms, plus quantification and other logical devices; the trick of accomplishing this is provided . . . by Russell's theory of descriptions. Thenceforward the variable of quantification becomes the sole channel of reference. For ontological commitment it is the variable that counts.[50]

32

Fear of Primitives, Primitive Fears
Anthropology in the Philosophies of Heidegger and Levinas

These are the words of Percy Mumbulla, from Ulladulla, an Australian aborigine in a long line of guardians of tribal memory about the arrival of Captain Cook at Snapper Island, as set down by Roland Robinson, a collector of oral traditions:

> Tungeii, that was
> her native name:
> She was a terrible tall woman
> who lived at Uladulla
> She had six husbands and buried the lot. . . .
>
> She was tellin' my father
> They were sittin' on the point
> That was all wild scrub
> The big ship came and anchored
> out at Snapper Island
> He put down a boat
> an' rowed up the river into Bateman's Bay. . . .
> When he landed he gave the Kurris clothes
> an' those big sea biscuits.
> Terrible hard biscuits they was.
>
> When they were pullin' away to go back
> to the ship, these wild Kurris
> were runnin' out of the scrub.

They stripped right off again
They were throwin' the clothes an' biscuits
back at Captain Cook
as his men were pullin' away in the boat[1]

I shall not try to assess the complex hermeneutical issues that the cross-cultural transmission process generates but want only to note the claim that, coming from the sea, a place of danger in Koori thought, Cook and his men disrupted the Koori order of cosmic and social law, which derives from the land. In an inversion of this disruption, one that philosophy has largely failed to disclose to itself, late-nineteenth- and early-twentieth-century Western thought is fissured by the "primitive" as derived from the new science of anthropology, construed early on in Kantian terms as the science of man. I shall focus upon Ernst Cassirer's account of myth and mana, the magical sacred of the Australian aborigines as depicted by Western ethnographers, and Lucien Lévy-Bruhl's description of the "savage mind" as these accounts bear upon the philosophies of Heidegger and Levinas. The political and cultural critique of the primitive as a mytheme in the larger narrative of modernism has received considerable attention, so I shall not rehearse what has been argued cogently elsewhere.[2] At its nadir, the primitive has been inscribed in the history of physical anthropology as racial morphology.[3]

For Heidegger, the received view of Dasein's lineage leads to its respectable origin in his favored figures of pre-Socratic philosophy: Anaximander, Empedocles, and Heraclitus, an origin that is not for him a mere beginning (*Beginn*) but an inception (*Anfang*), a sending forth of the thinking of Being.[4] For Heidegger's Hellenes, to ponder the truth of Being is to think the meaning of truth as an uncovering that is a concealing-revealing. The patrimony of Dasein is to think in accordance with method (*meta hod*), not in the modern sense, which for him "holds all the coercive power of knowledge,"[5] but etymologically: to think both within and beyond the way of the logos. Thus, to think is to do so errantly yet without departing from the philosophical etiquette of Greek thought.

Why, then, touch upon the Dasein of "wayward" primitives unconstrained by the logos? "Primitive Dasein speaks to us more directly in terms of a primordial absorption in phenomena," says Heidegger (*BT*, 76). Is it possible that Western Dasein is the bastard child for whom "the absorption in phenomena" supplements the existentialia uncovered through phenomenological analysis? Bastard, *enfant naturel*, child of nature, wild child, illegitimate and improper, the progeny of anthropologists' dreams.

What lack in Heidegger's *Daseinsanalyse* could be supplemented (giving the term its Derridean resonances) by cultural anthropology's representations of "primitive man"? The destruction of metaphysics, already far along in *Being and Time*, precludes the positing of transcendental conditions of experience in the Kantian sense, yet at the same time prohibits the description of a purely factical Dasein from passing as a phenomenologically clarified analysis of human existence, one that would be sufficiently general to possess its own *Notwendigkeit*, its necessity, without hypostatizing the subject. Primitive Dasein, the wild child, unconstrained by the Western mittance of Being, would come to fill this role. How, for example, can a Dasein always already ahead of itself be phenomenologically exhibited, how be brought out of time "in" time? By "going primitive." By scraping away the veneer of civilization, Dasein is both hidden and disclosed in an aleuthetic movement that allows it a certain abstractness without destroying its *Leibhaftigkeit*, its sense of embodiment.

I shall, however, consider the primitive in another light. Through a genealogical exhuming of the anthropological deposit in the primordial Dasein, the primitive can be seen as a disruption of philosophy. Heidegger's early writings on Christian mystics wend their way errantly into the domain of anthropology, so that the latter becomes a pressure chamber, as it were, that transforms the self-emptying and silence of the mystic into the desacralized existentialia of Dasein. Just as Descartes peeled away previous epistemic assumptions in order to uncover the cogito as the foundation of knowledge and state-of-nature theorists hoped to expose primal human nature without social encumbrance, so, too, a congeries of ethnography, linguistics, and comparative mythology would provide for Heidegger a scarcely acknowledged model for primordiality conditions that would both shape and trouble his account of Dasein.

Levinas is one of the few philosophers who has tracked the spoors of the primitive in Heidegger. In Levinas's own thought, the primitive provides a counterfoil to one of the driving forces of his ethics, the idea of the infinite, an idea that both abjures and mimics its own expressions. The primitive that he attributes to Heidegger provides an indispensable experiential and proto-axiological level in the stratigraphy of his own major work, *Totality and Infinity*. Levinas's Heidegger is largely the ontological thinker of *Being and Time*, but *Ereignis, aleutheia*, and the fourfold, as developed in the later Heidegger, also enter into Levinas's critique. The infra-rational and the anagogical that precedes language and challenges ethics, the un-Jewish, un-Christian underside of Being, which a transcendent alterity will contest and which Levinas attributes to Heidegger, is refracted for Levinas through the prism of Lévy-Bruhl's anthropology to enter into a new chain of *echt* Levinasian signifiers: paganism, autochthony, faceless Being. I hope to show too that, for Levinas, there is another sense of the primitive, one that points to a double alterity, that of the face and that of the innocence of one who has been extruded from history and thus from the guilt of the historical process.

Although the polysemy of the term *primitive* defies preliminary clarification, it must suffice simply to note that the works under discussion use "the primitive" to denote an essence subject to phenomenological explication as well as the one who instantiates this essence.

From Savages to Dasein

In tracing the ancestry of social science, Durkheim fastens upon Rousseau's account of the state of nature. Neither an actual historical period nor "a figment of sentimental reverie," the state of nature is for Rousseau "a methodological device" for understanding what man is like when stripped of what is owed to society.[6] Far from seeking a factual account of origins, Rousseau hypothesizes the natural state in order to illuminate what is essential in man, thereby providing an imaginary laboratory for the observation of human nature under controlled conditions. Because Rousseau's state of nature (unlike that of Hobbes) has so little in common with life in society, for Durkheim, Rousseau's position founders on its inability to explain the transition from atomized individuals to social existence.

Durkheim is struck by the methodological affinities between Descartes and Rousseau in that for both knowledge is secured through "a kind of intellectual purge" through which judgments not demonstrated scientifically are eliminated and the indubitable axioms that are to secure the propositions deriving from them are brought to the fore.[7] The contemporary reader will be impressed by the resemblance to Husserl's phenomenological reduction as a cordoning off of factual existence in order to disengage the pure essence of the phenomenon as a residue of the process. More important, it may be asked whether this is not Heidegger's strategy when he proclaims that the Dasein brings itself before itself by becoming "simplified" so that its "structural totality" is exhibited in "an elemental way?" (*BT*, 226).

But man in the state of nature is not yet the "savage" discovered through the voyages of Europeans. Closer to nature than modern human beings and therefore providing a better image of the human, free from the taint of a corrupt society, the savage is nevertheless seen as furnishing only a "debased image" of "natural man." Lacking nothing, man in the state of nature has no conception of the future, is not suspended over the abyss of his own nonbeing—in short, has not yet been penetrated through and through by the negative. Rousseau's *homo naturalis* will undergo considerable transformation before he is changed into the savage that will incise its traces in Dasein.

When mediated through the work of Cassirer, the study of primitives focuses upon mythical thought derived from ethnographic reports—for Cassirer those of William Jones, W. J. McGee, J. N. B. Hewitt, Robert M. Marett, Karl Beth, and such well-known propounders of theories about primitive societies as Marcel Mauss, Lévy-Bruhl, and Henri Hubert.[8] In Cassirer's neo-Kantian recasting of their work, he argues that mythic consciousness lacks the capacity to frame the ideal and therefore transposes meanings into material substances, so that image and object, rite and the reality it represents become indistinguishable. For Cassirer, mythical thinking is an infracognitive image-making encounter with the world distinct from that of science, conclusions transparently indebted as much to Hegel, Schelling, and Humboldt as they are to concrete ethnography.

Because its Kantianism fails to go all the way down, Durkheimian sociology collapses for much the same reason that, in Heidegger's view, Cassirer's own position will founder: in the quest for origins Durkheim attributes primordiality to that which is merely derived. Thus Cassirer declares that space, time, and causality, which Durkheim derives from social reality, actually constitute its foundations. Similarly, society is not the cause of the spiritual and religious categories but is grounded in them.[9]

In what might be construed as an act of unconscious mimicry, Heidegger, in a footnote about primitive Dasein, laments Cassirer's failure to clarify what is essential to primitive Dasein. He asserts: "From the standpoint of philosophical problematics it remains an open question whether the foundations of this interpretation are sufficiently transparent—whether . . . the architechtonics of Kant's *Critique of Pure Reason* can provide a possible design for such a task, or whether a new and more primordial approach might not here be needed" (*BT*, 490 n. xi). Sure of the rectitude of the principles of phenomenology, Heidegger goes on to note that, in a 1923 discussion with Cassirer in the Hamburg section of the *Kant Gesellschaft*, Cassirer conceded that a grasp of mythical Dasein requires the support of phenomenological analysis. For Heidegger, the pedigree of the natural child (primordial Dasein) will be in order, his lineage straightened out, once the unruly primitive is brought within the phenomenological horizons disclosed by Husserl.

But can myth ever be straightened out? Does Heidegger not inveigh against myth when brought to the assistance of philosophy as the king rails against writing as a supplement to memory when offered by the God Thoth in Plato's *Phaedrus*? "Our first philosophical step consists in not *mýthōn tina diogáïsthai*, 'not telling a story,'" Heidegger remarks early in *Being and Time* (*BT*, 26). Is this a warning to head off those who might identify philosophy with myth? Heidegger's suspicion appears to be founded on the view that myths are aetiological and supply causes for that to which causal thinking cannot be applied: the question of Being can never be understood by tracing entities back to Being as their origin, as if Being had the character of an entity. This (from Heidegger's perspective) debased view of myth is virtually formulaic for the neo-Kantian Cassirer: "Mythical thinking is by no means lacking in the universal concept of cause and effect . . . one of its very fundamentals,"[10] Cassirer writes.

Yet shortly after the appearance of *Being and Time*, in a 1928 review of Cassirer's work, Heidegger contends that when Cassirer identifies mythic life with mana, the primal sacred, he has found "not a being among beings but the how of all mythic actualities, i.e. the being of beings . . . as the holy."[11] How can we account for Heidegger's disparate interpretations of myth? It would seem that myths just are ambiguous, that their dangerous ambiguity as explanation and as primordial relation to Being can contaminate the meaning-revealing inquiry into the structure of Dasein. Is it an accident that Roland Barthes repeats this gesture when he writes in criticism of a master signifier, "In an author's lexicon, will there not always be a word-as-mana . . . whose sacred signification gives the illusion that by this word one might answer for everything"?[12]

Affect and Action: Gateways to the Worldhood of the World

Despite these caveats about myth as the semblance of philosophy, the affective and ritual dimensions of mythical thought will enter into descriptions of Dasein as mood and worldedness, often in virtually the same language as in Cassirer's account of them. These relations, even within the confines of *Being and Time*, are immensely complex and can only be suggested here, and then only insofar as they bear upon Dasein's "tainted" lineage. I shall point first to the affinities between Cassirer's primitives and the Dasein before commenting on Heidegger's heeding of and flight from a certain call of autochthony, as it were.

Consider, first, Cassirer's description of the affective stage of mythico-religious consciousness: "Things only are for the I if they affect it emotionally, if they release in it a certain movement of hope or fear, desire or horror, satisfaction or disappointment. . . . Before objectivization has begun, before the world as a whole has split into determinate, enduring and unitary forms, . . . it exists for man in unformed feeling."[13]

What has been encoded in the framework of Kantian metaphysics is decoded in the phenomenological key of affective intentionality by Heidegger when he writes of anxiety (*Angst*): it "does not know what that in the face of which it is anxious is. . . . That which threatens cannot bring itself close from a definite direction within what is close by; it is already there, and yet nowhere. It is so close that it is oppressive and stifles one's breath, and yet it is nowhere" (*BT*, 231).

Like the indeterminate of Cassirer, the awesome and the unknown are not anywhere, are always already there in a preobjectivating relation to Dasein, asphyxiating Dasein in an asthmatic encounter with the world. Are these not traces of the comportment of Cassirer's primitives in the affective relation of Dasein to its world, despite Heidegger's disclaimer that Being-in-the-world can in no way be illuminated by attending to exotic cultures? I shall return to both this claim and Heidegger's repudiation of it.

Consider next the phenomenon of action in the world of myth, different in Cassirer's view from that of modern man in that, for the primitive, a wish, if forceful enough, attains its goal. What is more, the influence the primitive exerts on his body is extended directly to the world in that nothing, neither image nor concept, intervenes between the body and its sphere of action. Just as my will moves my arm, so too my will can affect the actions of nature. No intermediate links leading from the beginning to the end of the process of causality are needed.[14]

Is the aborigine's mythical relation to the entities of his world as thus described the same as what Heidegger, in another connection, calls "merely talking such aspects into the entities . . . as if some world stuff present at hand were given subjective coloring" (*BT*, 101), or is there a more originary experience that has left its traces in Dasein's relation to equipmental being and the worldhood of the world? Is Cassirer's interpretation of primitive Dasein merely an example of an analysis that is only spuriously basic, one that manifests its Kantian lineage and therefore cannot provide the basis for an understanding of primitive Dasein? More to the point, is the converse true: that ethnology cannot provide the basis for a phenomenologically clarified grasp of Dasein? In his 1955–56 lectures, Heidegger summarized in remarkably succinct fashion the difficulty he had had all along with Kant's account of the subject, Kant's a priorism. Thus:

> The phrase "a priori condition for the possibility" is the leitmotif that reverberates throughout the whole of Kant's work. . . . Concealed behind [this] formula is the rendering of sufficient reasons, of *ratio sufficiens*, which as ratio is pure Reason. It is only by having recourse to reason (ratio) that something can be determined as to what it is and how it is a being for the Rational creature called "man."[15]

Had Kant's identification of man with rationality not brought to a climax the movement of subjectivization characterizing modem philosophy? And was Cassirer's description of the primitive not merely a manifestation of the same universal structure?

Cassirer's anthropology is indeed often formulaically Kantian. He explicitly endorses the transcendental deduction of time, space, and number, the positing of these as the conditions of all human experience, and the claim that the logical schemata mediate between sensory particulars and the universal laws of thought. Mythical thinking is not exempt from the constraints of the schemata. Instead, Cassirer contends, myth articulates them in its own way as sacred and profane. But how is its own way manifested? Sacredness, Cassirer avers, must appear as a kind of thing.[16] But is not the thing-being of the sacred gainsaid by Cassirer's own accounts of it? Are the manifestations of the sacred not too wild to be contained within the bounds of the transcendental deduction, which itself derives from the framework of mathematical cognition? Cassirer writes, in this vein, that the mythical "lives in the immediate impression, which it accepts without measuring it by something else."[17]

Is it possible that Heidegger too is blind to the primitive's undermining of the "legitimacy" of the existentialia in a gesture mimetic of the contamination of Cassirer's neo-Kantian discourse, even if Dasein's "impurity" differs in its expression from that of Cassirer's Kantian subject? For Heidegger, to be sure, Dasein's primordial encounters with the world can be neither acts of will, as in the case of Cassirer's aborigines, nor spectatorlike envisagements, in the manner of the modern subject. A Dasein that is always already ahead of itself differs from itself, is related to itself futurally. This will be reflected in its manner of encountering entities instrumentally, as something-in-order-to (*BT*, 96–97). Entities thus encountered are not dead objects, merely beheld, but have an intimate connection to Dasein, as having been freed for one of Dasein's possibilities (*BT*, 98). Such entities are gear or equipment and have the being of readiness-to-hand. To this account Heidegger adds: "That wherein Dasein relates itself [to the ready-to-hand] is the worldhood of the world with which it is primordially familiar. This familiarity with the world does not necessarily require that the relations constitutive of the world as world should be theoretically transparent" (*BT*, 119).

Have tools or equipment not undergone a certain quasi-sacralization or fetishization in their noncognitive, world-revealing character? Does this not introduce the primitive into the heart of Dasein? Heidegger sees the danger. Turning to the being of signs, Heidegger says that signs are equipment whose character is to show or indicate (*BT*, 108), but for primitive man the sign is not different from the thing, not only represents but *is* what is indicated. This does not mean that the sign has thereby become a thing, but rather that the sign has not yet become free from what it indicates. But if this is so, then for the primitive neither signs nor equipment can have the being of readiness-to-hand in that neither would be what it is if the other were imbricated in it. Heidegger concludes: "Perhaps even readiness-to-hand and equipment have nothing to contribute as ontological clues in interpreting the primitive world" (*BT*, 113). Does Heidegger mean that there is something ontologically prior to readiness-to-hand in Dasein's relation to entities? Heidegger does not say. But already the fused sign-thing that is neither object nor equipment has slipped outside the confines of existential analysis.

Only later, especially in Heidegger's 1957 "A Dialogue on Language," a conversation between Heidegger as inquirer and a Japanese friend, is a purview opened for addressing these questions. What is at stake in that context is no longer Dasein and the question of Being, but rather Appropriation, *Ereignis*, that which grants to mortals "the abode within their nature so that they may be capable of being those who speak."[18] To attempt an explication of this text would entail a digression that lies beyond the scope of my present remarks. Suffice it to say that the dialogue can be interpreted as holding that each site from which Dasein speaks—Japanese or Western—will determine its identity and thereby its difference from every other Dasein. Is difference, then, not what is most primordial in the Dasein? It is worth noting that difference, as construed in this dialogue, emerges in Heidegger's contention that, in Wilhelm van Humboldt's view, languages originate in distinct and separate acts of spirit, each of which generates a world view. Heidegger worries not only about reinstating the idealist subject but also about how language thus generated is riddled by difference.[19]

That the primordiality of difference is both revealed and concealed in *Being and Time* is clear from the doubleness of Heidegger's comment that access to "the most exotic and manifold cultures and forms of Dasein" does not assure a proper conception of the world unless there is a prior ordering principle, "an explicit idea of the world as such . . . and an insight into Dasein's basic structures" (*BT, 77*). By acknowledging that there are multiple forms of Dasein, on the one hand, and attributing a basic structure to Dasein, on the other, has not Heidegger discovered difference only to subordinate it to the universality of a certain essentialist conformation of the Dasein? The tension between these conceptions can be resolved only if the question of Being is no longer the orienting question for thought, if it is unsaid by that which is itself not an ordering principle yet more primordial, *Ereignis*. Only in the context of an originary Saying and Appropriation can such thinking come about. Thus Heidegger: "Appropriation is different in nature [from Being] because it is richer than any conceivable definition of Being. Being however, in its essential origin, can be thought of in terms of Appropriation."[20]

Is it possible that the primitive that taints the Dasein and, through it, the question of Being as an issue for thinking, wends its way, as it were, toward Saying as determined by Appropriation? And can this Saying be unsaid? Levinas's account of language is devoted to just such an unsaying (*dédire*). But can the primitive ever be unsaid?

Unsaying Heidegger: The Primitive as Other in Levinas

When, in *Being and Time*, Heidegger affirms the priority of Being over the existent, he has, for Levinas, decided the essence of philosophy to be ontology. By stressing the relation of the existent to Being rather than that of one to the Other, Heidegger subordinates justice to freedom, a freedom that is not an exercise of will but rather an obedience to Being. For Levinas, the relation with Being cannot be primordial, not principally because Being can never be the content of a thought, but rather because the relationship with the Other is anterior to thought and being. The existent in his or her Otherness is the interlocutor questioning my being, in what Levinas calls a Saying of one to the Other that precedes both discourse and ontology (*TI*, 45–48). The sharp contrast between Levinas and Heidegger with regard to originary Saying is revealed in the pair of statements that follows.

Heidegger writes:

Language is monologue. This now says two things: it is language alone which speaks authentically; and language speaks lonesomely.[21]

But Levinas says:

Contemporary philosophy and sociology have accustomed us to undervalue the direct social relations between persons speaking. . . . [a] disdain for the word derived . . . from the possibility of its becoming idle chatter. . . . But it is a disdain that cannot gainsay a situation whose privileged nature is revealed to Robinson Crusoe, when in the tropical splendor of nature, though he maintains his ties with civilization through [its artifacts and customs] he experiences in meeting man Friday the greatest event of his insular life — in which a man who speaks replaces the ineffable sadness of echoes.[22]

Heidegger's remarks should not be construed as a denial of sociality, of the belonging together of human beings, but rather as an affirmation that the essence of language is not a Saying of that which is held in common. Instead, language is being claimed by a Saying that must be brought forth in speech. The primordial relation for Heidegger is that between man and language, and not between one and the Other.

With the introduction of the Other, Levinas unsays the Heideggerian account of Saying as a seizure by language. The Levinas text cited is noteworthy from the standpoint of my theme in that its view of alterity leans on Defoe's proto-anthropological parable of civilization and savagery, *Robinson Crusoe*. As Levinas says elsewhere,

Crusoe achieves independence only by exploiting what he has salvaged from civilization.[23] It is worth noting that Baudrillard, in the context of demonstrating that there is nothing natural about use value, that "in fact the whole system and its mystery . . . were already there with Robinson on his island, and in the fabricated immediacy of his relation to things" is in this point in agreement with Levinas.[24] What is crucial for Levinas, however, is that, bereft of human presence, Crusoe is led by the trace or tracks of another to the "savage," Friday, the one who is uncontaminated by the culture and customs of civilized man, the Other who unsays the Heideggerian Saying, a Saying that is subservient to language. To be Other is to challenge Crusoe's right to an earthly paradise not because the hedonism of paradise is evil but rather because the Other's existence reduces the individual's rights to what there is to the null point, including the right to one's own life, which must be placed at the Other's disposal.

It is noteworthy that, following the text cited, Levinas comments about the Other as teacher. Like Kierkegaard, Levinas rejects the view that teaching is a Socratic-maieutic relation; rather, it is "wrenching experience away from its self-sufficiency, from its *here*" (emphasis in original).[25] Although Levinas often interprets teaching as the transmission process of rabbinic tradition through the person of a unique and irreplaceable teacher, the nudity of the face, the aniconic indicator of the Other, is prior to such transmission. Although the widow and the orphan are often tropes for the vulnerable other, in Defoe's text the Other is the savage, Friday. Unimpeded by the trappings of civilization, he is the primitive, whose face is a paradigm of nudity. *Robinson Crusoe* has long been a theme for French literature, from its inclusion as a pedagogical model in Rousseau's *Emile* to the critique of Rousseau's Crusoe in Michel Tournier's *Vendredi*.[26] But for Levinas, is Friday not the disfiguring figure of Rousseau's natural man, whose simplicity and purity is both expressed and traduced through his enslavement?

It might be asked whether the primitive is not doubly other. Not only does the primitive appear as a human countenance and thus as Other, but also as one who is infra-historical, who is extruded from the totality, the institutional and material culture that is the subject of history. There are, to be sure, those whom history will have forgotten. But if primitives are not forgotten—the forgotten are always subject to an anamnesis—but overlooked, theirs is a double alterity and a double innocence, that of the face and of those unimplicated in historical guilt.

Being and the Crucible of Anthropology: Levinas and Lévy-Bruhl

To speak of the primitive as the Other, as I have done, is to think at the margins of Levinas's discourse. When Levinas thematizes the primitive, however, he identifies primitivity with a chain of Heideggerian signifiers, the fourfold, pretechnological Being, autochthony, and paganism. Thus he writes that in the fourfold "Heidegger, with the whole of Western history, conceives of the relation with the Other as enacted in the destiny of sedentary peoples, possessors and builders of the earth. . . . In denouncing the technological powers of man, Heidegger exalts the pre-technological powers of possession. Ontology becomes ontology of nature, impersonal fecundity . . . matrix of particular beings, inexhaustible matter for things" (*TI*, 45). For Levinas, to award primacy to Being is to highlight an undifferentiated proto-ground, a faceless landscape against which entities are exhibited. This backdrop becomes an indispensable stratum in the complex layering of *Totality and Infinity*.

As early as his prewar study "Existence without a World," Levinas describes the indeterminateness of Being that would ensue if one imagined the disappearance of all beings. Levinas calls this impersonal, anonymous residue, the Being that wells up when there is nothing, the *il y a*, the "there is."[27] Just as mood is determinative for Heidegger's account of Dasein's relation with the world, so too the *il y a* is disclosed through horror, an unmediated, impersonal participation in Being akin to the primitive's relation to the magical sacred described by Lévy-Bruhl. It is consciousness, the emergence of the individual, that effects a break with the *il y a*. Contrary to what might be imagined, the *il y a* is not linked to a fear of death in that it is not an absolute nihil but a proto-immortal Being. A far cry from Durkheim's view of the sacred, according to which the subject-object relation is maintained and which evolves toward "higher" religions, the *il y a* "leads to the absence of God."[28]

The primitive mind as described by Lévy-Bruhl is specifically identified with contemporary existential philosophy by Levinas, although, far from endorsing the mentality that is his subject, Lévy-Bruhl acclaims a liberation from it. Still, Levinas argues, by reorienting standard epistemological discourse, Lévy-Bruhl undermines straightforward naturalistic ontologies. No longer does representation afford a privileged access to the world, in that now unmediated contact affords another entryway into the sensible. Thus, Levinas writes: "Precisely that which passes for what is blindest and deafest in us goes the longest way. . . . The very existence of the existent does not unfold as the tranquil subsisting of a substance, but as seizure and possession, as a force field, where human existence . . . is engaged . . . or, in Lévy-Bruhl's terms, participates."[29] In Levinas's reading, there is nothing celebratory about the experience of the sacred: it is, rather, an anguished encounter with anonymous Being, akin to a tribal social participation in the sacred.[30] What is significant for Levinas is, first, the fear that nostalgia for the primitive, which this deconstructive, antiepistemic move breeds, initiates a new form of cruelty and, second, his acknowledgement that immersion in the sacred is more originary than representation.

Despite the few references to the sacred in *Totality and Infinity*, I should like to fasten upon the originary character of this immersion as an indispensable element in the stratigraphy of that work. In a section devoted to enjoyment, Levinas turns to the backdrop from which entities arise, a terrain that cannot be possessed—the spatiality of earth, air, street, and road that he terms the "elemental." It is as if the horizon of which Husserl speaks faded from representational consciousness and was transformed into a medium. To be in the element is to be engulfed, like the surfer by the wave, to live in pure quality as enjoyment. One lives sensible qualities: green, loud, soft, dark (*TI*, 132). The primordial orientation to the world as elemental is a far cry from the suspension of Dasein over the abyss of its own nothingness. The elemental is not a hieroglyph for the primal sacred; rather, the elemental issues from a formless nowhere. Phenomenologically, the primal sacred can be linked to the terrifying chaos (*tohu v'vohu*) that precedes biblical creation. What is crucial for Levinas is that the element constitutes a separation from the infinite. But we shall see that this separation is itself fissured by duplicity and mimicry.

It is not my intent to consider in detail the role of the *il y a* in Levinas's complex late work *Otherwise than Being; or, Beyond Essence*, in part because such an analysis would, of necessity, wind through the absurdist legacy of existentialism—Merleau-Ponty's account of babbling, or Blanchot's descriptions of the rustling that goes on beneath language, to name only two possible paths.[31] By contrast with *Totality and Infinity*, however, it is worth noting that in *Otherwise than Being* the *il y a* is explicated in relation to philosophy. A discursive formation within which the order of justice is given linguistic articulation and rational form, philosophy bears the mark of a Saying that is anterior to ontology. The placement of philosophy, between alterity and being, renders it an effective bulwark against the slippage of Being back into the *il y a*.[32] No longer the obverse of the elemental in its materiality, the *il y a* is now the nonsignifyingness, the nonsense, that stalks language. Yet, paradoxically, it is the *il y a* that advances the de-nucleation of the self: "The incessant murmur of the there is strikes with absurdity the active transcendental ego, beginning and presence. . . . Behind the anonymous rustling of the there is subjectivity reaches [pure] passivity" (*OB*, 164). The displacement of the *il y a* from the material context of the elemental to the analysis of justice merits close study but lies outside the scope of the present chapter.

In *Totality and Infinity*, the elemental leads in two directions. On the one hand, the insecurity of the future in the elemental can be mastered by labor. On the other, when the sheer quality of the elemental is lost in the nowhere, in the *apeiron*, its tempo of existence, as it were, is other than and prior to the flux of time. Becoming "disintegrates" into "that time prior to representation—which is menace and destruction" (*TI*, 141). Like the question of time before creation that terrifies Augustine, the time of the *il y a* is that of the *nunc stans*, prior to the hypostatization of time in Parmenidean Being, prior to Heracleitian flux and to the ecstases of Dasein. Time in the elemental is that of Lévy-Bruhl's primitives, the anthropologist's time, or, as Levinas sees it: "mythical divinity . . . faceless gods, impersonal gods to whom one does not speak" (*TI*, 142). Temporalization presupposes separation and indeed is its very condition. But, like the *il y a*, the infinite challenges the self-manifestations of the separated self as egoity, undoes them into biorhythms: the time between heartbeats, the time of exhalation. Does not the a/temporality of the infinite repeat the a/temporality of the *il y a*, of the time that is prior to the emergence of the separated self as a temporal being?

The exploration of Levinasian time can lead away from the *il y a* to an entirely different manifestation of the primitive. Against Heidegger, Levinas defines time not as a being toward death but as "'not yet' which is the way of being against death, a retreat before death" (*TI*, 224). This "not yet" is itself subject to an inner scission: postponement and menace, It would seem that, as menacing, death would lead to the nowhere and nothingness of the *il y a*. But, surprisingly, Levinas guides the notion of the primitive along another path, into the heart of alterity itself. Thus Levinas: "Death, in its absurdity, maintains an interpersonal order, in which it tends to take on a signification—as in the primitive mentality where, according to Lévy-Bruhl, it is never natural, but requires a magical explanation" (*TI*,

234). Death, in this context, is one of the modalities of the relation with the Other in that death is envisaged as an opponent, as a hostile will, to which appeal can be made. Death is always already an act of violence, a potentiality of the Other. In this astounding claim, death is predicated as always already conceived *d'une manière sauvage*, so that the menace of death is not only for the primitive but for everyone fear of a hostile Other. I can die either "as a result of someone" or "for someone" (*TI*, 239). Does not death grasped as the threat of an alien other that reduces me to passivity, the perspective of Lévy-Bruhl's primitives, reproduce in its structure the various Levinasian tropes: substitution, persecution, desire for the Other?

In/conclusions

In a trajectory that leads from man in the state of nature to the emergence of the primitive in the science of anthropology, the generalizations of ethnography have infiltrated the philosophical discourses of Heidegger and Levinas. In a series of complex mimetic gestures and equally complex unsayings, each has appropriated the work of his anthropologically minded predecessors. Cassirer's neo-Kantian account of mythic consciousness is repudiated by Heidegger for its Kantian interpretation of time, space, and causality but is appropriated in all of its shocking ambiguity to manifest the *Urnatur* of Dasein and to unsay it as difference. Levinas identifies the Being of beings with Lévy-Bruhl's primitive sacrality, thereby unsaying Dasein understood in terms of its originary structure.

The implications of anthropological tropes for Levinasian discourse are considerable. His depiction of the primitive points to the Janus face of some motifs in *Totality and Infinity*: as lying beneath and beyond representation and cognition. The primitive, when identified with the *il y a* as sensory inundation, replicates the uncontainability and excessiveness of the infinite. More originary than the temporalization of separated being, it repeats the non-time of alterity. As formless, the *il y a* mimics the an-iconicity of the face.

Even more astonishing is the release of the primitive into the space of alterity. When the encounter with death as a menacing Other, as described by Lévy-Bruhl, is adopted as the mode of death's disclosure *tout court*, *Totality and Infinity* can no longer be seen as the gradual building up and articulation of a life-world fissured by the Other but rather becomes a complex of relations configured and disfigured by the anthropologist's dream.

Notes

Introduction

1. For an account of vanity as seeing all that is as though it were not, see Jean-Luc Marion, *God without Being*, trans. Thomas A. Carlson (Chicago: University of Chicago Press, 1991), 119–38.

2. Ludwig Wittgenstein, *Tractatus Logico Philosophicus* (London: Routledge and Kegan Paul Ltd., 1958), 181, 6.371.

3. Ibid., 6.372.

4. G. W. F. Hegel, *Phenomenology of Spirit*, trans. A. V. Miller (Oxford: Oxford University Press, 1977), 1. All essays mentioned in the Introduction as written by myself are included in the present volume.

5. Wittgenstein, *Tractatus Logico Philosophicus*, 121, 5.43.

6. Hegel, *Phenomenology of Spirit*, 17.

7. Ibid.

8. Ibid., 19.

9. Ibid.

10. Friedrich Nietzsche, *Thus Spoke Zarathustra*, in *The Portable Nietzsche*, ed. Walter Kaufmann (New York: Viking Press, 1965), 127.

11. Thomas Nagel, *The View from Nowhere* (New York: Oxford University Press, 1986), 14–15.

12. Ibid.

13. Ibid., 1, 162–63.

14. Nietzsche, *Thus Spoke Zarathustra*, 128.

15. See Edith Wyschogrod, *Spirit in Ashes: Hegel, Heidegger and Man-made Mass Death* (New Haven: Yale University Press, 1985), esp. chaps. 1 and 2.

16. Jean-François Lyotard, *The Differend: Phrases in Dispute*, trans. George Van Den Abeele (Minneapolis: University of Minnesota Press, 1988), 88–89.

17. Ibid.

18. Ibid., 96.

19. See Jean-Claude Beaune, "The Classical Age of Automata: An Impressionistic Survey from the Sixteenth to the Nineteenth Century," in *Fragments for a History of the Human Body*, Part I, ed. Michel Feher, with Ramona Naddaff and Nadia Tazi (New York: Zone Books, 1990), 435–37.

20. This paragraph is an altered version of a paragraph in my article "Errant Concept in an Age of Terror," in *Strike Terror No More*, ed. Don Berquist (St. Louis: Chalice Press, 2002), 106–7.

1. Intending Transcendence

1. *Inside/Outside* was exhibited in a retrospective of Clemente's art at the Solomon R. Guggenheim Museum, from October 8, 1999, to January 9, 2000. Composed on handmade Pondicherry paper, 63 inches high and 164 inches wide, the work was completed in 1980. The locking of hands appears to be an ironic visual commentary upon the linked hands in the creation as well as the temptation and expulsion scenes of Michelangelo's famous Sistine Chapel ceiling. For a reproduction of the work, see *Clemente* (Guggenheim Museum Publications, 1999), plate 115.

2. Paul Ricoeur, *Husserl: An Analysis of His Phenomenology*, trans. Edward G. Ballard and Lester E. Embree (Evanston: Northwestern University Press, 1967), 216.

3. Ibid., 87–88.

4. Ibid., 12.

5. Edmund Husserl, *Cartesian Meditations: An Introduction to Phenomenology*, trans. Dorion Cairns (The Hague: Martinus Nijhoff, 1960), 151.

6. Rudolf Boehm, "Husserl's Concept of the Absolute," in R. O. Elveson, *The Phenomenology of Husserl: Selected Critical Readings* (Chicago: Quadrangle Books, 1970), 183.

7. This interpretation, including that of *nulla "re" indiget ad existendum*, follows that of Rudolf Boehm in ibid., 181ff.

8. Immanuel Kant, *Critique of Judgement*, trans. J. H. Bernard (New York: Haffner Press, 1951), 294, writes: "If now we meet with purposive arrangements in the world and, as reason inevitably requires, subordinate the purposes that are conditioned to an unconditioned supreme, i.e. final purpose, then we easily see that . . . we are thus concerned not with a purpose of nature (internal to itself) . . . [but] with the ultimate purpose of creation. . . . It is only as a moral being that we recognize man as the purpose of creation [and have a ground for] regarding the world as a system of purposes."

9. James G. Hart, in "A Précis of an Husserlian Philosophical Theology," in *Essays in Phenomenological Theology*, ed. Steven W. Laycock and

James G. Hart (Albany: State University of New York Press, 1986), sees the Absolute's transcendence as different from the transcendence of the world and of the I-pole; it remains a single but dipolar principle (p. 141).

10. Boehm, in Elveson, *The Phenomenology of Husserl*, 199, suggests that the key question for Heidegger is "Why is there something rather than nothing?" whereas for Husserl it is "To what end is everything that is?"

11. See Jacques Derrida, "How to Avoid Speaking: Denials," trans. Ken Frieden, in *Derrida and Negative Theology*, ed. Harold Coward and Toby Foshay (Albany: State University of New York Press, 1992), 73–77. Hereafter cited in the text as *DNT*. In a subtle account of apophasis, Michael A. Sells, *Mystical Languages of Unsaying* (Chicago: University of Chicago Press, 1994), 1–33, writes: "The authentic subject of discourse slips back beyond each effort to name it or even deny its nameability." He shows how this strategy initiates a language of apophasis, a Greek term meaning "negation" or "un-saying or speaking away" (ibid, 2).

12. For a comparable claim in Kant, see note 8, above.

13. The citation by James G. Hart in *Essays in Phenomenological Theology* is from Husserl's *Nachlass*, B II, 2, 54, 146.

14. Anselm, *Proslogion, a Scholastic Miscellany*, ed. E. R. Fairchild (Philadelphia: Westminster Press, 1966), 70.

15. *The Portable Nietzsche*, ed. Walter Kaufmann (New York: Penguin Books, 1976), 340.

16. Ibid., 198.

17. The citation by Derrida is from Pseudo-Dionysius, *The Mystical Theology*, in *The Divine Names and Mystical Theology*, trans. John D. Jones (Milwaukee: Marquette University Press, 1980), ch. 3:1033bc. See *DNT*, 81.

18. Jacques Derrida, "Post-Scriptum: Aporias, Ways and Voices," trans. John Leavey, Jr., *DNT*, 321.

19. In *G*, 215, the supplement is seen as a refractory element that destabilizes a theory. Derrida writes: "There must (should) have been plenitude and not lack, presence without difference. . . . The dangerous supplement . . . [then] adds itself from the outside as evil and lack to happy and innocent plenitude, . . . an outside that would simply be the outside." But according to the logic of supplementarity "the logic would be inside . . . the other and the lack add themselves as a plus to replace the minus, . . . what adds itself to something takes the place of a default in the thing."

20. Jacques Derrida, "*Sauf le nom*," trans. John P. Leavey, Jr., in *On the Name*, ed. Thomas Dutoit (Stanford: Stanford University Press, 1995), 55.

21. Ibid, 69.

22. Ibid, 68.

23. *Kiddushin*, 71a in C. G. Montefiore and H. Lowe, eds., *A Rabbinic Anthology* (New York: Schocken Books, 1974), 14.

24. *Tanhuma*, Shemot, 20, f.88b (cp.[9]), ibid., 11.

25. *Kiддuуbin*, 40a, ibid., 304.

26. Jacques Derrida, *"Sauf le nom," DNT*, 37.

27. Levinas's critical but appreciative relation to Husserl's phenomeno-logical method, especially as explicated in *Ideas I*, has been explored in stud-ies too numerous to list exhaustively here. The following are especially relevant: Silvano Petrosini and Jacques Roland, in *La verité nomade* (Paris: Editions la Découverte, 1984), describe Levinas's thought as an an-archeol-ogy of meaning in which "meaning precedes essence" and thus is anterior to constituting consciousness (p. 146). Theo de Boer, in "An Ethical Tran-scendental Philosophy," in Richard Cohen, ed., *Face to Face with Levinas* (Al-bany: State University of New York Press, 1986), 83–115, sees Levinas's thought as transcendental philosophy in that it works back from objectify-ing knowledge to what precedes it (see esp. 106–7). Adriaan T. Peperzak, in "From Intentionality to Responsibility: On Levinas's Philosophy of Lan-guage," in *The Question of the Other*, ed. Arlene B. Dallery and Charles E. Scott (Albany: State University of New York Press, 1989), 3–22, traces Levinas's path from intentionality to language and responsibility as it un-folds in his *Otherwise than Being* (OB). In *Emmanuel Levinas: The Problem of Ethical Metaphysics*, 2d ed. (New York: Fordham University Press, 2000), 28–55, I show that Levinas cannot accept analogical appresentation as an account of the relation to the Other.

28. The notion of height is stressed in Richard Cohen's *Elevations: The Height of the Good in Rosenzweig and Levinas* (Chicago: University of Chicago Press, 1994).

29. Ibid., 197.

30. *GP*, 53. Some of these meanings attributed to faciality are referred to in Susan Handelman, *Fragments of Redemption: Jewish Thought and Literary Theory in Benjamin, Scholem, and Levinas* (Bloomington: Indiana University Press), 359 n. 4.

31. Levinas offers a brief overview of various accounts of infinity in the history of Western thought. See "Infinity" (*AT*, 53–76).

2. Corporeality and the Glory of the Infinite in the Philosophy of Levinas

1. The meanings attributed to the face in Maimonides, found also in Levinas, are mentioned in Susan Handelman, *Fragments of Redemption: Jewish Thought and Literary Theory in Benjamin, Scholem, and Levinas* (Bloomington: Indiana University Press, 1991), 359 n. 4.

2. For the extensive bibliography here, see Chap. 1, n. 27, above.

3. Personal communication in 1982.

4. Emmanuel Levinas, *The Theory of Intuition in Husserl's Phenomenology and Existential Philosophy* (Evanston, Ill.: Northwestern University Press, 1973), 155.

5. Ibid., xxxiv. Levinas's approach to Husserl throughout this work reflects an ontologization of consciousness and an approval of Heidegger's historization of the subject. See esp. 153–58.

6. See Edith Wyschogrod, *Emmanuel Levinas: The Problem of Ethical Metaphysics*, 2d ed. (New York: Fordham University Press, 2000), 94–101.

7. See Jacques Derrida, "Violence and Metaphysics," trans. Alan A. Bass, in *Writing and Difference* (Chicago: University of Chicago Press, 1978), 152.

8. Ibid. Robert Bernasconi comments about Derrida's reading of this problem in "Rereading *Totality and Infinity*," in *The Question of the Other: Essays in Contemporary Continental Philosophy*, ed. Arlene B. Dallery and Charles E. Scott (Albany: State University of New York Press, 1989), 25–26. He states that Derrida first appears to welcome Levinas's appeal to experience but then notices that experience is a term already determined by philosophy, so that to deconstruct the logos it is necessary to station oneself within it.

9. See Robert Bernasconi, "The Question of the Other," 28–29.

10. Robert Gibbs, *Correlations in Rosenzweig and Levinas* (Princeton: Princeton University Press, 1992), 213–16, speaks of the absolute accusative of alterity as a gnawing away at one's own body.

11. See Chapter 1, n. 9.

12. James G. Hart, "A Précis of an Husserlian Philosophical Theology," in *Essays in Phenomenological Theology*, ed. Steven W. Laycock and James G. Hart (Albany: State University of New York Press, 1986), 146. The citation by Hart is from Edmund Husserl, *Nachlass* B II, 2,54.

13. Charles Sanders Peirce, *The Philosophy of Pierce: Selected Writings*, ed. Justus Buchler (New York: Harcourt Brace and Company, 1950), 104.

14. Levinas takes up the question of enigma in detail in "Enigma and Phenomenon," in *BPW*, 65–78.

3. Postmodern Saintliness

1. The indiscriminate juxtaposition and appropriation of historical elements has been seen as a danger even in postmodern architecture. Thus Charles Jencks, in *What Is Postmodernism?* (New York: St. Martin's Press, 1986), 20, writes that postmodern architect Leon Krier's plan for the reconstruction of Washington, D.C., has been unfairly compared with the urban planning of Albert Speer under National Socialism. This characterization of Krier misses the "irreducibly plural reality" of Krier's work.

2. Michael Theunissen, *The Other: Studies in the Social Ontology of Husserl, Heidegger, Sartre, and Buber*, trans. Christopher Macann (Cambridge: MIT Press, 1984), situates the notion of alterity as a critical focus in the history of phenomenological and dialogical philosophy.

3. Mary Douglas, in *Purity and Danger: An Analysis of Concepts of Pollution and Taboo* (Harmondsworth, Middlesex: Penguin, 1970), addresses the

problem of liminality in terms of the fear aroused in nonliterate societies by borderline forms of life.

4. Jean-Paul Sartre, *Being and Nothingness: An Essay on Phenomenological Ontology*, trans. Hazel Barnes (New York: Philosophical Library, 1956), 600–15, analyzes such qualities as the soft, the sticky, and the slimy as revelations of being.

5. Mark C. Taylor, *Altarity* (Chicago: University of Chicago Press, 1987), 167.

6. Ibid., 167–68.

7. Cited in ibid., 9.

8. Ibid.

9. On violence as productive of beauty, see Yukio Mishima, *Sun and Steel*, trans. John Bester (Tokyo: Kodansha International, 1970), 50: "To combine action and art is to combine the flower that wilts and the flower that lasts forever."

10. That the body becomes a hieroglyph can be seen in Kafka's "The Penal Colony," trans. Willa and Edwin Muir, in Kafka, *The Complete Stories*, ed. Nahum Glatzer (New York: Schocken Books, 1976). The Harrow inscribes into the flesh of the condemned man a script "that cannot be deciphered with the eyes" but is deciphered, as it were, with his wounds (p. 150).

11. After completing my account of saintly corporeality, ecstasy, and self-giving, I had the opportunity as Dickinson Scholar at Dartmouth College, May 2–5, 2003, to enter into lively discussions about these themes in the lives of medieval women saints with interpreter of medieval hagiographic texts Amy Hollywood, feminist scholar of Judaism Susannah Heschel, and process philosopher Nancy Frankenberry. As guest lecturer at Drew University Theological School, I had a similar opportunity for discussion with medievalist Virginia Burrus and constructive theologian Catherine Keller, and, in the context of the American Academy of Religion meeting in 2002, with biographer of Jeanne d'Arc Françoise Melzer — exchanges that helpfully expanded upon gender-related issues.

12. Edmund Husserl, *Experience and Judgment: Investigations in a Genealogy of Logic*, trans. James S. Churchill and Karl Ameriks (London: Routledge and Kegan Paul, 1973), 350.

13. Ibid.

14. MT, 462.

15. The title of this section is found in Levinas, *TI*, 40. Levinas denies the primordiality of negativity because, for him, negativity requires a being that is prior to it. Thus negativity has its place in the world of totality, for example, in connection with work that transforms the world that sustains it, but "metaphysics does not coincide with negativity" (*TI*, 40–41).

16. Emmanuel Levinas, *Time and the Other*, trans. Richard A. Cohen (Pittsburgh: Duquesne University Press, 1987), 83.

17. Milan Kundera, *The Unbearable Lightness of Being* (New York: Harper and Row, 1987).

4. Levinas and Hillel's Questions

1. See the excellent analysis of Judaism's relation to philosophy as one of correlation, the transformation of a term through its relation to another term, in Robert Gibbs, *Correlations in Rosenzweig and Levinas* (Princeton: Princeton University Press, 1992). Gibbs argues that not only does Levinas aver in his philosophical works that ontology is non- or even antiethical, therefore requiring Judaism as its other, but that Levinas's Hebrew writings are infiltrated by the Greek—that Judaism needs philosophy. See esp. 155–75. Susan Handelman, in *Fragments of Redemption: Jewish Thought and Literary Theory in Benjamin, Scholem, and Levinas* (Bloomington: Indiana University Press, 1991), 263–305, argues powerfully that, for Levinas, the Jew is not an abstraction, a trope for alterity, but an essential event of being. For this reason, the Jew must be understood philosophically. If this is the case, Levinas is suggesting a postmodern inside/outside relationship. The connections of philosophy with nonphilosophy in a general context in Levinas's thought have been thematized in numerous quarters. See esp. articles by Paul Davies, Theo de Boer, Merold Westphal, and myself in *Ethics as First Philosophy: The Significance of Emmanuel Levinas for Philosophy, Literature and Religion*, ed. Adriaan T. Peperzak (New York: Routledge, 1995).

2. R. Travors Herford, in his introduction to *The Ethics of the Talmud: Sayings of the Fathers* (New York: Schocken Books, 1962), notes that *aboth*, a term meaning "fathers," refers to the name of the tractate and not to persons specified as fathers. When the tractate was singled out for commentary as an individual text, the term *pirke* (the plural of *perek*, or "chapter") was added, so that the tractate came to be known as *Pirke Aboth*. The titles "Sayings of the Fathers" and "Ethics of the Father" can be misleading if they are thought to translate *pirke*. The teachers mentioned represent a historical chain of transmission of the tradition and determine the organization of the tractate, while its content consists of ethical maxims. The sixth chapter of *Pirke Aboth* is not part of the Mishnah, generally agreed to have been compiled in the early part of second century, and was assembled after the closing of the Talmud (pp. 3–6). *Aboth* is included in the prayer book as a text that is studied between the afternoon and evening prayers on certain Sabbaths.

3. The translation of Herbert Danby, *The Mishnah* (London: Oxford University Press, 1933), reads: "He used to say: If I am not for myself who is for me? and being for mine own self what am I, and if not now, when?" (p. 447). I have cited R. Travers Herford's more contemporary rendering, although Danby's translation, despite its somewhat archaic language, implies a certain hardening, when one is for oneself, that more clearly suggests Levinas's account of egoity.

4. The relevant source is *RRSJ*. For a comparison of Levinas and Cohen, see Chapter 29 in the present volume.

5. Emmanuel Levinas, *Beyond the Verse*, trans. Gary D. Mole (Bloomington: Indiana University Press, 1994), 132.

6. Ibid.

7. Gaston Bachelard, *The Poetics of Space*, trans. Maria Jolas (Boston: Beacon Press, 1969), 150.

8. Ibid., 152.

9. Ibid., 151.

10. Ibid., 153.

11. Ibid., 152.

12. Ibid.

13. Ibid., 155

14. Levinas, *Beyond the Verse*, 130.

15. Ibid., 103.

16. Herford, *Ethics of the Talmud*, 15.

17. Levinas, *Beyond the Verse*, 109.

18. According to the introduction by Judah Goldin to his translation of *The Fathers According to Rabbi Nathan*, Yale Judaica Series, vol. 10 (New Haven: Yale University Press, 1955), xx–xxi (hereafter cited in the text as *ARN*), the work was probably compiled between the seventh and ninth centuries, whereas its date of composition may go back to the third century. The identity of Rabbi Nathan remains obscure. He may have been an older contemporary of Rabbi Judah the Prince, compiler of the Mishnah.

19. *Chapters of the Fathers*, trans. and commentary by Samson Raphael Hirsch (New York: Philipp Feldheim Inc., 1967), 17.

20. Adriaan Peperzak, *To the Other: An Introduction to the Philosophy of Emmanuel Levinas* (West Lafayette, Ind.: Purdue University Press, 1993), esp. 11–14, 138–41. Peperzak writes: "Levinas's philosophy cannot be separated from its polemical connections with Western ontology and its greatest contemporary representative [Heidegger] in particular" (p. 14). John Llewelyn, in *Emmanuel Levinas: The Genealogy of Ethics* (London: Routledge, 1995), argues that Levinas sees himself in continuity with Heideggerian ontology but calls into question the primacy of fundamental ontology, of the ontological difference, and turns instead to the concrete realm of the ontic (p. 108). The genealogical relation of Levinas to Franz Rosenzweig does not so much challenge the received view as show how Rosenzweig provided the resources for undermining Heideggerian ontology. By shattering the all, Rosenzweig demonstrates the uniqueness of each human. Thus Gibbs writes in *Correlations*, "Even Heidegger's ontology subordinates the being of each person to the question of Being. Levinas finds in Rosenzweig the requirement that each person is an infinite end" (p. 24). Stéphane Mosès, in "Rosenzweig et Levinas: Au delà de la Guerre," *Philosophie et la religion: Entre Ethique et l'ontologie*, Proceedings of the Colloque "E. Castelli," University of Rome, 1996, ed. Marco M. Olivetti (Milan: CEDAM-Casa Editrice Dott. Antonio Milani, 1996), shows that, for both Rosenzweig and Levinas, the totality is the realm of war, one that for Levinas is bound up with ontology. The question for both is "how to get out of the totality . . . beyond being . . .

[to] a place of pure transcendence, where man can mean outside all context?" (p. 796, translation mine).

21. See Gibbs, *Correlations*: "Even Heidegger's ontology subordinates the being of each person to the question of Being. Levinas finds in Rosenzweig the requirement that each person is an infinite end" (p. 24). See also Mosès, "Rosenzweig et Levinas."

22. Llewelyn, *Emmanuel Levinas*, 105.

23. Robert Bernasconi, "Rereading *Totality and Infinity*," in *The Question of the Other: Essays in Contemporary Continental Philosophy*, ed. Arlene B. Dallery and Charles C. Scott (Albany: State University of New York Press, 1989), 24.

24. Ibid.

25. This relation anticipates that between the Saying (*le dire*) and the said (*le dit*) and their unsaying by way of the *dedire* in *OB*.

26. *Chapters of the Fathers*, 16.

5. Recontextualizing the Ontological Argument

1. Anika Lemaire, *Jacques Lacan*, trans. David Macey (London: Routledge and Kegan Paul, 1977), 250.

2. St. Anselm of Canterbury, *Proslogion* II, from "St. Anselm," in *The Ontological Argument: From St. Anselm to Contemporary Philosophers*, ed. Alvin Plantinga (New York: Doubleday, 1965).

3. Ibid., *Proslogion* III.

4. Karl Barth, *Anselm: Fides Quarens Intellectum* (Richmond, Va.: John Knox Press, 1958), 73.

5. Ibid.

6. Jacques Lacan, "The Function of Language in Psychoanalysis," in Lacan, *Speech and Language in Psychoanalysis*, ed. and trans. Anthony Wilden (Baltimore: The Johns Hopkins University Press, 1968), 18; *Écrits*, 45; John Muller and William J. Richardson, *Lacan and Language: A Reader's Guide to 'Écrits'* (New York: International Universities Press, 1982), 70.

7. Arthur C. McGill, "Karl Barth: A Presupposition of the Proof: The Name of God," in *The Many-faced Argument*, ed. John H. Hick and Arthur C. McGill (New York: Macmillan, 1967), 97–98.

8. Barth, *Anselm*, 171.

9. Lacan, "Function of Language," 72.

10. René Descartes, "Meditations on First Philosophy," in *Philosophical Writings*, ed. and trans. Elizabeth Anscombe and Peter Thomas Geach (Indianapolis: Bobbs-Merrill, 1971), 87.

11. Lemaire, *Jacques Lacan*, 197. An ordinary use of metaphor in unpacking abstractions is described by linguistics scholar George Lakoff. He writes, "Abstractions and enormously complex situations are routinely understood via metaphor. There is an extensive and mostly unconscious system of metaphor that we use automatically and unreflectively to understand

complexities and abstractions." An example given is "social organizations are plants." See "Metaphors and War," <lists.village.virginia.edu/sixties/ HTML_Texts/scholarly/Lakoff_Gulf_Metaphor_l.html> p.1

12. Norman Malcolm, "Anselm's Ontological Arguments," in *The Many-faced Argument, ed. Hick and McGill*, 308–10.

13. Gaunilo's objection is said to be found in his *On Behalf of the Fool*, para. 2, I, 126.4 and is generally included with Anselm's reply in standard editions of the latter's *Proslogion*. See Hick and McGill, eds., *The Many-Faced Argument*, 16.

14. Lemaire, *Jacques Lacan*, 174.

15. Ibid.

16. Jacques Lacan, *The Four Fundamental Concepts of Psychoanalysis*, ed. Jacques-Alain Miller, trans. Alan Sheridan (New York: W. W. Norton and Company), 113.

6. Asceticism as Willed Corporeality

1. See Otto Pöggeler, *Martin Heidegger's Path of Thinking*, trans. Daniel Magurshek and Sigmund Barber (Atlantic Highlands, N.J.: Humanities Press International, 1989), 191.

2. Ibid., 210.

3. In the interest of imagining Heidegger in engagement with Foucault, I use the term *self-formation* in relation to the thought of both. It should be noted, as Theodore Kisiel, in *The Genesis of Heidegger's 'Being and Time'* (Berkeley: University of California Press, 1993), warns, that the compound *self-world*, used in the lectures of 1919–20 and 1925 to mean "the origin of the around world and with-world" through which one has oneself, is abandoned in *BT*, 510. Kisiel sees this abandonment as reflecting Heidegger's move to the "transcendence of the world to original temporality" (388).

4. For an excellent brief account of changes in Foucault's thought and informed suggestions for further reading, see Mark Poster, "Foucault and the Problem of Self-Consciousness," in *Foucault and the Critique of Institutions*, ed. John D. Caputo and Mark Yount (University Park, Pa.: Pennsylvania State University Press, 1993), 63–80. Heidegger bibliographies abound. The work of Theodore Kisiel contains selected bibliographic references.

5. Kisiel, in *The Genesis of Heidegger's 'Being and Time,'* pinpoints the difference between formalized inquiry and existential asking. In the former, the "trivial question" of *ens commune* is that of "a remote I and not the distressed question of *ens proprium* of a fully engaged I" (513 n. 13).

6. *Melete* is a term used in rhetoric to indicate the "work of preparing a discourse" or "an improvisation"; *gymnasia* is an activity in a real situation, including sexual abstinence and physical privation. See *TS*, 36–37.

7. For a description of these changes, see Hubert Dreyfus's preface to Michel Foucault, *Mental Illness and Psychology* (Berkeley: University of California Press, 1962), esp. xxv–xl.

8. For an account of the young Heidegger's interest in the medieval roots of "an attunement to the immediate life of subjectivity," see Kisiel, *The Genesis of Heidegger's 'Being and Time,'* 81.

9. Pöggeler, *Martin Heidegger's Path of Thinking*, 126.

10. Ibid., 76.

11. Michel Foucault, "The Masked Philosopher," in *Politics, Philosophy, Culture: Interviews and Other Writings* (New York: Routledge, 1988), 330.

12. Michael David Levin concedes in "The Ontological Dimension of Embodiment," in *The Body*, ed. Donn Welton (Oxford: Blackwell, 1999), "Discussion about seeing and hearing, posture and gesture, bearing and handling are not regarded as discussions about the body" (127). But Levin concludes that "caring is contingent upon openness to what is other and the extent of such openness to alterity is the measure of . . . the ontological dimension of our embodiment" (146).

13. Accounts of the young Heidegger's relation to the Christian mystical tradition now abound. Among them are: Kisiel, *The Genesis of Heidegger's 'Being and Time'*; John van Buren, *The Young Heidegger: Rumors of the Hidden King* (Bloomington: Indiana University Press, 1994); John D. Caputo, *The Mystical Element in Heidegger's Thought* (New York: Fordham University Press, 1986); and Thomas Sheehan, "Heidegger's Early Years: Fragments for a Philosophical Biography," in *Heidegger: The Man and the Thinker*, ed. Thomas Sheehan (Chicago: Precedent Press, 1981), 3–19.

14. For an account of premodern transgressiveness as a violation of limits established by ecclesiastic authority, see my *Saints and Postmodernism: Revisioning Moral Philosophy* (Chicago: University of Chicago Press, 1990), 12–13.

15. Foucault, "The Masked Philosopher," 326.

16. For a discussion of medicine in the classical period, see *CS*, 99–104.

17. The useful expression *ethical heuristic* has been coined by James Faubion to describe this and related constructions of the subject.

18. In a severely critical reading of the biographical relevance of Foucault's descriptions of mystical experience by James Miller, in his *the Passion of Michel Foucault* (London: Harper Collins, 1993), Jeremy R. Carrette argues that Miller conflates Foucault's accounts of Christian mysticism with his sexual practices in an effort to effect a "normalizing judgment" of Foucault. See *RC*, 13–24.

19. Heidegger's way of proceeding is explicated in his winter semester 1920–21 lectures in the *Phänomenologie des Religiosen Leben*, *Gesamtausgabe*, Vol. 60 (Frankfurt a. M.: Vittorio Klostermann, 1995), Part 1.

20. Kisiel, *The Genesis of Heidegger's 'Being and Time,'* 200–201.

7. Blind Man Seeing

1. Brian Friel, *Molly Sweeney* (New York: Plume Books, Penguin, 1994), 11–12.

2. Ibid., 15.

3. Roger Penrose, *The Emperor of the New Mind: Search for the New Science of Consciousness* (Oxford: Oxford University Press, 1994), 385.

4. Friel, *Molly Sweeney*, 53.

5. Jacques Derrida, *Memoirs of the Blind: The Self-Portrait and Other Ruins*, trans. Pascale-Anne Brault and Michael Naas (Chicago: University of Chicago Press, 1993).

6. Ibid., 109.

7. Ibid., 128–29, citing Andrew Marvell, "Eyes and Tears," in *The Complete Poems* (New York: Penguin, 1986).

8. Jean Baudrillard, *Simulations*, trans. Paul Foss, Paul Patton, and Philip Beitchman (New York: Semiotext[e], 1983), 2.

9. Nicholas Negroponte, *Being Digital* (New York: Alfred A. Knopf, 1995), 14.

10. Bill Gates, *The Road Ahead* (New York: Penguin, 1996), 30–31.

11. Negroponte, *Being Digital*, 14.

12. Jean Baudrillard, *The Illusion of the End*, trans. Chris Turner (Stanford: Stanford University Press, 1994), 1.

13. Jean Baudrillard, *The Transparency of Evil*, trans. James Benedict (London: Verso, 1993), 118.

14. Charles Siebert, "The Cuts That Go Deeper," *New York Times Magazine*, July 7, 1996.

15. Gates, *The Road Ahead*, 131–32.

16. Paul Virilio, "The Last Vehicle," in *Looking Back on the End of the World*, ed. Dietmar Kamper and Dieter Lenzen (New York: Semiotext(e), 1989), 112.

17. Friel, *Molly Sweeney*, 69–70.

8. The Howl of Oedipus, the Cry of Héloïse

1. This point is stressed in Vincent L. Wimbush, "Rhetorics of Restraint: Discursive Strategies, Ascetic Piety and the Interpretation of Religious Literature," *Semeia* 57 (1992): 1–9. In the two volumes *Semeia* 57 and 58, entitled *Discursive Formations, Ascetic Piety and the Interpretation of Early Christian Literature* (1992) and devoted to social, cultural, historical, and literary manifestations of asceticism, this diversity is exemplified.

2. Sophocles, *Oedipus the King*, trans. R. C. Jebb, in *The Complete Greek Drama*, eds. Whitney J. Oates and Eugene O'Neill, Jr. (New York: Random House, 1938), 1:410.

3. Claude Lévi-Strauss, *The Elementary Structures of Kinship*, trans. James Harle Bell, John Richard von Sturmer, and Rodney Needham (Boston: Beacon Press, 1969), 25.

4. Ibid., 32.

5. Anaximander, frag. 1, in Philip Wheelwright, *The Pre-Socratics* (New York: Odyssey Press, 1966), 34.

6. The term is Wheelwright's. See *The Pre-Socratics*, 5.

7. Ibid.

8. *The Hellenistic Philosophers*, ed. and trans. A. A. Long and D. N. Sedley, 2 vols. (Cambridge: Cambridge University Press, 1987), 434.

9. Plato, *Phaedo* 66, in *The Dialogues of Plato*, ed. Benjamin Jowett (New York: Random House, 1920), 1:450.

10. Plato, *Phaedo* 67, in *Dialogues of Plato*, 1:450.

11. *Phaedo* 80, in *Dialogues of Plato*, 1:465.

12. Plato, *Republic* V, 456, in *Dialogues of Plato*, 1:717.

13. *The Hellenistic Philosophers*, 1:185–86.

14. Heraclitus, frag. 29, in *The Pre-Socratics*, 71.

15. Ibid., frag, 30.

16. Ibid., frag. 31.

17. For an excellent account of this controversy, see Marilyn Nagy, "Translocation of Parental Images in Fourth-Century Ascetic Texts: Motifs and Techniques of Identity," in *Semeia* 58 (1992): 3–23.

18. Plato, *Timaeus* 27, in *Timaeus and Critias*, trans. Desmond Lee (London: Penguin, 1977), 40.

19. Ibid. 30, 43.

20. Peter Brown, *The Body and Society: Men, Women and Sexual Renunciation in Early Christianity* (Chicago: University of Chicago Press, 1988), 111.

21. Ecclesiastes 1:12–14, in *The Oxford Annotated Bible, Revised Standard Version* (New York: Oxford University Press, 1962), 805–6.

22. Ecclesiastes 1:17–18, in ibid., 806.

23. Ecclesiastes 11:5, in ibid., 813.

24. Ibid.

25. Jean-Luc Marion, *God without Being*, trans. Thomas A. Carlson (Chicago: University of Chicago Press, 1991), 127.

26. Ecclesiastes 1:8, in *The Oxford Annotated Bible*, 805. The predominant view of Greek philosophy, with which the creationist biblical view is often contrasted, is challenged in Derrida's novel interpretation of Plato's *Timaeus*. Derrida focuses on Plato's account of *khōra*, the womblike receptacle in which are inscribed the sensible likenesses of intelligible forms. The *khōra* is itself neither an intelligible nor a sensible object, and its liminality opens the way for overcoming the received view that Plato's philosophy posits two worlds, that of intelligible forms illuminated by the idea of the good, and that of sensible likenesses, of change or becoming. *Khōra* is thus useful for overcoming what Derrida sees as the binary logic of Western philosophy. A clear exposition of these issues (discussed by Derrida in numerous contexts) can be found in his "Khōra," trans. Ian McLeod, in Jacques Derrida, *On the Name*, ed. Thomas Dutoit (Stanford: Stanford University Press, 1995), 87–127.

27. The term *dénégation* is used by Jacques Derrida to describe the meaning of the term *secret*: that which "denies itself because it appears to itself in order to be itself" (*DNT*, 95).

28. This is Marion's translation of Romans 8:20 in *God without Being*, 122. *The Oxford Annotated Bible* renders the verse: "For the creation was subjected to futility" (p. 1368).

29. Athanasius, *The Life of Antony and the Letter to Marcellinus*, trans. Robert C. Gregg (New York: Paulist Press, 1980), 42.

30. Michel Foucault, *The History of Sexuality*, Vol. 1: *An Introduction*, trans. Robert Hurley (New York: Vintage Books, 1980), 159.

31. Anders Nygren, *Erōs and Agapē*, trans. Philip S. Watson (London: S.P.C.K., 1953), 210.

32. For a concise account of the debate initiated by Nygren's account of *eros* and *agapē* in a contemporary psychological context, see Paul Rigby and Paul O'Grady, "Agape and Altruism: Debates in Theology and Social Psychology," *Journal of the American Academy of Religion* 57, no. 4 (Winter 1989): 719–37.

33. Simmel is cited in Nygren, *Erōs and Agapē*, 177.

34. A. Hilary Armstrong, "Platonic Erōs and Christian Agapē," in *The Downside Review* 82 (1964): 268. Reprinted in his *Plotinian and Christian Studies* (London: Variorum Reprints, 1979), 9:106–7.

35. The authenticity of the letters is contested by a number of scholars. See Jean Leclerq, *Monks and Love in Twelfth-Century France* (Oxford: Oxford University Press, 1979), 119. For the purpose of my argument, it is the textually constructed Héloïse that is significant.

36. *The Letters of Abelard and Héloïse*, trans. Betty Radice (London: Penguin, 1974), 133.

37. Ibid., 162.

38. Leclerq, in *Monks and Love in Twelfth-Century France*, notes the strong sexual imagery of St. Bernard of Clairvaux in his commentary on the Song of Songs and elsewhere. Bernard's adversarial relations with Abelard brought them into contact, and Bernard is cited as having been in touch with Héloïse when he visited the monastery of the Paraclete. For Abelard and Héloïse, "it is quite natural that in such an environment the language of chivalry and the court, and the love literature which flowed from them should be familiar to all. It was part of the very air of the province" (99). The literature on the personal relationship of the lovers, on the relations between Abelard and Bernard, and on ecclesiastical authorities of the day is vast. A relatively brief bibliography can be found in Enid McLeod, *Héloïse* (London: Chatto and Windus, 1971), 305 ff. As romance, the tale of Héloïse and Abelard has found its way into Western literature from Petrarch and Pope to the present.

39. *The Letters of Abelard and Héloïse*, 67.

40. Ibid., 65.

41. Ibid., 135.

42. Ibid., 134.

43. Sigmund Freud, *The Ego and the Id*, trans. Joan Rivière (New York: W. W. Norton), 15–16.

44. Ibid., 16 n. 1.

9. From the Death of the Word to the Rise of the Image in the Choreography of Merce Cunningham

1. David Vaughan, *Merce Cunningham: Fifty Years* (New York: Aperture Books, 1977), 66.

2. I have followed Sally Banes in depicting the shifts in dance from the 1960s to the present, as they are described in her *Terpsichore in Sneakers: Postmodern Dance* (Middletown, Conn: Wesleyan University Press, 1986), xii–xxxiv.

3. Ibid., xv.

4. Merce Cunningham, "Cunningham and the Freedom in Precision," interview with Meredith Monk, *The New York Times*, September 7, 1997, sec. 2, 13, 35; 13.

5. See Susan Leigh Foster, *Reading Dancing: Bodies and Subjects in Contemporary American Dance* (Berkeley: University of California Press, 1986), 78–85.

6. Cunningham, "Freedom," 35.

7. Vaughan, *Merce Cunningham*, 66.

8. Ibid., 66–67.

9. Foster, *Reading Dancing*, 40–41.

10. Ibid., 41; cf. Vaughan, *Merce Cunningham*, 80–81.

11. Mark C. Taylor, *Disfiguring* (Chicago: University of Chicago Press, 1992), 168.

12. Robert Rauschenberg's statement is cited in James Fenton's "The Voracious Ego," a review of "Robert Rauschenberg: A Retrospective," an exhibition of his work at the Guggenheim Museum, both at its main location and at its locales in SoHo and at Ace Gallery, September 19–November 19, 1997, written for *The New York Review of Books*, November 6, 1997, 12.

13. For a brief account of Steve Paxton's work, see Banes, *Terpsichore in Sneakers*, 57–74.

14. Cunningham, "Freedom," 13.

15. Anna Kisselgoff, "From Baffling to Familiar to Startling Anew," *The New York Times*, October 16, 1997. E 1, 7; 7.

16. Taylor, *Disfiguring*, 171.

17. Ibid., 172.

18. Francis Sparshott, *Off the Ground: First Steps to a Philosophical Consideration of the Dance* (Princeton: Princeton University Press, 1988), 394.

19. Martha Graham, *Blood Memory* (New York: Doubleday, 1991), 3.

20. John Norman Davidson Kelly, *Early Christian Doctrines* (New York: Harper and Row, 1978), 120.

21. Cited in Foster, *Reading Dancing*, 41.

22. Friedrich Nietzsche, *The Portable Nietzsche*, ed. and trans. Walter Kaufmann (New York: Viking Penguin, 1968), 336.

23. Vaughan, *Merce Cunningham*, 86.

24. Maxine Sheets-Johnstone, who follows Husserl, is described by Sparshott (*Off the Ground*, 363) as holding something like this position. A good short account of Sheets-Johnstone's *The Phenomenology of Dance* (New York: Dance Books, 1979) is provided by Helen Thomas, *Dance, Modernity and Culture: Explorations in the Sociology of Dance* (London: Routledge, 1995), 170–75.

25. Maurice Merleau-Ponty, "Eye and Mind," trans. Carleton Dallery, *The Primacy of Perception* (Evanston, Ill.: Northwestern University Press, 1964), 163–64.

26. Kisselgoff, "From Baffling to Familiar to Startling Anew," 7.

27. Cited in James Klosty, ed., *Merce Cunningham* (New York: E. P. Dutton, 1975), 12.

28. The comment from Kant's *Critique of Judgment* is cited in Mark C. Taylor, *nOts* (Chicago: University of Chicago Press, 1993), 222–24.

29. Klosty, ed., *Merce Cunningham*, 13.

30. Ibid., 14.

31. Ibid.

32. Taylor, *nOts*, 251.

33. Kisselgoff, "From Baffling to Familiar to Startling Anew," 7.

34. Guy Debord, *The Society of the Spectacle*, trans. Donald Nicholson-Smith (New York: Zone Books, 1994), esp. 11–24.

35. Jean Baudrillard, "Simulacra and Simulations," in *Selected Writings*, ed. and introd. Mark Poster, 2d ed. (Stanford: Stanford University Press, 2001), 169.

36. Ibid., 171.

37. Angna Enters, "The Dance and Pantomime: Mimesis and Image," in *The Dance Has Many Faces*, ed. Walter Sorrell (New York: Columbia University Press, 1966), 56.

38. Cunningham, "Freedom," 13; Vaughan, *Merce Cunningham*, 276.

39. Cunningham, "Freedom," 35.

40. Jean Baudrillard, "Fatal Strategies," in *Selected Writings*, 189.

41. Cunningham, "Freedom," 35.

10. Empathy and Sympathy as Tactile Encounter

1. M. Scheler, *The Nature of Sympathy*, trans. Peter Heath (Hamden, Conn.: The Shoe String Press, Inc., 1970), 9.

2. Ibid., 20; *PP*, 184; E. Stein, *On the Problem of Empathy*, trans. Waltraut Stein (The Hague: Martinus Nijhoff, 1964), 7.

3. Stein, *On the Problem of Empathy*, 20.

4. Walter Kaufmann, *Nietzsche: Philosopher, Psychologist, Antichrist* (New York: Random House, 1964), 268–69.

5. Stein, *On the Problem of Empathy*, 54–55.

6. Aristotle, *Poetics* 1453a, in Aristotle, *The Basic Works of Aristotle*, trans. W. D. Ross (New York: Random House, 1941).

7. R. Solomon, *The Passions* (New York: Anchor Press, 1977), 341.

8. Friedrich Nietzsche, *On the Genealogy of Morals*, 1, 14, trans. Walter Kaufmann and R. J. Hollingdale, in *On the Genealogy of Morals and Ecce Homo*, ed., with commentary, by Walter Kaufmann (New York: Random House, 1969), 46–48.

9. Scheler, *The Nature of Sympathy*, 90.

10. Friedrich Nietzsche, *The Will to Power*, trans. Walter Kaufmann and R. J. Hollingdale (New York: Random House, 1968), 342.

11. Nietzsche, *Ecce Homo*, trans. Walter Kaufmann, in *On the Genealogy of Morals and Ecce Homo*, ed. Walter Kaufmann, 273.

12. Erwin Straus, *The Primary World of the Senses*, trans. Jacob Needleman (Glencoe, Ill.: The Free Press, 1963), 281.

13. The nucleus of this historical section is suggested in my "Doing before Hearing," *Textes pour Emmanuel Lévinas*, ed. François Laruelle (Paris: Jean-Michel Place, 1980), 179–203. Although the issues raised by Derrida in *On Touching: Jean-Luc Nancy*, trans. Catherine Irizaray (Stanford: Stanford University Press, 2005), are not the subject of the present discussion, Derrida's comments on Nancy's treatment of touch are significant for understanding Derrida's view of religion. Nancy's work brings to the fore "the aporia of the *intangible* or the *untouchable* depending upon whether one *cannot* or *must* not *touch*" (298; emphasis in original). This claim should be understood in light of Derrida's interpretation of Nancy's project of the deconstruction of Christianity and the resulting perspectives on touch. What is and is not tangible can be seen in the context of the problems of immanence and transcendence.

14. A. Montagu, *Touching: The Human Significance of the Skin* (New York: Harper and Row, 1971), 1–2.

15. M. Morgan, *Molyneux's Question: Vision, Touch and the Philosophy of Perception* (Cambridge: Cambridge University Press, 1977), 1.

16. Ibid.

17. Ibid., 13–14.

18. George Berkeley, *Essays towards a New Theory of Vision* (London: Dent, 1910).

19. Morgan, *Molyneux's Question*, 62. Merleau-Ponty cites the conclusions of a recent experiment that supports Berkeley's account of why we do not perceive the retinal image: "If a subject is made to wear glasses that correct the retinal images, the whole landscape at first appears unreal and upside down; on the second day of the experiment, the landscape is no longer inverted, but the body is felt to be in an inverted position. From the third to the seventh day, the body progressively rights itself, and finally seems to occupy a normal position, particularly when the subject is active"

(*PP*, 244). He concludes that touch has stayed "the right way" while vision has altered, so that the subject has two irreconcilable representations. Activity teaches the subject to harmonize the new visual and the old tactile data. "What counts for the orientation of the spectacle is not my body as it in fact is, as a thing in objective space, but as a system of possible action" (*PP*, 260).

20. Etienne Bonnot de Condillac, *Treatise on Sensation*, trans. G. Carr (London: Favil Press, 1930), 82.

21. Ibid., 85.

22. Ibid., 88.

23. Ibid.

24. Ibid., 148–49.

25. Stein, *On the Problem of Empathy*, 39.

26. Ibid.

27. Ibid., 40.

28. Straus, *The Primary World of the Senses*, 231.

29. H. Jonas, "The Nobility of Sight: A Study in the Phenomenology of the Senses," in his *The Phenomenon of Life: Towards a Philosophical Biology* (New York: Dell, 1966), 145.

30. Martin Buber, *Between Man and Man*, trans. Ronald Gregor Smith (Boston: Beacon Press, 1955), 97.

31. Touching in order to obtain cognitive yield or to create aesthetic form is touching as one sees. Diderot, in his "Letter to the Blind," already recognizes the possibility of one sense "going proxy" for another. In his interrogation of a blind man, he asks the man to imagine what seeing is by presenting him with a mirror. The blind man concludes that "vision is a kind of touch that extends to distant objects other than our face." See Morgan, *Molyneux's Question*, 33. This principle has been used in devising the "Tactile Visual Substitution System" (TVSS) of Collins and Bach-Y-Rita, which throws an image of objects on to the skin of the blind person, using electrically driven vibrators to provide the stimulation. A television camera sends signals to the vibrators. Each vibrator covers a small area of the image in the manner in which news photos represent a scene by means of dots (ibid., 201–202). Here we have an extreme instance of tactile data experienced in the manner of the visual image.

11. Levinas's Other and the Culture of the Copy

1. Humberto R. Maturana and Francisco Varela, *The Tree of Knowledge: The Biological Roots of Human Understanding* (Boston: Shambala, 1987), 47; as cited in N. Katherine Hayles, *How We Became Posthuman: Virtual Bodies in Cybernetics, Literature, and Informatics* (Chicago: University of Chicago Press, 1999), 152.

2. *SG*, 35. This work is more radical in its claims for the longevity and selfishness of genes than the later *EP*.

3. *EP*, 81–96. I consider the relation of gene and phenotype described in this paragraph in relation to Neoplatonism in Chapter 12, pp. 199–201, above.

4. Stephen Wolfram, *A New Kind of Science* (Champaign, Ill.: Wolfram Media, Inc., 2002), 383.

5. Christopher G. Langton, "Artificial Life," in *The Philosophy of Artificial Life*, ed. Margaret A. Boden (New York: Oxford University Press, 1996), 47.

6. Ibid., 50.

7. Ibid., 58.

8. Keith Ansell Pearson, *Viroid Life: Perspectives on Nietzsche and the Transhuman Condition* (London: Routledge, 1997), 113.

9. As cited in ibid., 118.

10. Ibid., 183.

11. Ibid., 183–84.

12. There are a number of references to Kierkegaard in the Levinas corpus. Pertinent to the present context is his positive view of Kierkegaard's account of the desire for God. See "Hermeneutics and Beyond," in *OG*, 109. Also worth noting is his claim that "the Kierkegaardian God is not simply the bearer of certain attributes of humility; he is a way of truth . . . not determined by the phenomenon" ("Enigma and Phenomenon," *BPW*, 71).

13. See Edward F. Mooney, "Repetition: Getting the World Back," in *The Cambridge Companion to Kierkegaard*, ed. Alastair Hannay and Gordon D. Marino (Cambridge: Cambridge University Press, 1998).

14. Søren Kierkegaard, *Repetition: An Essay in Experimental Psychology*, trans. Walter Lowrie (Princeton: Princeton University Press, 1941), 3–4.

15. Ibid., 5.

16. Quoted in Mooney, "Repetition," 294, from "Selected Entries from Kierkegaard's Journals and Papers Pertaining to *Repetition*."

17. See Jean-Pierre Dupuy, *The Mechanization of the Mind*, trans. M. B. DeBevoise (Princeton: Princeton University Press, 2000), 102–7.

18. See C and http://www.enolagaia.com/M78bCog.html, 30–31/4–5. Notes cite the online reprinted translation; original page numbers are followed by page numbers of the online document.

19. Hayles, in *How We Became Posthuman*, points out that the early work of Maturana and Varela allows for construing the metadomain of the observer as though it were a separate entity, whereas in the later work the observers are integral to the network of processes that produced them (145–46). In a perceptive analysis of the autopoietic school, Mark C. Taylor tracks the Hegelian implications of its account of the complexity of living systems. See his *The Moment of Complexity* (Chicago: University of Chicago Press, 2001), esp. 92–93.

20. Hayles, *How We Became Posthuman*, 144–45.

21. Paul Ricoeur writes that, in the first of the *Cartesian Meditations*, Husserl is "shifting the privilege of primary evidence from the presence of the world to the presence of the ego. This challenge to the pseudo-evidence (*Selbstverständlichkeit*) attaching to the presence of the world is the transcendental *epochē* itself [putting out of play or bracketing the existence of the

world]." The belief in being is dispelled so that I gain the "for-me-ness of the world" (*Husserl: An Analysis of His Phenomenology*, trans. Lester Embree [Evanston, Ill.: Northwestern University Press, 1967], 87–88).

22. Levinas is quoting here from Edmund Husserl, *Méditations cartésiennes*, trans. Gabrielle Pfeiffer and Emmanuel Levinas (Paris: Vrin, 1969), 19.

12. From Neo-Platonism to Souls in Silico

1. Rainer Maria Rilke, *Fifty Selected Poems*, trans. C. E. MacIntyre (Berkeley: University of California Press, 1947), 24.

2. Jean-Luc Nancy, Introduction, *Who Comes after the Subject*, ed. Eduardo Cadava, Peter Connor, and Jean-Luc Nancy (London: Routledge, 1991), 4.

3. John C. Avise, *The Genetic Gods: Evolution and Belief in Human Affairs* (Cambridge: Harvard University Press, 1998), 3–4.

4. *SoM*, 126 (emphasis in original).

5. P. F. Strawson, "Persons," in his *Essays in Philosophical Psychology*, ed. Donald E. Gustafson (New York: Doubleday, 1964), 388.

6. Jean Baudrillard, *The Illusion of the End*, trans. Chris Turner (Stanford: Stanford University Press, 1994), 95–96.

7. Ibid., 99–100.

8. Ibid., 111–12.

9. Derek Parfit, *Reasons and Persons* (New York: Oxford University Press, 1986), 215.

10. Ibid., 225 (emphasis in original).

11. Baudrillard, *Illusion of the End*, 2.

12. Ibid., 290.

13. Jean Baudrillard, *The Ecstasy of Communication*, trans. Bernard and Caroline Schutz (New York: Semiotext[e], 1988), 17.

14. Baudrillard, *Illusion of the End*, 122.

15. Parfit, *Reasons and Persons*, 446.

16. Martin Heidegger, *Early Greek Thinking: The Dawn of Western Philosophy*, trans. David Farrell Krell and Frank A. Capuzzi (San Francisco: Harper and Row, 1984), 16.

17. Ibid., 23.

18. Ibid., 26.

19. Martin Heidegger, *The Principle of Reason*, trans. Reginald Lilly (Bloomington: Indiana University Press, 1991), 120.

20. Ibid., 108.

21. Ibid., 104.

22. Martin Heidegger, *Basic Problems of Phenomenology*, trans. Albert Hofstadter (Bloomington: Indiana University Press, 1982), 249.

23. Stephen Gersh, *From Iamblichus to Eriugena: An Investigation of the Prehistory and Evolution of the Pseudo-Dionysian Tradition* (Leiden: Brill, 1978), 17–18.

24. Daniel C. Dennett, *Darwin's Dangerous Idea: Evolution and the Meaning of Life* (New York: Simon and Schuster, 1995), 115.

25. R. T. Wallis, *Neoplatonism* (London: Gerald Duckworth, 1972), 65–66.

26. Ibid., 61.

27. Eric Alliez, *Capital Times: Tales from the Conquest of Time*, trans. George Van Den Abbeele (Minneapolis: University of Minnesota Press, 1996), 48–49.

28. Eyjolfur K. Emilsson, *Plotinus on Sense-Perception: A Philosophical Study* (Cambridge: Cambridge University Press, 1988), 24.

29. In other contexts, Plotinus reverses this order and refers to soul as in the body. See Emilsson, *Plotinus on Sense Perception*, 34–35.

30. Jacques Derrida, *Of Spirit: Heidegger and the Question*, trans. Geoffrey Bennington and Rachel Bowlby (Chicago: University of Chicago Press, 1989), 112.

31. Dominic O'Meara, "La question de l'être et de non-être des objets mathématiques chez Platon et Jamblique," in *The Structure of Being and the Search for the Good: Essays on Ancient and Early Medieval Platonism*, ed. Dominic O'Meara (Brookfield, Vt.: Ashgate, 1998), 406.

32. Wallis, *Neoplatonism*, 126–27.

33. For a comparable use of numbers in Neoplatonism generally, see Stephen Gersh, *From Iamblichus to Eriugena: An Investigation of the Prehistory and Evolution of the Pseudo-Dionysian Tradition* (Leiden: Brill, 1978), 139–41.

34. O'Meara, "La question de l'être et de non-être des objets mathématiques chez Platon et Jamblique," in *The Structure of Being and the Search for the Good*, 414. The importance of number is extensively explored by Alain Badiou. In an essay on Platonism in his *Theoretical Writings*, trans. Ray Brassier and Alberto Toscano (London: Continuum, 2004), he writes in support of his view that mathematics is to be identified with thinking: "There is a coordinated movement of thought coextensive with being, which mathematics envelops" (54). In an essay on the being of number as "a form of multiple being," he contends that number is to be interpreted as "Neither an object nor an objectivity. It is a gesture in being. Before all objectivity, before all bound presentation, in the unbound eternity of its being, it makes itself available to thought as a form carved-out within the maximal stability of the multiple" (ibid., 64). In describing the identity of thinking and being, Badiou considers the ways in which the conception of the One comes to dominate the meaning of being, thereby altering their relation. Badiou's thesis requires extensive analysis of his work, which cannot be undertaken in the present context.

35. See Iamblichus, *The Exhortation to Philosophy, Including the Letters of Iamblichus and Proclus' Commentary on the Chaldean Oracles*, trans. Thomas S. Johnson (Grand Rapids, Mich.: Phanes Press, 1988), 30–31. For a detailed account of this controversy, see Gersh, *From Iamblichus to Eriugena*, 289–304.

36. See Carlos G. Steel, *The Changing Self, A Study on the Soul in Later Neo-platonism: Iamblichus, Damascius, and Priscianus* (Brussels: Verhandelingen van de Koninklijke Academic, Weternschappen, Letteren en Schone Kunsten van Belgie, 1978), 58–59.

37. Carlos G. Steel, "L'âme, modèle, et image: Philosopher and Man of Gods," in *The Divine Iamblichus: Philosopher and Man of Gods*, ed. H. J. Blumenthal and E. G. Clark (London: Bristol Classical Press, 1993), 21. My translation.

38. Ibid.

39. Gregory Shaw, *Theurgy and the Soul: The Neoplatonism of Iamblichus* (University Park: Pennsylvania State University Press, 1995), 192–93.

40. Iamblichus, *The Exhortation to Philosophy*, 78.

41. The view is that of D'Arcy Thompson, cited in *EP*, 2.

42. Dennett, *Darwin's Dangerous Idea*, 76.

43. Holmes Rolston, III, *Genes, Genesis, and God: Values and Their Origins in Natural and Human History* (Cambridge: Cambridge University Press, 1999), 79.

44. Ibid., 80.

45. Edward O. Wilson, "Biological and Social Bases of Altruism and Sympathy," in *Altruism, Sympathy, and Helping: Psychological and Sociological Principles*, ed. Lauren Wispe (New York: Academic Press, 1978), 11.

46. Christopher G. Langton, "Artificial Life," in *The Philosophy of Artificial Life*, ed. Margaret A. Boden (New York: Oxford University Press, 1996), 47.

47. Ibid., 50.

48. Dennett, *Darwin's Dangerous Idea*, 212.

49. See Langton, "Artificial Life," in *The Philosophy of Artificial Life*, 42–47. For an additional account of humanoid automata, see Jean Claude Beaune, "The Classical Age of Automata: An Impressionistic Survey from the Sixteenth to the Nineteenth Century," in *Fragments for the History of the Human Body*, part 1, ed. Michel Feher, Ramona Nadoff, and Nadia Tazzi (New York: Zone Books, 1990), 431–80.

50. Langton, "Artificial Life," in *The Philosophy of Artificial Life*, 88.

51. See his "An Approach to the Synthesis of Life," in Boden, ed., *The Philosophy of Artificial Life*, 136.

52. Langton, "Artificial Life," 58.

53. Jacques Derrida, *On the Name*, ed Thomas Dutoit, trans. David Wood, John P. Leavey Jr., and Ian McLeod (Stanford: Stanford University Press, 1995), 108.

54. Leviticus 27:20.

55. Derrida, *Of Spirit*, 113.

13. The Semantic Spaces of Terror

1. I shall capitalize *Terror*, as is the practice in regard to the French Revolution's Reign of Terror.

2. Martin Heidegger, *The Principle of Reason*, trans. Reginald Lilly (Bloomington: Indiana University Press, 1991), 28–29.

3. Ibid., 28.

4. For a discussion of the subordination of faith to ontology, see Merold Westphal, *Overcoming Ontotheology: Toward a Postmodern Christian Faith* (New York: Fordham University Press, 2001), 1–28, esp. 18–19.

5. Heidegger, *The Principle of Reason*, 128.

6. Martin Heidegger, "Building, Dwelling, Thinking," in *PLT*, 150.

7. I use the terms *historial* and *nonhistorial* following the usage of Michel Haar in *Heidegger and the Essence of Man*, trans. William McNeill (Albany: State University of New York Press, 1993), to distinguish an epoch of history from the dimension of "natural immediacy" (180–81).

8. Ibid., 179–80. Haar's claim that the nonhistorial dimension of existence remains constant can be contested in light of changes in basic corporeal structures engineered by modern genetics. See Chapter 12 in this volume.

9. Martin Heidegger, "Why Do I Stay in the Provinces?" in *Heidegger: The Man and the Thinker*, ed. Thomas Sheehan (Chicago: Precedent Publishing Inc., n.d.), 28.

10. Haar, *Heidegger and the Essence of Man*, 181.

11. Rudiger Safranski, in *Martin Heidegger: Between Good and Evil*, trans. Ewald Osers (Cambridge: Harvard University Press, 1998), summarizes and assesses the work of Victor Farias and Hugo Ott and others whose research critical of Heidegger's view of National Socialism and his role in the university in the Nazi period sparked heated discussion.

12. Jacques Derrida, "Autonomy, Real and Symbolic Suicides," in *Philosophy in a Time of Terror: Dialogues with Jürgen Habermas and Jacques Derrida*, ed. Giovanna Borradori (Chicago: University of Chicago Press, 2003), 99.

13. Ibid., 97.

14. Martin Heidegger, "The Turning," in *QCT*, 49.

15. Ibid., 37ff.

16. Martin Heidegger, *Identity and Difference*, trans. Joan Stambaugh (New York: Harper and Row, 1969), 40.

17. Derrida, "A Dialogue with Jacques Derrida," in *Philosophy in a Time of Terror*, ed. Borradori, 90.

18. Ibid., 105.

19. Ibid., 105–6.

20. Ibid., 96.

21. Ibid., 119.

22. Ibid., 120.

23. Ibid., 120–21.

24. Ibid., 123.

25. Heidegger, *The Principle of Reason*, 124.

26. Derrida, "A Dialogue with Jacques Derrida," in *Philosophy in a Time of Terror*, ed. Borradori, 99.

27. Ibid., 124.

28. Jacques Derrida, "Faith and Knowledge: The Two Sources of 'Religion' at the Limits of Reason Alone," in *Acts of Religion*, ed. Gil Anidjar (New York: Routledge, 2002), 70.

29. Ibid., 80.

30. Ibid., 82.

31. Ibid., 88.

32. Ibid., 91.

33. Ibid., 100.

34. Dominique Janicaud, *Powers of the Rational: Science, Technology, and the Future of Thought*, trans. Peg Birmingham and Elizabeth Birmingham (Bloomington: Indiana University Press, 1994), 65. See also Chapter 16 in this volume.

35. Ibid., 75.

36. Dominique Janicaud, *Rationalities: Historicities*, trans. Nina Belmonte (Atlantic Highlands, N.J.: Humanities Press International, 1997), 58.

37. Ibid., xvii.

38. Ibid., 46. Janicaud offers a more positive assessment of Heidegger as one of several thinkers who move in the direction of a minimalist phenomenology. By developing a "phenomenology of the inapparent," Heidegger departs from a spectator view of truth and instead "inhabits the world." See Janicaud's "Towards a Minimalist Phenomenology: The End of Overbidding," 98. http://ot.creighton.edu/u/otd521/Readings/Janicaud.

39. Janicaud, *Rationalities: Historicities*, 29.

40. Friedrich Nietzsche, *Human, All Too Human*, trans. Marion Farber, with Stephen Lehmann (Lincoln: University of Nebraska Press, 1984), frag. 251, as cited in Janicaud, *Powers of the Rational*, 251.

41. Ibid., 20.

42. Ibid., 238.

43. Ibid., xviii.

44. Laurie Williams and Alistair Cockburn, "Agile Software Development: It's about Feedback and Change," *Computer* 6, no. 6 (June 2003): 39.

45. Ibid., 40.

46. Kent Beck and Barry Boehm, "Agility through Discipline: A Debate," *Computer* 6, no. 6 (June 2003): 45.

47. Barry Boehm and Richard Turner, "Using Risk to Balance Agile and Plan-Driven Methods," *Computer* 6, no. 6 (June 2003): 59.

48. Nietzsche, *Human, All Too Human*, frag. 251 as cited in Janicaud, *Powers of the Rational*, 251.

14. The Warring Logics of Genocide

1. Dominique Janicaud, "Toward a Minimalist Phenomenology: The End of Overbidding," 100. http://ot.creighton.edu/u/otd521/Readings/Janicaud.

2. As an example, see a popular exposition of the conflicts within the cultural structures of Muslim countries. Ian Buruma, analyzing the work of Islamic scholar Bernard Lewis, points to Lewis's claim that there is simultaneously a war on modernity and an attraction to its "rock and roll" culture. The conflict with modernity occurs in numerous differing situations "from German Romanticism . . . that began as a reaction to the French Enlightenment . . . to nineteenth century Slavophiles in Russia who extolled the Russian soul." Despite their divergent perspectives, Buruma and Lewis appear to be accord on this matter. See Ian Buruma, "Lost in Translation: The Two Minds of Bernard Lewis," in *The New Yorker*, June 14 and 21, 2004, 190.

3. See "The Legal International Definition of Genocide," 1. http://www.preventgenocide.org/genocide/officialtext.

4. Ibid., 2.

5. See http://www.preventgenocide.org/law/icc/statute/part-a, p.3 for expanded text.

6. James E. Young, *Writing and Rewriting the Holocaust: Narratives and the Consequences of Interpretation* (Bloomington: Indiana University Press, 1988), 192.

7. Human Rights Watch document "'Ethnic Cleansing' in West Darfur." See http://www.hrw.org/english/docs/2004/05/datur8549, p. 1.

8. Ibid.

9. Marc Lacey, "White House Reconsiders Its Policy on Crisis in Sudan," *The New York Times*, June 12, 2004, A3.

10. Nicholas D. Kristof, "Dare We Call It Genocide?" op-ed, *The New York Times*, June 16, 2004, A21. These observations are offered in the context of his account of the experiences of a woman who survived the carnage she depicts.

11. See my *An Ethics of Remembering: History, Heterology, and the Nameless Others* (Chicago: University of Chicago Press, 1998),168.

12. Dominique Janicaud, *Powers of the Rational: Science, Technology, and the Future of Thought*, trans. Peg Birmingham and Elizabeth Birmingham (Bloomington: Indiana University Press, 1994), 65.

13. Ibid., 75.

14. Dominique Janicaud, *Rationalities: Historicities*, trans. Nina Belmonte (Atlantic Highlands, N.J.: Humanities Press International, 1997), 53.

15. Ibid., 45–47.

16. Ibid., 29.

17. Ibid.

18. *The Autobiography of Rudolf Hoess, Commandant of Auschwitz*, (London: Pan Books Ltd., 1961), 162. Cited in *Auschwitz, 1940–1945: Guidebook through the Museum* (Krakow: Panstwowe Museum, 1974), 40.

19. From the trial documents as cited in *Auschwitz 1940–1945*, 41.

20. Albert Speer, *Inside the Third Reich*, trans. Richard and Clara Winston (New York: Macmillan, 1970), 282.

21. Janicaud, *Rationalities*, 37.

22. Rudolph Hoess, Commandant of Auschwitz, 165, as cited in *Auschwitz 1940–1945*, 32.

23. G. W. F. Hegel, *Hegel's Logic*, Part One of *The Encyclopedia of the Social Sciences*, trans. William Wallace (Oxford: Oxford University Press, 1982), paras. 93 and 94, p.137.

24. *The Stroop Report*, facsimile edition and translation of the official Nazi report on the destruction of the Warsaw Ghetto, trans. and annotated Sybil Milton, introd. Andrzej Wirth (New York: Pantheon Books, 1979), p. 10 of first document generated, Warsaw, May 16, 1943. Preserving the sense of the original, the translated book is without page numbers.

25. *Auschwitz 1940–1945*, 109.

26. *The Stroop Report*, April 22, 1943.

27. Ibid.

28. *Auschwitz 1940–1945*, 73.

29. Aram Andonian, *The Memoirs of Naim Bey: The Turkish Armenocide* (the genocide of the Armenians by Turks), Documentary Series, Vol. 2, Fiftieth Anniversary Publication, 1965. Reprint by Armenian Historical Research Association, p. 46.

30. See my *An Ethics of Remembering*, 16–17.

31. *EE*, 58.

32. Ibid., 20.

33. Emmanuel Levinas, *Time and the Other*, trans. Richard Cohen (Pittsburgh: Duquesne University Press, 1985), 48.

34. *OB*, 161.

35. Primo Levi, *The Drowned and the Saved*, trans. Raymond Rosenthal (New York: Vintage Books, 1989), 38.

36. Philip Gourevich, "Letter from Rwanda: After the Genocide," *The New Yorker*, December 18, 1995, 92–93. In regard to the expansion of violence in the region, see Marc Lacey, "Life in Congo: Another Coup, Another Crisis," *The New York Times*, June 20, 2004, 4. He writes, "at its worst the Civil War in the Congo that appeared to be ended in 1998 drew in Angola, Zimbabwe and Namibia on the side of the government and Uganda and Rwanda as backers of rebel forces. In all an estimated three million people died. . . . Congo's relation with Rwanda remains tense."

37. Emmanuel Levinas, "God and Philosophy," in *BPW*, 139.

38. Janicaud, *Powers of the Rational*, 20.

39. Janicaud, *Rationalities: Historicities*, xviii.

40. Janicaud, *Powers of the Rational*, 238.

41. See Dominique Janicaud, "The Theological Turn of French Phenomenology," trans. Bernard G. Prusak, in Dominique Janicaud, Jean-François Courtine, Jean-Louis Chrétien, Michel Henry, Jean-Luc Marion, and Paul Ricoeur, *Phenomenology and the "Theological Turn": The French Debate* (New York: Fordham University Press, 2000), 16–103.

42. Janicaud, "Toward a Minimalist Phenomenology," 103.

15. Incursions of Alterity

1. Gregory Bateson, *Steps to an Ecology of Mind* (New York: Random House, 1972), 201.

2. The other-regarding ethic described is derived largely from Emmanuel Levinas, *Totality and Infinity*.

3. Cited in Jacques Derrida, *A Derrida Reader: Between the Blinds*, ed. Peggy Kamuf (New York: Columbia University Press, 1991), xxiii–xxv.

4. Emmanuel Levinas, *Outside the Subject*, trans. Michael B. Smith (Stanford: Stanford University Press, 1993), 94

5. Bateson, *Steps to an Ecology of Mind*, 205.

6. Ibid., 206–7.

7. Dominique Janicaud, *Powers of the Rational: Science, Technology, and the Future of Thought*, trans. Peg Birmingham and Elizabeth Birmingham (Bloomington: Indiana University Press, 1994), 5.

8. Ibid.

9. Ibid., 65.

10. Ibid., 75.

11. Friedrich Nietzsche, *Human, All Too Human*, trans. Marion Farber with Stephen Lehmann (Lincoln: University of Nebraska Press, 1984), section 251, as cited in Janicaud, *Powers of the Rational*, 251.

12. Janicaud, *Powers of the Rational*, 20.

13. Ibid., 238.

14. Ibid., 247.

15. Ibid., 249.

16. Ibid., 254.

17. Ibid., 25.

18. This citation, from Hume's *A Treatise of Human Nature*, is taken from Jon Elster and George Loewenstein, "Utility from Memory and Anticipation," in *Choice over Time*, ed. George Loewenstein and Jon Elster (New York: Russell Sage Foundation, 1992), 218.

19. George Ainslie, *Breakdown of Will: The Puzzle of Akrasia* (Cambridge: Cambridge University Press, 2001), 24.

20. George Ainslie, *Picoeconomics: The Strategic Interaction of Successive Motivational States within the Person* (Cambridge: Cambridge University Press, 1992), 362.

21. Jon Elster, *Sour Grapes: Studies of the Subversion of Rationality* (Cambridge: Cambridge University Press, 1983), 7. Elster had, early on, discerned the relation of rules of constraint to determining preference.

22. Ainslie, *Breakdown of Will*, 47. See also his *Picoeconomics*, 360–61.

23. Ainslie, *Breakdown of Will*, 28.

24. Ibid., 30.

25. Ibid., 40.

26. Ibid., 41; cf. Ainslie, *Picoeconomics*, 90–95.

27. In *Picoeconomics*, Ainslie speaks of a "private side bet" made when one stakes future behavior on precedent. An individual wagers on the basis of a series of similar choices seen as predictive of choices to come. See esp. 373.

28. Ainslie, *Breakdown of Will*, 89.

29. Ibid., 200.

30. Bateson, *Steps to an Ecology of Mind*, 272.

31. Ibid. At this point, Bateson provides an example of how contextual confusion can lead to differing consequences. Suppose, he speculates, that the operant training of a porpoise to raise her head when a whistle is blown is rewarded by food, and suppose further that to show how operant conditioning works in a broader context, quite different conditioned behaviors are rewarded. The heretofore compliant porpoise is befuddled by the rewarding of new behavior, but when she still receives rewards from her loving trainer for her efforts, she responds with new tricks in creative ways. In sum, pain and confusion are produced, but they can also be subverted in a wider context that allows for creative responses.

32. Ibid., 323.

33. Ibid., 336.

16. Memory, History, Revelation

NOTE: An earlier version of this essay was presented at the Enrico Castelli Colloquium, Rome, January 1994, and appears in its proceedings, *Revelation*, ed. Marco M. Olivetti, Biblioteca dell' "Archivio di Filosofia," CEDAM (Milan: Casa Editrice Dott. Antonio, 1994), 113–26.

1. Aristotle, *Poetics*, trans. Richard McKeon (New York: Random House, 1941), 1451b.

2. Cf. Hayden White, "The Historical Text as Literary Artifact," in *The Writing of History: Literary Form and Historical Understanding*, ed. Robert H. Canary and Henry Kozicki (Madison: University of Wisconsin Press, 1978), 59.

3. Ibid., 52.

4. Gilles Deleuze, *Proust and Signs*, trans. Richard Howard (New York: George Braziller, 1972), 138.

5. The question of the identity of the historian can be likened to the politics of the proper name as Derrida, in *The Ear of the Other: Otobiography, Transference, Translation*, trans. Peggy Kamuf (Lincoln: University of Nebraska Press, 1985), 5, develops this issue in the context of autobiographical writing. Speaking of the lives of philosophers he suggests: "A new problematic of the biographical in general . . . must mobilize other [than empirical psychological] resources, at the very least, a new analysis of the proper name and the signature. [What must be questioned is] the dynamic of that borderline between the work and the life . . . neither active nor passive, neither outside nor inside. . . . This divisible borderline traverses two 'bodies,' the corpus [of works] and the body, in accordance with laws we are

only beginning to catch sight of." The question of the relation of the identity of the historian to the narrative for which she or he assumes responsibility remains to be explored in the light of this Derridean problematic: the relation of the name, the signature borne by the written works, to the bearer of the name, the living individual.

6. Daniel Dennett, *Consciousness Explained* (Boston: Little, Brown, 1991), 153.

7. Ibid., 254.

8. Ibid.

9. Ibid., 279. Dennett dismisses both John Searle's and Hubert Dreyfus's well-known phenomenological defenses of consciousness in this brief passage: "Philosophers influenced by the Husserlian school of phenomenology have stressed the importance of [the] 'background' of conscious experience. But they have typically described it as a mysterious or recalcitrant feature, defying mechanical explanation, rather than the key . . . to providing a computational theory of what happens. [For them] consciousness is the source of some special sort of 'intrinsic intentionality'" (ibid.). The positions with which Dennett takes issue are first explicated in the earlier work of Hubert Dreyfus, *What Computers Can't Do* (New York: Harper and Row, 1979), and in John Searle, *Intentionality: An Essay in the Philosophy of Mind* (Cambridge: Cambridge University Press, 1983).

10. Ibid., 166.

11. Jean-François Lyotard, *The Inhuman: Reflections on Time*, trans. Geoffrey Bennington and Rachel Bowlby (Stanford: Stanford University Press, 1991), 62.

12. Ibid.

13. Ibid., 63.

14. Ibid., 64.

15. Ibid.

16. Plato, *Theaetetus* 191, in *Dialogues of Plato*, trans. Benjamin Jowett (New York: Random House, 1937), 2:195. Plato appears to be distinguishing recollection as remembering in the absence of the object from recognition, which occurs in the presence of the object. For puzzle cases and subtle variations on these modes, see Edward S. Casey, *Remembering* (Bloomington: Indiana University Press, 1987), 122–41.

17. Plato, *Theaetetus* 197–98, 201–2. For the subsequent use of the Platonic metaphors of seal imprint and aviary in medieval thought, see Mary Carruthers, *The Book of Memory in Medieval Culture* (Cambridge: Cambridge University Press, 1990), esp. 16–45. Janet Coleman, in *Ancient and Medieval Memories: Studies in the Reconstruction of the Past* (Cambridge: Cambridge University Press, 1992), 6, touches on but does not explicate the key problems of the *Theaetetus* as a focus for medieval accounts of memory.

18. Lyotard, *The Inhuman*, 65.

19. Ibid., 70.

20. Dennett, *Consciousness Explained*, 132.

21. David Lodge, *Nice Work*, quoted in ibid., 410.

22. Dennett, *Consciousness Explained*, 411.

23. Taking neither a semiotic nor a hermeneutical tack, Beth Preston, in "Heidegger and Artificial Intelligence," *Philosophy and Phenomenological Research* 53, no. 1 (March 1993): 52, argues that the role of the environment has been misunderstood in standard AI models that work with representational accounts of behavior. Such accounts miss the complex environmental structures and processes, the panoply of relations between organism and world, which cannot be described in representational terms. This argument is applicable, mutatis mutandis, to Dennett's view of consciousness.

The *Revue de Métaphysique et de Morale* (no. 2, 1992) contains a number of articles that compare or bridge the conceptual frameworks in terms of which the problem of consciousness is articulated. Claude Debru, in "La conscience du temps," considers the problem of how the constitutive phenomena of time differ from constituted objects in time in Husserl and William James. He finds suggestive answers less in Dennett's critical anti-Cartesian polemics than in his concrete account of "the intrinsic mechanisms that analyze information in accordance with parallel processes possessing distinct modes of temporalization" (293, my translation). Pierre Buser, in "Neurobiologie et conscience," argues for what he calls "emergent materialism." Steering a course between dualism and the radical reduction of mental phenomena to the smallest units at the physico-chemical level, Buser contends that the "mental is the product of the neural ensemble and not of the [particular] neurons" (17, my translation).

24. Martin Buber, letter dated June 5, 1955, in *On Jewish Learning*, ed. N. N. Glatzer (New York: Schocken, 1955), 118.

25. Jorge Luis Borges, "Pierre Menard, Author of the Quixote," trans. James E. Yarby, in Borges, *Labyrinths: Selected Stories and Other Writings*, ed. Donald A. Yates and James E. Yarby (New York: New Directions, 1964), 41.

26. Friedrich Nietzsche, *The Uses and Abuses of History*, trans. Adrian Collins (Indianapolis: Liberal Arts Press, 1957), 40.

17. Exemplary Individuals

1. Max Scheler, *Formalism in Ethics or Non-Formal Ethics of Values: A New Attempt toward the Foundation of an Ethical Personalism*, trans. Manfred S. Frings and Roger L. Funk (Evanston, Ill.: Northwestern University Press, 1973), 48–81.

2. See G. W. F. Hegel, *Logic*, Part 1 of *The Encyclopedia of the Philosophical Sciences*, trans. William Wallace (Oxford: Oxford University Press, 1975), 292ff. and Husserl, *Ideas*, 56ff.

3. Emmanuel Levinas, *The Theory of Intuition in Husserl's Phenomenology*, trans. André Orianne (Evanston, Ill.: Northwestern University Press, 1973).

4. Maurice Merleau-Ponty, *The Prose of the World*, trans. John O'Neill (Evanston, Ill.: Northwestern University Press, 1973), 20 n.

5. See: Rainer Maria Rilke, *The Notebooks of Malte Laurids Brigge*, trans. M. D. Herter Norton (New York: W. W. Norton, 1949), 15 ff.; Max Picard, *The World of Silence* (New York: Henry Regnery, 1961), 88–89; Jean-Paul Sartre, "Faces Preceded by Official Portraits," trans. Anne P. Jones, in *Essays in Phenomenology*, ed. Maurice Natanson (The Hague: Martinus Nijhoff, 1969), 157–64; and Levinas, *PN*, 119–23.

6. Maurice Merleau-Ponty, *The Structure of Behavior*, trans. Alden Fisher (Boston: Beacon Press, 1967), 167.

7. See Levinas's appreciative preface to Theodore F. Geraets in Emmanuel Levinas, *Vers une nouvelle philosophie transcendentale: La genèse de la philosophie de Maurice Merleau-Ponty jusqu'à la 'Phénoménologie de la Perception'* (The Hague: Martinus Nijhoff, 1971). For an analysis of the differences between dialogical and phenomenological constitution of the self in Husserl and Buber, among others, see Michael Theunissen, *The Other*, trans. Christopher MacAnn (Cambridge: MIT Press, 1984). Although the differences between Merleau-Ponty and Levinas are not treated, the discussion illuminates the strengths and weaknesses of Husserl's account of intersubjectivity.

8. Oliver Sachs, "The Twins," in *The New York Review of Books*, February 28, 1985, 36.

9. Ibid., 19

10. Ibid., 16.

11. See Robert Neville, *Soldier, Sage, Saint* (Albany: State University of New York Press, 1978) and Patrick Sherry, *Spirit, Saints, Immortality* (Albany: State University of New York Press, 1984). For an analysis of altruism, see Thomas Nagel, *The Possibility of Altruism* (Princeton: Princeton University Press, 1970).

12. See Steven T. Katz, "Language, Epistemology and Mysticism," in *Mysticism and Philosophical Analysis*, ed. Steven T. Katz (London: Oxford University Press, 1978), 22–75, and Carl A. Keller, "Mystical Literature," in *Mysticism and Philosophical Analysis*, ed. Katz, 75–101.

13. Teresa of Avila, *The Life of Teresa of Jesus: The Autobiography of St. Teresa of Avila*, trans. E. Allison Peers (Garden City, N.J.: Doubleday, 1960), 170.

14. Ibid., 191.

15. Ibid., 174.

16. Ibid., 127.

17. Catherine of Siena, *The Dialogue*, trans. Susan Noffke (New York: Paulist Press, 1980), 27.

18. Ibid.

19. Ibid.

20. Ibid., 29.

21. Friedrich Nietzsche, *The Will to Power*, trans. Walter Kaufmann and R. J. Hollingdale (New York: Random House, 1968), 484 and 543.

22. Teresa of Avila, *The Life of Teresa of Jesus*, 261.

23. Ibid.

24. Martin Buber, *Tales of the Hasidim: The Early Masters*, trans. Olga Marx (New York: Schocken, 1961), 77.

25. *The Questions of King Milinda*, trans. T. W. Rhys Davids (New York: Dover, 1963), 1:183.

26. Jean Genet, *Miracle of the Rose*, trans. Bernard Frechtman (New York: Grove Press, 1966), 171.

27. See Michel Tournier, *The Ogre* (New York: Pantheon Books, 1984).

28. See Jerome Shaffer, "Mind-Body Problem," in *The Encyclopedia of Philosophy* (New York: MacMillan, 1967), and Richard Rorty, *Philosophy and the Mirror of Nature* (Princeton: Princeton University Press, 1979), chaps. 1, 2, and 5. I do not mean to suggest that Levinas is an epistemological epiphenomenalist, but rather that body states predispose one to ethical relations.

29. Scheler, *Formalism in Ethics or Non-Formal Ethics of Values*, 582.

30. Alasdair MacIntyre, *After Virtue* (Notre Dame, Ind.: University of Notre Dame Press, 1981), 140.

31. An analysis of samples in the context of aesthetics can be found in Nelson Goodman, *Ways of Worldmaking* (Indianapolis: Hackett, 1978). For a description of Goodman's view of exemplification see Catherine Z. Elgin, *With Reference to Reference* (Indianapolis: Hackett, 1983), 90–93.

18. Interview with Emmanuel Levinas

NOTE: Interview conducted and translated by Edith Wyschogrod. Transcription from the original tape by Kinga Eremovitch. A special debt is owed to Ms. Eremovitch for her patience in dealing with the numerous difficulties of transcription. Square brackets indicate editorial additions, such as translation of words and expressions from the Hebrew or clarification of an obscure point.

19. Postmodernism and the Desire for God

1. Phillip Blond, *Post-Secular Philosophy: Between Philosophy and Theology* (London: Routledge, 1998); Graham Ward, *The Postmodern God* (Oxford: Blackwell, 1997).

2. See Derrida's highly autobiographical essay, modeled after Augustine's *Confessions*, "Circumfession," trans. Geoffrey Bennington, in Jacques Derrida and Geoffrey Bennington, *Jacques Derrida* (Chicago: University of Chicago Press, 1993), 153–55.

3. Mark C. Taylor, *Erring: A Postmodern A/theology* (Chicago: University of Chicago Press, 1984), is a landmark statement in the dialogue between religion and postmodernism. His latest works are *Hiding* (Chicago: University of Chicago Press, 1997) and *The Real: Las Vegas, Nevada* (CD-ROM) (Chicago: University of Chicago Press, 1998).

20. Heterological History

1. See Michel Foucault, *Ethics, Subjectivity, and Truth*, Vol. 1 of *Essential Works of Foucault*, ed. Paul Rabinow (New York: The New Press, 1997), 207–22.

2. Jean-François Lyotard, *The Differend: Phrases in Dispute*, trans. George Van Den Abbeele (Minneapolis: University of Minnesota Press, 1988), 10.

21. Between Swooners and Cynics

1. F. W. J. Schelling, *The Philosophy of Art*, trans. Douglas W. Stott (Minneapolis: University of Minnesota Press, 1989), 31.

2. Ibid., 154. Winckelmann is cited by Schelling.

3. Plato, *Theatetus* 155, in *The Dialogues of Plato*, trans. Benjamin Jowett (New York: Random House, 1937), 157.

4. Plato, *Philebus* 66, in *Dialogues of Plato*, 402–3.

5. Aristotle, *Metaphysics*, 982b, in *The Basic Works of Aristotle*, trans. Richard McKeon (New York: Random House, 1941), 692.

6. Ibid.

7. Jean Paul Friedrich Richter, "School for Aesthetics," in *German Romantic Criticism*, ed. Ernst Behler; trans Margaret R. Hale (New York: Crossroads, 1982).

8. Ibid., 50.

9. Ibid., 52.

10. J. H. W. Stuckenberg, *The Life of Immanuel Kant* (London: MacMillan, 1882).

11. Arseniz Glyga, *Immanuel Kant: His Life and Thought*, trans. Marijan Despalatovic (Boston: Birkhauser, 1985), 84.

12. In considering the unity of the system's parts in the *Third Critique*, Gary Banham, in *Kant and the Ends of Aesthetics* (New York: St. Martin's Press, 2000), 164, claims Kant resolves the problem of uniting nature and freedom through a procedure of analogy: "Critical analogy is analogy by type of comparison with form. Causality of freedom is not the same kind of causality as natural causality . . . the type of form is all that is involved in the procedure of analogy [and] is what permits unity between the three parts of the critical system."

13. Friedrich Nietzsche, *The Will to Power*, trans. Walter Kaufmann and R. J. Hollingdale (New York: Random House, 1968), 802, p. 421. For his criticism of Kant, see 101, p. 64.

14. Ibid., 844, p. 445.

15. A comparable view can be found in Immanuel Kant, *On History*, trans. Lewis White Beck (New York: Liberal Arts Press, 1963), 19. For the way in which the Kantian dynamical sublime figures in the conception of the historical subject, see Edith Wyschogrod, *The Ethics of Remembering: History, Heterology, and the Nameless Others* (Chicago: University of Chicago Press, 1998), 41–68.

16. Nietzsche, *The Will to Power* 1040, p. 535.

17. See Michael Frede, "The Sceptic's Two Kinds of Assent," in *The Original Sceptics: A Controversy*, ed. Myles Burnyeat and Michael Frede (Indianapolis: Hackett, 1997), 141.

18. Sextus Empiricus, *Outlines of Skepticism*, trans. Julia Annas and Jonathan Barnes (Cambridge: Cambridge University Press, 1994), Book I, iv–xiii, pp. 4–12.

19. This is the position of Michael Frede in "The Sceptic's Two Kinds of Assent," 153.

20. R. Bracht Branham, "Defacing the Currency: Diogenes' Rhetoric and the Invention of Cynicism," in *The Cynics*, ed. R. Bracht Branham and Marie Odile Goulet-Caze (Berkeley: University of California Press, 1996), 83–85.

21. Gilles Deleuze, *What Is Philosophy?* (New York: Columbia University Press, 1994), 64–65.

22. Luis E. Navia, *Classical Cynicism: A Critical Study* (Westport, Ct.: Greenwood Press, 1996), 94.

23. Ibid., 111.

24. Ibid., 103.

25. Ibid., 97.

26. Ibid., 100.

27. Heinrich Niehues-Probsting, "The Modern Reception of Cynicism: Diogenes in the Enlightenment," in *The Cynics*, ed. Branham and Goulet-Caze, 361.

28. Navia, *Classical Cynicism*, 81.

29. Friedrich Nietzsche, *Beyond Good and Evil*, trans. Walter Kaufmann (New York: Vintage Books, 1966), 26, 38

30. Ibid.

31. Niehues-Probsting, "The Modern Reception of Cynicism," 361.

32. Ibid., 362.

33. Throughout his work, Sloterdijk changes the spelling from *cynicism* to *kynicism* when speaking positively of the ancient version of cynicism.

34. Jean Baudrillard, *The Illusion of the End*, trans. Chris Turner (Stanford: Stanford University Press, 1992), 27.

35. I am indebted for the account of Boggs and the role of money as artwork to Mark C. Taylor, *Disfiguring: Art, Architecture, Religion* (Chicago: University of Chicago Press, 1992), 158–63.

36. Walter Benjamin, "The Work of Art in the Age of Mechanical Reproduction," in *Illuminations*, trans. Harry Zohn (New York: Schocken Books, 1969), 217–52.

37. See Taylor, *Disfiguring*, Plate 28.

38. Ibid., 281.

39. Ibid.

40. Nietzsche, *The Will to Power* 844, p. 445.

41. Ibid., 796 and 797, p. 419.

42. Augustine, *Confessions*, in *Basic Writings of Saint Augustine*, ed. Whitney Oates, trans. J. G. Pilkington (New York: Random House, 1948), 4.

43. Augustine, *On Free Choice of the Will*, trans. Anna S. Benjamin and L. H. Hackstaff (Indianapolis: Library of Liberal Arts, 1964), 74.

22. Facts, Fiction, *Ficciones*

1. John Ashberry, *Flow Chart* (New York: Alfred A. Knopf, 1991), 85–86.

2. Cited in J. Samuel Preus, *Explaining Religion: Criticism and Theory from Bodin to Freud* (New Haven: Yale University Press, 1987), 77. Preus's work is a clear and vivid historical account of some key figures in the scientific study of religion who exemplify the ontology of factuality that I am tracking.

3. Cited in ibid., 192.

4. Cited in ibid., 174.

5. Michel Foucault, *The Archeology of Knowledge*, trans. A. M. Sheridan Smith (New York: Pantheon Books, 1972), 91.

6. Ibid., 103.

7. Ibid., 38.

8. George Steiner, *A Reader* (New York: Oxford University Press, 1984), 398.

9. Plato, *Phaedrus*, in *The Dialogues of Plato*, trans. Benjamin Jowett (New York: Random House, 1937), 1:229.

10. Plato, *Republic*, in *The Dialogues of Plato*, 2:378.

11. Ibid., 3:414.

12. Steiner, *A Reader*, 406.

13. Jean-Jacques Rousseau, *Reveries of the Solitary Walker*, trans. Peter France (London: Penguin, 1979), 64–65.

14. Ibid., 66.

15. Ibid.

16. Ibid., 68.

17. Ibid., 69.

18. Ibid., 107.

19. Friedrich Nietzsche, "Twilight of the Idols," in *The Portable Nietzsche*, ed. and trans. Walter Kaufmann (New York: Viking Press, 1954), 485.

20. Ibid., 484.

21. Ibid., 486.

22. Nietzsche, *The Antichrist*, in *The Portable Nietzsche*, ed. and trans. Kaufmann , 640.

23. Nietzsche, "On Truth and Lie in an Extra-Moral Sense," in *The Portable Nietzsche*, ed. and trans. Kaufmann, 46–47.

24. Ibid.

25. Jorge Luis Borges, *Labyrinths*, ed. Donald A. Yates and James E. Irby, trans. L. A. Murillo (New York: New Directions, 1964), 171.

26. Ibid., 39–40.

27. Ibid., 40.

28. Ibid., 44.

29. Ibid., 43.

30. Ibid.

23. Eating the Text, Defiling the Hands

1. David Schiff, in "Exodus, 'Moses,' and a Lot of Caps," *The New York Times*, May 25, 1997, p. 25, recounts that Schoenberg superstitiously avoids a thirteen-letter title for his opera by spelling Aron with a single *a*. For the sake of consistency, I shall follow this practice.

2. Theodor Adorno, *Aesthetic Theory*, trans. C. Lenhardt (London: Routledge and Kegan Paul, 1984), 33.

3. Ibid., 70 ff.

4. See Alan Philip Lessem, *Music and Text in the Works of Arnold Schoenberg* (Ann Arbor, Mich.: UMI Press, 1979), 181. For an excellent account of the influence of these esoteric traditions upon modernist painters, see Mark C. Taylor, *Disfiguring: Art, Architecture, Religion* (Chicago: University of Chicago Press, 1992), esp. 52–73.

5. For an illuminating account of the transformation from oratorio to opera and of Schoenberg's use of text generally, see Pamela C. White, *Schoenberg and the God Idea* (Ann Arbor, Mich.: UMI Press, 1985), 93–112.

6. Alexander L. Ringer, *Schoenberg: The Composer as Jew* (Oxford: Oxford University Press, 1990), 36.

7. Ibid., 206.

8. Translation by Allen Forte, reprinted with permission of Mrs. Gertrud Schoenberg and B. Schott's Sohne, Mainz, 120. Translations cited are from the libretto accompanying the Pierre Boulez and BBC singers and orchestra version of *Moses and Aron*, SONY, 1975/1982.

9. Adorno, *Aesthetic Theory*, 219.

10. Gilles Deleuze, *Difference and Repetition*, trans. Paul Patton (New York: Columbia University Press, 1994), 60.

11. Ibid.

12. I am indebted to Dominic Crossan for his remarks at the Villanova conference "God and Postmodernism," September 25–27, 1997, concerning this episode.

13. Buber's account is from Martin Buber, *Moses: The Revelation and the Covenant* (New York: Harper and Row, 1958), 147–61.

14. This account can be found in George W. Coats, *The Moses Tradition* (Sheffield: Sheffield Academic Press, 1993), 125–34.

15. I am indebted to a member of the audience at the Villanova conference who asked how the bronze serpent might be interpreted in relation to the golden calf.

16. Louis H. Feldman, *Jew and Gentile in the Ancient World* (Princeton: Princeton University Press, 1993), 285–86.

17. Jacques Derrida, *Archive Fever: A Freudian Impression*, trans. Eric Prenowitz (Chicago: University of Chicago Press, 1996), 64.

18. Buber, *Moses*, 139–40.

19. Michael Broyde, "Defilement of the Hands, Canonization of the Bible, and the Special Status of Esther, Ecclesiastes, and Song of Songs," *Judaism* 173, no. 44 (Winter 1995): 66.

20. Saint Augustine, *Confessions*, trans. R. S. Pine-Coffin (London: Penguin, 1961), 256.

21. Ibid.

22. Ibid., 303.

23. Ibid.

24. Augustine, *Confessions*, 308.

25. Ibid.

26. Jacques Derrida, *Dissemination*, trans. Barbara Johnson (Chicago: University of Chicago Press, 1972), 350.

27. Ibid., 351.

28. In rejecting existence as a real predicate, Kant might have warned that because the second *Eyeh* adds nothing to the first any claim to polysemy is undermined.

29. Adorno, *Aesthetic Theory*, 212.

30. Ibid.

31. Ibid.

32. White, *Schoenberg and the God Idea*, 304–5.

24. Killing the Cat

1. Jean Genet, *Funeral Rites*, trans. Bernard Frechtman (New York: Grove, n.d.), 171.

2. Jean-Paul Sartre, *Saint Genet*, trans. Bernard Frechtman (New York: New American Library, 1963), 385.

3. Yukio Mishima, *Sun and Steel*, trans. John Bester (Tokyo: Kodansha International, 1980), 67.

4. Georges Bataille, *The Accursed Share: An Essay in General Economy*, Vol. 2 (New York: Zone, 1991), 105.

5. Ibid., 106.

6. Ibid.

7. Ibid.

8. Quoted in Henry Scott-Stokes, *The Life and Death of Yukio Mishima* (New York: Farrar, 1974), 235.

9. René Girard, *Violence and the Sacred*, trans. Patrick Gregory (Baltimore: The Johns Hopkins University Press, 1972), 222.

10. Friedrich Nietzsche, *The Will to Power*, trans. Walter Kaufmann and R. J. Hollingdale (New York: Random House, 1968), 419.

11. I take up the matter in connection with Genet in "The Double Language of Depravity: Teaching Jean Genet," in *Tainted Greatness*, ed. Nancy Harrowitz (Philadelphia: Temple University Press, 1993), 353–74.

12. Jean Genet, *The Thief's Journal*, trans. Bernard Frechtman (New York: Grove, 1964), 168.

13. Genet, *Funeral Rites*, 312.

14. Jean Genet, *Our Lady of the Flowers*, trans. Bernard Frechtman, introd. Jean-Paul Sartre (New York: Bantam, 1964), 283. (Sartre's Introduction is taken from his *Saint Genet*.)

15. Jacques Derrida, *Glas*, trans. John P. Leavey, Jr., and Richard Rand (Lincoln: University of Nebraska Press, 1986), 217.

16. Genet, *The Thief's Journal*, 168.

17. Jean Genet, *Miracle of the Rose*, trans. Bernard Frechtman (New York: Castle, 1966), 237.

18. Mishima, *Sun and Steel*, 49.

19. Ibid., 31.

20. Ibid., 50.

21. Genet, *Funeral Rites*, 85.

22. Ibid.

23. Ibid., 87.

24. Ibid., 247.

25. Genet, *The Thief's Journal*, 242.

26. Genet, *Funeral Rites*, 248.

27. Zenkei Shibayama, *Zen Comments on the Mumonkan*, trans. Sumiko Kudo (New York: Harper & Row, 1974), xiii.

28. Ibid., 107.

29. The summary of the novel's interpretations of the koan that follow are not citations from the novel but my own condensations of the lengthy renderings in the text. The glosses are numbered and reflect the order in which they occur in the novel. They will subsequently be referred to by number.

30. Nietzsche, *The Will to Power*, 273.

31. The term *inferential walk* is used by Umberto Eco in "Lecto Fabula," in *The Role of the Reader: Explorations in the Semiotics of Texts* (Bloomington: Indiana University Press, 1979), 214.

32. Yukio Mishima, *Temple of the Golden Pavilion*, trans. Ivan Morris (New York: Pedigree, 1980), 255.

33. Ibid.

34. *The Questions of King Milinda*, trans. T. N. Rhys David (New York: Dover, 1963), 1:63.

35. Genet, *Our Lady of the Flowers*, 75.

36. Zenkei Shibayama, *Zen Comments on the Mumonkan*, 112.

25. The Art in Ethics

1. Michel Leiris, *Manhood*, trans. Richard Howard (San Francisco: North Point Press, 1984), 42.

2. Ibid., 43.

3. Emmanuel Levinas, "On Maurice Blanchot," *PN*, 127–70.

4. Levinas cites from Maurice Blanchot, *L'attente l'oubli* (Paris: Gallimard, 1962), 35.

5. Maurice Blanchot, *When the Time Comes*, trans. Lydia Davis (Barrytown, N.Y.: Station Hill Press, 1985), 74.

6. Ibid., 6.

7. Joseph Libertson, *Proximity, Levinas, Blanchot, Bataille, and Communication* (The Hague: Martinus Nijhoff, 1982), 343.

8. Levinas, quoted in ibid., 156.

9. Levinas, quoted in ibid., 157.

26. The Moral Self

1. "A Discussion between Ernst Cassirer and Martin Heidegger," in *The Existentialist Tradition*, ed. Nino Languilli (Garden City, N.J.: Doubleday, 1971), 195. This piece is a translation of "Arbeitsgemeinschaft Cassirer-Heidegger," in Guido Schneeberger, *Ergansungen zu einer Heidegger Bibliographie* (Bern, 1960), 17–27. For other accounts of the Cassirer-Heidegger debate, see: C. Hamburg, "A Cassirer-Heidegger Seminar," *Philosophy and Phenomenological Research* 25 (December 1964): 208–22; Hendrick J. Pos, "Recollections of Ernst Cassirer," in *The Philosophy of Ernst Cassirer*, ed. Paul A. Schilpp (New York, 1949),67–69; T. Cassirer, *Aus Meinem Leben mit Ernst Cassirer* (New York, 1950), 165–67. Heidegger takes a more conciliatory tone than in the remarks cited in *BT*; see esp. 365–68. "In Cassirer's *Philosophie der symbolischen Formen*, Vol. 2, *Das Mythische Denken*, clues of far-reaching importance are made available for ethnological research. From the standpoint of philosophical problematics it remains an open question whether the foundations of the Interpretation are sufficiently transparent— whether in particular the architectonics and the general systematic content of Kant's *Critique of Pure Reason* can provide a possible design for such a task, or whether a new and more primordial approach may not here be needed."

2. Emmanuel Levinas, in *DEHH*, 53, writes: "Idealism has sought to purify the subject of this final contamination, by time, of this final mingling of being at the heart of the event summoned to found being. For the neo-Kantians as for Leibniz, time becomes a vague perception, foreign to the deep nature of the subject" (my translation).

3. By the "existential turn" I mean no more than a shift in focus from a disinterested spirit of inquiry to involved participation in the problems of human existence. The emphasis upon the split between religion and ethics is given prominence in Nathan Rotenstreich, *Jewish Philosophy in Modern Times* (New York: Holt, Rinehart, Winston, 1968), 64: "The meaning of the individual is real in relation to sensation. The breach in Cohen's conception of the nature of religion is connected, from the standpoint of method, to this

shift to logic, where the individual is stressed and religion is given an existential meaning." A contrary approach is taken in Stephen S. Schwarzschild, "The Tenability of Hermann Cohen's Construction of the Self," *Journal of the History of Philosophy* 13 (July, 1975): 368 n. 30: "It has been argued 'the old Cohen' made a turn away from the radical neo-Kantian idealism to religious metaphysics. But in fact this is not the case. At most one can speak of a shift in evaluative emphasis." Another instance cited by Schwarzschild as a variant of the two-Cohen point of view is Jacob Gordon, *Der Ichbegriff bei Hegel, bei Cohen und in der Suedwetdeutschen Schule* (Berlin: Akademie, 1927). Others who attest to the unity of Cohen's work include: Henri Dussort, *L'école de Marbourg* (Paris: Presses Universitaires de France, 1963), and H. Vuillemin, *L'héritage kantien et la révolution copernicienne: Fichte, Cohen, Heidegger* (Paris: Presses Universitaires de France, 1954). They do so on the grounds that the understanding of the noumenal at each level of analysis conceptually necessitates the next level for its resolution. Thus, there is an interlocking system of entailments between the thing-in-itself, the moral law, and God.

4. This view is rather more widely disseminated than is generally realized. It is held not only by European personalists (Buber, Marcel, et al.) but also by some American philosophers. In a letter to a friend, W. E. Hocking writes: "Kant was dead-right in finding a sense of obligation at the center of our consciousness: There's an aboriginal I-ought which goes with I-exist . . . The I-ought implies a Thou-art . . . That Thou is the self within the world, the One elemental Other." Cited in Louis Dupré, *Transcendent Selfhood: The Loss and Rediscovery of the Inner Life* (New York: Seabury, 1976), 109.

5. The influence of Franz Rosenzweig on Levinas's thought is strong and must be considered as partly responsible for his view of Hermann Cohen. Levinas shares Rosenzweig's antagonism to Cohen's uncritical admiration of the German spirit. In a letter to his mother apropos Cohen's death, Rosenzweig writes: "After hearing his lecture 'On the Peculiar Characteristics of the German Mind,' I was deeply disturbed. I thought he had fallen victim to chauvinism. . . . I behaved very crudely, starting with the accusation he had betrayed the Messianic idea." See Nahum Glatzer, ed., *Franz Rosenzweig: His Life and Thought* (New York: Schocken, 1953), 68–69.

6. Levinas's interpretation of Husserl presumes that phenomenology begins as an epistemological theory but ends as ontology. Thus he sometimes conflates Husserl and Heidegger. See André Orianne, "Translator's Forward," in Emmanuel Levinas, *The Theory of Intuition in Husserl's Phenomenology* (Evanston, Ill.: Northwestern University Press, 1973), xi–xxiii, and Edith Wyschogrod, *Emmanuel Levinas: The Problem of Ethical Metaphysics*, 2d ed. (New York: Fordham University Press, 2000), 26–50.

7. Levinas, *The Theory of Intuition in Husserl's Phenomenology*, xxxv; my italics.

8. Languilli, ed., *The Existentialist Tradition*, 193.

9. Cohen's method is not without a pragmatic aspect. The transcendental deduction can legitimate subjective principles, but one finds in the science of fact the empirical relevance of these principles. This view protects philosophical autonomy and uses science as a concrete control. See Dussort, *L'école de Marbourg*, 99 ff.

10. In Raymond Duval, "Exode et altérité," *Revue Scientifique de Philosophie et de Théologie* 59 (April 1975): 217–41. Levinas's work is viewed in terms of pairs of the oppositions oppression/deliverance and being/Other. It is being (and not nothing) that oppresses. Suffering (and not death) is the proof of freedom, for in suffering the will is undone.

11. Harold Durfee, "War, Politics and Radical Pluralism," *Philosophy and Phenomenological Research* (June 1975), comparing social contract and natural law theories of the state with Levinas's view, writes (551): "Community depends upon the linguistic communication of those who would otherwise be separated."

12. The idea of vulnerability is pervasive in Levinas. See esp. *TI*, 245: "The accomplishing of the I qua I and morality constitute one sole and same process in being: Morality comes to birth not in equality but in the fact that infinite exigencies, that of serving the poor, the stranger, the widow and the orphan converge at one point of the universe." The term *humankind* cannot, unfortunately, be substituted for *mankind* without affecting other concepts in Levinas's work.

13. It is in relation to separated individuality that Levinas remains most committed to phenomenological method. See Stephen Strasser, "Anti-phénoménologie et phénoménologie dans la philosophie d'Emmanuel Levinas," *Revue philosophique de Louvain* 75, no. 25 (February 1977).

14. It lies beyond the scope of this paper to canvas the extensive literature of British and American analytic philosophy on the question of personal identity. However, Terence Penulham's view in "Personal Identity," *Encyclopedia of Philosophy* (New York: Macmillan, 1967), puts forward criteria for reidentifying persons around which much of the debate has centered: the bodily criterion and the memory criterion. For Levinas, these would apply to the infra-ethical self of totality and interiority, respectively. The disadvantage of persons constituted on these criteria would (for Levinas) lie in their inability to grasp alterity. Levinas would see the relation of the ascription of responsibility to reidentification as a problem for jurisprudence rather than for philosophy.

15. Leo Strauss, Introductory Essay, in *RRSJ*, 17.

16. *TI*, 122–127; *DEHH*, 111–45 et passim. See also Wyschogrod, *Emmanuel Levinas*, 144 ff.

17. By de-structuring is meant bringing to the fore what has been concealed or forgotten. This process does not terminate in some point of origin but is the attestation in language of a beyond that is unreachable. See *SP*,

85, for an account of the "trace." In terms of a theory of truth as reference, the face is not a referring item.

18. The difference in thrust between Cohen's earlier *Ethik des Reinen Willens* (Berlin: Cassirer, 1904) and *RRSJ* can be attributed to differing conceptions of reason: in the former, reason is the instrument through which the concept of man is derived; in the latter, man is created a moral entity, as having moral reason, by a God of reason. See Schwarzschild, "The Tenability of Hermann Cohen's Construction of the Self," 366.

19. Strasser, "Anti-phénoménologie et phénoménologie dans la philosophie d'Emmanuel Levinas," 109, insists that Levinas's attack on Husserl's transcendental objectivism leads to a characterization of seeing itself as anti-ethical. Therefore the face does not appear. The form of the face is a disguise for its nudity.

20. It would not do to confuse Levinas's de-structuring with mere etymological reduction, as though an earlier signification were truer and the earliest the "most true." The word is a trace of a silent origin. Jacques Derrida makes the point (radically) in *G*, 61: "The trace is not only the disappearance of origin . . . It was never [even] constituted except reciprocally by a non-origin, the trace would thus become the origin of the non-origin." But if this is true, can ethics ever be incorporated into language? This question is the source of Levinas's *Otherwise than Being*. See Etienne Feron, "Ethique, langage, ontologie chez Emmanuel Levinas," *Revue de Métaphysique et de Morale* 82 (January-March 1977): 64–87.

21. Emmanuel Levinas, "Humanisme et anarchie," *Revue Internationale de Philosophie*, nos. 85–86, p. 331.

22. See Emmanuel Levinas, "La substitution," *Revue Philosophique de Louvain* 66 (August 1968): 487–508.

23. "Experience" is placed in quotation marks in this context, since Levinas insists, in "God and Philosophy," trans. Richard Cohen, *Philosophy Today* (Summer 1978): 144: "The adventure of knowledge which is characteristic of Being, ontological from the first is not the only mode of intelligibility of meaning. Experience as the source of meaning has to be put into question."

24. For an evaluation of Hegelianism in Cohen (despite his avowed anti-Hegelian posture), see Schwarzschild, "The Tenability of Hermann Cohen's Construction of the Self," 369 n. 31. For a dialectic, of sorts, in Levinas, see Raymond Duval, "Exode et altérite."

25. Ibid., 308–9.

26. Ibid.

27. Ibid.

28. Ibid., 323.

29. Ibid., 307. The actualization of the infinite task in Cohen does not pose the dilemma of Zeno's paradox of the infinite sequence of tasks, the

solution to which depends upon the condition that all points that must be passed over are bounded by a finite interval. If the points are not so bounded (and they are not in Cohen's conception), it would not be possible to pass over them (and it is not possible to do so in Cohen). For accounts of the paradox, see: James Thomson, "Infinity in Mathematics and Logic," *Encyclopedia of Philosophy* (New York: Macmillan, 1967),4: 188; and Gilbert Ryle, *Dilemmas* (Cambridge: Cambridge University Press, 1953), 36–53.

30. Levinas, in "God and Philosophy," 133, writes: "We are outside the order in which one passes from an idea to a being. Unlike every content, the idea of God is God in me, but already God breaking up the consciousness which aspires to ideas."

31. Jacques Derrida, "Violence and Metaphysics: An Essay on the Thought of Emmanuel Levinas," in Derrida, *Writing and Difference*, trans. Alan Bass (Chicago: University of Chicago Press, 1978), 83, interprets the uses of alterity in Levinas as a new empiricism. See also Wyschogrod, *Emmanuel Levinas*, 89–94.

27. Autochthony and Welcome

1. Jacques Derrida, *De l'hospitalité: Anne Dufourmantelle invite Jacques Derrida a répondre* (Paris: Calmann-Lévy, 1997), 135. Translations of direct citations from this work are mine.

2. In *Otherwise than Being*, Levinas writes: "In responsibility for another, subjectivity is only [the] unlimited passivity of an accusative . . . [reducible] to the passivity of a self only as a persecution . . . that turns into an expiation" (112). He goes on to say that "the self of this passivity . . . is a hostage" (114).

3. Derrida, *De l'hospitalité*, 44–45.

4. Ibid., 47 ff.

5. Dominique Janicaud, *Powers of the Rational: Science, Technology, and the Future of Thought*, trans. Peg Birmingham and Elizabeth Birmingham (Bloomington: Indiana University Press, 1994); see esp. chap. 3, 59–75.

6. Derrida, *De l'hospitalité*, 119.

7. The latter position is that of Levinas, *TI*, 73.

8. Martin Heidegger, "Building, Dwelling, Thinking," in *PLT*, 147.

9. Martin Heidegger, ". . . Poetically Man Dwells . . . ," ibid., 228–29.

10. *American Heritage Dictionary of the English Language*, ed. William Morris (Boston: Houghton Mifflin, 1981), 1518. See also Derrida's play on the ambiguity of his coined word *hostipitalité*, expressing both welcome and hostility, in *De l'hospitalité*, 45.

11. A brief account of Schmitt's membership in the Nazi party and for a certain time his articulation of juridical principles in consonance with its doctrines can be found in George Schwab, *The Challenge of the Exception*

(Berlin: Duncker and Humblot, 1970); see esp. Part II, "Schmitt and National Socialism 1933–1936." For engagement with Schmitt in a theological vein, see Jacob Taubes, *Ad Carl Schmitt Gegenstrebige Fugung* (Berlin: Merve, 1987).

12. Jacques Derrida, *The Gift of Death*, trans. David Wills (Chicago: University of Chicago Press, 1995), 103.

13. Ibid., 104.

14. Jacques Derrida, *Politics of Friendship*, trans. George Collins (London: Verso, 1997), 126.

15. Ibid., 116–17.

16. Ibid., 116.

17. Ibid., 120.

18. Ibid., 122–23.

19. Jacques Derrida, *Hospitality, Justice and Responsibility in Questioning Ethics: Contemporary Debates in Philosophy* (London: Routledge, 1999), 70.

20. Ibid.

21. Jacques Derrida, *De l'hospitalité*, 29.

28. Time and Nonbeing in Derrida and Quine

1. Richard Rorty, *Philosophy and the Mirror of Nature* (Princeton: Princeton University Press, 1979), 364. Despite his caveats concerning a *rapprochement*, Rorty's study is itself a step toward commensuration. Newton Garver makes a similar move in his suggestive remarks on Derrida and Wittgenstein in the Preface to Jacques Derrida, *Speech and Phenomena*. More guarded assessments of Derrida's work by Newton Garver and Richard Rorty, together with a brief note by Marjorie Greene, are found in *The Journal of Philosophy* 74, no. 11 (November 1977): 663–82. These papers were later presented to an American Philosophical Association symposium on the philosophy of Jacques Derrida. In an essay on the question of translation, Derrida himself argues that it is the sacred text that demands translation: "The sacred would be nothing without translation, and translation would not take place without the sacred; the one and the other are inseparable. . . . That event [the event of the sacred text] melds completely with the act of language. . . . And since no meaning bears . . . translating into another tongue as such (as meaning), it commands right away the translation that it seems to refuse. It is transferable and untranslatable." He concludes, quoting Maurice de Gandillac, that "all the great writings, but to the highest point sacred Scripture, contain between the lines their virtual translation. The interlinear version of the sacred text is the model or ideal of all translation" (Jacques Derrida, "Des Tours de Babel," trans. Joseph F. Graham, in Derrida, *Acts of Religion*, ed. and introd. Gil Anidjar [New York: Routledge, 2002], 133).

2. The pertinent epistemological essays are "Two Dogmas of Empiricism" and "Logic and the Reification of Universals," in *FLPV*.

3. Quine, "Two Dogmas of Empiricism," 44.

4. Three essays on linguistic theory are of particular importance in this context: "The Problem of Meaning in Linguistics" (PML); "Meaning and Translation" (MT), originally published in *On Translation*, ed. A. Brower (Cambridge: Harvard University Press, 1959), 148–72; and "Speaking of Objects" (SO), originally published in *Proceedings and Addresses of the American Philosophical Association*, 957–58 (Yellow Springs, Ohio: Antioch Press, 1958), 5–22.. MT, an adaptation of *Word and Object* (Cambridge: MIT Press, 1960), was written while the latter was a work in progress. Parts of this essay were delivered at the fourth Colloque Philosophique de Royaumont, April 1958, and were reprinted under the title "Le myth de la signification" in the proceedings of the colloquium, *La philosophie analytique* (Paris: Minuit, 1962). Derrida has himself, together with Roger Martin, translated Quine's "Les frontières de la théorie logique," in *Perspectives sur la philosophie nord-américaine, Les Etudes Philosophiques* 19, no. 2 (Paris: Presses Universitaires de France, 1964), 209–19. Although Derrida knew Quine's work, his thinking is, so far as I can tell, not marked by obvious Anglo-American influence. The exception is an essay on J. L. Austin, "Signature, Event, Context," trans. Samuel Weber and Jeffrey Mehlman, in *Glyph 1*, ed. Samuel Weber and Henry Sussman (Baltimore: The Johns Hopkins University Press, 1977), 172–97, and "Limited Inc a b c," (a reply to John R. Searle's criticism of this essay) in *Glyph 2* (Baltimore: The Johns Hopkins University Press, 1977), 162–254.

5. SO, 449. Quine cites *pou stoū* in Greek script.

6. Jacques Derrida, "Structure, Sign, and Play in the Language of the Human Sciences," in *The Structuralist Controversy*, ed. Richard Macksey and Eugenio Donato (Baltimore: The Johns Hopkins University Press, 1972), 260.

7. *SP*, 141. D. M. Armstrong, in *Nominalism and Realism*, Vol. 1 of *Universals and Scientific Realism* (Cambridge: Cambridge University Press, 1978), accuses Quine of "ostrich nominalism," a position that both denies universals and resorts to them. Michael Devitt, in "Armstrong on Ostrich Nominalism," *Pacific Philosophical Quarterly* 64, no. 4 (1983): 433–39, and D. M. Armstrong, in "A Reply to Michael Devitt," 440–49 comment further on these.

8. Quine appreciates the difficulties of the nominalist position. The "quixotic" nominalist "foreswears quantification over universals, for example, classes altogether." Quine prefers "conceptualism," a position that acknowledges that there are universals but holds them to be "man-made." "Tactically conceptualism is . . . the strongest position . . . for the tired nominalist can lapse into conceptualism, and still allay his puritanic conscience with the reflection that he has not quite taken to eating lotus with the platonists" ("The Reification of Universals," *FLPV*, 129). In what follows, I take Quine to be a "tired nominalist."

9. Derrida, "Structure, Sign, and Play," 24–25.

10. Jacques Derrida, "Ousia and Grammé: Note to a Footnote in Being and Time," in *Phenomenology in Perspective*, ed. F. J. Smith (The Hague: Martinus Nijhoff, 1970), 57.

11. Jacques Derrida, "Freud and the Scene of Writing," in *Writing and Difference*, trans. Alan Bass (Chicago: University of Chicago Press, 1978), 204.

12. Ibid., 205.

13. MT, 462. *Z* is used for Quine's SIGMA, *ѕ* for sigma. In what could be seen as a roughly parallel comment, Derrida speculates: "There is only the edge in language . . . That is, reference. From the supposed fact that there is never anything but reference, an irreducible reference, one can *just as well* conclude that the referent—everything save the name—is or is not indispensable" (Jacques Derrida, "*Sauf le nom*," trans. John P. Leavey, Jr., in Derrida, *On the Name*, ed. Thomas Dutoit [Stanford: Stanford University Press, 1995], 60).

14. Derrida, "Freud and the Scene of Writing," 203.

15. Jacques Derrida, "Plato's Pharmacy," in *Dissemination*, trans. Barbara Johnson (Chicago: University of Chicago Press, 1981), 63–171.

16. Quine, "Two Dogmas of Empiricism," *FLPV*, 42.

17. Quine, "On What There Is," *FLPV*, 2.

18. Quine writes on this point: "The nominalist has repudiated the infinite universe of universals as a dream world; he is not going to impute infinitude to this universe of particulars unless it happens to be infinite as a matter of objective fact—attested to, say, by the physicist" (see "Logic and the Reification of Universals," *FLPV*, 128–29).

19. Jacques Derrida, "Semiology and Grammatology: Interview with Julia Kristeva," in *Positions*, trans. Alan Bass (Chicago: University of Chicago Press, 1981), 35.

20. Quine, "Two Dogmas of Empiricism," *FLPV*, 43.

21. Ibid., 46.

22. Philip Wheelwright, ed., *The Presocratics* (New York: The Odyssey Press, 1966), 54.

29. The Logic of Artifactual Existents

1. An exception is John J. McDermott, *The Culture of Experience: Essays in the American Grain* (New York: New York University Press, 1976), 220 ff.

2. "Instrumentalism . . . constitute[s] a precise logical theory of concepts of judgments and inferences in their various forms, by considering primarily how thought functions in the experiential determination of consequences" (John Dewey, "The Development of American Pragmatism," *Studies in the History of Ideas* [New York: Columbia University Press, 1925], 2:21).

3. "Structure exhibits the characteristics of a system. It is made up of several elements none of which can undergo a change without effecting

changes in all other elements." But the total structure is invariant despite modifications of its elements: the *relata* change but the relations persist. (Claude Lévi-Strauss, *Structural Anthropology*, trans. Claire Jacobson and Brooke Grundfest Schoepf [Garden City, N.J.: Doubleday, 1967], 271 ff).

4. There is a tradition in philosophy cross-cutting methodological commitments characterized by the view "that some form of action precedes or grounds conceptions or that a theory of action is primitive with regard to knowledge" (Don Ihde, "Technology and Human Self-conception," *The Southwestern Journal of Philosophy* 10, no. 1 [Spring 1979]: 23).

5. This wider notion of philosophy is phenomenological in character and has been seen as Dewey's most important contribution to philosophy (Kenneth Chandler, "Dewey's Phenomenology of Knowledge," *Philosophy Today* 21 [Spring 1977]:44).

6. John Dewey, "In Defense of the Theory of Inquiry" (originally published as part of "A Letter to Mr. John Dewey concerning John Dewey's Doctrine of Possibility together with His Reply," by Albert G. A. Balz and John Dewey, *Journal of Philosophy* 64 [1949]: 313–42), in *On Experience, Nature, and Freedom*, ed. Richard J. Bernstein (Indianapolis: Bobbs-Merrill, 1960), 141.

7. Dewey is seen to hold that "scientific technology is the highest refinement of man's attempt to solve his problematic situation and needs" (Michael J. Zimmerman, "Dewey, Heidegger and the Quest for Certainty," *The Southwestern Journal of Philosophy* 14, no. 1 [1986]: 94). Such assessments are one-sided unless the alienation of science in its present form is borne in mind.

8. Chandler, "Dewey's Phenomenology of Knowledge," 51, suggests that "Dewey is not advocating a return to former innocence but seeks a post-reflective naivete."

9. "Artifacts then are human versions of the world acting as transactional mediations." McDermott, *The Culture of Experience*, 218.

10. Lévi-Strauss has frequently been criticized for failure to acknowledge conceptual changes when the level of discourse is altered. It has been pointed out that in the case of myth and science this failure results in a paradox: if there are forms of knowledge (such as science) that can articulate modes of thought cut off from self-knowledge (such as myth), there must be a radical distinction between scientific thought and myth (which Lévi-Strauss denies). If there were not, then knowledge would reveal its own impossibility (N. M. Geras, "Lévi-Strauss and Philosophy," *The Journal of the British Society for Phenomenology* 1, no. 3 [1970]: 56).

11. Claude Lévi-Strauss, *Myth and Meaning: The 1977 Massey Lectures* (New York: Schocken, 1979), 17.

12. Peirce's significance for the later Dewey is difficult to overestimate: "But I am quite sure that [Peirce] above all modern philosophers has opened the road which permits a truly experiential philosophy to be developed which does not, like traditional empirical philosophies, cut experience

off from nature" (John Dewey, "Qualitative Thought" [originally published in *The Symposium* 1 (1930): 5–32], in *On Experience, Nature and Freedom*, ed. Bernstein, 209–10.

13. *EaN*, 176; John Dewey, *Logic: The Theory of Inquiry* (New York: Henry Holt, 1938), 384–85.

14. In correspondence with Arthur C. Bentley, Dewey writes: "If I ever get the needed strength I want to write on *knowing* as the way of believing in which linguistic artifacts transact business with physical artifacts, tools, implements, apparatus, both kinds being planned for the purpose, and rendering inquiry of necessity and experimental transaction" (cited in McDermott, *The Culture of Experience*, 218).

15. While Dewey's notion of tools has something in common with Heidegger's view of equipment, Dewey does not take a radically antitechnological position, as is characteristic of Heidegger. For Dewey, scientific technology is alienated, while for Heidegger it represents the "final fruit" of a decadent metaphysics.

16. *EaN*, 122. Function is central to artifactual existence: "Form and matter become so integrally related to one another that a chair seems to be a chair and a hammer a hammer, in the same sense in which a stone is a stone and a tree is a tree" (Dewey, *Logic*, 385).

17. Dewey, "Qualitative Thought," 180 ff.

18. The pejorative meanings attributed to terms such as *savage* and *primitive* have now received significant criticism. See, esp., Marianna Torgovnik, *Gone Primitive: Savage Intellects, Modern Lives* (Chicago: University of Chicago Press, 1993).

19. Lévi-Strauss, *Myth and Meaning*, 15.

20. Edmund Leach, *Claude Lévi-Strauss* (Harmondsworth, Middlesex: Penguin, 1970), 39.

21. *SM*, 42. "Consciousness governed by emotions" etc. is a reference to Lévy-Bruhl's conception of "savage mind." In this interpretation, the consciousness of nonliterate societies is seen as infra-cognitive. Lévy-Bruhl's work was also known to Dewey. See "Interpretation of Savage Mind," *The Psychological Review* 9 (1902): 217–30, reprinted in John Dewey, *Philosophy and Civilization* (New York: Minton, Balch, 1931), 166–87.

22. Claude Lévi-Strauss, *Tristes Tropiques*, trans. John Russell (New York: Atheneum, 1961), 391.

23. Ibid., 390.

24. Ibid., 391.

30. The Mathematical Model in Plato and Some Surrogates in a Jain Theory of Knowledge

NOTE: This paper was first presented at the meeting of the International Society for the Comparative Study of Civilizations at Bradford College, Haverhill, Massachusetts, in April 1977.

1. Joseph Needham, *Science and Civilisation in China* (Cambridge: Cambridge University Press, 1954), 3:150.

2. Benjamin Nelson, "Sciences and Civilizations, 'East' and 'West,' Joseph Needham and Max Weber," *Boston Studies in the Philosophy of Science* 2 (1974):445–93.

3. *The Tathvārthādhigama Sūtra* of Śri Umāsvāti was composed as early as the period of the oldest Jain commentaries and crystallizes an early and much respected epistemological tradition. Its date is given as A.D. 300 The commentary of Śri Pujyapada is the oldest extant commentary on the sūtra and is accepted as definitive by the logician Śri Akalanka Deva in his *Rajavartika*. The sūtra, together with the commentary, will be taken as representative of the Jain epistemological literature. See the Preface to *The Tathvārthādhigama Sūtra* of Śri Umasvati, with the commentary of Śri Pujyapada, trans. S. A. Jain (Calcutta: Vira Sasana Sangha, 1960). An exhaustive list of translations of the sūtra can be found in Karl Potter, ed., *Encyclopedia of Indian Philosophies*, Vol. 1 (Delhi: Institute for Indian Studies by Motilal Banarsidas, 1970). This essay follows the translation of S. A. Jain cited above.

4. I do not allege the absence of mathematical speculation during the formative period of Indian philosophy or afterward, since such an assertion is both contrary to fact and beside the point. I do believe that the mathematical model does not provide the criteria governing the determination of truth in the Indian philosophical systems. Carl B. Boyer, in *A History of Mathematics* (Hoboken, N.J.: John Wiley and Sons, 1968), writes that our notation for integers and an equivalent of the sine function in trigonometry are significant ancient Indian contributions (237). There is a marked lack of continuity of tradition, however, so that such events are sporadic (229).

5. The nonliving (*ajīva*) encompasses an elaborate structure, including not only matter but time, space, and motion among its elements. For general accounts, see: Surendrenath Dasgupta, *A History of Indian Philosophy*, Vol. 1 (Cambridge: Cambridge University Press, 1963), 189–90 and 195–98; Sarvepalli Radhakrishnan, *Indian Philosophy* (London: George Allen and Unwin, 1923), 312–25; M. Hiriyanna, *Essentials of Indian Philosophy* (George Allen and Unwin, 1949), 62 ff.; and P. T. Raj, *The Philosophical Traditions of India* (London: George Allen and Unwin, 1971). For detailed accounts, see: S. T. Stevenson, *The Heart of Jainism* (London: H. Milford, 1915), 106 ff.; Walter Schubring, *The Religion of the Jainas*, trans. Amulachandra Sen and T. C. Burke (Calcutta: Sanskrit College, 1966), 16–18, and Mohan Lal Mehta, *Outlines of Jaina Philosophy* (Bangalore: Jain Mission Society, 1954), 26 ff.

6. The Jain doctrine of *anekānta* presumes that there is no privileged vantage point from which judgments may be made. All knowledge is relative to the standpoint of the observer: sense experience is only one of a variety of modes of experience. Jain epistemology holds that an object can be

viewed from different points of view: existent, nonexistent, one, many, identical, different, etc. Every object possesses indefinite attributes (dharmas), which are taken as actually existing in the object. When making a judgment, the observer selects an aspect of the object. The term *Syat* is used to designate a particular point of view, i.e., from this aspect the object is such and not otherwise. From the point of view of his father, for example, Anand is a son, but from the point of view of his brother, he is a brother, etc. The object itself is *anekānta*, a substratum that bears numerous characteristics.

Judgments regarding any object can be made in seven ways (*saptabhaṅgī*). Using the often-cited clay pot as an example, perspectival judgments can be schematized as follows:

1. Relatively the pot exists.
2. Relatively the pot does not exist.
3. Relatively the pot does and does not exist (although not in the same respect).
4. Relatively the pot is indescribable.
5. Relatively the pot exists and is indescribable.
6. Relatively the pot does not exist and is indescribable.
7. Relatively the pot exists, does not exist, and is indescribable.

Where the law of contradiction appears to be violated, the conjunctive expression is to be taken as designating different standpoints from which each conjunct can be seen to be true, i.e., true from that limited point of view. See Mehta, *Outlines of Jaina Philosophy*, 117 ff.

7. The Jain canons consider knowledge to be divided into five categories: *abhinibodhika, sruta, avadhi, manahparyaya,* and *kevala* (perception, scripture, clairvoyance, telepathy, and total knowledge, respectively). Two broad divisions are later added, under which these five are subsumed: *pratyaksa* and *paraksa* (direct and indirect, respectively). Perception is, in *The Tathvārthādhigama Sūtra*, counted as indirect, as is scriptural knowledge. See Mehta, *Outlines of Jaina Philosophy*, 85 ff., and Nathmal Tatia, *Studies in Jaina Philosophy*, Sanmati Publication no. 6 (Benares: Jain Cultural Research Society, 1951), 61–70.

8. The notion of what constitutes the mental realm is quite complicated in Indian systems. Suffice it to say that such functions as perceiving, deducing, willing, etc. are seen to be "mental" and belong to the materiality of the world as contradistinct from the power of spirit, which cannot be reduced to mental acts. See Mehta, *Outlines of Jaina Philosophy*, 97, for the Jain application of this principle.

9. See Norman Gulley, *Plato's Theory of Knowledge* (London: Methuen, 1962), 48.

10. Plato, *Republic* VII, 526

11. Plato, *Republic* VI, 510.

12. See Tatia, *Studies in Jaina Philosophy*, chap. 4, and Mehta, *Outlines of Jaina Philosophy*, chap. 6, for detailed discussions of the Jain doctrine of

karma. An older account can be found in Jagmanderlal Jaini, *Outlines of Jainism* (Cambridge: Cambridge University Press, 1916), 26 ff.

13. Plato, *Republic* VII, 529.

14. Śri Pujyapada, *Sarvarthasiddhi*, 1–2.

15. Mailisena Syadvamanjari, *A Commentary on the Examination of the Thirty-two Stanzas of Hemacandra*, xxiii. For general accounts of this view, see Dasgupta, *A History of Indian Philosophy*, Vol. 1, 179–80, and Radhakrishnan, *Indian Philosophy*, 2:294–95. Bimal K. Matilal, in *Epistemology, Logic and Grammar in Indian Philosophical Analysis* (The Hague: Mouton, 1971), contrasts the Jaina doctrine with that of the Advaitins and the Mādhyamikas. The latter two regard the character of the phenomenal world as indeterminable: it is not a merely fictive phenomenal realm but has a provisional existence, neither real nor unreal. Its character is logically indeterminable. For the Nyāya-Vaiśeṣika, any theory as to the character of phenomenality can be a valid theory concerning the character of the real: cause and effect are taken to be actual relations and the theory of causality a valid theory. The Mādhyamika not only reject the validity of the claims of any theory of the phenomenal world but claim, further, that no theory concerning its character can be demonstrated. All such theories can be shown to be internally inconsistent. The Jaina take a stand midway between these views, arguing that each theory of the phenomenal world is consistent with a standpoint, but is not absolutely valid. Thus if x is a particular theory of reality, given certain presuppositions from which x follows, an interpretation can be given to x such that x is true. For an account of the Jain doctrine of "tropes" or the acknowledgment of the validity of the positions of other Indian epistemological schools as partial views of the truth, see Raj, *The Philosophical Traditions*, 98 ff.

16. Since the mathematician may begin by studying sensible phenomena and then proceed to intelligible forms, the double interest results in a double function for mathematics: as propaedeutic to the knowledge of intelligible realities and as an instrument for describing and arranging the everyday world. See Robert Brumbaugh, *The Role of Mathematics in Plato's Dialectic* (Chicago: University of Chicago Libraries, 1942), 70.

17. I am indebted to Anders Wedberg, *Plato's Philosophy of Mathematics* (Stockholm: Almquist and Wiksell, 1955), 32, for this classification.

18. The Jain canons (see n. 7, above) do not change in the sūtra in this regard. The claim is made that this conception predates Lord Mahavira (the most recent founder and twenty-fourth *tirthankara* of Jainism).

19. Pujyapada, *Sarvarthasiddhi*, 33.

20. Ibid., 34 ff.

21. Plato, Meno.

22. Gulley, *Plato's Theory of Knowledge*, 28.

23. Plato, *Phaedo*, 75.

24. For the Pythagorean background of the physical representation of number, see W. K. C. Guthrie, *A History of Greek Philosophy*, Vol. 1 (Cambridge: Cambridge University Press, 1962), 242 ff. For the extent to which mathematical representation is said to characterize nonmathematical cases, see Brumbaugh, *Plato's Mathematical Imagination*.

25. See: T. Heath, *A History of Greek Mathematics*, Vol. 1 (Oxford: Oxford University Press, 1921), 290; Wedberg, *Plato's Philosophy of Mathematics*, 103 ff.; and Richard Robinson, "Hypothesis in Plato," in *Plato*, ed. Gregory Vlastos (Garden City, N.J.: Doubleday, 1971), 110–11. The position is summarized in Plato's *Republic* 511 thus: "And when I speak of the other division of the intelligible, you will understand me to speak of that other sort of knowledge which reason herself attains by the power of dialectic, using the hypotheses, not as first principles, but only as hypotheses—that is to say, as steps and points of departure into a world which is above hypotheses, in order that she may soar beyond them to the first principles of the whole; and clinging to this and then to that which depends on this, by successive steps she descends again without the aid of any sensible objects, from ideas through ideas, and in ideas she ends."

26. Pujyapada, *Sarvarthasiddhi*, 21.

27. This means only to apply to ideal entities as ideal number, but not to processes, which in Jainism include action, time, space, motion, rest, etc. See n. 5, above.

28. The passages in *The Philebus*, 56c–59d and 61d–62b, are interpreted by Wedberg, in *Plato's Philosophy of Mathematics*, as providing evidence for the accuracy of Aristotle's account in that they point to a separation between dialectic and philosophical arithmetic, the latter described as the study of numbers, which are not Ideas. These passages are also seen as pointing to eternal exemplars of geometrical Ideas.

29. Aristotle, *Metaphysics*, 1080 b, 11–14.

30. Ibid., 1080 a, 30–33. See Leon Robin, *La théorie platonicienne des idées et des nombres d'après Aristotle* (Paris: Felix Alcan, 1908), 625, and Wedberg, *Plato's Philosophy of Mathematics*, 116 ff.

31. Jacob Klein, *Greek Mathematical Thought and the Origins of Modern Algebra* (Cambridge: MIT Press, 1968), 90 ff. and 100–101, adds to this discussion by citing Aristotle's refutation of the Platonic view based on the mode of being Plato ascribes to mathematical objects (*Metaphysics*, 1076 a, 36 ff.). Aristotle argues for the natural meaning of *arithmos*: "To be present in number is to be some number of a given object" (*Physics*, A 12, 22, 1b). Attributes such as white, round, etc. are arrived at by disregarding certain other attributes of a thing, enabling one to extrapolate a quality apart from its contextual nexus. This quality can be predicated of other objects, where, in turn, certain other qualities had been similarly disregarded. By subjecting the *aesthete* to this procedure, numerical aspects of being can be ascertained. Number is no longer subject to the senses, yet it does not have any independent

ontological status. The mind tends to "think the mathematical objects which are not separate as if they were separate when it thinks them" (*DA*, 7, 431 b).

31. Soft Nominalism in Quine and the School of Dignāga

1. D. M. Armstrong, *Nominalism and Realism: Universals and Scientific Realism* (Cambridge: Cambridge University Press, 1980), 1:12.

2. Willard Van Orman Quine, "Logic and the Reification of Universals," *FLPV*, 129. Citations from Quine are largely from collections of his early essays (before 1960), in which the view of nominalism considered here may be found. Most of these are in *FLPV* and *WP*.

3. The principal works cited are: Dignāga's *Pramāṇasamuccaya*, with the commentary of Jinendrabuddhi; Dharmakīrti's *A Short Treatise of Logic*; the *Nyāyabindu*, with the commentary by Dharmottara; the *Nyāyabinduṭīkā*; Vācaspatimiśra's account of Buddhist nominalism from a Nyayika point of view, the *Nyāyavārtikatātparyaṭīkā*: all in *BL*. A useful summary of the *Nyāyavārtikatātparyaṭīkā*, by Bima Krishna Matilat, can be found in Karl H. Potter, ed., *Encyclopedia of Indian Philosophies, Indian Metaphysics and Epistemology: The Tradition of Nyāya-Vaiśeṣika up to Gangesa* (Princeton: Princeton University Press, 1977), 455–83. Dignāga, *On Perception*, the *Pratyaśapariccheda* of the *Pramāṇasamuccaya*, trans. Massaaki Hattori (Cambridge: Harvard University Press, 1968), has been consulted for purposes of comparison. To maintain consistency, texts cited are from *BL*. I use the term *Yogācārin* as shorthand for Dignāga and his followers. (This should not be construed as referring to the scriptural Yogācārins.) While there are differences among individual members of the school, there is an underlying unity in the nominalist thrust of its ontology that justifies this usage. In any case, specific works in which a doctrine is to be found are indicated in the notes.

4. Important misunderstandings result from translating Indian logical terms into an Aristotelean conceptual framework. Two essays of fundamental importance suggest that the Yogācārins were groping for the modern principle of extensionality. Hajime Nakamura, in "Buddhist Logic Expounded by Means of Symbolic Logic," *Indogaku Bukkyogaku Kenkyu* 8 (1958): 390, shows that the five-membered syllogism of Indian logic is condensed into one conditional sentence by Dignāga and is compatible with Russell's theory of apparent variables. H. Kitagawa, in "A Note on Methodology in the Study of Indian Logic," *Indogaku Bukkyogaku Kenkyu* 8 (1960): 380–90, shows that the Aristotelean syllogism depends on the subject-object-copula form, while Indian logic is framed in terms of property (*dharmin*) and possessor of the property (*dharma*). Like modern logicians, they distinguish between two uses of the copula, one denoting the relation of membership in a class, the other the relation of subclass to class, symbolized today as "E" and "C," respectively. Quine's criticisms of Aristotelean language are scattered throughout his work. See esp. "Two Dogmas of Empiricism,"

FLPV, 22; "Reference and Modality," *FLPV*, 155–57; and *Methods of Logic* (Cambridge: Harvard University Press, 1982), 94. For an account of the senses in which one can speak of a Buddhist logic, see R. Lance Factor, "What Is the Logic in Buddhist Logic?" *Philosophy East and West* 33, no. 2 (April 1983):179–88.

5. *Nyāyabindutīkā*, 6:12.14, *BL* II, 33. Compare Nelson Goodman's account of particulars in "A World of Individuals," in *The Problem of Universals*, ed. Charles Landesman (New York: Basic Books, 1971), 296: "No distinction of entities without distinction of content." No two distinct things have the same atoms; only from different atoms can different things be generated; all nonidentities between things are reducible to nonidentities between their atoms. Dharmakīrti and his successors stress that the point-instant is unique (*trailokya-vyvrtta*) and momentary (*kṣana*). The idea that the particular alone is capable of producing an effect is found in Dharmakīrti, but not in Dignāga. See Preface in Dignāga, *On Perception*, 14.

6. Ibid., 4:13.11, *BL* II, 36.

7. Ibid., 6:12.17, *BL* II, 34.

8. Compare Dignāga, *On Perception*, n. 1:40, p. 90. On the evils of term-by-term empiricism, see Quine's "The Pragmatist's Place in Empiricism," in Robert J. Mulvaney and Philip M. Zeltner, *Pragmatism: Its Sources and Prospects* (Columbia: University of South Carolina Press, 1981), 25–27.

9. *Nyāyabindutīkā*, 13.2, *BL* II, 35.

10. Ibid., 5:10.13, *BL* II, 26.

11. *Nyāyabindu*, 5:39, *BL* II, 26.

12. *Nyāyabindutīkā*, 7:15.8, *BL* II, 41. That determinate perception is constructed is Dignāga's contribution. See Dignāga, *On Perception*, 76.

13. *Nyāyabindutīkā*, 7:14.16, *BL* II, 39. One of Dignāga's original contributions, taken up also by his successors, is his rejection of the realist distinction between the means and results of cognition. See Dignāga, *On Perception*, 76.

14. *Nyāyabindutīkā*, 7:15.15, *BL* II, 42.

15. Quine, "From a Logical Point of View," *FLPV*, 40.

16. Ibid.

17. Ibid.

18. Quine, "On Mental Entities," *WP*, 226.

19. Ibid., 227.

20. Quine, "Posits and Reality," *WP*, 252.

21. Ibid., 250.

22. Ibid., 252. See also Willard Van Orman Quine, "The Pragmatist's Place in Empiricism," in Mulvaney and Zeltner, *Pragmatism*, 28.

23. Quine, "Posits and Reality," *WP*, 252.

24. The question is treated in considerable detail in *Nyāyabindutīkā*, 2:3.5–2:5.14, *BL*, II, 4–11.

25. Quine, "Two Dogmas of Empiricism," *FLPV*, 42.

26. Controversy persists as to whether Quine belongs to the pragmatic tradition. He claims to find little in common with it except for some tenets held by C. S. Peirce and C. I. Lewis. See Mulvaney and Zeltner, *Pragmatism*, 23–38. In the same volume, Ernest Gellner, "Pragmatism and the Importance of Being Ernest," 43–63, insists on a pragmatic strand in Quine. J. N. Jayatilleke, in *Early Buddhist Theory of Knowledge* (London: George Allen and Unwin, 1963), argues that the Buddha was not a pragmatist but a radical empiricist. This claim cannot, however, be extended to the School of Dignāga.

27. Quine, "On What There Is," *FLPV*, 10.

28. Jinendrabuddhi, 2:286.a.8–286b.2, *BL* I, 465.

29. *Nyāyabinduṭīkā*, 6:14.6, *BL* II, 37.

30. MT, 462.

31. Dignāga, *Pramāṇasamuccaya*, 2:ad. V.II, *BL* I, 461.

32. Jinendrabuddhi, 2:285.bl, *BL* I, 463. Nakamura, in "Buddhist Logic Expounded by Means of Symbolic Logic," 375, suggests that the doctrine of negative naming can be expressed as $p = \sim(\sim p)$. He comments that Quine reduces the process of logical thinking to denial and conjunction.

33. Jinendrabuddhi, 2:285.b.7, *BL* I, 464.

34. Ibid., 2:286.a.8, *BL* I, 465.

35. Vācaspatimiśra, *Nyāyavārtikatātparyaṭīkā*, 5:339.26, *BL* II, 412.

36. Jinendrabuddhi, 2:287.a1, *BL* I, 466.

37. Willard Van Orman Quine, "Identity, Ostension and Hypostasis," *FLPV*, 77.

38. Ibid., 65.

39. Ibid., 67.

40. Ibid.

41. Ibid., 68.

42. Ibid., 72.

43. Ibid.; Gustav Bergmann, "Frege's Hidden Nominalism," in *The Problem of Universals*, ed. Landesman, 83.

44. Quine, "Identity, Ostension and Hypostasis," *FLPV*, 75.

45. Karl H. Potter, in "Nature of a Philosophical System," *Encyclopedia of Indian Philosophies, Indian Metaphysics and Epistemology*, comments on the referentialism of Indian philosophy. Thus the Nayayikas construe even logical connectives as names.

46. Quine, *Methods of Logic*, 263–65; cf. "On What There Is," *FLPV*, 8–9.

47. *Nyāyabindu*, 9:46, *BL* II, 102.

48. Quine, *Methods of Logic*, 264.

49. Quine, "Identity, Ostension and Hypostasis," *FLPV*, 71.

50. Quine, "Carnap's Views on Ontology," *WP*, 205. For an elaboration of this point, see Chapter 28 in this volume.

32. Fear of Primitives, Primitive Fears

1. Cited in Chris Healy, "'We Know Your Mob Now': European and Aboriginal Histories of Captain Cook," *Oral History* 19, no. 2 (1991):28–29.

2. Examples include: Edward Said, *Orientalism* (New York: Pantheon, 1978); Marianna Torgovnick, *Gone Primitive: Savage Intellects, Modern Lives* (Chicago: University of Chicago Press, 1990); Tomoko Masuzawa, *In Search of Dreamtime: The Quest for the Origin of Religion* (Chicago: University of Chicago Press, 1993).

3. When asked about the studies of his youth, the chief of the SS medical staff at Auschwitz, Josef Mengele, declared: "Most exciting of all for me [was] anthropology." See Gerald L. Posner and John Ware, *Mengele: The Complete Story* (New York: McGraw Hill, 1986), 10. Mengele's doctoral thesis was titled "Racial Morphological Research on the Lower Jaw Section of Four Racial Groups," work that, according to the authors, contains no racial or antisemitic overtones.

4. The distinction between beginning and inception is made in Rainer Marten, "Heidegger and the Greeks," in *The Heidegger Case*, ed. Tom Rockmore and Joseph Margolis (Philadelphia: Temple University Press, 1993), 167–87.

5. Martin Heidegger, "A Dialogue on Language," in *On the Way to Language*, trans. Peter D. Hertz (San Francisco: Harper and Row, 1971), 74.

6. Emile Durkheim, *Montesquieu and Rousseau: Forerunners of Sociology*, trans. Ralph Mannheim (Ann Arbor: University of Michigan Press, 1960), 69.

7. Ibid.

8. Ernst Cassirer, *Philosophy of Symbolic Forms*, Vol. 2: *Mythical Thought*, trans. Ralph Mannheim (New Haven: Yale University Press, 1955), 76 nn. 1–3.

9. Ibid., 192–93.

10. Ibid., 43.

11. Cited in John van Buren, *The Young Heidegger: Rumor of the Hidden King* (Bloomington: Indiana University Press, 1994), 372.

12. *Roland Barthes by Roland Barthes*, trans. Richard Howard (New York: Hill and Wang, 1977), 129.

13. Cassirer, *Philosophy of Symbolic Forms*, 200.

14. Ibid., 212.

15. Martin Heidegger, *The Principles of Reason*, trans. Reginald Lilly (Bloomington: Indiana University Press, 1991), 72.

16. Cassirer, *Philosophy of Symbolic Forms*, 80–81.

17. Ibid.,73.

18. Heidegger, *On the Way to Language*, 128. Heidegger insists that his thought about the *Ereignis* is not new, that he had been thinking about and using the term for at least twenty-five years before the essays on language, thus dating his concern with the matter to a time roughly contemporaneous with his *Daseinsanalyse* (129 n.), Even if Heidegger's own chronology is not to be trusted, as recent scholarship attests, it is clear that the theme is longstanding. On Heidegger's recollections, see Theodore Kisiel, "Heidegger's Apology," in *The Heidegger Case*, ed. Rockmore and Margolis, 32.

19. Heidegger, *On the Way to Language*, 119.

20. Ibid., 129 n.

21. Ibid., 134.

22. Emmanuel Levinas, "The Transcendence of Words: On Michel Leiris's *Biffures*," in *Outside the Subject*, trans. Michael B. Smith (Stanford: Stanford University Press, 1994), 148.

23. Emmanuel Levinas, "The Ego and the Totality," *CPP*, 30.

24. Jean Baudrillard, "For a Critique of the Political Economy of the Sign," *Selected Writings*, ed. Mark Poster, 2d ed. (Stanford: Stanford University Press, 1988), 75.

25. Levinas, *OS*, 148.

26. The literary itinerary of Robinson Crusoe in France is tracked in Martin Green, *The Robinson Crusoe Story* (University Park: Pennsylvania State University Press, 1990). Rousseau makes *Robinson Crusoe* the one book in Emile's education, which is otherwise to be derived from the facts of the world. See 39–42. Harold Bloom, ed., *Daniel Defoe's Robinson Crusoe* (New York: Chelsea House Publishers, 1988), includes essays on such disputed questions as whether Crusoe is intended to demonstrate a commitment to solitude, thus marginalizing the Friday relationship, Friday's utilitarian value, or his salvation, See especially the essays of G. A. Starr, 43–66, and Leopold Damrosch, Jr., 81–110.

27. Levinas, *EE*, 57.

28. Ibid., 61.

29. Emmanuel Levinas, "Lévy-Bruhl et la philosophie contemporaine," *Revue philosophique contemporaine de la France et de l'Étranger* 147 (1957): 559, my translation.

30. Ibid., 567.

31. See esp. Maurice Merleau-Ponty, *Consciousness and the Acquisition of Language*, trans. Hugh J. Silverman (Evanston, Ill: Northwestern University Press, 1973). A good example can be found in Maurice Blanchot, *When the Time Comes*, trans. Lydia Davis (Tarrytown, N.Y.: Station Hill Press, 1985), 19–20: "The strangeness of that silent creaking . . . out of our sight, engrave upon the reality of the space of the night that undivulged strangeness of what we had been looking for beneath our words."

32. See a succinct formulation of this relation in Adriaan T. Peperzak, *To the Other: An Introduction to the Philosophy of Emmanuel Levinas* (West Lafayette, Ind.: Purdue University Press, 1981), 230.

Index

Carneades, 338
Cassirer, Ernst, 489, 492–96, 503
Catherine of Siena, Saint, 272–73
Céline, Louis-Ferdinand, 51–53
Certeau, Michel de, 319, 325
Clemente, Francesco, 13–14, 22, 27
Cohen, Hermann, 63, 361, 405–9,
    411–12, 414–16, 418–21, 545n9
Condillac, Étienne Bonnot de, 115, 164,
    167, 168, 170
Cunningham, Merce, 141–53

Darwin, Charles, 181, 190, 199, 204
Dawkins, Richard, 10, 177–80,
    199–200, 202
Debord, Guy, 119, 151
Deleuze, Gilles, 9, 46, 47, 48, 49, 51, 54,
    57
Delsarte, François, 146, 147
Dennett, Daniel, 199–201, 256–59
Derrida, Jacques, 3, 6, 7, 8, 12, 15, 18,
    20–23, 34, 51, 57, 60, 143, 148, 152,
    202, 204, 208, 212–17, 220, 221, 230,
    237–38, 253, 259, 294, 295, 298, 300,
    301–3, 305–7, 313–14, 316, 317, 320,
    322, 323, 349, 350, 356, 360, 364,
    366, 367, 369, 371, 372, 374, 423,
    425–30, 432–48
Descartes, René, 17, 27, 80, 162, 286,
    490, 491
Dewey, John, 449–52, 453–63
Dharmakīrti, 474, 481
Dharmottara, 474, 481
Dignāga, 474, 482–83, 486
Diogenes of Sinope, 338–40, 341, 342
Dostoyevsky, Fyodor, 292, 321
Duncan, Isadora, 143
Durkheim, Emile, 349, 354, 491–92, 500

Eckhart, 288–89
Elster, Jon, 242, 243
Enters, Angna, 151

Fokine, Michel, 146, 147
Foucault, Michel, 9, 53, 95–109,
    131–32, 136, 295, 324, 327, 349–50,
    352, 358

Freud, Sigmund, 49, 82, 128, 138–39,
    270, 300, 304, 349, 435, 439–40
Friedrich, Caspar David, 337, 343
Friel, Brian, 112

Gaunilo of Marmoutiers, 5, 78, 80, 83,
    84, 87–91
Genet, Jean, 9, 51, 274, 375–81, 386
Girard, René, 376
Goodman, Nelson, 264, 277–78
Graham, Martha, 141, 143, 146–47, 149
Guattari, Félix, 46–47, 49, 51

Haar, Michel, 210, 527n8
Hegel, Georg Wilhelm Friedrich, 1–4,
    6–7, 50–51, 226, 228, 251, 291, 314,
    320
Heidegger, Martin, 4, 8, 12, 21, 34, 36,
    40, 49, 62, 69–71, 74, 75, 95–111,
    123, 128, 176, 181, 192, 193, 208–21,
    226, 230, 233, 239, 240, 243, 245,
    246, 251–52, 283, 289–90, 294, 298,
    317, 318, 324, 325, 389, 392, 395,
    396, 397, 405, 406, 409–10, 414, 426,
    434, 435, 439, 447, 489–503
Héloïse, 126, 135, 137–38, 140
Heraclitus, 131
Hillel, 61–75
Hirsch, Samson Raphael, 63, 68, 72, 73,
    75
Hoess, Rudolf, 227, 228
Hölderlin, Friedrich, 292, 294
Hume, David, 242
Husserl, Edmund, 9, 12–19, 22, 24, 34,
    36–39, 56, 116, 174, 176, 185, 186,
    252, 265, 267, 286, 296, 406, 444,
    447, 491, 493, 501

Iamblichus, 190, 193, 196–98, 201

Janicaud, Dominique, 7–8, 208,
    217–21, 223, 226–28, 232–35, 237,
    239–41, 246
Jeroboam, 364, 365
Johns, Jasper, 144, 145, 150
Joshu (koan cited in Mishima, *Temple of
    the Golden Pavilion*), 382–85, 387

Rosenzweig, Franz, 69–70, 75, 260
Rousseau, Jean-Jacques, 295, 352–53, 463, 491–92, 499

Sacks, Oliver, 269–70
Sartre, Jean-Paul, 35, 38, 43, 49, 74, 81, 291
Scheler, Max, 59, 161, 263, 278
Schelling, Friedrich Wilhelm Joseph von, 331, 332
Schmitt, Carl, 427–30
Schoenberg, Arnold, 29, 360–62, 364–65, 367, 370–74
Sextus Empiricus, 338
Silesius, Angelus, 21, 100, 101
Sloterdijk, Peter, 46, 47, 48, 53, 54, 339, 340, 344
Socrates, 108, 129, 130–32, 202–3, 333, 340, 351, 354, 468
Sophocles, 127
Sparshott, Francis, 146
Speer, Albert, 227–28
Steel, Carlos, 198
Stein, Edith, 169

Steiner, George, 350, 352
Stone, Oliver, 121
Strawson, Peter Frederick, 190, 191
Stroop, Maj. Gen. Juergen, 228, 229

Taylor, Mark C., 50, 145, 150, 309, 316
Teresa of Avila, Saint, 270–73, 306, 307
Tharp, Twyla, 141
Theatetus (in Platonic dialogue), 332–33
Theodorus of Asine, 197
Theresa of Avila, Saint. *See* Teresa of Avila
Tournier, Michel, 274

Vācaka Umāsvāti, 465
Varela, Francisco, 175, 183, 188
Vico, Giovanni Battista, 349, 354

Weinstein, Donald, 48
White, Hayden, 249
Wittgenstein, Ludwig, 2, 3, 5, 7, 141, 145, 277
Wolfram, Stephen, 180–81

Perspectives in
Continental Philosophy Series

John D. Caputo, series editor

14. Mark C. Taylor, *Journeys to Selfhood: Hegel and Kierkegaard*. Second edition.

15. Dominique Janicaud, Jean-François Courtine, Jean-Louis Chrétien, Michel Henry, Jean-Luc Marion, and Paul Ricœur, *Phenomenology and the "Theological Turn": The French Debate*.

16. Karl Jaspers, *The Question of German Guilt*. Introduction by Joseph W. Koterski, S.J.

17. Jean-Luc Marion, *The Idol and Distance: Five Studies*. Translated with an introduction by Thomas A. Carlson.

18. Jeffrey Dudiak, *The Intrigue of Ethics: A Reading of the Idea of Discourse in the Thought of Emmanuel Levinas*.

19. Robyn Horner, *Rethinking God as Gift: Marion, Derrida, and the Limits of Phenomenology*.

20. Mark Dooley, *The Politics of Exodus: Søren Keirkegaard's Ethics of Responsibility*.

21. Merold Westphal, *Toward a Postmodern Christian Faith: Overcoming Onto-Theology*.

22. Edith Wyschogrod, Jean-Joseph Goux and Eric Boynton, eds., *The Enigma of Gift and Sacrifice*.

23. Stanislas Breton, *The Word and the Cross*. Translated with an introduction by Jacquelyn Porter.

24. Jean-Luc Marion, *Prolegomena to Charity*. Translated by Stephen E. Lewis.

25. Peter H. Spader, *Scheler's Ethical Personalism: Its Logic, Development, and Promise*.

26. Jean-Louis Chrétien, *The Unforgettable and the Unhoped For*. Translated by Jeffrey Bloechl.

27. Don Cupitt, *Is Nothing Sacred? The Non-Realist Philosophy of Religion: Selected Essays*.

28. Jean-Luc Marion, *In Excess: Studies of Saturated Phenomena*. Translated by Robyn Horner and Vincent Berraud.

29. Phillip Goodchild, *Rethinking Philosophy of Religion: Approaches from Continental Philosophy*.

30. William J. Richardson, S.J., *Heidegger: Through Phenomenology to Thought*.

31. Jeffrey Andrew Barash, *Martin Heidegger and the Problem of Historical Meaning*.

32. Jean-Louis Chrétien, *Hand to Hand: Listening to the Work of Art*. Translated by Stephen E. Lewis.

33. Jean-Louis Chrétien, *The Call and the Response*. Translated with an introduction by Anne Davenport.

34. D. C. Schindler, *Han Urs von Balthasar and the Dramatic Structure of Truth: A Philosophical Investigation*.

35. Julian Wolfreys, ed., *Thinking Difference: Critics in Conversation*.